STRATEGIC ORGANIZATIONAL COMMUNICATION

Harcourt College Publishers

Where Learning Comes to Life

TECHNOLOGY
Technology is changing the learning experience, by increasing the power of your textbook and other learning materials; by allowing you to access more information, more quickly; and by bringing a wider array of choices in your course and content information sources.

Harcourt College Publishers has developed the most comprehensive Web sites, e-books, and electronic learning materials on the market to help you use technology to achieve your goals.

PARTNERS IN LEARNING
Harcourt partners with other companies to make technology work for you and to supply the learning resources you want and need. More importantly, Harcourt and its partners provide avenues to help you reduce your research time of numerous information sources.

Harcourt College Publishers and its partners offer increased opportunities to enhance your learning resources and address your learning style. With quick access to chapter-specific Web sites and e-books . . . from interactive study materials to quizzing, testing, and career advice . . . Harcourt and its partners bring learning to life.

Harcourt's partnership with Digital:Convergence™ brings :CRQ™ technology and the :CueCat™ reader to you and allows Harcourt to provide you with a complete and dynamic list of resources designed to help you achieve your learning goals. Just swipe the cue to view a list of Harcourt's partners and Harcourt's print and electronic learning solutions.

C 62 00 00 00 00 00 00 25 20

http://www.harcourtcollege.com/partners/

STRATEGIC ORGANIZATIONAL COMMUNICATION

In a Global Economy

Fifth Edition

Charles Conrad
Texas A&M University

Marshall Scott Poole
Texas A&M University

Harcourt College Publishers

Fort Worth   Philadelphia   San Diego   New York   Orlando   Austin   San Antonio
Toronto   Montreal   London   Sydney   Tokyo

Publisher	Earl McPeek
Acquisitions Editor	Steve Dalphin
Market Strategist	Laura Brennan
Project Manager	Elaine Hellmund

Cover image provided by PhotoDisc © 2002.

ISBN: 0-15-506348-0

Library of Congress Catalog Card Number: 20011087291

Copyright © 2002, 1998, 1994, 1990, 1985 by Harcourt, Inc.

Figure on p. 322: From "Conflict and Conflict Management," by Kenneth Thomas. *Handbook of Industrial and Organizational Psychology,* Marvin Dunette, ed. Copyright 1976, p. 1128. Used by permission of Marvin Dunnette.

Address for Domestic Orders
Harcourt College Publishers, 6277 Sea Harbor Drive, Orlando, FL 32887-6777
800-782-4479

Address for International Orders
International Customer Service
Harcourt, Inc., 6277 Sea Harbor Drive, Orlando, FL 32887-6777
407-345-3800
(fax) 407-345-4060
(e-mail) hbintl@harcourt.com

Address for Editorial Correspondence
Harcourt College Publishers, 301 Commerce Street, Suite 3700, Fort Worth, TX 76102
Web Site Address
http://www.harcourtcollege.com

Printed in the United States of America

1 2 3 4 5 6 7 8 9 0   076   9 8 7 6 5 4 3 2 1

To:
Helen and Cecil
who gave me a love of knowledge,
BJ
who has given me knowledge of love,
and
Travis and Hannah,
our gifts of love.

To:
Ed, Helen, and Kim
who are the foundation,
Lisa,
who built the home,
and
Sam,
who keeps it warm
with all my love.

PREFACE

From its beginning almost 20 years ago, the goal of *Strategic Organizational Communication* has been to provide a unified description of the incredibly diverse array of ideas that make up our rapidly expanding field. Responses to the first four editions have been especially gratifying. Readers have been particularly complimentary about the level of sophistication of the book and its ability to integrate research from a number of academic disciplines. Responses to the later editions also have praised our efforts to place organizations and organizational communication within a broader social, economic, and cultural context and have appreciated our relaxed, engaging writing style. Of course, we have retained or expanded each of these characteristics.

We also have tried to maintain and strengthen the theoretical framework that has been central to the book since its inception. Each edition has focused on the two-level concept of *strategic choice making*. We believe that people make choices about the overall strategies that they will use to operate the societies and organizations they will live within. Ironically, people tend to normalize and naturalize these choices, transforming them from a conscious selection of one of a number of available options into taken-for-granted assumptions. These overall choices, in turn, create the specific situations that people encounter every day—the challenges they face, the resources they have available to manage those challenges, and the guidelines and constraints that limit the options that are available to them. People adapt strategically to the situations that they create, but in adapting, they tend to reproduce those situations, creating a complicated cycle of acting, creating situations, and adapting to them.

Understanding this action-situation-adaptation cycle requires people to realize these things:

- *Organizations are embedded in societies and cannot be understood outside of a society's beliefs, values, structures, practices, tensions, and ways of managing those tensions.* For example, U.S. society is defined in part by a tension between **community** and **individuality.** This tension is due to many of the challenges faced by contemporary U.S. organizations—challenges as diverse as the attitudes of "Generations X and Y" (Chapter 1); blending of traditional (Chapter 2) and cultural (Chapter 4) strategies of motivation and control; implementation of feminist and other so-called alternative forms of organizing (Chapter 5); and understanding non-Western forms of leadership (Chapter 7).
- *Each overall strategy of organizing includes a characteristic organizational design, a system of motivation and control, and a particular form*

of leadership. Each strategy of organizing is a choice, however; for example, bureaucracies are bureaucracies because people in them *choose* to act like bureaucrats. Each strategy also includes opportunities to *resist* the organization's strategy of organizing.

- *Members of organizations can manage organizational situations strategically.* They can exploit fissures and contradictions in social and organizational power relationships. Even in the turbulent world created by the new, global economy, members of organizations can manage organizational situations in ways that achieve their personal goals and the goals of other members of their organizations.

RESPONDING TO READER SUGGESTIONS

Readers also have been very open about changes that they would like to see us make. As a result, each new edition really has been a *new* edition. This one is no exception.

The New and Improved

The most obvious change involves our efforts to locate organizational communication within the new, global economy. This change is clearest in the addition of Chapter 12, on globalization, but readers will find examples and illustrations from non-U.S. organizations and non-Western cultures throughout the book. For example, of the 11 new case studies in this edition, 7 deal with non-U.S. settings.

Other changes are more subtle, and each one reflects recent advances in organizational communication theory and research. Our discussion of new forms of organizing and of communication technologies has been expanded to encompass two chapters (Chapters 5 and 6). Our treatment of feminist and critical theories continues to grow and deepen, as does the impact that those perspectives have on our discipline's understanding of communication in organizations. The chapters in Unit I have been streamlined and reorganized to increase readability. Our analysis of organizational emotions has been revised and expanded (Chapter 7), and the analysis of how people enter organizations has been revised to reflect recent research and theory. The material that we labeled "micro-ethics" in the fourth edition has been moved to the chapter on Power and Politics (Chapter 8), where the theoretical background for the case is developed; the material previously labeled "macro-ethics" is the core of Chapter 12. We also streamlined our discussion of issues related to race, gender, and ethnicity and have contextualized them within our analysis of globalization.

Many of the case studies that have been retained from the fourth edition have been revised, some substantially (for example, the case about the Challenger disaster in Chapter 2 and the case about managing emotions in Chapter 4). We have replaced some of the case studies included in the fourth edition with new ones, but we have retained the old ones in the Instructor's Manual in case instructors prefer to use them.

Oldies but Goodies

There are two aspects of *Strategic Organizational Communication* that we never want to change. One is the extensive research base for the book. The Bibliography for this edition is abbreviated in comparison to earlier editions, but like them it identifies readings that are especially appropriate for graduate students. In general, we have cited only classics in organizational communication and works published after 1990. Still, the endnotes for each chapter provide a number of additional readings on virtually every facet of contemporary organizational communication research and theory.

The second aspect that we hope always to retain is the conceptual coherence of the analysis. Two beliefs underlie all that we say in this book. The first is that organizations (and societies) are *sites* in which various tensions and contradictions are negotiated through communication (this idea is explained at length in Chapter 1). The second belief is that understanding organizations and organizational communication requires an analysis of *both* symbolic *and* structural processes. We realize that this both-and perspective is an anomalous position in a discipline that relishes either-or distinctions between functionalism and interpretivism, qualitative and quantitative research methods, and so on. We also realize that advocates of each of these polar terms often will feel that we are too sympathetic with the opposite pole and spend too little space examining their favored position. But we have consistently tried both to balance various perspectives and to indicate how each can be enriched by the key concepts of the others. Life is simply too complex for either-or thinking to capture its nuances; organizations are far too fluid and complicated for bimodal or trimodal paradigms to reveal much of importance.

ORGANIZATION OF THE BOOK

Like earlier editions, this book is divided into two units. Unit I introduces the theoretical framework that unifies the book, and it develops the concept of *strategies of organizing* in detail. Unit II examines a number of challenges that employees are likely to encounter in contemporary organizations, and it discusses the communicative strategies that they might use to *strategically manage* those situations. Chapter 7 provides an extended discussion of communication technologies, treating them not as a separate topic but as processes that modify and expand the strategies of organizing available to members of organizations. Chapter 8 examines strategies for managing membership in organizations, including the complex process of entering an organization. Subsequent chapters examine organizational power and politics; individual, group, and organizational decision making; organizational conflict; issues related to workforce diversity; and globalization.

THANKS

If they are to be effective, all communicative acts must be interactive. This dictum includes the writing of books. Consequently, our greatest vote of thanks goes to the many readers of the earlier editions who made thoughtful and valuable suggestions for improvement.

Of the advice that we received on the different drafts of this edition, the comments of many colleagues were exceptionally helpful: Brenda J. Allen, University of Colorado; James Anderson, University of Utah; Richard Ice, St. John's University; Angela Tretheway, Arizona State University; and Frederico Varona, San Jose State University. Brenda Allen provided valuable input into our discussion of feminist organizational communication theory and issues of race and ethnicity. Linda Putnam is a constant source of support, providing insight, expertise, and resources that only she can provide, while Kathy Miller's superb teaching of our organizational communication course constantly challenges us to be at our best. George Cheney, Ted Zorn, Steve Corman, Bob McPhee, Gerry DeSanctis, Peter Monge, and Joe Folger are constant sources of exciting new ideas. Huiyan Zhang was an invaluable source of insight into cross-cultural issues and is also the author of the Instructor's Manual. Amy McGaughey, Lisa Huebner, Laura Brennan, and Elaine Hellmund have made working with Harcourt College Publishers a joy—we have never encountered more supportive and capable people in any organization. Private encouragement was provided by Betty Webber Conrad and Lisa O'Dell, and in even the most hectic of times, Travis, Hannah, and Sam help us keep our priorities straight.

Charles Conrad
Marshall Scott Poole
College Station, Texas
January, 2001

CONTENTS

UNIT 1

Strategies of Organizing

Chapter 1

STRATEGIC ORGANIZATIONAL COMMUNICATION

Don't ask me. I just work here.
—ANONYMOUS

CENTRAL THEMES

- Organizational communication is strategic in two senses. Organizations emerge from strategic choices about how they will be designed and operated. These choices create the situations that employees encounter at work. Employees must then make their own strategic choices about how to manage those situations.
- Societies and organizations face a fundamental dilemma. They must control and coordinate the activities of their members. But, doing so frustrates their members' needs for autonomy, creativity, and sociability.
- All organizations are structured, but their individual structures differ in terms of how centralized, formalized, and specialized they are.
- Organizational communication is both like and unlike communication in non-organizational relationships.
- Organizations exist within societal contexts. The beliefs, values, and expectations that people bring into their organizations influence organizational communication in important ways.
- Organizations are systems, and viewing them as systems helps people understand the complex communication processes that take place within them.

KEY TERMS

Bureaucracy	Centralization
Chain of command	Specialization
Blended relationships	Hegemony
System wholeness	Networks

2

Uniplex relationships   Multiplex relationships
Self-regulation   Self-renewal

At one time or another almost everyone has responded to the question, "How did this (disaster) happen?" with a statement like, "Don't ask me. I just work here." In some cases the excuse is legitimate. The person giving the answer is not allowed by his or her organization to make even simple decisions or take any initiative. "I just work here" means that the person knows the answer or is aware of a solution to the problem but has too little power to make the necessary changes. In other cases, someone else failed to inform the person of the policy, problem, or procedure that is in question. "I just work here" means that the speaker simply does not have the information needed to answer the question. But sometimes the person did act in ways that caused the problem and the response is merely an excuse. Although viable excuses are often available in organizations, in the final analysis it is an employee's own choices that create the situations she or he faces.

This book is about the choices and choice-making behaviors of members of formal organizations. It concentrates on communication because it is through communication that employees obtain information, make sense of the situations they encounter, and decide how to act. And, it is by communicating that employees translate their choices into action. Organizations must maintain at least an adequate level of communication effectiveness to survive and prosper. People who have developed an understanding about how communication functions in an organization, who have developed a wide repertory of written and oral communication skills, and who have learned when and how to use those skills seem to have more successful careers and contribute more fully to their organizations than people who have not done so.

As a result, the number of college courses and professional training programs concerned with organizational communication has mushroomed. Of course, employees cannot function effectively unless they possess the technical skills that their positions require. But more and more it appears that being able to recognize, diagnose, and solve communication-related problems is vital to the success of people in even the most technical occupations. Accountants must be able to gain complete, accurate, and sometimes sensitive information from their clients. Supervisors of production lines must be able to obtain adequate and timely information on which to base their decisions. Managers of all divisions must be able to give their subordinates clear instructions, make sure those instructions are understood, create conditions in which their commands will be carried out, and obtain reliable feedback about the completion of the tasks that they have assigned. [1]

Understanding organizational communication has advantages above and beyond career advancement. At many times during their careers people feel powerless because they simply do not understand the events that are taking place around them. In some cases they are victimized by those events. And often, they simply do not understand how they became victims. As the title of a popular book says, bad things do happen to good people (and vice versa), both in our lives as a whole and in our organizations. People need to be able to take a critical perspective on organizational events; that is, they need to be able to examine the situations they find themselves in and understand the many pressures and constraints that make up those situations. People can learn from their experiences only if they understand the situations they face and the communicative strategies that they might use to manage them effectively. In short, understanding organizational communicative processes is itself empowering— it allows people to determine which events are their responsibility and which events are outside of their control and to discover new strategies that they could have used successfully and will be able to use in the future.

The primary goal of the book is to give readers a sense of how organizational communication is used strategically, that is, how employees can analyze the organizational situations they face and choose appropriate communication strategies. It assumes that all employees are goal-oriented and that if they understand how communication functions in their organizations they will be better able to achieve their objectives and those of their organizations. It explains when it is appropriate to use a variety of communication strategies, including the denial of responsibility and the claim of ignorance ("Don't ask me. I just work here"), and as important, when not to use them.

In this chapter, we will introduce the two concepts that underlie the rest of the book. First, we will observe that organizational communication is *strategic* and explain the two dimensions of that concept. Then we will explain that organizational communication is *multidimensional.* It is *structured, relational, contextual,* and *systemic.* Each of these concepts *is* complicated. Consequently, we will introduce them briefly in this chapter. As the book progresses they will become more and more clear; examples and expanded explanations will help you understand even the most complex of the ideas that we will present. Good things will come to those who wait, and read.

ORGANIZATIONAL COMMUNICATION AS *STRATEGIC* DISCOURSE

One way to understand a complicated phenomenon is to begin with definitions of key terms. The simplest definition of organizational communication is that it is communication that occurs within organizations, but that definition is not very informative. Communication is generally defined as a process through which people, acting together, create, sustain, and manage meanings through the use of verbal and nonverbal signs and symbols within a particular context. Of course, the key terms in this definition are people, acting together, meaning, and context. In even a simple conversation, individuals bring a number of things with them. They each have histories of past conversations with one another or with people they perceive as similar to the other person. For example, conversations with one's boss are in some ways influenced by one's past conversations with bosses and other authority figures. They also bring expectations about future conversations with one another, goals for the conversation and for their relationship, assumptions about how people are supposed to communicate with one another, different kinds and levels of communicative skills, and so on. During every conversation people create and exchange a complex set of messages with one another and in doing so create meanings for each message and for the interaction. Some meanings that emerge are consistent with what the communicators intended their messages to mean; others are not. The systems of meanings that individuals create together influence their impressions of one another, their interpretations of their relationship, and the meanings that they attach to their communication. As their conversation continues, their goals may change as they discover that the other person is more (or less) sympathetic to their position than they expected the person to be. Similarly, people's assumptions about how civil they should be toward one another may change when they notice others are more civil than ever before, and so on.

For example, one of our graduate students studied a committee that was charged with designing guidelines for the sex education program of a city school district. To represent both sides of the issue, the committee was composed of some members who were "liberal" in the sense that they supported a fairly extensive sex education program and others who were "conservative" and were opposed to most types of current sex education programs. Both the liberal and conservative subgroups came to the first meeting of the committee with little direct knowledge of one another. But each thought they knew what the others would be like based on their interpretations of the public debate in the United States over teenage sexuality and abortion. Conservatives feared that the liberals would want a program that encouraged sexual promiscuity among teenagers and would advocate abortion as a primary method of birth control; liberals were convinced that the conservatives would want a program that gave students little information and a great deal of fear and guilt.

During an early meeting the conservative group gave a number of long speeches arguing that the district's sex education program should persuade students to abstain from sexual activity. To both the liberal and conservative group's surprise, everyone in the room agreed. Although it took a while for the two groups to recover from the shock of finding that they agreed on something important, the rest of the committee's deliberations were different than they otherwise would have been. They continued to be suspicious of one another throughout the next six months, but at least they listened to one another. In doing so, they discovered many other areas of disagreement and some additional areas of agreement. In the process of communicating with one another, members created, sustained, and modified a system of meaning that was uniquely their own. Their discussions were always influenced by the context in which they took place, both the local situation faced by the school board and the national debate over sexual issues. But the messages they exchanged and the meanings that they attributed to those messages could only be understood within the communicative process that they created.[2] In short, people with varying degrees of communicative skills acted together through the use of verbal and nonverbal cues to create, sustain, and modify systems of meaning. That is, they communicated.

Our definition of organizational communication differs from this definition of communication primarily in terms of the complexity of the context and people dimensions. Organizational relationships are both like and unlike "normal" interpersonal relationships. We communicate with people at work because we like them and because our tasks require us to do so. Thus, our relationships at work have both an interpersonal and an organizational dimension. As later chapters will explain, we constantly have to negotiate an appropriate mix of these two dimensions. We may have a strong personal relationship with our supervisor, but have to maintain the kind of relational distance, detachment, and subservience that is appropriate to our organizational relationship. We may like one of our subordinates very much, but his or her inability to do the job well creates constant stresses in our interpersonal relationship. Consequently, the process of creating shared meanings is more complicated in organizational relationships than in those that occur naturally.

Defining *Strategic* Organizational Communication

The concept of strategy enters into our perspective on organizational communication at two levels. One level is that of the organization. Most people have learned to think of organizations as places where large numbers of members efficiently cooperate with one another to achieve some shared objectives. But organizations also are sites in which multiple tensions exist—tensions that must be managed successfully if the organization is to succeed in meeting its member's goals. Some tensions are specific to individual organizations; others are characteristic of the relationship between organizations and the surrounding society. But all organizations face at least one fundamental tension: a tension between individual members' needs and the needs of their organizations. People have needs for autonomy (the feeling that they are in control of their actions and destinies), creativity (feelings of pride that comes from making something that did not previously exist or in doing something better than or in a different way than anyone else), and sociability (the feeling that they have meaningful interpersonal relationships with other people). They also need an adequate degree of structure, stability, and predictability in their lives. They need to know who they are, where they fit in their organizations and society, and how they and their peers are likely to act in different circumstances.

Organizations also have needs that must be met. The most important of these are control and coordination. Organizations exist because the tasks that people must perform are sufficiently complex that members must cooperate with one another to achieve their goals. In essence, organizations require us to sacrifice some of our independence—our ability to be self-sufficient—and replace it with interdependence. In modern societies, few persons have the skills, experience, or opportunities to do everything personally that is necessary to live a productive life. Most modern people actually can do very little. We are constantly at the mercy of electricians, plumbers, appliance-repair technicians, auto mechanics, and organizations in which we work. What people can do, we do very well. Modern human beings have traded independence for **specializa-**

tion and have become far more efficient as a result. But our efficiency depends almost wholly on coordinating our activities with the activities of others. Different cultures vary in the degree of interdependence that exists within them, as do different organizations and the various departments within them. Research-and-development divisions usually have low interdependence, relying only on computer operators, purchasing and receiving departments (which order and deliver raw materials), and the physical plant operators (who keep equipment secure and functioning). For them, coordination within the division is crucial; coordinating their activities with outsiders is less important. For other divisions, coordination is a more complex and critical problem. But to some degree, all organizations need coordination.

Organizations also need to control their members' interpersonal relationships, both in terms of who they form relationships with and how they communicate within their work relationships. Some version of the military command that officers cannot fraternize with enlisted personnel exists within almost all organizations. For example, Intel Corporation forbids dating between supervisors and their subordinates and enforces the rule by transferring offenders to different departments, but does not restrict relationships among peers. Often the command is never spoken because it need not be. Associates (recent graduates) in law firms learn by observation that they should not initiate conversations with senior partners, but should respond immediately when partners initiate communication with them. Assembly workers at Dana Corporation learn that they are expected to have lunch with upper management, and individuals in upper management learns that they are expected to have friendly but relatively superficial interpersonal relationships with rank-and-file workers. In both cases, the organization subtly controls the kind of interpersonal relationships that employees form and maintain. Organizations do vary in how tightly they control their members' actions and relationships, but all organizations must exercise some level of control if they are to survive.

However, these two sets of needs—those of a society/organization and those of their individual members—create a fundamental dilemma. If a society or organization successfully controls its members, the individual needs for autonomy, creativity, and sociability are frustrated. But, if the society/organization fails to control its members, it loses the ability to coordinate its members' activities, and fails. So, societies/organizations must find ways to meet their members' individual needs while persuading them to act in ways that meet the society/organization's needs. They do so through adopting various *strategies of organizing*. In Unit I of this book, we will discuss the major organizational strategies that are employed in modern organizations. Each strategy has a different design and structure, a different system of employee motivation and control, and different communication systems. Of course, no organization corresponds perfectly to any organizational strategy. No strategy works exactly like it is supposed to work; and all organizations have a mixture of strategies in place. But, thinking about real organizations in terms of the available strategies of organizing can help members make sense out of their particular organizations.

Organizational Life as Strategic Communication

The second sense in which organizational communication is strategic involves the actions of individual employees. For more than 2000 years, communication scholars have believed that people communicate most effectively if they adapt their communication strategies to the situations they face.[3] To communicate effectively, employees must be able to analyze the situations they encounter in their organizations, determine which communication strategies are available to them in those situations, select the best of those strategies, and enact them effectively. However, selecting appropriate communicative strategies is a complex process. Strategies of organizing create particular kinds of organizational situations. All organizational situations contain *guidelines* that tell employees how they are supposed to act and communicate and *constraints* that tell them how they are not to act and communicate. Fortunately, organizational situations also provide *resources* for acting—potential lines of argument, acceptable forms of persuasive appeal, and so on—that allow employees to pursue their goals strategically. The relative importance of guidelines/constraints and resources differs in different situations. In most organizational situations, employees have the resources available that they will need to meet at least some of their goals and at least some of their organization's objectives simultaneously. In these cases, choosing productive communication strategies is not particularly difficult.

In other situations, however, choosing appropriate communication strategies is more difficult, perhaps impossible. Organizational situations sometimes paralyze employees, at least momentarily. One kind of paralysis occurs when the guidelines and constraints in a situation are clear, but the resources available to meet them are unclear, unknown, or insufficient. For example, organizational situations may include commands for psychotherapists to "do good work," hospital administrators to "cut costs," or elementary schoolteachers to "stimulate all the students' interests." These "guidelines" may tell employees what they are supposed to do, but they tell them little about how they are supposed to do those things. As a result, employees may become paralyzed while they make sense out of their situations and discover the resources that are available to them. For example, a newly graduated student who had become a stockbroker once called and asked "What do I do next?" after being given a desk and a "training session" that included only the comment "I hope you'll like it here. Just don't screw up like George (your predecessor) did." This kind of paralyzing situation seems to be common for new employees and has been shown to be a major source of organizational stress.

A more extreme form of paralysis occurs when action is called for, but constraints leave the employee with no available resources. Presumably, Linus' purpose (in Figure 1–1) is to gain the childlike fun that comes from a friendly snowball fight. But Lucy's comments leave him with both a command to act (since dropping the snowball is an act) and no productive way to achieve his purpose. Throwing the snowball will fail, so will not throwing it. Lucy has taken the fun out of snowball fights and has robbed Linus of any opportunity for meaningful choice.

FIGURE 1–1

PEANUTS reprinted by permission of United Feature Syndicate, Inc.

Organizational situations sometimes parallel the Peanuts situation. Supervisors may find that they have only one position to allocate and two departments that desperately need help, have equally strong claims on the position, and will be justifiably angry if they do not receive it. Subordinates may be told to do one thing by one superior and the opposite by another. They may know that one supervisor has a higher rank than the other and that in their organization they are always expected to follow the orders given by the higher-ranking person. But they may also know that the lower-ranking supervisor might retaliate against them, in ways that will never be detected by anyone else, for violating his or her order. In this kind of situation, the subordinate has no realistic options because no adequate resources are available. Between the two extremes of simple situations and paralyzing ones are the situations that employees normally face at work: situations that provide a range of options that can serve both the employees' purposes and those of their organizations, and situations in which employees can act and communicate strategically.

Finally, and perhaps ironically, employees' strategic choices create, reproduce, and in some cases, change the guidelines/constraints and resources that they face. For example, bureaucratic strategies of organizing continue to exist only because employees act like bureaucrats. The organizational strategy of making decisions by applying established, written policies and regulations (a key element of the bureaucratic strategy) exists only because members of those organizations actually make decisions based on established policies and regulations and have come to believe that decisions should be made in this way. In doing so, they choose to follow a rule that limits their actions to those prescribed by the organizational situation. And, in doing so, they use that rule as a resource for managing demanding people. But, in the process they reproduce and legitimize the guidelines and constraints that they face.[4]

DIMENSIONS OF ORGANIZATIONAL COMMUNICATION

All human communication is complex and multidimensional. Organizational communication has its own distinctive set of complications. It is like naturally occurring interpersonal communication, but it also is different. Understanding the unique dimensions of organizational communication helps people understand how communication functions in organizational life.

Organizational Communication as *Structured* Discourse

All organizations are structured. Indeed, it is structure that distinguishes organized enterprises from disorganized ones. Structure is important to members of organizations. It makes life predictable. It clarifies each member's areas of responsibility; it makes formal authority relationships clear to everyone involved in the organization; and it lets everyone know where different kinds of organizational knowledge are located. It makes life predictable, and with predictability come feelings of stability and trust.[5]

helps do these things

When most readers see the word "organization" the image that usually comes to mind is a specific kind of structure—the triangle-shaped organizational chart. It shows all the different tasks performed in the organization, and the responsibilities of each of the positions that make up the organization—people located in the marketing department devise strategies for selling the goods or services produced in the organization; people in the research and development division design new products or services, and so on. The labor that must be performed in the organization is *divided* among various groups of employees who have the *specialized* skills necessary to complete their assigned tasks efficiently and effectively. The organizational chart also shows how the various positions are arranged, so that lines of authority are clear to all. Usually this arrangement is *hierarchical*; supervisors are directly responsible to their own immediate supervisors for their own actions and for those of their immediate subordinates. It also implies that decision making and control are **centralized.** This means that all the major decisions facing the organization are made by the people who occupy the positions located at the top of the organizational hierarchy. Of course, all members of the organization are responsible for making *routine* decisions in their areas of responsibility. But, they must base their decisions on *policies* and *procedures* that are established at the top.

The organizational chart also suggests that communication will function in a specific way. The most important characteristic involves following the

chain of command. Employees are expected to communicate directly only with people located immediately above or immediately below them in the hierarchy. Lower-level employees simply do not communicate directly with their supervisors' supervisors, or employees located in other divisions of the organization. Instead, they take concerns to their supervisors, who take them to their supervisors, who take them to the supervisors of the other divisions involved, and so on. When communication does take place outside of the immediate work group, it is formal, both in tone and in terms of the way in which it is communicated.

Because this particular organizational structure is so widespread, it is easy to forget a number of basic facts about it. The most important fact is that structure is a choice. There are a large number, perhaps an infinite number, of ways in which an organization can be structured. The kind of structure that we have just described—a *hierarchical* organization in which tasks are highly *differentiated* and *specialized,* decision making is *centralized* at the top of the organization, and communication and interpersonal relationships are highly *formalized*—is characteristic of Western (European and North American) organizations. It is a **bureaucracy,** which, as sociologist Max Weber noted a century ago, is appropriate to Protestant, capitalistic, democratic societies. To people raised in those societies, bureaucratic structures do *seem* to be *natural, (*that is, inevitable) and *normal (*which means morally acceptable, among other things). As members of these societies mature, they learn that formal rules are necessary for the efficient operation of societies and organizations because they protect people from arbitrary or harmful treatment by more powerful people. They are taught that societies "of law" are better than societies of "men [sic]." They come to value individuality, to believe that individuals have rights, and that individuals are responsible for their actions. They learn to accept what Weber called *legal authority,* the notion that societies and organizations should be organized around a formal, objective (and thus impersonal), written set of rules, policies, and procedures. They come to value themselves in terms of the formal roles that they play in their societies and organizations and to accept the notion that with different roles come different rights and obligations. So, for people who have learned these lessons well, bureaucratic structures seem to be natural and normal. But, these perceptions mask the fact that the bureaucratic structure is only one of a large number of options and obscure the fact that they have distinctive strengths and particular weaknesses.

The second fact about organizational structure is that it simultaneously is *influenced by and influences* communication. For example, people located near the top of an organizational hierarchy tend to communicate more often, more openly, and more directly than people located lower in the hierarchy. As a result, they better understand the positive effect that communication has on organizational performance, tend to see organizational life as less political, and rely more on their peers than their supervisors for advice. Organizations that are highly differentiated experience more frequent communication breakdowns and conflicts than less differentiated organizations; highly centralized and/or highly formalized organizations have less communication, less flexibility, less effective communication, and less face-to-face communication than those that are less centralized.[6] In short, organizational structure influences communication in many ways. (Chapter 2 explains these ideas in more detail).

Communication also influences organizational structure. *Communication structures* always develop in organizations because people do not act or communicate at random. Task requirements lead them to seek out or share information with some people and not others. They form friendships with some of their colleagues, but not all of them. As a result, their communication is patterned—they talk with the same people about certain topics and communicate with other people about other topics. And, they may talk with a small number of people about everything (these relationships are called "multiplex" relationships). Sometimes the communication structure that emerges may actually look like the organization's formal structure—the organizational chart. People do actually communicate along the chain of command; people do actually take responsibility for their assigned tasks and refuse to do others' jobs; employees do actually accept their supervisors' authority over them (see Chapter 8 for more detail). In these cases the organizational chart actually represents the communication structure of the organization—the map really does represent the territory. But in other cases, the actual communication structure may be very different. People may develop close, effective communication relationships with their immediate supervisors, co-workers, and members of other divisions in the same strata of an organization, but have no contact with people farther up or down the chain of command. What matters are the communication patterns they develop and how those patterns fit together, not what is prescribed in the organizational chart.[7] In time, the formal chart may change to approximate the actual communication structure more closely. In the interim, the two may be very different. This does not mean that there is no structure; it just means that the structure is different than the organizational chart suggests. However, in all cases, it is the way that people communicate that creates and reproduces the structure. In the process, structure provides members of the organization with the stability and predictability they desire. (Chapter 5 develops these ideas in more depth).

Organizational Communication as Interpersonal Discourse

In the modern world, people can accomplish relatively little acting alone. In fact, the reason formal organizations developed after the agricultural revolution was because the everyday tasks that societies needed to perform could not be accomplished efficiently by individuals or family groups acting on their own. Organizations are made of people involved in complex webs of relationships with one another. In some ways, these working relationships are like the other interpersonal relationships that all people form throughout their lives. But in other ways they are different.[8]

Natural relationships seem to be voluntary—we encounter people, find some reasons to be attracted to one another and begin to develop a relationship with them. We learn about them, develop expectations about how they will act, and begin to trust them when those expectations are fulfilled. If they violate our expectations, we interpret their behavior as a negative comment on them—they're either crazy or evil—or as a negative comment on our relationship, in which case we consider whether we should retaliate for the slight, end the relationship, let it develop more slowly and carefully, and do more to protect ourselves while we are in it. If the relationship continues, we develop psychological contracts about how we will act and communicate toward one another, and we make sure that those contracts are understood by both parties. The nature of our relationships is influenced by our relational histories and our anticipated future, and by our expectation that our relationships should be mutually fulfilling.

Being members of the same organization complicates the relational development process in many ways. Some organizational relationships are imposed on us; to do our jobs, we must cooperate with other members of the organization. We may find some of those people unattractive, and, if given the choice, we would never form friendships with them.[9] But, organizations are made of interdependent roles, and if we are to play our organizational roles successfully, we must develop at least minimally productive working relationships with the people who play those roles on which we depend. It also is difficult to form and maintain relationships with people who have different levels of organizational power and status. As Chapter 7 will explain in more detail, these differences complicate the reciprocity that serves as the basis of natural relationships; buying lunch for someone in the next cubicle simply does not mean the same thing as buying lunch for the vice-president of sales. We communicate differently with people of different power/status, and we expect to be treated differently by them. Friends usually provide comfort and support to one another. But supervisors are required to evaluate their subordinates' work (and in some organizations, subordinates also evaluate their supervisors), and those evaluations may involve uncomfortable assessments of one another's competence, performance, and personality. Working relationships are also complicated by a "fishbowl" effect; they are public in a way that natural relationships are not. People at work know about friendships and observe them at close range. If the friends try to add a degree of privacy to the relationship, by gossiping with one another about nonwork topics, excluding coworkers from lunch or other social events, or engaging in a private communication style (whispering to one another, telling inside jokes, or communicating nonverbally with signals that others do not understand), they make their coworkers feel awkward or angry because they are being excluded.

The work situation also complicates normal aspects of relationships. All friends have to balance autonomy and connectedness. If friends work together, they may be forced to spend *too much* time together or to work too closely. They may expect special support or treatment from one another, leading to perceptions among coworkers that they are playing favorites if they provide it, or violated expectations and hurt feelings if they do not. Friends also tend to be more open and honest with one another because of their higher levels of trust. But, organizational roles often require people to keep information secret, even from their closest friends. Some of today's organizational practices add more complications. Employees of organizations that use "project teams," in which groups of people are assigned to work together on a specific project but assigned to other teams once the project is complete, develop different expectations about the future of their relationships than those who work with the same people on multiple projects. Organizations that use large numbers of short-term or part-time workers create divisions among employees that complicate relational development. For a number of reasons, the **"blended relationships"** that people form at work simply are more complicated than natural relationships.

However, being part of an organization can also provide relational advantages. Work roles and task requirements may lead people to form meaningful relationships that they otherwise would not have formed. Employees meet people they otherwise would not have met; they discover similarities in interests, backgrounds, or abilities that they otherwise would have overlooked, and have opportunities to develop loyalty and emotional support that they otherwise would not have had. Consequently, it is not surprising that the quality of work relationships, both with supervisors and with coworkers, is a strong predictor of overall job satisfaction. (Job satisfaction will be developed in more detail in Chapter 3.) Friends communicate more efficiently with one another and experience fewer misunderstandings and communication breakdowns. People who trust one another are more willing to discuss new ideas and to test out the ideas they have, which can benefit their careers and their organizations.

However there are also complications. These are easiest to see in romantic relationships at work. Although most experts on office etiquette flatly advise that if you care about your career, you should keep romance out of it, about 40 percent of workers admit to dating a colleague. With 50–60 hour workweeks, people simply do not have the time or opportunity to look elsewhere for romantic partners. Perhaps more importantly, people can gather accurate information about a potential mate by working with him or her—much more than they can learn at a singles' bar or in a classified ad. A few organizations (about 15 percent in 1999) had written policies forbidding dating between supervisors and their subordinates, and more than 70 percent of employees said that people should never date their bosses or people who report to them. In spite of these policies and attitudes, most office romances involve supervisors and their subordinates (about 70 percent), often married, male supervisors and single, female subordinates. Most seem to be based on "true love" rather than on job- or advancement-related motives (about 80 percent). In general, research indicates that romances do not harm organizational performance, unless they generate such a high level of gossip that interferes with task performance. In fact, romances may increase the performance of the couple because it makes them more approachable and may encourage them to perform at their best because they know they are being watched closely by their coworkers. But, obviously, perceptions of favoritism are more likely for employees involved in a romantic relationship with their supervisors. Gossip and discomfort among coworkers are extremely likely. If the relationship is terminated, it is difficult to see one's ex every day.[10]

Organizations are made of people. They provide their members with the "stuff" of interpersonal relationships—opportunities to meet and interact, intense emotions, and shared experiences. But, they also guide, constrain, and complicate those relationships.

HOW TO HANDLE THE SCARLET EMAIL?

There are a number of common-sense steps that people can take to manage the complications created by office romances. First, all employees should learn their organization's view of workplace relationships. Seventy percent of organizations have no official policies, so it is sometimes difficult to obtain this information. But, once a relationship becomes serious, a frank conversation with one's supervisors is warranted. Second, decide when and how to go public. Advisors differ on this issue. Some say that it's best to come clean about the relationship as soon as it gets serious. Others say that keeping it private is the best strategy. Your goal should be to minimize hearsay and innuendo, and especially to make sure your relationship doesn't interfere with your work. In some situations, those goals can best be achieved by keeping quiet; in others the honest approach is less disruptive. Third, have an exit plan. Discuss what the two of you will do if the relationship ends. Then do it. Finally, be discreet. Maintain a professional relationship at work. Richard Phillips, a career counselor in Palo Alto, California reminds employees that "what you consider to be lovely-dovey between the two of you may make your co-workers retch. You're forcing them into a situation they don't want to be in." Don't hold hands in the hallway, play footsie at meetings, or anything else that is perfectly appropriate in romantic relationships but completely inappropriate in professional relationships. And make sure your partner knows that your "aloof" behavior at work is not an indication that you're cold and uncaring toward him or her.

Washington Post columnist Marc Fisher once wrote a column that vividly described how awkward office romances can be to coworkers. One of his coworkers accidentally sent him an email that was meant for her romantic partner, probably by clicking the wrong line of her address directory. The message started out in a friendly tone, but very quickly became erotic. To make things worse, Marc knew the woman and her husband (who was **not** the recipient of the message); in fact he had been invited to their home for dinner. What should he do? Respond in a businesslike tone: "your message of 9:46 on Sunday morning was misdirected to me. Cheers." Notify the husband of what was going on? Keep quiet? Find some excuse for canceling the dinner date? He asked his friends for help. Most of the women told him to stay out of it; most of the men wanted him to find out all the sordid details and then let them in on it. He decided to do nothing.

Then, another message arrived, one that was more intimate than the first. He went to dinner, sat between husband and wife, and felt very nervous throughout the evening. He squirmed during a private after-dinner conversation when the

(continued)

(continued from the previous page)

husband told him about his dreams for their future years together. He went home rattled and vowed to not have anything more to do with either of them. Then he went to a stationery store and bought note cards and envelopes—the appropriate media for private messages.[†]

Applying What You've Learned

1. In what ways did the characters in Fisher's account violate the advice typically given to romantic partners in organizations? In what ways did they follow it?
2. Would a formal organizational policy about office romances have prevented this problem? What effects did the romance seem to have on the functioning of the organization?

Questions to Think About and Discuss

1. What would you have done had you been in Marc Fisher's place? What should you have done had you been in his place?
2. What does your answer to question 1 reveal about your personal values? About your view of the extent to which you have different values for working relationships at work than for non-work relationships?

---

[*]Sherri Eng, "Love In the Office Can Be Risky Affair," *Houston Chronicle*, March 14, 1999, C1.
[†]Marc Fisher, "What's the Proper Etiquette for a Scarlet E-mail," *Houston Chronicle*, June 1, 1999, C1.

Organizational Communication as *Contextualized* Discourse

Organizational communication is multidimensional. It is structured and creates structure, and it is relational. It also is contextual. Organizations do not exist in a vacuum. A century ago sociologist Max Weber observed that when people enter organizations, they bring with them a long history of living within their society, and of learning how members of their societies make sense out of events and respond to the situations they encounter. Conversely, experience in a society's organizations reinforces the overall values of the overall society.[11] Of course, every member of a given society has had unique experiences, has been involved in relationships with different people who have influenced their development in different directions, and has interpreted these experiences through her or his own unique personality. People with similar backgrounds and experience bring similar expectations to their organizations; people with diverse backgrounds may share some expectations, but differ in others. But no one enters an organization *tabula rasa*—everyone brings a particular world view.

Communication and Societal/Organizational Beliefs and Values   As people mature, they participate in many conversations—with parents, friends, teachers, and others—about what they should expect from life and from their careers and organizations. Those expectations guide the ways in which people communicate at work and the ways in which they make sense out of the information they obtain. Some people have repeatedly heard business described as being like the military—a clear chain of command with strict regulation of thought and behavior and a premium placed on following orders without question. These people have different expectations about organizational life than those who have learned to think of organizations as being like families, in which there is a high concern for one another and a commitment to group rather than to individual achievement, and so on.[12] Other conversations involve the act of working. People who have learned that work is boring, unending toil with few rewards other than a paycheck expect different work experiences than those who have learned that work is and should be one's primary route to self-fulfillment.

Other conversations involve people and their relationships to one another. For example, intercultural communication scholars note that the taken-for-granted assumptions of various societies differ from one another along a relatively small number of values. One of the most important differences involves the extent to which members of the society value "collectivism" or "individualism." Asian, Latin, Middle-Eastern, and African cultures tend to be collectivist, which means that people in those societies learn to place a high value on solidarity, cooperation, and concern for others. Their communication tends to be guided and constrained by concerns about hurting the other person's feelings, minimizing impositions placed on the other person, and avoiding negative evaluations of the other person. In contrast, Western European and North American societies tend to be individualistic, and people learn to value competition and independence from other people or groups. They learn to value communication that is clear, efficient, and effective and adapt their own communication to correspond to those guidelines/constraints.[13] It is not surprising that organizations in collectivist societies (and organizations located in individualist societies but dominated by people from collectivist societies) tend to operate according to collectivist principles; while organizations in individualistic societies operate in accord with the core values of those societies.[14] This does not mean that everyone from a particular society has the same core beliefs and values; gender, age, economic background, educational level, and individual experiences all influence the way in which people interpret and incorporate the messages that they receive into their own views of the world and ways of communicating. But, the complete package of beliefs and values that people bring with them into their organizations exert a powerful influence on their communication and are difficult to change.

The society from which an organization draws its members provides a context—a complex web of taken-for-granted assumptions, meanings, expectations, and sense-making processes—through which people make sense out of their experiences at work. This context guides and constrains their actions at work and in turn guides and constrains the kinds of organizational strategies they will enact.

As a result, members of organizations must find ways to manage what often are complex webs of differences in beliefs, values, and modes of communicating.

Communication and Societal/Organizational Tensions   Core beliefs and values make up only one dimension of the context surrounding organizations. Just as societies shape dominant values and beliefs, they also are composed of tensions and contradictions within and among those beliefs. For example, although Anglo-U.S. society is highly individualist, a number of social scientists have long observed that even there, a fundamental tension exists between individuality and community. Alexis de Tocqueville toured the United States soon after it became a nation. He observed that Anglo-U.S. people were so committed to the idea of individual achievement and individual responsibility for their success or failure that they had little basis for recognizing their common needs and interests and for developing a sense of community. Almost 200 years later, sociologist Robert Bellah and his associates interviewed hundreds of people from all walks of life. They found that European-Americans' obsession with individualism and their isolation from one another had expanded and deepened since the end of World War II. Warren Bennis and his associates noted that this same tension characterizes many societies, including those that are predominantly communitarian.[15]

Of course, tensions between and within a society's core values can be managed. Sometimes they are organizationally managed. For example, de Tocqueville concluded that the United States remained cohesive because so many people were involved in informal nonwork organizations that provided a sense of community—churches, lodges, and so on. These organizations compensated for the extreme individuality that European Americans face in their work organizations. Historically U.S. firms seem to have adjusted their strategies of organizing to compensate for this tension, oscillating between a highly individualistic strategy that focuses on unemotional, rational decision making and individual rewards for performance (see Chapter 2) and communitarian strategies that focus on relational ties and shared beliefs and values (see Chapters 3 and 4).[16] Societal/organizational tensions are also managed communicatively. All societies have characteristic myths, expressions of the core beliefs and values of the society that are rarely even questioned, much less tested, by their members. Myths may or may not be true in an empirical sense, but they are treated as if they are true by members of a society. Articulated in stories and rituals, societal myths both express the core values and beliefs of a society and manage its core tensions. (Chapter 4 discusses this concept in depth). For example, two of the most important myths in Euro-U.S. society are the Horatio Alger myth and the myth of the United States as a melting pot. The former myth is named after the writer of a series of short books published during the late nineteenth century. In them, the key character, always someone from a highly disadvantaged background, faced a series of challenges; but, thanks to personal grit, talent, and determination, and the unbounded opportunity provided by the U.S. economy, the character eventually overcame the challenges to become an economic and social success. Unlike Europe, the stories go, the United States is a classless society in which the only limit to success is an individual competence. Modern versions of the story, with a high-tech twist, are Apple Computer's Steve Jobs, Microsoft CEO Bill Gates, and Dell Computer's

Michael Dell. The melting pot myth suggests that all people—regardless of their race, gender, or ethnicity—can become Horatio Alger figures if they only embrace the distinctively Anglo-U.S. values of hard work, determination, and loyalty. When combined, the two myths manage the tension between individuality and community by telling us that the United States is an economic and social *community* unified by *individual* opportunity. [17]

Societal myths are important because they function as a powerful form of control. Social theorists have labeled this kind of control **hegemony,** a concept that is quite complex. It begins with the observation that societies are hierarchical in many ways, the most important of which are race, ethnicity, gender, and class. As we learn our society's assumptions, we come to accept its hierarchies uncritically, to see them as normal and natural. Societal assumptions often lead to some very concrete differences in the ways in which people are treated by a society and its organizations. For example, in the United States women have long been and still are paid substantially less than men for the same or comparable work. This situation exists partly because women tend to be concentrated in sectors of the economy that have relatively low salary rates (for example, teaching or nursing). Over time, as the proportion of women in these occupations increased, the level of prestige afforded the occupations, and the wage rates paid to the people in then fell steadily until the occupation was approximately 50 percent women. When the proportion exceeds 50 percent, wages plummet. There are two possible explanations for this phenomenon: First is an explanation based on societal myths, in this case the myth that women's work is worth less than men's work. The second myth is an economic explanation that says that when the number of applicants for a particular type of job increases, the heightened competition forces wages down. The cultural explanation has been shown to be more valid. Women are paid less than men in comparable jobs because their work is perceived to be less valuable, and our society has taught us that women's work is less valuable because they are paid less. The taken-for-granted assumptions of our society/organizations lead us to believe that hierarchical relationships are normal and natural. In turn, we act and think in ways that support those assumptions. [18]

Similarly, supervisors tend not to offer married women managers promotions that require relocation because they *assume* that wives will not ask their husbands and families to endure the stresses of moving, even when accepting transfers is necessary for promotion. Eventually these supervisors, their supervisors, and their employees notice that women managers do not move very often and in turn assume that this is because women managers value their families more than their careers (when it is more closely related to the lower number of offers they receive). There is little objective evidence to support any of these assumptions. Today women managers do not turn down promotions that involve relocating any more often than men do. [19] But, as long as managers *assume* that their beliefs are accurate, they will act on those assumptions.

In other cases, it is a combination of societal myths that is important. For example, the dominant ideology among Anglo-U.S. people is still that white men are more rational than women (and that women and African Americans and Latinos[20] are more emotional than Anglo or Anglo-U.S. men). These assumptions alone have little relevance to organizations. But a second societal myth is that organizations are (and should be) rational enterprises, especially at managerial levels (in spite of substantial evidence to the contrary, as summarized in Chapter 9). This assumption, in itself, has little relevance for race, gender, or ethnicity; but, when the two assumptions are combined, they generate a further assumption that Anglo men are inherently better managers than white women, African Americans, or Latinos. Whether they are direct or indirect, the dominant assumptions of a culture establish hierarchical relationships, and as long as the members of a culture believe that the hierarchies are normal and natural, they tend to act in ways that perpetuate those hierarchies.

Of course, no set of assumptions is accepted by all of a society's members all the time. Some people will constantly question some of the assumptions, and during times of social change large numbers of people may question many of the taken-for-granted assumptions of a society. But taken-for-granted assumptions are amazingly stable because we are constantly exposed to messages that support them, interpret ambiguous information so that it confirms them, and tend to ignore or rationalize information that disconfirms them. By doing so, by learning and accepting the assumptions of our society and organizations, we become qualified to participate in them. We learn how we should think and act. But at the same time, we subject ourselves to them; we accept limitations on how we think and act.[21] In summary, organizations exist within societal contexts. The communication strategies that their members choose are strongly related to the taken-for-granted assumptions of the societies from which they come. Those strategic choices in turn lead us to act in ways that make their taken-for-granted assumptions seem normal and natural, and accurate, and legitimate. Societal myths provide people with stable and predictable lives, both inside and outside of their organizations. This concept often is difficult to understand because doing so forces us to quit taking for granted the taken-for-granted assumptions of our society. It asks us to treat our most basic beliefs about what is natural and normal as societal choices, not as absolute truths. Normally we do not think about such things, and as a result, the assumptions provide powerful guidelines and constraints on our actions and the actions of our organizations.

CASE STUDY:
CAN YOU TRUST ANYONE UNDER THIRTY?

When managers, professors, and reporters think about workforce diversity, they usually think in terms of race, gender, ethnicity, or nationality. But, in modern organizations one of the most important differences involves age, and the experiences that accompany being part of a particular generation. The most common contrast is between the baby boomers, who were born between 1946 and 1964, and Generation X, born between 1969 and 1979. Boomers were raised in the post-WWII era of social stability and relative prosperity. Divorce was relatively rare; schools were safe, and jobs secure. Single-earner households with a clear division of labor

(continued)

(continued from the previous page)

between men and women were normal, for perhaps the only time in U.S. history. Their parents/role models were the "organization men" described in William Whyte's 1956 book by the same name. They were loyal and committed to their organizations, learned to pay their dues patiently and wait for the opportunity for advancement, and largely defined themselves and their success in terms of their organizational rank. It was an era during which white-collar workers in U.S. organizations believed and acted as if they had an unspoken contract with their organizations. If they worked hard, were loyal and productive employees, and followed the rules of their organizations, they expected to stay with their organizations as long as they chose to do so, to be rewarded for their contributions, and eventually, to be supported during their golden years by an adequate pension.*

In contrast, Xers, who now make up about one third of the U.S. workforce, grew up in two-career families, where divorce rates were increasing rapidly. They are the products of technology, including television, daycare, and perhaps most important, downsizing. From 1985 until 1995, the Xers' formative years, two-thirds of white-collar employees experienced downsizing or major restructuring. The fastest growing sector of the labor market between 1990 and 1995 was the category of temp/employment agencies. (The next fastest growing categories were restaurants and bars, local government, recreation, and hospitals.) Richard Florida, a Carnegie Mellon University professor who studies employee retention, observes that "my students expect corporate disloyalty. A 24- or 25-year old says 'I am responsible for my own life. No one's going to take care of me, because they threw my dad out of work.'"† Adding to the fear and insecurities that Xers' parents felt was a growing resentment that stems from the disparity between sky-rocketing firm profits and upper-management incomes and the experiences of both white-collar and blue-collar workers. Average worker pay rose 28 percent between 1990 and 1998, only 5.5 percent faster than the inflation rate. But average compensation of the top two managers in large companies rose 481 percent over the same time period. Consequently, the ratio of the base salaries of CEOs of U.S. firms to their average employee's salary in 1992 was 140:1 compared to 15:1 in Germany, 13:1 in Japan, and 40:1 in the United States twenty years earlier. In 1995 the ratio in the United States rose to 187:1 overall and 212:1 at the 30 largest U.S. companies; in 1999 the ratio was approximately 350:1.†

As a result everywhere Xers are advised to "consider themselves to be free agents," keep their resumes polished and their network connections alert to opportunities in other firms. They must plan their own careers, and seek out opportunities to develop new, marketable skills and opportunities to grow. And they seem to be listening. Traditional values like long-term commitment and loyalty to the firm aren't very popular with them. They refuse to make the kinds of sacrifices that their parents made—being subservient to their bosses, accepting multiple cross-country moves, putting in long hours, or accepting overnight travel. They are fiercely independent, aggressive, hard-working entrepreneurs, even if they are working in corporate structures. They concentrate on developing

(continued)

(continued from the previous page)

computer, leadership, and communication skills, in part to make them valuable to their current firms, but also as a means of going out on their own as soon as possible. They move on quickly, changing jobs 9 times by the time they're in their thirties. They are willing to take the risks of self-employment or job changes to get the greater rewards and freedom that accompanies being their own bosses. But they also tend to form relatively superficial and inauthentic relationships in the workplace. Knowing that they may not be around very long, they make little investment in getting to know their supervisors and coworkers as people, and their supervisors and coworkers spend little energy getting to know them. This makes it easier to exit the organization—they can do so without leaving close friends or commitments behind—and makes it more likely that they will do so. Ironically they need to be given clear road maps about organizational life, and want lots of performance feedback.

Some supervisors call them slackers—one J C Penny manager complained that "when I started out, I worked long hours. I did whatever they wanted me to do. They come in at 8 and leave at 5." The Xers are unrealistic about how long it will take them to be promoted—"if they don't get what they want, they'll leave—they're just not loyal." They question their supervisors' decisions and authority. They ask questions that are unheard of to the boomers, such as *if I don't like what my boss says, can I go to the next level,* and even do so during job interviews. Xers often view their Boomer bosses as burned out relics of a bygone era. They want rewards to be based on performance, not seniority. They want to know what those rewards will be, and know them in advance of taking on a task. They communicate in ways that Boomers find excessively blunt—a direct, bold, cut-to-the-chase style. Boomers like to think that the Xers are just in a passing phase, that in time they'll settle down into a traditional mold. But, Xers plan to retire long before they settle down. Some organizations are already encountering serious conflicts between the two groups. A U.S. Army report, scheduled to be released in early 2001, predicts that the service will find it difficult to fill leadership positions within a few years. In 1989 6.7 percent of the Army's captains left the service voluntarily. The figure rose to 10.6 percent in 1999 and is predicted to reach 13 percent in 2000. Why the increase? Tensions between Baby Boomer senior officers and Gen X junior officers. Leonard Wong, a retired lieutenant colonel who authored the report said, "Today's senior officers do not understand today's junior officers or their perspectives."[§]

Before that happens, the Xers also will have to deal with a new generation with different experiences, expectations, and demands. Tentatively labeled the "Y Generation" or "Millennials," they were born between 1980 and 1988. They have more disposable income and are more technologically sophisticated than any group of teenagers in U.S. history. As a result they are highly optimistic and see a world of opportunities in front of them. They are already trying to distance themselves from the Xers—softer music, different clothing. Like the Boomers, they are maturing in a time of sustained economic growth, have become accustomed to material possessions—cars, stereos, phones, computers, the right

(continued)

(continued from the previous page)

clothes—and believe in working hard in the short term for the promise of a big payoff in the long term. They have watched people make millions in the dot.com organizations and believe that they can do the same. They take risks, and like the Xers are highly individualistic. Some observers say they are cynical and disconnected from their communities and the political process. Others say that they do not trust institutions and really are socially active—more than any generation since the 1960s—and will bring their activist values to the workplace. But they do not trust existing political institutions to bring needed social changes. There are so many of them—the teen population is growing twice as fast as the rest of the U.S. population—that they will inevitably impose their tastes and values on the society as a whole. Within five years, they will enter the workforce, and will become the Xers' subordinates.-

Applying What You've Learned

1. What expectations do each of these generational groups have about life and about organizations?
2. What messages and experiences have contributed to those expectations?
3. Over what issues are the three groups likely to have conflicts? Why?

Questions to Think About and Discuss

1. To which, if any, of the three generational groups do you belong? How do your expectations and experiences correspond to theirs? Over what issues are you likely to have conflicts with members of the three groups? Why?
2. Are the strategies chosen by Generation Xers appropriate to the situations they face?
3. What effects are their strategies likely to have on their relationships with their supervisors in traditional firms? with their coworkers? with their subordinates? Why?

---

* Chip Walker and Elissa Moses, "The Age of Self-Navigation," *American Demographics* (September, 1996); Shelly Donald Coolidge, "Boomers, Gen-Xers Clash," www.abcnews.go.com/sections/business, September 1, 1999; Maggie Jackson, "Business bends to include Generation X Workforce," *Bryan/College Station Eagle*, E1, January 31, 1999. For analyses of these trends see Patrice Buzzanell, "The Promise and Practice of the New Career and Social Contract," in *Rethinking Organizational and Managerial Communication from Feminist Perspectives*, P. Buzzanell, ed. Newbury Park: Sage, 2000; David Neumark, ed., *On the Job: Is Long-term Employment a Thing of the Past?* (New York: Russell Sage Foundation, 2000).
† Stephanie Franken, "Corporations' Quest to Create a Happy Workplace," *Houston Chronicle*, 15 Oct., 2000, 3D.
‡ "Executive Pay Remains Tops," abcnews.go.com/sections/business, August 30, 1999; Joel Blau, *Illusions of Prosperity* (New York: Oxford University Press, 1999). These trends will be analyzed in more detail in Chapter 12.
§ "Top, Junior Officers Vie, Study Says," *Houston Chronicle*, 19 Nov., 2000, A11.
- Jim DeBrosse, "The Y's Have It," *Houston Chronicle*, February 17, 1998, D1; Gerald Celente, "The Millennial Generation," *Parade Magazine*, September 10, 2000, p. 19.

Organizational Communication as *Systemic* Discourse

A system is a network of interdependent components. Organizations are systems of individuals pursuing multiple goals by creating and interpreting messages within complex networks of interpersonal and task relationships. Organizational communication is *systemic* because it is simultaneously influenced by all the pressures that comprise an organizational system and is the key process through which those pressures, and the system, are maintained. Although these concepts will be explained at length in Chapter 5, a basic understanding of systems is important for understanding organizational communication. It is easiest to understand systems by thinking about their four key attributes: *wholeness, hierarchy, networks,* and *process.*

System Wholeness   Systems are made up of components, but they are much more than the sum of their parts. A cake is created from separate ingredients, but once baked (i.e., once the ingredients are joined to each other) the cake is an entity totally different from any of its ingredients. In the same way, an organizational system is more than the sum of its individual members and units or their particular relationships to one another. For example, most charitable fundraising agencies are composed of office staff, telephone and personal fundraisers, advertising and promotion staff, accountants and bookkeepers, managers, and a board of directors. Each individual member has particular skills, values, strengths, and weaknesses. Joined into units, such as the accounting department, individuals' skills and strengths can compensate for others' weaknesses, and together, they can achieve things they could not on their own. The units become wholes in their own right; they evolve their own goals and operating procedures, and they develop a set of values and culture of their own. Joined into an organization, the units, too, can achieve different outcomes and have different values than they could on their own. Accounting units keep the fundraisers honest. Advertising and promotion keeps the whole charity visible in the community, increasing revenues. But advertising and promotion would have no budget for their operations without the fundraisers (nor would the accountants be paid without those they monitor). In a very real sense, the charity functions as it does only because of its entire configuration of people and units. But the people and units would not be what they are without the whole. It is through their place in the charity that they realize their potential. This process, through which a dynamic interdependence of parts and whole creates a unique overall system, has been called emergence by systems researchers.

System Hierarchy   The concept of system hierarchy is the notion that every system is embedded in a group of larger systems (suprasystems) and that every system is made of a number of smaller, interdependent subsystems—in short, a system is more than the sum of its parts. For example, the loading crew of a freight company is a system made up of a number of subsystems (workers, their interpersonal relationships, and so on), which are made up of smaller subsystems (each worker's perceptual processes, tasks, information-processing activities, memories, expectations, family, church, and social ties, and so on). But the loading crew is only one part of the production suprasystem of the organization, which is only one part of the freight company (supra-suprasystem), which is part of the even larger trucking industry, and so on. At any given time, the actions of any of the many employees or subsystems of employees in the organization (the loading crew, for example) may be influenced by the actions of any of the other interrelated subsystems or suprasystems of people. Information is *input* into a system through one or more of its subsystems. As information moves through the system, it is interpreted, acted upon, and communicated to other members of the system. In systems-theory language, it becomes *output* that is interpreted, acted upon, and communicated to other systems and subsystems.

It is important to remember that organizational subsystems, systems, and suprasystems are made of people, not things. Each organizational member brings a complex set of beliefs, values, history, and expectations into the system. These beliefs, values, histories, and expectations have an important effect on how members interpret, respond to, and communicate the information they obtain. For example, if employees believe that dishonesty is the normal way of conducting interpersonal relationships in their organization, inevitable communication breakdowns (like those discussed in Chapter 2) are likely to be interpreted as dishonest manipulation. It matters little that the breakdowns may be the result of harmless organizational processes. Within the interpretive frameworks of employees of this organization, they will be interpreted as intentional manipulation. Conversely, in an organization whose employees value openness and honesty, the same breakdowns might be interpreted quite differently; employees will act differently on that information, and they will communicate it to others in very different ways.

Consequently, employees define the situation(s) they face at work in their own ways. Those definitions change as the employees perform new and different tasks, participate in interpersonal relationships that develop and grow, receive and interpret new information, and confirm or disconfirm interpretations. Their strategic choices are influenced by the entire matrix of pressures, goals, and concerns that they experience, all of which also are emerging and changing. As a result, individual employees may make decisions that are difficult for other employees to understand. From the position they occupy in their organizational system, their choices probably make perfect sense to them, but they may not make sense to someone in a different position.

System Networks   Every member of an organizational system is connected to other members of the system in one way or another.[22] Even *isolates,* people who have few network connections, communicate with people when they must interact to do their jobs. Usually people are members of multiple networks simultaneously. They are part of networks based on friendships (affective networks), part of other networks based on goal-achievement (power and influence networks), and part of *ad hoc* networks that are created to deal with an immediate crisis, challenge, or task. These networks overlap to some extent because some of our friends also have power in our organizations. So, our affective and power networks are connected.

Some networks involve people who are tightly connected with one another. In them, everyone knows how members of the network are supposed to think and act; people talk about how one another behaves and reward one another based on the extent to which they communicate and act in approved ways. People who are members of only tightly connected networks tend to resist change and fall prey to "groupthink" processes. Expertise tends to be limited and shared, that is, everyone knows everything that everyone else knows, but not much of anything else. Other networks are more diverse, more loosely connected, more contentious.

Within each network we have strong ties to some members and weaker ties to others. We talk more frequently with people with whom we have strong ties, and they provide us with emotional support and the resources needed to accomplish everyday tasks. They reinforce our beliefs, values, and ways of perceiving reality, and make it less likely that we will adopt new attitudes or actions. Those with whom we have weak ties are more likely to provide us with new ideas and expertise, and encourage us to take risks and break out of old patterns of behavior. They also tend to have more extensive connections with people who are outside of our own networks. For example, Mark Granovetter found that white-collar employees are more likely to hear about job opportunities through weak ties than through strong ones.[23]

Some relationships are **uniplex**, which means that the parties always talk about the same topic (for example, work or sports). Others are **multiplex** relationships in which the parties communicate about a wide variety of topics and play a number of different roles with one another (for example, boss, collaborator on a key project, tennis partner, and so on). Multiplex relationships tend to be long-term, emotionally intense, influential, trusting, and more predictable than uniplex relationships. Communication tends to be deep, involving a good deal of self-disclosure and rich, providing much emotional and cognitive detail. Multiplex relationships provide parties with social support and opportunities to vent frustrations, thus helping manage stress and make positive changes. They also may increase stress because it takes time and emotional energy to maintain intense relationships.

Networks can open organizations up to new ideas and new members. Or, they can close them down. Networks tend to be homogeneous. People are apt to invite people who are like themselves to join in their activities and not to issue invitations to people perceived as different. As a result, networks tend to be made of people of the same race, gender, ethnic and socioeconomic background, citizenship, residence (even in terms of the same suburban subdivision), and education (degree, major, and school), professions, and divisions of their organizations. It simply is easier to communicate with people who are similar. People who are alike provide one another with information that they all think is important, in a form that they all can easily understand, and they base their choices and actions on the same beliefs, values, and interpretive processes. When we are surrounded by similar people, our lives are more stable and predictable, and misunderstandings are less likely. When we encounter complex problems or situations that require quick decisions, these advantages are multiplied.

But, for organizations, this preference for forming network ties with similar people may cause problems. Similarity-based networks tend to be tightly connected and thus have all the related problems. In addition, such networks often create artificial advantages for some employees and artificial disadvantages for others. Since the members of elite networks in most modern U.S. organizations tend to be Anglo males, the network emergence process tends to close out women and members of minority groups. (This idea is developed at length in Chapter 11.) And, because homogeneous networks are made up of people who think alike and have similar experiences and expertise, these networks often result in lower quality decisions than more diverse groups would.[24]

Sometimes, networks may even interfere with an organization achieving its goals. Steve Corman and Robert McPhee have illustrated these concepts in a study of a local church. People who study religious organizations have long recognized that participating in church activities is interrelated with commitment to the organization; members who actively participate in the church's activities are highly committed to the church, and people who are highly committed to the church are actively involved in activities. But, Corman and McPhee found that the networks that emerged in the church also influence members' commitment and activity levels. Some church activities involve only an "elite" group of members. Sometimes this elite group was formally defined; for example, deacons (elders) met together without other people present. But sometimes the elite group resulted from the amount of effort required by the activity itself. Only certain people become Sunday School teachers because it requires so much time and effort; a very different group joins the church basketball team because it requires a different level (and kind) of effort. Eventually networks form around these activities among the elite participants. Although these networks help create commitment to the church and its activities by those who participate in them, they also make it difficult for people who are not part of the elites to become involved. Unless individuals participate in an activity, they are excluded from the network; unless they are part of the network, it is difficult to be involved in the activity. Of course, new people are sometimes able to enter into the network. Someone who is already a member invites them to join in the activity, where they meet highly committed members who encourage them to make the effort to be involved in demanding activities, and they become part of the network. But, people who do not receive these invitations find it difficult to enter into the core activities; they do not become part of influential networks and are unlikely to develop the level of commitment needed to participate in even more demanding activities. Eventually they give up and the churches lose many potentially valuable members.[25]

Systems in Process   The first three aspects of the systemic nature of organizational communication involve the concepts of wholeness, hierarchy, and networks. The final key concept is that of system process—the ways in which communication systems adapt, change, or remain the same. Three types of processes can be distinguished: self-regulation, adaptation, and self-renewal.

Self-regulation refers to the process by which systems remain stable (survival goals) or achieve certain objectives (purposive goals). Survival is the basic, lowest-order goal of all systems. Survival involves maintaining the system's integrity and, in some cases, reproducing the system. To survive, a fast food restaurant chain must keep customers coming in so that it can generate the revenues it needs. But in today's competitive environment, it is also important for chain restaurants to be located in as many cities and towns as possible because this wins customers who will patronize other outlets for the chain when they travel or move. So fast food restaurants not only want to ensure patronage, but they also want to "reproduce" themselves by setting up franchises far and wide. Systems also have purposive goals, that is goals or standards set up to go beyond survival. For example, a fast food chain might set two goals: 10 percent profit per annum and 15 percent growth in number of franchises per year. Goals help the chain act purposively and, if attained, ensure its growth and continued existence in the future.

The second major systemic process is *adaptation.* To thrive, and sometimes to survive, organizations must adapt to their environments. If the environment changes, or if they move into a new environment, the organization must change as well. During the early 1990s fast food chains adapted to the healthy-lifestyles movement by adding salad bars, vegetarian burgers, and moving into high schools and colleges, where their customers were not as concerned with health issues and regularly go through french-fry withdrawal. Some chains shut down their outlets in health-conscious areas and reopened new ones where health was not such a hot issue. Now that the healthy-lifestyles movement has faded, many of the salad bars and almost all of the veggie burgers have disappeared (except in India).

In adapting to environmental pressures, an organization must balance the need for change and the stability provided by the older systems. Because organizational systems are made up of people and not parts, they cannot always change on a dime. People who have worked in the organization may resist some types of changes, and they may be slow in adopting even those they accept. The organization's culture may preclude some types of change, or at least make them difficult to implement. Organizations that successfully adapt are able to acknowledge that stability as well as change is needed.

A vigorous, adaptive organizational system remains so because of the third process, **self-renewal.** Organizations, made up as they are of people and machines, need to replace these parts as they grow old, unable to perform, or unwilling to adapt. One way in which organizations renew themselves is by making sure to bring in fresh, new people and technology (see Chapter 6). The danger in this case is that the new people and machines will too radically challenge a structure and culture that has worked well. In many cases, self-renewal is most effective if it replenishes and refreshes rather than changes the organization. How new members can be integrated into organizational relationships and how cultures can be produced and sustained are important topics discussed in later chapters.

However, an organization must learn too, and this is also an important part of self-renewal. It is not only important to maintain, but to expand perspectives, to try out new things, to experiment. For years 3M Corporation has maintained a reputation for being one of the most innovative firms in the United States. A standard policy at 3M is to give its members license to "steal" time to work on new ideas and to reward people even for failures, as long as they keep trying to generate new ideas and products. Another form of learning is to take advantage of unexpected opportunities and events. Open systems expose themselves to their environments and thus are open to many unanticipated happenings. They can use these surprises to make themselves stronger and more adaptive. Sometimes these unexpected opportunities come by accident. The story is told that one of 3M's biggest successes, the ubiquitous Post-It Note, came about because of an accident that produced an adhesive that held only temporarily and could be easily peeled off. Rather than throwing out this batch of adhesive, creative 3M staff members tried to figure out what it could be used for. The result has replaced many a thumbtack, paper clip, or piece of tape. Opening up organizational systems to learning is critical to their growth and survival. Remaining open to new ideas and opportunities to learn is not always easy or even pleasant. But the organizations that are able to do so reap great benefits

SUMMARY: THE COMPLEXITIES OF ORGANIZATIONAL COMMUNICATION

All societies, and all organizations, must find ways to successfully deal with a fundamental paradox: If they are to survive they must control and coordinate the actions of their members. But, control and coordination frustrate individuals' needs for autonomy, creativity, and sociability. Historically, a number of strategies of organizing have been developed that strive to achieve the organization's goals while managing this fundamental paradox. Each of these strategies relies on communication because it is through communication that organizations emerge, are maintained, and change. The remaining chapters in Unit I describe each of those strategies of organizing, and indicate how they influence and are influenced by organizational communication. Chapter 2 examines what we call the *"traditional"* strategy of organizing, a perspective that focuses on the *structural* dimension of organizational communication. Chapters 3–5 cover *"relational," "cultural,"* and *"networking"* strategies of organizing, strategies that focus on the *relational, contextual,* and *systemic* dimensions of organizational communication. Although we will strive to present each strategy as clearly as possible, we will also continually caution readers to not lose sight of the complexity of organizational life. No strategy of organizing appears in a pure form in any modern organization. This is partly because every organization has its own unique history, membership, and mode of operating. As a result, they are distinctive mixtures of traditional, relational, cultural, and networking strategies. It also results from the strategies themselves. Each strategy focuses on one dimension of organizational communication while de-emphasizing the others. But, the de-emphasized dimensions cannot be ignored completely; they are integral parts of organizational communication and have an important impact even if they are not central to the dominant strategy that is used in the organization. As a result, organizational life is much messier than any overall strategy envisions. That messiness makes organizational life interesting, and makes strategic communication especially challenging.

Regardless of how messy one's organization might be, members of that organization must find ways to cope strategically with the situations they encounter. Strategies of organizing create organizational situations; the ways in which members of the organization interpret and respond to those situations implement and sometimes change the dominant strategy of organizing. Members of modern organizations face an increasingly complex array of challenges. Some of them result from characteristics of the organizations themselves; others result from rapid changes in the environments surrounding modern organizations. The chapters in Unit II examine what we believe are the most important of those pressures and processes. Chapter 6 examines the influences that communication technologies have on organizational situations and the communication strategies available to their members. Chapter 7 discusses strategic communication at different stages of a person's membership in an organization. Chapters 8–10 deal with three of the greatest challenges facing members of modern organizations—dealing with organizational power and politics, making effective decisions, and managing conflicts. Chapters 11 and 12 deal with the biggest challenge facing U.S. organizations in the early twenty-first century—diversity and globalization.

At this point, all of these ideas may seem a little overwhelming. At least, at this point we hope that most readers feel a little overwhelmed. Communication is an exceptionally complex process; organizational communication is an especially complex type of communication. There are a depressingly large number of books, training programs, and consultants' gimmicks that depict effective organizational communication as the simple application of "five foolproof techniques" or some equivalent. Unfortunately, these depictions are as glib as they are misleading. There are a number of principles that employees can use in most organizational situations. But they are neither simple, foolproof, nor applicable in every case. Our goal in this book is to explain those principles and indicate how people can analyze the complexities they face at work and choose appropriate strategic responses, recognizing all the while that the choices they make often reproduce the situations they face.

NOTES

[1] See, for example, Patricia Hayes Andrews and Richard T. Herschel, *Organizational Communication* (Geneva, IL: Houghton-Mifflin, 1996, pp. 16–18). For similar results in studies of Australian organizations, see Henry Irwin, *Communicating With Asia* (Sydney, Australia: University of New South Wales, 1997).

[2] See Nina Anderson Legg, Other People's Kids: Decision-making About Sexual Education, (Master's Thesis, Texas A&M University, 1992).

[3] See George Kennedy, *Classical Rhetoric in Its Christian and Secular Traditions from Ancient to Modern Times* (Chapel Hill: University of North Carolina Press, 1980). A similar concept has been developed by rhetorical theorist Lloyd Bitzer in "The Rhetorical Situation," *Philosophy and Rhetoric, 1* (1968): 1–14 and "Functional Communication," in *Rhetoric in Transition,* Eugene White, ed. (University Park, PA: Pennsylvania State University Press, 1980), especially pp. 27, 36–37.

[4] For a case study of how face-to-face communication reproduces strategies of organizing, see Teresa Harrison, "Communication and Interdependence in Democratic Organizations," *Communication Yearbook 17,* Stanley Deetz ed. (Newbury Park, CA: Sage, 1995, pp. 247–274).

[5] D.A. Morand, "The Role of Behavioral Formality and Informality in the Enactment of Bureaucratic Versus Organic Organizations," *Academy of Management Review, 20* (1995): 831–872; C. Handy, "Trust in Virtual Organizations," *Harvard Business Review, 73* (1995): 40–48. This section is based on two sources, Robert McPhee, "Vertical Communication Chains: Toward an Integrated View," *Management Communication Quarterly, 1* (1988): 455–493 and Robert McPhee and M. Scott Poole, "Organizational Structure, Configurations, and Communication," *The New Handbook of Organizational Communication,* F. Jablin & L. Putnam, eds. (Newbury Park, CA: Sage, 2000).

[6] McPhee, "Vertical Chains;" F.J. Yammarino & A.J. Dubinsky, "Superior-Subordinate Relationships," *Human Relations, 45* (1992): 575–600.

[7] Phil Clampitt & Cal Downs, "Employee Perceptions of the Relationship Between Communication and Productivity," *Journal of Business Communication, 30* (1993): 5–28; Henry Mintzberg, *Mintzberg on Management* (New York: Basic Books, 1989).

[8] See K. Bridge & L.A. Baxter, "Blended Relationships," *Western Journal of Communication, 56* (1992): 200–225 and B.A. Winstead, V.J. Derlega, M.J. Montgomery, & C. Pilkington, "The Quality of Friendships at Work and Job Satisfaction," *Journal of Social and Personal Relationships, 12* (1995): 199–215.

[9] Jon Hess, "Maintaining Nonvoluntary Relationships with Disliked Partners," *Human Communication Research, 26* (2000): 458–488.

[10] See James Dillard and Katherine Miller, "Intimate Relationships in Task Environments," in Steve Duck (Ed.), *Handbook of Personal Relationships* (pp. 449–465); James Dillard, J.L. Hale, and Chris Segrin, "Close Relationships in Task Environments," *Management Communication Quarterly,* 7: 227–255; Sue DeWine, Judy Pearson, and Carol Yost, "Intimate Office Relationships and Their Impact on Work Group Communication," in Cynthia Berryman-Fink, D. Ballard-Reisch, and L.H. Newman eds., *Communication and Sex Role Socialization* (pp. 139–165) (New York: Garland Publishing Company, 1993); Dennis Powers, *The Office Romance* (New York: American Management Association, 1999).

[11] K.R. Phillips, The Spaces of Public Dissension, *Communication Monographs, 63* (1996): 231–248. Also see Stewart Clegg, *Modern Organizations* (Newbury Park, CA: Sage, 1990). The most important of Weber's works on the relationship between the characteristics of Western societies and its organizations is *The Protestant Ethic and the Spirit of Capitalism* (New York: Charles Scribner's and Sons, 1958).

[12] Clifford Geertz, "Common Sense as a Cultural System," in *Local Knowledge* (New York: Basic Books, 1983).

[13] For summaries see Khalid Alkhazraji, William Gardner, Jeanette Martin, & Joseph Paolillo, "The Acculturation of Immigrants to U.S. Organizations," *Management Communication Quarterly, 11* (1997): 217–265; Taylor Cox, S. Lobel, & P. McLeod, "Effects of Ethnic Cultural Differences on Cooperative and Competitive Behavior on a Group Task," *Academy of Management Journal, 34* (1991): 827–847; and M. Kim, J.E. Hunter, A. Miyahara, M. Horvath, M. Bresnahan, & H. Yoon, "Invididual vs. Culture-Level Dimensions of Individualism and Collectivism," *Communication Monographs, 63* (1996): 29–49.

[14] See N. Adler, *International Dimensions of Organizational Behavior, 2nd ed.* (Boston: Kent, 1991), and Cox, Lobel, & McLeod.

[15] See Robert Bellah, et. al., *Habits of the Heart,* 2nd ed. (Berkeley: University of California Press, 1995), C.W. Reynolds and R.V. Norman (Eds.), *Community in America: The Challenge of Habits of the Heart* (Berkeley: University of California Press, 1988), and Warren Bennis, Jagdish Parikh, and Ronnie Lessem, *Beyond Leadership: Balancing Economics, Ethics, and Ecology* (Cambridge, MA: Basil Blackwell, 1994), especially Chapter 10. For a summary of de Tocqueville's observations and their applicability today, see John Cawelti, *Apostles of the Self-Made Man* (Cambridge, MA: Harvard University Press, 1974) and Stanley Deetz, *Democracy in the Age of Corporate Colonization* (Albany, NY: SUNY Press, 1992).

[16] Stephen Barley and Gideon Kunda, "Design and Devotion: Surges of Rational and Normative Ideologies of Control in Managerial Discourse," *Administrative Science Quarterly, 37* (1992): 363–399. Although we not agree with all of Barley and Kunda's conclusions, their arguments about the tension between individuality and community are compelling.

[17] Sonia Ospina has persuasively argued that the central tension in U.S. culture is this conflict between the myth of individual opportunity and merit and the realities of different opportunities

based on one's race, gender, class, and ethnicity (*Illusions of Opportunity* [Ithaca, NY: ILR/Cornell University Press, 1996]).

[18] Jeffrey Pfeffer and Alison Davis-Blake, "The Effect of the Proportion of Women on Salaries," *Administrative Science Quarterly, 32* (1987): 1–24; Robin Clair and Kelly Thompson, "Pay Discrimination as a Discursive and Material Practice," *Journal of Applied Communication Research, 24* (1996): 1–20.

[19] Lynn Martin, *Pipelines of Progress* (Washington, D.C.: U.S. Department of Labor, August 1992, p. 12); also see "Corporate Women," *Business Week* (June 8, 1992) and Korn/Ferry International, "The Decade of the Executive Woman" (New York: 1993).

[20] In general, we have chosen to use the terms that we do to refer to different groups of non-white employees because they seem to be preferred by members of each group. The reasons for our choice of terminology for persons of Spanish descent is a bit more complex. We use the terms *Latino* and *Latina* as *generic* terms to refer to men and women of Spanish descent respectively. We use the term Mexican American to refer to residents of the United States who were born in Mexico or whose families immigrated from Mexico. We do not use the term Hispanic at all because it is used in so many different ways, even in the scholarly literature, that its use is inevitably confusing. These terminological distinctions are important because the experiences of Latino persons in American organizations are very different depending on their heritage. In particular, people who immigrated from or whose families immigrated from Central and South America or the Caribbean face different attitudes and have had different experiences than those with roots in Mexico.

[21] Goran Therborn, *The Ideology of Power and the Power of Ideology* (London: Verso, 1980) and Dennis Mumby, *Power in Organizations* (Norwood, NJ: Ablex, 1988), especially Chapter 4.

[22] For an extended discussion of systems and networks see Chapter 5 of this book and Cynthia Stohl, *Organizational Communication* (Thousand Oaks, CA: Sage, 1995).

[23] Mark Granovetter, *Getting a Job* (Cambridge, MA: Harvard University Press, 1974).

[24] Rosabeth Moss Kanter, *Men and Women of the Corporation* (New York: Harper & Row, 1977) and *A Tale of "O:" On Being Different in an Organization* (New York: Harper & Row, 1980). For analyses of how network inclusion/exclusion is related to organizational power, see Robert Jackall, "Life Above the Middle," *Harvard Business Review* (September-October, 1982): 47–54, and Jeffrey Pfeffer, *Power in Organizations* (Marshfield, MA: Pitman, 1981).

[25] Robert McPhee & Steve Corman, "An Activity-Based Theory of Communication Networks in Organizations, Applied to a Local Church," *Communication Monographs, 62* (1995): 132–151.

Chapter 2

TRADITIONAL STRATEGIES OF ORGANIZING

*The foreman should never be authorized to enforce his discipline
with the whips if he can accomplish it with words.*
—VARRO OF ROME, C. 100

*If the words of command are not clear and distinct, if orders are
not thoroughly understood, the general is to blame.*
—SUN TZU OF CHINA, 500 B.C.

CENTRAL THEMES

- By the early 1900s a number of scholars and practicing managers realized that Western organizations faced serious problems. Their search for an alternative led to the development of "traditional" strategies of organizing.

- Traditional strategies of organizing attempt to control employees through rules, norms, and systems of rewards and punishments, all of which rely heavily on communication. But all control systems lead to resistance.

- If information is filtered as it passes through the formal chain of command, decision makers may have too little relevant information to make good decisions; if it is not filtered, they may be too overloaded with information to make good decisions.

- Both structural and personal/interpersonal factors lead to omission and distortion of information as it passes through formal channels.

- When the environment surrounding an organization is stable or not competitive, traditional strategies of organizing may function well; when the environment is turbulent or competitive, weaknesses in formal communication systems make it difficult for traditional strategies to succeed.

- In traditional strategies of organizing, leadership primarily involves managing, that is, designing and implementing formal systems of communication, motivation, and control.

KEY TERMS

Scientific job design	Time-motion studies
Scientific selection	Information overload
Decentralized decision making	Trained Incapacity
Legal authority	Legitimacy
Surveillance	

As the ancient comments at the beginning of this chapter suggest, neither the study of organizations nor of communication in organizations is terribly new. Whenever people have depended on one another to complete tasks or meet their needs, they have formed organizations. By the time human beings joined together into families and clans, they had become involved in the economic activities of hunting and gathering. They had started to organize, which required them to communicate with other workers. After humans had become farmers, they developed more complex organizations with more complicated communication needs. With farming came villages and the need to govern large groups of people; with villages came the concepts of citizenship and community welfare, which created the dual needs of defense and the management of the village's economy.

As villages became city-states, it became necessary for their managers to plan the operation of the society and to keep permanent records of the rules and procedures that they developed. The oldest written documents in existence deal with religion, management, and government, a combination that makes great sense when one realizes that the earliest managers also were governors and priests. As ancient religious and political civilizations expanded, their needs for effective economic organizations and effective organizational communication multiplied. As early as 2000 B.C. leaders recognized the importance of communication. Pharaoh Ptah-hotep instructed his sons and managers in the importance of listening skills, the need to seek advice and information from their subordinates, the importance of staying informed about what was taking place around them, and the necessity of clearly explaining each worker's tasks and documenting these instructions in writing. The Chinese emperors Yao and Shun (c. 2300 B.C.) also searched for ways of opening communication channels between themselves and the peasants and advocated consulting their subordinates about the problems faced by the government. By the time of Christ, Greek and Roman scholars had suggested many of the key concepts of modern organizational communication theory. But it was the growth of the nation-state and the mercantile system that created separate roles for governors, managers, and priests. The large and complex firms of the Industrial Revolution made it clear that control and coordination could be achieved only through effective communication.[1]

Unfortunately, the people who operated these organizations had few reliable guidelines. They had some experience in business and could rely on hunch and intuition. But peoples' memories often omit or redefine their failures and overemphasize successes, so experience is often an unreliable guide. Managers also could try to apply the principles used to run military organizations, which were the major large, complex organizations that existed before the Industrial Revolution. But, overall, owners' decision making suffered from a lack of concern for efficiency, and a virtual absence of reliable information.

In addition, owner-managers often treated their employees in arbitrary, capricious, and even inhumane ways. Proslavery politicians of the 1800s defended that institution by arguing that the lives of slaves were better than the lives of workers in Northern textile mills. There was enough of a parallel to make the argument credible. As a result, workers began to organize politically and form unions. Labor–management relations became increasingly hostile and confrontations between labor and management were often violent. The broad, rapid economic growth of the 1800s came to a screeching halt in a series of economic depressions during the 1890s. By the early 1900s, both managers and scholars recognized that Western organizations faced serious problems in design and operation. In response to these observations, a group of organizational theorists proposed an alternate strategy of organizing, one that sought to manage the paradox between organizational and individual needs by enhancing efficiency, creating stable and predictable organizational situations, eliminating arbitrary supervisory behavior, and motivating workers through economic rewards and a sense of personal achievement.

TRADITIONAL STRATEGIES OF ORGANIZATIONAL DESIGN

A large number of people were involved in the development of the traditional strategy of organizing. One group, who developed *scientific management,* tried to improve organizations from the bottom up, by reforming workers' tasks, efficiency, and rewards. They were inspired by an engineer, Frederick Taylor. A second group, the *bureaucratic theorists,* attempted to improve organizations from the top down, by improving the effectiveness of administrative employees. They are associated with sociologist Max Weber. Both groups had the same primary concern—replacing the arbitrary, capricious, and inefficient practices of contemporary organizations with systematically designed, objective, and fair systems of management and supervision.

Traditional Structure and the Structural Dimension of Communication

Both the scientific managers and the bureaucratic theorists believed that organizations should be segmented into a matrix of formal positions that are defined by the specific tasks for which their occupants are responsible. Those positions should be arranged in a hierarchy. Applicants would be hired for a position solely because they demonstrated the special expertise needed to perform their required tasks. Employees would base their decisions solely on the written policies, procedures, and rules of the organization, and all their actions should be documented in writing. Employees would be empowered to make decisions in their areas of expertise, as long as they followed established policies and procedures. Only those employees at the top of the organization would be empowered to actually establish policies and procedures or make major decisions. To prevent favoritism, all employees would be expected to maintain detached, impersonal relationships with clients and coworkers and keep emotional considerations from influencing their decisions and actions. Communication was to be formal and restricted to the chain of command because only then could responsibility for communication breakdowns be assessed and remedies taken.

The bureaucratic theorists valued this kind of structure primarily because they thought it would bring fairness and accountability to organizations, although they also believed that it would increase organizational efficiency. People would be hired based on their abilities, not their political or personal connections. Everyone involved in the organization would know who was responsible for each task that needed to be performed. If those tasks were performed well, the correct people would be rewarded; if not, the responsible people would be punished. Every employee would also be held responsible for communicating relevant information up and down the chain of command. After they successfully completed a probationary period, employees would be guaranteed a job for life (assuming their performance continued to be adequate), and an adequate pension. As a result, they could not be pressured to show favoritism to powerful clients or supervisors. Organizations, and all their members, would be accountable for their actions, and the organization would be efficient.

Advocates of scientific management were also concerned with accountability. In fact, Frederick Taylor was very disturbed by a common managerial practice of blaming and punishing workers for management's bad decisions. The practice inevitably drove a wedge between labor and management, and management's primary goal should be to create a cooperative relationship between management and workers. It also reduced organizational efficiency because managers who are not held accountable for *their* errors have no incentive to improve. For Taylor, accountability bred efficiency.[2]

Although these attitudes may not seem to be all that radical today, they were to Taylor's contemporaries. They were palatable to them only because Taylor coupled them with a set of efficiency-enhancing techniques that had significant economic benefits. Through these techniques, firms would be able to increase their profits and the incomes of all their employees (including managers) and reduce their prices, thus benefiting all consumers. Taylor labeled the first technique *scientific* **job design.** It started with a survey of all the tasks that needed to be performed in the organization. Managers then talked with workers about the best ways of doing their jobs. After the consultation phase was completed, tasks were redesigned through **time-motion studies**, in which a supervisor or consultant observed workers completing each task, broke the process down into its elements or motions, and then redesigned it so that the number of movements necessary to complete the task was minimized. Today a number of consulting firms, armed with sophisticated video technology, still conduct time-motion studies and make recommendations that improve effi-

height
example

ciency and reduce worker strain and fatigue. For example, Charley Conrad helped fund his college education by working summers and vacations in a metal processing foundry. Initially he operated a drill press. But, the company conducted a time-motion study and found that workers taller than six feet could not efficiently operate the equipment. They had to bend over to reach some of the levers and as a result got tired sooner than the shorter workers did. Like every other operator who was taller than six feet, he was transferred to a section that had tasks that could be efficiently performed by people of his height. When time-motion studies are used without first consulting workers, they generate strong resistance, especially if there is a low level of trust between labor and management. But, if used openly and in a cooperative atmosphere, they can have the positive effects that Taylor envisioned.

A second element of scientific management was **scientific selection**. Workers would be selected solely on the extent to which they possessed the necessary attributes for their tasks. (After the study, the foundry hired only drill-press operators who were less than six feet tall.) Once selected, workers are trained in the most efficient techniques of completing their assigned tasks and rewarded for their individual productivity. Taylor believed that under this system everyone involved would reap financial rewards from the increased efficiency that came from these techniques, and that workers also would feel a sense of achievement from succeeding in their tasks. Through a combination of scientific job design, careful selection, effective training, adequate incentives, and performance feedback, both organizational productivity and labor-management cooperation could be enhanced.

Today firms such as the ones Taylor envisioned are often viewed as sweatshops where workers are treated like inhuman cogs in a giant industrial machine. The term "bureaucracy" has a number of negative connotations—images of inefficient bureaucrats producing little save exhaustive expense accounts; of customers and employees alike being buried in red tape and treated as nonhuman cogs in a vast administrative morass; and of stubbornness when action is required, blind obsession with unchangeable policies when flexibility is necessary, and interminable delays when speed is crucial. These images of the traditional strategy of organizing are really quite ironic. The original purpose of this strategy was to create efficient and productive organizations in which people were treated fairly and equitably. The arbitrariness and capriciousness that Taylor and Weber observed in the organizations of their time were to be replaced by policies and procedures that treated everyone—workers and customers/clients—in the same way. The inefficient decision making of early firms was to be replaced by careful, data-based considerations. Although the strategy focused on meeting the organizations' needs for coordination and control, it also was intended to meet individual employees' needs for stability and autonomy. Bureaucratic structure is clear, stable, and predictable. But the traditional strategy is also problematic in two ways. Perhaps most important, its key elements—specialization, hierarchicalization, and centralization—place a great deal of pressure on an organization's formal communication system. Consequently, communication breakdowns are highly likely. Second, the strategy sacrifices flexibility and responsiveness for consistency and predictability. Although this is an appropriate trade-off for some organizations, it creates serious problems for others.

Communication Breakdowns in Formal Communication Systems

NOT ONLY RECEIVE — BUT ACCEPT + BELIEVE ACCURATE

For the traditional strategy of organizing to succeed information must flow freely through the chain of command. The decision makers at the top of the organization must receive accurate, complete, concise, and timely information about the extent to which orders have been carried out and tasks have been completed. They must also be informed about problems that have developed or are likely to develop in the future. In addition, decision makers must benefit from the specialized expertise of each employee along the chain of command. If that expertise is not available to individuals in upper management, their decision making will suffer. Similarly, information must flow from supervisors to subordinates, including information about policies, procedures, reward/rule systems, and the optimal means of performing each subordinate's assigned tasks. If any of these communication processes breaks down, the organization will function at less-than-optimal efficiency. If the margin of error available to the organization is small, these communication breakdowns may threaten its survival.[3]

The Filtering Paradox   Unfortunately, processes of information exchange create a fundamental paradox. On the one hand, upper-level decision makers depend on a free flow of information from employees located lower in the hierarchy. However, if information were to flow freely through the chain of command, the upper-level managers would soon be overloaded and overwhelmed by the information generated in their organization. For example, envision a moderate-sized hierarchical organization (one in which each supervisor has only four subordinates and the organization chart has seven levels). Each employee sends only one message a day up the chain of command. If no messages are filtered out, 4,096 messages would reach upper management each day, creating serious problems of *information overload*.[4] But, if every employee screens out only half of the information received, 98.4 percent of the information generated in the organization would never reach its decision makers. Consequently, the traditional strategy of organizing requires employees to rely on formal channels for the information they need while simultaneously restricting the flow of information through these channels.

Structural Barriers to Information Flow   A number of factors complicate the filtering paradox. Some of these barriers to information flow involve the people who make up the organization—their background and training, personal characteristics, and interpersonal relationships. But others involve the formal structure of the organization and the nature of human communication. These structural barriers would exist regardless of who worked in the organization.

When one person communicates a message to another, each of them interprets it. The words that make up the message are meaningless until some human being makes sense out of them.[5] When people communicate, they exchange their *interpretations* of information, not information in a "pure" form. When they interpret messages, they alter the message's meaning. People *condense* messages, making them shorter and simpler; people *simplify* messages into good or bad, all or none, or other extreme terms; they *assimilate* new messages so that their meaning is consistent with information received in the past; they *whitewash* messages, so that they will not upset the people to whom they are sent; and people *reductively code* messages by combining them with other information to form a sensible overall picture. In the process of interpreting a message, people simplify and clarify it. They absorb some of the uncertainty and ambiguity in the message. But, they also change it. Interpreting information is inevitable because all messages carry some degree of ambiguity, and some degree of uncertainty about how they should be interpreted. When messages are interpreted, they are changed.

Interpersonal Barriers to Information Flow A number of personal and interpersonal factors also complicate information flow (see Table 2-1). The amount of communication flowing through the chain of command is reduced by power and status differences among members of an organization. Messages are communicated in writing instead of face to face, and they focus on tasks, with little informal or social content. Written messages are more ambiguous than those exchanges in open, face-to-face encounters, making differences in

TABLE 2–1
Factors That Distort Vertical Communication

STRUCTURAL	PERSONAL AND RELATIONAL
1. Processes of interpreting messages Condensation Accenting Assimilation to past Assimilation to future Assimilation to attitudes and values Reduction	1. Power, status differences between parties
2. Number of links in communication chain	2. Mistrust between parties
3. Trained communication Incapacity Perceptual sets Language barriers	3. Subordinates' mobility aspirations
4. Large size of the organization	4. Inaccurate perceptions of information needs of others
5. Problems in timing of messages	5. Norms or actions that discourage requests for clarification
6. Problems inherent in written communication	6. Sensitivity of topics

interpretation more likely.[6] Differences in interpretations tend to reduce trust, which leads employees to rely even more heavily on written communication to protect themselves, and so on in a downward spiral. Supervisors can offset these effects by de-emphasizing status differences, training their subordinates in communication skills, rewarding their subordinates for keeping them informed, and encouraging them to seek clarification of ambiguous messages. However, they often do the opposite by verbally or nonverbally communicating, "*I don't want to hear about it now.*" They may talk only while on the run, use an annoyed tone of voice, physically move away from the subordinate, and allow other people to interrupt the conversation. Or they may simply fail to acknowledge or act on the information their subordinates provide.[7] If subordinates do not trust their supervisors, other factors come into play. Subordinates who wish to be promoted or recognized for past achievements and believe that the supervisor will have an influential voice on promotions are especially prone to withhold negative information from supervisors they do not trust. Those effects are increased when subordinates believe that their supervisors do not pass negative information on to them. They are especially unlikely to communicate negative information or information that deals with controversial or sensitive issues—precisely the kind of information that supervisors most need to have. In highly political organizations, withholding information is even more likely, especially when it is negative. As Chapter 8 explains, information is a potent source of power, but only if it is not widely available. Political battles—among individual employees and among units of the organization—often are information battles, and the side that has obtained and exploited secret information wins.[8]

Although this section has focused on barriers to the upward flow of information through the chain of command, downward communication also is limited by the same factors and processes. One of the most consistent findings in research on organizations is that subordinates want their supervisors to keep them informed and feel that they receive too little relevant and useful information from their supervisors, especially about events, policies, and changes directly involving them or their jobs. Many supervisors simply do not provide their subordinates with sufficient amounts of job-related information, especially feedback about the subordinates' performance. Downward communication is selected, filtered, and interpreted in much the same way as upward communication. In addition, when supervisors believe that they should give their subordinates only the absolute minimum necessary amount of information, they filter an even higher proportion of downward communication, frequently withholding even crucial information.

Destructive, or productive, cycles are formed and perpetuated. Supervisors whose communication is considerate, frequent, and reliable tend to have subordinates whose communication is similar. Because they better understand their supervisors' information needs, they can better summarize the information they receive without leaving out important details. These subordinates keep their supervisors informed, which makes them seem trustworthy, and perceptions of trustworthiness reduce the distorting effects of status differences. Conversely, supervisors who withhold information from their subordinates have subordinates who withhold information from them. The subordinates may interpret their own actions as an appropriate way to defend themselves against an untrustworthy supervisor; the supervisor may see the subordinates' actions as compelling evidence that they are hostile or unmotivated, which justifies the supervisor's withholding information, and so on. No individual is to blame (or should receive credit) for these patterns of action, although supervisors' higher formal power means that they have a greater effect on the direction the cycle will take. These patterns result from complex, interacting systems of meaning-creation and should be understood as complex systems of communication.

How Traditional Strategies Complicate Information Flow   Each of the sources of communication breakdowns described in this section are present in all organizations. But, they are more of a problem in organizations that employ traditional strategies of organizing than in organizations that rely on other strategies. One of the key characteristics of traditional strategies is centralization of power and decision making . If an organization is highly centralized (that is, if its organizational chart is "tall") messages will be exchanged, interpreted, and altered many times before they reach the decision makers at the top of the organization. The decisions that are made—the policies and procedures that are created—will be exchanged, interpreted, and altered many times before they reach the people at the bottom of the organization who will implement them. If decision making is distributed throughout the organization (that is, if it is **decentralized**) messages will be exchanged fewer times before action is taken on the information they contain. Fewer exchanges mean less interpretation and less alteration. In addition, communicating through the chain of command is very time-consuming, as any student who has needed to change a registration for a course or searched for a "lost" student aid check is painfully aware. In highly centralized organizations, information may reach decision makers (or implementers) too late for it to be useful.

A second element of the traditional strategy of organizing is *specialization.* It increases organizational efficiency by making sure that tasks are performed by people with the relevant expertise. But, specialization also complicates information flow. As people are trained in an increasingly specialized set of skills, they become less and less capable of performing other tasks. They develop a kind of **trained incapacity.** The most obvious incapacity involves differences between upper management and lower-level workers. Managers often become incapable of understanding the processes through which their workers perform their tasks and are rarely able to actually do those jobs themselves. Conversely, lower-level workers become less able to understand complex, abstract thought. But, trained incapacity permeates the entire organization. Employees who play specialized roles interpret the messages they receive in a manner appropriate to those roles. Personnel officers interpret messages in terms of what they imply about future needs for hiring, firing, or training employees; and financial officers attribute meaning to messages based on the economic impact that they imply. As their training and experience progress, employees become less capable of taking the perspectives of other members of the organization when interpreting or sending

Navy shipyard example

messages. Sometimes they may even create their own languages. As employees become literate in the artificial language of their position or unit, they become less capable of translating their ideas into a language that other people can understand.[9] As a result, misunderstanding across specialties often is more common than understanding. The size of an organization in itself does not seem to increase problems of trained incapacity, but when an organization is highly specialized, trained incapacity can create severe problems.

Finally, traditional strategies of organizing attempt to formalize communication, which highlights power and status differences, and stipulates that relationships between supervisors and subordinates should be impersonal and governed by established policies and procedures. As a result, trust and shared interpretations of information are reduced and written communication dominates. It is precisely in this kind of situation that the personal and interpersonal sources of distortion are most potent. In short, traditional strategies rely heavily on formal, chain-of-command communication and paradoxically create a number of barriers to successful information flow. If organizational communication really did function as it is supposed to in the traditional strategy, most people would not know what was going on most of the time.

CASE STUDY:
THE CHALLENGER CASE

Almost everyone knows the story of the January 28, 1986, launch of the space shuttle Challenger. Although the story tells us some important things about how difficult it is to design complicated equipment, it tells us a great deal more about how breakdowns occur in the formal communication systems of complex organizations. In fact, the Challenger case is not especially notable in itself—virtually all traditional organizations have the same kind of problems every day. What is notable is that the effects of NASA's communication problems were made public on national television. The immediate cause of the disaster was the failure of two O-rings, which were used to seal one of three joints in each of the two solid-fuel booster rockets produced by the Morton Thiokol company in Utah. From the moment of liftoff the damaged seals allowed a stream of superheated gas to escape, burn a hole in the main fuel tank, and ignite its contents, turning the most technically advanced vehicle ever produced into a flaming coffin. Less well known are the events leading up to the tragedy, especially the communication breakdowns that led up to the decision to launch. The Presidential Commission on the Space Shuttle Challenger Accident concluded tersely that "the testimony reveals failures in communication that resulted in a decision to launch [mission] 51–L based on incomplete and sometimes misleading information" (Commission, p. 82).* This case explores those communication processes.

Safety had always been a major concern at NASA. Initially separate safety oversight divisions were created in the shuttle project. This step was taken to ensure that the safety officers would be independent of the people they moni

(continued)

(continued from the previous page)

tored. But independence carries a price. It means that the safety officers had to depend on workers in the divisions they monitored to provide them with the information that they needed to do their jobs. Of course, those people had all the incentives to withhold or reinterpret negative information that exist in any organization. Independence also means that safety information had to pass through a lengthy chain of command before reaching the decision makers in upper management. In addition, the safety officers were so independent that they were perceived as being unimportant. When NASA faced budget constraints after 1970, it fired most of its safety officers—the total number declined 71 percent between 1970 and 1986. As a result, no safety officer participated in the prelaunch decision-making process for *Challenger.*

Finally, independence meant that the safety oversight groups had no power to reward or punish employees for their actions. In fact, NASA's overall reward/punishment system encouraged people to value speed and low costs more than safety. These trade-offs are not unique to NASA—all technological organizations in competitive environments face them. They became crucial at NASA after it made commitments to Congress to make the shuttle program financially self-sufficient (Vaughn, 1996, pp. 24–30). Even after the *Challenger* disaster, no managers at NASA "were terminated or even publicly castigated by NASA" (Vaughn, 1990, p. 247). Similarly, there had been more than 25 occurrences of O-ring erosion and related SRB anomalies [booster rocket equipment problems] at the time of the accident.

Thiokol had never been penalized, nor was there any evidence that punishment had been threatened. . . . Even after these [and other] violations became public, Thiokol was not penalized. . . . When rewards were great for cost savings and meeting deadlines and punishment was not forthcoming for safety infractions, contractors [like Thiokol] would tend to alter their priorities accordingly. Thiokol did comply, but with NASA production interests, not with safety standards (Vaughn, 1990, p. 248).

In December 1982, the O-rings were added to NASA's list of "criticality 1" features, a term meaning that a failure in this part could "cause a loss of life or vehicle" because it had no or insufficient backup systems for the O-rings. Unfortunately, this change was not communicated to all of NASA's division managers, so many of them believed that there were adequate backup systems. On at least three previous shuttle flights (in January, April, and October 1985) the seals had failed significantly. Lawrence Mulloy (manager of the Solid Rocket Booster division at the Marshall Space Flight Center) testified that "everyone" in NASA knew of these partial failures and the concern that they raised about the safety of the shuttles, especially when launched in cool weather (around 50 degrees). But everyone did not know. NASA had no centralized procedures or rules for reporting in-flight problems or any system for detecting trends across different launches. Consequently, each division and manager knew about problems in her or his area, but not about the overall picture of problems. Similarly, no one seems to have recognized that there had been O-ring problems on more than half of the

(continued)

(continued from the previous page)

flights. Presumably the safety group would be responsible for gathering, consolidating, and communicating the overall picture, but it had no way of extracting the information from the various divisions of NASA. After 1983, middle managers were no longer required to report safety problems to upper management, and when they did report problems Mulloy routinely waived the requirement that the problems be solved before the next flight (Vaughn, 1990, p. 236). Consequently, each of the subsystems designed to facilitate effective communication in the traditional strategy of organizing—the chain of command, centralized decision making, and reward/punishment processes—was in some way missing at NASA. Other communication breakdowns occurred during the hours immediately before the launch. At 6 PM on January 27, a teleconference was held between NASA and Morton Thiokol. Weather forecasts were for a low temperature of 22 degrees during the night, rising to 26 degrees by launch time. Lawrence Ebeling, manager of Thiokol's booster engineering division, testified that "the meeting lasted one hour, but the conclusion of that meeting was that Engineering . . . were very adamant about their concerns on this lower temperature, because we were way below our data base" (Commission, p. 86). The lowest temperature for a successful flight had been 53 degrees, and at that temperature the O-rings had experienced serious problems. The lowest temperature for a successful laboratory test had been 25 degrees (Vaughn, 1996, p. 290). The engineers' initial recommendation: "O-ring temp must be > 53 degrees F at launch" (Commission, p. 90).

However, key figures remembered different interpretations. Committee member Keel asked Dr. Judson Lovingood of the Marshall Center, "So as early as that first afternoon conference at 5:45, it appeared that Thiokol was basically saying delay. Is that right?"

LOVINGOOD: That is the way it came across to me. . . .

DR. KEEL: Mr. Reinartz [manager of the shuttle project, Marshall Center], how did you perceive it?

MR. REINARTZ: I did not perceive it that way. I perceived that they were raising some questions and issues which required looking into by all of the parties, but I did not perceive it as a recommendation delay" (Commission, p. 87).

Three hours later, a second teleconference began. It started with Thiokol's engineers presenting a set of charts on the "history of O-ring erosion" on previous flights and in tests that had been forwarded to the Kennedy Space Center. The engineers were worried that if the rings were too cold they would not be flexible enough to instantly seal the joint if they were needed. Engineer Boisjoly explained, "It would be like trying to shove a brick into a crack versus a sponge" (Commission, p. 89). He summarized the conversation:

> There was never one positive, pro-launch statement ever made by anybody [the engineers]. There have been some feelings since then that folks have expressed that would support the decision, but there was not one positive statement for launch ever made in that room.

(continued)

(continued from the previous page)

At about this time Hardy [NASA] was asked what he thought about the MTI [Thiokol engineers'] recommendation, and he said he was appalled. Hardy, also asked about launching, said that if the contractor recommended not launching, he would not go against the contractor (Commission, p. 90). Soon after, Thiokol managers asked for a brief recess so they could caucus with their engineers in private. A 30–minute conversation followed. Boisjoly continued:

> Those of us who opposed the launch continued to speak out, and I am specifically speaking of Mr. [Arnie] Thompson and myself. . . . Arnie actually got up from his position which was down the table, and walked up the table . . . in front of the management folks, and tried to sketch out once again what his concern was with the joint, and when he realized he wasn't getting through, he just stopped (Commission, p. 93)

However, there were good reasons to question the analysis provided by Boisjoly and the other anti launch engineers. In the first place, laboratory tests conducted by Thiokol found that the seals were pliable down to 25 degrees. Because of these tests, NASA managers were surprised that the Thiokol engineers chose 53 degrees as the bottom-line number. They did so because of their training—engineers learn to prefer field tests over lab tests and they knew that the O-rings had serious erosion problems at 53 degrees. But, the charts that the engineers presented to support their case were inconclusive. The most serious launch failure **had** been at 53 degrees, but the next most serious failure had been at 75 degrees. Other failures of comparable severity took place at temperatures ranging from 56 degrees to 70 degrees. The charts presented by the engineers simply did not seem to support their argument that there was a direct correlation between temperature and O-ring failure, or their selection of 53 degrees as a magic number. In fact, if anything it suggested that even at 53 degrees the secondary seals would work, giving the needed margin of safety.

(continued)

CHART A   SHUTTLE LAUNCHES WITH SOME O-RING FAILURE.

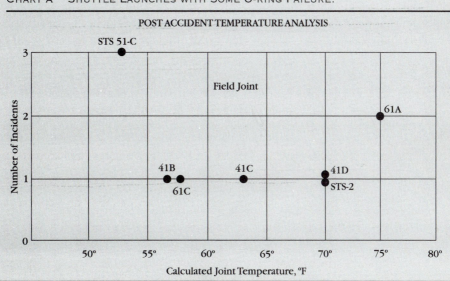

POST ACCIDENT TEMPERATURE ANALYSIS

(continued from the previous page)

Ironically, had the engineers based their analysis on **all** shuttle launches instead of just the ones that had experienced O-ring problems, they could have made a stronger case for their position. As Chart B shows, there **is** a strong relationship between temperature and O-ring failures, but the magic temperature is 65 degrees, not 53. Vaughn concludes, "*of the flights launched above 65 degrees F, three out of seventeen, or 17.6 percent had anomalies. Of the flights launched below 65 degrees F, 100 percent had anomalies* (1996, p. 382, emphasis hers).

CHART B   ALL SHUTTLE LAUNCHES BEFORE "CHALLENGER" ACCIDENT

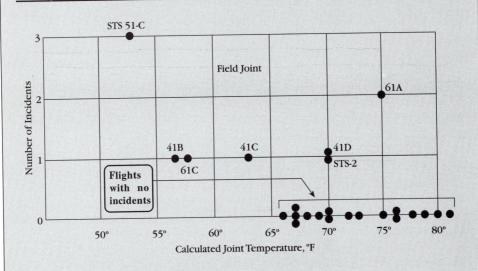

However, Chart B was prepared for a U.S. House of Representatives investigation, which took place months after the launch. It made perfect sense for the Thiokol engineers to focus their attention on instances of O-ring failure. But, doing made it difficult for them to build a persuasive case against launching the *Challenger.*

> [Later] Mr. Mason [Thiokol management] said we have to make a management decision. He turned to Bob Lund [Thiokol vice-president of engineering] and asked him to take off his engineering hat and put on his management hat. From this point on management formulated the points to base their decision on. . . . [Boisjoly complained that] I was not even asked to participate in giving any input to the final decision. . . . This was a meeting where the determination was to launch, and it was up to us to prove beyond a shadow of a doubt that it was not safe to do so. This is in total reverse to what the position usually is in a preflight conversation or a flight readiness review. It is usually exactly the opposite of that (Commission, p. 93).

(continued)

(continued from the previous page)

It was not unusual to ask Thiokol engineers to put on managers' hats. Every man in the room was both an engineer and a manager. Neither was it unusual for the engineers to have lively debates among themselves or with representatives of NASA. The questions asked by the NASA managers raised serious doubts about the accuracy of the anti launch engineers' scientific assessments. As Boisjoly testified to the Commission, eventually the highest-ranking caucused and changed their recommendation from no-launch to launch. All but two of the other engineers—Boisjoly and Thompson—voted with their bosses. Every engineer who changed his vote later said that they did so because of the technical arguments presented by NASA, although they also admitted that they felt that NASA was pressuring them toward a pro-launch decision. Lund explained why Thiokol management had interpreted NASA's comments as pressure to launch:

> We have dealt with Marshall for a long time and have always been in the position of defending our position to make sure that we were ready to fly. . . . But that evening I guess I had never had those kinds of things come from the people at Marshall. We had to prove to them that we weren't ready, and so we got ourselves in the thought process that we were trying to find some way to prove to them that it wouldn't work, and we were unable to do that (p. 94).

> At approximately 11:00 P.M.. Thiokol rejoined the conference and recommended that the shuttle be launched. NASA managers were surprised by the change of heart:"They assumed that Thiokol was reworking their technical arguments, doing further calculations, and would return with a stronger engineering analysis that supported their [no launch] stance" (Vaughn, 1996, p. 321). After recovering from the surprise, Hardy [NASA] requested that the recommendation be put in writing and sent by fax immediately to Marshall and Kennedy. No one at either NASA site knew that anyone at Thiokol still objected to the launch (Vaughn, 1996, p. 323).

However, at the Cape new concerns arose. Icicles had formed on the launch pad and the manufacturer of the shuttle, Rockwell International, was worried that falling icicles at launch would damage the shuttle, its main engine, or its fuel tank. After a lengthy discussion with NASA, Rockwell made a recommendation that the Commission found to be highly ambiguous. Even that recommendation "was not clearly communicated to NASA officials in the launch decision chain" (Commission, p. 116).

Applying What You've Learned

1. Which of the sources of withholding/distorting information discussed in this chapter were present in the Challenger case? How were they related to the reward/punishment structure of the organization? How did they influence the decision to launch?

2. Did any of the participants show characteristics of trained communication incapacity? If so, how?

(continued)

(continued from the previous page)

3. How did formal roles and reliance on the chain of command influence the events?

Questions to Think About and Discuss

1. Are the communication problems that led up to the launch decisions inevitable in complex, hierarchical organizations?
2. What changes could be made to prevent recurrence? Are these changes feasible in this kind of organization?

---

*This case is based on the report of the Presidential Commission, especially Chapter V, "The Contributing Cause of the Accident," Diane Vaughn, "NASA and the Challenger," *Administrative Science Quarterly, 35*(1990): 225–257 and Diane Vaughn, *The "Challenger" Launch Decision* (Chicago: University of Chicago Press, 1996). For an extended analysis of changes in NASA throughout its history, see Phillip Tompkins, *Organizational Communication Imperatives: Lessons from the Space Program* (Los Angeles: Roxbury House, 1993).

Compensating for Communication Problems of Traditional Strategies of Organizing

So far in this chapter, we have argued that traditional strategies of organizing rely heavily on formal systems of communication and that it is normal for these systems to break down. That analysis may lead readers to wonder just how these organizations manage to survive. The answer is that many organizations have minimal needs for rapid and accurate task-related communication. Some organizations exist in extremely stable environments that place limited demands on communication. Problems can be anticipated and situations can be understood rather easily because they almost always are like those faced in the past, and tried-and-true solutions are generally available. Expertise, decision making, and authority can be centralized; communication can be restricted to the chain of command; and so on. Information can usually be obtained through formal channels, and the kinds of communication breakdowns that are discussed in this chapter can be anticipated and offset. In stable environments, traditional strategies of organizing cope quite well with the limited amount of uncertainty that they face. In contrast, organizations in highly competitive, rapidly changing, turbulent environments are effective when their work and communication structures allow a free, open, and rapid flow of information, not the restricted, formal, and slow chain of command. Organizations in turbulent environments often face complicated problems unlike any they have faced in the past. Lynda St. Clair, Robert Quinn, and

Regina O'Neill state the case simply: "Both practitioners and theorists agree that organizations today face enormous competitive pressures and must be highly responsive to rapid changes in the external environment if they are to survive."[10] Open communication structures (such as those of the "relational," "cultural," and "networking" strategies described in Chapters 3, 4 and 5) allow information about sudden environmental changes to be rapidly diffused throughout the organization.

Fortunately, there are a number of steps that members of organizations can take to compensate for the communication problems that are inherent in the traditional strategy of organizing. Since competition and turbulent environments magnify these communication problems, managers can take steps to reduce those pressures. Large firms can pay other organizations not to produce competing products. They can purchase, and then dissolve, competitors, or they can become even larger. Monopolies and oligopolies are able to influence (perhaps even control) the prices and availability of inputs and sales in ways that reduce the environmental turbulence they face. Pharmaceutical firms have used all these strategies to prevent the development or production of low-cost generic drugs.[11] Managers also can often persuade government to insulate them against environmental pressures, by placing patent or copyright restrictions on their competitors, or by using tariffs or other restrictions to make foreign competitors' products excessively expensive. Or they can focus some of the organization's activities on sectors of the economy that have relatively stable environments. For example, the largest U.S. tobacco firms diversified their activities during the 1980s, often linking with stable industries such as food production. Not only does diversification reduce the impact of a volatile environment, it allows firms to apply political and financial pressure on potentially problematic elements of their environment. For example, television news organizations might be tempted to air highly popular *exposés* of the tobacco industry if not for the massive advertising revenues that they receive from the tobacco companies' food subsidiaries. Of course, in a society that presumably values "free and open competition," many of these activities raise important ethical and legal questions (see Chapter 12). But, they reduce the environmental pressures that organizations face.

Managers can relax organizational rules about following the chain of command during crises or when rapid flows of information are important. Subordinates can also compensate for problems of the traditional strategy. Once they isolate recurring patterns of communication breakdowns, they can offset problems of filtering and structural distortion by building *redundancy* into their own communication networks. They offset personal and interpersonal barriers through *counterbiasing,* in which they determine the probable biases of each person who communicates with them, adjust their interpretation of the message to compensate this bias, and then talk about the topic with people who have different biases. Fortunately, these compensating networks seem to emerge quite naturally unless managers actively suppress them.[12] By acting strategically in their own interests, employees compensate for the weaknesses of traditional strategies of organizing.

TRADITIONAL STRATEGIES OF MOTIVATION, CONTROL, AND SURVEILLANCE

One of the goals of the traditional strategy of organizing was to replace the arbitrary and capricious treatment of workers that often took place in turn-of-the century organizations with a scientifically designed and rationally implemented system of incentives and disincentives. All employees work to achieve goals, primarily economic ones, and a system that rewarded them for following established rules and procedures and maximizing their individual performance would be in everyone's self-interest. If appropriate rule-and-reward systems could be created, workers would choose to act in ways that met their needs and the needs of their organizations. Labor–management hostility would be replaced with cooperative, mutually rewarding relationships. But rule-and-reward systems succeed if and only if they are supported by effective communication.

Motivation and Control through Rules and Rewards

Many people find rule-and-reward systems an acceptable means of influencing their actions. Max Weber noted that in Western democracies, children learn to accept rule and reward-based control systems as a natural and normal way for a society and its organizations to function. Rule/reward systems increase efficiency and protect people from arbitrary or harmful treatment by more powerful people. They ensure that the rights of *individuals* will be protected and that *individuals* will be fairly rewarded for their contributions. Members of western democracies learn to believe in **legal authority,** the notion that societies and organizations should be organized around a formal, impersonal (and thus objective), written set of rules, policies, procedures, and rewards.

Rule-and-reward systems also make our worlds stable, predictable, and in some ways simpler. Organizational theorist Karl Weick has noted that rules place parameters around our interactions with other people. Without those rules, we would constantly have to negotiate and renegotiate how we will act toward one another, leaving little time and energy for accomplishing tasks or pursuing goals. For example, when hospitals provide parents of pediatric patients with a written list of rules about who (parents or nurses) would be responsible for different aspects of their child's care, both the parents and the nurses were more satisfied. The rules made an ambiguous and stressful situation less difficult and allowed the parties to spend their time and energy making detailed decisions about their child's special needs.[13] But, even with these advantages, it is still difficult to implement rule-and-reward systems successfully. Doing so depends on communication and on being able to persuade members of an organization that the rules and rewards in the system are *legitimate* and *fairly administered.* Success also depends on the systems themselves, and how they deal with *unintended consequences.*

 Rules, Rewards, and Persuasive Communication   To succeed, rules must be clear enough to be easily understood, specific enough to give employees precise guidelines for acting, and general enough so as not to seem overly particular. Rules will be seen as **legitimate** only if members believe that they are applied fairly equally to everyone in the organization and are produced by the organization, rather than by an individual supervisor acting on his or her own whim. Rules will be perceived as illegitimate if they are applied outside an accepted range of activities. For example, rules about employees' private lives will not be accepted if employees perceive that their employer does not have a legitimate right to enforce them. At one time employees, especially managerial and supervisory personnel, gave their organizations the right to control much of their private lives. Today employees often refuse to accept company rules about where they should live, how they should spend their income, or what they should do with their leisure time. For example, the management of Dell Computer Company recently created an uproar when it distributed a memo informing employees that their "Code of Conduct" for behavior at work also applies to the games of the local AA baseball team, the Round Rock Express (who play their home games at the Dell Diamond). Heckling visiting players or booing members of the home team are forbidden because they are "disruptive, unprofessional, offensive, or potentially slanderous;" acting "responsibly with respect to consumption of alcohol" is required. Dell employees are accustomed to rules that impinge on their private lives—60 hour work weeks for its sales staff or mandatory overtime for tech support people—and generally view those intrusions as legitimate business requirements. But, many of them believe that this rule goes too far.

Rules systems succeed only if they are supplemented by a credible reward system. Employees must perceive that the rewards they receive are both substantial and important. Pay seems to have these characteristics, especially for employees whose incomes are low, whose tenure in the organization has been brief, whose commitment to the firm is low, and who feel that their pay is inappropriate when compared to the pay of other workers. The promotions and status that usually accompany pay increases also seem to be important to most people, especially those with a high need for achievement. Praise also is salient to most people and is positively related to both improved performance and job satisfaction.

Employees must also be persuaded that the reward system is fair. They must believe that rewards are based on performance, rather than on friendships or biases, and that individual employees are primarily responsible for their level of performance, and the rewards they receive. This is a difficult undertaking because people tend to attribute their successes to themselves or to factors within their control and their failures to others or to factors they cannot control.[14] These problems are reduced when objective, quantifiable measures of an employee's performance are available. But, in the end, the key is a supervisor's ability to provide persuasive performance feedback.[15] Feedback should both clearly confront a problem (or clearly encourage continuation of excellent performance) and allow all parties to maintain face (see Chapter 7). Face management is complicated by an employee's status, race, gender, and ethnicity. For example, providing clear, detailed feedback to a person with higher status (for example, one's supervisor) may in itself threaten his or her face. Face-saving is especially important to people who have communitarian orientations (recall Chapter 1)—women and people from Latin, Asian, and Middle-Eastern backgrounds.[16]

At least for people from Western societies, a reward system is seen as fair only if it also is seen as *equitable.* They do not evaluate the rewards (or punishments) they receive in a vacuum; they compare them to what others receive and what they believe others *should* have received. If they perceive that the *rewards* allocated by the organization are *just,* their job satisfaction is higher than if they believe the distribution of rewards are unjust (labeled *distributive justice*). If they perceive that the *process* through which the rewards are allocated is fair (*procedural justice*), their trust in and evaluation of their supervisors, and their commitment to the organization will be higher.[17] If they perceive that the reward system is not just they will be frustrated and may respond by reducing their effort, attempting to increase their rewards, leaving the organization, or rationalizing the inequity.

Supervisors have a number of persuasive strategies available to convince their subordinates that the reward system is just. Some strategies are overt—giving workers information that proves that they are being treated equitably; others are covert—withholding information about the other employees' rewards, for example. It is difficult to employ the first strategy successfully, as professors remember each time they try to respond to a student's complaint that "I worked much harder than so-and-so and received a lower exam grade." It is equally difficult to implement the second strategy, although organizations often try to do so through rules that forbid employees from discussing their raises (or salaries) with others. The primary effect of these rules seems to be to encourage employees to obtain the forbidden information, since the very existence of the rules creates the impression that the reward system is inequitable. Thus the confidentiality rules give employees incentive to share salary information covertly. The fact that these rules often fail may be the best evidence in support of the equity theory's assumption that people are very much concerned with the equity of reward systems.[18]

Evidently, supervisors recognize the importance of issues about equity when they make decisions about rewards. When they believe they have reliable performance information on their employees, and they can realistically determine which employee was responsible for which outcomes (positive and negative), they do try to allocate rewards based on performance, although they realize that doing so can create competition and hostility within a work group. Equity considerations are especially important in large departments in which people work alone and do not have close personal ties with one another. But when the situation is less clear-cut, or when the supervisors are concerned about "team building," they tend to give approximately equal rewards to each of their subordinates. As a result, in departments in which people work closely together and are similar to one another in backgrounds, experience, and interests, rewards are more alike and there is less difference among the salaries of the various employees.[19]

To complicate matters even further, employees' responses to issues of equity seem to be culture-specific. In a study of employees in two individualistic and masculine cultures (the United States and Japan) and a culture that is less individualistic and less masculine (South Korea), Kim and his associates found that all three groups of employees preferred equity-based reward systems over across-the-board systems, although the preference was stronger with the U.S. and Japanese employees. Weber noticed that in traditional Catholic European peasant communities, raising the sum that workers received for each item they produced often actually *reduced* their output. Workers found that with the increased pay rates, they could maintain the same income with less effort. Since leisure time was more important to them than increased income, increasing their pay had a paradoxical effect. With the coming of Protestantism, and its emphasis on wealth and consumption as evidence of moral goodness, increases in pay have a more predictable effect on performance.[20] In sum, there is no doubt that organizational control systems influence employees' actions and attitudes. However, there also is a great deal of evidence that control systems may have many unanticipated consequences. Implementing control systems requires that a number of requirements—communicative and otherwise—be met, and even if these requirements are met, employees will still make their own decisions about how to interpret and respond to them.

CASE STUDY:
THE POWER OF REWARDS AT INDUSTRY INTERNATIONAL*

Industry International is a manufacturing firm with about 2,500 employees in a number of plants. It is often touted as a monument to the power of financial reward systems. In an industry that has been battered by foreign competition for three decades, it has remained highly profitable, in large part because its workers are 2 1/2 to 3 times as productive as those of its competitors. Their compensation is also three times the average salary for U.S. manufacturing employees. They are not unionized, have no paid vacations, and work 45–50 hours per week. Much of their income comes from a year-end cash bonus. Each year, after company taxes and dividends have been paid, the board of directors determines the size of the bonus pool, which is divided among the employees based on their base salary and individual merit ratings. From 1943 to 1994 the bonus percentage ranged from 55 percent to 104 percent; in 1994 it was 61 percent, meaning that an employee earning a $30,000 base salary and receiving a 100 percent merit rating would receive a bonus of $18,300. The bonus is kept secret from October until a meeting/celebration in December. When the meeting ends the employees rush to their cars, bonus checks in hand, and tie up traffic for hours going to their favorite places of celebration.

(continued)

(continued from the previous page)

Most employees use the money to pay accumulated bills, in fact many spend far in excess of their base salaries and then put off paying bills and loans until the bonus checks come in. Other employees use the money for less mundane activities. One got his bonus in $100 bills, spread them on the living room floor and, along with his wife, rolled around on them (among other activities) in celebration. Some made major purchases like houses, cars, and luxury items in cash. A few (mostly younger employees) used the money to gamble, hire prostitutes, or buy illegal drugs. When asked why they spend the money as they do, three answers were commonly given—to live the good life so valued in the United States, to assert their autonomy (one said "spending bonus money is the one thing they [management] ain't telling me what and how to do"), and for the social status that money provides:

> "As soon as they [friends and neighbors] find out you work there, they think you have money coming out of your ears"; [another said] "They think I'm the richest s. . .o. . .b [ellipsis mine] in the world"; [another recalled that] years ago we made more money than professional football players."

What they don't tell their envious neighbors is what they went through to get the bonus. Merit points are based on output, quality, dependability, and personal characteristics. The first two can be quantified, leading employees to "work like dogs" until dangerously exhausted by long hours and difficult working conditions; the latter two cannot, creating a highly political atmosphere in the plant: [most echoed one worker's conclusion that]

> "if you don't go along with the system [managers], you could be the hardest worker in the world . . . and you would still be way short because you have not gone with the flow and you would be blackballed, and they give you what they want to give you."

But, things have changed for Industry International. The recession of the mid-1980s led to low bonuses (55 percent). Many workers lost their homes and cars because they were relying on large bonuses to pay mortgages and loans. Workers attributed the decline to many things, but primarily to management greed and incompetence—a "fat managerial level and more men at the top," embezzlement, and mismanagement of overseas accounts. Whatever the reason, the recession made it clear to workers just how dependent they were on Industry International, and how much things had changed: "The whole philosophy [established by the founder and maintained until 1983] was that you worked hard and got compensated for it. You busted your ass, but you got compensated. Now you bust your ass and you don't get compensated for it." But, they have very few options. Most are too old to start over somewhere else and are limited by their education and training to manufacturing jobs, and high-paying manufacturing jobs are becoming very rare in the United States (see Chapter 12).

So, they talk about resisting management. They fear that management will eliminate the bonus system, replacing it with a form of profit-sharing that is not

(continued)

(continued from the previous page)

as lucrative for the workers. Many predict a massive walkout or work stoppage if that happens. Others talk about unionizing the firm. Management has persuaded them that the bonus system relies on a non-union shop, but if the bonus system is eliminated they have no reason not to unionize. Others predict that employees would quit the company; still others predict plummeting productivity and quality, others threaten physical violence against management and sabotage of the plant. "If they got rid of bonus, they wouldn't have the control over anyone. Bonus is what they have to keep the hold on you."

Applying What You've Learned

1. A number of factors need to be present for rule-reward systems to succeed. Which of those factors were present at Industry International? Which, if any, were absent?
2. What resistance strategies are available to these employees? What could they do to keep from being so dependent on the system? What effects would those actions have on the system? Why?

Questions to Think About and Discuss

1. There is a substantial amount of research evidence indicating that pay is the most powerful motivator for U.S. workers, more so than for workers in some other countries.† Why?
2. Would this kind of motivation/control system work differently in different societal contexts, for example, in a society that was not as consumption-oriented as the United States or in a country with extensive social support systems for unemployed workers and their families?††
3. If you were the CEO of Industry International, what kinds of public economic policies would you want the government to follow? (Would you want the Federal Reserve Board to focus on keeping inflation low or keeping unemployment low? Would you want corporate income taxes to be a primary source of government funding or personal income taxes)? Why?

---

*This case is based on Melissa Hancock and Michael Papa, "Employee Struggles with Autonomy and Dependence: Examining the Dialectic of Control through a Structurational Account of Power," Paper presented at the International Communication Association Convention, Chicago, 1996.

†See John Campbell and Robert Pritchard, "Motivation Theory," in Handbook of Industrial and Organizational Psychology, Marvin Dunnette, ed. (Chicago: Rand-McNally, 1976) and Charles Greene and Philip Podsakoff, "Effects of Withdrawal of a Performance-contingent Reward on Supervisory Influence and Power," Academy of Management Journal, 24(1981): 527–542.

††This question is examined in Richard B. Freeman, ed., *Working Under Different Rules* (Washington, D.C.: The Russell Sage Foundation, 1994).

Avoiding Unintended Consequences of Rule-Reward Systems   Unfortunately, rule-reward systems may inadvertently reward behaviors other than those they are designed to encourage. In what has become a classic essay on reward systems, Steven Kerr has provided a number of examples of "the folly of rewarding A while hoping for B." For example, in politics, U.S. citizens presumably want candidates for office to make their goals, proposals, and funding systems perfectly clear so that they can make informed choices. But, repeatedly, voters reject candidates who do so and reward those who deal with images and personalities rather than issues and solutions. Citizens want state adoption agencies to place children in good homes, but enact regulations that base their administrators' budgets, prestige, and staff size on the number of children enrolled (that is, the number *not* placed). Consequently, they are encouraged to make it difficult to adopt these children—requiring prospective parents to not smoke, be of the same religion, have never been divorced, have a separate bedroom for the child, and so on. Universities are supposed to teach students, but reward research activities that have only an indirect positive effect on teaching quality. Students are supposed to go to college to learn something, but are rewarded by employers and graduate schools largely based on the grades they receive regardless of what they have learned, thereby encouraging them to take easy classes (which reduces their opportunities to learn), obtain and study for passing exams in a course instead of for mastery of the material, and so on. Lower-level employees in a manufacturing firm perceive that they are rewarded for "apple-polishing" and "not making waves" when upper management sincerely believes that they are encouraging all employees to be creative and innovative.[21]

Reward systems may also ignore the intangible rewards that employees receive from their jobs. Some professors in research universities actually do spend time and effort on undergraduate teaching, in spite of the organization's formal reward system, because they receive intangible rewards from their interactions with their students. Kerr studied a medical insurance company that rewarded claims adjusters for quickly and accurately paying good claims and rejecting bad ones. But the size of the reward was too small to offset the hassles they received from turning down a claim. So, newcomers quickly learned "when in doubt, pay it out!"

Finally, some tasks are complicated in ways that make it virtually impossible to design an effective reward system. For example, William Ouchi examined the reward systems in a number of retail stores.[22] He found that those salespersons paid on a commission basis sold a lot of merchandise, but did no other necessary tasks—ordering and arranging inventory, or training new salespeople. In contrast, people paid an hourly wage completed all the necessary tasks, but didn't sell much merchandise. People paid on commission also had strong incentives to engage in unethical behavior. Presumably, management can discourage unethical activities and encourage employees to complete support tasks. But, if salespersons receive no rewards for maintaining high ethical standards or completing support activities, especially in the short term, they will do what they *are* rewarded for doing.[23] In sum, rule-reward systems are complicated because human beings are complicated. People actively perceive, interpret, and strategically respond to the guidelines and constraints they face. The people who design the systems clearly do not *intend* the systems to have these effects; indeed they cannot even *predict* that they will do so. Reward systems are powerful motivating agents, but their impact is determined more by the employees who interpret them than by the systems themselves.

Surveillance and Rule-Reward Systems

All organizational control systems require some form of **surveillance**, some process through which supervisors can determine the extent to which employees conform to policies, procedures, rules, and motivational systems. This is particularly true of traditional strategies of organizing because the primary function of supervision is worker control and because they exercise control over everything from major policies and procedures to microscopic elements of task design and completion. The simplest form of control involves supervisors constantly looking over the shoulders of their subordinates. This kind of surveillance is still common in newly industrialized economies. In a Malaysia-based microchip plant, male supervisors constantly pressured female workers to increase their productivity; even trips to the locker-room were penalized. Workers complained about being constantly spied upon and felt that they had no place to hide. The company set up an in-house "union" to serve as an additional watchdog.[24] However, simple surveillance systems have two important disadvantages. First, they are highly inefficient, requiring organizations to hire and pay large numbers of supervisors to watch over their employees. This managerial overhead is especially large in U.S. firms (almost three times as large as in Japanese organizations, and almost four times as large as in European firms), and it has steadily increased since the end of World War II. Second, they are very *obtrusive* (visible and "in your face"), which generates a great deal of antagonism between supervisors and subordinates.[25]

Direct Surveillance and Electronic Technologies   Today supervisory surveillance is made much easier by the advent of sophisticated computer technologies. A 2000 study by the American Management Association found that almost 80 percent of U.S. firms used some form of electronic surveillance during the previous year, a number that had increased by an astonishing 67 percent over the previous year. The most common activities were monitoring Internet use, listening in on or recording telephone conversations, storing and reviewing computer files, and recording computer use (number of keystrokes per minute, time taken between entries, etc.) Indeed, computer monitoring is more common in the workplace than in any other part of society, in part because modern organizations are technology-intensive, making it easy to monitor employees, and partly because of widespread acceptance of the doctrine of "employment at will," which means that employers have the right to set almost any condition of employment and to fire workers for almost any reason. Women are more likely to be monitored than men, and minority women are the most heavily monitored group. This is because it is easiest to monitor people whose jobs can

be quantitatively measured—clerical work, data entry, or routine computer programming—and those tasks are largely performed by minority women. Some
computer monitoring is widely accepted (for example, videotaping for security
purposes), some is widely condemned (monitoring and posting the number of
bathroom breaks employees take and the amount of time they spend in the
bathroom), some involves normal managerial activities (keeping track of inventory), but most involves employee control.

Assessing the effects of computer surveillance systems is difficult. They
have often been linked to a number of negative outcomes—lower job satisfaction, higher absenteeism and turnover, adverse health effects (including
increased stress and anxiety), feelings of lost privacy, lower commitment to the
organization, and high levels of resentment about being monitored. Heavily
monitored employees often perceive that management does not trust them and
treats them like children and fear that they are being set up for punishment or
dismissal. Some systems are interactive and flash messages like "work harder" or
"concentrate" on the workers' computer screens when they slow down. All the
negative feelings and attitudes are increased when these systems are used. Surveillance systems can also harm performance, especially for employees who
perform complex tasks. Employees begin to believe that management is concerned with quantity of output, *but not quality,* and respond accordingly. They
provide lower-quality service to customers and find ways to bypass complicated or otherwise time-consuming clients or activities.

However, properly designed and implemented electronic surveillance may
have net positive effects. Monitoring is perceived favorably if it is restricted to
legitimate, performance-related activities, if it increases the fairness of the organization's rule-reward system, and if it is linked to effective performance feedback. In these senses, employee responses to computer monitoring are very
much like employee responses to rule-reward systems in general.[26]

Resistance to Rule-Reward Systems   Resistance is an inevitable aspect of
social or organizational control because control systems inevitably reduce
members' autonomy and creativity (recall the dilemma discussed in Chapter
1).[27] The simplest forms of resistance are withdrawal and open rebellion. The
former leads people to be progressively less involved in and committed to their
jobs; the latter can culminate in sabotage. The disastrous chemical leak at
Bhopal, India, in 1985 resulted in part from an employee's rebelling against
being punished (fired) for breaking what he perceived as illegitimate rules. A
cleaning woman once admitted that she retaliated against an especially controlling employer by using her employers toothbrush to clean her commodes—for
years. Employees also may resist rules by *regressing,* that is, by reducing their
performance to the minimum acceptable standard that the rule-reward system
allows. Employees resist electronic surveillance systems by finding ways to fool
the computers, sabotaging the systems, or filing lawsuits.

Other forms of resistance are more complex. Employees sometimes rebel
against their organizations by following rules exactly, robbing their organizations of the common sense and flexibility to make rule systems work. In Mexican *maquiladoras* workers covertly resist pressures to speed up production by

engaging in *tortuosidad,* literally "working at a turtle's pace." Since their supervisors (U.S. and Mexican) viewed their workers as "lazy," they often failed to recognize that the slowdowns were strategic.[28] During 1991, a small number of American Airlines pilots resisted management by following FAA regulations to the letter—filing very complete flight plans, requesting detailed weather reports, and engaging in other activities that are completely legal but rarely absolutely necessary for flight safety. The number of flight delays and cancellations skyrocketed. Management retaliated by giving the pilots assignments that reduced their income (while denying in public that they were doing so). Pilots countered by following the rules even more exactly, eventually paralyzing the airline through their strategy of malicious obedience. Similar actions in 1997 and 2000 cost American $70 million and $225 million respectively. In 1997, United Airlines pilots virtually shut that airline down by obeying rules regarding overtime exactly; in 2000 the same strategy cost the airline $225 million. Even flight attendants, who have substantially less bargaining power, were able to force concessions from U.S. Airways in 2000 after costing the company $40 million by working to rule.[29]

Whether the consequences are massive or minor, all forms of resistance serve the same purpose: They allow employees to rebel against rule-reward systems. Unfortunately for organizations, supervisors often respond to resistance by tightening the rule-reward system, which increases the probability of further resistance. The organization then finds itself immersed in destructive cycles of disobedience and dictatorial management. Unfortunately for employees, resistance rarely leads to major changes in organizations or organizational rule-reward systems. The nature of the traditional strategy makes it difficult to locate and resist real sources of organizational control. When resistance actually does threaten to force changes on an organization, high-powered members are usually able to change the rules/rewards. For example, strikes have long been a potent way for unionized workers to resist management. But, first in the 1981 air traffic controllers' strike and increasingly since then, management has been able to hire (or threaten to hire) permanent replacements for striking workers, thus virtually eliminating strikes as a viable means of resisting management. In addition, resistance is exhausting, much more so than is enforcing rule-reward systems. Eventually workers lose the strength necessary for further resistance. Finally, resisting rule-reward systems focuses attention on them and can in effect legitimize them. Resistance usually raises questions about the legitimacy of a particular rule-reward system or the way in which it is being implemented. But it also accepts the legitimacy of *some* system of organizational control. Thus the relationship between control and resistance is paradoxical: Control inevitably creates resistance, which often supports systems of control.[30]

TRADITIONAL STRATEGIES OF LEADERSHIP

Most contemporary organizational theorists view "leadership" as a process of developing a vision that challenges an organization to excellence and change, a concept that contradicts the traditional strategy of organizing (see Chapters 3 and 4 for more detail on contemporary views of leadership). The traditional strategy dictates that supervisors will be "managers," people who implement an existing set of plans, or "administrators," people who develop routine techniques for accomplishing particular tasks. One of the early proponents of the traditional strategy of organizing, Henri Fayol, argued that managing consists of five key activities, four of which directly involve communication:

Organizing includes explaining employees' duties clearly, controlling the use of written communication, and providing clear and effective statements of managerial decisions.

Commanding involves conducting both periodic assessments of the organization's success through systems of performance feedback and conferences with employees to direct and focus their efforts.

Coordinating depends on making certain that all employees understand the nature and limits of their responsibilities.

Controlling involves administering rewards and punishments and persuading employees that their rewards are based on the quality of their performance.[31]

But the traditional strategy also implies that managers are not to be "leaders" in the modern sense of that term.[32] This criticism may be the result of very different definitions of what leadership means. Traditional strategies create situations that produce a particular kind of leadership. Traditional organizations are comprised of a kind of class or caste system that fosters clear distinctions among a managerial power elite, a "new working class" composed of lower-level managers and people with technical skills, and lower-level workers. To advance through the organizational hierarchy, employees must concentrate on conforming to the demands of upper management. Most of these demands involve creating and maintaining a certain kind of impression (a process that is discussed in more detail in Chapter 7). Successful workers work hard at being "like" upper management both in terms of overall attitudes and behaviors and in terms of microscopic image management. They must learn to please their superiors by accommodating their every whim and meeting their every need. Subordinates should anticipate superiors' demands, prevent or solve the problems they encounter, and "help a superior perform well and look good," even if doing so involves taking blame for the superior's errors and giving him or her credit for the subordinate's successes.[33] They must demonstrate loyalty, both to the organization and to their sponsors in the power elite. They must keep their distance from people below them in the hierarchy and develop a near obsession with following rules because rules are their only source of protection. People who advance through traditional hierarchies come from the same schools, wear the same clothes, and develop the same communication styles and mannerisms of their higher ups. Above all, they do not make waves; creative approaches and new ideas threaten the stability and predictability that are hallmarks of the traditional strategy of organizing. Since these values permeate organizations, they dominate selection decisions. As a result, the people who are hired for upwardly oriented jobs tend to already have the appropriate credentials and behavioral styles. But, even those people must refine their impression management as they move through the organization because fitting in gets progressively more important as one moves up the organizational hierarchy.

Omar Aktour has provided an excellent example of these processes in a study of two breweries, one in Montreal and one in Algiers. Although there were some differences in the two settings, there were striking similarities in how one became promotable in these two very traditional organizations. From the day they arrived in the organization, employees who eventually became worthy of promotion engaged in a particular pattern of behavior. They were obsessed with doing more—a machinist who used his breaks to clean his machine or a quality-control officer who repeatedly phoned the plant on his days off to make sure things were going well. They showed a strong capacity to keep lower-level workers in line and showed unconditional obedience and submission to their superiors. They kept their distance from the regular workers and took care to master the language of the elite—managerial jargon, including the most recent managerial fads, and upper-class accents. They zealously enforced rules and quotas, boycotted all unionizing activities (or informed on pro-union workers), appeared to suffer from their workload and worries, and constantly stayed on their bosses' coattails. In both plants the formal job descriptions of managers and the official reward/evaluation system focused on objective performance criteria such as production per machine or number of equipment breakdowns. But, upper management described a "good" (promotable) subordinate in terms that had little to do with technical expertise or objective performance. To them, good subordinates are submissive, punctual, serious (absorbed in their tasks), malleable, and ambitious. As a result it is not surprising that the workers in these plants complained about the technical incompetence of their supervisors as well as about their untrustworthiness and political game-playing.[34]

Consequently, by the time people are promoted to managerial positions in traditional organizations, they have developed ways of thinking and acting that preclude their being "leaders" in the contemporary definition of that term. The only legitimate vision is that of maintaining the existing systems and structures; the only possible challenge is to do what the organization has always done more rapidly and efficiently. Such people are likely to be excellent "managers" and "administrators," but not leaders.

CONCLUSION: COMMUNICATION AND TRADITIONAL STRATEGIES OF ORGANIZING

We have spent a substantial amount of space discussing traditional strategies of organizing because they are so relevant to modern employees. The traditional strategy, with its tight hierarchy, focus on the structural dimension of communication, and written policies and procedures, is still the dominant strategy used in the United States for governmental agencies, educational institutions, and many private firms. Bureaucratic modes of management are the norm rather than the exception throughout the world. Although very few organizations conform completely to the strategy, many employees entering organizations today find themselves in situations much like the traditional bureaucracy. Procedures and policies are documented in writing; job-related communication flow through the chain of command; positions require specialized skills and are filled at least in part because applicants fulfill established, written criteria; and decision making is centralized near the top of the organization. Of course, real organizations—even those in which the traditional strategy is in evidence—deviate in a number of important but predictable ways from what the traditional theorists envisioned. But, understanding the traditional strategy is important because many people will spend most of their lives working in organizations that are "traditional" in many ways.

NOTES

[1] Claude George, *The History of Management Thought* (Englewood Cliffs, NJ: Prentice-Hall, 1972), p. 52. The quotations from ancient managers that appear in this chapter and some of the historical summary are from this work.

[2] For excellent summaries of Taylor's ideas see Frederick Taylor, "The Principles of Scientific Management," in *Classics of Organizational Theory*, Jay Shafritz and Philip Whitbeck, eds. (Oak Park, IL: Moore, 1978) and Edwin Locke, "The Ideas of Frederick Taylor," *The Academy of Management Review, 7* (1982) 14–24.

[3] Robert Snyder and James Morris, "Organizational Communication and Performance," *Journal of Applied Psychology, 69* (1984): 461–465.

[4] This is why computerized management information systems, recently installed in virtually every major organization, have had perplexing effects. Computer information systems do not filter information. In theory, they allow every employee, no matter where in the organization, to instantly access any part of its information base. However, no one can process all the information. Unfiltered formal communication will literally bury upper-level managers in information, at least until they learn to use the equipment to screen out messages. High-speed computer systems may only allow them to be buried more quickly. The "solution" to the problem of communication overload is for upper management not to use the systems, which defeats the purpose of installing them in the first place. See Ron Rice and Urs Gattiker, "Communication Technologies and Structures," in *The New Handbook of Organizational Communication*, F. Jablin and L. Putnam, eds. (Thousand Oaks, CA: Sage, 2000. Also see Fredric Jablin, "Formal Organizational Structure," in *Handbook of Organizational Communication*, Fred Jablin, et al., eds. Newbury Park, CA: Sage, 1987).

[5] Eric Eisenberg, "Ambiguity as Strategy in Organizational Communication," *Communication Monographs, 51* (1984): 227–242

[6] Terrance Albrecht and Betsy Bach, *Organizational Communication* (Ft. Worth, TX: Harcourt, 1996).

[7] Cal Downs and Charles Conrad, "A Critical Incident Study of Effective Subordinancy," *Journal of Business Communication, 19* (1982): 27–38; Gail Fairhurst, "Dialectical Tensions in Leadership Research," in *The New Handbook of Organizational Communication*, F. Jablin and L. Putnam, eds. (Thousand Oaks, CA: Sage, 2000). For an extended analysis of how one's nonverbal cues influence interpersonal communication, including communication by the other members of the relationship, see Judee Burgoon, David Buller, and W. Gill Woodall, *Nonverbal Communication: The Unspoken Dialogue* (New York: Harper & Row, 1995); and Valerie Manusov and Julie M. Billingsley, "Nonverbal Communication in Organizations," *Organizational Communication: Theory and Behavior*, in Peggy Yuhas Byers ed. (Boston: Allyn and Bacon, 1997).

[8] Janet Fulk and Sirish Mani, "Distortion of Communication in Hierarchical Relationships," *Communication Yearbook 9,* Margaret McLaughlin, ed. (Newbury Park, CA: Sage, 1986).

[9] Larry Spence, *The Politics of Social Knowledge* (University Park, PA: Pennsylvania State University Press, 1978); Fredric Jablin, "Communication Competence and Effectiveness," in F. Jablin

and L. Putnam, eds., *The New Handbook of Organizational Communication* (Thousand Oaks, CA: Sage, 2000).

[10] "The Perils of Responsiveness in Modern Organizations," in Robert Quinn, et al., eds., *Pressing Problems in Modern Organizations (That Keep Us Up at Night)* (New York: AMACOM, 2000, p. 244. An excellent summary of the underlying research for this section is available in Kathy Sutcliffe, "Information Processing and Organizational Environments," in F. Jablin and L. Putnam, eds., *The New Handbook of Organizational Communication* (Thousand Oaks, CA: Sage, 2000).

[11] Sheryl G. Stolberg & Jeff Gerth, "Drug Makers Fight Generic Rivals and Raise Questions of Monopoly," Houston *Chronicle*, July 23, 2000, 4A.

[12] See Peter Monge and Noshir Contractor, "Emergent Communication Networks," in *The New Handbook of Organizational Communication*, F. Jablin and L. Putnam, eds. (Thousand Oaks, CA: Sage, 2000).

[13] Karl Weick, *The Social Psychology of Organizing*, 2nd. ed. Rebecca Adams and Roxanne Parrot, "Pediatric Nurses' Communication of Role Expectations of Parents to Hospitalized Children," *Journal of Applied Communication Research, 22* (1994): 36–47.

[14] Explanations of these processes are part of "attribution theory," a model summarized effectively and applied to organizational reward systems in J. Bettman and B. Weitz, "Attributions in the Board Room," *Administrative Science Quarterly, 28* (1983): 165–183; and B. Staw, P. McKechnie, and S. Puffer, "The Justification of Organizational Performance," *Administrative Science Quarterly, 28* (1983): 582–600.

[15] Karen Tracy and Eric Eisenberg, "Giving Criticism," *Research on Language and Social Interaction, 24* (1990/1991): 37–70.

[16] Barry Nathan, Allan Mohrman, and John Milliman, "Interpersonal Relations as a Context of the Effects of Appraisal Interviews," *Academy of Management Journal, 34* (1991): 352–369.

[17] Dean McFarlin & Paul Sweeney, "Distributive and Procedural Justice as Predictors of Satisfaction with Personal and Organizational Outcomes," *Academy of Management Journal, 35* (1992): 626–637.

[18] An excellent summary of the importance of equity in Western societies is available in Edward E. Sampson, "Justice, Ideology, and Social Legitimation," in *Justice in Social Relations*, H.W. Bierhoff, R.L. Cohen, and J. Greenberg, eds. New York: Plenum, 1986); a fine cross-cultural comparison is available in Ken Kim, Hun-Joon Park, and Nori Suzuki, "Reward Allocations in the United States, Japan, and Korea," *Academy of Management Journal, 33* (1990): 188–198. Summaries of the effects of perceived distributive and procedural justice are available in J. Brockner, T.R. Tyler, & R. Cooper-Schneider, "The Influence of Prior Commitment to an Institution of Reactions to Perceived Unfairness," *Administrative Science Quarterly, 37* (1992): 254–271 and Dean McFarlin and Paul Sweeney, "Distributive and Procedural Justice as Predictors of Satisfaction with Personal and Organizational Outcomes," *Academy of Management Journal, 35* (1992): 626–637.

[19] James Meindl, "Managing to Be Fair," *Administrative Science Quarterly, 34* (1989): 252–276; Jeffrey Pfeffer and Nancy Langton, "Wage Inequality and the Organization of Work," *Administrative Science Quarterly, 33* (1988): 588–606.

[20] Cited in Francis Fukuyama, "The End of History?" *National Interest,* 1989.

[21] Steve Kerr, "On the Folly of Rewarding A While Hoping for B," *Academy of Management Journal, 19* (1975): 769–783.

[22] William Ouchi, "The Relationship Between Organizational Structure and Control," *Administrative Science Quarterly, 22* (1977): 95–113. This concept is developed in greater detail in the final sections of Chapter 9.

[23] Jeffrey Kerr & John Slocum, "Managing Corporate Culture Through Reward Systems," *Academy of Management Executive, 1* (1987): 99–108.

[24] Aihwa Ong, "The Gender and Labor Politics of Postmodernity," *Annual Review of Anthropology, 20* (1991).

[25] The best source for data on managerial overhead is David Gordon, *Fat and Mean* (Cornell, NY: Cornell University Press, 1996). Superb summaries of these ideas are available in Stanley Aronowitz, *False Promises* (New York: McGraw-Hill, 1973); Harry Braverman, *Labor and Monopoly Capital* (New York: Monthly Review Press, 1974); Michael Burawoy, *Manufacturing Consent* (Chicago: University of Chicago Press, 1979); and Richard Edwards, *Contested Terrain* (New York: Basic Books, 1978).

[26] G. Stoney Adler & Phil Tompkins, "Electronic Performance Monitoring," *Management Communication Quarterly, 10* (1997): 259–288; J.R. Aiello, "Computer-based Work Monitoring,"

Journal of Applied Social Psychology, 23 (1993): 499–507; J.R. Aiello & C.M. Svec, "Computer Monitoring of Work Performance," *Journal of Applied Psychology, 23* (1993): 537–548; Balitis, Jr., J.J. (1998). Care needed with electronic monitoring. *Business Journal (Phoenix), 18* (21), 71; Carl Botan, "Communication, Work and Electronic Surveillance," *Communication Monographs, 63* (1996): 294–313; Carl Botan, "Examining Electronic Surveillance in the Workplace," paper presented at the International Communication Convention, Acapulco, MX, 2000; R.E. Kidwell, Jr. & N. Bennett, "Employee Reactions to Electronic Control Systems," *Group and Organization Management, 19* (1994), 203–219.

[27] Hannah Arendt provides an explanation of the inevitability of resistance in *The Human Condition* (Chicago: University of Chicago Press, 1958). Michel Foucault, a theorist whose work we will cite frequently in this book, draws similar conclusions in Michel Foucault, *Discipline and Punish* (Harmondsworth, U.K.: Penguin, 1977), *Power/Knowledge,* ed. C. Gordon (Brighton, U.K.: Harvester Press, 1980), and *The Practice of Everyday Life* (Berkeley: University of California Press, 1984). Foucault's work is difficult to understand. An excellent summary is available in James Barker and George Cheney, "The Concept and Practices of Discipline in Contemporary Organizational Life," *Communication Monographs, 61* (1994): 20–43.

[28] D. Pena, "Tortuodidad" and G. Young, "Gender Identification and Working-Class Solidarity Among *Maquila* Workers in Cuidad Juarez," in *Women on the U.S.-Mexican Border,* V.L. Ruiz & S. Tiano, eds. (Boston: Allen & Unwin, 1987).

[29] Laura Goldberg, "Slowdowns Hit Airlines," Houston *Chronicle,* 6 Dec., 2000, p. 1C.

[30] Charles Conrad summarizes the research underlying these conclusions in "Was Pogo Right? Communication, Power and Resistance," in *Communication Research in the 21st Century,* Julia Wood and Richard Gregg, eds. (Creskill, NJ: Hampton Press, 1995). The most important sources are Michel de Certeau, *The Practice of Everyday Life* (Berkeley: University of California Press, 1984); Michael Burawoy, *Manufacturing Consent* (Chicago: University of Chicago Press, 1979); and Stewart Clegg, "Power, Theorizing and Nihilism," *Theory and Society, 3* (1976): 65–87, and Kathy Ferguson, *The Feminist Case Against Bureaucracy* (Philadelphia: Temple University Press, 1984).

[31] Henri Fayol, General and Industrial Management (London: Pitman, 1949). The other functions were regulating technical processes, purchasing and marketing, obtaining and using capital, protecting employees and property, and accounting.

[32] Marlene Fine & Patrice Buzzanell, "Walking the High Wire," in *Rethinking Organizational and Managerial Communication From Feminist Perspectives,* P. Buzzanell, ed. (Newbury Park: Sage, 2000).

[33] Roy Smith, "How to Be a Good Subordinate," *The New York Times,* November 25, 1970, p. 16F. The primary source for this section is Kathy Ferguson, *The Feminist Case Against Bureaucracy* (Philadelphia: Temple University Press, 1984).

[34] Omar Aktouf, "Defamiliarizing Management Practice," in *Understanding Management,* Stephen Linstead, Robert Grafton Small, & Paul Jeffcutt, eds. (London: Sage, 1996).

Chapter 3

RELATIONAL STRATEGIES OF ORGANIZING

*If thou art one to whom petition is made, be calm as thou
listeneth. . . . Do not rebuff him before he has . . . said that
for which he came. . . . It is not [necessary] that everything
about which he has petitioned should come to pass, [but]
a good hearing is soothing to the heart.*

—PHARAOH PTAH-HOTEP TO HIS MANAGERS, C. 2700 B.C.

*If a leader maintains close relationship with his soldiers
they will "be more eager to be seen performing some
honorable action, and more anxious to abstain from
doing anything that was disgraceful."*

—A LESSON LEARNED BY ALEXANDER THE GREAT
FROM THE PERSIAN KING CYRUS, C. 325 B.C.

CENTRAL THEMES

- Relational strategies of organizing substitute decentralization and participatory decision making for the centralized, hierarchical, specialized organizational design of the traditional strategy. Employees sometimes resist these strategies, and their effects depend on a number of factors.
- Informal communication networks are an inevitable aspect of organizations and they can benefit organizations and their members in many ways.
- Teams are a basic building block of the relational strategy. Teams enable relational organizations to respond flexibly to their challenges, but they may also function to control their members rather than empowering them.
- Relational strategies rely on creating open and supportive supervisor-subordinate relationships, achieved through "transactional" leadership tactics.
- Critical theories of organizational communication argue that relational strategies obscure differences among the interests of owner, managers, and workers.

KEY TERMS

Empowerment	Rumors
Hygiene factors	Motivators
Deskilling	Teams
Ratebusters	Quality circles
Systematically distorted communication	Pacification
Disqualification	Co-oriented

Like Chapter 2, this chapter discusses organizational design, motivation/control/resistance, and leadership. However, the amount of space that we devote to each of these topics is quite different than in Chapter 2, in which we examined organizational design and motivation/control/surveillance at length, but de-emphasized leadership. This chapter de-emphasizes organizational design and deals more extensively with motivation/control/surveillance and leadership. This difference in focus results from the strategies themselves. Traditional strategies focus on organizational design and assume that if those things are taken care of, everything else is pretty simple. Relational strategies are much less concerned with design and instead focus on intangible aspects of control and on interpersonal relationships between supervisors and their subordinates and among members of work groups. As a result, relational communication is much more important.

RELATIONAL STRATEGIES OF ORGANIZATIONAL DESIGN

There is one important design-related difference between relational and traditional strategies—*decentralization.* Two key features of the traditional strategy were centralization and hierarchicalization—the notions that organizations should be shaped like a multilevel triangle. Only those employees at the top would make decisions about policies, procedures, and so on. Lower-level employees are allowed to make decisions, but only about implementing the rules, policies, and procedures that are established on high. The relational strategy relaxes both assumptions, asserting instead that organizational hierarchies should be "flattened" and decision making should be decentralized. There would be far fewer exchanges of messages between the sources of information and the people who use that information. This means that lower-level employees would be empowered to make decisions about a wide range of issues that directly affect them and their jobs, and that there would be far fewer links in the formal chain of command.

Decentralization and Participation

Decentralization and participatory decision making(PDM) are two sides of the same coin. If an organization adopts a decentralized organizational structure, the number of managers drops significantly, as does the number of levels of management. As a result, lower-level employees must be allowed to make every-day decisions because there is no one else available to do so. In addition, the managers that are left in the organization are required to supervise much more "loosely" than are managers in the traditional strategy. "Tight" supervision is alienating and increases the likelihood that workers will resist management's efforts. Loose supervision involves granting workers more autonomy, allowing them to determine how to accomplish their assigned tasks, and expecting them to make the decisions that influence them most. Supervising loosely would allow each supervisor to manage a much larger span of control. Furthermore, decisions would be made by the employees who are most directly concerned with them and most expert in the day-to-day activities of the organization. For-mal communication would cross fewer levels, thus reducing the potential for distortion (recall Chapter 2).

Necessary Features for Successful PDM   Participatory decision making is time-consuming and costly for organizations, but these costs are often more than offset by the increased morale, improved decision quality, and enhanced infor-mation flow that results. PDM comes in a variety of different forms and a number of different labels. (Workplace democracy, employee involvement, and Total Quality Management are some common examples.) But, for PDM to increase organizational performance a number of requirements must be met:

1. Subordinates must want to be involved in decision making, must be involved in complex tasks, and must be given substantial control over how they complete their tasks.
2. Supervisors must be willing to allow their subordinates to participate legitimately and must listen and respond to their ideas, and to encourage them to contribute.
3. The issues being discussed must be important to the participants. Workers usually believe that any decisions that directly affect them or their jobs are important and that decisions about more general company policies are less important. They especially would like to have influence over deci-sions about how to do their own work, scheduling of work, awarding raises and promotions, and hiring and firing of coworkers.
4. All the participants must have expertise and information relevant to the problems being discussed.
5. Managers must foster and support the beliefs, values, and attitudes neces-sary to legitimize participatory systems. Publicly recognizing employees' contributions and creating positive feelings of success make employees feel that they really do have the authority to act on their own, and thus are important determinants of feeling empowered.[1]

Sometimes resistance is grounded in the societal context surrounding an organization. In some societies, people learn that supervisors should make and enforce decisions simply because they are supervisors (a concept that Max Weber labeled *traditional authority*). For example, Asian Americans often find it difficult to challenge higher-status members of their organizations. For them, PDM can be alien and frustrating. Sometimes resistance is based on a lack of trust or skill. Many workers, especially blue-collar workers, do not wish to participate in decision making because they would rather not share the responsibilities that accompany the systems. This is especially true early on, before workers are persuaded that management will not use the systems to penalize them when they make inevitable mistakes. People with high levels of expertise but weak communication skills are often frustrated by PDM. They expect to have a great deal of impact on decisions because of their expertise. But, their limited communication skills reduce their impact and they become frustrated. People with high levels of communication anxiety may also find participation threatening and may respond by withdrawing. The organization loses the expertise of such employees and their satisfaction with their jobs drops. In less participatory arrangements, these people would have opportunities to communicate privately with a single supervisor. Since privacy provides back stages where they can plan and rehearse their messages for this single, known listener, their anxiety may be reduced. For them, nonparticipatory decision making may be more satisfying and may allow the organization to benefit more from their expertise.

Participation may also increase employee stress by creating communication overload. When participatory strategies are used, everyone involved is required to increase his or her communication. Some PDM systems ask employees to meet after work or on weekends. Especially when their jobs place extreme demands on them, they may not be able to handle the increased communication and the time it takes away from other activities. The problem is even greater when employees, for whatever reasons, wish to participate less than they are asked to do. When the amount of participation is either more or less than employees desire, they have higher stress, lower job satisfaction, and poorer performance than when participation matches their preferences.[2]

Supervisors also resist PDM. People become supervisors, at least in part, because they have a desire for power and an ability to obtain and use it to their advantage. They gain substantial rewards from their superior positions—salary, status, and most important, the legitimate right to exercise authority over others. People maintain positive self-images by comparing themselves, their positions, their power, and their achievements to others. Power-sharing strategies, including PDM, are designed to reduce the power "gap" between supervisors and their subordinates. If the strategies succeed, they threaten the superiority, and thus the self-esteem and self-images, of powerful people. Thus, PDM threatens precisely those people who hold power most dear and who have the greatest personal and practical reasons to want to hold on to the power they have gained over the years.

Power holders may resist sharing their power overtly by refusing to use participatory strategies; using them only for trivial issues; acting in ways that split the group or otherwise impede its ability to make effective decisions; refusing to carry out the group's decisions; or sabotaging the decision when it is implemented. Other methods are more subtle, for example, withholding valuable information from subordinates. Doing so leads their subordinates to make bad decisions. Based on this withheld information supervisors can (accurately) predict that their subordinates' decisions will fail. When their self-fulfilling predictions come true, their subordinates perceive that they are exceptionally expert and competent. Thus their ability to control the group's decisions in the future is increased. In this way, power holders may actually be able to use participation to increase their influence and enlarge the power gap between them and their subordinates.[3]

In a series of studies of power-sharing strategies in European firms, Mauk Mulder found that in addition to having greater access to information, supervisors typically also have greater communication skills than their subordinates. They are more persuasive, argue positions more effectively, and are more adept at interpreting other employees' communication and responding appropriately. In participatory systems, these advantages allow them to influence the views of other employees. In time a "power elite" develops whose membership seems to be determined by their greater communication skills, but also is related to their formal positions. Eventually less powerful members communicate less and less and more powerful members begin to dominate the decision-making process. Thus, the opportunity for more open communication, which is the strength of participation, may lead to increased power gaps rather than to power sharing. In a study of communication in a lumberyard, Michael Huspek found that workers were often left powerless by their inability to express their concerns in the technical language of management; they were often literally unable to say a word during grievance sessions. As important, their inability to express themselves led them to believe that they did not know enough to have the right to challenge their supervisors.[4]

CASE STUDY:
NO PILLSBURY DOUGH BOYS HERE*

Resistance is both an individual and a group phenomenon. Different groups of people interpret and respond to the same organizational strategies in different ways. This concept will be discussed at length in Chapter 4, but its relevance to the concept of resistance can be discussed now. For example, let's look at a quality of working life (QWL) program in a large food processing company.*

QWL programs are focused participatory decision-making systems. They are designed to improve productivity and the quality of working life by encouraging labor and management to cooperatively find solutions to everyday concerns that are not addressed in formal labor contracts. But, like every other aspect of organizational life, the way a QWL program is perceived, interpreted, and enacted depends on the frames of reference of the different groups of employees who

(continued)

(continued from the previous page)

are involved. At Foodcom (a pseudonym, of course) various groups interpreted the program in terms of their own short-term interests, and in doing so probably doomed the program to failure from the beginning.

Top management saw the program as a threat to its control of the organization and to short-term profitability. It took months for the consulting group that was hired to help create the program to negotiate seemingly minor issues. Upper management, which operated on the basis of a strict accounting procedure, had institutionalized an obsession with minimizing costs. Because, like all participatory systems, QWL programs incur initial costs greater than their short-term returns, department heads were placed in an impossible situation: They were expected to make the system work while being punished for allowing their employees to spend the time necessary to make it work.

Plant managers described their organization as a "family," but defined that word in paternalistic terms: managers were parents, workers were children. Managers were supposed to control all aspects of "children's" lives. Dress codes and arrival times were strictly enforced, regardless of their actual effect on productivity, and no one was allowed to communicate with anyone else in the plant without the manager's explicit approval. The QWL committees were expected to serve as rubber stamps for the plant managers' projects rather than propose or implement their own solutions to the problems they encountered. Just as the plant managers enacted the role of dictatorial parents, the workers accepted their place as dependent children. They saw the QWL committees as a mechanism for getting perks—new uniforms, better cafeteria food, athletic facilities, and so on—instead of a way to resolve problems encountered at work. Even the workers' union representative accepted this version of the family metaphor: "I'm not saying they're children; I'm saying, you know, that sometimes you gotta police it like they were children." Just as plant managers refused to give their employees any power or responsibility, workers were unwilling to accept any responsibility, instead expecting that someone else would solve their problems for them. For both groups, the QWL program was simply a mechanism for continuing their paternalistic family.

But one group of workers, the machinists (who constructed, repaired, and maintained the plant and its equipment) saw the program differently. There were two unions in the plants, one representing the bakers and packers (FWIU) and one representing the machinists. The FWIU, long dominated by women, had successfully pressed for wage equality. The machinists were all men and resented the women and their salaries. They regularly engaged in sexually harassing communication and made it as difficult as possible for the FWIU employees to do their jobs. Their primary objective seemed to be to assert their power whenever possible. When equipment broke down, they refused to repair it until the request went through the entire chain of command; when the FWIU asked that a holiday be changed from Thursday to Friday to create a three-day

(continued)

(continued from the previous page)

weekend, the machinists refused. They also refused to participate in the QWL project out of fear that they would be outvoted by nonmachinist members. When the committee developed proposals that required the use or adaptation of machinery, the machinists refused to go along unless the proposal benefited them alone. As a result, most of the QWL group's proposals were never implemented or were implemented in a way that doomed them to failure. Through each of these processes, the competitive relationships among upper management, plant managers, FWIU workers, and machinists were maintained through the implementation of a program that was supposed to foster labor-management cooperation.

Applying What You've Learned

1. According to Chapter 3, why do people resist programs of participatory decision making?
2. Why did the various groups resist the QWL program at Foodcom? Which of those reasons were overlooked in the summary of resistance presented in Chapter 3?

Questions to Think About and Discuss

1. Given all that you know about traditional organizations and the accepted assumptions that support them, is it realistic to expect power-sharing systems to ever be accepted without intense resistance?
2. Given all that you know about control and resistance, what are the likely effects of attempting to implement a power-sharing system and failing to do so? Why are those effects likely?

*This case study is based on Michael K. Moch and Jean Bartunek, *Creating Alternative Realities at Work* (New York: Harper Business, 1990). A summary of this book is available in Jean M. Bartunek and Michael Moch, "Multiple Constituencies and the Duality of Working Life," in *Reframing Organizational Culture*, Peter Frost, et al., eds. (Newbury Park, CA: Sage, 1991).

The Effects of PDM and Decentralization   Participatory systems have a number of positive effects. In U.S. firms, formal, company-wide programs of participation still are rare, although their popularity has increased during the last decade (see Chapter 8). Informal programs of participation, where supervisors ask their most productive employees for advice or information, are more widespread. Subordinates respond with useful advice, which increases their supervisors' trust in their judgment and encourages them to seek further advice, and their job satisfaction increases, which reduces absenteeism and voluntary turnover. Somewhat surprisingly, these positive effects do not result from subordinates feeling that participation gives them greater power. Instead, it results from their being better informed about what is going on in the organization. During participatory interactions, supervisors provide information and a more open and satisfying communicative relationship is created.

Systems of participation have more limited effects on performance and productivity. In general, the quality of decisions made by participatory groups is better than that of decisions made by the "average" member of the group but is worse than the decision that would be made by the group's most expert individual. This does not suggest that better decisions would be made by a supervisor acting alone, for the simple reason that the supervisor may or may not be the most expert member of a work group. It just suggests that the positive effects of PDM depend on a number of factors, including the distribution of expertise in the group. Research on the effects of participation on productivity is less favorable. Some studies have found that participation does motivate workers to perform more effectively and more efficiently. In other cases, participation gives supervisors an opportunity to persuade their subordinates to accept high performance goals. But, overall, research on participation indicates that participation does not automatically increase organizational productivity.[5]

The Organization as a Tier of Groups

The relational strategy does not do away with managerial structure altogether. There are still top managers and some middle managers, as well as line-level work groups. However, the concept of the hierarchy so critical to the traditional strategy is replaced with the concept of the organization as a tier of groups.

One of the primary advocates of the relational strategy, Rensis Likert, developed a model of relational organizational design that may help clarify these concepts. He proposed that organizations should be structured around overlapping groups of employees instead of with the independent divisions of the bureaucratic model. Each group would make any decisions that affects it or its members. Each group would be linked to every other group with which it was interdependent by a "linking pin," an employee who was a member of both groups (see Figure 3–1). In this structure, each group could better understand the needs and problems of the other groups. The groups would minimize the problems of trained communication incapacity and specialized languages (discussed in Chapter 2) because they would always have a translator available. Intergroup conflict could be reduced because communication breakdowns between the two groups would be less frequent. Group decision making would be enhanced because each linking pin would have access to different kinds of information as a result of his or her contact with other groups. In effect, this system (which Likert called System Four) created an organizational structure designed around the concept of PDM. Unfortunately, linking pins are placed in difficult and stressful positions. When things go wrong, they are handy scapegoats, and they are often not rewarded for their efforts.[6]

FIGURE 3–1
Likert's Multiple Overlapping Groups

$\bigotimes$ *Linking pins.*

Developing Informal Communication Networks

Chapter 1 explained that informal communication networks emerge in every organization. They were present even in the prisons and concentration camps of World War II. Traditional strategies of organizing largely ignore communication networks other than the formal chain of command. Indeed, because communication through informal ties is outside management's control, supervisors often try to suppress their development. Relational strategies suggest that supervisors should encourage the development of informal networks to supplement the linking-pin structure. Through them employees form meaningful interpersonal relationships, gain a sense of self-respect, meet their sociability needs, and exercise some degree of control over their working lives. People who are actively involved in informal networks have higher morale, job satisfaction, and commitment to their organizations; know more about how their organizations operate; and are better able to meet other peoples' communication needs than employees who are not actively involved.[7]

However, it takes effort to develop and sustain informal networks. It takes time for people to find one another and much successful communication for them to come to understand and trust one another. Sometimes they must learn to compensate for the problems of trained incapacity that were discussed in Chapter 2. Informal networks must regularly be used or they will disappear. Unless two people communicate on a fairly regular basis they will forget the language and frame of reference used by the other person. Just as competence in a foreign language wears off with disuse, learning the frame of reference of other employees also wears off. Then, when a crisis occurs in which employees need to communicate, they find it difficult to do so. Typically informal networks are maintained through gossip,—the sharing of personal information that is irrelevant to specific tasks or organizational decisions. But without gossip, informal networks dissolve.[8]

Generally speaking, informal networks help organizations in three ways: by compensating for the weaknesses in formal communication, by improving organizational decision making, and by fostering innovation. Formal communication networks allow people to handle predictable, routine situations, but they are inefficient means of meeting unanticipated communication needs, for managing crises, for dealing with complex or detailed problems, sharing personal information, or exchanging information rapidly. In a now classic study, Keith Davis found that during a quality-control crisis in a large firm, the information that was needed to solve the problem was rapidly disseminated using informal networks, not formal channels. Informal communication may also be more reliable than formal communication. Because informal communication is less restricted by differences in power and status, it is richer in content than formal communication. Mutual give and take is less inhibited in informal communication, so communicators provide more detail in their messages and are more willing to give and receive feedback. Even gossip and **rumors**—messages whose accuracy cannot immediately be determined by management—usually provide accurate information. Job-related rumors occur because employees are not adequately informed through formal channels. Although some gossip and rumors may be false, when compared to formal communication, with its inherent problems of withholding and distortion (recall Chapter 2), informal communication may even be *more* accurate. Informal networks also tend to be self-correcting. Once an employee is caught spreading false rumors, his or her credibility is reduced. Formal communication networks are not based on interpersonal relationships, so they tend not to self-correct.[9]

Informal networks can also foster innovation. Sometimes people have access to a wealth of valuable information that they are not "officially" supposed to possess. Informal relationships with those people provide an invaluable source of information, especially information that is not supposed to be public knowledge. Employees can release "trial balloons" and monitor employees' reactions while never having to admit officially that the proposal was even being considered. Being able to talk off the record seems to improve organizational decision making, especially when organizations are in the early stages of defining problems and searching for solutions. Through his twenty-year study of bureaucratic organizations, Peter Blau found that informal communication allowed employees to obtain advice and assistance without "really" admitting that they needed it and provided them with politically safe opportunities to think out loud about new ideas or experiences. As a result, informal networks foster innovation. In general, the more open, rapid, and complete an organization's communication system is, the more innovative its employees can be. Through informal networks, people share innovative ideas, obtain feedback that allows them to improve those ideas, and eventually obtain support for those innovations. Informal networks allow (but do not guarantee) people to come to a shared understanding of new ideas and their importance to the organization and thus stimulate them to take collective innovative action.[10]

RELATIONAL STRATEGIES OF MOTIVATION, CONTROL, AND SURVEILLANCE

Traditional strategies of motivation and control are based on the assumptions that workers are motivated primarily by the promise of economic gain. Relational strategies are based on a very different view of human beings and work. As Chapter 1 noted, people have important needs for autonomy, creativity, and sociability, needs that are frustrated by organizations' (and societies') needs for control and coordination. Traditional strategies largely overlooked those needs in a view of human beings that Douglas McGregor has labeled "Theory X." In contrast, relational strategies are designed to fulfill these individual needs through three approaches: persuading supervisors to adopt a radically different view of human beings and the role that meaningful work plays in their lives (a perspective that McGregor calls "Theory Y"; see Table 3-1), enlarging and enriching jobs, and adopting relationship-oriented leadership strategies.[11]

TABLE 3–1

McGregor's Theory X and Theory Y

THEORY X

1. Workers must be supervised as closely as possible, either through direct oversight or by tight reward and/or punishment systems.

2. Work is objectionable to most unless it is made offensive by the actions of organizations.

3. Most people have little initiative, have little capacity for being creative or solving organizational problems, do not want to have responsibilities, and prefer being directed by someone else.

4. People are motivated by economic factors and a need for security.

THEORY Y

1. People usually do not require close supervision and will, if given a chance to control their own activities, be productive, satisfied, and fulfilled.

2. Work is natural and enjoyable to people.

3. People are ambitious, desire autonomy and self-control, and can use their abilities to solve problems and help their organizations meet their goals. Creativity is distributed "normally" across the population, just as is any other characteristic.

4. People are motivated by a variety of needs only some of which involve economics or security.

Job Enrichment and Enlargement

Three of the most influential advocates of this approach to motivation and control were Abraham Maslow, Frederick Herzberg, and Chris Argyris. Maslow's model of human motivation is widely known—people have five kinds of needs that are arranged in a hierarchy: *physiological* (expressed in feelings of thirst, lust, and so on), *safety* (feeling free from danger, harm, and the fear that physiological needs will not be met), *belongingness* (a desire for meaningful relationships with other people), *esteem* or *ego* (feelings of accomplishment and recognition), and *self-actualization* (a concept that Maslow never explained clearly but that seems to be related to the feeling that one has done or is doing what one is meant to do). Once lower-level needs are fulfilled, upper-level needs become salient. Herzberg refined Maslow's model by differentiating "lower-level" needs (which he called **hygiene** *factors*) and "higher level" needs (which he called **motivators**). Hygiene factors motivate people by allowing them to avoid pain. When these needs are not met, people feel discomfort; when they are met, the discomfort is reduced, but once an adequate level of fulfillment is reached no additional pleasure is felt. Motivators create pleasure when they are provided but their absence does not cause frustration or pain. Although neither Maslow's nor Herzberg's conclusions have been supported consistently by subsequent research, their perspective became the basis of a number of strategies for increasing workers' job satisfaction by enlarging and enriching their jobs.[12]

One of the earliest and most influential advocates of job enrichment/enlargement was Chris Argyris. He argued that many of the key characteristics of traditional models of organizing frustrated the needs of normal, psychologically healthy people. Jobs that are specialized or routinized (performed in the same way day after day), supervisors who control their employees "tightly", and highly competitive, individualistic atmospheres are especially alienating. People respond to these situations by acting in ways that are counterproductive for their organizations—becoming defensive (attacking or withdrawing from coworkers) or apathetic (for example, daydreaming), socializing with other frustrated workers instead of focusing attention on their work, leaving the organization, or attempting to advance to positions that are less frustrating. The traditional strategy focuses on creating precisely these kinds of situations. Managers are charged with segmenting, simplifying, and routinizing jobs—making them as "impoverished" and "small" as possible.

Presumably, this **deskilling** of jobs is designed to increase organizational efficiency. But, it is so alienating for employees that it often leads to a net loss in individual and organizational productivity. The real reason for deskilling may be to enhance supervisory control. Direct surveillance is easiest when jobs are deskilled. In addition, organizations with many deskilled jobs can hire employees who have few alternatives and thus cannot resist management regardless of how alienated they are—high school students, disabled people, or, most recently, residents of Third World countries (including children). Deskilled tasks can easily be outsourced (contracted to outside organizations who use their own workers to do the job, often at much lower rates of pay) or assigned to part-time or other "contingent" workers (people who are hired for a specific project only). And, because workers perform tasks requiring few skills, they are easy to replace when they are fired. Arraying deskilled tasks along an assembly line provides workers with little or no opportunity to communicate with one another and forces them to adjust the pace of their activities to the pace of the machines. This keeps them from sharing grievances, comparing the way management treats them, or making plans for collective action. New technologies can be developed solely for the purpose of simplifying and routinizing jobs even further. For example, at one time the service jobs of grocery-store checker and fast-food sales clerk required at least minimal arithmetical, keyboarding, and memory skills. Today computerized cash registers—that, as all other deskilling technologies, can increase output per person hour—make it possible to hire people without these skills. The next time you visit your local McDonald's, look closely at the keyboard on the cash registers and ask yourself what skills are necessary to operate it. To see just how deskilled these jobs are, order something that is not represented by a button on the keyboard and see what happens. By the mid-1960s most production workers in the United States were involved in this kind of routine, repetitive, deskilled activity, which failed to fulfill individual needs for creativity, autonomy, or sociability. By the mid-1980s many white-collar workers were involved in similar jobs.[13]

Although deskilling does increase productivity for a time, it also decreases job satisfaction and encourages resistance. Sometimes resistance is informal. For example, salesclerks have long resisted deskilling by creating and using their own informal relational strategies. They are friendly and supportive of one another, huddle together on the floor to foster in-group communication, ignore management's efforts to make them compete against one another, share duties that management assigns to individuals, and meet together outside of work to engage in "rituals of women's culture", such as wedding and birth showers.[14] Other forms of resistance involve more overt hostility between labor and management.

An alternative to deskilling is for management to do just the opposite—to "enlarge" or "enrich" jobs. Doing so increases efficiency because it allows organizations to decentralize. It also increases profitability by substituting the upper-level rewards of enhanced creativity and autonomy for expensive lower-level rewards, such as salaries and wages. But, successful enlargement/enrichment relies heavily on relational communication. If a job is too complex, it is frustrating and unsatisfying. If it is too simple, it is boring. Successfully matching workers and jobs, as Fredrick Taylor realized a century ago, requires a high level of open communication and feedback between supervisors and their subordinates. In addition, workers seem to figure out how rich their jobs are both by monitoring what they do and by talking with other workers. Unless people believe that their tasks are stimulating, they will not be stimulating. Workers develop these beliefs when other workers tell them that they envy their jobs. In fact, job satisfaction in general is influenced both by the objective features of employees' jobs **and** by what their coworkers say about their jobs. Thus, successful job enlargement/enrichment requires both careful job design, and active and supportive relational communication.[15]

Teams and Team-based Surveillance

The relational strategy takes groups as the basic formal unit of the organization. A variety of groups and teams can be found in most organizations. A "**team**" is a formally established group that has a clear focus and an effectiveness-driven structure in which members are aware of their own and others' roles and are motivated to work together to help the team succeed. As this definition implies, not all groups are teams, and becoming a team is something of an accomplishment[16].

Larson and LaFasto conducted an in-depth study of 50 teams, ranging from a field team from the Centers for Disease Control to the 1988 Notre Dame football team. They found that effective teams have seven common characteristics:

A *clear, elevating goal* that is meaningful and significant to members, clearly stated in familiar terms, measurable, and challenging. Larson and LaFasto concluded that the main reason for failure in the 50 teams they studied was that personal goals superceded group goals.

A *results-driven structure* with clear role definitions, accountability, methods for monitoring performance, and an effective communication system that fosters fast and complete information exchange and documentation of issues and decisions.

Competent team members who have technical knowledge and skills necessary for the team's work. Members must also have *social* competencies as well. They must be able to work with others, desire to contribute to the group, and appreciate others' differences and contributions.

Unified commitment to the team and its success. This is fostered, first, by promoting participation of all members in making important and day-to-day decisions. Second members must develop "high expectations for each other, expect that everyone else on the team will contribute to the extent that each is capable, and will become disturbed if a member pursues individual objectives at the expense of the team goal."[17]

A *collaborative climate,* characterized by open communication operating on the following principles: honesty—bringing all issues before the group and not hiding problems or exaggerating what one has done; willingness to share and receptivity to ideas, opinions, and positions; consistency in behavior; and respectful and dignified treatment of all people.

Standards of excellence that create pressure to perform at very high levels. Pressure to perform stems from having members who have a high motivation to excel, encouragement by other members to perform, a clear sense of the positive consequences of success and the negative consequences of failure, and external pressure from the organization. High standards are encouraged by models of excellence, especially other high performing teams. Effective teams also continuously upgrade their standards as they meet or exceed them.

External support and recognition from the larger organization. The team must be given the resources and authority to succeed and the organization must recognize and reward high performance.

Principled leadership that establishes a vision for the team and empowers members. The leader must also create change by realizing the need for change, reminding members that change is normal, and helping members through the change process. The goal of the effective team leader is to unify the team and enable members to "unleash their talent" in the team's work.

A group that organizes itself around these principles is designed to galvanize its members but also to enable them to improve their knowledge and skills. Teams such as these do not just spring into being with little or no work, but instead are cultivated over a period of time.

The most common form of team is the *formal, on-going work group,* such as a hospital emergency room or a sales team. Work groups have definite goals and tasks, and their relationships with other work groups and the larger organization are often specified in formal terms. For instance, the group in a chair-manufacturing firm that draws up contracts for delivery of the company's products must carefully coordinate its actions with the group that plans production and the shipping department to ensure that there will be enough chairs and that they can be delivered at the desired time. Under the relational strategy this coordination is carried out through direct communication between the groups, sometimes through linking pins and sometimes via informal representatives. The informal communication system may also play a role in coordinating work groups.

Project teams are temporary groups set up to carry out a specific task within a specified time frame, which may vary from a few months to several years. Members are typically assigned to project teams on a limited basis and are often on loan from their home department or group. Organizations often create project teams to develop new products and activities or to solve persistent problems, as when McDonald's Corporation formed the Chicken McNugget team to bring this interesting fast food to market.[18] The Chicken McNugget team had members from the product development and marketing departments, which made it a *cross-functional project* team. Cross-functional teams are constituted to ensure that the perspectives of different departments or functions are brought to a project and that all aspects of the organization that must participate in the project are involved. Other examples of project teams include *quality circles* and *quality-improvement teams,* which are charged with studying and solving problems in some organizational process and *task forces,* which focus on important, high-profile problems or issues and are composed of high-status members who bring credibility to the group.

In addition to work groups and project teams, there is one other important type of group in most organizations, the *integrating team.* Integrating teams are set up specifically to coordinate activities of different teams or departments in an organization. Examples of integrating teams include the executive committee of a college within a university, which is comprised of department heads who discuss issues that affect more than one department or the college as a whole, and a merger team, composed of members from two organizations that are set to merge, which attempts to coordinate the combination of the organizations and address problems as they develop. (We will discuss integrating teams in more depth in Chapter 5.)

The employee's work group is the single most important influence on his or her attitudes and actions. Attention to work-group influences on motivation goes back at least as far as the Hawthorne studies of the 1930s. Groups "tell" their members how to make sense out of their experiences at work. For example, if a work group interprets an organization's attempts to motivate employees as exploitative, its members are likely to reject these programs, no matter how attractive they may seem to those who devise them. On the other hand, if groups buy into job enrichment or other programs, it may significantly increase their motivational impact.

Many organizations, including corporations such as Xerox and Proctor and Gamble, are attempting to promote the development of teams by setting them up so that they are "self-managing." Self-managing teams are intended to empower team members by enabling them to organize and govern themselves as they see best. In many cases, the team is also allowed to set its own goals. In a real sense, the team members serve as their own manager and leader. The philosophy behind self-managing teams takes a page from the book on empowerment discussed previously: If members are told what to do and kept in dependent positions, they are unlikely to develop the skills and motivation needed to create an effective team. If, on the other hand, members are given power and responsibility, they will see them as a privilege and rise to the occasion, learning the skills and attitudes of leaders by making their own mistakes and correcting their course. The self-managing team is currently the pinnacle of the relational strategy of organizing.

Teams influence their members' productivity. In some cases, these pressures lead individual members to be less productive. **Ratebusters**, people who produce too much or who go along with management too readily, may be punished by coworkers. Sanctions can range from "tutoring," to warnings, to the "silent treatment," and even to physical violence. But, in other cases the pressures may be to increase production. Leonard Sayles notes that "We have other instances on record where the group has sanctioned increasingly high productivity, rejected fellow workers who could not maintain high output, and resisted threats to existing high quality standards." This line of thought is behind recent advocacy of team-based organizations. In theory, properly composed and motivated teams may create a more effective organization than more traditional forms of organizing.[19]

CASE STUDY:
EMPOWERMENT, OR IRON CAGE?

Xel Communications, a telecommunications manufacturing company located in the Denver suburbs, changed its manufacturing plant from a traditional hierarchy to a flattened design that depended on self-managed teams.* Xel made this change because Vice President Joe Painter became convinced that the company could survive in the highly competitive telecommunications market only if it was adaptive and innovative. He concluded that self-managed teams that harnessed all employees' energy and creativity were the most effective way to increase Xel's flexibility.

Self-managed teams are peer groups of 10 to 15 people totally responsible for the manufacture of major components. Members of the team make all the decisions and undertake all the work involved in manufacturing the components; they are also responsible for hiring and firing, obtaining materials, and for general management of the team. If a self-managed team has a problem coordinating with another team, members of the two teams meet to come to a workable decision. Barker, Melville, and Pacanowsky observe, "These teams fit best in organizations characterized by interdependent tasks, complex processes, time sensitivity, and the need for rapid change and adaptation."

Xel implemented the new program gradually starting with a trial team that performed well beyond anyone's expectations. This success led Painter and his managers to speed up training the other employees and within eight months the plant had been reconfigured to accommodate three self-managing teams, labeled the red, white, and blue teams. Painter's role was changed by this transformation into that of "coach," a consultant the teams could call on for advice and problem-solving suggestions. The teams ultimately, however, called their own shots. It took all three teams about three months to work out a routine for their operations, and each worked out their own procedures for making decisions, managing their work, and coordinating.

One milestone in the life of the white team occurred when it ran into an unexpected problem. A component in a circuit board that was part of a very important order had not come in due to an inventory order error. One of the basic principles the group had decided on was "Do not build a board unless all the parts are in" (the logic behind this was that adding a part at a later time could result in damage to already installed components). The team sent its coordinator, Alma, to Joe Painter to ask his advice. Alma interpreted Joe's suggestion that the team should build the boards and add the part later as an order; she had some trouble making a transition from the old hierarchical structure to the new self-managing organization. When Alma brought what she saw as Joe's directive back to the white team, the members of the team rebelled. They expressed anger and resentment that Joe would "order" them, a self-managing team, to do anything.

(continued)

(continued from the previous page)

They scheduled a meeting with Joe and aired their grievances, at which time Joe told the white team that they were absolutely correct that they should make their own decisions and that Alma had misinterpreted his suggestion as an order. The members of the white team were pleased when their independence was confirmed. They felt they had learned to stand on their own two feet and to take responsibility. They had developed their own procedures and structure in the coordinator role, and Joe had accepted it.

Another aspect this incident underscored was the strong identification team members had with the organization. As the team began to manage itself, members realized that the fate of the company rested in their hands. They were responsible for decisions that could make or break Xel. They were free from direction from the top, but with this came a weighty responsibility. This shift resulted in an increased feeling of ownership of their work among team members. They had the same desire for the success of Xel as Joe Painter and the other top management had once felt.

Over time the team's empowerment confronted it with a thorny issue: what was it to do with members who had their own ideas about work and did not go along with the group's sense of what should be done? The move to self-management had done away with the managers who formerly would have written up employees whose behavior detracted from the team's ability to get its work done. One particular problem was employees who arrived late and left work early. In theory members could set their own hours now that the team managed itself, and a degree of flexibility was seen as desirable by some members. However, when these members worked fewer hours than (but received the same pay as) other members, it impaired the white team's ability to deliver orders in a timely fashion.

At the white team's daily 7 A.M. meeting, when the day's activities were planned and other decisions made, the members of the team decided that everyone should arrive before the 7 A.M. meeting and work until 5 P.M. to meet the backlog of orders. A worker who arrived five or more minutes late would be docked a day's pay. When one late-arriving member protested the penalty, team members scolded her and refused to relax their rules. This and similar incidents had an interesting effect on the members of white team. They noted their fellow members' strictness and became afraid of it themselves. Moreover, having seen the team be hard on its own members, they were also not inclined to let other members "get by" by relaxing the norms. Over time, some members began to resent the rigidity of the white team to some extent. However, they reinforced it as well by enforcing team rules tightly, for fear that any relaxation would lead to an erosion of team standards. Over time, the white team focused more and more on its control system. Members spoke less about values of teamwork and more about the need to obey the team's norms and they worked to write unambiguous rules that strangely resembled bureaucratic regulations.

(continued)

(continued from the previous page)

Applying What You've Learned

1. What forms of control are characteristic of relational strategies of organizing?
2. How do those forms of control differ from control in traditional strategies?

Questions to Think About and Discuss

1. Were the members of white team empowered, or trapped in a control system of their own creation?
2. Barker et al. conclude that employees who strongly identify with a firm are generally tougher managers for each other than hierarchical supervisors are. Do you agree or disagree with this?
3. Why might employees entrusted with managing their own team develop this strong surveillance and control system over other members?
4. Barker et al. argue that excessive (and even exploitative) control of self-managing teams over their members is harder to recognize and resist than the same type of control by managers. This is because members believe that rules they are enforcing that are legitimately made by a democratic process. As a result, they see the rules as more objective and legitimate than they might if a manager imposed them from outside. Could the white team break out of the spiral of control it has fallen into? What recommendations do you have for how it could do this?

---

*This case is based on J. R. Barker, "Tightening the Iron Cage: Concertive Control in Self-Managing Teams," *Administrative Science Quarterly, 38* (1993): 408–437; and J. R. Barker, C. W. Melville, and M. E. Pacanowsky, "Self-Directed Teams at Xel: Changes in Communication Practices During a Program of Cultural Transformation," *Journal of Applied Communication Research, 21* (1993): 297–313.

While teams can be quite rewarding to participants, as the Xel case shows, they also exert their own form of control over their members, control that may cause stress and even lead members to act against their best interests. Several characteristics of teams—their stress on unity and commitment, their emphasis on high levels of performance, ever-increasing standards, and high levels of mutual responsibility among members—can set the stage for the development of extreme pressure to conform on members who are out of line with the group. When groups strongly identify with the organization, as at Xel, this pressure can serve as a stronger controlling force than a traditional hierarchical manager exerts. Tompkins and Cheney call this concertive (or "unobtrusive") control because although it has many of the same results as control by top managers, it arises from the concerted action of peers.[20] In such cases, the team becomes just another body that represents managerial interests at the expense of worker development, empowerment, and other desirable results of the relational strategy. Members of controlling teams tend to fall back into a cycle of doing things the organization wants them to do, powerlessness, and in some cases the same type of resistance to the team that is common in hierarchical structures. However, concertive control is particularly effective because it is often much harder to recognize than control by managers or top-down rules. This is because members of the team have inadvertently developed the control system themselves, and they see it as a normal outgrowth of their work and tend not to recognize how it undermines participation. (We will discuss concertive/unobtrusive control at more length in Chapter 4.)

Other kinds of teams, such as **quality circles,** have been criticized for similar reasons. Cynthia Stohl argues that though quality circles are often intended to enable employees to improve their work through participation, they frequently become tools of managerial control.[21] Only those suggestions that management is comfortable with are implemented, which in effect takes participation out of employee hands and turns quality-improvement efforts into instruments of organizational control. Scott Poole found examples of this in a large medical organization; several members of quality teams commented that had they known that their efforts would be used to promote the agendas of management, they would not have participated in the first place. However, this reaction was not uniform: Other members found the quality teams a great source of satisfaction and felt their voices had been heard; some also believed participation helped them develop their leadership skills and would help their careers. As with all systems of surveillance and control that develop in participative programs, control is less than perfect; resistance is possible; and some participation is real and meaningful

RELATIONAL STRATEGIES OF LEADERSHIP

Although there are a large number of different relational strategies of leadership, they all focus on improving supervisor-subordinate relationships through making them more trusting and more predictable. These goals are achieved by fostering open and supportive communication and by engaging in **transactional leadership.**

Fostering Open and Supportive Supervisor–Subordinate Communication

Early research on relational strategies of leadership found that high-producing organizations had supervisors who were both highly competent in the technical aspects of their jobs and were employee-centered and considerate. Effective supervisors express respect for, trust in, and a genuine concern about their subordinates. They set high but achievable performance goals for their units and communicate a kind of contagious enthusiasm about achieving them. They supervise loosely and actively encourage their subordinates to participate in decision making. They do not engage in superficial "pat-on-the-back" or "first-name" gimmicks, but emphasize a deeper concern for the group members' needs. They also do not make their subordinates feel uncomfortable or *defensive*.

When people feel that they are being judged (even praise creates discomfort if it is excessively strong or too public), manipulated (tricked into believing that they have an important role in the organization when they do not), controlled, or "preached at," or otherwise treated as an inferior, they become defensive and withdraw from the relationship. Supervisors can create supportive, nondefensive climates by communicating in ways that are *descriptive* and *objective* rather than *evaluative;* that focus on working *together* to solve important problems; that are *spontaneous,* open, and honest; that *affirm* the subordinates' competence; and that *encourage* them to initiate communication, even if doing so involves negative topics or information. Even orders can be given in a supportive way. The orders themselves need to be clear and specific, be perceived as logical and appropriate, and be legitimate in the sense that Weber used that term (that is, accepted as normal and proper by workers). Orders also need to be communicated in a way that allows subordinates to retain a sense of personal pride, self-respect, and autonomy (to "save face," a concept that will be developed in Chapters 7 and 11)—to feel that they are making a free and open choice to obey the order.[22]

Supportive communication also depends on the supervisor's listening skills and his or her ability to avoid disconfirming communication. Messages carry meaning at both content and relational levels—they provide information and they make a statement about the interpersonal relationship that exists between the communicators (see Chapter 7 for a more detailed discussion). **Disconfirming communication** occurs when a supervisor communicates in a way that does not acknowledge a subordinate's worth. For example, a young accountant waited two weeks to see her supervisor. After having meetings canceled, rescheduled, and canceled again; telephone calls cut off; and chance meetings in the hallway in which the supervisor did not even stop walking to say hello, the accountant finally got into a meeting. After explaining that she did not understand new tax laws on capital gains rates, her supervisor said, "This isn't my problem. Talk to the training department." Her long-awaited meeting lasted three minutes. Clearly, she concluded, her supervisor does not recognize that she exists, much less that she is an important part of the team. This does not mean that supervisors cannot disagree with their subordinates, because one can reject or question the content of persons' communications without rejecting their identities.[23] Open and supportive communication enhances trust, reduces withholding and distortion of information, and serves as a basis for transactional leadership.

Transactional Leadership

Supervisor–subordinate communication is a two-way, interactive process. Although supervisors tend to have a greater impact on communicative relationships than their subordinates because of their formal authority, interpersonal relationships develop because of the *mutual* exchanges that take place *between* the parties. This is the primary assumption underlying transactional views of leadership. Leaders, according to this model, must legitimize their position—formal rank alone does not make one a leader—but legitimation is a two-way street. Leaders and each of their followers negotiate working relationships. (Chapter 7 examines the negotiation process in more detail.) Both parties align themselves with one another; they converge toward the same set of values, are able to solve complex and unprecedented problems together, and have a relaxed, mutually supportive relationship. Eventually, they become **co-oriented**—they reach agreement on the rules that guide their relationship (for example, what topics they will discuss and what topics they will avoid, whether they must schedule meetings or can just pop in to one another's office, whether to use first names or titles, whether they interrupt one another or quietly wait until the other is finished talking to respond). They negotiate a trusting relationship, one in which their motives, intentions, openness, and integrity are consistent, in which they are dependably competent, willing, and able to help one another with job-related problems, and in which the judgment is reliable.

Even supportive communication is mutual and transactional. Trust, respect, and task factors, such as risk-taking and innovation, have all been shown to be greatest when supervisors are supportive of their supervisors *and* their subordinates perceive that they receive high levels of support. In other words, both the level of support and the level agreement about the level of support are important factors. Supervisors and subordinates support *one another* in a number of ways: by talking about how organizations work (for example, discussing potential career moves and their likely effects); by helping develop new skills or giving one another tangible assistance when it is needed (for example, a director of programming jumping in to help solve a knotty language problem and doing so cheerfully without a this-will-cost-you-later attitude); by providing an outlet for venting anger or frustration (serving as a sounding board); or by offering praise, acceptance, or reassurance. Regardless of the specific technique that is used, it is the *mutual* support that supervisors and subordinates give one another that is important.[24]

In sum, transactional views of leadership focus on the development of particular kinds of supervisor–subordinate relationships. It recognizes that neither person is wholly in charge of the process and that supervisors will often have different kinds of relationships with different subordinates.

ASSESSING RELATIONAL STRATEGIES

There are many criteria that might be used to evaluate a strategy of organizing and its associated motivation and control strategy and approach to leadership. Two commonly used criteria are employees' job satisfaction and organizational performance and profitability.

Relational Strategies and Employee Job Satisfaction

Relational strategies do lead to increased job satisfaction. This impact has been shown to be rather small from a practical standpoint, but it does seem to occur consistently regardless of the kind of organization being studied or the specific research method employed. The relationship is strongest for employees near the bottom of the organizational hierarchy and with people who need large amounts of information to do their jobs well. But, regardless of the specifics of a work situation, employees in open, supportive communication climates are satisfied employees.[25]

Creating and maintaining high levels of job satisfaction is important for a number of reasons. Perhaps most important, work groups composed of satisfied people simply are more pleasant places to work. Since most people spend much of their lives at work, this may be sufficient justification for the use of relational strategies. There also are some more tangible benefits. Job dissatisfaction has consistently been linked to high levels of absenteeism and voluntary turnover. When employees who perform important tasks are missing, other employees feel increased stress and organizational performance declines. When the costs of searching for and training replacement personnel are high, voluntary turnover is costly. When the economy is strong, as it has been in the United States for the past decade, voluntary turnover can be extremely expensive. For example, in 1999 Ford Motor Company agreed to establish thirty round-the-clock "Family Service and Learning Centers" at their largest locations. These centers will provide child and elder care, formal and informal education programs, health screenings and limited health care. They are primarily designed to address the lack of affordable child care for working parents, especially for those who work the night shift. Ford President, Jacques Nasser, said, "It's not low cost, but we're not wasting a cent. This is an effort to attract and retain talent because turnover costs money."[26] Of course, other factors also influence turnover. Relationships with coworkers are important, especially to lower-level employees. So are factors such as the legacy of downsizing and the end of loyalty described in Chapter 1. But, the primary factor seems to be satisfaction with supervision. In a 1999 survey by Lou Harris associates, employees who were dissatisfied with their supervisor-subordinate relationship were four times as likely to be looking for other jobs than were satisfied employees. A 1999 Gallup poll found that a caring boss is a more important determinant of job satisfaction than either money or fringe benefits. The researcher in charge of the study concluded that "people join companies, but they leave managers."

Relational Strategies and Individual/Organizational Performance

Relational strategies of organizing are based on the assumption that improving communication will increase morale and motivation, which in turn will increase individual and organizational performance. Ironically, at least in production-oriented firms, relational strategies do have positive effects on performance *but not for the reasons described in the strategy.* First of all, the primary assumption of the relational strategy does not seem to be accurate: *High levels of job satisfaction do not inevitably lead to high levels of individual or organizational performance.* Of course, it does makes sense intuitively that satisfied workers will work harder and perform better than dissatisfied workers; if people are happy at work, they *should* be more committed to their organization and thus *should* want to work harder to make sure their organizations succeed. However, fifty years of research on the relationship between job satisfaction and performance has not found strong relationships between the two. The average correlation is 0.14, which means that about two percent of differences in employees' performance can be attributed to differences in their job satisfaction. Instead, this research indicates either that high performance leads to high job satisfaction (because workers feel pride in a job well done) or that other factors simultaneously increase both satisfaction and performance. For instance, if workers value hard work and high levels of performance for its own sake, or if they believe they will receive tangible rewards from high performance, they tend to be both satisfied and productive. If they do not hold these beliefs, they tend to be both dissatisfied and relatively unproductive regardless of the strategy of organizing used in their organizations. People who are trapped in an autocratic, alienating organization because they have few employment opportunities, because of their race, gender, ethnic background, lack of education, disabilities, or because of the general economic situation, are often dissatisfied but highly productive because they are afraid of losing their jobs. Conversely, people whose nonwork lives are fulfilling may expend only the minimum amount of effort necessary to keep their jobs regardless of how satisfied they are at work. In short, the work world seems to be relatively full of people who smile a lot and do very little and people who smile not at all and do a lot.[27]

So, relational strategies do not necessarily improve productivity by increasing morale. But, they do seem to pay off for other reasons. Open and supportive supervisory communication helps compensate for the problems in formal communication that were described in Chapter 2. Openness creates trust, and trust reduces the withholding or distorting of information. Supervisors give trusted subordinates more attention, support, and sensitivity than they do to subordinates they do not trust, and they use persuasion or information-giving instead of coercion as a means of influence. In turn, this kind of communication gives subordinates a great deal of information about their jobs, organizations, and their supervisor's needs. This knowledge allows them to know what information is important to their supervisors and enables them to better filter the information that they exchange with their supervisors. Trusted subordinates provide more information and more accurate information and thus give their supervisors incentives to trust and be open with them. Nontrusted subordinates grow to mistrust their supervisors and withdraw (withhold or distort communication), giving their supervisors evidence that they cannot be trusted. Through this kind of reinforcing communication cycle, openness begets openness; closed and defensive communication perpetuates closed and defensive communication. Open and supportive communication is especially valuable for subordinates who have complex and ambiguous jobs. They need a great deal of task-related information and advice that only their supervisors can provide. It is difficult to ask for help from a closed and unsupportive supervisor. If they do not ask for information or help, it is more difficult for them to master their complex tasks, which makes it more likely that they will make errors. Subordinates who make frequent mistakes lose their supervisors' trust, which perpetuates the negative cycle.[28]

Relational strategies also seem to have a positive influence on the perfor- mance of service-related organizations, which now comprise more than half of U.S. firms. When employees communicate with clients or customers, they tend to mirror their communication relationship with their supervisors. If their supervisors are not warm, supportive, and open with them, they will not be with their clients and customers. Alienated subordinates create alienated cus- tomers, who may take their business elsewhere. For example, the late 1990s were a disastrous time for Northwest Airlines, the fourth-largest carrier in the United States. Beginning with serious labor problems in 1995, the public's opinion of the airline plummeted, culminating in a 1999 snowstorm in Detroit when angry passengers were left sitting in planes for eight hours. Faced with economic disaster, Northwest's management asked some of its best customers (then a small and rapidly declining number of people) to tell them what they could do to turn the airline around. The customers blamed the airline's image problem on poor supervisor-subordinate relationships. One told them that "your employees do care and a lot of them are frustrated by lack of response from Northwest's management;" another advised them to "focus on respect for your employees and they will undoubtedly deliver." Management responded by trying to improve supervisor-subordinate communication. Within a year, North- west's regular customers saw a difference. Tom Bagget, a customer from Mem- phis, TN, noted that "Northwest is going from an almost adversarial relation- ship with employees to cooperation." It is too early to tell whether the improved relationships will continue, but Northwest's experience makes it clear that improving superior-subordinate communication pays immediate div- idends in improving employee-customer relationships. For service organiza- tions, high customer satisfaction yields bottom-line benefits: It increases profit margins, reduces marketing costs while increasing them for the competition, enhances the organization's reputation, and lowers many of the costs of doing business.[29]

Finally, relational strategies enhance the performance of organizations in highly competitive, turbulent environments. Decentralized structures, PDM, and supportive supervision combine to create open, relatively free-flowing communication systems. Boundary-spanners can obtain information from the environment and rapidly disseminate that information to other employees who will be able to draw on multiple kinds of expertise to solve complicated, unprecedented problems. For example, Taiwan and Hong Kong, and more recently mainland China, have built their economic success around family businesses. These organizations have thrived in highly competitive, global environments because they are more flexible, less bureaucratic, and have greater employee commitment than large private or state-owned companies. They also innovate more rapidly and are quicker to adopt new product lines.[30] In short, for the same reasons that traditional strategies tend to fail in competitive, turbulent environments (recall Chapter 2), relational strategies thrive.

A DIFFERENT TYPE OF ASSESSMENT

Throughout this chapter we have examined relational strategies largely in terms of organizational performance and effectiveness. There is a very different way to evaluate strategies of organizing, one proposed by a number of scholars who call themselves "critical theorists." They argue that relational strategies may seem to create better work situations than traditional strategies, but that impression masks some important realities about all strategies of organizing. Two key concepts are especially important for understanding critical theories of organizing—*interests* and *legitimate participation*.[51]

At one level, owners, managers, and workers all *seem* to have many interests in common, including the long-term survival of their organization. On a closer look, it becomes clear that all three groups have some self-interests that are different from, and contradictory to, the interests of the other groups. For example, workers almost always have a strong vested interest in the continued operation of their firms in a particular locale and with stable or increasing real (adjusted for inflation) wages. When plants are closed or relocated, workers usually lose their jobs and find it difficult to find comparable employment elsewhere. Even if they are offered employment in other plants, relocating is psychologically and financially costly, especially when the workers have not previously moved. Similarly, reductions in wages or benefits can be devastating for workers, and programs to increase organizational productivity through technological innovations often lead to layoffs or a lowered standard of living.

Managers usually benefit little from maintaining the long-term viability of their organizations or increasing their workers' job security. This is because managers rarely are owners, especially in large firms. They are not entrepreneurs whose vision, ideas, and hard work built an organization to which they are psychologically and financially committed. Indeed, their careers usually involve moving rather quickly from one organization to another. Their rewards are based on the short-term profitability of the firm, especially now that a large proportion of managers' total income is based on year-end performance bonuses. Consequently, they may have little self-interest involved in the firm's long-term success and a great deal of interest in downsizing, reducing workers' wages and benefits, and replacing workers with new technologies. Since each of these steps is likely to increase the firm's short-term profitability, they will increase the managers' economic gains. They also may increase managers' salaries, bonuses, and job security because they also serve the financial interests of investors. For example, Alan Downs found that in U.S. firms during the 1990's, the number of jobs that a CEO eliminated was a better predictor of her or his compensation than the overall performance of his or her firm.[32] Similarly, successful strategies of motivation and control tend to serve management's interests much more than workers' interests. Even if they do lead to increased organizational effectiveness and profitability, most of the resulting rewards will go to management and investors, not to workers.

Owners (which means stockholders in most large firms) also are interested in limiting worker incomes and benefits. They also have an interest in limiting management's salaries and bonuses because all these limits serve to increase stock dividends. Because it is relatively easy to sell stock on the public market when an organization begins to decline, owners may also have little interest in the long-term survival of the firm. A similar analysis can be developed for organizations that are not in the private sector.

Two highly publicized cases illustrate this point. During the 1980s, Frank Lorenzo was the CEO of Texas Air, the parent company of Continental Airlines and Eastern Airlines. Although Continental and Eastern regularly lost $200 million or more each year and entered bankruptcy proceedings three times, Lorenzo regularly received annual performance bonuses of more than $1 million. When Eastern finally went out of business, its owners (creditors) received approximately three cents for each dollar they had invested in the airline. Similarly, during the late 1980s and early 1990s, Lee Iacocca decided to move much of Chrysler's production operation overseas (primarily to Mexico and the Far East). These steps cost thousands of autoworkers their jobs, but they also increased Chrysler's profits (or, initially, reduced its losses) and the value of its stock. Iacocca was rewarded with multimillion-dollar annual performance bonuses and one of the largest retirement bonuses in American history. Iacocca could have taken a different approach to revitalizing Chrysler—reducing stock dividends and reinvesting the funds in improved production technologies, as many German automakers did, or reducing the massive gap between worker income and managerial salaries as Japanese automakers did, or reducing overhead by restraining managerial salaries. There is little evidence that Chrysler's management (or the management of virtually any large U.S. organization) ever seriously considered these approaches. In sum, actions that may be in management's self-interest may violate the short- and long-term interests of workers and owners and vice versa. Because workers and owners have little influence on the everyday operations of an organization, it is the interests of the managers that take precedence. (Critical theorists use the term "privileged" to refer to those interests that are given prominence.)

However, the conflicting nature of these interests is often disguised by the discourse of modern organizations, a process that Jurgen Habermas has labeled **"systematically distorted communication."**[33] One way of disguising the contradictions is to treat one set of interests (for example, management's) as everyone's interests. Installing a computerized system for monitoring employees' work is usually justified in terms of its increased efficiency and the firm's enhanced ability to compete (recall Chapter 2). Efficiency and increased competitiveness are presented as being in everyone's interests. In the long run, they may or may not be, depending on a large number of economic considerations. But in the short term, the new system increases management's control and workers' stress and has no guaranteed effects on either workers' or owners' incomes, because the savings may not be passed on to either group. Another way of disguising the contradictions is to simply deny that they exist.[34] Simple forms of *denial* include refusing to discuss a topic or to deny that one's actions meant what they seemed to mean. ("Of course I wasn't trying to get rid of you. I just wanted you to have the excitement of working in Bosnia.") A more complicated mode of denial is

pacification, a process through which legitimate conflicts are treated as unimportant, or mere communication breakdowns, as when managerial discourse suppresses grievances through defining the organization as a team or family in which all the members are in it together. Another way of disguising contradictory interests is **disqualifying** some interest groups, as in "This is a managerial problem, and you just don't have the information necessary to understand it fully." If events are also defined as inevitable or unavoidable (layoffs during recessions, for example) or value-neutral ("We have to base our personnel decisions on the data, not on how we feel"), they cannot be discussed, much less challenged. (Recall the discussion of hegemony in Chapter 1.)[35] Whatever the specific technique, the effect of organizational discourse is to disguise or redefine the contradictory interests of workers, managers, and owners. Relational strategies disguise the contradictory interests of workers, managers, and owners.

The second key concept of critical theory perspectives is that systems of "empowerment," including PDM, have to have certain characteristics if they are to be legitimate. First, participation must be valued for its own sake, as a means of ensuring that the legitimate interests of all organizational groups are represented in decisions. This means that it cannot be justified solely because it increases organizational efficiency, because efficiency inherently fulfills the interests of managers and owners more than workers. Legitimate participation also provides equal opportunities to communicate. This sounds simple, as when women's consciousness-raising groups use "talking sticks" (objects that someone must be holding in order to be allowed to speak) to ensure that all members get an equal number of speaking turns. But, the research summarized earlier in this chapter on the strategies that supervisors use to resist participatory systems suggests that it often does not happen. Legitimate empowerment programs also ensure equal opportunities to influence the group's decisions. But legitimate empowerment includes giving all employees all the information that is relevant to their decisions. It also means that all conceptions of truth be considered by the group. For example, single parents' reports of their own frustrating experiences finding adequate child care will be respected as much as the results of management's surveys on child-care issues. Finally, it means that conflicts within the group will not be resolved through appeals to some external higher authority (as in, "It's a great idea, but the CEO will never buy it").

As empowerment programs are implemented in modern organizations, radical critics argue, they inevitably obscure conflicting interests. Legitimate participation rarely occurs. As long as participatory systems are used without making major changes in organizational power relationships, managerial interests will be privileged. The existence of the hierarchy and the right of management to make final decisions—including how, when, where, over what issues, and with what outcomes participation will occur—will continue to be treated as natural and normal. When workers are trained to participate in decision making (or quality-control programs or quality of working life groups), they are taught to make decisions on criteria (like efficiency) and through processes that favor the interests of management.[36] This may be true even when workers believe they are acting in their own interests, as when the machinists in the Foodcom case described earlier in this chapter sabotaged the QWL program. In maintaining their own power over the other workers, they supported management's interests in making the program fail. When managers use supportive communication to increase morale and productivity and reduce absenteeism and turnover, they fulfill their own interests more than those of workers or owners. When management determines what issues will be examined by participatory groups, what range of solutions they may choose among, and what information will be made available to them, they maintain unequal levels of power in the guise of power sharing. But the discourse surrounding relational strategies of organizing presents PDM as processes of fulfilling the interests of all stakeholders.

CONCLUSION: THE UNDERLYING PRINCIPLES OF RELATIONAL STRATEGIES

The relational strategy of organizing is based on several principles of communication.

Principle 1. Informal communication is just as important to organizational functioning as formal channels. Whereas the traditional strategy dictates that organizations should restrict communication as much as possible, the relational strategy advocates cultivating informal as well as formal communication. Relational organizations acknowledge the fact that informal communication is going to occur whether management wants it to or not and try to utilize informal channels for the good of the organization. This involves aligning the organization's structure, motivational strategies, and leadership so that it nurtures an informal communication system that promotes the organization. By empowering members, the relational strategy attempts to create a flexible, responsive organization that is open to innovation and change.

Principle 2. Emphasize both lateral and vertical communication. To create a communication system that helps the organization, the relational strategy emphasizes lateral communication as much as vertical communication. For groups and teams to promote flexibility and innovation, it is important that coworkers communicate openly with each other and that they make cross-unit linkages. This creates a problem-solving system that transcends the narrower perspectives of particular individuals or units and pools the best knowledge in the organization.

Rather than conceptualizing vertical communication as a chain of single superior-subordinate links, the relational strategy construes it as groups passing information to other groups through complex networks of connections. So vertical communication is not simply a matter of one-to-one, chain-of-command transmission. Instead it is influenced by the group surrounding both sender and receiver. How messages are interpreted and the reactions they elicit depend as much on group processes as on individual predispositions, beliefs, and attitudes. The other cliques to which group members belong also influence vertical communication. For example, a receiver who is a member of a clique interested in resisting automation of an organization might distort a message about a new technology in a negative direction rather than pass it down the chain faithfully.

Principle 3. Do not restrict communication to task matters only; expressive and relationship-oriented communication is just as important. The traditional strategy emphasizes information related to the task. The relational strategy argues that emotional, expressive, relationship-building communication is just as important. Building rich, multiplex relationships among members is critical to opening the flow of communication. Multiplex ties are also important because they help to build a sense of community that increases members' loyalty and willingness to remain with the organization. In the relational view, the purpose of communication is not only to help the organization, but to help its members develop their skills and meet their needs.

Principle 4. Realize that relational strategies may seem to change the fundamental nature of organizations, but they may do little to change the power relationships and contradictory relationships that exist among various organizational interest groups.

NOTES

[1] Angella Michelle Chiles and Theodore Zorn, "Empowerment in Organizations: Employees' Perceptions of the Influences on Empowerment," *Journal of Applied Communication Research, 23* (1995): 1–25. The concept of empowerment is popular in contemporary organizational theory, and will appear repeatedly throughout this book, especially in Chapters 4, 5, and 7. One of the most important lines of research underlying the relational strategy was conducted by Arnold Tannenbaum and his associates. They found that in many kinds of organizations in both capitalist and socialist countries, employees believe that they exercise far less influence over decisions that affect them directly than does upper management. In contrast, Tannenbaum found that the most productive organizations and departments were ones in which all employees, even those at the bottom of the organizational hierarchy, perceived that they had substantial influence over decisions (see Arnold Tannenbaum, "Control in Organizations," *Administrative Science Quarterly, 7* (1962): 17–42).

[2] David Jamieson and Julie O'Mara, *Managing Workforce 2000* (San Francisco: Jossey-Bass, 1991). Also see David Seibold and Christine Shea, "Participation and Decision-Making," in *The New Handbook of Organizational Communication,* Fredric Jablin & Linda Putnam, eds. (Newbury Park, CA: Sage, 2000); Virginia P. Richmond and K. David Roach, "Willingness to Communicate and Employee Success in U.S. Organizations," *Journal of Applied Communication Research, 20* (1992): 95–115; and Chris Foreman, "The Reality of Workplace Democracy: A Case Study of One Company's Employee Involvement Process," paper presented at the International Communication Association Convention, Chicago, IL, 1996.

[3] See Bernard Bass, *Bass and Stogdill's Handbook of Leadership,* 3rd. ed. (New York: The Free Press, 1993).

[4] See Mauk Mulder, "Power Equalization Through Participation?" *Academy of Management Journal, 16* (1971): 31–38; and Mauk Mulder and H. Wilke, "Participation and Power Equalization," *Organizational Behavior and Human Performance, 5* (1970): 430–448; and Michael Huspek, "The Language of Powerlessness," Ph.D. Dissertation, University of Washington, 1987. Also see Dennis Mumby, "Communication, Organization, and the Public Sphere," in *Rethinking Organizational & Managerial Communication from Feminist Perspectives,* Patrice M. Buzzanell, ed. (Thousand Oaks, CA: Sage, 2000).

[5] Bass; Teresa Harrison, "Communication and Participative Decision-Making," *Personnel Psychology, 38* (1985): 93–116.

[6] Dennis Organ, "Linking Pins Between Organizations and Environments," *Business Horizons, 14* (1971): 73–80. For an extended critique of Likert's model, see Alfred Marrow, David Bowers, and Stanley Seashore, *Management by Participation* (New York: Harper & Row, 1967).

[7] Terrance Albrecht, "An Overtime Analysis of Communication Patterns and Work Perceptions," in *Communication Yearbook 8,* Robert Bostrom, ed. (Beverly Hills, CA: Sage, 1984); Fredric Jablin, "Task/Work Relationships," in *Handbook of Interpersonal Communication,* Gerald Miller and Mark Knapp, eds. (Beverly Hills, CA: Sage, 1985); and Eric Eisenberg, Peter Monge, and Kathleen Miller, "Involvement in Communication Networks as a Predictor of Organizational Commitment," *Human Communication Research, 10* (1983): 179-201.

[8] James March and Guje Sevon, "Gossip, Information, and Decision Making," in *Advances in Information Processing in Organizations,* Lee Sproull and Patrick Larkey, eds. (Greenwich, CT: JAI Press, 1982), vol. I.

[9] See Sally Planalp, Susan Hafen, & A. Dawn Adkins, "Messages of Shame and Guilt," in *Communication Yearbook 23,* Michael Roloff, ed. (Thousand Oaks, CA: Sage, 1999). Davis' study is "Management Communication and the Grapevine," *Harvard Business Review* (September-October, 1953): 43–49.

[10] See Terrance Albrecht and Bradford Hall, "Facilitating Talk About New Ideas," *Communication Monographs, 58* (1991a): 273–288; Terrance Albrecht and Bradford Hall, "Relational and Content Differences Between Elites and Outsiders in Innovation Networks," *Human Communication Research,* 17 (1991b): 535–561; Betsy Bach, "The Effect of Multiplex Relationships Upon Innovation Adoption," *Communication Monographs, 56* (1991): 133–148; David Bastien, "Change in Organizational Culture," *Management Communication Quarterly, 5* (1992): 403–442; Beth Ellis, "The Effects of Uncertainty and Source Credibility on Attitude About Organizational Change," *Management Communication Quarterly, 6* (1992): 34–57; Ronald Rice and Carolyn Aydin, "Attitudes Toward New Organizational Technology," *Administrative Science Quarterly, 36* (1991): 219–244.

[11] McGregor found that supervisors really do tend to communicate to their subordinates in ways that are consistent with one of these two sets of assumptions. Also see John Courtright, Gail Fairhurst, and L. Edna Rogers, "Interaction Patterns in Organic and Mechanistic Systems," *Academy of Management Journal, 32* (1989): 773–802.

[12] Edwin Locke, "The Nature and Causes of Job Satisfaction," in *Handbook of Industrial and Organizational Psychology,* Marvin Dunnette, ed. (Chicago: Rand-McNally, 1976).

[13] See Richard Edwards, *Contested Terrain* (New York: Basic Books, 1978) and Christopher Dandeker, *Surveillance, Power and Modernity* (New York: St. Martin's Press. 1984). An excellent example of the alienating effects of deskilling is provided in "The Lordstown Auto Workers" in *Life in Organizations,* Rosabeth Moss Kanter and Barry Stein, eds. (New York: Basic Books, 1979).

[14] S. Benson, "The Clerking Sisterhood," in *Gendering Organizational Analysis,* A.J. Mills & P. Tancred, eds. Newbury Park, CA: Sage, 1992.

[15] Timothy Pollock, Robert Whitbred, & Noshir Contractor, "Social Information Processing and Job Characteristics," *Human Communication Research, 26* (2000): 292–330.

[16] Starting in the late 1980s, there has been an upsurge in the research and popular literature on teams in recent years. See Larson and LaFasto; Jon R. Katzenbach and Douglas K. Smith, *The Wisdom of Teams* (New York: Harper Collins, 1993); J. Richard Hackman, *Groups That Work (And Those That Don't)* (San Francisco: Jossey-Bass, 1990).

[17] Larson and LaFasto, pp. 82–83.

[18] Carl E. Larson and Frank M. J. LaFasto, *TeamWork: What Must Go Right/What Can Go Wrong* (Newbury Park, CA: Sage, 1989).

[19] Elton Mayo, *Social Problems of an Industrial Civilization.* (Boston: Graduate School of Business Administration, Harvard University, 1945). In *The Human Group* (New York: Harcourt Brace, 1950) George Homans gives a readable account of the information provided by the Hawthorne Studies on work group influences on members. For examples of the processes described in this paragraph, see Leonard Sayles, "Work Group Behavior and the Larger Organization," in *Research in Industrial Human Relations,* W.F. Whyte, ed. (New York Harper, 1957) and Susan A. Mohrman, Susan G. Cohen, and Allan M. Mohrman, *Designing Team-Based Organizations: New Forms for Knowledge Work* (San Francisco: Jossey-Bass, 1995).

[20] Philip K. Tompkins and George Cheney, "Communication and Unobtrusive Control in Organizations," in *Organizational Communication: Traditional Themes and New Directions,* Robert D. McPhee and Philip Tompkins, eds. (Beverly Hills, CA: Sage, 1985).

[21] Cynthia Stohl, "Bridging the Parallel Organization: A Study of Quality Circle Effectiveness," in *Communication Yearbook 10,* Judee Burgoon, ed. (Beverly Hills, CA: Sage, 1985).

[22] Much of this foundational research is summarized in Rensis Likert, *New Patterns of Management* (New York: McGraw-Hill, 1961) and in the first and second editions of *Studies in Per-*

sonnel and Industrial Psychology, Edwin Fleishman and Associates, eds. (Homewood, IL: Dorsey, 1961 and 1967). An excellent summary of research on leadership communication is provided by Gail Fairhurst in "Dialectical Tensions in Leadership Research," in F. Jablin & L. Putnam eds., *The New Handbook of Organizational Communication* (Thousand Oaks, CA: Sage, 2000).

[23] Virginia P. Richmond & James C. McCroskey, "The Impact of Supervisor and Subordinate Immediacy on Relational and Organizational Outcomes," *Communication Monographs, 67* (2000): 85–95; Martin Remland, "Leadership Impressions and Nonverbal Communication," *Communication Quarterly,* 19 (1987): 108–128; Fredric Jablin, "Superior-subordinate Communication," in *Communication Yearbook 2,* Brent Ruben, ed. (New Brunswick, NJ: Transaction Books, 1979) and "Communication Competence and Effectiveness," in *The New Handbook of Organizational Communication,* Fredric Jablin & Linda Putnam, eds. (Thousand Oaks, CA: Sage, 2000).

[24] Terrance Albrecht and J. Halsey, "Mutual Support in Mixed Status Relationships," *Journal of Social and Personal Relationships,* 9 (1992): 237–252; Terrance Albrecht and Mara Adelman, *Communicating Social Support* (Newbury Park, CA: Sage, 1988).

[25] Ruth Guzley, "Organizational Climate and Communication Climate," *Management Communication Quarterly, 5* (1992): 379–402; Dominic Infante and William Gordon, "How Employees See the Boss," *Western Journal of Speech Communication, 55* (1991): 294–304.

[26] "Ford, Union to Open 30 Child-Care and Family-Service Centers for Workers," *Houston Chronicle,* 22 Nov., 2000, C1; Amy Zipkin, "Bosses Become Nice to Try to Keep Employees from Leaving," *Houston Chronicle,* June 4, 2000, 5D. Denise Segura argues that what satisfies workers varies with their level in the organization, but not with their gender or ethnicity ("Chicanas in White-Collar Jobs," in *Situated Lives,* Louise Lamphere, Helena Razone', and Patricia Zavella, eds. [New York: Routledge, 1997]). Craig R. Scott and his associates ("The Impacts of Communication and Multiple Identifications on Intent to Leave," *Management Communication Quarterly, 12* (1999): 400–435) and Mike Allen ("The Relationship Between Communication, Affect, Job Alternatives, and Voluntary Turnover Intentions," *Southern Communication Journal, 61* (1996): 198–208) both found that there also is a direct relationship between communication and turnover—communication in itself influences turnover intentions **and** also influences satisfaction which has an additional effect on turnover.

[27] Cynthia Fisher, "On the Dubious Wisdom of Expecting Job Satisfaction to Correlate with Performance," *Academy of Management Review, 5* (1980). Also see Barnard Bass, *Bass and Stogdill's Handbook of Leadership* (Greenwich, CT: JAI Press, 1993). For summaries of the relationship between organizational communication and voluntary turnover, see Myria Watkins Allen, "The Relationship Between Communication, Affect, Job Alternatives, and Voluntary Turnover Intentions," *Southern Communication Journal, 61* (1996): 198–209.

[28] Dennis Gioia and Henry Sims, "Cognition-Behavior Connections: Attribution and Verbal Behavior in Leader-Subordinate Interactions," *Organizational Behavior and Human Performance,* 37 (1986): 197–229. Also see Gail Fairhurst, "Dialectical Tensions in Leadership Research," in *The New Handbook of Organizational Communication,* Fredric Jablin & Linda Putnam, eds. (Newbury Park, CA: Sage, 2000).

[29] Karen Mills, "Northwest on a Flier-Satisfaction Mission," *Houston Chronicle,* May 14, 2000, 6D; Kim Cameron & Michael Thompson, "The Problems and Promises of Total Quality Management," in Quinn, ed., *Pressing Problems in Modern Organizations* (That Keep Us Awake at Night) (New York: AMACOM, 2000).

[30] L.P. Dana, "Small Business as a Supplement in the People's Republic of China (PRC)," *Journal of Small Business Management, 37* (1999): 76–81.

[31] The best analysis of the development of critical theory and its many versions is David Held, *Introduction to Critical Theory* (London: Hutchinson, 1980). An excellent application to organizational theory is Mats Alvesson and Hugh Wilmott, eds. *Critical Management Studies* (Newbury Park, CA: Sage, 1992); and to organizational communication is Stan Deetz, "Critical Theories of Organizational Communication," in *The New Handbook of Organizational Communication,* Fredric Jablin & Linda Putnam, eds. (Thousand Oaks, CA: Sage, 2000) and *Transforming Communication, Transforming Business* (Creskill, NJ: Hampton Press, 1995).

[32] Alan Downs, *Corporate Executions* (New York: AMACOM, 1995); also see Stanley Deetz, *Democracy in the Age of Corporate Colonization* (Albany, NY: SUNY Press, 1992), especially Chapter 9.

[33] See *Knowledge and Human Interests* (London: Heinemann Educational Books, 1972) and *Communication and the Evolution of Society* (London: Heinemann Educational Books, 1979).

³⁴ See John Forester, *Planning in the Face of Power* (Berkeley: University of California Press, 1989. The foundation of the ideas presented in this section is Goran Therborn, *The Ideology of Power and the Power of Ideology* (London: Verso, 1980). A fine summary of issues regarding the concept of ideology is available in Astrid Kersten, "Culture, Control, and the Labor Process," in Stanley Deetz ed., *Communication Yearbook 16* (Newbury Park, CA: Sage, 1993).

³⁵ Richard Jehensen, "Effectiveness, Expertise, and Excellence as Ideological Fictions," *Human Studies, 7* (1984): 3–21. For analyses of how seemingly objective organizational "data" are manipulated symbolically to privilege management's interests, see S. Ansari and K. Euske, "Rational, Rationalizing, and Reifying Uses of Accounting Data in Organizations," *Accounting, Organizations, and Society, 12* (1987): 549–570 and David Sless, "Forms of Control," *Australian Journal of Communication, 14* (1988): 57–69.

³⁶ See, for example, Mats Alvesson, "Organizations, Culture and Ideology," *International Studies of Management and Organization, 17* (1987): 4–18 and *Organization Theory and Technocratic Consciousness* (New York: Walter de Gruyter, 1987). Classic studies of non-legitimate participatory systems are available in B. Abrahamsson, *Bureaucracy or Participation* (Beverly Hills, CA: Sage, 1977); Charles Perrow, *Complex Organizations,* 3rd ed. (New York: Random House, 1986); and Stewart Clegg, *Power, Rule and Domination* (London: Routledge and Kegan Paul, 1975).

Chapter 4

CULTURAL STRATEGIES OF ORGANIZING

*The reality of the [social] world hangs on
the thin thread of conversation.*
—PETER BERGER AND THOMAS LUCKMANN

CENTRAL THEMES

- Cultural strategies of organizing assume that managers can influence employees' beliefs, values, and perceptions of reality and that employees actively create their own beliefs, values, and perceptions.
- Organizational cultures are communicative creations, embedded in a history and a set of expectations about the future. They are usually heterogeneous, composed of multiple subcultures.
- Cultural strategies of motivation and control rely on self-surveillance, which is accomplished through systems of unobtrusive control, emotional regulation, and discursive practices.
- Cultural strategies of leadership focus on "transformational" processes through which leaders communicate a vision of the organization and help employees "frame" everyday events.
- Organizational symbolism—metaphors, stories, myths, and rituals—facilitates unobtrusive control.

KEY TERMS

Obtrusive Control
Externalization
Internalization
Metaphors
Mythologies
Charisma

Self-surveillance
Objectification
Identification
Subcultures
Story-telling
Framing

In Chapter 1 we suggested that a central tension in all societies is between *individuality* and *community*. The traditional strategy of organizing focuses on the individual pole of this tension and relies on the structural dimension of communication to manage it. The traditional strategy assumes that rewarding employees for their *individual* competence and performance will motivate them to act in ways that meet their organizations' needs for control and coordination. Feeling connected to one's coworkers is either ignored or treated as a potential threat to organizational control. Although some versions of the traditional strategy noted that people do feel pride from successfully performing their tasks, traditional strategies view human beings as predominantly rational, not emotional, beings. In contrast, relational strategies retain the rational, individualistic focus of traditional strategies, but also recognize that human beings are emotional, community-oriented creatures. Relational strategies focus on how the relational dimension of communication can create job satisfaction and improve the quality of interpersonal relationships at work. For this reason they offer a more complete view of human experience. Their recognition of the power of work groups and teams admits that sociability and interpersonal relationships are important aspects of working life. But even these changes offer an impoverished view of the rich texture of feelings and personal connections that characterize life in modern organizations.[1]

The cultural strategy suggests that humans are emotional beings and that feelings of connectedness and community are important aspects of all social structures, including organizations. The contextual (and relational) dimensions of communication are central to organizational life. Emotional ties, both to one's organization and to one's co-workers are powerful influences on how people choose to act and communicate at work. Cultural strategies do not ignore individuality or rationality. Indeed, they suggest that employees make reasoned, strategic choices based on their individual beliefs, values, and sense-making processes. Motivating and controlling employees' behavior depends on persuading them to accept the organization's core beliefs, values, and frames of reference as their own. Creating a sense of community within work groups is depicted as a primary means of managing the tension between individual and organizational needs.

CULTURAL STRATEGIES OF ORGANIZATIONAL DESIGN

Although most advocates of cultural strategies of organizing[2] were comfortable with relational conceptions of organizational design—decentralization, participation, and so on—issues of organizational design were relatively unimportant to them.[3] The values, beliefs, language, symbols, and meaning systems that hold the organization together are much more significant. Initially they argued that organizational cultures could be managed strategically, and rather easily. Upper management merely had to communicate persuasively the core values of the organization to all employees and provide tangible and intangible rewards to employees who act in accordance with those values. Eventually, a homogeneous and harmonious "strong" culture would emerge, one in which employees throughout the organization—regardless of their rank, tasks, networks of interpersonal relationships, or formal roles—would share the same goals, have the same kinds of feelings about the organization, and interpret the culture in the same way. This strong culture would be the key to managerial control, worker commitment, and organizational effectiveness.[4]

Typical of this early view was Tom Peters and Robert Waterman's conclusion that "excellent" firms—those that for long periods had exceptional productivity, profitability, and stability—differed from "nonexcellent" firms in terms of the strength of their cultures. Of course, this perspective was attractive to managers in U.S. organizations. It suggested that *they* are the key to making organizations succeed and it provided them with some seemingly simple tools that they could use to increase control over employees' behaviors. It offered some relatively inexpensive ways of increasing employee morale, commitment, and productivity; and promised significant short-term increases in the competitiveness and profitability of their firms. Consequently, it rapidly became the dominant view of organizational cultures among managers and scholars alike.[5] But almost as soon as the perspective was presented, critics began to question its core assumption that employees' beliefs, values, and views of reality could be strategically controlled by upper management.

Organizations are composed of active, thinking human beings. Employees sometimes interpret management's attempts to mold beliefs, instill values, and manipulate perceptions and emotions as offensive and manipulative (regardless of how management interprets them). Even if they are not offended, they may interpret and respond to management's messages in completely unanticipated ways. In other cases, they may resist even positive changes in their organization's culture, and generally make culture management or planned cultural change exceptionally difficult. Even if a strong culture exists, not all employees will participate in it equally or in the same ways. Employees tend to form communicative ties with people who share their view of their organization. Different **subcultures** emerge—groups of people whose shared interpretation of their organization helps bind them together and differentiate them from other groups of employees. Consequently, it is more likely that an organization will be composed of many distinct and different subcultures rather than a homogeneous culture consciously defined and guided by upper management.[6]

For example, Charley Conrad once visited the technical writing division of a major computer firm as part of a consulting project. He entered through the front door and was examined by the security team at the front desk. Then he was led down corridor after corridor past each of the major divisions of the firm into a separate building that housed the writing staff. One of the first things he noticed was the staff's coffee room. On the wall was a poster of the firm's newest product, an exceptionally powerful portable computer that was not yet on the market. But unlike the hardware division, which had an entire wall covered with the posters, or the software group, which had arranged to have one of the posters professionally framed and displayed in the center of their workroom, the technical writing group had only one poster and displayed it in a dark corner. In front of the poster was a Norfolk pine that all but obscured it from view.[7]

Prominently displayed in the center of the room was a poster of a penguin jumping off an ice cliff into the ocean with a long row of penguins following it. Someone had written the division head's name next to the lead penguin and the other writers' names next to the others. Significant symbols reveal a great deal about the culture (or subculture) of an organization. In this organization the poster-symbols suggested that Technical Writing was a subculture—a strong and stable one—that was separate from the other units of the organization. They perceived themselves as writers, not as employees of Computer Firm X. They proudly told Conrad that they were in their isolated building because they had asked to be there. Sometimes the different subcultures make up an organization, but coexist peacefully; in other cases their values, patterns of acting, sense-making processes, and so on are conflicting and irreconcilable. Subcultures, like the communication networks that underlie them, are fluid and changing.

The existence of multiple, ever-changing organizational subcultures does not mean that implementing cultural strategies of organizing is impossible. In some cases, the subcultures may be so similar that tensions among them are minimal. In other cases, the organization's core beliefs and values are so powerful and communicated so persuasively that subcultural differences can be managed or overwhelmed. But whatever the particular pattern of subcultures that emerges in a particular organization, the important point is that subcultures do emerge. They are not designed by upper management, or by anyone else for that matter. Cultures are communicative creations. They emerge and are sustained by the communicative acts of all employees, not just the conscious persuasive strategies of upper management. People interact with one another as if they shared culture. Through trial and error, and through conversation and negotiation, they act together to achieve their goals. Successful use of cultural strategies depends on understanding how all employees perceive and respond to their organization's culture and to efforts to manage it.[8]

CULTURAL STRATEGIES OF MOTIVATION, CONTROL, AND SURVEILLANCE

Both the traditional and the relational strategies of organizing relied on systems of motivation and control that are **obtrusive,** that is, known by and visible to workers. Indeed, if reward and punishment systems, "technical" factors such as assembly lines, and policies and procedures are not obtrusive, they will not succeed.[9] Similarly, surveillance in traditional strategies is direct, involving supervisors monitoring their subordinates through some system. In relational strategies, surveillance is less direct and is usually accomplished by work groups rather than by individual supervisors. Employees may often choose to resist motivation/control/surveillance systems, particularly when they are obtrusive. In contrast, cultural strategies of organizing focus on "unobtrusive" forms of control—on creating situations in which employees choose to act in ways desired by the organization while perceiving that they are freely choosing to do so. In effect, surveillance is *self-surveillance* rather than surveillance by supervisors or coworkers. Self-surveillance has three components, *unobtrusive control, emotional regulation,* and *disciplinary practices.*

Organizational Communities and Unobtrusive Control

Unobtrusive control is self-surveillance through employees' cognitive processes, their thoughts and decisions. It relies on successfully persuading employees to accept the core beliefs and values of the organization and to base their decisions about how to act at work on those beliefs and values. Employees are persuaded to accept these values in a number of ways—through particular kinds of leadership strategies (examined later in this chapter) and through socializing newcomers into the organization (examined in Chapter 6). But, if employees can be persuaded to accept the beliefs and values of upper management, they can be counted on to make the same kinds of decisions that upper management would make. Thus employees, especially managers, can be allowed a great deal of freedom of action because they will choose to act in desired ways.

Sociologist Peter Berger has described the process through which people learn and accept the core values and beliefs of their society or organization. In the first phase, **externalization,** people notice the ways in which others interpret and respond to their surroundings. To fit in, they begin to act as the "locals" do. Eventually, they may enter the second phase, **objectification.** They begin to believe that the way the people in their societies/organizations act is the only correct (that is, normal and natural) way of acting. They begin to "objectify" the thought processes and action patterns of their society/organization and to not be consciously aware of how those societal/organizational assumptions influence their everyday lives. Eventually they forget that the people in their societies/organizations *choose* to act as they do, and that they could have chosen any number of different courses of action. The concept of objectification implies that societies (and organizations) are maintained nonconsciously, as much through habit as through conscious deliberation. Routine decisions can be made automatically, and with little expenditure of time or energy. In the final, **internalization** phase people begin to evaluate themselves and their actions in terms of the society/organization's assumptions. They begin to see themselves as good, productive, or righteous only if they think and act in accordance with the core beliefs and values of their organization. Their self-concept begins to depend on their continually thinking and acting in ways that are normal in their organizations. Their self-esteem depends on doing what is valued by their society/organization. If they ever do act in ways that violate those core beliefs and values they will view themselves negatively and be motivated to change their behavior. Their sense of who they are as people is tied to their society/organization and its accepted assumptions.

In organizational settings, some employees never reach the objectification or internalization stages. They continually realize that their organization operates on the basis of a particular set of assumptions, but that any number of alternative core beliefs and values are possible. Even those employees who do internalize the accepted assumptions of their organizations, may at times question those assumptions and identify with their organizations less than they did before. But, when members of an organization truly identify with it, they are likely to act in precisely those ways that are desired by the organization.

Identification and Unobtrusive Control   Perhaps the best way to explain **identification** is through examples. In Chapter 2 we introduced Industry International, an organization with an especially powerful system of financial rewards. But, Industry also relies on identification and unobtrusive control. Industry's employees learn to accept its core beliefs and values long before they ever enter its doors. The organization hires its workers, which are frequently relatives of its current employees, from the local blue-collar communities. From childhood, they learn that Industry is a stable and highly successful organization. By the time they are adolescents, they have learned a strong work ethic—to be dependable, conscientious, concerned about the quality of their work, and to work very, very hard. They learn that real men put food on their family's table, and that only "real men can make it at Industry International."[10] In fact, being able to withstand the body-punishing rigors of blue-collar life and being willing to celebrate the strength, stamina, and manual dexterity required by Industry work is the source of the worker's identity and self-esteem. For Industry's employees, these attributes make them superior to people who make a living by shuffling papers. Industry's employees internalize the organization's values at their dinner tables and look forward to someday becoming one of "the mud, the blood, and the beer guys."

By the time people apply to work at Industry, they know what will be expected of them, what it means to be part of a cohesive work group, and what kinds of financial rewards they can obtain. This pre-employment indoctrination makes it easy to adopt the core beliefs of the organization. As Roy, a 17-year old employee notes:

> You walk in there and you know you're not going to get days off. You know you're not going to get sick days. You know that you don't just say 'I'm not feeling well and I'm going home'. If the person after you doesn't show up [for the next shift], you know that you're not leaving. Your group depends on you to keep the line going.

And employees know that if they ever slack off, if they ever forget, they will be reminded by the men with whom they are working. Deon (an old-timer at 25) explains, "When I see these kids in here who do not know how to work, I kinda' take them under my wing. I show them how to work hard." Jim personalizes the issue: "If my kid or relative went there and wasn't working hard, I'd go down and kick his ass. No way he's shamin' me by not working as hard as I said he could." Some of the most powerful identification messages come from employees' supervisors and coworkers.[11] But, if workers really have identified with their organizations, few messages are necessary. They act as the organization wants them to because they believe that it is natural and normal to do so.

However, most people enter organizations with less complete preparation than the employees at Industry International receive. As a result, organizations must encourage employees to identify with the organization. They sometimes do so through formal organizational discourse—newsletters, annual reports, and so on. Some identification messages laud a *team atmosphere* between workers and the organization. Other identification strategies involve *expressing concern for individual employees* and *recognizing contributions* made by individual employees or work groups to the organization or to the larger society. Other messages *invite* employees to become involved (or remain involved) in some worthwhile organizational activity, or *brag* about the dedication shown by an individual or work group successfully completing a task. The Bank of America newsletter includes a regular feature in which employees talk about their contributions to the company.

Sometimes employees are encouraged to identify with their organizations by messages that identify a common enemy. When Steve Jobs served his first term as head of Apple Computer; he expressed respect for IBM as a "national treasure" but galvanized Apple's employees by telling them that he was concerned that Apple was the only thing that kept IBM from "total industry domination." Each of these communicative strategies create a corporate "we" between workers and the organization—a feeling that "we" are inextricably tied together, teammates in the struggle against common enemies. Through overt persuasive efforts, organizations attempt to move employees toward identifying with them.[12]

However, employees may respond to these efforts in a number of ways. Many do identify with their organizations. They feel close ties to the employees who are mentioned in the messages and feel connected to the organization through their positive feelings about those people. They may feel as though they really are part of the organization or feel pride in being involved in an organization that cares for its members. Or they may feel a strong connection to their peers or to their organizational community. Other employees may interpret the messages as mere sources of information or entertainment and even complain that they don't achieve either of those goals very well. Others actually may "disidentify" with the organization because of the messages. They may feel that their own experience contradicts the messages, may see the messages as a waste of organizational resources, or feel that their work group or its members are not given enough recognition.

Identification messages fail for a number of reasons. First, to be successful they must be consistent with the messages that members receive from their overall society. While growing up, employees may have learned that people work solely for functional reasons. Members of the United Automobile Workers who work for Ford may perceive that they do so only because they can't get anywhere near $18 an hour anywhere else. They have a vested interest in seeing the organization succeed, but only because its success provides them with tangible rewards. Messages glorifying the Ford team are not likely to be effective and may even be offensive.[13]

Second, people may resist identification pressures because people have complex and multifaceted identities. For example, both authors of this book simultaneously are husbands, fathers, researchers, teachers, organizational communication scholars, members of a rather unique communication department, part of a College of Liberal Arts and a university with a distinctive culture and tradition, and a number of other people. Our selves are constantly being created and re-created as we receive and interpret messages from people who see only one or two of our many identities. The boundaries between those selves are blurry and constantly changing.[14] As a result, it is unlikely that we would ever identify completely with any of the organizations or groups of which we are members. We tend to identify most closely with the social groups that include the people who are most central in our communication networks—our immediate families and our immediate work groups (our department). And we identify most closely with organizations that we have been involved with for a long time, because we have developed closer communicative relationships within them. We interpret each identification message we receive through lenses that are made of complex webs of attachment and identification.

Finally, people may not identify with their organizations for a number of tangible reasons. If they are dissatisfied with their pay, their working conditions, or the degree of autonomy they have at work, they are less likely to identify with their organizations and are more likely to interpret identification messages as manipulation.[15] As a result, employees differ in their degree of organizational identification. Some identify completely and constantly. Others may identify only in part, for example when their own beliefs, values, and interests happen to coincide with those of the organization. They understand where they fit in the organization, take pride in their contributions to its success, and feel commitment to its continuation. They may accept some of the accepted assumptions of the organization; but they do so because they actually believe in those values, not because the organization tells them they should. They may believe and proudly say "I am an IBMer" in a way that suggests that they have identified completely with the organization and at the same time realize that their commitment is primarily based on coinciding goals and functional ties. Even true-blue IBMers call their generous retirement programs and benefits packages "golden handcuffs" (because they would lose so much money by moving to another firm that they are effectively tied to IBM). They learn the assumptions of the organization but do not accept them uncritically. An employee's level of identification also varies across time and with different organizational experiences. A handsome reward or especially moving integration ceremony may lead an employee to temporarily identify more strongly with the organization; a negative performance evaluation or conflict with a coworker may reduce such identification. But even during those times, identification is a powerful mode of organizational control.

Organizational Symbolism and Unobtrusive Control   Symbolic forms—metaphors, stories, myths, and rituals—have a dual relationship to cultural strategies; they express the taken-for-granted assumptions of the culture and, when articulated, reproduce those assumptions. Some advocates of the cultural strategy of organizing assume that upper management can motivate employees to act in desired ways by strategically managing organizational symbolism. Unfortunately, this view seriously oversimplifies the nature of symbolic acts and organizational cultures. Employees are human beings, and humans actively perceive, process, and choose to respond to messages in their own often idiosyncratic ways. They interpret stories and other symbolic forms precisely as they interpret identification messages, terms of their own needs, experiences, and frames of reference. Different employees or different "subcultures" of employees may interpret the same symbolic act in different ways. They also may tell different stories about management, create their own independent rituals, or describe their organization or unit through the use of different metaphors. Upper management may tell a different story to explain an organizational disaster (or success) than production employees do; employees in a subculture dominated by marketing employees may tell a story that blames the research and development division for a failed product line, while research and development employees may tell the same story in a way that satirizes members of the marketing. In these cases, organizational symbolism may actually reduce managerial control and motivate employees to act in ways that are not preferred by management.

Metaphors are symbols in which one image is used to describe another one. They are often used to describe an entire organization. Frequent organizational metaphors are military machines (working here is like being in the army), families (these people are my closest friends, my family or this desk is my home away from home), and games (to survive here you have to play the game, pretend to be what the big shots want you to be).

Of course, metaphors should not be interpreted literally. The metaphorical family is not patterned after any real family, but is a construct based on someone's idea of what a family is or should be like—the Taylors (*Home Improvement*) or Camdens (*7th Heaven*) or Hills (*King of the Hill*) or any other mythical family whose attributes are like those of the employee's organization. Metaphors are important, because they guide and constrain peoples' interpretations of everyday events. They also provide stability because people tend to perceive reality in ways that confirm their metaphors. If they believe their organization is a family, they will perceive employees who behave in unfamily-like ways as being bad family members. Only in rare cases do these events lead us to question the accuracy of the metaphor itself.

For fifty years, a large West Coast toy manufacturer has been described by its employees as an "army under siege." Although the enemy has changed many times, from profit-hungry East Coast companies during the 1950s to wily foreign importers who keep their workers in poverty during the 1960s and 1970s to computer firms that care about wires and chips, not children in the 1980s, the guiding metaphor has remained the same. Employees talk about "fighting the battle," which means constantly working hard to maintain efficiency; "taking no casualties," which means having everyone constantly monitor quality (including a company program in which samples are donated to employees provided they take them home and see how long it takes their children to destroy them); "everyone being a spy," which leads most employees to regularly take their children to toy shops just to see which of their competitors' products are popular and ought to be duplicated; and "foot soldiers in the battle," which both involves every employee in the mission of the organization and justifies a hierarchical, rule-governed style of management. But the most powerful expressions of the metaphor are borrowed from the larger culture: "Be all that you can be" is used to justify voluntary overtime, and "lean, mean fighting machine" is used to explain reductions in the number of middle managers. Almost every normal work experience is explained in language reflecting the army-under-siege metaphor; almost every behavior desired of workers can be justified by referring to the metaphor. In cases like this one, management and employees share the same metaphorical description of their organization and define that metaphor in the same way. Motivation and control are enhanced. But, metaphors are highly ambiguous—they can be interpreted in a number of different ways.[16] If employees think their organizational family is like the Simpsons, using the metaphor has very different effects than if they think it is like the Camdens. Finally, metaphors are not static. They emerge, change, become dominant for a time, and eventually are replaced by other metaphors. When metaphors are interpreted in different ways, or when management relies on an outdated metaphor to motivate and control their employees, the power of metaphor may lead to very different outcomes.

Human beings are *storytelling* animals. From childhood fairy tales to the tales told during executives' weekend retreats, stories provide concrete, vivid images of what life is or will be like and what behaviors our culture values or prohibits.[17] Stories present events in sequence rather than in a list or chart, which makes some events seem to be the causes and effects of other events. At least in Western cultures, stories are based on a dramatic conflict between a protagonist and an antagonist. Stories are relevant to the needs and experiences of members of the organization. Stories are told most often and are most powerful, when people are confused and concerned about what is going on in their organizations (for instance, when a person is entering a new organization or when the organization is undergoing major changes). They provide explanations of events, policies, procedures, and so on that are beyond doubt or argument. They function as social *myths,* not in the sense that they are untrue (although they may be), but in the sense that their "truths" are taken for granted by the people who tell and listen to them. Like stories, the power of myths stems from their coherent, vivid details, their ability to help people make sense of their surroundings, and their consistency with other organizational stories and myths.[18]

Stories and myths usually coalesce to form **mythologies,** groups of interconnected symbols that support one another. In short, stories and myths tell people how things are to be done in a particular group and provide a social map that points out potentially dangerous topics, events, or persons present in at least one of an organization's subcultures. To be credible, stories must express a value, purpose, or philosophy that is consistent with the taken-for-granted assumptions of the culture or subculture and must provide employees with guidelines for acting. They often tell employees what management wants them to believe is valued and rewarded in the organization; they sometimes tell employees what management really rewards and who really has power. And, sometimes they may do both. Stories and myths also gain power from the processes through which they are told. **Storytelling** (and mythmaking) is an interactive process in which the teller presents his or her version of a story, usually leaving out many details, while others jump in and challenge, reinterpret, and revise the storyteller's version. The process allows each of the storytellers to link his or her own experiences to the experiences and interpretations of other storytellers. Through this process of mutual interpretation and re-interpretation the accepted assumptions of the group are shared and reproduced. During the storytelling process, differences and tensions among interpretations may be expressed and managed. Thus, through a complicated process, the values and accepted assumptions of the group are produced, reproduced, and revised.[19]

Of course, the observation that organizational symbolism can be powerful does not imply that its effects are always positive. Tom Hollihan and Patricia Riley's study of a "Toughlove" group provides an excellent example. Toughlove is a self-help voluntary organization composed of parents who have troubled teenagers. Toughlove meetings are like "testimonial services" in Protestant churches. Members come to tell stories about their experiences and their successes in overcoming their problems. Their individual stories combine to form a complicated mythology that unifies the members through their common experiences. The core experience is suffering brought on by the actions of their delinquent children; the common salvation is recognizing that adolescent children choose to behave as they do, realizing that parents have rights to peaceful homes and productive lives, and taking action to regain control of their lives instead of remaining victims of the tyranny of their children. Their stories are filled with villains and nostalgic images of a peaceful past. The villains are child-service professionals—teachers, social workers, therapists, and counselors—who are too quick to blame the parents for their children's delinquency and who are responsible for the modern "permissive" view of child-raising that the parents believe has created the problem of delinquent children. The nostalgia is of their childhoods when visits to the woodshed led them to both fear and respect their parents and learn to behave in socially acceptable ways. Hollihan and Riley conclude:

> Shared stories [and myths] respond to people's sense of reason and emotion, to their intellects and imagination, to the facts as they perceive them, and to their values. People search for stories that justify their efforts and resolve the tensions and problems in their lives. . . . Those who do not share in the storytelling . . . might view particular stories as mere rationalization, but this is to miss the very nature of the storytelling process.[20]

By listening to stories members of organizations learn the values that bind the culture together and discover what they must say and do if they are to become accepted members of the culture.

CASE STUDY:
TROUBLE IN THE HAPPIEST PLACE ON EARTH

The metaphors and stories that people use to describe their organizatio... reveal a great deal about the effectiveness of a system of unobtrusive control. If everyone uses the same metaphors, tells the same stories, and interprets them in the same way, control is maximized. But, if they use different symbolic forms for interpreting the same symbols in different ways, control is weaker. If members of different subcultures use contradictory symbols or interpret official symbols in contradictory ways, unobtrusive control is failing.

On the surface, Disneyland and Disney World seem to be perfect examples of a homogeneous "work hard/play hard" culture. Employees are selected to correspond to the image of all-American boys and girls—clones of Annette Funicello and Frankie Avalon. They are hired because they have exceptional people skills, although few of them have much direct contact with customers and all of them are taught to refer all but the simplest questions to supervisors or security people. If they just practice common courtesy, they can perform their jobs successfully. Like the workers at Industry International, they have been prepared to work for Disney since they were children, not by their parents but by the media. Bill Ingram recalls that "I was raised with the characters. I was raised with the songs. I was raised with all of the good feelings that go along with Disney. So to have an opportunity to work and help create that magic for new generations of kids. I thought that was a great opportunity."†

There is a hierarchy among the clones, however. Bilingual tour guides are at the top of the hierarchy, followed by skilled ride operators, unskilled ride operators, sweepers, and finally, the lowly food and concession workers. No one really knows how an individual worker gets assigned to his or her place in the hierarchy (central casting makes these decisions in secret), but salary and perks such as the frequency of rest breaks go along with a higher rank. There is *very little* movement up the hierarchy, although it happens often enough for dishwashers to dream of becoming pirates in Captain Hook's band. The employees enforce the hierarchies strictly. Romances are common among Disney employees but, of course, people do not date, mate with, or marry people from the wrong status level.

The employees also create their own hierarchies. Among women, uniforms convey status—the sexier the uniforms, the greater the status (all this is relative, since the sexiest uniform in the Disney empire would bore a healthy teenaged boy to tears). In fact, a story told at Disneyland tells how the tour guides were offended by new uniforms given to ride operators because they included shorter skirts and more revealing blouses. The tour guides pressured management to give them new, even sexier uniforms that returned them to the top of the hierarchy.

According to management, Disneyland relies on unobtrusive control. All the employees believe that "the customer is king" and are personally committed to making the parks the happiest places on earth. If there are any efforts to control workers, they are unobtrusive. After a lengthy training process, new employees

(continued)

(continued from the previous page)

leave Disney University with deep pride in themselves and their organization, and with an even deeper commitment to doing things "the Disney way." But workers tell a different story. According to it, Disneyland is a hotbed of simple control. At Disney University workers learn that supervisors are in park "only to help." The workers' story says that supervisors also are there to monitor and punish them when they make mistakes or violate park policies. Infractions, no matter how trivial, are met with instant and harsh discipline. Workers who supervisors decide are "malcontents," "troublemakers," or simply "jerks" are often fired on the spot. Disneyland is an unarmed camp, in which each group in the status hierarchy coalesces into a tightly knit subculture committed to defending one another against the supervisors, although there are "finks" and "stool pigeons" among each group. Ironically, this close camaraderie among employees is one of the main attractions of working at Disney and one of the main reasons that employees return year after year. But in 1984, these tensions and hostilities erupted in ways that made Disneyland seem to be the "unhappiest place on earth."

Early in its history Disneyland management consciously propagated a "drama" metaphor which depicted the Magic Kingdom as a giant performance in which every employee played a "role" in making customers happy. Dress codes were labeled "costuming," rules about how to look, talk, and behave were depicted as "all part of the show," and the personnel department was called "casting." The drama metaphor turned even the most mundane of employees' activities into a calculated fiction designed to please customers. The workers were living Walt Disney's dream: "I don't want the public to see the real world they're living in. I want them to feel they're in another world." But, management's version of the metaphor had another dimension. Acting is fun, they noted, but "each member must have a clear understanding of the business of show business."

Eventually the drama metaphor started to be replaced by a "family" metaphor. Disneyland was known as a "friendly place to work" where keeping everyone on a "first-name basis" was valued and teamwork was essential. Organizational stories reported that Walt (who insisted that workers call him by his first name) was a caring family man who reserved his Saturdays for his two daughters and designed the park to give all families a safe, clean, enjoyable place to go. Initially management supported the family metaphor because it strengthened the workers' commitment to providing excellent service to the guests. But, the employees soon began to interpret the metaphor as meaning that managers would treat workers like family members. The friendly, family atmosphere was so appealing that most employees and many managers started to believe it uncritically, forgetting that Disneyland was a for-profit business. The inherent ambiguity of metaphors and stories allowed employees and mangers to develop their own preferred interpretations of what "drama" and "family" meant to them.

In good times there was little need to be clear about exactly how a term like "family" might be interpreted or about how it would influence employee behavior.

(continued)

(continued from the previous page)

But, as financial problems grew, business considerations became increasingly important. Employees started to resent this new concern: "It used to be, 'Let's try to make the employees as happy as possible so that they make the public happy,' and now it's 'Let's save as much money as we can and make a buck'" (a ride operator with thirty years' experience) or "There was a time when the employee was very important to the company; now they're more of a company. It's getting more like a business, and I don't think the park should be run like a business" (service employee, twenty-five years' experience). In 1984 management cut wages and benefits for some employees. Shocked, the employees argued that management's decisions were not true to the spirit of Disneyland, to Walt's original dream. They held a candlelight vigil, printed bumper stickers that said "Disneyland—Walt's dying dream," and eventually went on strike. Employees claimed that management was unfair, that this was not the way to treat their family: "It's just totally business. They are not worried about the family thing" (twenty-four years' experience); "It's not fun to work at Disneyland anymore. They gave us a cold slap in the face" (thirty-two years); "Walt wanted family, but it's a business now, not Walt's dream. That's shot, it's not what he wanted" (twenty-three years). Management responded with its interpretation of the family metaphor: sometimes family life is hard, and truly close families make sacrifices if they are to survive.

Fifteen years later, after Disney management broke the strike and eventually returned to profitability under the leadership of Paul Pressler, a "no-nonsense," "bottom-line-oriented" manager, the drama metaphor seems to be back. Cynthia Harris took over at Disneyland in January, 1999, when Pressler was promoted to president of Walt Disney, Co.'s entire theme park division. She's a breath of fresh air, say many workers. Cruz Revelas, a Disneyland custodian, says that "we finally have a leader who truly believes that we're the ones who make things happen, and she's trying to improve our environment on the job." Harris spends a great deal of time in the park, talking with employees. And she talks in familiar metaphors:

> We're building a whole new resort here, and it's important to stay close to the cast and know what's on people's minds. Our responsibility here is to provide an extraordinary experience for our cast so they can provide it to our guests.††

Applying What You've Learned

1. How did the stories and metaphors told at Disneyland function as unobtrusive control?
2. Were the workers' interpretations of the organizational stories and metaphors ever really under management's control? Did that control eventually dissolve? If so, why?
3. How did changes in the dominant metaphors influence the attitudes and actions of employees and management?

(continued)

(continued from the previous page)

Questions to Think About and Discuss

1. Why did the dominant metaphors change?
2. What does the Disneyland experience imply about the stability of organizational symbols? Of cultural strategies of organizing?
3. Will the revival of the drama metaphor revive Disneyland's management-worker relationships? Why or why not?

---

*This case is adapted from John van Maanen, "The Smile Factory," in *Reframing Organizational Culture,* Peter Frost, et al., eds. (Newbury Park, CA: Sage, 1991) and Ruth C. Smith and Eric Eisenberg, "Conflict at Disneyland: A Root-Metaphor Analysis," *Communication Monographs, 54* (1987): 367–380.

†Mike Schneider, "Life Isn't So Magical for Some Workers," Houston *Chronicle,* 2 Jan., 1999, p. C4.
††Bernard Wolfson, "For Disneyland, Boss's Wish Upon a Star Come True," Houston *Chronicle,* 5 Dec., 1999, C4. For a critical analysis of Disneyland's management see David Koenig, *Mouse Under Glass* (Irvine, CA: Bonaventure Press, 1997) and *More Mouse Tales* (Irvine, CA: Bonaventure Press, 1999).

Rituals and ceremonies gain their power from the act of participating in them, as well as from the meaning that people extract from them. Because the meaning of rituals and ceremonies is located in the doing, they can be especially powerful symbolic acts. Rituals are informal celebrations that may or may not be officially sanctioned by the organization, and ceremonies are planned, formal, and ordained by management. When a work crew gets together at a local bar on Friday evenings, it is a ritual—an informal gathering. When all the employees of a department store are asked to appear at a media event designed to kick off a new line of clothes, it is a ceremony.

Participating in rituals and ceremonies helps individual employees understand the political and interpersonal nuances of their organization. If they perceive that the ritual or ceremony is meaningful, participating may increase their commitment to the organization because it makes them feel like they are a part of the organizational community. Harrison Trice and Janice Beyer have observed that there are five primary types of organizational ceremonies. *Ceremonies of passage* tell everyone that a person has changed organizational roles and now has a new set of responsibilities, behavioral guidelines and constraints, and interpersonal relationships. *Degradation ceremonies* assign responsibility for errors or problems, refocus attention on the kinds of performance that is expected by management, and remove the guilty party from the power structure of the organization (usually through demotion, reassignment, or resignation). *Enhancement ceremonies* (for example, Mary Kay Cosmetic seminars) reemphasize the goals of the organization and create instant heroes who symbolize those goals. Regular awards ceremonies for the top salespersons can serve this function. *Renewal ceremonies* (such as annual executive retreats complete with motivational speakers) create an image of action and deflect attention from underlying organizational problems. *Integration ceremonies* (for example, giving every employee an identical Thanksgiving ham) redefine the organization as a community and tell each employee that she or he is a part of it.[21]

Of course, the power of ceremonies to motivate and control employees depends on the meaning that employees extract from them, and the extent to which they are meaningful. Like all symbolic forms, ceremonies can be interpreted in many different ways. The foundry that Charley Conrad worked in during his undergraduate years (recall the time-motion study described in Chapter 2) had a Christmas ceremony during which hams were distributed by the owner to each worker from the back of a truck—every worker except him. After his first Christmas ceremony, the owner quietly took him aside and explained that he was excluded because he was a part-time employee (summers and holidays). The owner feared that giving Conrad a ham would make the ceremony less meaningful (or might even cause resentment) for the full-time workers. Ironically, a group of workers later took him aside and told him that they felt bad that he had been left out. They explained that they thought the oversight was because he was not the head of a family as they were and thus didn't need the gift. And, they presented him with a ham that they had purchased during lunch with a pool of money they had collected from one another after the ceremony. Interestingly, although the two meanings were very different, they both recognized that the ceremony was meaningful to the owner and workers alike.

Some office holiday parties may provide an opportunity for a closely knit group of people to celebrate their commitment to a common goal and their legitimate emotional attachments to one another. Others may only be command performances that people attend because the plant manager takes roll. People participate only in the sense of going through the motions; they are never emotionally involved in the ceremony. The meaningfulness of key ceremonies as well as the meanings extracted from the experience may reveal the strength of the organizational culture. Ceremonies that are meaningless to employees, or ceremonies that mean something very different to managers and workers may reveal a culture or subculture that is in the process of decay.

Rituals have some of the same characteristics as ceremonies. Their power stems from the emotional commitments created by the act of participating in them, and they may also vary in meaningfulness and in the meanings that are extracted from them. Some rituals provide opportunities for workers to express their independence from (or hostility toward management); others may provide a means of fulfilling sociability needs that are not met on the job; others may help people deal with job-related changes and the interpersonal changes that they require. For example, wives of major league athletes usually form a close-knit, supportive unofficial family. A key ritual for them is to sit together during home games. When it appears that a wife's husband is about to leave the team through a trade or being sent down to the minors, the unofficial family begins to dissolve. Other wives begin to spend less time with her and begin to sit away from her during games, and so on. The new ritual signals to her—and to her husband—that they must prepare themselves psychologically for a major change and a new informal family.[22] In some cases, rituals reinforce the meanings of ceremonies, as when organizations die, enhancing motivation and control.[23] In other cases, they help meet employees' needs for autonomy, creativity, and sociability, thereby reducing the alienation that comes from unfulfilling jobs, also enhancing motivation and control. But, in other cases they may contradict or redefine the meanings of ceremonies, undermining managerial control, or serve as opportunities for resistance.

Emotion Regulation and Unobtrusive Control   So far we have discussed unobtrusive control in terms of employees' thoughts—the ways in which they come to identify with the dominant beliefs and values of their organizations. But, human beings are not only thinking creatures; they also are emotional beings. Chapters 7 and 9 will examine emotions in more depth, but they must also be discussed in this chapter. Emotions are relevant to cultural forms of motivation and control in three ways. At the simplest level, supervisors can use their positions to manipulate employees' emotional responses. The emotions may be positive, as in ceremonies of enhancement or they may involve the negative emotions of degradation ceremonies. Often the recognition is based as much on complying with the organization's control system as on making tangible contributions; often the recognized employee is chosen because he or she has in some way enhanced or threatened the power of the supervisor. But, in any case, public recognition solidifies the supervisor's power position, because she or he makes the decision about whom to recognize and how to do so. When employees want to be recognized (or want to avoid embarrassment), management's ability to fulfill (or frustrate) those desires serves as a potent basis for control.

Negative emotions serve the same control functions. Steven Fineman, an expert on organizational emotions, concludes that "the socially constructed emotions of embarrassment, shame, and guilt are central to many aspects of organizational order. . . the motivational springs to self-control." Many observers of the trends toward downsizing and contingent workers that have dominated the 1990s are designed more to control workers through fear and anxiety than to enhance organizational efficiency. Some strategies are even designed to keep employees for leaving for better jobs. Manipulating negative emotions reduces employees' self-esteem and makes them more compliant; they follow orders more readily and are less likely to see emotional manipulation as a control strategy. For example, Pan American airline stewardesses who had been made to feel shame about their age, weight, or sexual orientation refused to go along with a union slowdown and voted against their coworkers because of their internalized emotions. Supervisors who are made to feel embarrassed for mixing with their subordinates tend to withdraw from them and become more autocratic.[24]

Unobtrusive control is also exercised when employees learn to interpret emotional responses in ways that are preferred by the organization. Emotional responses are highly ambiguous. Fear and excitement *feel* very much the same, so they must be interpreted. The core beliefs and values of an organization often tell employees how to interpret their emotional responses. They may learn to feel pride only when the organization's goals are met, not when their own objectives are fulfilled. For example, stewardesses may be successfully taught to interpret their anger at obnoxious passengers as care and concern for their helpless and dependent charges. Employees may also begin to interpret their responses to organizational changes (for example, downsizing) as excitement about new opportunities rather than as fear that they may be the next victim.

Finally, employees in many organizations are involved in "emotion management" as part of their jobs. For example, people who work in the leisure/tourism industry are required to constantly display positive emotions and to elicit them in their clients or customers. Stewardesses and cruise ship employees are expected to be happy, perky, and concerned about meeting their customers' needs and to make those customers feel the same positive emotions. In contrast, bill collectors are expected to display negative emotions, such as disgust, to elicit other negative emotions (guilt) from the people they contact. Still other employees must display neutral (or no) emotions, even in crisis situations, to calm other people. No matter how trivial a call to 911 might seem to be (the Chicago-area 911 gets many calls regarding parking just before Bears' home games), or how much of a crisis is involved (people who actually have a burglar in their homes), operators are expected to remain calm, collected, and emotionally distant. Employees can manage these demands in three different ways. They may pretend that they feel the emotions that they display, a process that usually is labeled "surface acting." Or, they may draw on their training or past experiences to actually feel the required emotions, a kind of deep acting. Or, in extreme cases they may learn to feel only what they are supposed to feel in work situations.

For example, Arlie Hochschild's study of stewardesses found that emotions often are not just responses to work, but emotion control is the work. Stewardesses learn to experience only the feelings that are required by their organizational roles and to suppress other feelings. They create a package of emotions and emotional displays in which genuinely felt emotions are transformed into organizationally acceptable emotions. In a way, this is the easiest response to organizational demands for emotion regulation. Acting, in either its surface or deep forms, creates dissonance. It is uncomfortable to feel one thing (for instance, disgust at a client's lifestyle) and display another (warmth and concern). And, it is exhausting to continually do so—acting takes a great deal of effort. This dissonance is lowest, and the amount of effort is reduced, when someone actually feels the emotions that he or she is supposed to feel and express. Emotion management can lead to burnout, reduced self-esteem, depression, and cynicism. But, if employees learn to deal with it, emotion management can increase job satisfaction, and enhance feelings of connectedness and community at work, and worker's beliefs that they are performing their tasks well and having a major impact at work. This is why employees who have been in careers that require emotion management for a long time experience less dissonance and less effort than newcomers to a profession.[25]

Dissonance and effort are greatest when the organization focuses on quality rather than quantity of service, when it provides employees with extensive training on how to "do" the proper emotional displays, and when employees are given very little latitude in emotional expression. They are least severe when employees find their own ways of dealing with the stresses they encounter. For example, 911 operators cope by joking with one another about their craziest callers and telling and retelling their favorite stories. Since some callers are regular customers, the operators may actually create relationships with these people and enjoy their conversations, just as some grocery store clerks develop friendships with their regular customers. Operators also gain satisfaction from knowing that they are helping people who are in need and they talk with one another about their altruistic motives. And, since some of their calls really do involve life-and-death crisis situations, they get an adrenaline fix from helping people who desperately need it. Human service workers choose their careers at least in part because of the satisfaction and excitement that comes from their jobs. But, ironically, they also may be precisely those people who are most susceptible to systems of unobtrusive control. And the more an employee identifies with his or her job and organization, the more likely she or he is to accept emotional labor as a fair and equitable requirement.[26]

Unobtrusive Control and Self-Surveillance   Throughout this book we have examined the ways in which surveillance, control, and resistance go hand in hand. In traditional forms of control, the source of surveillance and control was obviously outside of the worker. Supervisors oversee their workers directly, by enforcing rules of behavior, or through reward systems. Sometimes control is built into work processes themselves. Assembly lines guide and constrain workers' behaviors, even if a supervisor is not looking over their shoulders. In relational forms of control, surveillance is imbedded in interpersonal relationships and in team-based pressures. But, no control system is automatic or completely external to employees. Rule and reward systems work only if employees perceive them as legitimate and value potential rewards/punishments; relational systems are successful only if employees seek satisfying jobs and feel psychological connections to their teams. Unobtrusive control is even more internal. It relies on **self-surveillance,** a process in which employees act in ways that are desired by the organization, because they have accepted its core beliefs and values, and because they feel positive emotions when they comply with its commands. But, even it is not completely internal. Core beliefs and values will not be seen as legitimate if they contradict the experiences and messages that workers have had outside of the work setting. Negative events at work lead people to un-identify with their organizations, just as positive events encourage further identification. Resistance occurs regardless of the kind of control system in place in the organization, although the extent and form of resistance varies across different control systems.

CASE STUDY:
THE HIDDEN EMOTIONS OF TOURISM*

As we have indicated throughout this book, resistance is an inevitable aspect of systems of motivation and control. This is true even of cultural forms of control, although if unobtrusive control is working, it is largely invisible. Consequently, resistance is less likely than in other forms, but it still is possible. Some modes of resistance may be overt and public. For example, some of the stewardesses in Hochschild's study admitted "accidentally" spilling hot coffee in the laps of especially obnoxious travelers. But, it is more likely that resistance to unobtrusive control will occur in private places and times. This case is about emotional control and resistance in three tourism-related organizations, an airline (FWA), a cruise ship (the *Radiant Spirit*), and *Pairs,* an upscale, all-inclusive Caribbean resort. The names have been changed to protect the innocent—and guilty. *Pairs* and *Radiant* cater to people from all over the world, but primarily from Europe and North America. FWA has a less exclusive clientele, but also operates largely in North America. Their marketing rhetoric, from brochures to television ads, depict all three organizations as places where tourists are catered to in every way. At *Pairs* front-line employees, all of whom are black, are taught that they are to display the "happy-go-lucky" attitude that tourists expect of Caribbean people. Employees on the *Radiant,* all of whom are white, learn to mimic the behaviors of the crew of the television series *The Love Boat,* which above everything else means to constantly be smiling and "perky". In all three, employees learn that the customer is always right, and that employees will always be smiling, happy servants. They also learn that these commands have no limits. One *Pairs* staff member said, "A guest coming here could be a thief or a murderer, but we have to be nice to them no matter what." Cassie, a *Radiant* employee, told about a man at the ship disco who

> asked me to dance. He was grabbing and holding me close . . . and saying these weird things . . . [like] 'have you ever thought of coming over to the dark side?" I just played dumb . . . In this type of situation you don't want to piss someone off. . . I didn't know what I could get away with and what I could not. I was so frustrated that I had no control (p. 110).

When Cassie reported the incident to her supervisor she was told to walk away when things like that happen. But, after a training program that included the motto "We never say no," she really didn't know what to do, and blamed herself for not knowing.

All three organizations use a variety of mechanisms to enforce their behavioral rules. At *Pairs* each guest is given an evaluation sheet that includes a section where she or he is asked to comment on the performance of the staff by name. Twice a month the public relations office posts the comments for all employees to see. Cash rewards are given to employees who receive many positive comments, and punishments are given those with negative comments. The *Radiant*

(continued)

(continued from the previous page)

uses a similar system, and it works so well that employees believe that the passengers are their "second bosses," who control the employees' actions and emotions. But their cash awards seem to focus on control as well as service—one employee won an award to suggest that mirrors be installed throughout the ship so that employees could constantly monitor their appearance. FWA uses "ghost riders," supervisors who fly disguised as customers.

The employees themselves help discipline one another. *Pairs* posts summaries of customer comments. When the sheets are posted all the desk staff excitedly huddle together behind the reception desk to read the results. Workers read positive comments aloud for all to hear; workers with the highest points received congratulations from their peers; workers with negative comments and low points were talked about behind their backs for the rest of the week. When Ken, a bellman, walked by the desk, Simone teased him by saying "I don't see your name here." He immediately turned the pages of the report until he found a remark that included his name: "It only takes one," he said. If any of the *Radiant's* workers complain, their coworkers will tell them "it's a tough job. If you can't handle it, go home."

The control system does *seem* to work. Most of the workers are like Trendy, about whom *Pairs* workers commented, "I have never seen Trendy get mad. I'm not telling a lie. In all the years I've been here I've just seen her smile [when guests or supervisors are present]." A *Radiant* employee said, "Our job is to be happy, and there will be times when you don't feel that way. You have to put it aside and look as though you're enjoying your job (p. 106)." The employees' performances are so fluid and so convincing that they seem to be scripted. One script welcomes new guests: "Hi, I'm Laura your concierge [big smile]. I am here to help. If you have any questions don't hesitate to call. If any situations arise (I won't say problems because we don't have problems at *Pairs*), please call. We are out of the office a lot but we have a radio, so just call the operator and he will get in touch with us." Even the actor's voice is scripted. When the staff members talk to one another or to guests from the Caribbean they use the local patois, with its rhythmic tone and colorful metaphors. But with most guests only standard English is used.

Perhaps most important, most of the workers see their act as just that, a strategic way of behaving that fulfills management's commands while making their lives easier. *Radiant* employees complained bitterly that management shoved the customer service program down their throats. And, behind the scenes—in the galleys of airliners, the back rooms of resorts, and the tiny employee staterooms on cruise ships—"servanthood" is a different thing entirely. When safely out of the hearing of guests or management *Pairs* staffers talk about anything and everything, and they often complain about the customers, making it clear that it simply isn't true that the customer is always right. A *Radiant* employee told all his peers about a customer who asked if the ship generates its own electricity, and wondered "what if I would have told him, 'No, we run an

(continued)

(continued from the previous page)

extra long electric cord back to port." Simone was working at the *Pairs* registration desk with Sandy one day and a U.S. tourist interrupted and asked Sandy if he could mail his postcards with U.S. stamps. Sandy, in his best British English, explained that he would have to use local stamps "because each country uses its own stamps and postal system." As the guest departed he immediately shifted into his local dialect and we talked at length about how little U.S. residents, including his friends at school, knew about Caribbean or West Indian culture. In fact, one of the dominant topics of conversation involved the various failings of the guests—their stupid questions ("Why is it raining?" or "What language are the staff members speaking?" [the answer is English]), their arrogance (for example, one U.S. resident who repeatedly demanded that the desk clerk check his bill for unauthorized long-distance calls after seeing his maid using his phone, even after being told that the maids *always* use the room phones to notify the desk when they have finished cleaning a room), their paranoia (the German couple who would not leave their luggage for a moment lest a staff member steal the tacky palm leaf hat and the couple who demanded to know the location of the American embassy in case of civil unrest, something that had not happened on this island in almost a century), and their racism (all staff members are black; almost all guests are white). Telling these stories to one another seemed to have three purposes—they place the worker in a superior role vis-à-vis the guest, thus reversing the complete subservience demanded by their organization; they help cushion the worker from negative comments by the guests, making it less likely that they will blame themselves when they encounter rude behavior; and, paradoxically, they allow the worker to continue to play his or her assigned role while simultaneously rejecting it.

Employees also share strategies for resisting the control system with one another. FWA old-timers tell new employees how to detect ghost riders and how to use privacy laws to short-circuit managerial strategies, such as making random checks of the flight attendants' bags. They teach one another to follow the most alienating rules only when management is around. Terry was told to never again wear her Santa earrings on flights during the holidays. To get around the policy she took them off when management was around and put them on when she stepped on a plane. They fulfill the requirement to wear makeup only during their annual performance reviews and wear the required high-heeled shoes only when flying through a hub city where managers are likely to be hanging around. They teach one another to use humor to keep overbearing pilots in their places and to combat the sexism that often accompanies their jobs. Or they devise systems that allow them to escape the housemothers who are assigned to women's dormitories during training, which they satirically label "Barbie Bootcamp."

The goal of this case study has been to contrast employees' public performances—those that take place in the view of people who have the organizational right to control them, supervisors and customers—and their private or "hidden" performances. The greater the power gap between controllers and controlled,

(continued)

(continued from the previous page)

the more different these two types of performances will be. If one looks at public performances alone, it seems that unobtrusive control is total—employees' beliefs, values, and feelings correspond with the desires of their organizations. But, if one also examines their hidden messages a much more complex picture emerges. Workers in all three organizations do seem to have internalized the core beliefs and values, of their organizations and do seem to be willing to enforce behavioral constraints on themselves and their peers. This is especially true in public but also seems to be true to some degree in private. But, they also engage in complex processes of resisting sometimes in public, and often in private. Organizational life seems to involve a "dance of resistance and domination" (Tracy, p. 99).

Applying What You've Learned

1. What evidence is there that the employees of these tourist organizations have identified with their organizations and roles in them? What evidence is there that they have not done so?
2. How does surveillance work in these organizations? Who does it? How do they do it, and with what effects?

Questions to Think About and Discuss

1. How do the various forms of control used at *Pairs, Radiant,* and FWA support one another? How would the points/bonus system work differently if there was no system of managers watching the employees? No system of guests being encouraged to watch and report on the employees? No training program or messages that support the organizations' core beliefs and values?
2. What functions does resistance play for the workers? What effects does it have on the functioning of the organization? On the organizational control system? Why?
3. Some theorists argue that unobtrusive control soon will go the way of the dinosaurs. Recent trends toward short-term employment (recall Chapter 1) mean that employees will not be in a company long enough to even learn its core beliefs and values, much less identify with it. Others argue that people are getting more and more isolated from one another, so that their workplace is the only source of community that is available to them. As a result, unobtrusive control will be even more powerful. What do you think? Why?

This case is based on Simone Carnegie, "The Hidden Emotions of Tourism: Communication and Power in the Caribbean," M.A. Thesis, Texas A&M University, 1996; Alexandra Murphy, "Hidden Transcripts of Flight Attendant Resistance," Management Communication Quarterly, 11(1998): 499–535; and Sarah J. Tracy, "Becoming a Character for Commerce," Management Communication Quarterly, 14 (2000): 90–128. The key source for all three studies is James Scott, Domination and the Arts of Resistance (New Haven, CT: Yale University Press, 1990). For an analysis of resistance in a very different kind of organization see D. Collinson, Managing the Shop Floor (New York: DeGruyter, 1992).

CULTURAL STRATEGIES OF LEADERSHIP

We noted earlier in this chapter that there is a key tension within cultural strategies of organizing. On the one hand they assume that organizational cultures can be managed strategically. But, on the other hand they assert that employees actively perceive, interpret, and strategically respond to their organizational situations. Thus, employees may come to believe, feel, and act in different ways than management assumed they would. Cultural strategies of leadership recognize that this tension exists and strive to deal with it through what have been labeled "transformational" processes. The most important of these processes are called visioning and framing.

Visioning and Transformational Leadership

Both transformational and transactional leaders are characterized by their consideration for employees and their needs, by their willingness to actively involve their subordinates in decision making (even encouraging them to question the basic assumptions of the organization or unit), and by their willingness to supervise loosely. Both forms of leadership involve similar communicative strategies: Leaders clarify the challenges that the organization or unit faces while encouraging, supporting, and inspiring their subordinates to use their own abilities to meet those challenges. Transformational and transactional leaders both maintain close communicative ties with their subordinates.

But, transformational leaders also differ from transactional leaders. Their authority is based on what Max Weber called "**charisma,**" the image that they possess some divine, supernatural, or otherwise special talents or attributes. At the heart of charismatic leadership is the ability to create a vision of where the organization or unit is going and how it is to achieve those goals and persuade others to accept that vision.[27] Visionary leadership involves communicating a mission for the organization or unit that is noble or otherwise meaningful for employees. The vision encompasses each employee's hopes, desires, and so on (even if it requires the leader to sacrifice some of her or his own gains). Visionary leadership involves a great deal of impression management—displays of personal integrity and a willingness to take reasonable risks and give of oneself for the good of the organization and demonstrations of personal warmth and charm, including showing concern for employees and their nonwork lives.[28] Transformational leaders are able to transform their subordinates' creative ideas and actions so that they further the mission of the organization or unit and do so without embarrassing them or claiming ownership of their ideas.

Of course, not just any vision will do. A transformative vision is realistic and credible. It is consistent with the history of the organization or unit and fits the realities of the current situation, and it is attractive. It provides targets that beckon. The genius of transformational leadership is the ability to "assemble—out of all the variety of images, signals, forecasts, and alternatives—a clearly articulated vision of the future that is at once simple, easily understood, clearly desirable, and energizing."[29] Visions provide a picture of the future, an explanation and sense of purpose, and guidelines for acting on an everyday basis. They allow each

retention rates

employee to find his or her own role in the organization, his or her own way to contribute to the mission, and in doing so, they release new energies and enthusiasm. They emerge over time, with experience, and through mutual consultation with subordinates. They are flexible and adaptive. They include long-term goals that help define a series of short-term goals, which in turn both guide and are influenced by goals that emerge out of everyday experience. For example, when Dr. Barbara Barlow was appointed chief of pediatric surgery at Harlem Hospital Center, her goals focused on successful treatment of patients. But she and her staff noted that many patients were hospitalized because of injuries suffered from falling out of buildings, playing on unsafe playground equipment, and improperly operating their bicycles. So, her goals changed to focus on preventative care as well as acute care—increasing the number of window gates in apartment buildings, teaching children safety rules and street smarts, and so on. Her unit now pursues long-term, short-term, and emergent goals simultaneously, and each kind of goal influences the pursuit of the others.[30]

Finally, visions are *appropriately* ambiguous. It is somewhat ironic that transformation leadership *relies* on ambiguity, because ambiguity complicates cultural strategies of motivation and control. When situations and symbolic acts are ambiguous, employees have much more freedom to reinterpret them and act in ways that differ from what the leader intended. But, ambiguity may be intentional and strategic. This may seem to be a somewhat strange concept for members of Western societies, because they have been taught to value clear communication. In many non-Western societies, ambiguity is treated as something that should be managed strategically. Some situations call for a high level of clarity and specificity—communicating technical standards for precision equipment or delivering negative performance feedback, for example. But, in other cases, ambiguity can actually be helpful. It allows different people to interpret the same message in different ways, helping to maintain a diversity of viewpoints within the same organization. When the organization faces problems that are new or particularly difficult, or when it goes through major organizational changes, this diversity can lead to innovative solutions. Ambiguity may also allow parties involved in conflicts to avoid having to blame anyone for an impasse or escalation, thus saving face. "Teamwork," an important dimension of both transactional and transformational leadership, is an ambiguous but appealing concept in many societies. In Japan it is associated with loyalty to one's company; in Sweden it refers to one's membership in a work group; in Anglo societies it evokes images of team sports—rugby, cricket, futbol (soccer), baseball, or basketball. Good visions are both sufficiently focused to energize employees and give them a sense of direction, but ambiguous enough to allow flexibility. According to cultural/transformational strategies of leadership, this dilemma is managed through processes of framing.

Framing and Transformational Leadership

In addition to persuading employees to accept a particular set of beliefs and values, transformational leadership involves persuading them to see their organizational world in a particular way. It may be as simple as persuading them to view a new situation as a challenge rather than a problem. The ambiguities of organizational life create spaces within which transformational leaders can act. Framing begins when a leader develops her or his own view of reality and makes sense of the organization's past, present, and future in terms of that view. It continues when she or he communicates that view to subordinates. In this sense, the key to framing lies in employees' memories. If a leader's interpretation makes sense and seems to be spontaneous and honest, it may be credible (recall Gibb's discussion of supportive communication in Chapter 3). When employees later encounter a new situation, they will automatically approach it through the supervisor's frame of reference. Eventually the entire work group or organization begins to share the same way of making sense out of the world.

In some cases, members of the organization may develop a language that is consistent with their frame of reference. They will think in terms of a particular set of metaphors and categories, interpret events in accord with stories and myths that they share, and infuse their new language with beliefs and values that are especially meaningful. So, the key to persuading subordinates to accept a transformational leader's frame of reference is not overt persuasion. Instead, persuasion occurs when a leader uses a particular frame in his or her everyday activities to make sense out of events. By paying attention to some things and ignoring others, expressing honest emotions of anger in response to some things and joy in response to others, and reacting to critical incidents and crises in particular ways, we let other people know how we make sense out of life, and in the process we let them know what we really value. The supervisor-subordinate relationships that emerge can be empowering for workers, because they capitalize on enthusiasm and create feelings of significance, competence, and connectedness to others who share a common purpose.[31]

For example, a new resort was about to open. They employees were anxious because they knew about a neighboring resort that had recently experienced a disastrous opening day; everything that could have gone wrong did. Recognizing how nervous everyone was, the CEO convened a meeting of all employees and said:

> We have all noticed the bad press about [other resort's] opening day. You can't help but feel the pressure. Despite our confidence and all that we've done to get ready for tomorrow, you can be sure that something will go wrong. But that's not what makes a bad opening day. It's how you deal with what goes wrong that makes the difference. Tomorrow, you will see people walking around looking lost. You'll be lost too. Instead of sitting there feeling insecure, walk up to our guests and introduce yourself, Say, "I'm new here too, but I'm going to do my best to try to help you.

He went on to tell other stories about people bringing order out of chaos and thereby replaced the failure scenario that the employees had been circulating with a more positive one. The exchange helped put people at ease and contributed to a successful opening day.[32]

Of course, leaders do communicate their frames of reference in more formal ways. During planning sessions, a leader sets an agenda for a group by guiding the discussion toward a certain set of priorities or suggesting that the group view a particular event or problem in a certain way. Leaders also send powerful messages about what they actually value when they appraise employees' performance and distribute rewards. But, the most powerful way to communicate a frame is by everyday behavior, by seizing what Fairhurst and Sarr call "leadership moments," opportunities to suggest a particular way to view events, messages, and communication.

CASE STUDY:
"NUTS!" DOWN UNDER*

The 1990s were the era of planned organizational change. The new century seems to be continuing the focus on change, especially in governmental organizations. Throughout the world agencies are being asked to do more with less, to become less bureaucratic and more flexible and adaptive. Citizens have become consumers, demanding the same quality and responsiveness from public sector and voluntary organizations that they demand from the private sector. The discourse about change now is so extensive that it is accepted uncritically—opponents are immediately dismissed as being out of touch with the reality of the 21st century.†† The problem faced by change-oriented managers is that their employees are often not as closely attuned to management fads, change-oriented or not. They sometimes like things the way they are and are deeply suspicious of efforts to transform their lives. One way to overcome this resistance is to point to an exemplar, to mimic the "best practices" of a highly successful organization. This case study is about a transformational leader, known only as Ken, who transformed a governmental agency in New Zealand by persuading his subordinates to emulate Texas-based Southwest Airlines.

There is no question that Southwest deserves to be copied. For a decade it has had the highest customer satisfaction rates of any U.S. airline, and consistently high profits. It has thrived in spite of cut-throat competition from much larger airlines (primarily American), aided by their allies in the U.S. government. The key to its success has been superb strategic decision making in the executive suite, exceptional morale and commitment among its employees, and a rather quirky mode of operating. Employees dress casually, have frequent parties (which upper management attends), and joke with or otherwise entertain customers. Ken encountered Southwest through a biography of its CEO, Herb Kelleher, entitled *Nuts!* (Southwest flies short hops, too short to serve meals. Instead, it serves drinks and peanuts, a metaphor that it also uses to publicize its low fares. Hence the title of the book. Ken has never actually flown Southwest, since it doesn't get within 12,000 miles of New Zealand, but in a recent telephone conversation said that he's looking for an opportunity to do so.) His department, which provides support functions like processing license applications for the local government, has been undergoing planned change since 1996. The organization was restructured, some staff members were transferred to other departments,

(continued)

(continued from the previous page)

and an organization-wide development program (called FIT, for *focus* on the customer, *invest* in the process, and *teamwork*) was established. The department is made up of Ken and eight women who vary in age from their early 20s to their mid-50s. As part of the restructuring, the department was moved to a new building where team members were located in full view of everyone who entered, staff and customers alike. Ken told his workers that he saw the changes as an opportunity to increase the importance of the department to the entire organization, and purchased them new "stewardess-like" uniforms to enhance their image.

Ken's vision involved being the best, in every sense of the term, but especially regarding customer service and teamwork. He implored them to "grasp a new challenge with both hands." Then he read *Nuts!* He gave a copy to every woman and asked them to present the section that they found to be most meaningful at the weekly staff meeting. He created slogans (like "positively outrageous service," lifted directly from Southwest) and continuously uses the word "outrageous" to describe ideas and actions that are consistent with his philosophy. He prominently displays the awards won by the department, which includes a nation-wide award for customer service. Workers were given gold-colored name tags instead of white ones like everyone else, a ring binder that has the department's code on the front and newspaper clippings on service and the weekly *Nuts!* presentations on the inside. Several weekend activities focused on teamwork and customer service. These included visits to government agencies that were known for their service and, once they were exhausted, to exemplars in the private sector. These visits were designed to foster continuous improvement; something that Ken framed as "learning from the best."

He took every opportunity to recognize, reward, and highlight service, quality, and teamwork. In meetings that resemble high school pep rallies or religious revivals, he lauds them for being winners, heroes who "go the extra mile" to "get the work done at the highest standard." Bread is broken, testimonies are given in ritual sharing and bonding. Christine chose the following passage from *Nuts!* for her presentation:

> In [good] organizations . . . relationships are based on covenants, people are bound by a deep sense of loyalty to each other; instead of simply trading a fair day's work for a fair day's pay, they share a common set of values, norms, and guiding philosophy.

Another recounted a *Nuts!* metaphor of geese flying together. There is strength and safety in numbers, as long as all of the geese fly in the same direction toward a common goal. At each meeting the women make presentations that persuade one another, and persuade themselves, to believe in Ken's vision. The women see themselves as being "special," and as members of a team that wants everyone to feel involved. They offer ideas for improving the department, knowing that Ken will support them even if they "step on some toes." They are an intimate family that supports and takes care of one another during difficult times, a family that is united by their heroic mission to reform local government. One of the advantages

(continued)

(continued from the previous page)

of the family metaphor is its vagueness, but Ken defines it in terms of trust and collaboration. He is a little paternalistic, as when he encouraged the team to help take care of Natalie, a young, single team member whose pregnancy had elevated her blood pressure to a dangerous level. Sometimes he scolds the workers, not like a command-and-control manager but like a father whose daughters really should know better.

Of course, there is resistance. Elsie complained that the weekend meetings took time away from family and domestic duties, something that Ken probably didn't understand since he is a man. Others noted that "teamdom" wasn't equal, that some members helped others out much more often than they were helped. But, when complaints are raised, the topic of conversation is changed very quickly. And they have won all of those awards.

Applying What You've Learned

1. What elements of cultural strategies of organizing has Ken incorporated into the Business Services Department? What has he ignored? What elements of transformation leadership has he employed?
2. Ken's employees seem to have accepted their new situation rather easily. Why? To what extent are the factors you have identified necessary for transformational leadership to work?

Questions to Think About and Discuss

Critical theorists (you first met them in Chapter 3) would argue that the Business Service Department provides a classic example of manipulating workers through the use of hidden mechanisms of control. In fact, at one meeting Ken explicitly admitted that the system has been "put into place for self-monitoring" by employees. While workers may gain prestige and self-esteem through these strategies, they really are not any more empowered than they would be in a traditional bureaucracy. Unobtrusive control and transformational leadership only lead workers to toil longer and harder for no increases in power or tangible rewards.

1. How would you respond to this criticism?
2. Is unobtrusive control less ethical than systems that are not hidden (e.g., simple control)?
3. Is it more manipulative to create situations in which employees engage in self-persuasion than it is to create tangible reward systems like the one at Industry International?
4. Why or why not?

---

*This case is based on Theodore Zorn, Deborah Page, & George Cheney, "Nuts about Change," *Management Communication Quarterly, 13*(2000): 515–566.

†See E. Abrahamson, "Management Fashion," *Academy of Management Review, 21*(1996): 254–285.

A Retrospective Look at Traditional, Relational, and Cultural Strategies of Organizing

Throughout Chapters 2 through 4 we have examined strategies of organizing in isolation of one another. We did so because each strategy is so complicated that it is impossible to treat them together. But, doing so may be a little misleading, because it separates the three strategies, making them seem to be mutually exclusive alternatives. There are very few (if any) real organizations that use only one strategy of organizing. Organizations emerge and develop in their own, distinctive ways as their members collaborate (and compete) to deal with the situations they face. They develop their own mixes of traditional, relational, and cultural strategies. Sometimes these strategies are in tension with one another, as when retail organizations develop cultural strategies that focus on flexibility and customer service, but operate in a traditional bureaucratic structure. In other cases, the strategies are more congruent with one another, but even then there will be other tensions and contradictions. For example, at Wellblown Manufacturing Company, an English subsidiary of a U.S. multinational firm, employees learn to believe in and value the traditional chain of command. Management does not talk about the chain very often because doing so might alienate the workers. But, when things at work get especially complicated, it is used to clarify authority relationships and bring things down to earth.

Similarly, communication is multidimensional. It is at once structural, relational, contextual, and systemic. Even though one strategy of organizing may feature one dimension of communication, the other dimensions are always present. This multidimensionality complicates organizational communication and processes of organizing in many ways. Consider two examples. From its inception the W.L. Gore Company has focused on a cultural strategy of organizing. In 1969, Bill Gore founded W.L. Gore and Associates and started making a variety of products out of Dupont Teflon—everything from outdoor clothing and camping gear to vein grafts and filters for blood transfusions. Gore decided to keep his plants relatively small—never more than 250 "associates," as employees are called—and to arrange them in clusters. Gore was convinced that when organizations or units become too large, it is difficult to make cultural strategies of organizing succeed. Members are so isolated from one another and from upper management that they tend not to share in the vision and values of their cultures. He also believed that the kinds of communication breakdowns described in Chapter 2 become increasing problems as organizational size increases. Instead of being structured like a bureaucratic triangle, Gore plants look like a lattice, a crosshatch that represents unrestricted communication (no chain of command), and no formal authority. Associates communicate with whomever they need to talk with to get the job done. The lattice survives partly because management does not interfere with the natural emergence of informal communication networks and partly because it assists in the process. But the overall strategy works because structural and cultural choices are congruent with one another and are based on a concern for maximizing organizational effectiveness in a competitive, turbulent environment.

In other cases, an organization implements a strategy whose components render it dysfunctional. After a number of apparently avoidable airline crashes during the late 1990s, a number of think tanks examined the Federal Aviation Administration, whose many missions include maintaining airline safety. The studies found that the organization, as many government agencies, had developed a highly bureaucratic structure that made it virtually impossible to affect change or help the agency learn from its mistakes. As a result, there was little accountability in the system—one division of the organization could easily shift responsibility for errors to another division and so on. But, the FAA is also "a culture that does not recognize or serve any client other than itself."[33] The organization is adequately funded and full of capable, hard-working people, but it has chosen a structure and developed a culture that combine to make bad decision making almost inevitable. So, the key question facing organizations and their members is not whether to rely on traditional, relational, or cultural strategies of organizing. It is to determine the combination of strategies that best meets the organization's needs and the needs of the people and groups it serves. This question becomes even more pressing as new strategies of organizing emerge and are implemented. As Chapter 5 will explain, these alternatives may be appropriate to the situations that organizations face in the competitive, global economy of the early 21st century, but they are no less complicated than the traditional, relational, and cultural strategies.

NOTES

[1] Stephen Fineman, "Emotion and Organizing," in *Handbook of Organization Studies,* Stewart Clegg, Cynthia Hardy, & Walter Nord, eds. (Thousand Oaks, CA: Sage, 1999).

[2] Joanne Martin, *Cultures in Organizations: Three Perspectives,* (New York: Oxford University Press, 1992).

[3] Karl Weick has argued that decentralization and participation are necessary for cultural strategies to succeed ("Organizational Culture and High Reliability," *California Management Review, 29* (1987): 112–127).

[4] For an extended analysis of the development of the cultural strategy see Eric Eisenberg and Patricia Riley, "Organizational Culture," in L. Putnam and F. Jablin eds., *The New Handbook of Organizational Communication* (Thousand Oaks, CA: Sage, 2000). The primary proponents of this view were Tom Peters and Robert Waterman, *In Search of Excellence* (New York: Harper & Row, 1982); Terrance Deal and Alan Kennedy *Corporate Cultures* (Reading, MA: Addison-Wesley, 1982); and William Ouchi and A. Jaeger (see "Type Z Organization," *Academy of Management Review, 3* (1978): 305–314 and William Ouchi, *Theory Z* (Reading, MA: Addison-Wesley, 1981)). *In Search of Excellence* was the most popular book on organizations ever published (selling more than 5 million copies in its first three years). It generated a series of follow-up books, videotapes, and consulting programs and by 1987, three years after its publication, Peters' consulting firm was grossing about $3.5 million per year.

[5] The popularity of the perspective is explained in Charles Conrad, "Review of *A Passion for Excellence,*" *Administrative Science Quarterly, 30* (1985): 426–429. The dominance of the perspective is examined by Stephen Barley, G.W. Meyer, and Debra Gash, "Cultures of Culture," *Administrative Science Quarterly, 33* (1988): 24–60.

[6] William Ouchi and Alan Wilkins, "Efficient Cultures," *Administrative Science Quarterly, 28* (1983): 468–481; Kathleen Gregory, "Native-view Paradigms," *Administrative Science Quarterly, 28* (1983): 360–372.

[7] For examples of subcultural differences, see Michael Rosen, "Breakfast at Spiro's," *Journal of Management, 11* (1985): 31–48; and Ed Young, "On the Naming of the Rose," *Organization Studies, 10* (1989): 187–206 and Leslie Baxter, "'Talking Things Through' and 'Putting It In Writing'," *Journal of Applied Communication Research, 21* (1994): 313–328.

[8] Alan Wilkins, *Managing Corporate Character* (San Francisco: Jossey-Bass, 1989).

[9] The ideas that we will present in this section are similar to those of Mats Alvesson, "Cultural-Ideological Modes of Management Control: A Theory and a Case Study of a Professional Service Company," in Stanley Deetz ed., *Communication Yearbook 16* (Newbury Park, CA: Sage, 1994, pp. 3–42).

[10] Cited in Melissa Gibson & Michael Papa, "The Mud, The Blood, and the Beer Guys," *Journal of Applied Communication Research, 28* (2000): 78. For a similar case study in organizational control at the U.S. Forest Service see Connie Bullis and Phil Tompkins, "The Forest Ranger Revisited," *Communication Monographs, 56 (*1989): 287–306. For analyses of the processes through which identification occurs see Michael Pratt, "The Good, The Bad, and the Ambivalent," *Administrative Science Quarterly, 45* (2000): 456–493.

[11] Michael Kramer & Vernon Miller, "A Response to Criticisms of Organizational Socialization Research," *Communication Monographs, 66* (1999): 362

[12] These examples are from George Cheney & Greg Frenette, "Persuasion and Organization," in *The Ethical Nexus,* Charles Conrad, ed. (Norwood, NJ: Ablex, 1992) and James DiSanza & Connie Bullis, "Everybody Identifies with Smokey the Bear," *Management Communication Quarterly, 12* (1999): 347–399.

[13] See DiSanza & Bullis; Robin Patric Clair, "Ways of Seeing," *Communication Monographs, 66* (1999): 374–381.

[14] See George Cheney, *Rhetoric in an Organizational Society: Managing Multiple Identities* (Columbia, SC: University of South Carolina Press, 1991); Craig Scott, Steven Corman, & George Cheney, "Development of a Structurational Model of Identification in the Organization," *Communication Theory, 8* (1998): 298–336; Linda Larkey & Calvin Morrill, "Organizational Commitment as Symbolic Process," *Western Journal of Communication, 59* (1995): 193–213; Traci Callaway Russo, "Organizational and Professional Identification," *Management Communication Quarterly, 12* (1998): 72–111; Craig Scott, "Identification with Multiple Targets in a Geographically Dispersed Organization," *Management Communication Quarterly, 10* (1997): 491–522; James Barker & Phillip Tompkins, "Identification in the Self-Managing Organization: Characteristics of Target and Tenure," *Human Communication Research, 21* (1994): 223–240; and Neil Paulson, et al., "The Intergroup Context of Communication in Organizations," Paper presented at the International Communication Association Convention, Acapulco, MX, June, 2000.

[15] Russo.

[16] Louis Pondy, "The Role of Metaphors and Myths in the Organization and the Facilitation of Change," and Joanne Martin and Melanie Powers, "Truth or Corporate Propaganda: The Value of a Good War Story," in Pondy, et al., *Culture;* Kenwyn Smith and Valerie Simmons, "The Rumpelstiltskin Organization," *Administrative Science Quarterly, 28* (1983): 377–392.

[17] A number of sources have investigated the relationship between stories and cultures, organizational and otherwise. A treatment that has become popular among communication scholars was presented by Walter Fisher, "Narration as a Human Communication Paradigm," *Communication Monographs, 51* (1984): 1–22; an extended treatment of the relationship between stories and societal control is available in Dennis Mumby, ed., *Narrative and Social Control: Critical Perspectives* (Newbury Park, CA: Sage, 1993). For extended analyses of organizational stories, see Harrison Trice and Janice Beyer, *The Cultures of Work Organizations* (Englewood Cliffs, NJ: Prentice Hall, 1993). For an extended distinction between lists and stories, see Larry Browning, "Lists and Stories in Organizational Communication," *Communication Theory, 2* (1992): 281–302 and Karl Weick and Larry Browning, "Argument and Narration in Organizational Communication," *Journal of Management, 12* (1986): 243–259.

[18] Fisher.

[19] The distinction between stories and storytelling is developed at length in Michael Pacanowsky and Nick O'Donnell-Trujillo, "Performance," and in Michael Pacanowsky, "Creating and Narrating Organizational Realities," in *Rethinking Communication,* vol. 2, Brenda Dervin, et al., eds. (Beverly Hills, CA: Sage, 1989). Also see Joachim Knuf "'Ritual' in Organizational Culture Theory," in Stanley Deetz ed., *Communication Yearbook 16* (Newbury Park, CA: Sage, 1994) and

David Boje, "The Storytelling Organization," *Administrative Science Quarterly, 36* (1991): 106–126.

[20] Thomas Hollihan and Patricia Riley, "The Rhetorical Power of a Compelling Story," *Communication Quarterly, 35* (1987), 15.

[21] See Harrison Trice & Janice Beyer, *Cultures,* and "Studying Organizational Cultures through Rites and Ceremonials," *Academy of Management Review, 9 (*1984): 653–669. For an excellent analysis of the ritualized nature of the concept of communicating via the chain of command, see David Golding, "Management Rituals," in *Understanding Management,* Stephen Linstead, R.G. Small, & P. Jeffcutt (London: Sage, 1996).

[22]. Betty Webber Conrad, "The Moving Experience," *The Waiting Room, 2* (1985): 12–18.

[23] Stanley Harris and Robert Sutton, "Functions of Parting Ceremonies in Dying Organizations," *Academy of Management Journal, 29* (1986): 5–30.

[24] H. Flam, "Fear, Loyalty, and Greedy Organizations," in *Emotion in Organizations.* Stephen Fineman, ed. (Newbury Park, CA: Sage, 1993). For the examples presented in this section, and others, see Sally Planalp, Susan Hafen, & A. Dawn Adkins, "Messages of Shame and Guilt," in *Communication Yearbook 23,* Michael Roloff, ed. (Thousand Oaks, CA: Sage, 2000).

[25] Emotion management is a relatively new topic for organizational communication scholars. The classic study is sociologist Arlie Hochschild's study of stewardesses in *The Managed Heart* (Berkeley: University of California Press, 1983). Alexandra Murphy revisited flight attendants in "Hidden Transcripts of Flight Attendant Resistance," *Management Communication Quarterly, 11* (1998): 499–535. And Sarah Tracy and Karen Tracy examined 911 operators in "Emotion Labor at 911," *Journal of Applied Communication Research, 26* (1998): 390–411. A recent special issue of *Management Communication Quarterly* summarizes recent trends. See Susan Kruml & Deanna Geddes, "Exploring the Dimensions of Emotional Labor," *14* (2000): 8–49; Sherianne Shuler and Beverly Davenport Sypher, "Seeking Emotional Labor," *14* (2000): 50–89; and Sarah J. Tracy, "Becoming a Character for Commerce," *14* (2000): 90–128.

[26] B.E. Ashford & R.H. Humphrey, "Emotional Labor in Service Roles," *Academy of Management Review, 18* (1993): 88–115 and Gideon Kunda, *Engineering Culture* (Philadelphia, PA: Temple University Press, 1992).

[27] See J. Kevin Barge, *Leadership* (New York: St. Martin's, 1994); Bernard Bass, *Leadership and Performance Beyond Expectations* (New York: Free Press, 1985); M.Z. Hackman and C.E. Johnson, *Leadership: A Communication Perspective* (Prospect Heights, IL: Waveland Press, 1991); and C. Pavitt, G.G. Whitchurch, H. McGlurg, & N. Peterson, "Melding the Objective and Subjective Sides of Leadership: Communication and Social Judgments in Decision-Making Groups," *Communication Monographs, 62* (1995): 243–264; and Warren Bennis, Jagdish Parikh, and Ronnie Lessem, *Beyond Leadership: Balancing Economics, Ethics, and Ecology* (Cambridge, MA: Basil Blackwell, 1994, p. 58).

[28] William Gardner & Dean Cleavenger, "The Impression Management Strategies Associated with Transformational Leadership at the World-Class Level," *Management Communication Quarterly, 12* (1998): 3–41.

[29] Warren Bennis, Jagdish Parikh, and Ronnie Lessem, *Beyond Leadership: Balancing Economics, Ethics, and Ecology* (Cambridge, MA: Basil Blackwell, 1994, p. 58); Peter Senge, *The Fifth Discipline* (New York: Doubleday, 1990).

[30] The example and the analysis of different kinds of goals is from Gail Fairhurst and Robert Sarr, *The Art of Framing: Managing the Language of Leadership* (San Francisco: Jossey-Bass, 1996) who based their analysis on Steve Wilson and Linda Putnam, "Interaction Goals in Negotiation," in James Anderson, ed., *Communication Yearbook 13* (Newbury Park, CA: Sage, 1990) and Pamela Hellman, "Her Push for Prevention Keeps Kids Out of ER," *Sunday Examiner and Chronicle Parade Magazine,* April 19, 1995, pp. 8–10. An excellent discussion of the need for visions/goals to be adaptive and flexible is available in Michael Hitt, B.W. Keats, H.F. Harback, and R.D. Nixon, "Rightsizing: Building and Maintaining Strategic Leadership and Long-Term Competitiveness," *Organizational Dynamics, 23* (1994): 18–32.

[31] Marlene Fine & Patrice M. Buzzanell, "Walking the High Wire," in *Rethinking Organizational and Managerial Communication from Feminist Perspectives,* Patrice Buzzanell, ed. (Thousand Oaks, CA: Sage, 2000).

[32] Ellen O'Conner, "Discourse at our Disposal," *Management Communication Quarterly, 10* (1997): 395–432.

[33] Wellblown is discussed by David Golding in "Management Rituals," in *Understanding Management,* Stephen Linstead, Robert Grafton Small, & Paul Jeffcutt, eds. (London: Sage, 1996); W.L. Gore is examined in Michael Pacanowsky, "Communication in the Empowering Organization," and Terrance Albrecht, "Communication and Personal Control in Empowering Organizations," in James Anderson (Ed.), *Communication Yearbook 11,* (Beverly Hills, CA: Sage, 1987) and the F.A.A. is profiled in Don Phillips, *Houston Chronicle,* July 12, 1996, 6A.

Chapter 5

NETWORK STRATEGIES OF ORGANIZING

*New organizational forms arise to cope
with new environmental conditions.*
—RAYMOND E. MILES AND CHARLES C. SNOW

*The connective mechanism that enables parts of the
[network] organization to coordinate with one another
and with other organizations is communication.*
—JANET FULK AND GERARDINE DESANCTIS

CENTRAL THEMES

- Over the past fifty years, there has been a transition from a production economy based on physical production of goods in factories to a knowledge society, in which most value is added through information and knowledge-related activities.
- The knowledge society gives rise to different types of organizations than did the production economy and to two new types of workers, knowledge workers and information workers.
- Along with the knowledge society came an increased rate of change in the growth of knowledge and in markets, products, and competition, much of it spurred by the globalization of the economy.
- The increased complexity and required speed of response has led organizations to emphasize flatter structures with more lateral links; a number of different types of integrating mechanisms have been developed to coordinate these organizations.
- The network organizing strategy has evolved to handle very high levels of uncertainty due to complexity and rapid change in the environment.
- The network organization has four characteristics: flexible modular structures, team-based units, flat organizational design, and use of information technology to integrate the organization.

- Motivation and control in network organizations is handled through developing trust, engaging, significant tasks, and formal control systems.
- Network strategies of organization rely on leaders to be symphony conductors rather than top-down managers. The manager must be coach, negotiator, problem solver, and improviser, rather than simply a director.
- Several problems confront network organizations, including their complexity, a tendency for power to "recentralize" despite efforts at empowerment, and the disadvantages of permanent "temporariness."
- The effectiveness of an organization's structure and communication system depends on the nature of the organization's work, its interdependencies with other organizations, and its environment.
- Contingency-design theory attempts to explain which structures are most effective under various conditions and gives advice on how to design an effective organizational communication system.

KEY TERMS

Knowledge society	Environmental stability
Knowledge work	Information work
Integrating roles	Liaison roles
Task forces	Integrating teams
Managerial linking roles	Dual-authority systems
Matrix	Network organization
Trust	Full-disclosure information systems
Broker	Formalization
Centralization	Span of control
Technology	Routine technology
Nonroutine technology	Interdependence
Pooled interdependence	Sequential interdependence
Reciprocal interdependence	Environmental complexity

Peter Drucker, an astute observer of society and of organizations, wrote in 1994:

> No century in recorded history has experienced so many social transformations and such radical ones as the twentieth century. . . . In the developed free-market countries—which contain less than a fifth of the earth's population but are the model for the rest—work and work force, society and polity, are all, in the last decade of this century qualitatively and quantitatively different not only from what they were in the first years of this century, but also from what has existed at any other time in history: in their configurations, in their processes, in their problems, and in their structures.[1]

Perhaps the most far-reaching change has been the transformation of the United States and most of the developed world to a **knowledge society.** For most of this century and the last, the economy focused largely on production, on the laborious work in farm and factory that resulted in tangible products. Before

World War I, farmers were the largest single group of workers in most countries. From 1920 to 1950, the farm population declined, although the production of food increased. In the 1950s, blue-collar workers accounted for 40 percent of the American workforce, representing the emphasis on factory production through manual labor of that period. However by 1990, blue-collar workers accounted for less than 20 percent of American workers and farmers less than 5 percent. The largest classes of workers in 1990 were those employed in what Drucker terms "knowledge work" and what has been called "information work."

Knowledge work involves creating and applying knowledge. Examples range from research scientists, engineers, attorneys, and financial analysts on the high end of the scale to teachers and X-ray technicians on the low end. Several things differentiate knowledge work from production work. Working with knowledge involves performing abstract operations and its product—knowledge—is intangible. Indeed, the only tangible outcome of much knowledge work is a document. However, despite its intangible nature, knowledge is the critical factor in the development of new products and the delivery of services such as legal and financial advice. Knowledge work organizes other forms of work, including production work. Knowledge work adds value to materials and to information, making them more useful or desirable or effective. An engineer's designs turn sand, copper, and aluminum into computer chips; an attorney's interpretive and negotiation skills create business partnerships from indecipherable (to any ordinary person) legal tomes and discussions among the parties involved. Knowledge-based work requires formal education (as opposed to apprenticeships or trade school) and an ability to acquire and apply abstract theoretical and analytical knowledge. It also requires a commitment to continuous learning; the knowledge worker's best and only asset is his or her expertise, which must be developed constantly through experience and further schooling.

Information work supports knowledge work. It involves gathering, entering, formatting, and processing information. Examples of information workers include clerical jobs, data entry, and telemarketing. These jobs are generally lower paying than the lowest rungs of knowledge work. They have been called "pink-collar" work, because they are often office positions staffed largely by women.

Together knowledge and information workers comprise about 40 percent of the workers in manufacturing firms and up to 80 percent in service organizations. They have become the largest class of workers in our society. This does not mean that production work is no longer important. It is, after all, what actually creates the products that knowledge workers design and that information workers catalog and sell. However, production work has become subsidiary to knowledge work in the new social arrangements. Advances depend far more on increases in knowledge than on production per se.

A second development has been increased instability, complexity, and turbulence of organizational environments. The growth of knowledge in recent years has resulted in an increased pace of change. Products now change much more quickly. Product life cycles—the time from introduction to the point at which the product is outmoded or dated—have grown increasingly shorter. The life cycle of a computer chip has decreased from five years to one. Even refrigerators have product life cycles of only three years now, as opposed to ten or more years ago. Services are also changing rapidly. The difference in the number of options for telephone or banking service today compared with ten years ago is striking.

The pace of change in products and services is driven in part by the rapidly increasing pace of technological advance. The stunning advances in medical technology in the past three years—the sequencing of the gene, new understandings of the roots of diseases such as arthritis, Alzheimer's disease, and addiction, and new therapies such as noninvasive surgery—clearly show the ever-accelerating growth of knowledge, know-how, and innovation. To keep up with their competition, organizations have to improve their operations and innovate continuously. Rapid technological change makes the continuous learning characteristic of knowledge work particularly important.

Along with increased instability has come increased complexity of organizational environments. The globalization of the economy has introduced many new competitors into the United States and, in turn, made opportunities available in many more places than was previously envisioned by most U.S. organizations. (We will discuss these changes in more detail in Chapter 12.) The rapid change and growth in knowledge and technology has increased competition as well, as companies strive for advantage. The public, too, has become more aware of the impacts of organizations on the quality of life in general. As a result, organizations have to deal with increasing regulation, lawsuits from disgruntled parties, and consumer protests. As time goes by, the environment of many organizations becomes more crowded with stakeholders who are more tightly interconnected.

While organizations in the private sector, such as manufacturers, food companies, and retailers have been most immediately affected by these changes, they are reverberating through the government and nonprofit sectors as well. Vice President Gore implemented the "Reinventing Government" initiative that promoted innovation and work redesign in more than half the U.S. federal government agencies. Governments at all levels are implementing information technologies and going on-line. The same tendencies can be seen in nonprofit hospitals, charitable organizations, consumer advocacy groups, and many other organizations in the nonprofit realm. Indeed, the first decade of the twenty-first century seems likely to bring about changes in public and nonprofit sectors comparable to those in the private economic sector in the 1990s.

The upshot of these cumulating and accelerating changes is that many organizations must deal with extremely uncertain conditions. They employ changing technologies and face environments that are unstable and highly complex. None of the strategies for organizing that we have introduced is well suited for this situation. The most flexible of the three strategies, the relational strategy, is appropriate for organizations facing moderately high rates of change, but not the rates of flux that a significant number of today's organizations confront.

In the "good old days" organizations would have had to throw up their hands and cope as best they could. However, now there is a wild card—information technology.[9] It opens many options to organizations that were previously simply too time-consuming or costly. The advent of information technology is also one of the enabling forces behind the emergence of the knowledge society. It facilitates both the management of existing knowledge and the growth of knowledge. Information technology has also facilitated the emergence of the network strategy of organizing as a major trend in the twenty-first century.

NETWORK STRATEGIES OF ORGANIZATIONAL DESIGN

Network strategies of organizing are premised on the need to balance integration and change. As previous chapters have observed, a major purpose of organizations is to integrate the activities of many people and units to achieve goals too ambitious for smaller, informal groups or individuals. Organizations achieve this coordination by integrating members and their work through structures, relationships, and cultures, using means discussed in Chapters 2 through 4. But as the world changes around them, organizations must change how they operate if they are to achieve their goals, and this often means that they must change their structures, relationships, and cultures.

A major problem faced by organizations is balancing these two opposing tendencies. An organization faced with a low to moderate amount of change in its environment can often effectively change by simply tinkering with and altering structures, relationships, and cultures as described in the chapters on structural, relational, and cultural strategies. A bureaucratic organization could amend its procedures and rules to take new circumstances into account. An organization using a relational strategy could involve its employees in a change program whereby they would diagnose needed alterations and implement them. Organizations also undertake steps—sometimes more and sometime less successfully—to alter their cultures. However, tinkering has its limits, and when the need to change passes a certain point, it becomes difficult to use the three strategies to integrate organizations.

There have been other times when organizations faced the need to integrate in the face of great change and uncertainty. The Manhattan Project which created the atomic bomb in World War II, and NASA's project to put a human on the moon in the 1960s both confronted these conditions and had to develop new techniques for integration. These have continued to develop, culminating in the growth of the network strategy from a specialized approach to a common form of organizing in the 1980s and 1990s. To understand the network strategy it will be useful first to make a short detour to consider ways of integrating organizations.

Methods for Integrating Organizations

Methods for integrating organizations are a response to uncertainty due to changes in technology, the organization's environment, or internal problems. Jay

Galbraith discussed a number of methods organizations use to cope with uncertainty, and based on recent developments in information technology, we can add several others.[2] Galbraith was concerned with how the organization can reduce uncertainty to manageable levels while maintaining as low a cost in money and time spent communicating as possible. Of particular interest to us are methods for creating lateral relationships, relationships that facilitate communication and coordination across different units.

In this section we will concentrate on nontechnological mean of intergrating organizations. Email, teleconferencing, computer conferencing, and videoconferencing can all be utilized to integrate organizations, but they will be discussed in Chapter 6. While they facilitate integration, they build on types of human relationships involved in the methods discussed in the next section.

Lateral Linkage Methods   There are several methods for creating lateral linkages in organizations. Since some methods are more costly to implement than others, we have arranged them in order of increasing cost:

Liaison roles. Personnel are assigned specifically to link two units. This may be a part-time or full-time assignment. For example, the assistant to the director of a local social service agency was asked to be liaison to the County Health Department. This assignment took one day a week and involved keeping contact with the Health Department to ensure that the social service agency's soup kitchen and homeless shelter complied with codes and to represent the agency to the Health Department. By having a "person on the spot," the social service agency ensured that it had some input on the writing and enforcement of regulations. Filling the liaison role usually has beneficial career development consequences, because it broadens the liaison's outlook and sharpens his or her communication skills. The major disadvantage is that the liaison may come to identify more with the unit he or she visits than with the home unit or organization.

Task forces. As mentioned in Chapter 3, these are short-term teams set up to deal with a specific problem or project. Members are drawn from several different units based on special knowledge about the issue and the interests their units have in it. Task forces typically dissolve after a set time or when the project is finished. A key challenge for the team is to overcome communication barriers posed by the fact that its members come from different units (and sometimes different organizations) and have to overcome differences in experiences, terminology, and interests. If this problem can be surmounted, task forces often outperform other teams. When Texaco, Inc. faced charges that it systematically discriminated against black managers, it formed a blue-ribbon task force to find the roots of this problem and work out a solution. The task force went to work, quickly made some recommendations and was dissolved.

Integrating teams. Sometimes a problem or project continues indefinitely or recurs regularly. In this case, a dedicated team is formed on a permanent basis. Assignments to this team become a permanent part of the members' jobs. Many universities have ongoing committees dedicated to increasing the number of women and minorities they hire. These integrating teams have representatives from all parts of the university.

Managerial linking roles. Often the integrating team has a special in-between status. Everyone agrees it is dealing with an important problem and upper management agrees to back up its recommendations and actions; but the team itself is still not regarded as a legitimate unit on a par with long-established departments or units. To give the integrating team more legitimacy and power, a formal manager may be added. This managerial integrator is directly connected into the hierarchy of authority and has a budget. He or she represents the team to the organization and serves as a symbol. Having an integrating manager gives the team more legitimacy and resources to work on its own.

One company that designed integrated computer hardware and software systems had several teams working on different parts of its new System Alpha. To deliver System Alpha on time and in shape, it was vital that each team's work be compatible with that of the others. The company created an Alpha Management Team whose assignment was to coordinate the work of the System Alpha teams. An engineer who had informally worked on coordinating the teams involved in System Alpha was appointed manager of the Management Team. She was given a budget for personnel to test the compatibility of products that the different teams were creating and to provide extra help for teams having problems. This extra heft that the manager had enabled her to stimulate the teams to action, and System Alpha was delivered on schedule.

Dual-authority systems. Sometimes organizations face tasks of high complexity that require them to constantly adjust and coordinate the activities of a great many specialties and departments. In these cases it is useful to shift to a dual-authority system in which members of specialized departments are assigned to one or more projects and report to both the integrating manager of their project team and to their department manager. The most common type of dual-authority structure is called the **matrix.**[3] As Figure 5-1 illustrates, the matrix is literally a matrix structure in which members of project teams report to two managers: the project manager and their department manager.

Matrix Organizations. To accomplish the incredibly complex and daring feat of landing a person on the moon, NASA developed one of the first matrix organizational forms. Members of various departments were assigned to one or more special projects. For example, a materials engineer specializing in forming parts from metal alloys might be assigned to the Nosecone Team for 50 percent of his or her time, to the Booster Team for 30 percent and spend the remaining 20 percent back in the Materials Engineering Laboratory. On both teams, the engineer would lend her or his special expertise in materials to creating the best possible nosecone or booster, working closely with other engineers and scientists with different

FIGURE 5–1

Diagram of a Dual-Authority Matrix Structure

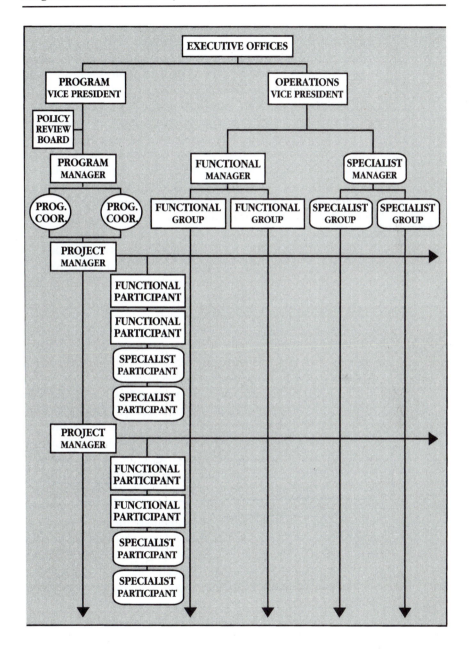

specialties. Back at the home lab, the engineer could consult with other materials engineers about problems that needed solving on his teams and catch up on the latest knowledge in materials engineering.

The advantage of dual structures, such as the matrix, for the organization is that teams keep the work focused on tangible products and outcomes (nosecones and boosters). Reporting back to their home department helps members keep their skills sharp and keep up to date on the latest developments in their fields. So our engineer is kept focused on nosecones by the project emphasis of the Nosecone Team. Other members of this team keep the engineer from applying only a materials perspective to the problem and she or he will keep other team members "honest" by making sure that materials issues are considered each time the team makes a decision. Upon return to the materials department, the engineer is able to consult with other materials engineers about the materials-related problems that the team has encountered. This sharpens the engineer's own expertise and makes her or him more valuable to the project team.

The matrix structure as a whole also helps ensure that the various project teams and departments are coordinated. The project managers meet as a team and with their integrating managers to ensure that the various projects come together into an effective whole. Using a structure such as this, NASA succeeded in putting a man on the moon by 1969, after starting almost from scratch in 1961. No one, not even NASA managers, thought it could be done. But the matrix organization was up to the task. Giant corporations, such as Dow-Corning, have put permanent matrix structures into operation to integrate their international operations.

The matrix structure attempts to ensure effective performance on complex tasks by dividing them among highly focused project teams. However, to ensure that the personnel on these teams are highly qualified and current in their fields, they are drawn from specialized departments with which they keep in touch. The overall structure of the matrix coordinates the work of the various project teams. The glue that holds the matrix together is intensive communication. Through many team meetings, liaisons between teams, integrating teams across projects, and communication with functional departments, members of the matrix create a deep and complicated flow of information and ideas throughout the organization. For the matrix to work, communication within project teams and in specialized departments must create team and organizational cultures that promote open communication, innovation, constructive criticism, and high standards of excellence.

This communication-intensive organization has costs as well. Serving more than one supervisor can create ambiguities in the chain of command and tensions for workers who are torn between the mandates of two or more bosses. The requirement of continuous open communication can cause overloads and stress in its own right. Meetings, meetings, meetings can drive workers to distraction. And the solution to these problems is often even more communication. The matrix keeps all workers on their toes, but can be exhausting as well. In addition, this form works only if the integrating managers can coordinate the various projects, bringing them to completion on schedule so that one project does not hold up other interdependent ones.

Which Integration Mechanism to Use?   How does one choose among and combine these integration mechanisms? One thing to consider it the *cost of the method* compared to the benefits it offers. Benefits depend on the method's effectiveness in handling the level of uncertainty the organization experiences. Liaisons and task forces are effective for moderate to moderately high levels of uncertainty. Organizations facing high levels of uncertainty will be more effective if they utilize approaches further up the list, including integrating teams, managerial linking roles, and matrix designs. But costs must also be considered: These include personnel expenses, time spent learning to use the method and getting it to work smoothly, information load imposed by the method, and the amount of stress members experience.

From the cost-benefit standpoint, an organization should select the least costly mechanism that meets its needs. For example, an organization in a very complex, unstable environment with a highly difficult task may have to choose a highly flexible, yet costly form, such as the matrix. On the other hand, an organization in a more stable situation that has one difficult problem may be able to handle things with a task force.

Another variable to consider in choosing a linking mechanism is the *cultural strategy* in place in the organization. The values, traditions, and history of an organization may predispose it to be more comfortable with some integration methods than others. Selecting a method the organization is not accustomed to requires a period of learning and change. For example, implementing a task force is not simply a matter of assigning people. More important is getting people from different departments that have very different views on an issue to work together. In organization that emphasize teamwork and inclusion, this will be easier than in those built around competition and individualism.

No single integration method will work under all circumstances or for all organizations. The balance among cost-benefit considerations, geographical dispersion, and culture depends on which is more important to the organization or the task at hand. In many cases, organizations settle on integration modes after a period of experimentation in which different methods are tried and rejected.

Limitations of Integrating Mechanisms   The integrating mechanisms have proven extremely useful. However, they do not offer a complete solution to problems of uncertainty. All these mechanisms except for the matrix are essentially patches, suitable for fixing individual, temporary problems, but not capable of integrating organizations as a whole. The matrix is a solution for the whole organization, but it works best for moderately high uncertainty and not for extremely uncertain conditions. The matrix tends to become inflexible after it is used for some time. Members learn to think of it as a framework much like the bureaucracy, and the matrix is flexible as long as managers keep it so; but once they start to think about it as a standard operating procedure, it can become as much of a cage as a bureaucracy. DuPont developed a standardized three-dimensional matrix for its formal structure. Units were classified in three dimensions according to function (engineering, production) project (agro-chemicals, industrial solvents) and geographical area (Africa, Northern Europe). Although effective as a means of organizing DuPont, this matrix structure is hardly flexible enough to promote fast innovation. A different, more flexible network structure is needed to deal with highly uncertain situations.

The Network Organization

Network organizations are aggregates of organizations whose component units are assembled to meet a particular set of demands. They are referred to by a number of names including *dynamic networks, federated organizations, "cloverleaf" forms, virtual organizations,* and *post-bureaucracies.* Most of these forms have not been described in definitive terms at this time, primarily because their mechanics are still being worked out by the organizations that use them. However, their roots in networks are clear. Network organizations take a wide variety of forms: In some cases the units are from the same organization, whereas in others, different organizations comprise the network; some network organizations are assembled on a long term basis; but others are set up for temporary projects. The Japanese *keiretsu,* a dense network of interrelated organizations that develops lasting and stable business relationships, is a good example of a long-term networked organization. In the Japanese automobile industry, firms such as Nissan and Toyota develop networks of suppliers, ship-pers, and financial institutions that depend on the central firm's business for their livelihood and in turn give the central firm exceptional quality, effort, and dependable support.

Some textbook publishers offer examples of temporary, project-centered networks, illustrated in Figure 5–2. Older publishing companies have tradition-ally consolidated the acquisition of new books, their design and layout, printing, and sales in a single organization. More recently publishers have been farming out some, and in some cases all, of these functions. The publisher may acquire the book and then hire a graphics firm to handle layout, an independent printer to produce the books, and several firms, including the publisher's own staff, to market the book. Special types of books are produced for the publisher by smaller independent firms, themselves dynamic networks, often founded by for-mer employees of the publisher who have gone out on their own. Publishing is a very different game today than it was thirty years ago.

Whereas the example of textbook publishers shows how a number of dif-ferent organizations can be combined into a network, large firms often create networks within themselves for special projects. One common case is when firms assemble temporary dynamic networks to develop a new product and bring it to market. The network might be put together by an integrating project manager who would assemble units for the project: Design might be carried out by a team assigned from engineering; production would be from a particular plant with excess capacity; inventory would be handled by suppliers on a just-in-time basis; marketing would be the responsibility of a sales team reassigned from a downsizing division; and the accounting department would handle bookkeep-

FIGURE 5-2

Here: A Network Organization: Textbook Publishing

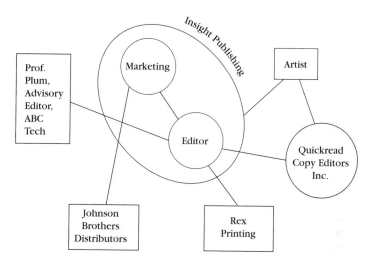

This is a network for the publication of a new chemistry textbook by Insight Publishing. The editor, with advice from Professor Plum, accepts the textbook, which is sent to the copy editor and artist, who develop materials that Rex Printing puts into final form. Once the book has been printed it is shipped to Johnson Brothers Distributors, who handle shipping to book stores and in response to Web purchases. Johnson Brothers coordinates closely with the Marketing Department at Insight Publishing, which is in charge of publicity and the sales force.

Note how the component firms, assembled specially for this project, relate in a network which is assembled and coordinated by the Editor. A different set of firms might be assembled for the next textbook project.

ing. The project manager would start with no organization and through negotiation and competitive bidding get units together to bring the product out. After the product was out and sales had begun, it might be transferred to an existing functional unit of the organization and the dynamic network disbanded.

Characteristics of Network Designs   The network is not a new organizational design[4]. Building contractors have long employed this structure. They assemble reliable subcontractors into a temporary structure that they coordinate to the needs of each unique project. Before the 1980s, network structures were utilized mostly by specialized industries such as construction; but in the past twenty years, they have become ubiquitous. The modern network organization generally has four characteristics:[5]

   1.   *Flexible, modular organizational structures* that can be readily reconfigured as new projects, demands, or problems arise. As noted previously, these structures may be composed of units of a single larger organization, or they may be different organizations joined through various types of interorganizational

alliances. Rearrangement of organizational units is important to the ability of networked organizations to adapt. For example, a network of community mental health agencies might find that its clients need help with job placements. It could then approach a job-training and placement agency and arrange for it to join the network.

2. *Team-based work organization* that emphasizes autonomy and self-management. This is generally combined with emphasis on quality and continuous improvement. To be effective, network organizations must be designed so that they promote effective teamwork, as discussed in Chapter 3. So they must work to define clear goals that specify the overall mission of the organization and the contribution of each unit, so that units can manage their own processes to contribute to the overall mission. Team-based work organization also involves empowerment of employees, just as in the relational strategy, because only if they have the necessary resources and authority can teams adapt to the needs of the situation. Cross-functional teams that bring together people from different units and organizations are particularly important in network organizations.

3. *Flat organizational structures* that rely on coordination and negotiation rather than hierarchy to manage relationships among teams and units. As organizations move to network structures, they lose layers of middle managers and generally have fewer employees than traditional organizations.

4. *Use of information technology to integrate* across organizational functions and geographically dispersed units to reengineer production and service processes, and to create tighter interdependence among activities. Technologies, such as email and telecommunications, discussed in Chapter 6, can be used to ensure that people from different units coordinate their activities. These units may be different departments in a single location, units spread across a wide distance, or a combination.

One pharmaceutical company Scott Poole worked with used a computer conferencing system and teleconferences to develop a team of 11 salespeople, each stationed in a different Asian or African country. The team members met face-to-face a few times a year, but conducted all other business through the Internet and teleconferences. Members of the team not only had to manage their own sales strategy, but they also had to coordinate with other sales teams that had responsibility for other geographical areas and with production units in Europe and the United States on a frequent basis. Without information technologies, this team could not possibly have managed its work.

Information technologies also enable organizations to redesign and rethink how they do their work. As networked organizations rely more and more on information technology, their work is changed. For example, an organization may decide to use an automated inventory-control system that relies on input of stock levels through hand-held computers. It also is likely to find that it does not have to keep as many parts on hand, since the computer system enables it to keep track of them easily and automatically reorders them through the Internet. As a result, it might enlarge the jobs of stockroom clerks so that they are also responsible for reordering needed parts, which eliminates some jobs in the procurement department, but greatly reduces the costs incurred in storing parts.

Finally, information technologies can also enable units to automate their coordination. For example, a group of companies planning a complex offshore oil project can automatically share updates to designs through computer networks. When a unit in charge of designing the pipes for bringing the oil from the seafloor to the platform changes its design and specification, the plans of each other unit would be instantly altered to reflect this. Unit members could then determine whether the alterations would cause any problems or require any action on their part. In all three functions, information technology speeds up production and response time and enables the organization to adapt to customer needs and environmental demands in highly specific ways.

Network Organizations and Boundaries   Peter Monge and Noshir Contractor have commented that, "network organizations create what have come to be called 'boundaryless' organizations."[6] In network structures, it is not always clear where one organization begins and the other leaves off . Organizations and units in networks share practices, knowledge, and often members. No longer is it necessary to think of organizations as self-contained entities with definitive structures. Instead they can be composed, rearranged, and stuck together by various integrating mechanisms, as the occasion demands. Organizations become "mix-and-match" systems. The network offers a good description of the various joint ventures, cross-firm alliances, and consortia that are becoming increasingly prevalent today. An example of this type of venture network is SEMATECH, the Austin, Texas-based research-and-development consortium developed by more than ten leading information technology companies.[7] Typically firms assign researchers to SEMATECH, where they work with employees of other companies to develop cutting-edge products and share insights into solving production problems. The rationale behind such a consortium is that the United States needs a prosperous, technically advanced group of information technology companies if it is to remain among the world leaders in this area. Such firms are usually seen as temporary ventures; but some are so successful that they exist for a long time. SEMATECH now is more than ten years old.

CASE STUDY:
EVOLVING INTO A NETWORK ORGANIZATION*

Industrial controls maker ICG has long been in the forefront of its industry. It had been among the first firms of its kind to implement a computer integrated design and manufacturing (CAD/CAM) system (explained in more detail in Chapter 6). The CAD/CAM system enabled engineering and manufacturing units to work on a common set of plans stored in a database; as the units made alterations and adjustments in either design or manufacturing they were automatically entered into the plans. This system was met with some resistance from engineers who

(continued)

(continued from the previous page)

were used to paper drawings, but their enhanced ability to consult with manufacturing noticeably improved the quality and time-to-market for the various product lines offered by ICG. These teams worked in a paperless environment with the CAD/CAM system as the linking pin for their efforts.

As ICG worked with the CAD/CAM system, top managers realized that the company was not capitalizing on its potential. To take advantage of the system, they felt, it would be necessary to develop cross-functional teams that would own product development from womb to tomb, so to speak. ICG constituted product teams with representatives from marketing, engineering, manufacturing, scheduling, and quality assurance that would be responsible for product performance in terms of quality, cost, time-to-market, and profit. These product teams were formed by top management and charged with managing a set of products and allocating resources among them. While many ICG employees were skeptical about the new teams because they had been ordered by top management, they were eventually won over as it became clear that management were going to give the teams full control over their own decisions. Working on product teams enabled employees to develop their skills in management, teamwork, communication, and leadership, as well as increasing their commitment to ICG.

Its experience as a leader in CAD/CAM led to ICG's next advance. It worked with a major computer maker to create the Pyramid Integrator, a computer system that incorporated CAD/CAM and had the ability to integrate all of a company's design and manufacturing across multiple products. The Pyramid Integrator facilitated standardization of designs across products, reducing costs and enabling companies to build on previous designs as they created new products in a rapid and flexible process. It also made it much easier to tailor products to customer needs, since customers could work with ICG personnel, in effect to design their own systems. The first product lines ICG designed with the Pyramid Integrator were a great success and won the company national recognition and an award from a manufacturing publication. The Pyramid Integrator also became a profitable product for ICG.

ICG had moved to a team-intensive organization, but it was still hierarchically organized around divisions that corresponded to product lines. The excessive amount of work entailed by the various teams and the fine-tailoring of products for customers put pressure on the product-oriented divisions, which were better suited for relatively large production runs of similar products. Moreover, the divisions tended to be concerned mainly with their own success and did not think in terms of the success of the entire enterprise of ICG. Each division focused on its narrow line of products, which utilized a certain technology, and sought to be a world leader in its products. This narrow focus sometimes put divisions at odds with each other, as they introduced products that conflicted or went in very different directions. It also confused the sales force and ran the risk of overstretching resources across too many product lines.

(continued)

(continued from the previous page)

The executive vice president decided that ICG needed to reorganize. He argued that the success no longer depended on technologies or new products, because technology was beginning to diffuse rapidly through the industry; rather success would depend on how well the company could respond to the particular needs of its customers. Therefore, ICG should be organized around its customers and projects for them rather than around product-focused divisions. After considerable analysis of customer needs, the management group determined that the core business for ICG lay in two product lines and that everything else the company did basically added value to these lines.

ICG was reorganized as a concentric organization with the two core control businesses at the center. A second ring, Communication and Information Systems, would focus on tying these core technologies together using information systems. The third and outer ring, application services, would package integrated control systems according to customer needs. General service functions, such as human resources, marketing, planning, and operations, were consolidated from the old divisions into single units in orbit around these three rings to provide support for them as needed.

The company reorganized its efforts to cut down the number of products it offered and focused on customer groups, reducing its number of projects to about one third of those in the old divisionalized structure. It developed a number of self-managed teams to handle various projects and customer groups. Teams sometimes operated at one layer of the concentric circles; for example, a team might specialize in controls for canning companies and work with teams in the control and communication and information systems layers to tailor these. In other cases, teams bridged layers; for example a team attempting to develop new control devices to combine with other company products in an integrated system might be composed of personnel drawn from the core and second layers of the ICG. Teams could be formed only with the approval of an upper-level management team, which was called an executive sponsor team. The executive sponsor team scanned for business opportunities and identified personnel and resources for the teams that undertook them. Once formed, the teams were largely self-managing. Supervisory business teams were formed to coordinate sets of related teams and to argue for and make decisions about resources and other organizational-level issues for their teams. The result was a network of teams and a shallow three-level hierarchy with little direct authoritarian control over the bottom-level teams. Just as teams were created at need, they were phased out when their projects had run their course, and the personnel were reassigned to other teams.

ICG also included personnel from its suppliers on some teams, creating networks with its suppliers. As it developed deeper relationships with some particularly effective suppliers, ICG reduced the total number of suppliers it dealt with by about 50 percent. Cross-organizational teams of ICG and supplier personnel embarked on quality improvement projects to ensure that parts and materials

(continued)

(continued from the previous page)

met the highest quality specifications; they also embarked on some joint ventures in which both the supplier and ICG developed parts of a new product. ICG also reached out to competing firms to engage them in developing standards and sometimes in joint ventures.

Over a fifteen-year period, ICG moved from a traditional divisionalized form to a networked organization best characterized as a team of teams.

Applying What You've Learned

1. What characteristics of a network organization does ICG exhibit? Which ones are missing, if any? Is ICG a "poster child" for network organizations?
2. Why did ICG evolve from a divisionalized form to a networked organization? Were any of the forces discussed at the beginning of this chapter in operation?

Questions to Think About and Discuss

1. Based on the discussion in Chapter 3, we would expect that teams in ICG are not always completely satisfactory experiences for their members. What are some of the problems that might arise in ICG's teams? How might these problems carry over into networks of teams?
2. The change at ICG was instituted on the initiative of top management. What measures did management take to ensure that employees accepted and cooperated with these changes? What might management have done to increase the probability that employees would go along with the changes at ICG? What would have happened to ICG if it had not changed? Would it have been as successful? Why or why not?

This case is based on Nitin Nohria and James D. Berkley, "Allen-Bradley's ICCG Case Study" in The Post-Bureaucratic Organization: New Perspectives on Organizational Change, Charles Heckscher and Anne Donnellon, eds. (Newbury Park, CA: Sage, 1994).

MOTIVATION, CONTROL, AND SURVEILLANCE IN NETWORK ORGANIZATIONS

The lack of hierarchy and the empowerment of members in network organizations poses new challenges for coordination and control. While members of the units that comprise the network are likely to feel loyal to their units, there is no intrinsic reason for them to feel the same loyalty toward the network. Consider the case of a computer programmer whose software firm contracted to develop a new inventory system for a major company. This software firm is part of a temporary network formed to bring a major new product to market. The programmer's future is with the software firm, not the company; any raises come from the firm, and personal ties exist with coworkers in the firm, not with "those other guys" in the big company. The software firm and the project itself form the programmer's frame of reference when planning work. The programmer uses the standards of her firm and profession when planning and evaluating work. The big company's standards are relevant only if her managers emphasize them. The programmer is influenced by the software firm's culture, and much less by the culture of the distant company. To the extent she orients to the big company at all, her main concern is to ensure that the software company delivers on its contract and is judged favorably by the larger firm.

Motivation in Network Organizations

How do network organizations motivate the members of individual units to collaborate and be innovative? This problem cannot be solved by a leader's dictates, because the flatter network organization does not have hierarchical authority over its constituent units or their members. Indeed, hierarchical authority would undermine the flexibility and adaptability that are the greatest advantages of the network form. Another challenge arises from the fact that the network gives units a degree of freedom in how they organize their work and the effort they put into the larger enterprise. This situation makes it possible for some units to take advantage of the others by "free riding" and taking shortcuts so they maximize their profit by putting in the bare minimum that others will accept.

Network organizations motivate and control their units and their units' members through three complementary routes. First, they attempt to cultivate **trust** in the network. Trust is the ideal cement for the network organizations. They have little or no hierarchy, so hierarchy cannot be the source of authority to coordinate and control. Moreover networks are often composed of numerous different organizations, each with its own culture, so culture cannot be the basis for control. Trust is a special property of the relationships among members of the network that enables them to act on the assumption that others will fulfill their own responsibilities in good faith. It is achieved through engaging in cooperative action with others and through observing their competence and their willingness to live up to their commitments. To cultivate trust, the managers of the new product network might ask the programmer to work in the field for a couple of weeks with programmers from other components of the network. If their work goes well, programmers from the various firms come to trust each other and carry back good reports to the rest of the network. Trust will also be built in this network as various units carry out their responsibilities on time and effectively.

Trust can also be based on reputation; we tend to trust people who are recommended by those we trust or who have a reputation for integrity. If the programmers report back to their managers that other firms' programmers are competent and good to work with, this in turn enhances the managers' trust in the network.

Generally trust is assessed informally through direct experience of others. Hence organizations are most likely to enter into networks with those they already know and respect. Research shows, for example, that managers and decision makers tend to turn first to well-established networks of associates and advisors, rather than broadly searching for "strangers" who might be competent.[8] However, there are also formal indicators of trustworthiness. Professional credentials and certifications, such as those a computer programmer is likely to have, can also form the basis for trust. Some have envisioned that in the future companies and professional associations will develop reputational rating systems that record the projects that individuals and firms participate in and the reactions of their managers and peers in the network to their work. Those interested in building network organizations could then consult the ratings for advice as to which individuals and companies might be suitable for a project.

A second source of motivation in network organizations is an *inspiring, meaningful task.* Network organizations are typically task or product focused, and this gives all members a common frame of reference. A meaningful task or goal can inspire the units and individuals in the network to work hard and ensure that they coordinate with other units. For example, the goal of the networked floral company, Calyx and Corolla, is to deliver the best possible flower arrangements faster than any other company and at a good price. This goal unifies the efforts of each part of the network: the flower growers try to deliver high quality flowers; the arrangers work out innovative designs; the express delivery companies configure their operations to make sure the flowers get there fresh; and the coordinating unit, Calyx and Corolla itself, works hard to make sure that the parts of the network connect smoothly with each other as the process moves from flowers in the field to flowers on the table.[9]

One important thing to bear in mind, however, is that an inspiring task can hold a network together only for so long; in the longer term, members must also develop trust in each other. If some part of the network does not deliver—for example, if a grower delivers poor quality flowers—the best efforts of other units will not succeed. In this case, the network either begins to malfunction and fall apart or finds another, better grower.

A third source of motivation and control in network organizations are *network-based formal systems for monitoring and control* of members and their activities. In addition to trust, networked organizations may also attempt to develop structures to formally coordinate unit activities. These systems are based on contracts among the units in the network that provide a formal, written understanding among the units concerning their responsibilities and compensation. Because contracts are legal documents, any unit that does not fulfill its contract can, of course, be sued. However, since legal actions often take years, they are not effective in coordinating ongoing activities. A more effective means of coordination is to first, develop a project or workflow plan that specifies what should be done and in what sequence, second, provide methods to enable units to monitor each others' activities, and finally, a full-disclosure information system that enables units to know what other units are contributing to the network and what earnings they are getting from it.

As we will discuss in Chapter 6, information technologies are often employed to keep track of project plans and to exchange information that allows units to monitor and coordinate each others' activities. For example, our programmer may want to know when code is due; the project plan would provide an expected delivery date; but he or she can also check the project-management software used by the members of the network to find out whether the units that need the software are ahead of or behind schedule. If the programmer sees a danger of not meeting the delivery date, she can contact her supervisor, who would meet with affected parties to determine how to minimize the problems caused by this delay.

A **full disclosure information system** is comprised of accounting-information system and electronic communication systems. The accounting-information system (see Chapter 6) is a set of open databases that shows participating units whether other units are meeting their responsibilities and the level of return obtained by the organization as a whole and by each unit. For example, units in the new product venture could determine from this data whether suppliers are on time with their deliveries, whether other units are putting in a fair effort (based on their expenditures and the payments they have received), and where they stand vis-à-vis other units in the network in terms of expenses and profits. This accounting-information system reassures units that others are holding up their end of the bargain and puts pressure on them to hold up their own end. As units see that others are faithfully fulfilling their obligations, they come to trust them and trust builds over time. Also important in this trust-building process are timely and effective use of electronic communication systems such as email, teleconferencing, and groupware, discussed in Chapter 6. Direct, rapid communication and response help the network coordinate work and iron out problems. Both the accounting and communication systems help to build trust, and trust is a self-reinforcing cycle: Open communication builds trust, which leads to more open communication and to more trust, in an ever-increasing spiral.[10]

Problems with Control Systems in Network Organizations

Systems for motivation and control in network organizations are an amalgam of methods used in the relational strategy (trust, an involving task) and the traditional strategy (formal control systems). The network strategy, however, extends relationships over a much greater distance than does the relational strategy, and it calls for more flexibility in the control system than is typically allowed for by the traditional strategy.

Just as team control sometimes becomes overwhelming in the relational strategy, control can be excessive and uncomfortable in the network. The project management system and full-disclosure information systems give information to all parties. This information can be used to make judgments about the effort of any given unit and bring pressure on that unit to get into line. The fact that these systems and their plans were approved by all units and are open to everyone gives negative information an objective force that can be used to embarrass and harass individuals or units. The resulting control structure can be just as oppressive as the team-based systems discussed in Chapter 3, creating defensiveness that makes the network less flexible than it could be if each unit were not holding all the others to strict standards of accountability.

There is also something of a mismatch between the types of rewards and incentives acceptable in U.S. culture and those needed to make a network organization function properly. Team-based organizations should give rewards to teams rather than basing salaries and promotions on individual performance. But most people are accustomed to expect rewards on an individual basis, as specified in the traditional strategy and passed on to the relational strategy. Anne Donnellon and Maureen Scully argue that organizations like the network form must move beyond traditional assessment and reward practices in which the manager assesses the employee, who receives an individual reward based on the assessment. Instead they argue for assessment by fellow team members and team-based rewards supplemented by individual rewards. In addition, they argue that organizations ought to avoid using terms like "merit," a symbol that implies that individual characteristics are responsible for good performance. Such a term is misleading in network organizations, where good performance is dependent on collaboration and teamwork among individuals and units. In such systems, performance cannot be traced to individuals, and it is a mistake to continue to use the language of merit, which implies that it can.

LEADERSHIP IN NETWORK ORGANIZATIONS

Leadership in network organizations is not as clear cut as it is in the traditional, relational, or cultural strategies, simply because they are more diffuse. It is useful to distinguish top leadership, in which there is a central figure who provides leadership for the network, and leadership at the unit and interunit levels.

In most networks there is a salient person or persons who can emerge as leaders. Many network structures are assembled by **brokers,** a manager or firm that identifies appropriate units and builds them into a network. The broker may be an integrating project manager, as in the new product development example introduced at the beginning of this chapter. Alternatively, the broker may be an independent agent or organization. Building contractors, who coordinate the work of carpenters, plumbers, electricians, and others, are a familiar examples of brokers. In other cases, leaders emerge as symbols or spokespeople for the central organization in a network. The president of SONY, for example, could serve a leadership role for the *keiretsu* that developed in association with SONY.

These top leaders may take either transformational or transactional roles in the networked organization. A *founder* or *renewer* of the network may play the role of a transformational leader, described in Chapter 4. The founder/renewer sets the values and basic directions for the network, and its members look to him/her as an inspirational model. A broker or manager of a network will take a transactional approach, as detailed in Chapter 3. The role of transactional manager in newer designs, such as the networked organization, has been described as more like that of a symphony conductor than anything else. The individual units and their members have high levels of specialized knowledge and skill, and, like individual musicians, they know best how to perform their part in the organization. A good leader, rather than telling them what to do—micromanaging—instead sets up conditions that enable units and members to perform up to their capabilities and helps them to coordinate their work with other units.

With respect to leadership within units, the network form poses several challenges for managers[11]. The team-based structure of network organizations implies that leaders must be able to promote teamwork as described in Chapter 3. Since teams are self-managing, leaders should take on the role of coach rather than directive leader, advising the team and helping it to solve problems. The flatness of networked organizations necessitates a negotiator role for the manager as well. The negotiator must be able to represent the unit and its interests in negotiations over schedules, division of labor, and problems between units. The flexibility of network organizations means that managers must be able to deal with workforce management in a responsive, creative manner. For example, if serving a client means that someone has to travel to a distant plant and fix something, who in the unit is to do it? How does that person get compensated for his or her time within a fixed budget without causing perceptions of unfairness on the part of other employees? These and other sorts of issues arise during the process of constant adjustment necessary for flexible response. So the manager in the networked organization must be coach, negotiator, problem solver, and improviser, rather than simply a director.

Managers and members of units in networked organizations must also manage relationships with other units and organizations. Some of the functions involved in boundary spanning were discussed in Chapter 3. In addition, units in network organizations face a new problem. Whereas previously the problem was how to relate to another set of units one is more or less stuck with, in the network it becomes how to maintain credibility in a network of units, some of which may be potential competitors seeking to replace your unit. The problem in this case is how to project an image of competence, efficiency, and quality. In a real sense each unit—even within intact organizations—becomes an independent small business vying with many potential competitors. This situation requires a very different strategy for communicating with other units than do the three strategies discussed in Chapters 2, 3, and 4.

Challenges and Problems for Network Organizations

Organizations employing network strategies face a number of problems. For one thing, network organizations—with their flexible structures and complicated relationships among units—are extremely complex. This complexity introduces problems. It is often not easy to determine who is responsible for what in network organizations. Unless units specifically work out how they coordinate activities and constantly communicate with each other, important things can fall between the cracks.

Another issue with complex systems is that it is often impossible to determine the cause of problems. Consider a relatively simple organization composed of three units: one that designs widgets, a second that produces them, and a third that markets and distributes them. The marketing unit may find that there is not enough of product X to meet the demands of an important customer. Its initial tendency is to blame production, which has immediate responsibility for making the X. But production may be having trouble due to a design problem that causes a part of the product to break when it is removed from the stamping presses. The blame then seems to shift to design. However, the design unit used the flawed plan for product X, because it had not gotten any feedback from production on the problem. Moreover, design understood from marketing that customers really appreciated the part of X that tended to break off in production's machines, so they wanted to keep it. Does the problem then trace back to production's lack of feedback or to marketing's insistence that the part of the design that caused problems be retained? The answer is that *none* of these can be said to be the sole cause of the problem. Causality in networks is ambiguous. The problems persist because of the organizational system as a whole, a system in which design does not communicate with the other units, in which production is not particularly proactive about problems it encounters, and marketing is out there selling stuff without considering whether other departments can meet the delivery schedules it sets. In cases where it is difficult to determine the causes of problems, it is also difficult to solve them. When eliminating the source of a problem means changing the entire system, the problem may recur, because systems change slowly at best.

Network organizations also face a tendency for power to centralize, which threatens to undermine their flexibility and their members' empowerment. In any communication network, the most central units—those with the most connections to other units—tend to be more powerful. They have information that other units do not have; they enjoy status due to their centrality, and they can control the flow of information. The extent of their power is in direct proportion to how much they control the key communication paths in the network. This slight (and sometimes not so slight) advantage can set up a self-reinforcing cycle whereby the more centralized units use their power to exert some control over the network, thereby increasing their reputation and power still more and so on. However, centralized control over the network weakens the ability of units to adapt flexibly to the demands of the situation, defeating the purpose of using a network system. Centralization also takes power away from some units, sapping the initiative that self-management gives them.

A fourth problem with network organizations is that, although they may enable their members to develop their own professionalism and careers, they do so at the expense of making "temporariness" permanent. No longer can employees assume they'll be working for the same company for 30 or 40 years. By their very nature, network organizations force their employees to think of a future in which they'll have to find new contracts and new positions in a new organization. This can undermine loyalty to the organization, making it hard to develop and sustain an organizational culture. It is also an uncomfortable situation for individuals who desire stability in their lives.

Summary

While the networked organization may appear novel at first sight, it also exhibits many of the same strengths and weaknesses of the traditional, relational, and cultural strategies. Rather than being a novel form, some scholars maintain that network organizations actually are not new at all. They argue that network organizations are similar to the types of organizations that were common prior to the 1850s, before bureaucracy became dominant and to alternative and international organizational forms that have sprung up since 1950.[12] It is hard to decide how new the network organization is, because the network strategy is still evolving. Notwithstanding, the network strategy is one of the four most important approaches to organizing in the early twenty-first century.

CONTINGENCY DESIGN THEORY

Now that we have defined four strategies for organizing, a key question arises: What conditions determine which strategy will be most effective? Advocates of traditional and relational strategies thought they had found the one best way to organize. So did the early proponents of cultural strategies, who viewed strong cultures as a universally applicable strategy. However, much research and practical experience has shown that they were mistaken. Under some conditions, the bureaucratic strategy works best; while under other conditions, the relational, cultural, or networking strategies are superior. This was first noted in the late 1950s by two English sociologists, Burns and Stalker.[13] They found that when conditions are stable, a well-planned, efficient organization, which is epitomized by the bureaucracy, outperforms all other types because it is the most efficient organization. Other types of organizations may do well for a while; but ultimately the bureaucracy outraces them, because it produces the best results with the least input. It will have superior profitability and efficiency and more funds to reinvest in improving its product or service.

However, as Chapters 1–3 indicated, Burns and Stalker found that when the environment is unstable and turbulent, the bureaucracy is too slow to adapt. Its formal structures, standard operating procedures, and centralized decision making limit its members' ability to recognize the need for change and make it inflexible when change is necessary. The relational strategy, which features decentralized decision making and informal structures, and cultural strategies that focus on change are much better at adapting. Of course, if employees become too committed to one another (as sometimes happens with relational strategies) or identify too completely with the organization's core beliefs and values (as in some strong culture organizations), they have trouble changing. Under conditions of high instability and turbulence, when adaptation is at a premium, the network strategy is more effective than the relational or cultural strategies. Contingency design theory helps to explain why some organizational systems are more effective than others. It also gives useful advice about the design of organizational structures and communication systems.

Design Features That Can Be Managed Strategically

Viewing organizations as systems suggests that they must adapt if they are to survive. Many features of organizational structures and processes can be altered in an effort to adapt to situational pressures. These include the following:

Formalization: As defined in Chapter 2, formalization is the degree to which the organization has well-defined roles, strict division of labor into relatively small tasks, and rules and procedures that apply to most activities. Bureaucratic structures are high in formalization. An organization lower in formalization would have more flexible role definitions, adjustment and redefinition of tasks, and few codified rules and procedures. The structures associated with the relational strategy are typically low in formalization. Network structures are intermediate in their degree of formalization, since they often have formal control systems but also need to have flexible response and therefore as few rigid rules as possible.

Centralization: This refers to the degree to which control is centralized in top management. As Chapter 2 noted, bureaucratic structures tend to be highly centralized. Power is more widely distributed in relational and network strategies and they are therefore less centralized.

Specialization: This is defined as the degree to which workers and staff have to obtain specialized training or degrees to carry out their work effectively. For example, engineering firms require a highly trained staff with a great deal of experience to function. In contrast fast food restaurants and department stores do not. Most employees are hired with minimal screening, because the organization believes it can easily train them to do an adequate job.

Span of control: This is the number of employees who report to a single manager or supervisor. Managers with wide spans of control supervise many employees; whereas those with narrower spans supervise fewer. Narrow spans of control are important when managers must check for details, special problems, or errors. Wider spans of control are workable when there are not many exceptions and the work is pretty much the same all the time.

Communication and coordination: Organizations may vary the frequency, formality, and medium of communication among members. If they frequently experience coordination problems, communication must also be more frequent, less formal, and more immediate. While a preset chain of command may be sufficient for routine communication, more direct and unregulated interaction is required to solve problems and deal with exceptional circumstances. While routine communication can be handled through written media (memos, email), communication about problems, exceptional circumstances, and nonroutine matters is more effectively dealt with through face-to-face discussion, telephone calls, and meetings.

Interorganizational relationships: Organizations may also vary the degree to which they form and maintain stable relationships with other groups or organizations. Some organizations have well-defined boundaries and remain self-contained; whereas others form relationships with other organizations in the form of contracts, joint ventures, or partnerships.

Variables That Must Be Considered When Choosing Organizational Design Strategies: Contingencies

Contingency design theory builds on the observations outlined in Chapters 1–3 about the organization-environment relationship. Research has identified three characteristics that are particularly important in determining organizational design: technology, interdependence between units, and the organizational environment.

Technology   In contingency design theory, technology is broadly construed as the tools, techniques, and actions used to transform organizational inputs into outputs.[14] This definition means that technology includes more than just machinery, computers, or chemicals; technology refers to the means by which the work of the organization is done. According to this way of thinking, a social service agency has a technology just as much as an automobile plant does. The social service agency's technology is comprised of the procedures followed for patient intake and record-keeping, the service procedures (for example, such things as client counseling or therapeutic methods), and procedures for discharge and billing. This technology enables the social service agency to serve its clients, which in turn ensures a flow of funds to the agency.

In general terms, technology varies along a continuum from *routine* to *non-routine*.[15] In a **routine technology**, the process by which the work must be done is well understood, and there are few unexpected problems or exceptions. *Routine* tasks can be broken down into steps and programmed. In many cases, routine tasks can be automated, reducing the organization's reliance on human labor. For example, fast food restaurants offer limited menus, so the procedures for preparing the food are highly standardized. Machines often do the cooking, and workers follow tightly regimented recipes and portion-control formulae. Routinization ensures a consistent product and good returns for the franchise. In fact, the primary appeal of McDonald's is that Big Macs taste the same almost everywhere in the world. Even exceptions can be easily planned for. "Having it your way" involves a relatively limited set of ingredient variations and preparation steps, each of which is planned well in advance. Workers have little or no discretion or control over the work. Engineers, operations management specialists, and other experts analyze the work and determine how it should be done.

At the other end of the scale are **nonroutine** tasks. Because there are many exceptional cases, and because the procedures for doing nonroutine tasks are not well understood, human judgment and discretion must be applied to each case. As the old phrase goes, the work is more of an art than a science. Skilled workers are needed to exercise finely trained judgments in solving problems and doing the work. Strategic planning requires extensive know-how and background. However, planners do not always understand exactly what the right way to respond to the situation they face is. Nor do they know what the situation will be like in the future. Hence they must improvise and project based on their own knowledge and experience.

Generally speaking, uncertainty increases as we move from routine to non-routine technologies. As a result, traditional strategies of organizing are most effective for routine technologies; whereas relational organizations are most effective for nonroutine technologies. Cultural strategies that emphasize continuity and stability are more effective for routine technologies; but those that emphasize change and innovation are more effective with nonroutine technologies. Intermediate cases are more difficult. In such cases, there is less-than-perfect knowledge of how to do the work and more than a few exceptions occur; however, these intermediate cases do not have the extremely high degrees of uncertainty that nonroutine technologies are designed for. Examples of intermediate cases are clothing design and pattern making, specialty steel manufacturing, legal work, and the performing arts. A typical intermediate strategy is to develop a repertoire of methods or techniques that can be mastered and applied to different cases. The challenge is selecting and combining the right routines to get the job done properly. So the surgical team knows many different procedures (anesthesia, opening the patient, tying off blood vessels), and combines different sets of them in different ways, depending on the type of operation being done and the particular characteristics of the patient.

Organizational communication is quite different in organizations with routine technologies from those with nonroutine technologies. The greater the uncertainty, the greater the need for direct, intensive communication and many adjustments. Although most people prefer face-to-face communication, direct and intense communication is costly. It takes a great deal of time to communicate and come to an understanding, to adjust work and plans, and to manage the conflicts that may arise along the way. For best results, a balance must be struck between communication needs and cost: The organization should enact the least costly communication system that can adequately meet its needs for communication and coordination. If people need to exchange only standard information, such as an order for a meal, placing the order through a more impersonal medium, such as a checklist or computer system, is adequate because it conveys the same information with less communication cost. (Of course, the computer system is costly in its own right, but for high volumes of communication the cost per message comes out to be quite low). For routine technologies, vertical, formal, written communication is most adequate. For highly analyzable tasks, there is usually a wealth of documented information and statistical analysis concerning how best to do the work and handle problems. This can be put in formal manuals or work procedures that substitute for direct communication between workers or between workers and managers. For routine tasks, most communication follows the chain of command as managers give orders to and solve problems for subordinates. Low levels of task variety suggest that exceptions requiring extended discussion will be rare and that instructions for handling those that do can be built into procedural manuals.

For nonroutine technologies uncertainty reaches very high levels. There is high variety and low analyzability, so each task must be approached with a great deal of direct, often unscheduled communication. Face-to-face consultations and long, intense meetings are often the only adequate form of communication to meet the needs of nonroutine work.

For intermediate cases, there is a need for higher levels of communication than routine organization allows for but less than the nonroutine case. The lowest cost method for increasing communication beyond formal channels in such cases is the scheduled meeting, because this can be planned into the work.

To sum up, depending on the nature of the technology employed in a unit, the unit will have different levels of uncertainty and different communication needs. To remain effective and viable, the organization must develop a communication system that is adequate for the demands placed on it. Assessing a unit's technology can help us understand why its communication is effective or not and what needs to be done to improve communication.

Interdependence   Technology influences the communication systems of intact units. However, units do not always work in isolation; they are interdependent with other units. Three different types of interdependence can be distinguished[16]: *pooled, sequential,* and *reciprocal.* Each imposes different communication requirements on the organization. In the case of **pooled interdependence**, work does not flow between units. Instead the units each work on their own product or services and the total output of the organization is the pooled work of the individual units. Franchise restaurants, such as Denny's or McDonald's, are good examples of pooled interdependence. Franchises in different locations do not need to coordinate with each other; each does its own work and contributes independently (more or less) to the return of the whole chain. Other organizations with pooled interdependence include personal tax-return preparation services and independent long-haul trucking firms.

Because the degree of interdependence is low, communication among units or people linked in pooled interdependence can be handled through standardization, and the creation of rules, and formal written plans to ensure that each of the parallel units is adequately supplied and turns out work of adequate quality. These plans and rules serve as substitutes for communication and reduce the need for other forms of communication. Managers above the pooled units provide sufficient coordination to keep them operating smoothly, and vertical communication between managers and units is the final ingredient in an effective coordination system. Units with pooled interdependence do not require strong communication links with each other; hence they do not have to be located together or linked by telecommunications.

Sequential interdependence exists when units are arrayed in a series and the output of one department is the input for another In this case, how well each successive unit can perform depends on how well the previous units have done their work. Sequential interdependence increases coordination needs and requires higher levels of communication than pooled interdependence (see Figure 5–3). Since one-way flow of materials, people, or information occurs, extensive planning and scheduling is required and feedback concerning problems is needed to ensure that earlier steps have been performed properly. The classic

FIGURE 5–3
Three Types of Interdependence among Organizations or Units

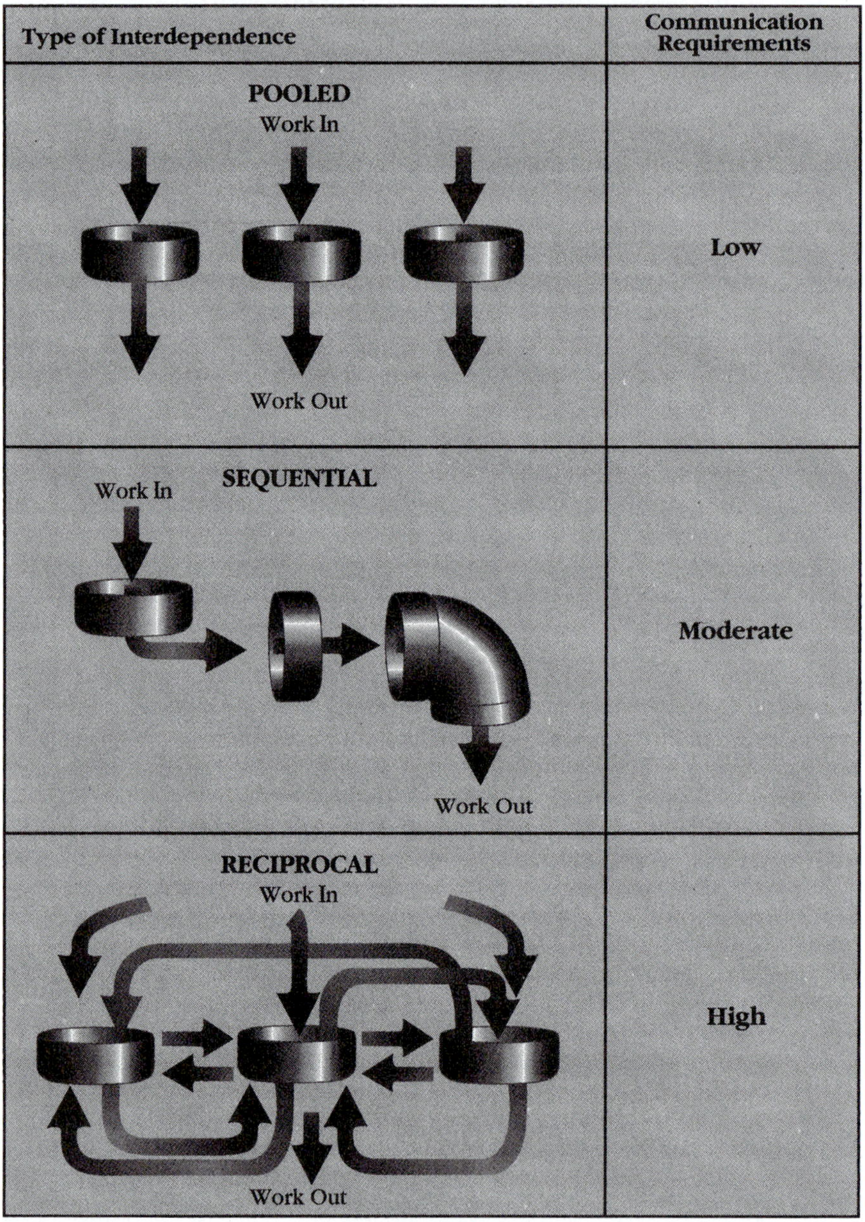

Type of Interdependence	Communication Requirements
POOLED Work In / Work Out	Low
SEQUENTIAL Work In / Work Out	Moderate
RECIPROCAL Work In / Work Out	High

example of sequential interdependence is the assembly line. Other examples include college admissions offices, financial institutions, and unemployment offices.

Sequential interdependence is best coordinated by active planning among participants, guided by management. Managers use vertical communication channels to do a great deal of the coordination work for sequential units. Under the auspices of management, representatives of these units also come together in scheduled meetings to form plans that ensure smooth operation and minimize problems. Problems that arise are dealt with either by management or through horizontal communication among units.

The highest level of interdependence is **reciprocal interdependence.** In this case, all units are involved together in the work; the outputs of each unit become the inputs of the others, and vice versa. Units work together intensively when there is reciprocal interdependence, so a great deal of communication and coordination is needed. It is not always possible to predict beforehand the types of operations or problems that will occur under reciprocal interdependence, so it falls to the units to manage coordination through direct interaction as the need arises. Reciprocal interdependence requires extensive coordination and is best handled through mutual adjustment of the units, though the modes of coordination employed for pooled and sequential cases standardization and planning can help as well. Coordination needs for reciprocal interdependence tend to arise on the fly and must be handled by horizontal communication via unscheduled meetings, face-to-face communication, and electronic channels. While managers can help resolve coordination problems for reciprocally linked units, the units themselves are in the best position to actually suggest and try out solutions.

To sum up, at low levels of interdependence, substitutes for communication are sufficient; as interdependence increases, plans, scheduled communication, and vertical communication are needed, until at high levels of interdependence, horizontal, unscheduled and continuous communication is required. Organizations that want to coordinate their units adequately (sufficient communication with minimum cost) would do well to follow these guidelines.

Environment   The third variable affecting organizational design and communication structures is the organization's environment. The notion of organizational environment has already been introduced in Chapter 1 and discussed in Chapters 2 and 3. In this section, we will define environment in more detail and connect it to the design of organizations and their communication systems.

Literally, *environment* refers to everything outside the organization's boundaries. However, for purposes of analysis, environment can be defined as those institutions, organizations, groups, and people outside the organization that affect it. Environments are made up of many elements, including domestic and foreign competitors, customers and clients, government agencies and regulators, general economic conditions, technological developments relevant to the organization, financial resources, the labor market, raw materials suppliers, and the general culture surrounding the organization. Not all these elements are similar or equally important for every organization; depending on its purpose and location, each organization has a particular mix of these elements as its environment.

Organizational environments can be described in terms of two basic dimensions, complexity and stability.[17] The **complexity** of an organization's environment refers to the number of elements in the environment with which the organization has to deal. An organization with a simple environment may have only a few elements to deal with; whereas one in a complex environment may deal with dozens or hundreds of elements. For example, a university library has a relatively simple environment; it has to deal with the university's administration, student and faculty clientele, publishers and other publication sources, and other libraries. Many of the library's dealings with other agencies, such as the Occupational Safety and Health Administration and the Social Security Administration, are handled for it by the university administration, greatly reducing the environmental complexity. On the other hand, a publishing house has to deal with a much more complex environment—stockholders or owners (who may change frequently as a result of mergers), competing publishers, authors (who often miss deadlines), customers, an assortment of government agencies, the financial institutions that provide its capital and operating monies, labor unions, and new technologies that compete with published books, magazines, and journals. Clearly, university libraries and publishing houses experience different environmental demands.

The other dimension of organizational environment, **stability,** can be defined as the rate of change in the elements of the environment and their relationships (recall Chapters 1–3). Some environments are stable and/or change in a predictable fashion. Before deregulation AT&T, the telephone company had a stable environment. Suppliers and customers were predictable; the telephone company's monopoly status gave it a guaranteed market, and its relations with the regulators ensured it would make a reasonable profit. Change came mainly in the form of new technologies and services that the phone company developed itself. On the other end of the continuum are organizations whose environments are changing rapidly and continuously. These organizations must adapt constantly, and unpredictability is expected and factored into their operation. To deal with instability, these organizations develop special positions and units to monitor and plan reactions to the environment. Firms in the information technology field offer a good example of life in an unstable environment. Driven by the fast pace of technological change and cutthroat international competition, they often change their products, their markets, and their own structures to survive and remain competitive.

Together environmental complexity and stability define four basic situations that can be arranged in order of increasing uncertainty. *Simple, stable environments* create relatively low levels of uncertainty. Organizations in these environments can focus on setting up the most effective and efficient organizational design. Examples of such organizations in this cell include soft drink distribution companies and law offices. *Complex, stable environments* offer medium levels of uncertainty. As a result, the organization must evolve special units or procedures for dealing with uncertainty and anticipate a certain amount of change. Examples of organizations with complex, stable environments include universities and chemical companies.

Moderate to high uncertainty is experienced by organizations in *simple, unstable environments.* Whereas these environments are relatively simple, they undergo continuous change, and organizations must change to survive in them. Examples of organizations with unstable, simple environments include firms in the clothing industry and manufacturers of personal computers who supply the big retail outlets. Finally, *unstable, complex environments* create the highest level of uncertainty. In these environments, the organization must constantly plan for change and react to circumstances beyond its control. To do this, special positions and units are created to monitor and guide reactions to environmental change, and a flexible organizational structure is needed to promote adaptation. Examples of organizations in this quadrant are software, telecommunications, and airline firms. (We will return to this concept in Chapter 12.)

To be effective, organizations in stable environments should adopt the traditional strategy; those in moderate to highly unstable environments should adopt the relational strategy, and those in environments with very high instability should adopt the network strategy.[18] Cultural strategies that value stability are more effective in stable environments; those that emphasize innovation and change are more effective in unstable environments. The traditional form is the most effective when the organization can plan its structure and procedures carefully because of its advantage in efficiency. However, when the environment is changing, the flatter, more interconnected relational form is preferred because of its adaptability.

As environmental complexity increases, the number of departments in the organization generally increases. Organizations typically have units to deal with critical aspects of their environments, and the more of these there are, the greater the number of units there must be. The only bank in a small rural town has a relatively simple internal structure: officers to deal with regulators and make major decisions, accountants and auditors to keep track of the money, tellers to deal with customers, and janitors to keep the place clean. However, if another bank moves into town, the first one may add a marketing unit to compete for customers; if a large plant relocates to the town, the bank may add a commercial lending unit. As the number and interrelationship of environmental elements increases, the structure of the organization becomes more complex. In the same vein, organizations facing complex environments may add boundary-spanning personnel who directly relate to various organizations or groups in the environment. The small-town bank, for example, may add a special position dedicated to contacting and serving the relocated plant.

As instability and complexity increase, organizations become more complex and have less stable structures. This situation increases the need for communication and integrating roles in the organization. Integrating roles are those that help different units coordinate their efforts and resolve actual and potential conflicts. Organizations with high levels of instability and complexity in particular have many integrating roles.

CASE STUDY:
STEELING AWAY INTO A DIFFERENT STRUCTURE*

From the days of Andrew Carnegie and the other steel barons to the late 1960s, the steel industry was dominated by large, vertically integrated companies. The industry existed in a stable environment and the rate of technological advance was steady and gradual. If steel manufacturers could produce steel of good quality at a reasonable price, it could be sold.

Excelsior Steel is 125 years old, employs 2,200 and makes 250,000 tons of steel a year. Located in Northern Indiana, it is housed in a huge plant that consolidated all operations under one roof. Excelsior had a centralized, hierarchical structure. From its offices in downtown Gary, top management, with the aid of engineering, made decisions regarding the products Excelsior would manufacture and the level produced. Separate departments handled manufacturing, marketing, metallurgy, field sales, and support for these units. Over the years, top managers forged close contacts with unions, and the unions often worked with Excelsior to determine work rates and how the work should be done.

But all that changed starting in the late 1970s. The inflation of that period, coupled with the recession that followed it and fierce competition from Germany, Japan, and Brazil, brought Excelsior to the edge of bankruptcy. Excelsior was in danger of following many of the other steel giants that lined the southern edge of Lake Michigan out of the steel business. But Excelsior did not become another of those huge abandoned buildings north of Hammond, Indiana. Instead it took aggressive steps to solve problems.

After extensive diagnosis, Excelsior's managers found that their products were no longer keeping pace with the market, 60 percent of the firm's orders ran behind schedule, and profits were eaten up by materials, energy, and labor costs. In this more turbulent environment, the stable, hierarchical structure was not nimble enough. Moreover, technological advances had rendered much of Excelsior's plant outdated. Smaller furnaces equipped with the latest computer-assisted manufacturing devices could turn out many of Excelsior's products at a much lower cost.

In conjunction with outside experts and the union, management at Excelsior concocted a strategy to save the plant. The strategy hinged on shifting production to high-value products tailored for separate markets, while upgrading technology and research.

To get started, Excelsior set up three product task forces: sheet metal, special alloys, and open-die forgings. These task forces had representatives from all departments involved in the products and their charge was to determine how each product could be produced in an independent product group. The task forces formed the basis for permanently integrating teams headed by product managers, each of which was responsible for all aspects of one of the three product areas, including sales. Each product area was also responsible for introducing new products and trimming products that were not successful.

(continued)

(continued from the previous page)

Over time, there were so many orders for different types of specialty steel that the special alloys group subdivided into multiple project teams, instituting a mini-matrix structure within the group. Since it was important to keep the personnel in the special alloys groups trained in the latest technology and metallurgical research, the functional departments assumed increased importance. Functional managers, such as the manger of metallurgy, were responsible for keeping abreast of the latest technical developments and for keeping personnel trained. These personnel were then assigned to one or more projects, under the supervision of the project manager. This structure greatly enhanced communication both within and between specialties.

Excelsior installed electronic mail and voice mail when it implemented an order and inventory tracking system. These greatly increased the ability of Excelsior's employees to keep in touch with each other and increased the flow of ideas. Along with this, Excelsior created a program to cultivate new ideas in which employees who had brainstorms could set up project teams to develop them, provided they could make a good case with the management team. From this program came several new product lines.

Implementation of this new structure was not painless. The company had to lay off workers, because the three product lines did not require as many employees as Excelsior had in its heyday. By the end of the reorganization, Excelsior had only 1,300 employees; however, as production increased it hired back about 300 more. Many of the laid-off employees were replaced by technology. The union still hung on, but union and management were much less adversarial than in the past. Union and management worked together to reorganize the plant. Middle managers and foremen were especially confused by the transition to product units and the matrix-based structure. Not accustomed to dealing with ambiguity, they initially resisted the increased number of meetings and negotiation required. Over time the most disgruntled managers and foremen retired, and the new structure, which emphasized horizontal and integrative links as well as vertical communication took over. Many of the managers who initially resisted this shift have found it to be a growth experience; they try to involve younger employees in new product development and problem-solving to develop them for the future.

Excelsior Steel is now back on track. Deliveries are on time better than 95 percent of the time. An average of twenty new products are introduced each year and profits are up. Market share has recovered as well. Excelsior employees gladly embrace their new motto, "Change or Die."

Applying What You've Learned

1. How did Excelsior respond to changes in its environment and technology? Which of the integrating methods did Excelsior use?

(continued)

(continued from the previous page)

Questions to Think About and Discuss

1. It is not clear that a company in Excelsior's position can ever stop changing. What are some of the disadvantages of continuous change? How could Excelsior minimize them?

2. What communication problems would you expect to occur as Excelsior moved from its old structure and culture to the new one?

---

*This case is a composite of several cases describing companies both inside and outside the steel industry. It was inspired by Richard Daft, *Organization Theory and Design,* pp. 244–245.

Interrelationships among the Variables   Each of the three variables affects somewhat different features of organizations and their communication systems. Technology influences the communication system within units; interdependence influences the communication between units within the organization, and the environment influences the communication system that crosses the boundaries of the organization. If we can assess the values of these variables for a given organization, we can know what an effective communication system should be like. Contingency theory can also help pinpoint possible problems in an organization's communication system and suggest ways in which it can be made more effective.

These variables also suggest a key problem: What if the variables are inconsistent with each other? An organization might, for example, have a nonroutine technology but confront a simple, stable environment. The technology suggests that the relational strategy should be used; but its environment suggests the traditional strategy. Two possible outcomes have been suggested for organizations in this situation. First, some scholars suggest that the organization should adopt the most complex organization indicated by the three variables. At the cost of some inefficiency, the organization would be able to deal with its toughest challenge. Second, other scholars suggest that cases when the variables are inconsistent represent instances when the organization must "suboptimize" or underperform, because it is faced with contradictions.

CONCLUSION

Organizations have always had a wide range of options for organizing themselves, and new technologies have broadened this range still further. The gradual evolution of the knowledge society in the last half of this century set the stage for the explosive rate at which the emphasis on knowledge and information work has developed over the past twenty years. Along with this came the globalization of the economy, rapid growth in knowledge and technology, and increased environmental turbulence. The rapid development of information technology has facilitated and fed on these changes. Computer and telecommunications technologies have permeated organizations and made many types of structures and communication systems possible that were only visions before 1980.

To deal with the increased pace of change and adapt to turbulent environments, organizations must incorporate integrating communication mechanisms for coordination. We discussed a number of different methods for integrating organizations and suggested that they be evaluated on the basis of benefits and costs to the organization, the degree of geographical dispersion of the organization, and the organization's culture. Ideally the least costly method that can adequately meet the organization's needs should be chosen. In practice this is not always possible due to limitations in member knowledge and willingness to use a given method and due to lack of fit with the organization's culture. These coordination methods will help organizations employing the traditional, relational, and cultural strategies to deal with changing technologies and environments; but they can only go so far. When uncertainty is high due to environmental change, internal complexity, or other factors, a different strategy of organizing is needed.

The network strategy of organizing is appropriate for organizations that must cope with high levels of uncertainty. It is a highly relational strategy that designs the organization as a network, with a flexible, modular structure that links units in a network, a relatively flat hierarchy, emphasis on teams and self-management, and use of information technology to coordinate units. Networks can be changed relatively easily to incorporate new units or to rearrange themselves to respond to new demands from their work or environment. The network organization relies on employees to be independent, knowledgeable and team-oriented. Rather than rigid structures, the network uses mutual trust among members, member's commitment to their work, contracts, and open communication systems to hold the network together. Units in the network coordinate through communication and negotiation rather than through authority.

Contingency design theory, which attempts to explain what makes different organizational structures effective, gives us some guidelines to use in determining which (or which mix) of the four strategies of organizing to use. It gives advice on how an effective organization and its communication system can be designed based on three variables: its technology, its interdependence with other organizations or units, and its environment.

In concluding, it is important to acknowledge that many organizations are a pastiche of more than one strategy. Many large transnational companies, for example, combine a (shorter) hierarchy built on the traditional strategy with a network strategy.[19] Organizations making a transition between strategies also usually exhibit characteristics of two (or more) strategies. As the case of ICG illustrates, organizations commonly maintain aspects of their previous strategy of organizing as they search for a new strategy that works for them. As ICG evolved toward a network form, it kept aspects of the traditional hierarchy in place and gradually shed some of the traditional structures as it networked. It is important to bear in mind that the four strategies are ideal types, and the "real world" is a blurry, confusing place. Many organizations we encounter will not display the strategies in the pure, clear way we have discussed them.

POSTSCRIPT: ALTERNATIVE ORGANIZATIONS

The network and other new organizational forms continue to evolve. However, as we have noted, they did not spring up new in the 1990s. Versions of the network organization have been around for decades if not centuries. A number of alternative organizational forms have also developed, but they have only recently been noticed by mainstream scholars and managers.

The most common types of truly alternative forms of organizing have emerged at the intersection of feminist theories of organizing (discussed in Chapter 7) and research on women's ways of leading (discussed in Chapter 11). Feminist theorists argue that masculine conceptions of reality, modes of organizing, and ways of communicating dominate the public realm in Western societies. Masculine organizations are dominated by metaphors suggesting hierarchy, rely on "power over" views of interpersonal influence, define effectiveness as achieving goals in spite of resistance by others, and privilege centralized expertise and decision making. In contrast, feminine (as well as feminist) organizations are defined by metaphors that describe webs of interconnected interpersonal relationships, define effectiveness in terms of achieving consensus among organizational members, and focus on systems of shared leadership and diffuse expertise. The distinction between feminine and feminist organizations is important because many alternative organizations, while composed primarily or exclusively of women, are not based on feminist goals regarding social change and their members may not espouse feminist values at all.

For example, Nancy Wyatt described a women's organization composed primarily of middle-class, conservative women who were unified by their common interest in sewing and weaving but never expressed an interest in feminist politics. But they created and sustained an organization that was fundamentally different from any of the strategies of organizing discussed in this book. The women provided one another with mutual support and opportunities to learn new skills from one another; they saw failure as an equally important part of learning as success; they were avidly noncompetitive and maintained diffuse and nonhierarchical power relationships and modes of decision making. Leadership was shared by eight members of the weavers' guild, some of whom were leaders because they were uniquely able to articulate a shared vision for the organization, and some of whom were leaders because of their ability to organize the group's activities. But all eight were very much concerned that they not dominate the others—they provided advice and direction only when asked, for example. This was in part because of the history of the group. At one time it had a strong, centralized leader, and when that woman left the guild it almost fell apart. But it also was because of their focus on maintaining a supportive community within the group. So, formal roles rotated among the group's members so that a variety of talents and interests were represented in decision making, and the guild's activities were orchestrated so that each member's goals were met. There were tensions within the group, usually over the organization's unique form of organizing. One member once had been a weaver by profession and tended to withhold her expertise from the other members, because doing so had been a successful political strategy in her previous organizations. Members who wished to use the guild as a stepping-stone for a future career in "typical" weaving organizations were frustrated by the shared responsibility and shared credit characteristic of the guild. In spite of these tensions, the weavers' guild was able to create and sustain a fundamentally different kind of organization—one that was able to simultaneously be a community and address the needs and desires of its individual members.[20]

Other feminist organizations have found it more difficult to maintain that kind of balance. Frequently, feminist organizations begin with an emphasis on consensus, equality, collectivity, and legitimate participatory decision making; but they emerge toward more traditional, hierarchical strategies of organizing in which representative democracy replaces participation. This shift seems to stem from environmental pressures on the organization. Feminist organizations face an important dilemma: How can an alternative organization maintain a collective, nonhierarchical, participatory, egalitarian strategy of organizing while simultaneously pursuing other goals like profitability? Some external pressures are overt and direct. In Western societies, organizations need funds to survive and especially to grow. A major donation or grass-roots political campaign may provide sufficient funding for an organization to be created and even to succeed at a relatively small size. But if it is to grow, other sources of funds become necessary, and significant funds are usually available only from traditional, bureaucratic organizations—government agencies, banks, and the financial markets. Decision makers in traditional bureaucracies are comfortable with organizations that operate on the basis of similar strategies of organizing. So they pressure alternative organizations to be less alternative or at least to appear to be. Alternative strategies of organizing become less alternative, and, if the organization is involved in social change efforts, those efforts are moderated or made less visible. For example, *MS* magazine faced a central tension from the day it was created: it drew its content from feminist publications but designed its format and marketing to be like mainline women's magazines. Its funding came from readers who were attracted to the magazine because of its feminist ideology, and from advertisers who saw it as an opportunity to reach women readers. Advertisers pressured the editorship to focus content on career feminists, who had the disposable income that they coveted. But career feminists were only part of the *MS* readership, and many of them were attracted to its feminist ideology. As competition and costs increased during the 1980s, advertising revenues became more necessary, and the advertisers' influence over content increased. Readers found many of the ads offensive and resisted the shift. The opposition crystallized around a 1987 issue on women and addiction, which included none of the tobacco and alcohol company ads that had become common. Readers were irate about what they saw as blatant hypocrisy, and the editors' argument that the *MS* policies had led to improvements in advertising directed toward women fell on deaf ears. Although the magazine's content had become progressively less political as the advertisers exerted increased control, advertisers abandoned the magazine during the highly conservative political climate of the late 1980s. In 1989 the magazine folded, only to be reborn the following year with no advertising.[21]

Environmental pressures may also be subtle. People, regardless of their gender and regardless of the strategy of organizing that is in place, bring the dominant assumptions of their societies with them into their organizations. Thus, people in Western societies tend to value efficiency, expertise, and experience. Consensus decision making and participation consume a great deal of time and energy (recall Chapter 3) and thus *seem* to be inefficient, especially in the short term; differences in expertise and experience *seem* to warrant hierarchical power relationships. Members of alternative organizations are pressured by the many different traditional organizations in which they also are involved— churches, schools, clubs, and so on. These competing organizations work on a schedule and through a process that contradicts the flexibility and adaptability of the alternative organization. Consequently, it is difficult for members to continue to support forms of organizing that seem to be so *non-normal*, so *unnatural*. A number of factors do help offset these pressures—small organizational size, common goals, relatively equal knowledge and experience, and a benign environment. As a result, there are a number of flourishing cooperatives and collectives that operate on the basis of alternative strategies; but sustaining them involves a constant process of managing tensions.[22]

Alternative organizations face a second dilemma: Can alternative strategies of organizing successfully include people from diverse racial, ethnic, class, and gender groups? Alternative organizations tend to begin with local, grass-roots organizing. These groups tend to have common interests and homogeneous backgrounds and experiences. For example, in the United States, feminist groups have primarily involved educated middle- and upper-middle-class Anglo women. Unless they actively reach out to men and to people of other classes, races, and ethnic origins, they tend to remain homogeneous. Since an alternative form of organizing does not in itself bridge racial, class, or ethnic differences, and since the concerns that bring middle-class Anglo women together in alternative organizations may not be salient to anyone else (and vice versa), diversifying alternative organizations is quite difficult. Doing so is more likely when the organization emerges from a multiclass, multiethnic community; but even then it takes a great deal of time and energy to sustain a truly diverse organization. Consequently, pressures for efficiency may be especially acute for these organizations, making factors like small size and common goals even more important.[23]

NOTES

[1] Peter Drucker, "The Age of Transformation," *Atlantic Monthly* (September, 1994): p. 53.

[2] Jay Galbraith, "Organizational Design," in *Handbook of Organizational Behavior*, J. Lorsch, ed. (Englewood Cliffs: Prentice-Hall, 1987).

[3] A readable account of the matrix organization can be found in Robert Youker, "Organization Alternatives for Project Managers," *Project Management Journal*, VIII (March, 1977): 18–24. Also see Galbraith.

[4] Susan J. Winter and S. Lynne Taylor, "The Role of Information Technology in the Transformation of Work: A Comparison of Postindustrial, Industrial, and Protoindustrial Organization," in *Shaping Organization Form: Communication, Connection, and Connectivity,* Gerardine DeSanctis and Janet Fulk, eds. (Newbury Park, CA: Sage, 1999).

[5] Marshall Scott Poole, "Organizational Challenges for the New Forms," in *Shaping Organization Form: Communication, Connection, and Community,* Gerardine DeSanctis and Janet Fulk, eds. (Newbury Park, CA: Sage, 1999). Deborah Ancona, Thomas Kochan, Maureen Scully, John Van Maanen, and D. Eleanor Westney, "The New Organization: Taking Action in An Era of Organizational Transformation" in *Organizational Behavior and Process* (Cincinnati: South-Western College Publishing, 1999).

[6] Peter Monge and Noshir Contractor, "Emergence of Communication Networks" in *The New Handbook of Organizational Communication,* Fredric M. Jablin and Linda L. Putnam, eds. (Newbury Park, CA: Sage, 2000).

[7] Larry Browning.

[8] Monge and Contractor.

[9] Henry C. Lucas, *The T-Form Organization: Using Technology to Design Organizations for the 21st Century* (San Francisco: Jossey-Bass, 1996).

[10] Dale E. Zand, "Trust and Managerial Problem-Solving," *Administrative Science Quarterly*, 17: 229–239.

[11] Ancona et al. Ch. 1.

[12] Susan J. Winter and S. Lynne Taylor, "The Role of IT in the Transformation of Work: A Comparison of Post-industrial, Industrial, and Proto-Industrial Organizations," *Information Systems Research,* 7 (1996): 5–21.

[13] Tom Burns and G.M. Stalker, *The Management of Innovation* (London: Tavistock, 1961).

[14] Charles Perrow, "A Framework for the Comparative Analysis of Organizations", *American Sociological Review,* 32 (1967), pp. 194–208.

[15] Perrow divides technology into two dimensions: analyzability and variety. Analyzability refers to the degree to which process the technology is designed to carry out, and is known and understood. The second dimension of technology is its variety and the number of exceptions encountered in the course of doing the work. In some work, exceptional cases are very rare; there are only small differences from case to case and the "inputs" to the organizational systems are relatively uniform. This defines four types of technology. Two are covered in detail in the main text: low analyzability coupled with high variety (nonroutine technologies apply) and high analyzability coupled with low variety (routine technologies apply). The other two cases are Engineering and Craft technologies. Engineering technologies, with high analyzability, but also high variety, are complicated, because many exceptions are encountered. However, because cause-effect relationships are well understood for these tasks, it is possible to develop a set of formulas that can then be applied to the different cases. For engineering technologies, uncertainty is somewhat higher. Manuals and standard procedures describe the various programs the unit can carry out, but members of the unit may need to consult regarding the specific programs that will be used, how they will be coordinated with each other, and what to do if problems arise. Hence, engineering technologies are most adequately served by a combination of written, standardized communication and verbal communication directed to coordinating work and problem resolution.

Craft technologies, with low analyzability and low variety, have a stable set of activities, but the transformation process is not well understood. Extensive training and experience is required to master work techniques and the judgment necessary for applying them. For example, a group of performing artists putting on a play, knows the script, but turning that script into a performance requires them to draw on years of slowly accumulated know-how that they cannot put into words. For craft technologies, uncertainty is still higher than for engineering technologies. Because these technologies deal with low analyzable work, the use of manuals and standard procedures is less feasible. The most adequate way of coordinating craft work is through horizontal verbal communication among those who have to work together. This can often be scheduled. For example, a specialty steel fabricating plant might have a scheduled weekly meeting to discuss formulations for new orders.

[16] This important distinction was developed by James Thompson, *Organizations in Action* (New York: McGraw-Hill, 1967).

[17] Robert B. Duncan, "Characteristics of Perceived Environments and Perceived Environmental Uncertainty," *Administrative Science Quarterly*, 17 (1972): 313–327.

[18] Daft, especially Chapter 2; Howard E. Aldrich, *Organizations and Environments* (Englewood Cliffs: Prentice-Hall, 1979).

[19] Janet Fulk and Gerardine DeSanctis, "Articulation of Communication Technology and Organizational Form," in DeSanctis and Fulk.

[20] Nancy Wyatt, "Shared Leadership in a Weavers' Guild," in B. Bate and Anita Taylor, eds., *Women Communicating* (Norwood, NJ: Ablex, 1988). An excellent, in-depth treatment of feminist organizations is Myra Marx Ferree and Patricia Yancey Martin, *Feminist Organizations* (Philadelphia: Temple University Press, 1995).

[21] Amy Farrell, "Like a Tarantula on a Banana Boat," in Marx Ferree and Yancy Martin, eds. *Feminist Organizations.*

[22] See Joan Acker, "The Gender Regime in Swedish Banks," *Scandinavian Journal of Management* (1994) and "Feminist Goals and Organizing Processes," in Marx Ferree and Yancy Martin (Eds.) *Feminist Organizations;* Joyce Rothschild-Whitt and J. A. Whitt, *The Cooperative Workplace* (Cambridge: Cambridge University Press, 1986); George Cheney, "Democracy in the Workplace," *Journal of Applied Communication Research, 23* (1995): 167–200.

[23] Acker, "Organizing;" Mary Pardo, "Doing It for the Kids," in Marx Ferree and Yancey Martin, eds. *Feminist Organizations.*

Unit II

Communication Strategies and Organizational Challenges

Chapter 6

COMMUNICATION TECHNOLOGY

The possibilities are endless.
—ADVERTISING SLOGAN FROM THE 1960S

To err is human; to really foul things up requires a computer.
—PROVERB FROM THE 1970S

CENTRAL THEMES

- Information and communication technology offers one way of dealing with the complexity of the knowledge society and its increased rate of change.
- Information technology has evolved from centralized computing, in which information processing was carried out in large mainframe computers, to today's emphasis on distributed, decentralized computing.
- Five types of information technology are important in today's organization: electronic data processing, management-information systems, decision-support systems, office automation, and expert systems.
- Telecommunications technologies are critical to integrating organizations and are currently converging with information technology to give rise to integrated technologies.
- Information technology opens up a wide variety of communication options to organizational members; in choosing among them, organizations should consider information richness, fit with the organization's culture, and the symbolic value of the medium.
- Information and communication technology (ICT) has given rise to novel organizational arrangements, including the virtual organization, telework, and knowledge management.
- Impacts of ICTs on organizations and their members are neither simple nor deterministic but are shaped by social processes in the organizations and by the strategy of organizing they utilize
- A number of ethical and policy problems arise due to organizational use of ICTs, including privacy issues and the degree of surveillance that organizations should be allowed to undertake.

174

KEY TERMS

Electronic data processing
Accounting information systems
Management information systems
Decision support systems
Group decision support systems
Electronic mail
Electronic calendaring
Voice mail
Audio conferencing
Videoconferencing
Computer conferencing
Videotex
Office automation

Desktop publishing
Expert systems
Networked computing
Distributed computing
Virtual organizations
Informate
Telework
Critical mass
Innovation adoption curve
Reinvention
Knowledge management
Information richness
Imaging

INFORMATION TECHNOLOGY: EXPANDING THE HORIZONS OF ORGANIZATIONAL STRATEGIES

The last twenty years of the twentieth century and the first years of this century will surely be remembered as the time when information and communication technology exploded. The most obvious indication of this is the phenomenal growth of the Internet. But, the Internet is only the tip of an iceberg of changes that include the spread of business transaction systems, the beginnings of an explosion in wireless telecommunications, the takeoff of videoconferencing, the advent of virtual organizations, and reengineering of countless private, public, and nonprofit organizations to incorporate information technology.

Some scholars argue that information and communication technology (ICT) does not really change organizations.[1] They regard it as simply another variable that influences organizational communication. To them, its main impact is to increase speed, efficiency, and integration of information exchange. However, we believe this is misleading, because in most U.S. organizations ICT has become so much a part of everyday operations that it is an integral part of the organization. It plays just as important a role in the organization and its communication system as a face-to-face conversation or a telephone call.

We use the term ICT to refer to computerized systems and to advanced telecommunication systems. Relevant computerized systems include those used to manage databases containing budget, order, or inventory information, to provide communication through electronic mail and conferencing, and to coordinate work processes. Advanced telecommunication systems include voice mail systems, fax technology, proprietary telephone systems (for example, PBX systems), teleconferencing, videoconferencing, and wireless communications. All these systems enable organizations to operate much more rapidly and (sometimes) adapt more quickly than they could if human communicators and traditional modes of communication (memos, letters, phone calls) made up the entire communication system. ICT gathers and transmits information so quickly, thoroughly, and reliably, that it enables human links in the communication system to focus more on quality thinking, reasoning, and service, the jobs for which they are best suited. However, along with the promise of ICT, there is concern about the impact that it has on organizations, their members, and their communication processes. We examine this issue later in this chapter.

A Quick Tour of Organizational Information Systems

Before exploring the impacts of ICTs on organizations and work, we will examine the history and variety of ITCs.

In the Beginning. . .Electronic Data Processing   When the first computers were developed in the late 1940s, many scientists predicted that the world would only need a dozen or so computing machines. They could not imagine the vast array of applications that would develop over the next fifty years and the ubiquitous spread of the computer throughout society. In the early years, computers were large boxes that had to be housed in special rooms to guard against overheating and other environmental stresses. The sale of "Big Iron"—large mainframe computers—catapulted IBM, Burroughs, Control Data, and other companies into the forefront of technological innovation. The first applications of mainframe computers centered around electronic data processing, and the tabulation and analysis of large amounts of data into meaningful form.[2] Applications of computers to process data include their use by the Census Bureau, by scientists, and by organizations for accounting purposes. The term **accounting information system,** mentioned in Chapter 5, refers to the use of information systems to manage data, such as sales figures, customer accounts, client records, and budgets for firms. These data-management functions can be integrated so that, for example, changes in customer orders can trigger changes in sales figures, update inventory records, and order stock to replenish depleted inventory. Integrated accounting information systems enable firms to coordinate their functions by managing the large amounts of data involved. Accounting information systems produce some meaningful information for the organization through summary analysis of the data.

Management Information Systems   Prior to 1964 most computers were constructed with vacuum tubes, which burned out easily and generated a great deal of heat. In 1964 a new generation of mainframe computers based on silicon chips was introduced. They were promoted with the concept of management information systems—the idea that in addition to data processing, computers could be used to actively support the work of managers.[3] A **management information system** (MIS) is a system that makes information available to management to help it plan, control, and evaluate the activities of the organization. The information describes the organization or one of its major units in terms of what has happened in the past, present performance, and what is likely to happen in the future. MISs use various models to analyze organizational databases and develop reports for managerial use. For example, an MIS might perform an analysis of the financial potential of a division of an organization based on its sales and costs and on information about markets and competitors. The analysis would be based on a formal mathematical model built into the MIS (and would only be as valuable as the model was accurate). This report would help managers make decisions about whether the division should expand, and if so what financing to seek and on what terms. Various types of MISs include executive information systems (which create special analyses for top management), marketing information systems, manufacturing information systems, financial information systems, and human resource information systems.

The value of all these MISs depends on the accuracy of the data in the databases and the validity of the models used to analyze the data. If the models make unrealistic assumptions or do not take important factors into account, the advice they give will be poor. Launched with much fanfare in the mid-1960s, early MISs often did not live up to expectations. One mistake that was often made was to try to integrate all the organization's information and analysis into one giant MIS, which often collapsed due to overcomplexity. But in many organizations, IT personnel and researchers persisted, and today MISs are widely used with a great deal of success.

Decision Support Systems　　One response to the problems with large-scale MISs was to design more limited decision support systems, "information-producing systems aimed at a particular problem that a manager must solve and decisions the manager must make."[4] The *decision support system* (DSS) is designed to help individual managers make special types of decisions. It differs from the MIS in that the MIS is designed for use by a group of managers to manage a whole organization or its unit, whereas the DSS is aimed at helping an individual decision maker with specific, localized decisions. DSSs also typically help the manager through all the steps of the decision process; whereas MISs are best for more restricted problem or opportunity identification. DSSs help managers and other members structure problems, gather data to understand and analyze the problem, and make decisions about the best course of action. Examples of DSSs include systems designed to assist in product-pricing decisions and plant investment decisions by managers, patient referral decisions by social service intake workers, and analysis of potential contributors by a charitable fundraiser.[5] Group decision support systems (GDSSs), described later, offer support for decision making by groups.

Like the MIS, the DSS is helpful only if the data is accurate and the model built into the DSS is accurate and applicable to the situation. Force-fitting a decision about ethical issues into a DSS designed for economic decision making would not lead to good outcomes.

Office Automation Systems　　In the late 1960s, about the time DSSs were evolving, a different application of computers emerged. **Office automation** (OA) includes "all of the formal and informal electronic systems primarily concerned with the communication of information to and from persons both inside and outside the firm."[6] People at all levels of the organization, as well as those outside the organization, utilize office automation. The application that drove office automation originally was word processing, introduced by IBM in 1964. Computers were used to enter, store, move, and print documents throughout the firm. As time passed, a number of other OA applications have been developed, including electronic mail, voice mail, electronic calendaring, audio conferencing, videoconferencing, computer conferencing, fax, videotex, imaging, and desktop publishing.[7]

Electronic mail (email) is the use of networked computers to allow users to send, receive, store, and forward messages in electronic formats. Users type in messages and send them to others' electronic mailboxes. Most email systems allow for automatic reply addressing, forwarding, and sending copies of messages to additional parties. Email greatly reduces the time spent in trying to contact others. Studies have shown that as many as 75 percent of business telephone calls do not reach the desired person; often two parties end up playing telephone tag, when each tries to call the other repeatedly, only to find the party out or busy.[8] Email eliminates this, enabling parties to have messages waiting for each other and to reply rapidly. **Voice mail** is like email except that messages are sent by voice and people use their telephones to retrieve messages instead of a computer. Voice mail messages can be stored and forwarded, just like email messages.[9]

Electronic calendaring is the use of a networked computer to keep and retrieve calendars for members of the organization. The person or a secretary can enter appointments on the calendar. Often members are allowed to call up each other's calendars to determine when they are free to meet. In principle, electronic calendaring enables the entire organization to coordinate scheduling. In practice it has met with less success, because it is difficult to get people to take the effort to keep their calendars current.

Audioconferencing is the use of voice communication equipment to establish a link among a set of people. The conference call enables a group to meet even when its members are in different locations. **Videoconferencing** is the use of video technology to link geographically dispersed people or groups. Unlike audioconferencing, which requires only telephone equipment and special linking software, videoconferencing requires cameras and video transmission channels. Many videoconferencing facilities are similar to television broadcast studios; but recent advances have made desktop videoconferencing through PCs possible. Videoconferencing has been tried and failed to get off the ground many times in the past due to problems of high cost and technological shortcomings.[10] For example, videoconferences used to yield only jerky pictures and the screen often went blank due to inability to transmit the images rapidly enough. However, recent advances have brought the price of videoconferencing units down considerably, and the availability of sufficient transmission bandwidth to carry good images has encouraged many organizations to implement videoconferencing.[11]

Computer conferencing is similar to email; but it facilitates communication among dispersed teams and organizes their discussion around specific topics.[12] A conference enables members to enter comments about various topics in a sequence, indicating which prior comment they are responding to. Members can sign on at any time to participate, and comments are kept permanently so that new members can catch up easily. The slower pace of conferencing, which allows team members to reflect on comments prior to entering them, often results in more thoughtful, deeper discussions. However, a key challenge for the conference is making decisions and coordinating activities; the slower pace of conferences makes them better for deliberation than for action. Newer conference tools incorporate workflow tools, action tracking, and automated reminders that pick up the pace of group work. An advantage of computer conferences over audio- and videoconferencing is that they can include large numbers of members. One of the largest computer conferences on record was formed at IBM to discuss the IBM PC; it included over 40,000 members and there were over 4,000 separate topic areas.[13] However, many users find computer conferences less personal and immediate than audio- and videoconferencing and some are reluctant to use them.

Several OA technologies allow users to work with graphics as well as text. **Fax** transmits document images from one place to another. This technology, perfected in Japan to transmit ideographic writing, has proven to be very useful to organizations. **Videotex** uses computers to access and display stored text and graphic material. Some organizations use videotex internally to make documents accessible to all members. However, a more common use is for organizations to purchase videotex services from firms that maintain large databases of useful information. Examples of these firms include Lexis®, which provides legal research and documents, and Lotus One Source®, which provides financial and other information on a wide variety of firms. Sometimes this material is accessed over a network and sometimes it is provided on CD-ROM. **Imaging** is the use of optical character recognition to create digital files of text and graphics that can be accessed and worked with on computers. Organizations that have large volumes of graphical material, such as maps or oil field diagrams, find imaging and document-management systems very useful. Applications of imaging are spreading rapidly as its technology becomes more workable and affordable. Desktop publishing is the use of computers to prepare output that is close in quality to that produced by typesetters and publishing houses. Many organizations are using desktop publishing to prepare documents for presentations and public relations purposes.[14]

The original vision for OA was integration of all these applications. For example, an oil exploration company in Houston uses imaging to store diagrams of geological formations, move these images into a videoconference with a client half the world away in Nigeria, process a contract negotiated in the videoconference and attach the geological images, send it via email or fax to the client, and then get the signed and authenticated contract back via email, and finally store it in the contract database, which has special links to various work notification messages sent via email that would inform exploration employees of the new job, who would then email back to verify assignments, call up the images to help plan drilling, and so on. The ideal OA system would link all the information processing and "paperwork" of the firm into a seamless whole. It would enable the organization to move information easily and quickly from one tool to another. And it would greatly reduce paper consumption and filing problems, because all this work is done in the so-called paperless office. This vision is still unrealized, for the most part, because people continue to want paper documents; but various vendors continue to work on it. The closest most of us have come to the paperless office is probably those advertisements for computer networks where happy employees are sitting at desks without a single slip of paper on them, keyboarding away. When integration can be achieved, it will offer great potential for organizational communication. Raymond McLeod calls OA the "sleeping giant" of information systems applications.[15]

Expert Systems The first four types of information systems move from an emphasis on processing data (electronic data processing) to providing information from that data (management information systems) to using that information to provide support for decision making (decision support systems) to communication in general (OA). The final type of information system goes beyond passive information presentation or communication support to provide active counseling to organizational members. **Expert systems,** first developed in the 1960s, attempt to capture expert knowledge in a computer model that can be used to "think through" problems just as the expert would. Typically this involves finding one or more outstanding experts in a specific area and studying their thought processes to build a *rule-based model* of how they reason and make decisions under different circumstances. If this is done effectively, every member of the organization can have on his or her desk the best advice possible on a given subject. Expert systems have been constructed to help brokers make investment decisions, to aid medical diagnosis, and to construct legal cases.

A different approach to modeling, *neural networks,* creates an expert system that can learn the optimal approach for various problems. Basically, neural networks simulate the structure of the brain and learn by building patterns and testing to see whether the outputs those patterns produce yield good results. So it is necessary to have a task for which there is plentiful, readily available feedback. Given this type of task, the network can take a set of input variables associated with the task and work out a pattern of associations among those variables that yields good outcomes. Neural networks have been used, for example, to deduce optimal operating conditions for oil refineries. They "learn" the proper temperatures, pressures, catalysts, and conversion rates to produce good products. Then they can play a major role in maintaining a smoothly running refinery.

Other approaches to the development of expert systems are being tried as well. This growing area promises to turn information technology from conduit and enabler to adviser, making it a much more active participant in the organization. As with all modeling efforts, the resulting system is only as good as the data it is based on and as the model that is utilized.

Networked Computing Data processing, MISs, DSSs, OA, and expert systems all germinated as applications during the age of mainframe computers. However, since the early 1980s a revolution has occurred in information technology that changed forever how it is used in organizations. As personal computers, microcomputers, and computer networks developed, a new paradigm for computing emerged—networked computing.[16] In networked computing, also called **distributed computing,** processing is no longer conducted in one large central processing unit but instead is spread out among many machines dispersed in a network. For example, in the older computing paradigm a DSS would be located in a large mainframe computer along with all the data it required. Input would come from terminals scattered around the organization and output could be displayed on these terminals; but the computing was done in the mainframe computer located in the information systems department. In the new paradigm, there would be a network, with perhaps a mainframe for storing data and many other types of personal computers and workstations located in the departments that use them. In this case, the DSS software might be located on the executive manager's PC. When an analysis is conducted, it would draw data from databases in the mainframe and also on two other minicomputers located in different departments. It might route its output to several other managers' PCs via email messages.

The differences between centralized and distributed (networked) information systems are significant for organizational communication. Centralized computing tended to keep information technology the preserve of a few highly skilled technicians in the information systems department. Maintaining and working with mainframes requires special skills and training, and so this arrangement gave power and control to the information systems people. As distributed computing spread, it became possible to locate computers in departments where the work was done and not just in the information systems preserve. To do this, it was necessary to develop computer programs that could be understood, configured, and operated by the end user. This has taken a while to accomplish; but programs and even programming are much easier now than they were ten or even five years ago. Scholars in the information technology area look forward to the time in the near future when programming can be done automatically in response to natural language descriptions by the user. (Indeed there are fairly good code generators right now; but they still require some specialized training in programming to operate.) The advent of networked computing and the user-friendly interfaces of personal computers made many communication applications, such as email, word processing, database management, desktop publishing, and even videoconferencing much easier and more accessible to all members of the organization. The result has been a significant opening of communication channels in many organizations.

Distributed computing has the potential to move control over information technology into all parts of the organization and society. The Internet is probably the best example of the impact of distributed computing. And as information technology becomes easier for nonexperts—more transparent in the terminology of the computing industry—the number of networks and the dispersion of computing through society will continue. Computer networks and the communication links based on them grow organically, rather than through formal planning only as was the case when central processors were the only option for design.

Distributed computing makes much more complex and flexible organizational structures possible and has contributed to the rise of the network strategy of organizing, discussed in Chapter 5. It is no longer necessary to take months or years to painstakingly design and build formal structures for information storage and processing, as it was in the days when paper or centralized processors were used to manage organizational information flows. Distributed information systems make rerouting information flows relatively easy; it is a matter of reconfiguring or expanding the arrangement of computers and telecommunications in the network. Communication can be managed quickly and with relatively low overhead, so altering the organization's structure is not likely to block the flow of command and coordination communication. Information systems also make it possible to monitor employees and work processes, so there is no longer the need to have employees or work done where supervisors can oversee it directly. Organizations can be dispersed over many locales and their members linked with high-speed information systems. Distributed information systems are well suited for the demands placed on organizations by the knowledge society, turbulent environments, and rapid change.

Organizational Information and Communication Technologies

The various types of information systems introduced in the previous section make up much of what we refer to as ICTs. Email, DSSs, OA, expert systems, and distributed computing are components of many ICTs. There are, in addition, more specialized applications that are discussed in this section, along with some of their immediate impacts on organizational communication.

Telecommunications   Simple forms of telecommunications, such as telephones, voice mail, conference calls, and fax have become standard integrating mechanisms. They enable people in different locations to coordinate work and make decisions much more rapidly than they could have thirty years ago. These modes of communication are now being bundled in single media—conferencing, phone calls, and fax can be handled over the Internet, for example, and high-speed Internet access is becoming possible through conventional phone lines.

Perhaps the most far-reaching change in ICTs is now occurring in telecommunications, namely the advent of wireless communications. Cell phones are the most familiar wireless devices for most people. While telephone service is the most common use for cell phones, use of cell phones for access to the Internet and private networks is an increasingly common application. Handheld computing devices, such as personal digital assistants and palm computers connected into wireless networks, take computer networks into the field in a very flexible way. Companies are now using such devices to take inventory and make medical records by the patient's bedside. For example, garment maker VF Corporation is using wireless devices to tie its entire production and distribution system together.[17] Wireless networks will be used to track sales rates of various garments, so that materials can be reordered and additional garments produced as needed. Wireless networks and factory input devices can ensure perfect color matching of the various pieces of fabric that go into garments, reducing quality problems. Wireless devices to be integrated into this system include mobile computers, wearable computers, bar-code scanners, and vehicle mounted computers. This array of devices will greatly increase VF's ability to innovate and respond to market changes.

Wireless has great promise to rapidly change how people communicate both privately and in organizations, because it does not require the laying of cable or optical fiber, which may take years and cost billions of dollars. The recent rash of mergers in the telecommunications industry now centers on wireless technology, so future growth for this technology seems probable.[18]

The line between telecommunications and information systems has been blurred in recent years by the fact that many computing applications can be transmitted through telecommunications devices. The Internet, which many of us get through a telephone modem in our homes, is a clear example. Wireless communications has been used to network computers as well, creating a convergence of technologies with great promise.

Electronic Mail   Email is a fast and effective linking mechanism, for several reasons. Email enables communication between people who are on different schedules, because it can be read and answered whenever convenient for the receiver. It is also less intrusive than a phone call or face-to-face contact; the recipient can reply on her or his own schedule. Hence, email encourages communication between people who do not know each other well, who differ in status, or who are in different units that do not have formal relationships. Email also allows the sending of broadcast messages—requests or memos sent to a large group of recipients, even to the whole organization. This capability enables people who do not know whom to ask to gather information and create links.

When email systems are implemented, the total amount of communication within an organization or work group increases and the use of the telephone and written memos does seem to decrease, although the use of face-to-face communication increases. Thus the electronic media seem to supplement, rather than replace, traditional media.[19] The information exchanged via electronic media does not seem to be any more or less accurate than information exchanged through other media, although people tend to be less confident of its accuracy. In face-to-face communication, we rely on vocal cues (pitch, rate of speech, loudness) and nonverbal cues to confirm our interpretations of the meanings of the words that people use. Because these cues are less readily available or are absent in mediated communication, we feel less secure in our interpretations.

Studies show that email often increases lateral communication, contacts across organizational levels, and the flow of ideas compared to more traditional communication media.[20] Sara Kiesler reports a case in which a broadcast request for ideas to solve a problem received over 100 replies in two days, several of which solved or significantly improved the problem.[21]

There are also costs to email, notably message overload. In email-intensive organizations, it is not unusual to receive more than fifty messages a day. (One manager in an information technology firm came back from a two-week vacation to find over a thousand messages waiting!) Sorting through this to separate the junk mail from the important messages can take much time and energy. Some have worried about the impersonal nature of computer-mediated communication. However, studies have generally shown that this medium can be as personal as any once users master it.[22] The style of electronic messages often is less formal than in written messages, and people seem to think less about social norms and hierarchical relationships when constructing electronic messages than when constructing messages for other media. Their communication may be less inhibited—they may express extreme emotions overtly (a process called flaming) and swear more often. Of course, groups of people develop and enforce cultural expectations that require users to refrain from flaming or to engage in other patterns of communicating, such as reading and responding to email messages within a specified period of time.[23]

The availability of electronic message networks also allows people to address messages by topic rather than by the name of the recipient. Employees who are unhappy about a recent management decision can instantaneously locate other people who also are unhappy, share their gripes, circulate resumes, and help one another look for new jobs, as Emmett observed in a large computer organization.[24] Of course, this highly efficient means of letting angry employees know that other people share their sentiments was probably not what upper management had in mind when they purchased the systems.

Electronic Workflow Linkage Several types of information technology help organizations integrate work processes. *Electronic data integration* (EDI) systems enable the management of data exchange among units, divisions, and companies that have to coordinate their work. Organizations use EDIs to set up automated exchanges of information needed to coordinate key tasks. For example, Chrysler Corporation has an EDI linking its suppliers and plants.[25] This EDI keeps track of inventory and is used for parts requests by managers; as parts are needed, suppliers are informed and orders arrive at the factory just in time to be installed. This just-in-time parts system eliminates the cost of keeping large inventories and helps avoid purchase of unneeded parts; as a direct link between suppliers and Chrysler, the EDI also helps the suppliers avoid manufacturing parts that go unsold and increases production quality through immediate feedback. Customers may also be included in EDI systems. American Hospital Supply was a leader in utilizing information technology for customer orders. It placed terminals into health care organizations to enable them to order supplies directly from AHS, resulting in huge sales growth. A second type of workflow integration, *Computer Aided Design/Computer Aided Manufacturing* (CAD/CAM) systems, integrate the design of parts and products with their manufacturing. In an integrated system, design and manufacturing are done in a seamless process mediated by the information technology. This enables much easier redesign and correction of problems than do traditional methods. Office automation systems, discussed previously, are another type of electronic workflow linkage.

The monetary cost of electronic workflow linkage is substantial, since it typically involves design of complex hardware configurations and integrating software across many applications. Even with substantial investment, problem-free integration of the various parts of a system is difficult. Many office automation projects, for example, remain unfinished, because incompatible software and hardware make it impossible to link the various subsystems together. There may also be human resistance to workflow integration. Automating integrating functions may eliminate jobs. It also tightens up surveillance, which may cause resentment, even as it increases quality and control. However, the gains from electronic workflow integration can be substantial, in terms of effectiveness and efficiency. So long as the process being integrated constitutes a substantial part of the organization's critical work and the implementation of the integration is competent, the gains outweigh the costs.

Groupware   Groupware refers to various technologies that support the work of groups or teams. Groupware is typically used for two purposes: to help groups generate ideas and make decisions and to help teams coordinate projects.

To help groups make better decisions, some groupware incorporates formal decision tools, such as idea generation (brainstorming), problem-solving sequences, analysis methods, and evaluation tools (such as voting and rating). These systems, called Group Decision Support Systems (GDSSs), have enjoyed increasing use over the past ten years. GDSSs are often used to help groups meeting face to face make important decisions or resolve conflicts; but they can also be used to help coordinate dispersed groups. FIGURE 6-1 shows a typical GDSS for relatively small face-to-face groups. Each member has his or her own computer and the group can view the results of activities such as brainstorming or a vote on a public screen. The menu for this GDSS gives the group a number of decision procedures to work with, including idea generation, idea evaluation, and decision procedures, such as multi-attribute decision analysis (which enables groups to evaluate options on many criteria), stakeholder analysis (which enables groups to conduct analysis of the political climate surrounding a decision), and problem formulation. GDSSs have been shown to increase the number and quality of ideas considered by groups, to enable more effective conflict management, and in some cases, to promote more effective decision making.[26] However, this depends on whether the group uses the GDSS to promote member input and participation. In groups that do not use the GDSS in this way, the benefits are not as likely to materialize.

A second, more common, use of groupware is to support workgroups in carrying out both short and long-term projects. A number of systems, including Lotus Notes and Microsoft Exchange, have been developed for this purpose. These systems combine features from office automation, electronic workflow linkage, and computer conferencing systems into a bundle of tools for a group; these tools can be used by groups working in the same office or building or by geographically dispersed groups. A typical workgroup support system, such as

FIGURE 6–1
Small Decision Room with Group Decision Support system

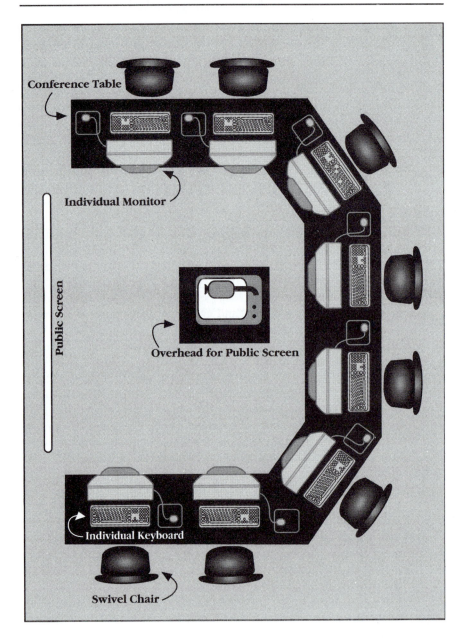

FIGURE 6–2

An Example of a Threaded Discussion from a Workgroup Support System.

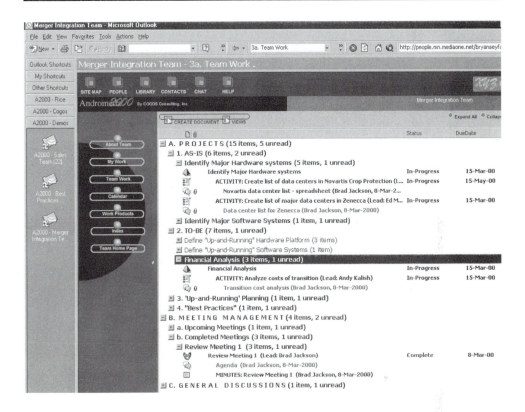

This is an example of a team work space in a groupware application called Andromeda (© Cogos, Inc.). This is a team at Cogos, Inc. whose members are in four different places, Boston, MA, Houston, TX, rural Pennsylvania, and Minneapolis, MN. there are two major topics in this space, Projects and Meeting Management. The entries under "Projects" refer to various companies that this team is working with. The entries under "Meeting Management" refer to virtual meetings the team will conduct on-line.

The Projects are divided into two types, "As-Is" and "To-Be", which reflect special meanings for this team's members. Under As-Is there are two major topics of discussion, which refer to actions the team is taking. "Identify Major Hardware Systems" has under it five comments. A comment is indented if it is a response to a previous comment. So "Activity: Create a list of data centes in Novartis Crop Protection. . . " is a response to the topic "Identify Major Hardware Systems". Items are labeled according to whether they are simply comments (which have no prefix) or refer to activities (which have the "Activity" prefix to the comment). To read a comment a team member would simply click on the heading and it would come up in his or her screen with options to reply, vote, etc.

This type of software also enables members to remind each other when an activity is due, update each other as to whether it has been done, enter items in a library, monitor other teams' work, and many other activities.

Lotus Notes, includes document management, scheduling features, email notification, and computer discussion groups. The discussion groups are similar to computer conferences in that they contain discussion threads, which are lines of discussion on a single topic arranged in statement-response format. Figure 6–2 contains an example of threaded discussions organized by topic. Under each topic a response to a statement is indented to indicate what it is addressed to. Discussion topics can vary widely, from a general discussion of policies to specific updates on a particular task. Other features that may be incorporated into a workgroup support system include audio- or videoconferencing over the Internet, project-management tools that keep a diagram of the project and monitor progress, and libraries to store commonly used documents. In addition, organizations may program their own specific applications into the system; an accounting firm, for example, may want to have its software connect with the workgroup system. At present, the most widely used workgroup softwares are Lotus Notes and Microsoft Exchange, which require organizations to buy and support specialized software. However, in the past year, several workgroup systems that can be used through Internet browsers have been developed.

Teams that use workgroup support systems typically have to change their mode of operation, because the systems require members to diligently check in and enter their own work and documents.[27] These systems generally encourage groups to be more structured in how they work and make decisions, because the group has to "think out loud" about how it is going to proceed as it decides how to break up its work into tasks and decides on discussion topics. While groups initially try to use their own typical procedures in the system, over time, their style of working adapts to the system itself. For example, a team that typically did not get feedback from all members on an idea would be likely to develop a norm favoring more input and feedback if it faithfully used the discussion features of a workgroup system.

While the most direct application of workgroup support systems is for the groups themselves, the systems can also be used to link teams and people across entire organizations. Teams can be given access to each other's discussions and timelines, and discussion groups that anyone interested may join can also be set up. For example, a major oil company used Lotus Notes to set up project support for over 30 teams and gave members of other teams limited access to most of these "team spaces." This enabled members of related teams to find out what other teams were doing, helped coordinate work between teams, and enabled teams to learn from each other. In addition, general discussion groups were initiated on various topics, including general interest topics, such as Movies and the company's Charitable Projects, and specific topics, such as Microsoft Office and Techniques for 3-Dimensional Analysis of Oil Deposits. These general discussion groups enabled people from all over the organization to get to know one another and share ideas; they also built organizational cohesiveness. A few executives complained that these general discussion groups wasted company time, because they were not related to specific project support. However, the Chief Information Officer argued for and succeeded in preserving the discussion groups on the grounds that they encouraged employees who otherwise might be unwilling to learn the new technology to try it out and generally led to a more connected organization.

Workgroup support systems are used by about 10 million people, according to the combined estimates of sales by Lotus and Microsoft. The actual number of users is probably a good deal smaller, however, because in most cases a number of team members either do not learn the software (which is difficult and confusing at first) or are low-level participators. These types of members are more common in teams located in the same facility than in teams dispersed over several different locations, because the co-located teams also have the option of meeting face to face. The browser-based systems, which are expected to be the future of groupware, are more likely to have larger proportions of members actually using them, because they are more familiar to people already using the Internet.

Using ICTs as Integrating Mechanisms   ICTs offer an additional; set of methods for integrating organizations that supplement and expand the integrating mechanisms discussed in Chapter 5. As described in chapter 5, one consideration in choosing ICTs as integration mechanisms is the ratio of benefits to cost. The benefits and capabilities, as well as some of the costs of ICTs, have been discussed in earlier sections. What has not been mentioned are the budgetary costs involved, which can be considerable. These costs include not only the purchase price of technologies, but also the expense of implementing them and integrating them with existing systems. A company that installs videoconferencing, for example, has to work out how this technology will operate with existing computers and telecommunications systems. This is not a trivial question, and getting new technologies to work together is often a matter of months or years. So the cost of using ICTs to integrate an organization depends on whether the organization already has the appropriate technological infrastructure; for example electronic mail requires the organization to have networked computers and support staff. If the expense of infrastructure is counted, then ICTs are very low-cost coordination mechanisms.

Another factor to consider in choosing between ICTs and the more traditional; integration is *geographical dispersion*. Organizations whose members are highly independent yet spread around a number of locations must utilize one of the electronic forms of integration. Before the advent of electronic modes of linking, organizations either had to situate employees working on highly independent tasks in the same place or allow for delays due to the time taken to manage interdependence via letter, memo, or phone. However, electronic linkages are so fast, reliable, and provide such rich interaction that organizations can now plan to have work dispersed to the locations where it can be done most effectively and integrate via electronic communication. For example, a sales team working with a firm purchasing industrial equipment can work directly with engineers back at the home office to determine if alterations desired by customers are feasible and to price the changes. Where this may have taken a week or more in the "old days," electronic linkages make it fast and relatively easy.

The fit of ICTs with organizational culture should also be considered. In some more traditional cultures, members may be uncomfortable with email, because it does not involve face-to-face, or at least verbal, contact. However, in a culture that stresses innovation, ICTs may be readily adopted, because they show that members are using the newest communication technologies available.

CASE STUDY:
WORKING IN THE VIRTUAL FUTURE: AN OPTIMISTIC VIEW

As her train picked up speed on its trip from Philadelphia to Boston, Tara Rodgers linked her personal digital assistant to the onboard computer linked into the armrest of her seat. Tara was on her way to Boston to facilitate a meeting for a scientific team that Worldwide Consulting Group was organizing for InuitAid International. InuitAid International (IAI) was a network organization of social service and health agencies that was being developed to address a health crisis among the Inuit peoples of Northern Canada. For the past three years, starting in 2008, Inuit children and elders had been contracting respiratory infections at 3 times the rate of 2007. Deaths in both groups had increased sharply, and a number of Native American tribes and organizations had urged the governments of Canada and the United States and the United Nations for help with this crisis.

Tara had a degree in communication, with a specialization in intercultural and group communication, and seven years experience working with international scientific teams. She had started with a major accounting firm, but soon left to set up her own private agency with two of her colleagues. They had begun working with medical research teams in Boston and later along the East Coast. They developed expertise in helping teams whose members worked in several locations develop virtual organizations. Tara specialized in teamwork and facilitation and her other two partners were experts in contract law and information technology, respectively. The partners learned from each other and each pitched in to help with all sides of the business, but having these three deep specialties enabled the partners to cover most of the important aspects of scientific collaboration. Tara's firm affiliated with Worldwide's group of consulting agencies three years ago and had worked on several contracts for Worldwide. Tara and her colleagues liked having their own independent firm, because it gave them flexibility to work on projects they believed in, like this one. Being one of Worldwide's affiliated partners had brought them a good deal of business, plus some wonderful opportunities like this one.

Tara's immediate job was to facilitate the organizing meetings of the diagnostic group of the IAI. She envisioned that the first set of meetings for this group would take about two months. Following this, Tara (and her associates if they were needed) would continue to work with the IAI to facilitate meetings, assist with problems and help manage conflicts and help to keep project teams were on schedule for the remainder of the project.

The IAI had been quickly assembled by Posi Sistrunk, the broker from the UN Agency for International Relief. She succeeded in getting commitments from

(continued)

(continued from the previous page)

the Centers for Disease Control, the UN Health Service, the Canadian Health System and the Novosibirsk Hospital in Russia. The Centers for Disease Control brought expertise in tracking down the causes of outbreaks of disease or mortality; the UN Health Service had years of experience in delivering care in rugged terrain; the Canadian Health System had first documented the problem and would be in the front line of care provision. The Novosibirsk Hospital had dealt with a similar incident among native peoples in Siberia four years before. In that case the cause had been found to be heavy metals from industrial sites in southern Siberia. Two major drug companies had agreed to provide medicines for the network, if any were needed. As with all network organizations, it was important that all partners commit themselves fully and develop good working relationships and clear ground rules from the beginning.

Using the onboard computer, which had a brighter and larger display screen than her personal digital assistant, Tara downloaded her email and found she had received biographies of the seventeen people who would attend the workshop. This was a diverse group, and Tara knew that their different nationalities and scientific backgrounds would make coordinating this group a challenge. From hard-won experience, Tara knew that it was particularly important that everyone agree on definitions of key concepts, such as quality control. Scientists from different disciplines often assumed that others assigned the same meanings that they did to terms. As a result, needless disputes could arise; one scientist might disagree with another's quality assessment, for example, because the two had different definitions of the type of data needed to measure quality. Tara knew that it was important to spend several meetings agreeing on definitions and standards, even though the scientists might grumble that all they were doing was agreeing on words.

Tara knew three of the scientists well, and had heard of several others. She patched through a video call to Stanley Marsh, an epidemiologist with another firm in Worldwide's network who knew most of the scientists. After inquiring about each others' families, Tara and Stanley discussed the members of the group. Tara realized that Stanley was getting more and more interested in the project, so she asked him if he'd like to come on board as cofacilitator; his scientific expertise and evident trust in Tara would give extra weight to Tara's attempts to guide this group. Following this, Tara put in a video call to Scientific Associates International, a nonprofit group dedicated to promoting scientific cooperation among nations, and downloaded case studies of effective scientific health teams and statistics on how long start-up periods for multidisciplinary scientific groups typically were. These would help her make her case for a slow but thorough start-up period for IAI.

In Boston Tara walked from the train station to Worldwide's telecommunications station. Participants would be linked into a virtual meeting tomorrow, and Tara wanted to familiarize herself with the meeting room. On one side of the room was a video screen that could hold full pictures of up to eighteen separate

(continued)

(continued from the previous page)

meeting sites; the three dimensional holographic technology made them seem as though they were just different parts of the same room. She knew that not all sites had this technology; the Russians in particular, had only two-dimensional videoconferencing walls with a capacity for four meeting sites. So she knew she would have to make sure to indicate carefully who wanted to be recognized to speak in the meeting so that the Russians could switch to that site if it was not up on their screen already. Tara also spent some time setting up the conferencing software that would link the group's work over the next year. It allowed textual and data transfer, on-line data analysis, and video links for impromptu meetings of a few of the scientists in the network. This conference environment would be the team's virtual home for the next year. Finally Tara arranged for a direct video interview of several Inuit leaders. She planned to lead off the meeting with this to highlight the plight of the Inuit, thus providing a common ground for fast, cooperative action in IAI.

Tara walked out the Worldwide a happy woman, looking forward to the meeting tomorrow. Sure, there would be some problems and unpleasant arguments, but she looked forward to tackling them. Making IAI work was a challenge, but it would help so many people.

Applying What You've Learned

1. What aspects of the virtual organization (see below) does Worldwide display?
2. IAI will bring together people from very different organizations, each of which will have a different organizational culture. What might Tara do to help these cultures work together? (Hint: Look back to the discussion in Chapter 3 on teamwork.)

Questions to Think About and Discuss

1. Are all virtual organizations also network organizations (see Chapter 5)? Are all network organizations also virtual organizations?
2. What might be the downside of working in this organization for Tara? Can you identify any problems she might face or stresses she might experience?

Choosing among Communication Modes: A Key Skill in the New Organization

To this point the discussion has made it clear that members of organizations now have many more options for communicating with one another than they previously did.[28] These options include face-to-face conversation, a face-to-face meeting, a speech to a large assembly, memos (handwritten and typed), formal reports and documents (similar to essays in form), telephone, fax, email, audio-conference, videoconference, and computer conference. How should we decide which mode to employ?

Trevino, Lengel, and Daft developed a framework for media choice based on the relative *richness* of the media.[29] Media richness depends on the number of cues the medium can carry, the timeliness of feedback via the medium, the variety of language that can be used in the medium, and the degree to which the medium allows the message to be personalized. A highly rich medium would carry many cues, and allow immediate feedback, a wide variety of languages, and a high degree of personalization of messages. Less rich media are deficient in one or more of these respects. Based on this definition, media can be ranked according to richness. The richest medium is face-to-face conversation, because it allows people to exchange a wide range of vocal, nonverbal, and verbal cues. Telephones screen out nonverbal cues and thus are less rich than face-to-face conversation. Email also screens out vocal cues. Personal written messages are even less rich than phone calls, and written messages sent to a number of people are the leanest medium of all.

Simple, routine messages such as requests for information (lunch at Fred's at 1:15?) can be communicated in either rich or lean media, and complex messages or sensitive processes, such as negotiating or managing disagreements and conflicts, need to be done face to face.[30] If the parties are unfamiliar with electronic media, people should use richer media than they would with people who are experienced and comfortable with the new technology. Of course, this assumes that the communicator wants to be understood as fully as possible. Employees who wish to be purposefully ambiguous may want to choose leaner media.[31] But, *in general,* when communicators want immediate feedback, need to monitor emotional responses or determine how a message influences their interpersonal relationships with the other person, or are communicating equivocal or ambiguous information, they should rely on rich media.[32]

However, media richness theory fails to take into account the ways in which organizational situations guide and constrain choices of communicative media. Like everything else, perceptions of what are appropriate media for different kinds of messages and different communication processes are socially constructed. Employees learn the accepted assumptions of their cultures or subcultures about media use the same way that they learn other assumptions—indirectly, by observing what other people do, and directly, through conversations with others, particularly those in their immediate groups.[33] After an advertising account representative lost an important account because the representative was offended by the brevity and impersonality of an email message, all the executives started using the telephone or face-to-face meetings with their clients. An engineer asked his associates how to deliver bad news to the manager of another division of the organization. One colleague advised using lean media for this message, another recommended using a written memo sent through the normal chain of command to signal respect for the other division, and still another told a story about what happened the last time an engineer communicated with the other division via a memo. Together, the engineers established a set of their own "rules" for choosing appropriate media. Although considerations such as the inherent richness of a medium are important, those considerations must be interpreted within the cultural context of the organization.

A final consideration is raised by Sitkin, Sutcliffe, and Barrios-Choplin: One should also consider the symbolic impact of media choice.[34] They note that immediate goals and norms are not the only influences on communicators' media choices. Instead, communicators also consider the *symbol-carrying capacity* of the medium. Symbol-carrying capacity manifests itself in at least two ways. First, media vary in their ability to transmit the core values of the organization. For example, an organization that values efficiency will find email, which can deliver a message almost instantaneously, a better device for signaling this value than snail mail: regular postal delivery that could take several days for the same message. Symbol-carrying capacity is also evident in the symbolic value that the medium itself comes to hold. During World War II, parents of a soldier serving at the front shuddered when they saw the Western Union delivery person, because the news of deaths was announced in telegrams; telegrams came to symbolize death and mourning. For many of today's communicators, using email symbolizes being technologically savvy and innovative; whereas sending the same message in a handwritten note indicates backwardness. Because the form of a message is often as important as its content, symbol-carrying capacity is an important criterion to consider in choosing a medium. Of course, organizational cultures and coworker attitudes also shape what a medium symbolizes. Symbol-carrying capacity may vary a great deal from organization to organization.

Together, richness, cultural norms, and symbol-carrying capacity provide a useful set of criteria to guide media choice. As was the case for the contingency-design variables, which were described at the beginning of this chapter, the only problem arises when the recommendations made by different criteria conflict with each other. Probably the most basic criteria is the organization's culture. There are indications that it shapes both perceptions of richness and symbol-carrying capacity.

IMPLEMENTING ICTs IN ORGANIZATIONS

Installing an ICT in an organization and getting its members to use it is not a simple process. Members of organizations do not all take to an innovation with the same degree of enthusiasm and willingness to experiment. Studies of successful innovations indicate that in any large group of people about one sixth are innovators who seek out innovations willingly and embrace them; about one third are early adopters, willing to try something out soon after they see its benefits for the innovators; another third are late adopters, who are more skeptical and take up the innovation only after a large number of people adopt, and the remaining sixth are laggards and nonadopters (see Figure 6-3).[35] So ICTs can take a while to spread through an organization, if they are adopted at all. (A number of innovations simply fail.) Research suggests that social influence from work groups and peers is critical in persuading people to adopt or reject ICTs.[36] Another factor, **critical mass,** also plays a role in the adoption and use of ICTs.

FIGURE 6–3

The Innovation Adoption Cure, with the Point of Critical Mass Indicated

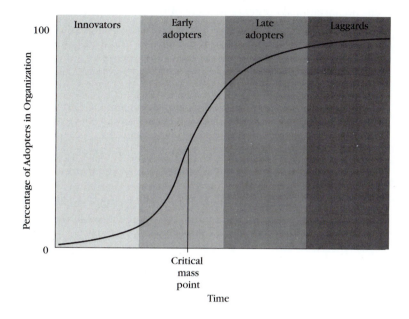

A critical mass refers to the point at which there are enough initial users to make the ICT useful and attractive to organizational members. For example, there is not much incentive for members to use email if few others are use it; however, when there are a large number of email users, it becomes an easy way to communicate with them, and there is more incentive to adopt. As Figure 6-3 indicates the critical mass is the point at which the adoption curve takes off as users are rapidly added to the system. The adoption of other ICTs, such as video-conferencing, the Internet, and instant messages is also stimulated by achieving a critical mass of users.

The tendency is to regard technologies as more or less objectively there. However, though the computer or the interface to our email system or a video-conference system seem hard and real to us, technologies are socially defined. Their use comes from the meanings and norms organizations and groups develop for them. For example, email may be seen by one group as too cold to use for personal messages, a business-only medium. Another group may see email as a great way to cultivate contacts, an ideal personal medium. Still another group may see email as backward, because it does not provide the support for teams that groupware does. Which picture of email is the true one? It depends on the group one is in. Rice and Gattiker comment, "[ICTs] are inherently ambiguous (because they can be interpreted in multiple and possibly conflicting ways), can rarely be fully understood and continue to be adapted, reinvented, and redesigned."[37]

A term in the last quotation requires further explanation. **Reinvention** refers to the changes a technology undergoes in the hands of its users. The same technology can be reinvented in very different ways as it is put to use in different organizational contexts. A study of the implementation of word processing in the insurance industry by Johnson and Rice revealed several different versions of word processing, depending on how the organizations reinvented it.[38] In some organizations, word processing was regarded as a fancy typewriter, and was used to replicate and automate typewriting. These firms tended to create typing pools in which word processors were used in a factory-like way to turn out documents brought in by different departments. Other organizations realized the potential of the word processor as a system for office automation. They used it not only for typing, but for filing, classifying, and moving documents around. In these firms, typists were upgraded to office professionals who handled many additional aspects of work. Both types of organizations reinvented word processing by developing their own interpretations of what the technology was and could do. This reinvention was accomplished as the organizations made sense of the technology and considered how it matched with current structures and cultures in the organization.

CASE STUDY:
TECHNOLOGY AND ORGANIZATIONAL CHANGE

After examining virtually every published case study of introducing new communication technologies into organizations (and surveying their own consulting experiences), Noshir Contractor and Eric Eisenberg* created a hypothetical typical case that explains the complexities of this kind of organizational change process.

The Chief Executive Officer (CEO) of a manufacturing company returned from a convention having been convinced that his firm needed a voice mail system, although this technology was rare in his city or industry. He had learned that voice mail was a prompt, personal, and accurate way for people (like himself) who were often away from their offices to keep in touch. At first the system was installed only for upper management, but it was an immediate success. Everyone used this tool that had been blessed by their boss, and everyone reported that the CEO had again come up with a brilliant idea. The CEO then announced that the system would be added throughout the company, because it was so personal, fast, and accurate. These attributes quickly became the criteria that the employees would use to evaluate the new system.

As expected, many employees quickly started to use the system. Salespersons found that it was a wonderful way to keep from feeling so isolated when

(continued)

(continued from the previous page)

they were away. Assembly line workers also used it, but not in the way the CEO anticipated. Instead of using it to keep in touch with their supervisors, they used it as a way to avoid talking to them face to face. Their primary use was to make contact with workers on other shifts. The engineers and accountants also surprised the CEO by resisting the new system. Engineers refused to use a system that precluded the use of visual aids (try sometime to describe the inside of your telephone to someone over the telephone); accountants were unable to adapt their usual ways of communicating numbers and texts to the new medium.

As a result, the sales department improved its contacts with upper management; while the relationships between upper management and the accounting and engineering divisions deteriorated. After noticing that their political standing in the organization was declining, the accountants started a campaign to discredit the system. They argued that the system was much more expensive than it had been projected to be and claimed that people had been passing private messages on to upper management. For both reasons, people reduced their use of the system, and management responded by restricting access to the system. Engineering reacted to their isolation by proposing that the organization purchase more technology—a LAN (local area network) system that would allow the transmission of both audio and visual information. Upper management, which was still enamored with the new technology, approved the purchase; this allowed engineering to again have direct access to them and led to additional changes in the way the various groups communicated with one another.

Applying What You've Learned

1. Is this case consistent with the concepts discussed in the section on Implementing ICTs?
2. Rice and Gattiker argued that ICTs are ambiguous. What does this mean? How does this ambiguity show up in the case and how did it affect the implementation of voice mail?

Questions to Think About and Discuss

1. Could the CEO have anticipated all of the different uses that the employees made of the voice mail system? Would the organization have benefited from the CEO's being able to anticipate these uses?
2. What effects did the installation of these systems have on the role that middle managers (the supervisors of the various divisions) played in the organization? Were they more important before or after the installation of the system?

*See "Communication Networks and New Media in Organizations," in *Organizations and Communication Technology* (Newbury Park, CA: Sage, 1991).

IMPACTS OF ICTS

ICTs have had far-reaching impacts in organizations, as Chapters 2 through 5 indicate. We will distinguish impacts on organizations themselves from impacts on their members and their work lives.

Impacts on Organizations

Decentralization, Empowerment, Participation   The advent of computing in organizations immediately raised the question of whether it would decentralize organizations (recall Chapter 3). Some scholars argued that computers would empower lower-level members of organizations, because computers could provide previously unavailable information and guidance about decision-making processes. Other scholars believed that the opposite tendency toward centralization of power would occur, because computerized MISs would enable top management to monitor and control employees.

A number of studies of the effects of computerization on organizational structure were conducted and they yielded decidedly mixed results. In some cases, organizations decentralized in response to the implementation of computer systems; in other cases they centralized. Careful reviews of the literature concluded that computers had no deterministic effects on organizational structure. Instead computers tended to enhance whatever culture and tendencies presently existed in the organization. In organizations that tended toward centralization, the introduction of computers led to increased centralization; in organizations that tended toward decentralization and empowerment, the introduction of computers increased empowerment and decentralization.[39]

Studies of participation indicate that ICTs typically increase it. As noted previously, the introduction of email tends to increase the range of ideas circulating in organizations and also brings groups that previously did not communicate into contact. Groups using GDSS have more equal interaction patterns and report greater equality than face-to-face groups.[40] Whether this participation actually translates into empowerment is an open question, because being able to participate does not mean that members have influence in the organization.[41]

Virtual Organizations   A virtual organization is one that has no physical existence.[42] It has no building, no campus, no office. Instead it exists across a computer network. Some dynamic networks are virtual organizations, but other types of organizations are as well. Many catalog companies' sales divisions are virtual organizations, with independent individual sales agents operating out of their homes. The catalog companies link them via high-speed computer lines to a central database that handles order delivery and other functions. Compaq Computer Corporation moved its sales force into home offices and reported a 50 percent reduction in sales expenses as a result.

The California flower company Calyx & Corolla, described as a network organization in Chapter 5, is also a good example of a virtual organization. The organization is really a virtual network composed of a negotiated agreement between three organizations. Calyx & Corolla mails catalogs showing flower arrangements to potential customers and takes orders using an eight hundred number and an order center located in a suburb of San Francisco. The orders are then forwarded via computer network or fax to flower growers who have also agreed to package the flowers in arrangements prior to shipping them. Calyx & Corolla has negotiated an agreement with Federal Express to pick up and deliver the arrangements the next morning to any place in the continental United States. Orders are tracked and monitored via a computer system that also handles accounting and distribution of payments to the various components of the organization. Calyx & Corolla itself is relatively small; but the virtual organization it has put together is much larger, and is comprised of the growers and Federal Express. Consumers cannot differentiate the different organizations that make up Calyx & Corolla; from the point of view of the customer, Calyx & Corolla looks like a traditional florist who delivers.

One characteristic of virtual organizations is that to outsiders they appear to be like older self-contained organizations. They deliver the same or better product or service with the same or better efficiency. Information technology and telecommunications enable these dispersed organizations to coordinate their activities and maintain coherent work processes. Each part of the virtual organization is able to focus on its particular function, resulting in competent and even excellent performance. By staying small, the component organizations keep their costs for management and overhead down, enhancing efficiency. Smallness also makes communication easier within the components, opening them up for fast development and testing of new ideas.

Like the network organization, the virtual organization requires the development of trust among members. However, unlike the dynamic network, in many virtual organizations trust is often cultivated by forming long-term relationships among component organizations. Kingston Technology, one of the most successful firms in Silicon Valley, has only 220 employees, with the rest of the organization spread out over a network of subcontractors.[43] However, rather than hiring subcontractors on a temporary basis, Kingston maintains long-term, solid ties with its partner companies. Kingston designs systems that speed up PCs and data transfer. These are assembled by Express Manufacturing, which works closely with Kingston, and then they are shipped by Federal Express. When Kingston needed more manufacturing capacity, Express Manufacturing built more because it knew it could depend on the business from Kingston. While Express has other customers, Kingston always comes first. When Kingston needed more advertising material shipped, it worked with its printer to expand that business, again guaranteeing work. As the companies work together and develop stronger and stronger communication ties, trust grows. Kingston often does business without contracts and pays ahead of time on its orders so its small affiliates will have the money to do their work. It also maintains open books, so that all its employees maintain trust in management. Kingston has built a virtual organization by building a family of firms and a family of its own employees. It has developed an enduring culture that spans a number of companies.

Impacts On Life and Work in Organizations

Different Ways to Use ICTs: Automating Versus Informating   Distributed computing may also contribute to significant shifts in the nature of work. Once applications are in the office or on the work floor, employees can begin to master computers themselves. They can use the computers to analyze their work and improve it. Shoshanna Zuboff argued that the preferred strategy for organizations is not simply to use computers to *automate* work and replace employees with machines.[44] Instead she advocated using information technology to *informate* work, to enable workers to learn which processes are effective and which are not. Informating is possible because computers—properly programmed and utilized—can generate information on how the work is done and the output associated with different configurations of steps or methods. This makes workers smarter about their work and also better able to suggest and make improvements. As the following case on the Electronic Sweatshop illustrates, computers are sometimes used in a very different way, to deskill employees and turn them into servants of the machine.

For informating to succeed, those at the top of the organization must be willing to share power with those lower down. Those at lower levels must feel some control over their work and some power to make changes before they are willing to take the initiative to change how they work based on the new information. While management often initiates the empowerment of workers, distributed technologies themselves may also shift the balance of power downward. Enhanced communication via email and other telecommunications facilities make it possible for lower-level employees to form coalitions and share information that increases their power in the organization. For example, a number of years ago, the email system in IBM, V-Net, also became known as "Gripe-Net," because lower-lever employees used its open architecture to engage in discussions about problematic managers and management practices; this consciousness raising can be the beginning of resistance at lower levels.[45]

CASE STUDY:
SCENES FROM THE ELECTRONIC SWEATSHOP

Barbara Garson, playwright and investigative journalist, investigated how computers were transforming office work. Her book *The Electronic Sweatshop* documented how some organizations were using computers to deskill work and render people redundant by some organizations.* Here are two vignettes based on her book that illustrate the dark side of ICTs:

Until the late 1970s, *airline reservation agents* were valued, long-term employees of the major airline companies. They had to learn and remember the

(continued)

(continued from the previous page)

companies' fares, routes, and policies and apply this knowledge to solve problems for customers on an individualized basis. This made them highly skilled employees who were difficult to replace. Some made as much as $15 per hour in the early 1980s, good money at that time.

However, once computerized reservation systems were developed, companies attempted to redefine the work of the reservation agent. Much of the problem-solving was built into the system: the agent simply had to type in the place of departure and destination and the computer listed the available times and seats. There was, however, still need for a human in the loop, because each customer's circumstances was so different that adjustments had to be made.

However, while the airlines still had to have people on line, they wanted to regulate their behavior as much as possible to maintain strict cost and quality control. Based on studies of the work process involved in making a booking, conversations between agent and customer were broken into typical segments, with recommended scripts and prompts assigned to each. For example, if a customer called up knowing what he or she wanted, agents were instructed in ways to get the reservation down as quickly as possible, so they could go on to the next customer. In cases in which customers were fare shopping, agents were taught ways to probe for a sale; for instance one strategy was to tell the customer that there were limited seats at the low fare and that the seat could be held for 24 hours at no cost, which insured that many customers would call back and offer another opportunity to close the deal. Agents were also told never to ask yes or no questions such as "Would you like to book?"; instead they were to ask "Would you like the 10 AM or the 2 PM?" All transactions between agents and customers were tightly scripted. Supervisors listened in without the agent's knowledge and graded them on how well they kept to the script and efficiently booked passengers. Too much small talk or empathy could get the agent a lower grade. The companies also set performance targets: in the company Garson studied, agents were supposed to make a sale during 26 percent of their calls.

Time on and off line was carefully monitored by the computer system as well: AHU ("after hang up") time, the time between calls, was supposed to be 14 seconds on average, if the agent wanted a raise. To keep one's job and get raises, the agent had to be available, plugged in, 98 percent of the time for bookings.

For this, the new agents were paid $5.77 an hour.

The Automated Social Worker

When New York State installed a computer system to keep track of its welfare system, it took a job that it would seem is impossible to automate and turned it into a series of steps. Most social workers take up the profession, because they want to help people. They are taught in school that every person is an individual and that it is important to take each individual's needs into account to help them. People attracted to this field typically enjoy working with others

(continued)

(continued from the previous page)

and hope to make a difference in people's lives. However, the computerization of work in New York did not take this approach.

Job analysis divided the social worker's tasks into units and assigned a time value to each. For example, making a food stamp change counted .5, authorizing funeral and burial expenses counted .7, and replacing a lost or stolen welfare check counted .4, where the numbers stood for tenths of an hour. As a worker does each of these tasks, they are toted up to give a figure for hours of work done. Once a worker reaches his or her allotted 160 hours (actually the target is about 120 hours per month, because 40 hours are required for staff meetings, maintaining work records, and other activities), he or she is done for the month. An experienced worker can do most of these tasks in much less time than the official time figure, so they can get credit for 160 hours with much less work.

So do the workers stop working when their credits reach their limit? Although we have not provided a full list of tasks here, suffice it to say that activities such as making exceptions for clients, trying to help them with their special problems when the help goes outside procedures, and providing sympathy are not among the officially-sanctioned list of tasks. The tasks list refers only to bureaucratic operations involved in registering parties for welfare and delivering their services, not to the human side of welfare. Garson found that the social workers spent the time they had left after satisfying their hourly credits on these other activities—coaching clients in how to get the best benefits, giving them sympathy and support, working around the system—and also in helping and counseling each other. The social workers made the system human by "gaming" the system.

Sadly, social workers who really try to help clients within the system often receive poor performance evaluations. If they diligently carry out their work, it takes more time than is allotted in the work analysis. One social worker commented,

> Now if you is a person with a problem, you don't want to just tell it to everyone. You want to feel it out first. 'This [social] worker, does she have some sensitivity to my problem? Can she hear me?' But I can't hear her. I can't listen to her. I'm just trying to get my points. The whole system is survival. And she goes away feeling as bad or worse than when she came down here. . . .[S]ome people come here, they are at the end of their rope. They think, 'You is a social worker. That's something. Maybe you can help me.' And they start telling me about a child that is getting out of hand, starting to drink, not coming home. . ."

This woman was a dedicated social service employee, who wanted to do the best she could for her clients. But engaging a client in this way was not efficient and did not earn her the points she needed to make her hours. She had been "written up for Corrective Action" three times in the previous four months. Garson concluded, "The fact is that Jo Martin is not an efficient [social worker]. But a human service department that's organized so it can't use her true skills is profoundly inefficient."

(continued)

(continued from the previous page)

The system used to organize social workers was very similar to the scientific management systems set up to control work under the traditional strategy of organizing. However, unlike the studies of physical labor conducted by management scientists, New York's studies made a profound error. Sympathy for the client and advocacy for his or her needs are an important part of the social worker's job that were simply omitted from the analysis; the system captured all the physical motions of being a social worker, but ignored the spirit of the profession. This may have been inevitable in a system that was intended to enable computerization of social work. Behaviors that could be counted were emphasized because number-crunching is what the computers at that time did best.

A good deal of the social worker's time was spent filling out papers that documented all the papers they filled out for clients, so that their work records could be entered into the computerized system. The next step was to set up the system so social workers could enter their activity records into networked computers themselves. As the system developed further, the workers would enter in data about their clients directly, and the system would guide the social worker through the steps of authorizing burial expenses and other activities. In theory this might eliminate the labor of filling in forms, freeing the social worker up to engage their clients. However, judging by how the system had been developed at the time of Garson's interview, it is doubtful that this was the direction it would take. Instead the social workers would simply have their case loads increased.

Ironically, the dedication of the workers to their clients kept this system going. Garson had the following conversation with one of the supervisors:

G: "What do you think of the time standards and point system?"

S: "I blame the union for the way it's operating."

G: "You mean because they're sabotaging it?"

S: "No, because they're *not* sabotaging it."

G: "What do you mean?"

S: "If they followed the rules the department issued them, this system would have collapsed in three months. . . .If I were a worker and a union activist, the first time I did 100 percent in the first three weeks of the month I'd stop work. And if they tried to make me do anything over 100 percent, I'd fill out an overtime form. The problem is that all the workers have developed systems of their own to get the points they need and still deliver timely service. That's what keeps this place going."

Applying What You've Learned

1. Are the airlines and the social work agency engaging automating or informating their work? (See the section below on Impacts of ICTs on work.)

(continued)

(continued from the previous page)

2. How do these organization apply the principles of the traditional bureaucracy in their systems? What are likely reactions of employees to the system controls?

Questions to Think About and Discuss

1. What are some of the benefits of the computerization of work discussed in these cases for the employees involved? For customers or clients?
2. Would you like to work in these jobs (assuming that pay was up to your standards?) Why or why not?
3. Do you agree with the supervisor's suggestion concerning how the social workers could shut down the system? What might management do if the social workers tightly conformed to rules?

---

*This case is based on Barbara Garson, *The Electronic Sweatshop: How Computers Are Transforming the Office of the Future into the Factory of the Past.* New York: Penguin.

Telework   **Telework** refers to a wide range of working arrangements in which employees work outside the traditional office and conduct a large portion of their work via computer or telecommunications linkages.[46] The nature of telework varies widely. Some teleworkers conduct all their business from home; the telephone salespersons for the catalog companies mentioned in the previous section are one example; but many other professional employees work out of their homes as well. Some employees telecommute only part time, working at home a few days a week or month, and going into a regular office the rest of the time. Another type of teleworker is the road warrior. The advent of reliable telecommunications makes it possible to coordinate complex work, such as sales of high ticket items with complex specifications, over fax and phone.[47] Many insurance firms have done away with central offices, assigning agents and underwriters to the field, where they work out of cars and hotel rooms via telecommunications and email. At AT&T, about 5 percent of the company's 373,000 employees do their work from cars or hotels. These road warriors save their companies millions in overhead each year. But they also complain of the lack of a feeling of belonging to their organizations and of the stress of living on the road many weeks a year. The number of teleworkers has been growing steadily from 4 million in 1990 to over 18 million in 1998.

Telework is feasible for any job that centers around paperwork and information processing. There are a number of incentives for telework. For organizations, the attraction stems from lower overhead since they don't have to maintain office buildings and, for the many teleworkers who work on a part-time basis, don't have to pay benefits. For the worker, advantages include closer contact with home and family (except for the road warrior), a more relaxed lifestyle away from the formality of the office, avoidance of office politics, and fewer long commutes. There are also advantages for the public, since less commuting means less expense for highways and other infrastructure and less automobile pollution. Evaluations of telework support its advantages. The majority of studies suggest that teleworkers are more productive and less costly than those based in the office.

There are several prerequisites for teleworking arrangements to succeed. First and foremost, the technological infrastructure must be developed. Often this means that high-speed transmission lines must be installed by the phone companies or other communication carriers. The organization must also purchase the proper technology (computers and high-speed modems) for processing and moving the information. Second, all involved must have developed "communication discipline," that is, they must be in the habit of using their email, groupware, and other communication technologies to stay in contact. These new media require users to develop new patterns of behavior based on different communication modes (usually written) than the verbal channels with which most people are accustomed. Managers must be able to trust that commands issued via communication technology will be followed; employees must learn to understand what managers mean over media such as email that do not offer the direct personal contact that often provides extra information and detail. A final prerequisite for effective telecommuting is that home workers must create a work environment in their homes. Provisions must be made so that family matters do not constantly intervene in work. Some employees take on considerable expenses in setting up and equipping home offices. Since some office equipment is too expensive to be installed in the homes of all workers, many companies have set up satellite offices where employees can come when they need office facilities. Satellite offices are also places where employees can work with information too sensitive to transmit over public media.

A major barrier to effective telework arrangements is the discomfort of managers who can no longer see what their employees are doing. Before they become accustomed to electronic media, many middle and upper managers are wary of supervising employees they cannot see. "Management by walking around" is premised on visual contact and face-to-face communication. Managers do not know what they will find, but walk around to see what is happening; in the process they see things that work and should be done more and problems that have to be addressed. Management is very different with teleworkers. The information technology provides ways to monitor work, but understanding and working with the information requires managers to learn new procedures and skills. Managers who do not have these, or who are uncomfortable with new technologies in general, are likely to perceive a loss of control due to telework.

Telework may also present some problems for the employee. The line between work and private or family time often blurs for teleworkers. Telework may be convenient in the sense that it gives the employee a more informal and flexible work environment; but it also makes it more convenient for others to reach the employee. Most teleworkers—and almost all road warriors—report that they work more hours. When work intrudes into the family space, there is nowhere for employees to escape work-related stress and get a break from the pressure. Teleworkers must exert considerable effort to keep their nonwork lives intact.

Despite these disadvantages, telework is here to stay. It is simply too attractive to both organizations and employees. Some futurists predict that telework will reverse the growth of cities and suburbs. If a travel agent can work as effectively from a farm 100 miles from Minneapolis as in the city, there is nothing to keep him or her in the city. A corporation that can locate satellite offices around the country in cheaper rural locales could be sorely tempted to vacate its high-priced suburban campus. It is possible that telework will encourage dispersion of the population and a general move away from the cities. The result may be further deterioration of cities and, eventually, suburbs, as those holding the highest paying jobs disperse more evenly around the country.

Surveillance, Privacy, and ICTs   As we noted in Chapter 2, ICTs offer an unprecedented opportunity for organizations to monitor their employees and control their behavior. For instance, it is possible for a secretarial supervisor to monitor every keystroke that employees take to make sure they are working up to standards. Some software sweeps through email to uncover messages counter to company policies or private use of email. Email systems often keep copies of erased messages, so there is no way for members to hide their activities, as Oliver North, President Reagan's aide who planned secret arms sales to the Iranians via email, discovered to his chagrin. Network software keeps records of all activity on the Internet from each computer station, enabling employers to discover when employees are surfing the net on company time. Chapter 2 discussed some of the negative effects of hidden surveillance on employees and the organizations.

These capabilities raise important ethical and policy questions. How far should organizations be able to go in monitoring employees? Some argue that if an organization provides the ICTs to employees they should be able to monitor and control everything that goes on in the system. The organization is not paying for personal facilities for its employees; they should use the system for work and nothing else. Further, if an employee engages in illegal or questionable behavior—sexual harassment of a coworker, fraudulent use of the Internet, lobbying a politician—the organization will be held liable, because it provided the means to the perpetrator. The other side of the argument holds that even in the workplace employees have some expectation of privacy. While it is true that the organization provides the ICT, personal use with reasonable bounds should be allowed, particularly since the company often expects employees to check their email or voicemail from home on their personal time and may request that employees work extra hours. Being able to take a few minutes to order Christmas gifts from the office is reasonable compensation for the organization's infringement on personal time and private life. The vast majority of employees do not engage in questionable activities using ICTs and they should not be penalized for the misdeeds of a few. Moreover, employees will always make some personal use of organizational resources; they make phone calls related to private matters and use the photocopier for their tax returns. Is there really any difference between this and some private use of the Internet? There is no clear resolution to this issue at present.

A recent study showed that an overwhelming proportion of employees report using the Internet for personal reasons.[48] This study indicated that costs to the organization of this behavior can be substantial. A company with 1000 Internet users who do personal Web surfing for one hour per day can lose more than $35 million in productivity costs each year. However, the study also indicated that the great majority of firms were not concerned about this type of cost, because they believed that increased morale among employees more than compensated for it. Most organizations in the survey indicated that they tolerate private use of the Internet as a perk for their employees. Over 80 percent of the firms surveyed indicated that they have a written Internet use policy to guide employees.

A second privacy-related problem concerns organizations' use of private information about customers and employees. The increasing integration of computer networks enables information from different databases to be linked and shared within and across organizations. Information about employees' health histories, for example, might be compiled and shared among companies. Since employees with health problems often result in higher insurance costs and more time missed from work, some organizations might use this information in their hiring decisions. There has long been a debate about the appropriateness and legality of compiling and using this type of information, and laws and standards have been proposed. This issue is clearly on the public's mind. Fear of having health problems included in a company database and ultimately disclosed has led some people to avoid seeking treatment for serious maladies or to seek private treatment that they pay for themselves.

Information about consumer preferences can also be captured by ICTs. A group of 70 electronic commerce companies, including IBM and First Union Corporation have been developing a data-sharing specification called Customer Profile Exchange.[49] This promises to enable companies to compile massive databases on customers and to comb through them to discover purchasing patterns, lifestyle information, and other information about customers. This possibility has raised concerns that the companies are overstepping the bounds of their customers' privacy. The chairman of the Senate Select Committee on Intelligence, Richard Shelby, has written to the Federal Trade Commission (FTC) regarding concerns for lack of privacy protection. It is unclear whether the FTC has legal authority to develop regulations for such efforts, and the debate continues. One part of the solution to this problem will come late in 2001, when Internet browsers incorporate Platform for Privacy Protection, a program allowing consumers to set privacy preferences in their Internet browsers. However, legal and policy issues still remain to be determined.

Knowledge Management   Networked ICTs have also promoted a move by large organizations and networked organizations to manage the knowledge that they develop and accumulate over years of operation.[50] Chapter 5 chronicled the development of the information society and the importance of knowledge and information work. As a result, one of an organization's greatest assets is the knowledge that its employees develop. Two kinds of knowledge can be distinguished. One important type of knowledge, *organizational knowledge,* consists of accumulated experience in an area, such as an extensive database of customers or experience with developing and operating a specialized product, for example computer-assisted inventory systems. A second type of knowledge is the expertise of employees. While this knowledge may seem to be solely the property of the employee, the organization has a stake in it as well, because it often pays for employee education and training and gives the employee a context in which to develop this knowledge. For example, an employee who develops expertise in Web-site design has done this using his or her talents and initiative; but the organization has supplied the computers and software and time for programming that enabled the employee to become an expert. Both organizational and employee-based knowledge have come to be regarded as assets that organizations can use to add value to their products and services, and organizations have attempted to develop knowledge-management processes to capitalize on these assets.

Knowledge management refers to the practices and procedures that organizations use to identify, catalog, harness, and utilize valuable knowledge. ICTs generally play an important part in knowledge management, because once an organization identifies key knowledge, it wishes to preserve it in a form that makes it easily available and manipulable. Knowledge-management systems can take a number of different forms. In some cases, organizations compile databases listing customers, problems that have occurred with products, and other organizational knowledge. Linking these together provides an elementary knowledge-management system. Expert systems that capture the expertise of a talented and successful employee can also be part of a knowledge-management system. Still other organizations actively solicit information and knowledge from employees, who enter it into a groupware system such as Lotus Notes. This, however, is quite time-consuming for employees and they are not always willing to comply fully with such requests. (Indeed, some are probably afraid that if they put everything they know into the system, they would be let go!) Noshir Contractor developed a system to identify knowledge networks that did not rely on cataloguing knowledge, but rather identified expertise among the members of an organization.[51] He used a two-part mapping strategy: The first part involves identifying networks of who-knows-what knowledge that is relevant to a project; the second step is to identify people "who know who knows what," that is individuals who are particularly knowledgeable about where expertise lies in the organization. If one could not locate a needed expert from the first map, one could use the second map to find someone likely to know someone else who had the knowledge you needed.

Knowledge management is in its infancy, and several problems must be solved before it can reach its full potential. As we have already mentioned, knowledge management requires cooperation of organizational members. In this time of overworked, overstretched workers, it may be difficult to obtain the needed inputs. Second, knowledge itself is often difficult to identify. Much knowledge exists in a form that can be expressed verbally and written down or stored in databases; just as much or more knowledge is tacit knowledge, know-how that cannot be put into words, but instead is in the hands of the experienced worker or the judgment of the manager or expert. Most organizational knowledge-management systems cannot capture this type of knowledge. It is possible that Contractor's approach is the best that can be done for tacit knowledge. Finally, some have doubted that effective knowledge management is even possible, given the fact that knowledge is a community property and changes constantly.

A Reflection on the Impacts of ICTs on Organizations and Their Members

If one thing is certain from the research on effects of ICTs, it is that there are no simple, clear-cut effects. The context in which the ICT is implemented—which include the organizational culture, the goals of the different parties involved in its implementation, the specific problems or opportunities the ICT is brought in to addresses, and social influence processes at workgroup and individual levels—all shape the impacts of the ICT on the organization and its members. To be sure, ICTs have certain potentials or tendencies that materialize in organizations, but they are just that—tendencies. This should also be a lesson to managers or planners. Technology is not a silver bullet that can be used to fix or reengineer the organization. Managers who assume it is will find that the bullet often hits different targets than those at which they aim.

CONCLUSION

ICTs have opened up a whole range of possibilities for organizations in the twenty-first century. The steady development of ICTs from stodgy mainframe computers of the 1960s to the dynamic, flexible network and wireless technologies of the 2000s have greatly enhanced organizations' ability to innovate and change. At this point it seems apparent that technology will continue to advance at a dizzying pace into the foreseeable future, so we should be ready for even more changes in work and organizations.

ICTs have promoted the emergence of new strategies for organizing, including the network form discussed in Chapter 5 and the virtual organization. These new forms are communication intensive and provide some features of control that the traditional strategy offered but have the flexibility, adaptability, and empowerment offered by the relational strategy. What is less clear is whether these forms can evolve coherent organizational cultures.

These technologies have also changed the way work is done. Telework, either on the road or from home, gives both organizations and employees more options. In addition, organizations are increasingly trying to harness their employees' knowledge. However, there are potential problems with both of these developments. Telework threatens to erode workers' private time even further. Knowledge management asks employees for something they have never had to provide before, their special knowledge and insights accumulated over the years. This represents a new extension of the organizational domain over the individual. Other contentious issues pertain to possible infringements on privacy and confidential information.

The impacts of implications of ICTs are not determined by the technology. They are worked out in human use of the technology, in the balance of organizational and individual forces that put the technology into action.

NOTES

[1] This opinion is expressed by Susan J. Winter and S. Lynne Taylor, who argue that new IT-supported organizational forms resemble those found in the pre-industrial era. See their article in *Information Systems Research, 7* (1996): 5–21.

[2] This section owes a debt to an excellent book by Raymond McLeod, Jr., *Management Information Systems,* 6th ed. The various types of information systems defined here are discussed in more detail by McLeod in Chs. 2, and pp. 12–21.

[3] McLeod, Chapter 13.

[4] McLeod, p. 19.

[5] The concept of decision support system was originated by G. Anthony Gorry and Michael S. Scott-Morton, "A Framework for Management Information Systems," *Sloan Management Review, 13* (Fall 1971): 55–70. In that article they define the various functions of decision support systems. An updated account can be found in McLeod, Ch. 14 and in David L. Olson and James F. Courtney, Jr. *Decision Support Models and Expert Systems* (Houston: Dame, 1998). Dozens of examples of decision support systems are described in the journal Interfaces.

[6] McLeod, p. 436.

[7] McLeod, p. 439

[8] Ron Rice, *New Communication Technologies* (Beverly Hills: Sage, 1984).

[9] Good descriptions of the development and state of voice mail and most other office technologies can be found in August Grant and Jennifer Harmon Meadows, eds., *Communication Technology Update VI* (Boston: Focal Press, 2000). This series of books gives readable, up-to-date descriptions of many communication technologies.

[10] Grant and Meadows, Update

[11] Grant and Meadows. See also, Bob Francis, "Tune in to Cheaper Videoconferencing", *Datamation, 39* (October 1, 1993): 48–51.

[12] The classic book about computer conferencing is by Starr Roxanne Hiltz and Murray Turoff, *The Network Nation: Human Communication via Computer* (Reading, MA: Addison-Wesley, 1978). Computer conferencing is also discussed in Ron Rice, The New Media; Robert Johansen, Jacques Vallee, and Kenneth Spangler, *Electronic Meetings: Technological Alternatives and Social Choices* (Reading, MA: Addison-Wesley, 1979); Elaine Kerr and Starr Roxanne Hiltz, *Computer-mediated Communication Systems* (New York: Academic Press, 1982).

[13] McLeod, p. 446.

[14] For an interesting account of facsimile (fax) development, see Jonathan Coopersmith, "Facsimile's False Starts," *IEEE Spectrum* (February, 1993): pp. 46–49. Rice, *The New Media*, discusses various uses of videotex; and McLeod, pp. 448–449 discusses imaging.

[15] McLeod, p. 453

[16] McLeod, Chapter 1.

[17] Bob Brewin, "Garment Maker Donning Wireless," *Computerworld,* September 11, 2000.

[18] Peter W.G. Keen, "Ready for 'new' B2B?," *Computerworld,* September 11, 2000.

[19] R. Johansen, *Teleconferencing and Beyond* (New York: McGraw-Hill, 1984).

[20] Ron Rice and Urs E. Gattiker, "New Media and Organizational Structuring," in *The New Handbook of Organizational Communication,* Frederic M. Jablin and Linda L. Putnam, eds. (Newbury Park: Sage, 2000).

[21] Sproull and Kiesler, *Connections;* Sara Kiesler, Jane Siegel, and Timothy W. McGuire, "Social Psychological Aspects of Computer-Mediated Communication," *American Psychologist, 39* (1984): 1123–1134.

[22] Sproull and Kiesler, op. cit.; Lee Sproull and Sara Kiesler "Reducing Social Context Cues," *Management Science, 32* (1986): 1492–1512; Tom Finholt and Lee Sproull, "Electronic Groups at Work," *Organization Science, 1* (1990): 41–64; Ron Rice, R. and G. Love "Electronic Emotion," *Communication Research, 14* (1987): 85–108; Joe B. Walther, "Interpersonal Effects in Computer-Mediated Interaction," *Communication Research, 19* (1992): 52–90.

[23] Joanne Yates and Wanda J. Orlikowski, "Genres of Organizational Communication," *The Academy of Management Review,* 17 (1992): 299–326. Also see Lee Sproull and Sara Kiesler, "Reducing Social Context Cues," *Management Science, 32* (1986): 1492–1512 and S. Rafaeli, *Electronic Message to Computer-Mediated Hotline* (Comserve Electronic Information Service, April 26, 1990); and Charles Steinfeld, "Computer-Mediated Communication in the Organization," in *Cases in Organizational Communication,* Beverly Sypher, ed. (New York: Guilford, 1991).

[24] R. Emmett, "Vnet or Gripenet," Datamation, 27 (1981): 48–58. This capacity sometimes can cause problems for new users of the systems. When Charley Conrad was first learning to use email he sent a relatively personal note to Ted Zorn (whose work is often cited in this book) congratulating him on his promotion to associate professor. He accidentally told his computer to send the message to everyone who is on the organizational communication network, which, of course, includes Charley. Conrad knows this because some kind people recognized what he had done and sent him instructions about how to keep from doing it again. He has never admitted his error to Ted, who may never know unless he reads this footnote.

[25] Lucas, T-Form, pp. 144–146.

[26] Gerry DeSanctis and Brent Gallupe, "A Foundation for the Study of Group Decision Support Systems," *Management Science, 33* (1987), 589–609; Brent Gallupe, Laura Bastianutti, and W.H. Cooper, "Unblocking Brainstorms," *Journal of Applied Psychology, 76* (1991), 137–142; Jay F. Nunamaker, Alan R. Dennis, Joe Valacich, Doug Vogel, and Joey George, "Electronic Meeting Systems to Support Group Work," *Communications of the ACM, 34* (1991): 40–61; V. Sambamurthy and Marshall Scott Poole, "The Effects of Variations in Capabilities of GDSS Designs on Management of Cognitive Conflict in Groups," *Information Systems Research, 3* (1993): 224–251; Janet Fulk and Lori Collins-Jarvis, "Wired Meetings: Technological Mediation of Organizational Gatherings," in Jablin and Putnam; Craig R. Scott, "Communication Technology and Group Communication" in Frey, Gouran, and Poole.

[27] Wanda J. Orlikowski, Joann Yates, K. Okamura, and M. Fujimoto, "Shaping Electronic Communication: The Metastructuring of Technology in the Context of Use," *Organization Science, 6:* 423–444.

[28] Excellent discussions of research on communication media choice can be found in Rice and Gattiker and Fulk and Collins-Jarvis.

[29] Linda Trevinio, Ralph Lengel, and Richard Daft, "Media Symbolism, Media Richness, and Media Choices in Organizations," *Communication Research, 14* (1987): 553–574.

[30] When messages are not complex, personal preferences seem to determine which media people use (Trevino, Daft, and Lengel). For example, people with high levels of oral communication anxiety seem to avoid face-to-face media unless the complexity of the message absolutely requires them to use it (Elmore Alexander, Larry Penley, and I. Edward Hernigan, "The Effect of Individual Differences on Managerial Media Choice," *Management Communication Quarterly, 5* [1991]: 155–173).

[31] Contractor and Eisenberg. There also is evidence that people quickly learn to manipulate the richness of a medium. Olgren and Parker found that employees who regularly use videoconferencing learn to control vocal and nonverbal cues, so that they put on a performance rather than communicate the substance of their ideas (Teleconferencing Technology and Applications, Dedham, MA: Artech House, 1983).

[32] Ron Rice, "Evaluating New Media Systems," in *Evaluating the New Information Technologies,* J. Johnstone, ed. (San Francisco: Jossey-Bass, 1984); Richard Daft and R.H. Lengel, "Information Richness," in *Research in Organizational Behavior,* vol. 6, Larry Cummings and Barry Staw, eds. (Greenwich, CT: JAI Press, 1984).

[33] Janet Fulk, Charles W. Steinfield, Joseph Schmitz, and J.G. Power, "A Social Information Processing Model of Media Use in Organizations," *Communication Research,* 14 (1987), 529–552.

[34] Sim B. Sitkin, Kathleen M. Sutcliffe, and J.R. Barrios-Choplin, "A Dual-Capacity Model of Communication Medium Choice in Organizations," *Human Communication Research, 18* (1992), 563–598.

[35] Everett M. Rogers, *Communication of Innovations,* 4th edition (New York: Free Press, 1994).

[36] Rice and Gattiker, pp. 553–556.

[37] Rice and Gattiker, p. 546.

[38] Bonnie Johnson and Ron Rice, *Managing Organizational Innovation: The Evolution from Word Processing to Office Information Systems* (New York: Columbia University Press, 1987).

[39] Rice and Gattiker, p. 563–564.

[40] This effect is clear in groups studied in the field. There are mixed results in laboratory experiments on GDSSs, probably because lab groups are set up ad hoc and respond to the experimental manipulation, tending to behave more equally when conditions promote it and less equally when conditions promote the emergence of status networks. See Fulk and Collins-Jarvis, p. 639.

[41] Guisseppi Mantovani, "Is Computer-Mediated Communication Intrinsically Apt to Enhance Democracy in Organizations?" *Human Relations, 47:* 45–62.

[42] Lucas, T-Form, describes virtual organizations in some detail.

[43] Michael Meyer, "Here's a 'Virtual' Model for America's Industrial Giants," *Newsweek* (August 13, 1993): p. 40.

[44] Shoshanna Zuboff, *In the Age of the Smart Machine* (New York: Free Press, 1988).

[45] Lee Sproull and Sara Kiesler, *Connections: New Ways of Working in the Networked World.* (Cambridge, MA: MIT Press, 1992).

[46] Peter Leyden, "Teleworking Could Turn Our Cities Inside Out," Minneapolis *Star-Tribune* (September 5, 1993): 15A-16A.

[47] Kirk Johnson, "Many Companies Turn Workers into High-Tech Nomads", Minneapolis *Star-Tribune* (April 3, 1994), 1J.

[48] Dan Verton, "Employers OK with E-Surfing," *Computerworld,* December 18, 2000.

[49] Dan Verton, "Senator Attacks Data Sharing," *Computerworld,* December 11, 2000.

[50] Knowledge management is one of the most rapidly growing areas of interest in information systems and management. The discussion in this section is based upon several sources, including Monge and Contractor; Bruce Kogut, W. Shan, and Gordon Walker, "Knowledge in the Network and the Network as Knowledge: Structuring of New Industries," in *The Embedded Firm: On the Socioeconomics of Industrial Networks,* G. Grabher, ed. (New York: Rutledge, 1993); Clyde Holsapple and K. D. Joshi, "In Search of a Descriptive Framework for Knowledge Management: Preliminary Delphi Results," *Kentucky Initiative for Knowledge Management, Research Paper No. 118* (Lexington, Kentucky: University of Kentucky).

[51] Noshir Contractor, *Inquiring Knowledge Networks on the Web. Conceptual Overview,* http://www.tec.spcomm.uiuc.edu/nosh/IKNOW/sld001.htm; Noshir Contractor, Barbara O'Keefe, and P.M. Jones, *IKNOW: Inquiring Knowledge Networks on the Web.* http://iknow.spcomm. uiuc.edu.

Chapter 7

MANAGING MEMBERSHIP
IN ORGANIZATIONS

CENTRAL THEMES

- Newcomers to an organization (or a new unit of an organization) face two important challenges: making sense out of their new surroundings and negotiating a role in the organization that satisfies their needs and the needs of their new coworkers.
- Sense making is an especially complex process for newcomers who are not middle-to-upper-class white males.
- Once newcomers have settled in to their organizations, their success depends on their ability to analyze organizational situations and strategically adapt to them. Doing so depends on mastering a variety of listening, image-management, and influence strategies.
- Work is a highly emotional activity. Managing emotions is closely tied to societal norms and expectations, as well as to communicative skills.

KEY TERMS

Reality shock	Indirect questions
Self-disclosure	Mentors
Role negotiation	Enacting peripheral roles
Role encapsulation	Public self vs. private self
Justifications	Rationalizations
Strategic ambiguity	

Everyone enters new organizations throughout their lives. Studies of voluntary job turnover and of the career aspirations of Generation X and Generation Y employees suggest that today's college students will change organizations more times during their careers than any other generation every has. The entry experience poses a distinctive set of challenges to newcomers. But, once they have settled in to their new organizations and organizational roles, life is still complex. Managing membership in organizations involves mastering a particular set of analytical skills and communicative strategies.

ENTERING ORGANIZATIONS: PRESSURES, AND COPING PROCESSES

When people enter a new organization or a new division of their existing organization they bring with them a lengthy and complex history.[1] They have learned to perceive their organizational worlds in their own ways and have developed patterns of acting and communicating that have succeeded in the past. But, every organization is unique in some ways. Consequently all newcomers experience some degree of *reality shock*—the sudden realization that what they took for granted in their previous organization is not what people take for granted in their new one. So, the first challenge that newcomers face is *making sense out of* their new organization, of coping with the surprises that their new experiences bring.

Newcomers face a second challenge. They understandably want to change as little as possible while adjusting to their new surroundings. But, they have entered an organization (or unit) that also has a complex history and a group of employees who have developed their own successful, stable, predictable, and comfortable ways of perceiving and acting. So, their news coworkers also want to change as little as possible to accommodate the newcomer. As a result, the parties must negotiate about their new relationship. If the negotiation succeeds, the newcomer will probably experience reduced stress, increased performance, and enhanced job satisfaction. If it fails, the newcomer's satisfaction and performance will be reduced and he or she is likely to leave the organization.

Making Sense of Organizational Situations

The key to coping with a new organization is to make sense out of it. Sense-making is a complicated process that relies on communication. When situations do not make sense, people seek out information and perspectives from other people. Through *interacting* with others, newcomers begin to manage the ambiguities and uncertainties that they feel. Eventually, the new situation begins to make enough sense that individuals can begin to seek out additional information about how the organization works.[2] Of course, some newcomers are better able to cope with new situations than others. Newcomers who have had many and varied work experiences deal with the reality shock of the entry experience more successfully than people with few work experiences. Among employees with limited experience, some personality characteristics may also influence their ability to cope. For example, people who are inner-directed, that is, who rely on their own beliefs, values, and analytical skills, cope more easily than people who are outer-directed, who usually rely on the opinions and interpretations of others.[3] But, for everyone, sense-making depends on communication.

Coping with Unmet Expectations   As we have suggested throughout this book, expectations are influenced by the accepted assumptions of a person's society, as well as by a person's individual needs and experiences. Some societal assumptions involve work and organizational life (recall the Generation X case study in Chapter 1). These assumptions create expectations that may or may not be fulfilled by a person's new organization. For example, students in U.S. universities seem to expect to someday get a real job, that pays well (the realest ones have six-figure salaries), is full-time, involves managerial tasks, perks (independence and a large private office), includes the possibility of advancement, and is with a reputable company.[4] In real jobs, supervisors are competent and do not mistreat their subordinates. Of course, these expectations are elitist, and they are stereotypically masculine because the realness of a job depends on traditionally male considerations, such as financial gain and upward mobility. Stereotypically feminine attributes like nurturing and caring for others, are characteristic of jobs that are not regarded as "real" jobs. Students' perceptions of real jobs include a particular kind of organizational life and a specific set of criteria for evaluating an organization, a job, and the people who fill them. But, some jobs are simply not real jobs, and these society-level expectations will not be fulfilled.

As soon as a person has accepted a new position she or he begins to anticipate what the new job will be like. For some people these expectations will be relatively accurate; for others they will not be. Sometimes selection processes and negotiations over terms of employment create inaccurate expectations. During these processes, the firm and the applicant engage in communication that is similar to romantic courtship, where each party strives to present the best possible image. But, as in many marriages, the reality may be quite different from the expectations.[5] For example, a new psychiatrist entered an international competition for a postdoctoral research fellowship at a major medical center in the southeastern United States. After being flown at the agency's expense to New York, Boston, and Washington for three rounds of extensive interviews, she learned that she had won the competition. Filled with justifiable pride and the expectation that she would arrive at the medical school as a respected colleague of an established research team, she was met by a secretary who escorted her to a hidden-away corner where she joined five other postdocs. Because of an error by the purchasing department, her desk and chair were not scheduled to arrive for two weeks. Three years later she angrily described her postdoc experience in a single phrase: "I didn't even have a chair."

Sometimes unfulfilled expectations involve organizational tasks and perks. But, just as often they involve the employees' family—their subdivision was not as welcoming, or their children's' schools were not as good, or the weather was not as balmy as they had anticipated. Organizations do a great deal to help newcomers prepare for their jobs, but they often fail to realize that people also have identities and lives that go beyond the workplace. Failing to adequately prepare newcomers for their nonwork lives is just as alienating, perhaps more so, than failing to prepare them for their tasks. The most memorable experiences that people have in their organizations involve their first few weeks. Unfortunately, if these memories involve unmet expectations, the hurt feelings may never disappear.[6]

Current employees' expectations about their newly hired colleagues also may not be met. When expectations are violated, people feel betrayed, and their trust in the other parties is reduced. As Chapter 3 explained, low levels of trust reduce the amount of and accuracy of communication. As the quality of communication between newcomers and old-timers is reduced, it becomes progressively more difficult for either side to understand the other. New expectations are formed, based on patterns of withholding or distorting information. Since these expectations are unrealistic they are easily violated. As employees become less predictable to one another they tend to withdraw, making it even more difficult for them to communicate effectively. Their expectations become less realistic, their orientations toward one another less trusting, open, or cooperative. Their access to the information they need to perform their assigned tasks effectively is reduced. Fortunately, this cycle of unfulfilled expectations, reduced trust, and isolation is not an inevitable part of the anticipation stage. Organizations can prevent it to some degree by attempting to create accurate expectations among new employees and old-timers. Newcomers can reduce it if they understand that their anticipation of a new job distorts their perceptions and if they adopt communication strategies that help them cope with reality shock.[7]

CASE STUDY:
JULIE'S EXPERIENCE, PART I

Julie was a project manager in an important support division of a major international firm. She had started as a temporary employee and was hired as a full-time project assistant when she received her degree. Although she did not have the title or salary of a project manager, she had so impressed her supervisor that she had been given many of the project manager's responsibilities. Her job was exciting and challenging. She had to understand the firm's entire line of products and have exceptional written and oral communication skills. Her advancement resulted from her willingness to work hard to improve her technical expertise and from her ability to take on and complete tasks that required sixty to eighty hours per week of complex work under severe time pressures. She very much enjoyed the communication element of her job, but she never really felt excited about the sophisticated computerized machinery that she was communicating about.

So she started to look for other jobs. Her workload had started to interfere in her family life, and the high stress and low morale of her department had started to make her dread going to work. She felt that she could do nothing about the workload, because in her company's culture working a sixty-hour week was normal and expected. In fact it was seen as evidence of loyalty to the firm. This was especially frustrating, because the extra load often was avoidable; it almost always resulted from poor organization, jumping into projects before thinking through the details, or changes in design because of communication breakdowns between units.

(continued)

(continued from the previous page)

She also was concerned about her ability to move up in the firm. Although she did not need to move immediately, she soon would be promoted to an official project manager position. After she was promoted, her salary would be high enough that it would be difficult to leave Widgets, Inc., without taking a major pay cut. Since other firms would be suspicious about why she was willing to sacrifice $10,000 a year to move, her promotion easily could trap her at Widgets. And her next promotion would probably be her last. There just were not many positions above the next level, and a large number of people would be competing for the few higher-level openings.

One afternoon a friend told Julie of an upcoming opening at a nearby firm whose products were similar. All she knew about Family, Inc., was that it was a major competitor of Widgets and was reputed to be a good place to work. Founded by an entrepreneur who still was the top manager, it had an exceptional number of perks—exercise room and indoor pool, gourmet food in the cafeteria, private offices, and comparable salaries to those at Widgets. When she first talked with people at Family she was impressed. Everyone seemed to have both technical and professional skills and worked as a team. The description of the new job was very much like her favorite assignment at Widgets. In the end she was not offered that position, but Family had been so impressed with her that they offered her a project leader position for a product that sounded interesting but somewhat outside of her expertise.

Impressed with the close, collegial relationships among her potential coworkers, the obvious concern for employees—everyone was virtually required to work no more than a forty-hour week, and Family was one of the few firms in the area with high-quality, on-site day care—and the large number of women in upper-management positions, she decided to make the move.

Applying What You've Learned

1. What were Julie's expectations? What were they based upon?
2. What would her organization have had to do to fulfill her expectations?

Questions to Think About and Discuss

1. How did Julie's situation at Widgets influence her priorities when she started looking around?
2. How did the situation influence her perceptions of Family? What factors were more important than they otherwise would have been? What might she have overlooked because of her frustrations with Widgets?
3. In what ways did her priorities shift during the selection process? (Focus particularly on the differences between the two jobs at Family.)

Learning About One's New Organization   In the best of all worlds, new-comers will be given opportunities to discuss their new duties with their supervisors and coworkers prior to making the move. Unfortunately, organizations often do not provide these opportunities, even when the employee is being transferred from one unit of the organization to another. Once they arrive in their new organizations or units, newcomers *should* be given information about the formal requirements of their job by their supervisor—the nature and relative importance of assigned tasks, key deadlines, and the newcomer's interdependencies with other employees or units of the organization. But some supervisors isolate themselves from their subordinates. They are less useful sources of information than supervisors who are open and who help newcomers get to know people in other parts of the organization. Fortunately, newcomers usually know within a month or so what kind of communicative relationship they will have with their supervisors. Relationships that are close and collegial at one month tend to be close and collegial long into the future; relationships that are cooperative but distant tend to stay that way.

When their supervisors are not effective communicators, newcomers may have to rely on their peers for job-related information. Through normal, everyday communication peers provide newcomers with cues that give them a sense of competence and achievement (or incompetence and failure). Peers are good sources of information about how to make sense out of strange organizational events and activities, about how they should and should not communicate (including what media to use), and how they are expected to behave. If the organization (or unit) has developed its own language (recall the discussion of trained incapacity in Chapter 2), peers can teach it to the newcomer. Peers also help newcomers learn about organizational power relationships. They explain when subordinates are expected to defer to their superiors; when they should remain quiet and let their supervisors accept credit for their work or blame them for their own errors; and when they should invite superior-grade personnel to dinner parties, show concern for their spouses and families, note their birthdays and anniversaries, and so on. However, since peers have only indirect insight into the supervisor's expectations for the newcomer, this information may be unreliable or it may contradict other available information, creating stress and uncertainty.

Although newcomers never are given an official script, they still learn how they are expected to play their part. They usually go through a honeymoon period when current employees do not overtly pressure them to conform. In fact, since newcomers generally want to fit in, overt pressure is not needed. New managers learn never to say anything negative about the firm or its products in public; officers (supervisors) usually learn that they do not fraternize with enlisted personnel (subordinates); employees learn to maintain the public images of their roles and their firms. They use its products, live in its neighborhoods, and subscribe to its dress code. Newcomers often learn that their job descriptions exclude some responsibilities that are actually mandatory and include others that are actually forbidden. Job descriptions for secretaries rarely include making coffee for their bosses, buying presents for their bosses' relatives, or lying to their spouses about their location or activities. But these behaviors are sometimes expected. Employees who have accepted a job because its official job description includes some desirable perk—representing the firm at trade conventions held in exotic ports of call, for example—may find that their bosses prefer to perform that task themselves. They learn to at least pretend that they have cooperative, friendly, and professional relationships with their associates. Team spirit is demanded by almost all organizations, and acting like a member of the team is expected of every employee. In many cases these expectations are easy to fulfill. Newcomers soon feel that they actually are part of a team. In other cases they have to pretend that they do. And because fulfilling expectations is important, the most successful new employees are often the most consummate pretenders.[8]

Just as there are a number of potential sources of information, there are a number of strategies that newcomers can use to obtain it. Asking overt questions is the most *efficient* way to obtain information; but it is awkward because doing so reveals one's ignorance. It is especially difficult for newcomers who have been transferred from other parts of the organization, because they are *supposed* to know what is going on. Consequently, newcomers ask direct questions only when they feel comfortable approaching a particular oldtimer and feel that there is little chance that they will be embarrassed by doing so. Similarly, oldtimers provide the requested information only when they feel comfortable with the newcomer and his or her request, and when it does not involve sensitive topics.

So, newcomers tend to avoid overt strategies of obtaining information until they perceive that the risks, including the possibility of being embarrassed, are small (see Table 7–1). Instead, they may devour all the written information that is available to them. Or they may ask **indirect questions** about a harmless topic that is related to what they really want to know. They may hint or ask other employees about their histories with the firm as a way of finding out about how people advance through the organizational hierarchy. *Joking* about key characteristics of the new organization or **self-disclosing** (revealing a relatively private aspect of one's experiences or identity) may generate informative responses from other employees. For example, a newcomer might tell a supervisor that she or he prefers all-nighters to missing deadlines in the hope that the supervisor will respond by revealing his or her preferences about deadlines and work styles. Newcomers also may simply *observe* other employees completing specific tasks and mimic their actions. As Chapter 4 pointed out, newcomers can obtain a great deal of insight into the beliefs and values of the organization by closely monitoring key symbolic forms—stories, myths, metaphors, rites, and rituals. Of course, they must be careful to remember that the official meaning of a symbol may be very different from the real meaning that employees attribute to it. Asking third parties is risky, because it may produce incorrect or misleading information, or may lead a newcomer to view the organization in ways that conflict with the supervisor's views. An even more risky are covert strategy involves *testing limits,* when newcomers intentionally violate the informal rules of the organization and observe and interpret other employees' responses to their actions.

TABLE 7-1
Types of Information-Seeking Behavior

	OVERT QUESTIONS	INDIRECT QUESTIONS (HINTING)	THIRD PARTY	TESTING LIMITS	DISGUISING CONVERSATIONS	OBSERVING	OBSERVATION
Newcomer comfort level	High	Low	Low with supervisors Medium with peers	High	Low	Low	Low
Fear of being embarrassed	Low	High	High	Low	High	High	High
Source availability/ competence	High	High	Low	High	High	High	High
Risks	High	Medium	Low	High	High	Moderate to High (depending on degree of culture shock)	Moderate (because relies on newcomers' perceptions)

The most effective way to make sense out of an organization may be to engage in normal processes of building interpersonal relationships—talking with people about the community, their families, their outside interests to find common ground with at least some of the old-timers. Most newcomers who leave their organizations early do so because they didn't fit in, which usually means they didn't form meaningful interpersonal relationships. As newcomers establish relationships, they begin to be accepted as part of the work group. Coworkers withhold less information and respond more positively to even very specific, overt questions than they did earlier in the relationship. Eventually they feel safe enough to reveal even sensitive information. In general, the information that newcomers receive during these informal, face-to-face conversations provides the most valuable clues for making sense out of their new situation.

Sense-Making and "Different" Newcomers   Unfortunately, there has been little research on how a newcomer's race, occupation, or gender affects the sense-making process. The evidence that does exist suggests that it is more difficult for women, members of minority groups, and people in occupations that are not central to the operation of the organization (for example, human resources officers in engineering firms) to obtain the information needed to make sense out of the organization. People interact with one another based on the whole person, which includes race and gender as well as organizational position, task assignments and professional expertise. Current employees in U.S. organizations are disproportionately white and middle-class, at least in the managerial and professional ranks. They often have not had much experience communicating with people who are different than they are and feel uncomfortable doing so. They may fear that if they do offer advice or help, the newcomer will view their efforts as patronizing, sexist, or racist. Or, they may perceive that she or he was an affirmative action hire who really does not deserve the position and want the newcomer to fail. So, they withdraw from him or her, and it takes longer for them to form effective interpersonal relationships, if they ever do. Current employees expect these newcomers to occupy low-power positions in their organizations, and as a result are less accommodating about providing inside information. In ambiguous situations, people rely on stereotypes to guide their interactions—stereotypes that may be very inaccurate and misleading. For example, black women are often viewed as experts on human relations, public relations, race and gender, not on nuclear engineering, even when that is their specialty.[9] Current employees may believe that white males are intellectually and/or professionally superior to everyone else and engage in more testing of a "different" newcomer's competence and abilities.

Conversely, a different newcomer may feel awkward and lack the confidence needed to use direct information-seeking strategies or initiate relationships with new peers. She or he also may be reticent about asking indirect questions because of a fear that doing so will threaten the current employees and lead them to provide misinformation.

Even quasi-formal systems of integrating newcomers into organizations may be complicated for employees who are not white males. There is widespread agreement that newcomers who successfully navigate the entry experience do so largely because they are able to establish close, personal mentoring relationships with one or more senior employees early in their careers.[10] From these *mentors* newcomers obtain all the different kinds of information discussed in this chapter. However, like all interpersonal relationships, mentor–mentoree relationships are difficult to form and maintain, especially when mentorees are of a different gender, race, or ethnic background than their mentors. Informal mentoring systems tend to exclude African Americans and Latinos/Latinas, and to a somewhat lesser degree, white women. A study by Catalyst, a New York based research organization, found that half of African American women had been unable to establish a mentoring relationship compared with a third of white women.[11]

Both mentor and mentoree may feel awkward, especially at first. Once the relationship is established it may be difficult to avoid creating an actual or perceived dependency relationship. In U.S. firms, so few women or members of minority groups occupy positions near the top of organizations that the vast majority of mentors will be European American men. In general, these supervisors seem to be willing to mentor or assist male subordinates if they are sufficiently competent. However, they seem to be willing to mentor European American women, Latinos, and African American men only if they are near the bottom of the organizational hierarchy. Once they are promoted and begin to become potential threats to the European American male supervisors, they withdraw their help, even if they espouse egalitarian attitudes.

Traditional sex-role stereotypes also complicate mentoring relationships by making it difficult for the parties to know how to act toward one another or interpret one another's actions. The relationship may be strained and communication may be less open and spontaneous than in same sex relationships. Cross-sex (or cross-race/ethnicity) mentoring relationships also seem to be weaker, less stable, and more limited to discussions of task issues than are same-sex (and same-race/ethnicity) relationships. European American male mentorees also seem to obtain access to other relationships through their mentors, while this is much less true for women, African American men, and Latinos. As a result, establishing and maintaining positive mentoring relationships is more difficult for women, African American men, and Latinos than it is for Anglo men, and the mentoring relationships that they do establish seem to be less beneficial to their career advancement. The complicated nature of mentoring is one reason why women and minority men often do not become fully integrated into their organizations and eventually move on.[12]

Another mechanism for helping newcomers make sense of their organization is to encourage them to become linked to informal communication networks. For the reasons described in the previous paragraphs, "different" employees often find it difficult to become integrated into the informal networks that exist within their firms. An alternative is external networks. Most major cities and many smaller ones now have active networks for women, African American, and Latino managers and professionals. External networks have proven to be valuable to all three groups. Contacts made in networks provide a wide variety of information about how organizations work as well as social and emotional support. Employees who have experienced overt discrimination or racial or sexual harassment are supported by people who have had similar experiences and have learned how to deal with those problems. Networks share information about which firms have good (and poor) records of advancing women and minority employees. They provide advice about handling everyday work-related problems and exchange information about when and where vacancies are anticipated. At times, networks can become elitist, shifting their focus from aiding all their members to assisting a selected few. But, when they work effectively, they can provide members with all the information that European American men traditionally have gained through informal good-old-boy networks. In short, external networks help compensate for the fact that Latinos, Latinas, European American women, and African Americans are often excluded from the internal networks of their organizations.[13]

CASE STUDY:
JULIE'S EXPERIENCE, PART II

Julie: "Within a month of joining Family I knew I had made a mistake. It probably was the kick in the pants I needed to switch to do what I wanted to do. The project was even more boring than what I'd been doing at Widgets. Now I realize that I had much better tools to work with there. Our support equipment is antiquated and slow, something that took me completely by surprise because Family is internationally known for making precisely the kind of support equipment that we need but don't have—I didn't even bother to ask. And I made some errors. Although everyone seemed to be open and supportive, I once compared Family to Widgets and found that 'loyalty' in this corporate culture means that you don't criticize, not even in private. When it comes down to it, because Family gives you all of these benefits, they want your soul, they really want your soul. And I'm not willing to give it!"

"There's also this feeling (assumed and verbalized) that you must become part of the family. You feel these pressures to be sucked into the group and react by trying to stay apart and separate. It wasn't until then that I realized that I identified with Widgets more than I had known. It's frustrating—at Widgets we got the equipment we needed to do the job but not the people, here we get the people but no support equipment, even things that we make upstairs. Family is much more efficient and you waste so much less time. But it's all so informal. Basically it's a mismatch. I really shouldn't have made a move until I knew definitely what I wanted to do, or had it more focused, I guess."

"One of the good things about Family is that it has a much stronger commitment and flexibility to families. It got to a point [at Widgets] where you got to see your son for half an hour in the morning and ten minutes at night if you're lucky.

(continued)

(continued from the previous page)

And they really do seem to promote people on the basis of ability, not gender. I've never, ever heard a comment by anybody about somebody's competence based on gender. I knew that before I made the move. They're so flexible in some areas, but so very rigid in others. There are just some parts of the culture that are fixed in stone. You're expected to be there at 9:00 A.M. regardless of how late you work the night before, and sometimes everyone has to work over. But teamdom means that by God you're there as early as everyone else."

Applying What You've Learned

1. How did Julie obtain information about her new organization? How did she make sense out of it?
2. What information should she obtain about new firms before she makes a decision to move again?

Questions to Think About and Discuss

1. What surprised Julie about Family? Why was she surprised?
2. What are her priorities now? How do they differ from her priorities while she was looking to leave Widgets?
3. Pretend that you are in Julie's position. Will she/you stay with Family, Inc.? Why or why not?

Negotiating Organizational Roles

People who are already part of an organization have understandable reasons to want newcomers to mold themselves to fit existing roles; newcomers have equally understandable reasons for wanting to modify those roles to fit their individual needs and goals. *Role negotiation* involves using communication to create a shared set of expectations about how a newcomer will fit in the organization. It occurs whenever an employee's situation changes—entering a new organization, accepting a transfer within the same organization, taking maternity or paternity leave, returning to school to pursue an advanced degree or update training, or adapting to a merger or downsizing. Each of these events requires a renegotiation of one's organizational role. Role negotiation is more complicated for newcomers, because each party has only a limited amount of information about and commitment to the other party.

Sometimes newcomers try to avoid negotiating directly about their role by instead *enacting peripheral roles* (taking on tasks that are outside of their job descriptions or current employees' expectations), or by modifying existing roles (focusing their effort on the aspects of their role that they enjoy while ignoring the remaining features). Since these strategies are implemented without the supervisor's knowledge or consent, they are likely to provoke a response once they are discovered. The newcomer may be reprimanded (which usually leads to changes in behavior so that the supervisor's expectations are fulfilled), ignored (which means that the newcomer has successfully changed his or her role, although through very risky means), or even lauded because it in some way contributes to the organization. They are more risky strategies than openly negotiating about one's new role.

Role negotiation involves and affects everyone in a work group. However, because of organizational power and authority relationships, it focuses on supervisors. When supervisors have open communication relationships with their subordinates and are actively involved in helping their subordinates do their jobs, people feel comfortable negotiating about their organizational roles. In modern organizations, role negotiation is particularly difficult. One challenge involves *role encapsulation,* processes through which individual employees are perceived through racial or sexual stereotypes. For example, some women simply are not warm, supportive, nurturing people and do not want to be, in spite of what dominant stereotypes suggest. Nurturance, like any other behavior, is learned, not innate. But, the stereotype is so powerful that supervisors, and peers, often try to negotiate women into support-oriented organizational roles (both formal and informal), frequently without realizing that they are doing so. Some male engineers negotiate roles that allow them to focus on their families and avoid burnout, even in organizations where burnout and devaluing family life is both normal and a sign of masculinity.[14] Indeed, 75 percent of male employees say that they would exchange promotion opportunities and raises for more time to spend with their families. They are unable to do so, because of the negative impact on their careers, status, and job security.[15]

As a result of role encapsulation, role negotiation tends to be limited to *organizational* considerations. Career goals, task preferences, and work styles are part of every newcomer's preferences and do need to be negotiated. But, people simultaneously play other roles—parent, caretaker, spouse, church member—that affect and are affected by role negotiations. Historically, role negotiations have largely ignored those other roles, and have assumed that a newcomer is interested in negotiating for the long term. But, Generation X employees (and lots of other people) often do not anticipate being in an organization for the long term. They also tend to have strong commitments to their nonwork relationships. Trying to negotiate them into traditional, 1950s-type organizational roles is doomed to fail. Similarly, trying to persuade a supervisor whose entire life has centered on the 1950s model to allow subordinates to negotiate radically different roles may be virtually impossible. The concept of individualizing an organizational role may be completely foreign to him or her, even though it is what the negotiation is all about. In both cases, role-making is a constant process of resisting efforts to place a newcomer into a generic role based on the newcomer's membership in a particular group, and it requires a constant effort to be treated as an individual. Role negotiation may be the organizational process where the inevitable tension between organizational and individual needs (recall Chapter 1) is most clear.

THE CASE OF THE AGGRIEVED EXPATRIATE*

It is well known that expatriates—people who work in a foreign division of a multinational company—have high turnover rates (one fifth to one half of personnel sent overseas by U.S.-based multinational firms return early.) Since the costs of recruiting, relocating, and training expatriates is very high, this kind of turnover is a serious problem. Sadie Wagner seemed to be a perfect match for a middle-management position that recently had opened up in FPI's German division. She was an expert in strategic management, which is what the position required; she was fluent in the language and familiar with the culture as a result of being a foreign exchange student in Germany and spending a year doing graduate study there. The opportunity was a step up for her, and after telephone interviews with the director of human resources and her prospective boss, Mr. Reil, and a three-hour interview in Germany with the highest-ranking executive in the German division, Mr. Carstensen, she excitedly accepted the job.

Immediately after arriving she was introduced to two other expatriates, Charles (a single American male who had been in the finance division for only six months) and William (a single English male in marketing). Her first week was a little weird. Since her boss was leaving for a month-long vacation at the end of the week she went through a crash-course in the division's financial reporting system. She thought that it was a little strange that the company sent her to Europe when they did, knowing that her boss was going to be gone for a month. But, she used the time to handle routine financial postings and to learn more about the German division's operations and handled. Since she always had been taught that newcomers should actively form relationships in their new organizations, she met as many colleagues as possible and started to form alliances with them. Unlike the other expats, whose limited language skills forced them to socialize with one another, Sadie was able to get to know a larger group of people. Many of them were interested in getting an international assignment, so she was able to provide them with information about how to do so while they told her about the German division.

She learned that FPI's expats typically had mixed experiences. Most were upper-middle or senior-level managers and had been led to believe that the German assignment was a plum. So, they expected people to roll out the red carpet for them. They also were used to making decisions based on the best available data and with the best resources. When they got to Germany they found no red carpets, little data, and even fewer resources. For their part, the German senior managers were much less supportive of the expat program than Mr. Carstensen was. They were afraid that since the expats came from the home office, their jobs

(continued)

(continued from the previous page)

were secure. But, once they became familiar with the German operation, the head office might see the German managers as expendable. The home office wanted the expats to bring a bit more flexibility to the highly structured, rule-bound German office, but it seemed that all Carstensen really wanted was their language skills and knowledge of how the home office operated.

Once Mr. Reil returned from vacation things started to get uncomfortable. Sadie asked him for permission to take a refresher course in German language, but he refused, because all communication with the home office was in English (even though all internal memos, lunchtime conversation, and so on were in German). After talking to the Office of Human Resources, she decided to take the course anyway. While Riel was away, Sadie adopted a normal American workday, 8:00 a.m. until 5:30 p.m, different than the typical German white-collar schedule of 9:00 a.m. until 7:00 p.m. (except for senior managers who left at 6:00 p.m.). Sadie was single, and since German shops closed at 6:00 p.m. on every weekday except Thursday and were only open until noon on Saturday, she needed to leave early to take care of routine shopping. (This is not a problem for married German managers, because it is rare for wives to work outside of the home and they take care of the domestic tasks). Since Riel was known for being the first one to arrive and the last to leave, Sadie's schedule annoyed him. He talked with her about how it looked. She also was becoming annoyed because her workload was light, and she didn't seem to receive the managerial tasks that her job description called for. Even after the strategic planning process for the German division started, she still didn't receive managerial assignments, even though that presumably was why the company sent her to Germany in the first place. If she didn't get the right assignments, she wouldn't develop the skills necessary to move up in the organization, which is why she accepted the expat assignment.

Increasingly frustrated, she decided to talk with Charles and William. They too were frustrated, but for different reasons. They sought expat assignments because they are interesting, not because they wanted to move up in the organization. But, they felt that the company was not using their technical expertise. Sadie stayed in Germany until after the planning process was over, but left for another firm soon after returning to the United States.

Applying What You've Learned

1. What aspects of Sadie's experience result from typical processes of entering an organization?
2. What aspects can be attributed to her being an expatriate?
3. What aspects can be attributed to differences between U.S. and German culture?

(continued)

(continued from the previous page)

Questions to Think About and Discuss

1. What steps did Sadie take to negotiate a mutually acceptable role in her new organization? What steps should she have taken? Why?
2. What steps did FPI take to help Sadie develop an effective role? What steps should FPI take to help reduce turnover among their expatriate employees? Why?

---

*This case is based on Colleen Keough, "The Case of the Aggrieved Expatriate," *Management Communication Quarterly, 11*(1998): 453–459. For more information on expatriates' experiences see Philip Harris & Robert Moran, *Managing Cultural Differences,* 3rd. ed. (Houston, TX: Gulf Publishing Company, 1991); and Rosita Albert, "Cultural Diversity and Intercultural Training in Multinational Organizations," in *Communicating in Multinational Organizations,* R.L. Wiseman, & R. Shuter, eds. (Thousand Oaks, CA: 1994).

COMMUNICATION STRATEGIES FOR PEOPLE WHO HAVE SETTLED IN

Soon after their first days in a new job, newcomers begin to settle in to their new organizational worlds. They will "know" that they have settled in when they can make sense out of events and messages without having to consciously analyze them, understand their role in the organization, and no longer feel stress, because they do not know how to act. Even after they have settled in, new employees will continue to experience surprises. They may be surprised to learn that some parts of their jobs are less stimulating than they expected them to be. They may find that the experience itself is not what they thought it would be. Medical students know at an intellectual level that they will work sixty to eighty hours a week while in residency; mental health professionals know that they will be overloaded with complicated cases and buried in unnecessary administrative red tape. But they do not—indeed, they cannot—know what it will *feel* like until they actually do it. And, new employees may surprise themselves. They may have chosen a position, or even a career, because they thought they wanted independence, a sense of achievement, feelings of contributing to society, or some other goal. Once they are given an opportunity to achieve that goal, they discover that it was not what they wanted after all. Many of the our generation (the baby boomers) thought they wanted to "make the world a better place to live." Lots of us have discovered that what we really want is to retire early.

Learning to Analyze Organizational Situations

Once newcomers have settled in, they can begin to concentrate on communicating strategically. Doing so involves analyzing the situations they face at work, choosing communicative strategies that are appropriate to those situations, and implementing those strategies effectively. In the process they must learn to manage their emotions and the emotions of their coworkers.

Most of organizational life—including organizational communication—is habitual. But the most important organizational situations are ones that call for people to abandon habitual behaviors, to analyze a particular situation and make sense of it.[16] Some people are more capable of making sense out of situations than others. But all people can enhance their ability to do so by learning some basic principles of listening.

Listening is a complex and difficult process. Effective listening depends on understanding the nature of messages and developing a specific set of skills. Every message includes multiple levels of meaning. Messages "mean" on a *cognitive* level—they convey bits of information. They also "mean" at *emotional* and *relational* levels. It is possible to detect a speaker's emotional tone and intensity during face-to-face communication, even though communicators often attempt to hide their emotions, especially in organizations where rationality is valued and emotional displays are frowned on. It is more difficult to assess emotional tone when messages are communicated in modes that do not include nonverbal cues, for example, in written memos. Finally, messages "say" something about the sender's interpersonal relationship with the receivers, with other members of the organization, and with the organization itself.[17]

Simultaneously listening for cognitive, emotional, and relational dimensions of meaning is important for two reasons. First, it gives employees more complete and accurate information about the purposes that underlie communication from others. For example, when an old-timer tells a newcomer, "That's a pretty good idea, for a rookie," the comment may reflect a variety of purposes. It could be intended to focus attention on a good idea (primarily a content purpose), to express a mentor's pride in the accomplishments of a mentoree (an emotional purpose), to remind the newcomer that he or she is a subordinate (rookie, a relational purpose), or any combination of the three. The rookie can accurately understand the comment and its purposes only by thinking about what it means at content, emotional, and relational levels.

Second, listening for multiple levels of meaning also gives employees a sense of what responses are appropriate to different messages. For example, the effects of the rookie's responding "Yep. . . . Gee, I'm smart, aren't I?" will depend on the old-timer's purpose(s). If it was content, the response would have little impact. If it was emotional, the response could deny the old-timer's right to feel pride in the mentoree. If it was relational, it could challenge the hierarchical relationship that existed between them. In either case, the response would alienate the mentor.

However, listening for multiple levels of meaning is a skill that must often be learned. For example, in Western societies men often do not learn to listen at the relational level. They also learn not to be highly responsive to relational messages (for example, by saying yeah or umhumm) or to respond by giving the other person advice about how to deal with relational problems. This kind of response is comfortable, because it allows the person to maintain a superior position and to stay in control of the conversation; but it does not acknowledge the other person's feelings or relational concerns. It is also consistent with the norms of most organizations, because they tend to be speech communities in which masculine styles are dominant. But, such a response can easily lead to misunderstandings, frustration, and communication breakdowns, because it does not adequately acknowledge emotional and relational levels of meaning. In contrast, Western women typically learn to focus on the relational level of meaning and to respond by expressing understanding, sympathy, and emotional support. They learn to treat the content of the message as less important. But, focusing solely on the relational level of meaning can also create misunderstanding and frustration.[18]

Just as employees must listen for multiple levels of meaning, they also must listen for the *organizational functions* and *personal implications* that messages contain. Some messages serve a decision-making function. They call for a rational analysis of problems and give permissions to disagree with one another to some extent. Other messages only *seem* to serve a decision-making function but are really organizational ceremonies (see Chapters 4 and 8). For example, when upper-level personnel resign or retire, messages like "What can we ever do to replace Andy?" abound. They may sound like a call for analysis; but responses like "Well, Fred, Jennie, or Stanley could easily move up and do quite well" or "Ah, come on . . . anyone could handle Andy's job" would miss the point entirely.

Messages also include *personal implications*. Every message can influence employees' public images and their private conceptions of themselves. The challenge that new employees face is to understand that the organizational functions and personal implications of messages often do not coincide. It is difficult to construct messages that meet both goals simultaneously, as illustrated by research on organizational friendships. Work fosters the development of friendships, because it places people in sustained contact with one another; because it makes it easier to find common interests, backgrounds, and so on; and because it creates opportunities for people to demonstrate their loyalty to and concern for one another. Contact, similarity, and emotional commitment are the basis of strong interpersonal relationships, in part because they foster high levels of trust.

But work also creates tensions within friendships. One tension is between individuality and community. Friends enjoy contact and interaction; but too much contact can smother the relationships and create tension. Other tensions involve organizational roles. Friendships are most stable if both parties are open, honest, and nonjudgmental. But organizational roles often require people to evaluate one another's work, especially in supervisor–subordinate relationships and in work teams, and organizational situations usually limit the kinds of information that coworkers can share with one another.[19]

Learning to Choose and Use Appropriate Influence Strategies

As new employees settle in to their organizations, they learn to make sense out of the situations they face. Eventually, they learn how to manage those situations communicatively. They develop an image that is positive and accepted, and they learn how to construct messages that influence others. By learning to communicate strategically, they become effective parts of their organizations.

Image-Management Strategies   For millennia communication scholars have recognized the impact that a communicator's image has on her or his messages. As early as 330 B.C., Aristotle observed that the images speakers create of themselves are their strongest persuasive tools. Images are created through communication and can be altered by subsequent communication. The content of organizational communicators' messages, the justifications they provide for their recommendations, and the beliefs and values they espouse, all influence their images. Conversely, the images they create influence the way other employees interpret, evaluate, and respond to their messages. Employees cannot choose between creating an image and not creating one. They *can* choose between creating an image by chance or doing so by design. They can manage the images they present without being dishonest. Every person has a number of traits, abilities, and personality characteristics. Impression management means accenting some of those characteristics and de-emphasizing others. It involves putting on one's "best face" but not putting on a false face.

Because impression management is so pervasive in organizations, one employee rarely can know the "real" person of another employee. Erving Goffman, a sociologist whose research provides the most thorough analysis of image management, has differentiated a person's ***public self***—the image that the people around us have of us—and our ***private self***—the image that we have of ourselves. To feel comfortable in relationships with others, Goffman argues, people need to be able to keep some of their self private. In organizational relationships, the barriers to self-disclosure are even greater. Consequently, one employee can know only the surface person, the public image created by other employees.[20] Hiring decisions are based largely on selection agents' conclusions about the extent to which candidates match their images of the kind of person needed for a particular job. Promotions are granted or withheld primarily on the basis of how well an employee's image conforms to decision-makers' preferred images. Employees live in fishbowls (or given the size of most organizations, in aquariums) in which they are constantly observed and their actions analyzed and interpreted.

Once employees learn the attributes that are valued by members of their organizations, they can begin to create situationally appropriate images. If the gap between one's public and private images is too great, that person has to engage in a great deal of exhausting pretending. In these cases employees might be wiser to either change their aspirations or move to an organization in which their private image would be valued. For example, professors who enjoy performing in the spotlight probably should gravitate toward institutions that value undergraduate teaching; those who are most comfortable working alone or with small groups may be more successful and more comfortable in major graduate research universities.

Once an image has been created, it must be maintained. Doing so is made difficult by the dynamics of nonverbal communication. Some nonverbal cues are easy to manage; others are not. Personal appearance can be consciously managed and has been related to career success, although the size of the effect is small. In general, people who fulfill cultural assumptions about what constitutes attractiveness may be preferred over people who do not. For example, in U.S. organizations men who are tall (over 6 feet) and trim have been shown to have higher salaries than men who are short (5 feet, 5 inches) and overweight. Having long hair or beards is negatively related to getting an initial job offer, especially in organizations or careers in which having a particular kind of appearance is a strong taken-for-granted assumption (for example, accounting). For women, the dynamic is more complicated. Hair that is too short may seem to be unfeminine and violate traditional cultural assumptions about sex roles; but hair that is too long (or blonde) may be interpreted as sexy and contribute to perceptions of incompetence or low intelligence.

Other nonverbal cues are more difficult to manage consciously. Maintaining direct eye contact, active gesturing, a relaxed and open body position, responsive nonverbal cues (e.g., nodding in agreement), and leaning forward while talking are all perceived positively and can be consciously controlled. For example, in job interviews, interviewers' perceptions of an applicant's social skills seem to be more positive if the applicant is animated (gestures actively for a period of time during the interview), responsive (provides extended and relevant responses to questions), and conforms to expectations regarding attire and appearance (is moderately formally dressed).

Fortunately, "presenting an appropriate self" (as Goffman labels the image-maintenance process) is made easier by two elements of interpersonal communication. First, people usually establish working agreements to support one another's public images. If any participants violate the implied agreement, they risk having others retaliate by undermining their images. Image maintenance is also aided by the availability of front and back stages in interactions. Even in organizational fishbowls, there are times and places in which people can rehearse and perfect the communication patterns they are trying to establish. The need for back stages is one of the reasons that employees have resisted open-office arrangements: Walls and doors create back stages. Removing these physical barriers to communication robs employees of the vital process of rehearsing their images.

Image-maintenance strategies can also be used to defend one's image after making errors.[21] Of course, one can offer a legitimate apology—admitting error, accepting responsibility, and suggesting remedies or reparations. Doing so may assuage one's guilt and save one's face; but it also invites sanctions. Consequently, in organizational discourse, legitimate apologies are relatively rare. It is more likely that an employee will simply *deny* having made the error. One also may offer a *quasi-theory,* that is used to explain away errors. In our culture commonly used quasi-theories include boys will be boys, or we had a falling out. Or, one may offer an *excuse* in which one acknowledges making an error but denies any harmful intent or claims that she or he had no choice in the matter (the devil made me do it). One may *justify* one's actions by blaming them on some socially accepted rule or conduct, on organizational policies, or a higher authority. One can offer *counterclaims,* in which one denies intentions to influence or hurt anyone or asserts that he or she really had the other person's interests at heart (I really wasn't trying to sell you more life insurance, I was just telling you what I do for a living, or this policy is such a wonderful deal that I really had to share it with you). Another strategy is *bolstering,* in which the accused person (or company) accepts the charges but attempts to overcome them by linking himself or herself to relationships, concepts, or objects that the audience values.[22]

For example, during 1996 the Texaco Oil Company became involved in a highly publicized case of racial discrimination. A suit filed in 1994 claimed that Texaco systematically discriminated against minority employees in favor of less qualified whites in hiring and promotion decisions and fostered a racially hostile environment. Plaintiffs complained of being called uppity for asking questions about policies and procedures and of being called orangutans and porch monkeys. Texaco *denied* that any discrimination had taken place. Federal law requires plaintiffs to produce hard evidence that their treatment was both discriminatory and that the discrimination was because of their race. There are many ways for a company to hide evidence of discrimination—obscuring discriminatory decisions in larger downsizing moves, changing job descriptions to make a qualified minority applicant seem unqualified, or (as Texaco did) simply keeping one set of records for private use and another for government agencies, courts, and the public. As a result, it is almost impossible to obtain direct evidence of discrimination, so denial is a very effective strategy. Without direct evidence, the 1994 suit had languished, although in early 1996 the Equal Employment Opportunity Commission issued a preliminary decision in favor of the plaintiffs. This decision triggered what was to become a fateful meeting among Texaco executives.

It was a frank and wide-ranging discussion of issues related to Texaco's affirmative actions programs. Worried about the suit, David Keough (senior assistant treasurer) discussed ways to *carefully* destroy company documents so that evidence of discrimination was eliminated but evidence supporting Texaco's case was retained. The secret appraisal documents and minutes of meetings during which they were discussed were the biggest concern. Robert Ulrich, the company treasurer, concluded that "you know, there is no point in even keeping the restricted version anymore. All it could do is get us in trouble." After reviewing Texaco's promotion history, Ulrich noted that "all the black jelly beans seem to be glued to the bottom of the bag." Eventually the executives discussed their feelings about the suit and the employees who had filed it. Ulrich complained that those "niggers" were causing difficulties for them.

None of this would ever have been known except for two events. Richard Lundwall, the coordinator of personnel in Texaco's finance department, had been assigned to keep minutes on the meeting and had tape-recorded it to have an accurate record. In August 1996 Texaco fired Lundwall in a downsizing move, and he turned his tapes over to the plaintiffs' attorneys, who released them to the *New York Times.* They broke the story on November 4.

Denial was no longer a viable response; and there simply were no quasi-theories, excuses, or justifications readily available. Texaco immediately shifted strategies to a barrage of *bolstering*. Texaco attorney Andrea Christiansen was "shocked and dismayed" by the tapes; CEO Peter Bijur announced that "the rank insensitivity demonstrated in the taped remarks . . . offends me deeply. . . . This alleged behavior does not represent the way the company feels about any of our employees. This alleged behavior violates our code of conduct, our core values, and the law. . . .Wherever the truth leads, we'll go." He also announced that Texaco would hire an outside attorney to assist the authorities with the investigation, would spend $35 million on outside evaluations and enhancement of Texaco's affirmative action and diversity management programs, and had hired an outside expert to evaluate the tape. On November 14 Texaco announced a new scholarship program for minority students, but said that "the program has nothing to do with recent negative publicity concerning published reports of racial slurs used by company executives." Faced with a boycott of its products by civil rights groups, Texaco settled the two-year-old suit within two months and accepted external oversight of hiring and promotion programs as part of the settlement. Virtually everything that a company and its spokespersons can say or do to bolster its image as a nondiscriminatory employer was done between November 1996 and January 1997.

In addition, the company briefly offered a *counterclaim*. The independent specialist hired and paid by Texaco to analyze the tape reported that the word that had initially been translated as "nigger" really was "St. Nicholas." But this strategy was short-lived, because, as CEO Bijur admitted when the finding was announced, "these preliminary findings merely set the record straight as to the exact words spoken in the conversations; but they do not change the categorically unacceptable context and tone of these conversations."[23] Although it is too early to assess the extent to which Texaco has altered its discriminatory culture and practices, the organization's responses did succeed in diverting attention and rebuilding the organization's image.

Similar strategies can be used to maintain individual employees' images in the face of adverse events or errors. Shifting responsibility and changing perspectives allows employees to maintain images of rationality, expertise, and competence. But all image-management strategies involve presenting information to others that alters their interpretations of events. To maintain their images, employees must have access to and control of valuable information, and they must understand the strategies that can be used to maintain images. It is inevitable that employees develop images. The decision they must make is whether to allow their images to emerge through accident or as the result of careful strategic communication.

Choosing Appropriate Influence Strategies   Analyzing organizational situations provides guidelines about what communicative strategies to use and how to turn those strategies into messages. Of course, one aspect of the situations an employee faces is his or her image. A communicator's image influences the credibility of any message that she or he might construct, just as the credibility of the messages influence image.

Fortunately, employees have a wide variety of message strategies available to them; unfortunately they do not seem to strategically select from the available options unless specifically trained to do so.[24] These strategies can be grouped into three categories, *open persuasion, manipulative persuasion,* and *manipulation.* Open persuasion occurs when employees make their goals and methods clear to their target(s). Some open persuasion strategies are *cooperative,* as when an influencer bases appeals on rational arguments grounded in the available information. Bargaining may also be an open, cooperative strategy if both parties are interested in achieving a mutually beneficial outcome.

Other open persuasion strategies are *competitive,* as when an influencer simply orders someone to do something or threatens or promises sanctions. Threats, promises, and self-centered bargaining are available to all employees; even workers at the bottom of the organization can threaten to quit working or promise to work harder. As one might expect, subordinates rarely use competitive strategies to influence their supervisors; rational strategies are used instead. However, when resources are tight, and competition for them is intense, competitive strategies are more common.[25]

A second type of influence strategies involve manipulative persuasion, when influencers disguise their strategies but not their goals. *"Going over someone's head,"* seeking support from coworkers, and manipulating interpersonal relationships are competitive versions of this strategy. *"Wearing a target down"* with repetitive influence attempts is another. *Ingratiation,* making others feel important or humbling oneself, is a common cooperative form. Although ingratiation rarely influences decisions or outcomes, it does seem to make targets like influencers more, which may benefit them in the long run.

The final category involves manipulation, disguising one's goals and one's strategies. A complex version of manipulation involves overloading a target person with information until the target is confused. The influencer then offers a solution that she or he prefers. There is a substantial amount of evidence that manipulation is the most common organizational influence strategy. The reason is simple: the potential costs of failing to influence are smallest when one's intention to influence is hidden. If the influencer fails, he or she can merely claim not to have been trying to influence. Retribution then would be seen by others as arbitrary and capricious behavior.

Concern for retribution also seems to influence organizational persuaders' choices of *targets* for their efforts. The optimal target is someone who is sufficiently powerful in the organization to actually influence the outcome of an issue, but who cannot retaliate against an employee who tries to influence him or her but fails. Trying to influence one's immediate supervisor carries risks, because the superior can retaliate if the attempt is offensive. It is safer to choose a target who can impose smaller costs—a peer, group of peers, or employee in another unit of the organization. Thus, two supply sergeants at different bases will bargain with one another for desired materials more than they will bargain with their base commandants. If the negotiations go awry, neither one can punish the other. Thus, the optimal target for influence attempts is the weakest person in the organization who can give the influencer what she or he wants. But, regardless of the target choice, in general, the softer influence strategies (open persuasion or ingratiation) seem to be more effective in persuading other employees to change their beliefs or actions than harder strategies.[26]

Other factors that influence employees' choices of strategies include their *cultural backgrounds* and *goals,* and the *point in the influence effort.* For example, European American managers in U.S. firms seem to use different strategies depending on the issue. When the issue is clearly within the manager's formal authority (for example, a subordinate not coming to work on time), managers tend to use highly individualistic and dominating strategies—issuing ultimatums or threatening the subordinate with punishment. When the issue is less clearly within the manager's range of formal authority, managers tend to use softer individualistic strategies—requests (such as, I want you to feel free to ask me for help), promises (I reward people who have good ideas), and ingratiation (I really trust your judgment). In contrast, Japanese managers seem to use community-related strategies regardless of the issue—altruism and appeals to duty (such as For the good of the company, please do it) or counseling (Can I help you get here on time?). Of course, European American managers also occasionally use community-related strategies and Japanese managers also sometimes use individualistic strategies. In addition, there is no evidence that all Japanese (or all European American) managers are alike in their selection of influence strategies. But the tendencies of the two groups seem to be quite clear regardless of the kind of organization they work in and clearly related to their cultures of origin.[27]

Communicators' goals also seem to influence strategy selection, at least among European American employees. When the goal is to improve performance or meet organizational objectives, cooperative strategies are more common; when the objective is to get personal assistance or rewards, ingratiation is most common. When the target has high formal status, rational argument is most common; when the target is of low status, competitive and manipulative strategies seem to dominate. Supervisors' personal preferences seem to be a more important influence on their choices of influence strategies than strategic considerations: They use friendly and attractive compliance strategies with subordinates whose communication is friendly and attractive, and they use unattractive strategies with subordinates who communicate in unattractive ways.

Finally, communicators seem to use different influence strategies at different *"points in the influence effort."* Organizational communicators are similar to modern politicians, who do not try to sway voters with a single brilliant speech or television ad but instead hope to influence them through a lengthy persuasive campaign. Organizational politicians usually begin influence efforts with open and cooperative strategies and shift to competitive or manipulative communication when they encounter resistance or discover that more cooperative strategies have failed.[28]

Three conclusions can be drawn about research on choices of influence tactics. The first is that supervisors really do engage in preferential treatment—they communicate differently with those they like than with those they do not like. The second is that, as virtually everything else about organizational communication, the choice of influence strategies is reciprocal. Supervisors mirror the influence styles of their subordinates, who in turn mirror the supervisors' influence styles. Third, the influence strategies used in organizations reflect their masculine character. They are individualistic and emphasize competition and achieving goals, usually by gaining or asserting control over other people. They focus on protecting one's identity and feelings. Like any other organizational strategy, a preference for masculine influence styles is a choice, a choice that employees may not be aware they are making because it is a taken-for-granted assumption. Other influence systems are possible. For example, organizations could adopt feminine influence tactics, ones that value the ideas of all members of the organization, focus on equality and openness, and value tentativeness and flexibility. However, these tactics are appropriate only in particular contexts—where an organization makes sense to all of its members, where people feel *safe* to take risks and self-disclose, and where organizational control systems are not excessively constraining. These conditions do seem to exist in some alternative forms of organizing (see Chapter 8); but even there they are difficult to sustain because masculine strategies are viewed as normal and natural (recall Chapter 1) in organizations.[29]

Developing Effective Messages   Employees inevitably need to explain their recommendations, proposals, and positions on issues. Some explanations are ***justifications*** (reasons presented in public before an action is taken, a policy is implemented, or an issue is resolved); others are ***rationalizations*** (reasons presented after a decision or action). Both forms of explanation are essentially the same—they are presented by an image to an audience through some medium of communication and consist of reasons arranged in some order. In the best of times employees carefully choose the reasons, structure, medium, and image. In the worst of times they do not.

If employees notice that in their organization's rationalizations are often based on statistical data of a certain type, they can conclude that this kind of data is a place from which they can draw reasons for policies and actions. Conversely, if they find that statistical data are *never* offered successfully as reasons, they can eliminate this kind of information from their list of potential justifications. Of course, some of the items in the acceptable list are more powerful than others in particular organizational situations. For example, moral arguments like fairness, equity, and honesty may be used successfully in personnel decisions but not in budget decisions. In other situations, none of the usually acceptable reasons are viable, forcing the employee to employ a usually unacceptable reason and create some plausible explanation of why is it appropriate in this case and only in this case. Our point is that the actions of employees determine which reasons are acceptable; employees sometimes change their minds; and naive employees can get caught in the middle of the shift if they are not careful.

Once employees choose a set of situationally appropriate reasons to support their ideas, they still have to express those reasons in a message. In Western societies and organizations, messages are more influential if they are clear, organized, include extensive supportive evidence, and generally create an impression of rationality. Creating effective messages involves a great deal of editing. In general, messages that offer simple, straightforward *expressions* of one's feelings or thoughts tend to be minimally effective. Most organizational situations are complex and multidimensional, requiring people to pursue multiple goals simultaneously. For example, subordinates almost always want to construct messages that *both* preserve or strengthen their relationships with their supervisors and achieve one or more tangible goals. Even when a supervisor–subordinate relationship is hostile or otherwise negative, subordinates want to maintain at least the minimum level of civility needed to perform his or her assigned tasks.[30] Expressive messages tend to be too simple and blunt to achieve multiple goals simultaneously. And, they tend to lock relationships into us-against-them patterns, polarize positions on the issue(s) being discussed, and create ill feelings. If reciprocated they tend to create rapidly escalating conflicts (see Chapter 10).

Messages that draw on the *conventions* of a society or organization tend to be more effective than expressive messages. But by using the rules and resources that exist in a particular situation of a group, conventional messages reproduce situational rules and tend to create rigid, emotionally distant, formal work relationships. *Rhetorical messages* allow employees to pursue multiple objectives simultaneously—express feelings, create harmony, foster relational development, demonstrate sensitivity to others, and generate productive outcomes. They recognize the unique circumstances faced by the other person or the unique complications that exist in a particular situation. And, they also tend to be ***strategically ambiguous.***[31]

Students and employees are often told that clarity is a virtue. But in organizational situations, ambiguity can be strategic. It allows someone to speak without being held accountable for what he or she says. Employees sometimes may want to say, "Making a good decision on this issue is more important to this organization than pretending that we all get along." But they realize that the message must be presented in a way that ensures that only insiders will know its real meaning. One of the marvelous features of communication is that people can exchange a great deal of information without ever saying anything explicit. Items that are omitted often say more than items that are included. Messages can *imply* many things without ever saying them.

Strategic ambiguity also allows people to violate expectations—to say things that are not supposed to be said—without overtly doing so. For example, in contemporary organizations, recommendation letters are often left ambiguous for two reasons. Legal factors may make it impossible to keep recommendation letters confidential. If recommenders prefer not to spend time in court, they have three options: refuse to write a recommendation (which also may be cause for legal action), write only factual information (telling when a person worked at the organization, what jobs he or she held, and so on), or write a highly ambiguous letter. The second reason involves the circumstances surrounding a worker's termination. It is often in the best interests of the organization to persuade an employee to resign rather than be fired (the organization may be able to avoid paying unemployment compensation or fulfilling contractual obligations regarding severance pay). Typically, part of the arrangement that is negotiated involves giving future employers positive, or at least neutral, recommendations. Ambiguous messages allow these negotiations to succeed. But it works only when both sender and receiver understand its value and are willing to tolerate its use.

Ambiguity also allows different people to interpret the same message in different ways, helping to maintain a diversity of perspectives within an organization. When the organization faces new or particularly difficult problems, diversity of interpretations can lead to innovative solutions. Interpretations differing from what was intended often reveal problems in the organization and can eventually lead to organizational change. If goals and procedures set in the past are clear, they are also constraining. If they are ambiguous, they can be changed without anyone having to admit that they have abandoned the past.

Finally, ambiguity also may allow people to take actions that are necessary but forbidden by existing policies and procedures. A supervisor usually cannot openly tell his or her subordinates, "OK, do it that way, but if you get caught I'll never admit that we had this conversation." He or she can, however, leave instructions so ambiguous that a sensitive subordinate will get the message. Ambiguity provides flexibility, and in highly structured organizations, flexibility may be more important than clarity. However, ambiguity can also be used to manipulate employees. People are led to believe that commitments have been made that later are not carried out. They take risks and exert time and effort for promised rewards that do not materialize. They become angry and defensive, resorting to the destructive bureaucratic behaviors that were described in Chapter 2. Cycles of distorting and withholding information are established, and people become more concerned with creating a protective paper trail documenting their activities than in maintaining effective work groups.

In general, rhetorical messages are more effective than expressive or conventional ones. They are quite common in good working relationships, and uncommon in poor ones. This seems to be largely because of supervisors' biases. They seem to allow their preferred subordinates a great deal of latitude about the kinds of messages they can use. Preferred subordinates can pursue many objectives simultaneously—they can engage in small talk and informal discussions of a wide range of personal and nonwork-related topics. Preferred subordinates may even construct messages designed to negotiate a better relationship or to establish informal contracts about how the two parties act toward one another. In contrast, supervisors seem to require their nonpreferred subordinates to use expressive or conventional messages. Nonpreferred subordinates respond in kind, often by using protective strategies, such as withholding or distorting information (recall Chapter 2), further locking the relationship into a distant and tense pattern. In a complex cycle, relational factors guide and constrain message production and message effectiveness, and the types and effectiveness of the messages that people produce create and sustain relational factors.

Learning to Manage Emotions

Work is a very emotional activity; organizations are sites where the strongest emotions—anger, pride, satisfaction, frustration, irritation, gloom, excitement, and fear—are commonplace. This observation seems obvious; but it contradicts long-held notions that organizational success and efficiency depend on rational actions. In this view, good organizations are places where feelings are eliminated or managed in private. This bias toward rationality is deeply imbedded in Western culture, which has long separated feelings from thoughts, relegating the former to the private realms of home and family and the latter to public realms of commerce and politics. It is exaggerated in "scientific management-oriented" strategies of organizing (recall Chapter 2), and in masculine definitions of organizational life.[32]

But, as the chapters in Unit I indicated, this is simply untrue. From creating pride in a job well done to enhancing job satisfaction to encouraging organizational identification, strategies of organizing focus on worker's emotions, treating them as an outcome of effective leadership or as a means of fostering organizational control. In addition, feelings and thoughts simply cannot be separated—they are inter-related in complicated ways. Emotions influence what people think about and how they think about those topics. Emotional responses are triggered by thoughts. When normal processes of making sense out of a person's surroundings are upset or interrupted that person experiences a flood of emotions—confusion, insecurity, fear, and/or anger. And emotional responses continue until the person is able to think her or his way to a new system of sense making.

A Model of Organizational Emotionality   Our model of emotional response begins with *expectations* (see Figure 7-1). People learn rules about emotions from their families, religious organizations, and the mass media. These rules tell them what emotions are appropriate to feel, when it is appropriate to feel them, and how they should be interpreted. In Western societies, children usually learn that while positive emotions can be useful, negative ones are dangerous and destructive. European Americans prefer to hide anger, embarrassment, jealousy, fear, and guilt and to hide even positive emotions if they are too intense. Boys learn to interpret a wide variety of feelings they experience as hurt and they learn to remain stoic in public. While they are allowed to express anger, they learn to act physically on their feelings rather than display them communicatively. Girls learn to suppress displays of anger or to express that emotion through tears rather than by acting out. People generally believe that men focus their attention on the problem that leads to emotions while women focus on the emotions themselves. However, research indicates that Anglo Americans of both sexes tend to be problem or action-oriented, and differences in how they interpret feelings depends much more on the situation itself than on gender.

In all cultures some people learn to be highly adept at interpreting others' emotional states; others do not. In general people become more skilled at doing so as they mature, at least through midlife. Westerners also learn that emotions are located within individuals and interfere with reasoning. In other societies individual feelings are not even worth discussing; in still others children learn that emotions are "real" only when they are shared or built through interaction with others. For example, Chinese children typically learn that emotions are nat-

FIGURE 7–1

A Model of Organizational Emotions

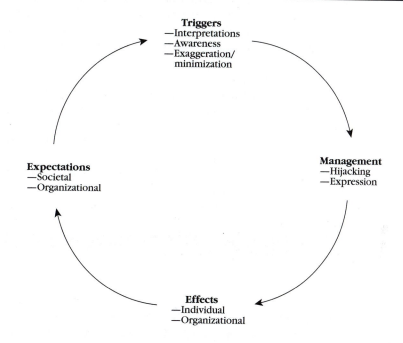

ural and normal, and are directly connected to reasoning processes. They also learn a complex set of emotion rules—to neutralize inner feelings and restrain overt expressions of emotions to maintain face and group harmony. Societal rules preclude expressing negative emotions in public and require expressions of positive emotions to be restrained. Getting in touch with one's inner feelings, a very popular concept in Western popular literature since World War II, is relatively unimportant. Tensions and inconsistencies between one's inner feelings and one's expressions of emotion are much less troubling than they are for Westerners and may even be viewed as an opportunity to learn to be more sensitive and responsive to the needs of the group. In fact, acting on one's feelings can undermine the community ties that give people feelings of security and connectedness. Reciprocity in actions and feelings is valued highly and it is more acceptable to express other-oriented emotions (for example, sympathy) than self-oriented ones (anger or pride). For example, when Chinese students were asked to describe a situation that made them angry, they described something that happened to another person significantly more often than they described an event that involved them. Non-Chinese American students did the opposite.[33]

However, the relationship between cultural expectations and emotion rules are very complex. One example involves black women in organizations that are dominated by white males. Two relevant stereotypes are black women as mammies and as matriarchs. The former focuses on the role of nurturing caretaker and creates the expectation that black women will serve as a mother confessor and comfort-giver for other members of the organization, and as an advocate for members of low-power groups, including other minority employees. The latter stereotype creates expectations that black women will be aggressive, overbearing, and confrontational. Since black women are aware of these stereotypes, they may be exceptionally careful to not display emotions such as anger, frustration, or disappointment, lest they perpetuate the stereotypes.[34]

Another example involves Chinese managers of plants in China. Bureaucracy dominates Chinese organizations and it emphasizes the virtue of *li*, which means correct behavior, the need to act in a way that is consistent with one's role in the bureaucratic hierarchy. But, unlike Western versions of bureaucracy in which employees are supposed to maintain distant, impersonal relationships, supervisors in Chinese bureaucracies are expected to look after and educate their subordinates. As a result, supervisors act in ways that are paternalistic and inequitable by Western standards. As a result, Chinese managers report that events that effect the social order in their plants are more emotionally involving than any other kind of event. One noted that, when the plant achieved its goals he felt a great deal of pride *in the group.* "when this comes true, because of the joint efforts of all employees. I realize that our employees are capable people . . . and that we are able to develop of production successfully. So I was very pleased." Another reported feeling sadness (not anger) when his superiors rejected his advice and made a bad decision that created a burden on his employees. When they experience strong emotions, they attempt to think the situation through with the employees who are involved:

> No matter how depressing or exciting it can be . . . one has to remind oneself to cool down, not to allow my emotion to influence subordinates or other employees so as not to affect the work. The thing to do in this kind of situation is stay away from everyone for a while, try to calm one's emotions and think up some ways of dealing with things.

But first:

> One has to look for one's own part in the problem . . . My experience is that as long as one treats himself firmly and with discipline, and treats others kindly and clearly distinguishes between right and wrong, one will not have bad moods.

Of course, in spite of the emotion rules of Chinese society, managers sometimes do feel and express strong emotions, just as Western bureaucrats sometimes find it impossible to maintain detached, unemotional relationships with their subordinates. But they recognize that doing so is improper, and resolve to manage those emotions in socially appropriate ways.

Organizations and organizational subcultures (recall Chapter 4) have their own emotion rules—they "bond people emotionally, while also defining the nature, form, and legitimacy of their emotionality."[35] These rules stipulate what emotions people can feel and what emotions they can express. They vary across different organizational roles, different kinds of work, and different audiences. Managers are supposed to feel commitment to the organization and excitement about their work and to express both emotions when subordinates are present. Disney workers are allowed more freedom to express negative emotions with coworkers, somewhat less with supervisors, and none with guests. Supervisors expect a certain level of deference from their subordinates and are allowed (or required) to feel anger or disdain when they do not receive it. Like any other organizational rules, feeling rules are introduced during selection processes, codified during training sessions, and enforced through the normal organizational reward system.

Emotions are *triggered* when people's normal processes of making sense out of their surroundings are upset or interrupted, when employees *interpret* an event or action as violating their expectations. When everyday routines are violated, feelings are aroused. It is not clear which comes first—the interpretation (thought) or the feeling—but it is clear that the bigger the violation of expectations, the more intense the resulting emotion will be. However, people are able to manage emotional triggers strategically by controlling their awareness of their feelings. They can minimize their emotional involvement by distracting their attention away from the emotional triggers. For example, construction workers on the tops of buildings can focus the attention away from their fears. Employees can minimize the significance of the situation or the trigger itself (for example, she or he is just tired and stressed out today; or that award is no big deal, so it doesn't really matter who won it). Or, they can use a variety of communication strategies to minimize the emotion. Students label exams quizzes instead of finals; construction workers refer to falling off of a building as falling in a hole, as if they are safely on the ground; or people find something *humorous* in even the most frightening or anger-inducing situations. Each of these strategies makes them feel that they are in control of the situation, and feeling in control tends to reduce other emotions.

Conversely, people may want to find ways to maximize their emotions. Acting on a problem takes energy, and emotions often provide that energy. For example, one of the greatest challenges faced by dual career couples is finding mutually acceptable ways of managing household chores. The available research indicates quite clearly that, although some change has taken place, women bear the bulk of household responsibilities. In couples where both parties believe that the wife is wholly responsible for housework, that husbands have no domestic responsibilities, and that wives should feel gratitude whenever their husbands do perform tasks around the house, the issue is not emotionally charged (although the wife probably is exhausted much of the time). However, in couples where the wife does not share these beliefs, she is likely to be angry much of the time. However, traditional societal norms and myths make it difficult for her to express that anger or to take steps to negotiate a more satisfying arrangement. When wives do focus their attention on their feelings that the arrangement was unfair and dwell on its importance to them, they can overcome those societal barriers. When they focus on their emotions they are able to act.[36]

Once employees choose to be aware of their emotions, they must *manage* them. Interestingly, there is evidence that managing emotional expressions manages the emotions themselves. People can hijack their emotions by responding in a certain way—remaining calm when the boss yells or continuing to be quietly supportive when a patient becomes hysterical actually can dissipate anger. People can seek out coworkers who respond to trigger events in the ways that they want to respond. And, they can learn to adapt their emotional responses to different audiences strategically. They may suppress their anger with people who have higher status or power in their organizations. Passions are real, but they can be used "tactically."[37] The challenge is to find some way to reconcile spontaneous feelings and strategic sensibilities. Like any other aspect of strategic communication, emotion management is learned, so some people do it much better than others. Some families and schools teach children emotion management more effectively than others do. There also seem to be differences in skills across different groups. For example, people who typically occupy low power/status roles in Western organizations (women and members of minority groups) seem to be more skilled at interpreting emotions and managing emotional expressions than are people who occupy high status/power roles (European American males). Errors in emotion management are potentially very damaging for low-power people, so they develop the skills necessary to protect themselves.

Finally, emotional management has effects, both for organizations and their members. Organizations in which people consistently suppress, redefine, or excessively manage their emotions tend to be resistant to change. If employees do not manage their emotions adequately, they tend to be dissatisfied, experience high levels of stress, are prone to burning out, and are generally ineffective. Employees who find ways to mange the tension between spontaneous and strategic emotions tend to have more productive and satisfying lives.

CONCLUSION

Organizational communication is *strategic*. It involves choosing communicative strategies for managing those situations. However, strategically managing organizational situations is not the same thing as *accommodating* oneself to organizational constraints. One of the recurring themes of this book is that while communication often does *reproduce* the guidelines and constraints that employees face, it does not have to do so. Communication can also be used to *resist* and even *transform* situational constraints.

We have included this cautionary reminder because many published discussions of communication competence equate competent communication with compliant or accommodationist communication. An entire industry of publications, consultants, and trainers has developed whose goal is to teach managers (and *only* managers) how to be effective communicators.[38] Like all forms of systematically distorted communication (recall Chapter 4), the rhetoric of communication competence *appears* to be equitable and neutral. But the goal of these programs is often to increase managerial control of employees, or to motivate workers to make sacrifices that promise few rewards for them. Competent *subordinates* would upset the system. Supervisors may *say* that they want their subordinates to be competent communicators, but *mean* that they want compliant communicators. In contrast, we have suggested that communication competence need not mean *accommodation* at all. It can involve the effective use of communicative strategies by all employees to create more meaningful and more fulfilling work situations and working relationships.

NOTES

[1] The entry experience usually is thought of as occurring in stages, but doing so can easily be misleading. It is made up of the processes that occur throughout a person's experience in an organization—they are continuous, overlapping, and do not occur in a fixed sequence. There do seem to be key "turning points" that, in retrospect, signaled the declining importance of some thoughts, emotions, and communication processes and the increased importance of others (J. Kevin Barge and G.W. Musambria, "Turning Points in Chair-Faculty Relationships," *Journal of Applied Communication Research, 20* [1992]: 54–77; Connie Bullis and Betsy Wackernagel Bach, "Socialization Turning Points," *Western Journal of Speech Communication, 53* [1989]: 273–293. Excellent summaries of research on the entry experience include Vernon Miller and Fredric Jablin, "Information Seeking during Organizational Entry," *Academy of Management Review 16* (1991): 92–120 and Fredric Jablin, "Organizational Entry, Assimilation and Exit," in *The New Handbook of Organizational Communication,* Fredric Jablin and Linda Putnam, eds. (Newbury Park, CA: Sage, 2000). Two classic articles are Meryl Reis Louis, "Surprise and Sense-making in Organizations," *Administrative Science Quarterly, 25* (1980): 226–251; and John van Maanen and Edgar Schein, "Toward a Theory of Socialization," in *Research in Organizational Behavior,* Barry Staw, ed. (Greenwich, CT: JAI Press, 1979), vol I.

[2] For fine summaries of newcomers' information-seeking tactics, see Vernon Miller and Fredric Jablin, "Information-seeking During Organizational Entry," *Academy of Management Review, 16* (1991): 92–120; Debra Comer, "Organizational Newcomers' Acquisition of Information from Peers," *Management Communication Quarterly, 5* (1991): 64–89; and Michael Kramer, R.R. Callister, & D.B. Turban, "Information-Receiving and Information-giving During Job Transitions," *Western Journal of Communication, 39* (1995): 151–170.

[3] A summary of these personality variables is available in Terrance Albrecht and Betsy Bach, Organizational Communication: A Relational Perspective (Fort Worth, TX: Harcourt Brace, 1996, especially Chapter 7); also see Renee Edwards, "Sensitivity to Feedback and the Development of Self," *Communication Quarterly, 38* (1990): 101–111 and Meryl Reis Louis, "Acculturation in the Workplace," in *Organizational Climate and Culture,* B. Schneider, ed. (San Francisco: Jossey-Bass, 1990). Personality variables seem to not be important for people involved in job transfers (see Fredric Jablin & Michael Kramer, "Communication-related Sense-making and Adjustment During Job Transfers," *Management Communication Quarterly, 12* (1998): 155–182.

[4] Robin Patric Clair, "The Political Nature of the Colloquialism, 'A Real Job,'" *Communication Monographs, 63* (1966): 249–267.

[5] Steven Ralston & William Kirkwood, "Overcoming Managerial Bias in Employment Interviewing," *Journal of Applied Communication Research, 23* (1995): 75–92. It also is disorienting when the organization changes around its employees, as in mergers (see David Schweiger & Angelo Denisi, "Communication with Employees Following a Merger," *Academy of Management Journal, 34* [1991]: 110–135.

[6] Bullis & Rohrbauck Stout; Cynthia Stohl, "The Role of Memorable Messages in the Process of Organization Socialization," *Communication Quarterly, 34* (1983): 231–249; Jablin & Kramer.

[7] For excellent analyses of communication surrounding job transfers, see Michael Kramer, "Communication and Uncertainty Reduction During Job Transfers: Leaving and Joining Processes," *Communication Monographs, 60* (1993): 178–198 and "Communication After Job Transfers: Social Exchange Processes in Learning New Roles," *Human Communication Research, 20* (1993): 147–174).

[8] Robert Nelson, *1001 Ways to Take Initiative* (New York: Workman, 1999); Robert Rosner, *Working Wounded* (New York: Warner Books, 1999). Rosner also has created a website which is available through the ABC News website or at workingwounded.com.

[9] Brenda Allen, "A Black Feminist Standpoint Analysis," in *Rethinking Management and Organization Communication from Feminist Perspectives,* Patrice Buzzanell, ed. (Thousand Oaks, CA: Sage, 1999); E.L. Bell, "The Bicultural Life Experience of Career-Oriented Black Women," *Journal of Organizational Behavior, 11* (1990): 459–477; P.H.Collins, "Comment on Hekman's 'Truth and Method'," *Signs, 22* (1997): 375–381; D.C. Hine, "The Future of Black Women in the Academy," in *Black Women in the Academy,* L. Benjamin, ed. (Gainesville: University of Florida Press, 1997); P.S. Parker & D. Ogilvie, "Gender, Culture, and Leadership," *Leadership Quarterly, 7* (1996): 189–214.

[10] See Kathy Kram, *Mentoring* (Chicago: Scott, Foresman, 1986) and R. Michael Bokeno & Vernon Gantt, "Dialogic Mentoring," *Management Communication Quarterly, 14* (2000): 237–270. For work on African Americans, see David Thomas and Clayton Alderfer, "The Influence of Race on Career Dynamics," in *Handbook of Career Theory* (New York: McGraw-Hill, 1989) and Floyd Dickens & Jacqueline Dickens, *The Black Manager* (New York: AMACOM, 1991) and on Hispanics, see Stephen Knouse, "The Mentoring Process for Hispanics," in S. Knouse, P. Rosenfeld, and A. Culberson, *Hispanics in the Workplace* (Newbury Park, CA: Sage, 1992).

[11] "Little Upward Help for Minority Females: Executive Women Say Mentors Needed," Houston *Chronicle,* 14 July, 1999: C3; M. Maynard, "Diversity Programs Work, Where They Exist," *USA Today,* 15 Sept., 1994, p. 5; R. Scherer, "First National Survey of Minority Views Shows Deep Racial Polarization," *Christian Science Monitor,* March, 1994. P. 4.

[12] Bullis & Rohrbacuk Stout; John Dovidio, et al., "Cognitive and Motivational Bases of Bias," in *Hispanics in the Workplace,* P. Knouse, P. Rosenfeld, & A. Culberson, eds. (Newbury Park, CA: Sage, 1992).

[13] "Little Upward Help;" Herminia Ibarra, "Personal Networks of Women and Minorities in Management," *Academy of Management Review, 18* (1993): 56–87 and "Race, Opportunity, and Diversity of Social Circles in Managerial Settings," *Academy of Management Journal, 38* (1995): 673–703; Judi Marshall, *Women Managers Moving On* (London: Routledge, 1995); B. Milwid, *Working with Men* (East Rutherford, NJ: Berkley, 1992); Audrey Edwards & Craig Polite, *Children of the Dream: The Psychology of Black Success* (New York: Doubleday, 1992).

[14] D.E. Eyer, *Mother-Infant Bonding: A Scientific Fiction* (New Haven, CT: Yale University Press, 1992); Gideon Kunda, *Engineering Culture* (Philadelphia: Temple University Press, 1992); Mumby, "Organizing Men," *Communication Theory, 8* (1998): 164–183.

[15] Julia Wood, *Gendered Lives* (Belmont, CA: Wadsworth, 1994).

[16] Frances Westley, "Middle Managers and Strategy," *Strategic Management Journal, 11* (1990): 339. Also see Barbara Czarniawska-Joerges, *Exploring Complex Organizations* (Newbury Park, CA: Sage, 1992) and Karl Weick, *Sensemaking in Organizations* (Thousand Oaks, CA: Sage, 1995).

[17] Paul Watzlawick, Janet Beavin, and Don Jackson, *Pragmatics of Human Communication* (New York: W.W. Norton, 1967).

[18] See Dennis Mumby, "Organizing Men;" Julia Wood, "Engendered Relationships,: in *Processes in Close* Relationships, vol. 3, Steve Duck, ed. (Beverly Hills, CA: Sage, 1993) and *Lives.*

[19] This section is based largely on Karen Bridge and Leslie Baxter, "Blended Relationships: Friends as Work Associates," Western Journal of Communication, 56 (1992): 200–225. Also see D.J. McAllister, "Affect- and Cognition-Based Trust as Foundations for Interpersonal Cooperation in Organizations," *Academy of Management Journal, 38* (1995): 24–59; Michael Kramer, "A Longitudinal Study of Superior-Subordinate Communication During Job Transfers," *Human Communication Research, 22* (1995): 39–64; Patricia Sias and Fredric Jablin, "Differential Superior-Subordinate Relations, Perceptions of Fairness, and Coworker Communication," *Human Communication Research, 22* (1995): 5–38; and Patricia Sias, "Constructing Perceptions of Differential Treatment," *Communication Monographs, 63* (1996): 171–187.

[20] Erving Goffman, *The Presentation of Self in Everyday Life* (New York: Doubleday, 1959) and Goffman, "On Face Work," *Psychiatry, 18* (1955): 213–231. Also see Anthony Giddens, *Modernity and Self Identity* (Palo Alto, CA: Stanford University Press, 1991).

[21] The key source for the following section is William Cupach and Sandra Metts, Facework (Newbury Park, CA: Sage, 1994). For detailed analyses of what we will label "counterclaims," see Joe Folger, Marshall Scott Poole, and Randall Stutman, *Working Through Conflict*, 4th ed. (New

York: Addison-Wesley,2000) and for "conversational repairs," see Michael McLaughlin, *Conversation* (Beverly Hills, CA: Sage, 1984). For an application to the communication of public figures, see B.L. Ware and W.A. Linkugel, "They Spoke in Defense of Themselves," *The Quarterly Journal of Speech, 59* (1973): 273–283.

[22] For a number of case studies in the strategies that organizational rhetors use to maintain the images of their firms, see Elizabeth Lance Toth and Robert Heath, eds., *Rhetorical and Critical Approaches to Public Relations* (New York: Praeger, 1992).

[23] This example is based on Kurt Eichenwald, *New York Times,* November 4, 1966, A1, C4 and "Texaco Reeling from Racial Scandal," Houston *Chronicle,* November 5, 1996, 1C; Sharon Walsh, "Plaintiffs Say Texaco Tough in Bias Cases," Houston *Chronicle,* November 14, 1996, 1C; L.M. Sixel, "Workplace Racism Cases Hard to Win," Houston *Chronicle,* November 13, 1996, 1C; and Salatheia Bryant, "Texaco Initiates Scholarship Program to Help Minorities," Houston *Chronicle,* November 12, 1996, 17A.

[24] See Steven R. Wilson, John O. Greene, & James P. Dillard, "Introduction to the Special Issue on Message Production," *Communication Theory, 10* (2000): 135–138.

[25] For a summary of subordinates' influence strategies, see Kevin Lamude, Tom Daniels, and Kim White, "Managing the Boss," *Management Communication Quarterly, 1* (1987): 232–259. Also see Nancy Roberts, "Organizational Power Styles," *The Journal of Applied Behavioral Science, 22* (1986): 443–455.

[26] Cecilia Falbe and Gary Yukl, "Consequences of Managers' Using Single Influence Tactics and Combinations of Tactics," *Academy of Management Journal, 32* (1992): 638–652.

[27] Randy Hirokawa and A. Miyahara, "A Comparison of Influence Strategies Used by Managers in American and Japanese Organizations," *Communication Quarterly, 34* (1986): 250–265. Also see Young Yong Kim and Katherine Miller, "The Effects of Attributions and Feedback Goals on the Generation of Supervisor Feedback Message Strategies," *Management Communication Quarterly, 4* (1990): 6–29). For an analysis of relational effects on supervisor strategies, see Michael Garko, "Persuading Subordinates Who Communicate in Attractive and Unattractive Styles," *Management Communication Quarterly, 5* (1992): 289–315.

[28] G.H. Morris et al., "Aligning Actions at Work," *Management Communication Quarterly, 3* (1990): 303–333.

[29] See Wood, *Lives* and Sonja Foss & Cindy Griffin, "Beyond Persuasion," *Quarterly Journal of Speech, 62* (1995): 2–18.

[30] See Vince Waldron and Kathy Krone, "The Experience and Expression of Emotion in the Workplace," *Management Communication Quarterly, 4* (1991): 287–309, and Vince Waldron, "Achieving Communication Goals in Supervisor-Subordinate Relationships, *Communication Monographs, 58* (1991): 289–306.

[31] Eric Eisenberg, "Ambiguity as Strategy in Organizational Communication," *Communication Monographs, 51* (1984): 227–242 and Eric Eisenberg and Steven Phillips, "Miscommunication in Organizations," in *"Miscommunication" and Problematic Talk,* N. Coupland, H. Giles, and J. Wieman, eds. (Newbury Park, CA: Sage, 1991).

[32] See Stephen Fineman, "Organizations as Emotional Arenas," in *Emotions in Organizations,* Stephen Fineman, ed. (London: Sage, 1993); Dennis Mumby & Linda Putnam, "The Politics of Emotion," *Academy of Management Review, 17* (1992): 465–486; and Mumby, "Organizing Men,"

[33] See Sally Planalp, *Communicating Emotion* (Cambridge, U.K.: Cambridge University Press, 1999) and "Communicating Emotion," *Communication Theory, 9* (1999): 216–228; H.C. Chang & G.R. Holt, "More than Relationship," *Communication Quarterly, 39* (1991): 251–271; and Kathleen Krone, et al., "Managerial Emotionality in Chinese Factories," *Management Communication Quarterly, 11* (1997): 6–50; Robert Bellah, et al., *Habits of the Heart, 2nd ed.* (Berkeley, CA: University of California Press, 1995); and

[34] Brenda Allen, "Feminist Standpoint Theory," *Communication Studies, 47* (1996): 257–271.

[35] Stephen Fineman, "Emotion and Organizing," in Stewart Clegg, Cynthia Hardy, & Walter Nord, eds., *Handbook of Organizational Studies* (London: Sage, 1996). Also see A. Rafaeli & R. Sutton, "The Expression of Emotion in Organizational Life, II," *Research in Organizational Behavior, 11* (1989): 1–42; John van Maanen & Gideon Kunda, "'Real Feelings,'" *Research in Organizational Behavior, 11* (1989): 43–103; Vincent Waldron & Kathleen Krone, "The Experience and Expression of Emotion in the Workplace," *Management Communication Quarterly, 4* (1991): 287–309; and Greg Fiebig & Michael Kramer, "A Framework for the Study of Emotions in Organizational Contexts," *Management Communication Quarterly, 11* (1998): 536–572.

[36] Arlie Hochschild, "Ideology and Emotion Management," in *Research Agendas in the Sociology of Emotions,* T.D. Kemper, ed. (Albany, NY: SUNY Press, 1990).

[37] The concept of emotional hijacking was introduced by D. Goleman, *Emotional Intelligence* (New York: Bantam Books, 1995). An excellent treatment of strategic uses of emotion is F.G. Bailey, *The Tactical Uses of Passion* (Ithaca, NY: Cornell University Press, 1983).

[38] See Stanley Deetz, *Democracy in an Age of Corporate Colonization* (Albany, NY: SUNY Press, 1992) and *Transforming Communication, Transforming Business* (Creskill, NJ: Hampton Press, 1995).

Chapter 8

COMMUNICATION, POWER, AND POLITICS IN ORGANIZATIONS

Whatever else organizations may be . . . they are political structures. This means that organizations operate by distributing authority and setting a stage for the exercise of power.
—ABRAHAM ZALZENIK

Insofar as knowledge is power, communication systems are power systems.
—DAVID BARBER[1]

CENTRAL THEMES

- Power usually is thought of as the "ability to dominate" other people. Not only does this perspective ignore the "accomplishment" aspect of power, but it also seriously oversimplifies its multifaceted nature.
- Power has two components: a "surface structure," which consists of overt displays of power and conscious but unspoken decisions about who, when, and how to challenge power relationships; and a "deep structure," which consists of unconscious elements of power relationships.
- Power is in the eye of the beholder. Whenever people are able to control resources that others perceive they need, they have a potential base of power.
- Employees can develop power through developing personal characteristics (expertise, interpersonal skills, and access to symbols of power) and through controlling key resources (information, rewards and punishments, roles in coalitions).
- One of the effects of social and organizational power relationships is to silence the voices of dissenting individuals. These processes help explain unethical and/or illegal organizational behavior.
- Power also serves to silence the voices of "different" employees. One of the most important sources of resistance to power relationships is raising those voices.

KEY TERMS

Sovereign power

Surface structure of power

Deep structure of power

Whistle-blowers

Hetrarchies

Disciplinary power

Hidden face of power

Politics

Technical vs. practical questions

Deconstruction

The words *power* and *politics* are used every day by almost everyone to explain much of what happens in life and at work. Consumers decry their powerlessness in the face of big business. Students complain that they are victimized by arbitrary professors and administrators, but can do nothing in response. Subordinates vow to change their organizations for the better as soon as they advance to positions of authority (but they rarely do). Power influences employees' choices about which audiences to address (and which to avoid) and how to communicate to them. Political considerations tell people what actions must be taken in particular situations and what actions and emotions should be suppressed.

If subordinates see their supervisors as powerful members of their organizations, their job satisfaction may increase and their tendency to withhold or distort may decrease. Similarly, if subordinates perceive that their supervisors are actively involved in organizational politics, they may trust them less and be more likely to withhold information.[2] Employees base their choices about how to communicate on their assessment of organizational power relationships and politics, and their choices about how to communicate reproduce power relationships.

A PERSPECTIVE ON ORGANIZATIONAL POWER

Many discussions of organizational power and politics are based on a misconception about what power is and how it functions in organizations. They focus on what Michel Foucault calls "**sovereign power**," the processes through which sovereigns (kings, dictators, prison wardens, or directors of mental institutions) dominate their subjects. Historically, this kind of "power" is connected to the phrase "abuse of" because having total power often leads to its misuse. However, "sovereign" (or "power over") definitions permeate Western society to such a extent that they also influence the way people conceive of power in organizations where control is less total.

There are a number of problems with this "power over" view. One is that it fails to recognize that power is dispersed throughout societies and organizations. It exists in every relationship and every interaction, not just those that cross levels of the organizational hierarchy. As Chapter 2 explained, organizational control does involve simple surveillance by supervisors and systems of control through rules and rewards. It also involves team surveillance/control (Chapter 3) and self-surveillance/control (Chapter 4), processes that Foucault calls "**disciplinary power.**" In modern organizations, disciplinary power is at least as important as sovereign power, so "power over" models seriously oversimplify organizational power relationships.[3]

Second, traditional views of power forget that it is abuse stems from *imbalances* of power, not power itself. The accent in Lord Acton's famous dictum that "absolute power corrupts absolutely" should be on absolutism, not on power. When people have a great deal of power over others they begin to believe that low-power people are inferior and untrustworthy. Conversely, being in low-power positions is also damaging. If people feel powerless, they tend to become depressed and helpless, feel higher levels of stress, develop physical symptoms such as headaches and hypertension, and impede valuable organizational change and innovation. Powerlessness creates feelings of vulnerability, and vulnerability leads to abuse. People need to feel that they have influence over their lives. One way to offset these effects is to help people understand the relationships between power and communication. All power relationships involve opportunities and strategies for resistance. Although knowledge is often used to dominate people, it also can lead to *empowerment*. Increasing the degree of balance in organizational power relationships reduces the potential for abuse.

Third, an "ability to dominate" view of power also makes people overlook the positive role that power plays in mobilizing people and resources to get things done. Power is necessary to accomplish goals, both individual and organizational. If members of an organization define power as "accomplishment" rather than "domination," nonproductive and personally destructive power games are less likely. But because the "domination" view of power is a taken-for-granted assumption in Western societies, it is difficult for people to change their frame of reference. The shift can happen, but only through understanding how communication, power, and politics are interrelated.

The final problem with "sovereign" views is that they focus on only the overt, conscious level of power. We will call this level the **surface structure** of power.[4] It has two dimensions. One involves an *open face* that is composed of overt displays of power—threats, promises, negotiations, orders, coalitions, gag rules and so on. The second dimension of the *surface structure* of power is its **hidden face.** This face works by regulating public and private issues. In organizational life, employees must often make difficult decisions about when and how to challenge power holders. Newcomers soon learn that some issues are not to be discussed in public; some potential solutions are not to be considered openly; and some arguments are not to be made. Open discussions are limited to safe topics (those that power holders are willing to have discussed in public), acceptable alternatives, and unofficially sanctioned premises for making decisions. As a result of these regulatory processes, consensus in open discussions is the rule, not the exception. When disagreements are voiced they tend to be over minor issues and serve the purpose of perpetuating the myth that open, rational, and objective decision making exists in the organization. If individuals violate these constraints, they may either be ignored or attacked by the rest of the group. If they persist they will be "educated" by an unofficial tutor. If they cannot be educated, they may be removed.

But, power also has a second level, a **deep structure** that operates below employees' conscious awareness. Throughout this book, we have discussed the processes through which the taken-for-granted assumptions of a society guide and constrain employees' actions. People act in ways that they have learned are *normal* and *natural* and usually do so without being aware of it. A society's taken-for-granted assumptions tell people who they are, what their role is in society, and where they fit in the formal and informal hierarchies that constitute their society. It is through these nonconscious parameters of action that power is normally exercised. People act in socially-approved ways, not because of overt threats, promises, or appeals, but because doing so is consistent with their non-conscious assumptions about who they are and what actions are normal and natural in their societies and organizations. Usually they never realize that these societal assumptions are part of organizational power relationships.

For example, in Western societies people take it for granted that experts on an issue should have the greatest influence over decisions about that issue. This assumption ensures that people who control access to information or who have had training in argumentation will have the greatest degree of power in decision-making situations. This is true even if the decision is one for which information and argument are largely irrelevant, for example, a highly value-laden issue. For example, deciding when to terminate life support for a terminally ill patient is a matter of values and emotion much more than one of information and exper-tise. But societal assumptions—codified into law in most states—lead people to treat it as an information-based decision to be made by medical experts.[5] By deferring to expert opinions, people support the societal assumption that experts should dominate decision making. In doing so, they reproduce the deep structure of power.

doctors

The taken-for-granted assumptions of societies and their organizations dic-tate that some people will have power over others. But power is not hierarchi-cal; it is diffuse and dispersed. Some source of power is available to every mem-ber of a society or organization. Our goal in this chapter is to examine potential *sources* of power and to describe the communicative strategies that can be used to manage organizational power relationships. In the process, we will discuss the ways in which power is exercised in organizations, a process that we label *organizational politics*.

SOCIETAL ASSUMPTIONS AND THE BASES OF ORGANIZATIONAL POWER

Power is in the eye of the beholder.[6] It is the belief by some members of a soci-ety or organization that they should obey the requests or commands and seek the favor and support of other members. Power is not possessed by a person. It is granted to that person by others. One person may order another to act in a certain way. But the person giving the command has no power over the other until she or he accepts the first person's right to dominate. In this sense, power is a feature of interactions and interpersonal relationships, not of individuals or

simplistic

organizational roles. People have power only when other people perceive that they do and act accordingly.

Creating perceptions of power is important to every employee. But creating perceptions of power is particularly important for people who depend on other people to help them do their jobs. Even employees located near the bottom of an organization can have power if other employees depend on them. If an employee is relatively autonomous and independent, creating and maintaining power is less important. But only completely self-sufficient workers need not be concerned with developing power.

Traditional strategies of organizing assume that power and power relationships could be built into the formal structures of organizations; relational strategies assume they could be imbedded in particular forms of leadership and tasks; cultural strategies inculcate beliefs and values that create distinctive kinds of power relationships; and networking strategies conceptualize power as stemming from one's position in the network and alliances among parties. But there are fissures, gaps, and contradictions in all systems of power. Employees can maneuver within these gaps and manipulate these contradictions by acquiring power on their own, independent of their formal position in their organizations.[7] They can do so by demonstrating that they possess one or more valued *personal characteristics* or that they have the ability to control the distribution of resources valued by other people. But resources cannot be transformed into power unless they are *scarce* (available in supplies that are smaller than the existing demand), *significant* (employees depend on them to do their jobs), and *irreplaceable* (depletable and not easily replaced).

Gaining Power through Personal Characteristics

In Western societies two kinds of personal characteristics are assumed to be a legitimate basis on which some people can obtain and exercise power—*expertise* and *interpersonal relationships.*

Expertise as a Source of Power   In Western societies expertise has at least two dimensions. The first is a person's organization-related *knowledge*.[8] However, knowledge provides power only if other people depend on it and it is scarce, significant, and irreplaceable. This explains why people sometimes do not want to hire the most competent applicant for a job. If the newcomer has the kind of expertise that an old-timer has used to gain power, the newcomer is threatening. When you are the only person who can operate the computer system, you have almost complete power. When you are one of two people who knows how to do so, you have little power unless you can form and sustain an alliance with the other expert. It also explains why employees sometimes develop equipment or procedures that only they understand. Secretaries have known for millennia that if they devise filing systems that only they understand, they may be irreplaceable. In a group of tobacco processing plants the mechanics who repaired machines realized that they had a great degree of power; without their cooperation the plant would come to a grinding halt. Over time they trained new mechanics orally, making sure that there were no written diagrams of equipment or repair instructions around. They modified the equipment in ways that would make it difficult, if not impossible, for outsiders to repair it. As a result, as long as they cooperated with one another, they could virtually force management to act as they wanted. Although their power was fragile, it could be maintained as long as management depended on them to keep the equipment running.[9] More recently middle managers who fear that the installation of computerized management information systems would eliminate their jobs have used similar strategies to increase their organizationally relevant expertise. They may create files that only they can locate, design systems that only they can operate, or enter data in forms that only they can interpret.

Communication is necessary to transform expertise into perceived power. Sometimes other employees do not understand why a particular employee's expertise is important to them and to their organization. This is one of the reasons why it is more difficult for staff personnel to obtain and maintain power than it is for line personnel to do so. The people who occupy the top positions of organizational hierarchies determine what "counts" as expertise, how much value is attached to different kinds of knowledge, and how it is supposed to be used. The upper managers of chemical firms are usually chemists, not human resource specialists. Engineering firms are usually controlled by engineers, not former directors of personnel. They can understand the value of being able to develop new chemicals or design new equipment. They often find it more difficult to understand why the ability to design and administer a new appraisal system is significant.

The second dimension of expertise is an employee's ability to *articulate* positions effectively, to argue successfully in favor of preferred courses of action. Anyone can find facts and arguments to support a position on complex issues. But, as Chapter 7 explained, influence depends on articulating situationally appropriate reasons. In addition, choosing *appropriate* arguments creates an image of expertise. Being able to present masterful, logical arguments in support of a proposal is a wonderful skill. But if the proposal is rejected, the advocate's credibility is reduced, regardless of how brilliant his or her arguments might have been. Good proposals often fail solely for political reasons. They may involve scuttling a powerful member's pet (but failing) project or shifting the staff and budget of a powerful department to a less powerful one. Especially good proposals may even provide evidence that a subordinate is more expert than a supervisor. In all of these cases, the proposal threatens power holders and is likely to be resisted and, ultimately, rejected. In what may seem to be a kind of perverse logic, expert people are those whose ideas are accepted, and people whose ideas are accepted are perceived as experts.

Interpersonal Relationships as a Source of Power   The second primary source of personal power is the creation of *interpersonal relationships.* People have learned that it is natural and normal to comply with the wishes of people with whom they have good relationships. If we believe that refusing to comply with a friend's request may threaten the relationship, we are more likely to comply. Maintaining effective interpersonal relationships also increases a person's power in less direct ways. People view those with whom they have good relationships as being more expert, powerful, and trustworthy than others. They communicate more freely with friends and give them information they can use productively. An employee who has many friends in the organization eventually knows a lot about what is going on and can use that information to create an impression of expertise and power. Because people are attracted to expert, powerful people, they form friendships and share information with them. Sharing provides them with additional information and expertise. In a complex cycle, creating and sustaining interpersonal relationships also enhances an individual's access to other bases of power.

Interpersonal relationships with groups of people also can provide power.[10] Coalitions are particularly important for employees or departments that lack other bases of power. Having allies includes the additional benefits of increasing employees' self-confidence and reducing their stress. Alliances are based on common interests—policies that each party wants to see enacted, threats that each party has received and cannot overcome alone, resources that each party wants to obtain and are willing to share. But coalitions are flexible and ever-changing. When the conditions that created the common interests change, the coalition becomes temporarily inactive or dissolves. Coalitions are inherently unstable, because issues and interests change and every member has the option of defecting and joining a different alliance. They are also unstable because of the dynamics of size. Alliances are based on the expectation that some form of spoils will be divided up if the coalition is victorious. Each member's reward will be increased and obligations to the other members decreased if the alliance is of the smallest winning size. But employees also must think about the future and the need to implement the decision once it is made. Implementation often requires the cooperation of a large number of people. Their support will be stronger if they are part of the alliance that got it enacted. To gain their support, coalition members must give up some of their potential rewards to these persons. Each member of the coalition thus may be ambivalent about the presence of each other member. Coalitions are unstable, although for many people they may be the only available base of power.

Gaining Power through the Control of Key Resources

People control resources when they are *key communicators* or *gatekeepers* in communication networks, occupy formal positions that allow them to distribute *legitimate rewards* and *punishments,* or can obtain access to the *symbols* of power.

Controlling Information   In societies that value rational decision making, information is a potent source of power. In fact, people who appear to be experts often have no more knowledge than anyone else, but have superior access to information. Information allows people to anticipate organizational problems and either prevent them or be ready with solutions when they do occur. It helps them locate and exploit weaknesses in potential adversaries and locate employees with whom they have common interests. But knowledge is usually acquired only from other employees, primarily through informal communication networks. Employees who occupy a central role in these networks (the key communicators described in Unit I) have access to more information than people who occupy peripheral roles.

Being a key communicator and possessing information reinforce one another. When people are confused, they seek out people who are reputed to be in the know. Key communicators can also control the flow of information through their organization. Information gives people power only if it is scarce. If it is disseminated selectively, it can enhance an individual's image as an expert. For example, in a classic study of how an organization chose between two computer systems, Andrew Pettigrew revealed the strategies a middle manager used to see that his preference was purchased. The manager gathered information about both systems from his subordinates, passed little information about the system he opposed on to his supervisors (unless that information was negative), and sent on favorable information about the system he favored. In effect, he created uncertainty about one system and then provided the information needed to resolve that uncertainty. Since he was in a central position in the formal communication network and was able to prevent his subordinates from "going over his head," he was able to control communication. This control gave him influence over both the computer decision and subsequent decisions. Of course, in an organization with an active informal communication network, controlling information flow is very difficult. But since key communicators in formal networks also tend to play central roles in informal networks, it may not be impossible.[11]

Employees also can gain power by processing information about an organization's environment. As the chapters in Unit I indicated, organizations must adapt to the pressures imposed on them by their environments. They must obtain accurate and timely information, but in obtaining information, they create ambiguities and uncertainties for their decision makers. Boundary spanners obtain and interpret this information. They create a dependency relationship between themselves and their organizations. One's place in overall communication networks provides a basis of influence. In fact, it may be the most potent source.[12] Power is perception. What appear to others to be personal characteristics—expertise, relational skills, and so on—often, perhaps most often, are the result of using information skillfully.

Formal Control of Resources   Some positions in formal hierarchies involve officially sanctioned control of scarce resources. Resource control gives people power by enabling them to reward or punish (promise gains or threaten losses to) other employees. As long as they threaten subtly or promise tactfully, they will be able to exercise power. Resource control also allows employees to persuade others to share some of the assets that they control. Most societies have deeply ingrained norms of reciprocity. When people voluntarily give something to someone else, the recipient feels pressure to reciprocate.

Although any scarce resource can be used to threaten or promise, the most important is money. Employees and groups who control funds invariably are the most powerful parts of an organization. In all organizations a substantial proportion of the budget is fixed. The allocation of the remainder (usually less than 10 percent) is flexible and can be distributed at someone's discretion. Once it is distributed, recipients begin to depend on it. They start payments on new equipment, hire new staff, or expand sales territories. If the discretionary funds are suddenly withdrawn, the person or unit faces serious problems. Payments will not be met, new staff will have to be fired, and new clients will have to be abandoned. Controlling discretionary funds is a potent source of power, and it provides an exceptionally strong basis for making threats, promises, or bribes. It's a golden rule: "The one who has the discretionary gold makes the rules."[13]

Obtaining Access to the Symbols of Power   At first glance it may seem strange to think of symbols as a resource. But power depends on perceptions, and symbols are powerful influences on perceptions. In all societies tangible materials symbolize power: large offices, large desks, royal blue carpets, the keys to the executive washroom, invitations to social events that include high-status people, and even office windows. Symbols create the impression that the person who possesses them should be honored and obeyed. They take on meaning disproportionate to their "real" value.

As a result, some of the most intense and humorous battles ever observed involved an office with a large window or office space that neither combatant really needed. While Charley Conrad was an undergraduate working in the foundry described in Chapters 2 and 4 the key symbol of power was a hard hat—lower-level workers had none; foremen had blue ones; supervisors white ones. One day Charley and a friend started wearing yellow plastic, nonprotective hard hats that they had borrowed from one of his neighbor's children. For two weeks the foremen and supervisors puzzled over what to do about the toy hats, although they agreed from the outset that *something* must be done. Since there was no official rule about wearing toy hard hats, he and his friend were violating no policy, but they were upsetting the power relationship by violating (and making fun of) its most important symbol. Finally, after a one-hour high-level meeting, a new policy was enacted that forbade the wearing of unapproved hats, "because they provided no added safety for workers," of course. Possessing symbols of power creates the perception of power, but only if some people are denied access to them.

Summary   Power is in the eye of the beholder. In this chapter, we have discussed a number of potential sources of power as if they were independent of one another. In real organizations they are interrelated. For example, people who occupy central positions in communication networks also tend to be perceived as experts and generally are part of many interpersonal relationships. Individuals who are supposed to have powerful allies are often seen as being more expert and having access to more information than other people. Perceptions of others are not separate and discrete. They merge together and overlap into complicated overall images. The communication strategies that employees can use to establish one base of power also influence other bases. Individuals or units of organizations are seen as being powerful or powerless depending on the *composite image* that their communicative acts establish in the minds of other members of their organization.

ORGANIZATIONAL POLITICS: OVERT POWER IN COMMUNICATIVE PROCESS

Politics is power in communicative action.[14] In its simplest form, organizational politics involves using the image management and influence strategies described in Chapter 7 to pursue one's interests. Open politicking is relatively rare in organizations. Employees must appear to be cooperative members of their organizations or units, lest they be perceived untrustworthy. If they undermine their trustworthiness, they risk destroying their credibility and undermining their ability to gain cooperation from others.

I disagree

When open politicking does occur, it usually is in situations that are confusing or ambiguous. Uncertainty and ambiguity create power vacuums that invite political activity. This explains why organizations are most politically active when changes are taking place—reorganization, personnel assignment (hirings, firings, and promotions), and budget allocation. These issues are directly related to organizational power, partly because they are important and partly because they involve high levels of uncertainty. But open politicking creates uncertainty and ambiguity, which feeds political activity. Politics depends on power, but power often depends on not seeming to be political.

Managing Organizational Politics

Politics is a central element of virtually all organizational situations. The greatest complication in managing organizational politics is their game-like nature.[15] In some ways game is an unfortunate metaphor. When used in the popular press, it tends to trivialize political action. It also suggests that there are stable rules that govern organizational politics. Neither notion is accurate. Even what seem to be incredibly trivial political games—fights over corner offices, the largest cubicle, and so on—often are serious processes of negotiating organizational power relationships. Similarly, while organizational political games may *seem* to have rules, the rules are always negotiable and can change at any moment. The old adage that "when English gentlemen can't win playing by the rules, they just change the rules" should not be limited to people from the U.K. or to gentle-*men*. In all organizations manipulating the rules is an important part of political action.

Ed's private

Some political games involve the surface structure of power. The strategies used may be relatively transparent, or they may be more covert. As Chapter 7 explained, sense making is an inherently political process. When employees interpret events or actions, they label them as either legitimate or illegitimate.

Actors who act in ways that are perceived to be legitimate tend to garner support from others, and because they act "legitimately" they tend to maintain or increase their power. People who act in ways that are defined as "illegitimate" generate opposition and reduce their power. As a result, much of organizational politics is covert and subtle, as the following case study illustrates.

CASE STUDY:
IT'S MY PARTY AND I'LL DO WHAT I WANT TO*

Subtle and covert political games often take place in settings that on the surface do not seem to be political settings at all. Chapter 4 explained that organizational ceremonies function to maintain the assumptions of an organization. Since those assumptions underlie the view of "reality" that its members take for granted, and since power relationships are grounded in employees' views of reality, maintaining an organization necessarily involves maintaining its power relationships. In a study of annual ceremonies at a Philadelphia-area advertising agency—a Christmas party and an annual breakfast—Michael Rosen has shown the subtle and powerful ways in which ceremonial events serve as covert power games.

Organizational ceremonies are part party (a celebration of a sense of community that binds people together) and part work (a reminder of the status and power hierarchy that separates people from one another). Shoenman and Associates' annual Christmas party had characteristics of both. Although it was held after hours on the Friday before Christmas, attendance was required. No spouses or family members were allowed to attend (except the boss's family), and a formal program—a four-page list of the evening's activities printed on heavy yellow paper—was provided. But it also is a party. It was held at a rustic bar away from work, where people seem to eat, drink, and "make merry" with one another as equals regardless of their formal rank, and where the boss acts more like a host than like a supervisor—wearing casual clothes and circulating from table to table making small talk at each stop. But the tension between the two identities is also quite clear. As one married member put it, the structure of the event tells employees that "your work is your life, and these are your friends. It's so f—— weird. There's dancing later. I don't want to dance with people that I work with." The party *did* require employees to be away from their families for an extended period during the most family-oriented time of the year. But, perhaps because of the timing—the holiday season—or the location, most of the employees seemed to think of the event as more party than work.

After dinner was over, the program began—a series of jokes and skits that are carefully prepared and professionally executed. All of them were funny; all were ambiguous; most made fun of the higher-ups in the firm. Together they created a joking relationship that seemed to help bridge or flatten the hierarchy of the firm. They celebrated the bosses' problems. All three top managers were

(continued)

(continued from the previous page)

going through divorces. The employees joked about the divorces and presented a skit entitled "The Mating Game" (a take-off of the TV series "The Dating Game") that included a voluptuous blonde asking pointed questions about the sexual appetites and exploits of the three divorcing upper managers. Other jokes and skits made fun of the managers' status symbols and of one manager's inability to keep secretaries because he was so obnoxious. The humor also commented on the crazed pace and work hours of the agency—one skit raffled off a coupon for electroshock psychotherapy treatments and many of the jokes were about the craziness of the work environment. They also made fun of other workers. One skit spoofed the large number of female employees who dyed their hair blonde; another made fun of the different attire of the business side of operation (dark blue suits and ties) and the creative side (almost anything else).

At one level, the humor made it seem that the organization's hierarchy had disappeared and it was a community of equals. After the program ended, the participants adjourned to the bar and dance floor. During this very informal part of the ceremony bosses and subordinates buddied around the bar, arms on shoulders, joking and laughing. Workers commented on how the humor had skewered the bosses. Some were even honest with management. The obnoxious manager asked the office manager what people thought of him. Thinking "what the h——," she told him that he is considered to be a bastard and is the most disliked person in the agency, something she admitted that she never would have said at work. She could get by with saying it, because they were at a party. In Western societies eating signals community, and drinking alcohol symbolizes freedom, especially from the drudgery of work. Parties are times of unusual license, and frictions encountered in the presence of alcohol tend to be forgiven. It *seemed* that the rules of the game were very different at the party than they were at work.

But, behind the scenes things were different. Hierarchy and formal power/ authority relationships were subtle, but still in place. People seemed to dance with one another as equals; but even during the most informal part of the party, the women (most of whom are secretaries) danced with males who were their own age or older and who occupied higher positions in the organization. The skits that skewered upper management were written by a skits committee only after a lengthy negotiation process, and were revised many times before being approved by the committee chair. As one member put it, "We really had to watch our asses, but we had a f—— ball putting this thing together." A skit at the previous year's party had superimposed a picture of the boss over a picture of a farmer in overalls, boots, and pitchfork, with the title "Big Wally (boss) Sells B—— s—— (advertising) Cheaper." Walter had made it very clear that the picture was out of bounds, primarily because it was a permanent record that could leave the party, not a joke or skit that could be remembered but not reproduced. Through censorship, the rules of the work game invaded the party game, and actions that were permitted under the party rules were not allowed to be carried back to the work game. In addition, much of the party celebrated and legitimized the rules of

(continued)

(continued from the previous page)

the work game. One of the most important work rules was that work comes before anything else—that all employees were expected to sacrifice their personal and family lives to meet deadlines and satisfy clients' every whim. Much of the humor at the party focused on the frenetic pace of the organization—even divorces could be celebrated, because everyone knew that they resulted, at least in part, from the demands of the workplace. Even the party itself required employees to sacrifice time that could be spent with outside relationships.

Interactional rules were constantly being negotiated, but negotiated in a way that maintained the underlying power relationships. Subordinates *could* make fun of their supervisors, but only in approved ways. Supervisors *could* fraternize with their subordinates, but only in ways that maintained the hierarchy of the firm. Supervisors *could* ask for frank reports on how they were perceived by others; but they alone could decide what to do with that information. Subordinates *could* give frank responses, but only in private and only when asked. Some kinds of communication were out of bounds and other kinds were permitted. Although the bounds were different at the party than they were at work, boundaries did exist, and in negotiating them everyone was reminded that underneath it all was a power relationship that could not be challenged.

While the Christmas ceremony was a party that retained vestiges of the power and authority relationships at work, the breakfast ceremony was work with some of the trappings of a party. Held at one of Philadelphia's most posh hotels, everyone—even the servers—were dressed in formal attire. In one way everyone was alike—even the lowliest employee could experience opulence at least once a year just by being part of the team. For a moment, even they were being served instead of serving. But in other ways the opulence focused attention on hierarchy—most of the employees could never have afforded this place on their salaries, and for a short time everyone was looking and consuming *as if they were managers,* not as if they were regular employees. It also obscured differences between the business and artistic sides of the organization.

After breakfast, the speeches started. Unlike the Christmas party, the boss (Walter) was in control of the entertainment part of this ritual. Walter congratulated everyone for the firm's success and noted that it occurred in spite of the recession, in spite of "problems" in the public relations division, and because of their hard work and sacrifice (late hours and frenetic work pace). Walter gave gifts to retirees and recognized their loyalty to the firm. Walter talked about the "things the agency does for *us*," like funding the pension program (not mentioning that the "agency" [that is, Walter] has a legal obligation to do so, that "it" did so instead of giving year-end bonuses that were customary in other advertising agencies and had been customary in their firm, or that it could do so because of the work and skills of the workers). After a slide show that made fun of the creative side of the firm, Walter announced that the money that would have gone to bonuses reluctantly had to be retained "for the good of the firm." Although managers would benefit from the decision, because it would increase the value of their

(continued)

(continued from the previous page)

stock in the firm, it meant that the workers' incomes actually fell because of the effects of inflation. And, raises and bonuses would occur only when management decided that they should be given, and no one knew when that might happen. One accountant referred to this tendency to leave potentially troubling details out of his announcements about the munificence of management as a "Walterism."

Finally, the vice-president of public relations spoke. He talked about how important the division was, admitted that it had problems and failures, and confessed that all of those problems were his fault. After the confessional, Walter returned to the podium and led the celebrants in a pep rally, focusing on telling versus listening ("If everyone in this agency told and listened, we'd have fifteen percent more revenue"); me versus we ("If we can get all of the ambitions of the Me under the We, Shoenman and Associates could add another 15 to 20 percent to our revenues"); and drive/win ("Laid-back people have no place in this agency. . . drive is what it takes to win . . . let's get back to work").

Although still subtle, the discourse at breakfast enacted the organization's power relationships in a much more overt form than the Christmas party. *Walter* decided who would be rewarded, who would be chastised, and who would be allowed to talk. *Walter* defined and celebrated the values of the organization and legitimized them in terms of increased revenues. And *Walter* decided how those revenues would be distributed. Although at least some of the employees understood all of these things, they said nothing, for saying nothing is how *they* play the Walter game.

Applying What You've Learned

1. What were the rules of the power game at Schoeneman's?
2. How did the behaviors at the parties enact those rules? How did they undermine them?

Questions to Think About and Discuss

1. Rosen argues these political rituals are important because they obscure the organizational power relationships while enforcing them. How would the employees' interpretations and responses have been different if Walter had been overt and direct about his expectations about employee performance and his evaluations of their work? Why?
2. What would have happened if an employee who understood what was going on had spoken up? How would the other employees have responded? Why?

---

*This case is based on Michael Rosen, "You Asked for It: Christmas at the Bosses' Expense," *Journal of Management Studies, 25* (1988): 463–480 and "Breakfast at Sprio's," in Peter Frost, et al., eds., *Reframing Organizational Culture* (pp. 77–89) Newbury Park, CA: Sage, 1991.

The Biggest Game of All: Taking and Silencing Voices

During the 1990s organizational communication theorists started to focus on the concept of *voice,* recognizing that a crucial element of social and organizational power relationships is regulating who gets to speak (and who does not), what they may speak about, and how they must speak in order to be heard. The process of regulating voice occurs at an individual level when organizations suppress dissent, but it also occurs at a broader level. Organizational discourse tends to be discourse by and for a particular group of people—primarily educated white male managers—and tends to exclude the voices of other groups— women, nonmanagement workers, and members of racial and ethnic minority groups. Since these concepts are developed in more detail in Chapters 11 and 12, we introduce them only briefly in this chapter. But since processes of privileging some voices and muting others are essentially political processes, it is important to think about them in terms of organizational power relationships.

Muting Individuals' Voices   W. Charles Redding, generally viewed as the father of organizational communication, once summarized a speech given to his class by a high-ranking officer of a *Fortune* 500 firm:

> A single dominant theme emerged from the speaker's lecture. . . . Although the company needs people who, of course, are intelligent and competent, our overriding objective is to find people who will *fit in.* . . . "Will this applicant become a Company Man or a Company Woman?" (a "loyal" employee who internalizes corporate goals and values). . . . To be sure we heard the conventional wisdom that the company needed college graduates with "ideas," with "creativity and imagination." However class questions elicited the caveat that generating innovative ideas did *not* extend to challenging "basic corporate policies" or "managerial prerogatives." I wrote down at one point the speaker's exact words, which he emphasized with appropriately vigorous gestures: *We don't particularly need boat-rockers.*[16]

Fifteen years later, Redding's point still is appropriate—in most organizations dissent is forbidden, regardless of how principled or correct it might be. Employees are expected to speak in the organization's (that is, upper management's) voice, both inside and outside of the organization.

Of course, in most organizations, most of the time, dissent is not even an issue. Every strategy of organizing (recall Unit I) has its own system of controlling employees. Every system of control covers what employees do *and* what they say. But no control system is perfect; there is always some space for resistance, and dissent is a potent form of resistance. When resisting voices are raised, surface-level power strategies come into play. These overt strategies of suppressing dissent typically take place in graduated phases. Initially, organizational power holders attempt to persuade the dissenters that they are wrong or mistaken (a process sometimes called nullification). If that fails, the dissenters are isolated from coworkers—disconnecting telephones or revoking computer access codes, removing the dissenters' names from invitation lists for social events, or transferring them to the corporate version of Stalin's Siberia. If isolation fails (and it rarely does, because most people decide that dissent is not worth the costs), direct sanctions are applied—defaming the dissenters or expelling them from the organization.

The processes through which organizations suppress dissent is illustrated clearly by research on "unethical actions" in organizations and by the experiences of **whistle-blowers,** people who report unethical or illegal activities within their organizations to the authorities or the press. During the 1980s and 1990s repeated cases of fraud, embezzlement, and other illegal activities (for instance, insider trading of stocks) created the impression that many members of the business community had abandoned the values of honesty and fair play that are so important to society. But, in many of these cases the employees were part of organizations that had systematically and strategically planned to act in illegal or unethical ways. Thus, moral decay was much more than the result of isolated activities by a handful of ethically challenged individuals. In fact, between 1975 and 1990, two-thirds of the *Fortune* 500 firms were *convicted* of serious crimes ranging from price fixing to illegal dumping of hazardous wastes. In late 1996 Archer Daniels Midland ("supermarket to the world," according to its commercials) was fined a record $100 million by the U.S. Justice Department for illegally fixing prices of citric acid and lysine (an additive in animal feeds). Many other organizations reached out-of-court settlements or were convicted of misdemeanors. In some sectors of the economy, pressures to engage in illegal or unethical actions are so intense and the actions are so frequent that they have come to be seen as the normal way of doing business (for example, financial fraud in defense contracting, sexism in the military, and racism in the petroleum/petrochemical industry).[17]

In addition, many studies find that managers believe that their jobs require them to compromise their own values. In a typical study, Posner and Schmidt found that 72 percent of employees face pressure to engage in actions that they perceive to be unethical, and that 41 percent admit that they have succumbed to those pressures. A 1995 study of thirty Harvard MBAs revealed that 29 of them had been ordered to violate their own personal ethical standards at least once during the previous five years. Consequently, the key ethical question is not what kinds of people act in unethical or illegal ways and what has happened to their individual sense of integrity? It is what organizational factors encourage people to decide to act in illegal or unethical ways and how do those processes operate?[18]

Three aspects of organizational power and politics seem to explain much of this illegal and unethical behavior. First, upper management often discourages employees from discussing ethical issues, especially when possible illegal activities are involved. In fact, upper management is even willing to fire employees for *talking about* ethical issues. Then, if employees *do* act in unethical or illegal ways, management can plead ignorance of the activities and escape responsibility. Operatives in the administration of President Reagan gave the name "plausible deniability" to this strategy. Although more and more companies are stating publicly their commitment to ethics in management, few of their employees find it comfortable to raise such concerns in public or in the privacy of their offices. Toffler concluded that "there seems to be a sense among managers that talking about ethics is 'just not done here.' And, unfortunately, they are usually right."[19]

The existence of these gag orders means that employees must make complicated and difficult ethical decisions alone, in private, and in an atmosphere of ambiguity and uncertainty about the organization's values. In addition, if one employee acts in ways that are ethically questionable, it is difficult for other employees to challenge or resist that person's decision. Most employees really do have strong personal moral codes; but because they are not allowed to talk to one another about ethical issues they rarely *realize* that other people share their values and would support a decision to resist an unethical or illegal order. So they acquiesce, making it *seem* to everyone else that they do not oppose the unethical action. When all the employees in a unit acquiesce, it *seems* that immoral or unethical decisions are supported by all the employees. When communication about ethical issues is suppressed, the resulting ambiguities make it more likely that employees will act in ethically questionable ways.[20]

Second, the structure or standard operating procedures of many organizations encourage unethical actions. For example, bureaucratic structures (recall Chapters 1 and 2) allow employees to avoid taking responsibility for unethical actions. Lower-level employees are allowed only to *implement* established policies and procedures, not to make them. As long as they act in ways that are consistent with those policies, they can claim not to be responsible for their actions, even if they are illegal or unethical. Upper-level employees also are able to deny responsibility, because they only establish policies and procedures (which almost never are illegal or unethical in themselves), not make the illegal or unethical decision. As a result, in bureaucratic organizations, it is easy to rationalize ethical considerations as "someone else's responsibility."[21]

In addition, in extremely large or complex organizations, tasks are usually broken into small components. Each employee deals with such a small part of an overall process that she or he may not realize that the activity as a whole is improper. Secretaries shred paper, not knowing that the documents have been subpoenaed by a grand jury. Truck drivers dump their loads in a county dump, not knowing their vehicles are filled with toxic wastes. Accountants approve allowable cost increases in defense contracts, not realizing that some of the money will be used as kickbacks. Not only does the structure of large, complex organizations diffuse responsibility, it also diffuses the information necessary to realize that activities are illegal or unethical.

A final, "hidden" factor involves what earlier chapters called identification and unobtrusive control (recall Chapter 4). One characteristic of so-called "strong culture" organizations is the high level of commitment shown by their employees. During the late 1970s a group of employees of the Revco Drug Company in Indiana defrauded the state welfare department of millions of dollars. Interestingly, although the organization gained a great deal from their actions, the workers got little or no individual benefit from doing so. They acted illegally, largely because they were loyal to their organization. They believed that the monies were legitimately owed to Revco, that a history of stalled negotiations between the firm and the welfare department proved that the company was being victim-

FIGURE 8–1

NON-SEQUITUR reprinted by permission of Universal Press Syndicate

ized by the bureaucracy, that the cost of correcting the situation through legal channels was greater than the likely return, and that they could significantly increase the firm's short-term profits if they were successful. They were, in short, precisely the kind of employees that are "created" through cultural strategies of organizing—highly capable individuals committed to their organization and its success and willing to take risks and act creatively to ensure that it succeeded. Unless prohibitions against illegal or unethical activities are core organizational values, cultural strategies of organizing may actually encourage illegal or unethical action.[22] Of course, neither bureaucratic structures or cultural strategies of organizing are *intended* to encourage employees to act in illegal or unethical ways. But, when combined with organizational power relationships that discourage dissent, they create opportunities and incentives for them to do so.

The processes through which organizations suppress dissent is also illustrated clearly by the experiences of whistle-blowers. Examples of whistle-blowers are easy to find—every major newspaper publishes at least one story every month. Whistle-blowers' stories are amazingly consistent with one another. They detect something going wrong in their organization. It often involves illegal activity and always involves something that the potential whistle-blower fervently believes is unethical. She or he then uses the organization's internal processes in an attempt to get the practice changed. When internal appeals fail, the whistle-blower goes public. After that the organization's response is easy to predict. A typical case is John Kartak, who reported fraudulent activities in a Minneapolis Minnesota Army recruiting office. Soon after he filed his report, he was ordered to report to a Veterans Administration hospital for psychological evaluation. After being declared fit for duty, he returned to his unit. He was constantly watched by his supervisors and ostracized, threatened, and intimidated by his coworkers (many of whom were later proven guilty of fraud). Then he was ordered back to a military hospital for another psychological evaluation, which also declared him fit for duty. Studies in the United States have found that 90 percent of whistle-blowers lost their jobs or were demoted, 27 percent faced lawsuits, and 26 percent experienced psychiatric or medical referrals. Australian whistle-blowers have similar experiences.

The decision to "go public" is a very difficult one. The risks to a whistle-blower's personal life, advancement, relationships with coworkers, and personal safety often are quite large and the potential gains quite small. One quarter become alcoholics; 17 percent lose their homes; 15 percent subsequently are divorced; 10 percent attempt suicide; and 8 percent go bankrupt. But the personal costs of not doing so—reduced self-esteem, guilt, and fear that someone else will report it, leaving the employee in the role of an accomplice—may also be quite large. For potential whistle-blowers merely deciding whether to communicate is in itself a complicated problem. Most people do not speak up even when doing so promises equivalent gains and risks; very few do so when speaking involves substantial risks with little opportunity for gain. For example, after reflecting on his experiences, Richard Lundwall, the manager who blew the whistle on Texaco's racist promotion policies (recall Chapter 7), now says "if there are other Richard Lundwalls out there who have information contrary to their employers' best interest, they would be rather foolish to put themselves at risk." As a result of the experiences of people like Lundwall, whistle-blowing is relatively rare, and whistle-blowers' complaints are often withdrawn before any corrective action is taken.[23]

CASE STUDY:
SUPPRESSING DISSENT IN THE NUCLEAR INDUSTRY*

Because of the obvious risks to public health and safety, the nuclear industry has one of the strongest whistle-blower protection systems in U.S. industry. Since 1974, if a nuclear organization is convicted of discriminating against an employee for raising safety concerns, the U.S. Department of Labor can order reinstatement, back pay, promotion, and other compensation and the Nuclear Regulatory

(continued)

(continued from the previous page)

Commission (NRC) can fine the company and refer the matter to the Justice Department for criminal prosecution. But the power relationships between nuclear organizations and their employees mean that "the system is stacked against you . . . if you've got the law and the facts and God on your side, you've got a 50 percent chance of winning," says Larry Simmons, a former contact welder who blew the whistle at Florida Power Company's Crystal River plant in 1988. The results of the many complaints filed against nuclear firms seem to support Simmons' conclusion. (In January 1993, 142 such cases were pending nationwide, a figure that almost certainly underestimates the number of violations, since most people do not blow the whistle on their employers.) It is nearly impossible to win a case against a multimillion-dollar firm with a battery of skilled attorneys who can drag a case out for years while the plaintiffs' savings and resolve are depleted and their careers destroyed. Even in the relatively rare cases when plaintiffs receive a settlement, the vast majority of the money goes to cover their legal expenses, and fines levied against the organizations are small relative to the firm's size. (Fines of $25,000 to $250,000 are common for violations at plants that generate $1 million a day in revenues.)

Three cases are illustrative of the experiences of nuclear industry whistleblowers. In March 1989, Len Trimmer (who had worked for the University of California division at Los Alamos National Laboratory since 1962, receiving numerous promotions) was assigned to inspect drums of radioactive material to see that they met safety standards. He complained that his test equipment was malfunctioning and later discovered about 20 leaking drums. The drums tested with the flawed equipment were labeled "certifiable" and the leaking drums were left to leak. He complained to the NRC and subsequently experienced a number of events that he believed were in retaliation: One coworker kicked a chair out from under him, and he was ordered to move heavy drums, aggravating an old back injury. While he was on disability leave, his desk and locker were broken into, and on the day that the local newspaper ran a story about him a large rock bounced off his parked car. He was never called back to work.

Martin Marietta Energy Systems, the primary contractor at Oak Ridge National Laboratory, transferred Charles Varnadore to a high radiation chemistry lab and assigned him the task of manipulating radioactive materials with mechanical arms, something he couldn't do well because he had been blind in one eye since birth and didn't have the depth perception necessary to operate the equipment properly. After he made a number of messes, he complained. From then on he was a *persona non grata,* being transferred so often that he earned the nickname "technician on roller skates." He returned to work in July 1989 after surgery for colon cancer to find that his job had been filled by a younger man, and his new office was a room "with mercury all over it" where drums of radioactive waste were stored. In June 1993, Judge Theodor Von Brand ruled in Varnadore's favor and wrote a blistering criticism of Martin Marietta that concluded that "they inten-

(continued)

(continued from the previous page)

tionally put him under stress with full knowledge that he was a cancer patient . . . particularly vulnerable to the workplace stresses to which he was subjected." Since the court decision, Varnadore has filed additional complaints, one of which accuses a company labor relations officer of saying during a training session that "someone should get a gun and take him out and shoot him."

One of the longest and most complicated cases involves Vera English, whose eight-year battle against General Electric's nuclear fuel plant in Wilmington, North Carolina, has included favorable rulings by the U.S. Supreme Court, NRC, Department of Labor, and a number of other judges; $250,000 in lost wages and legal fees; no financial gain; and a $20,000 fine paid by GE. In March 1984, after two years of complaining to GE management about safety-related violations, English charged GE with violations of company policy regarding safety. In April, GE told her that she would lose her job unless she applied to be transferred to the non-nuclear section of the plant. In July she was fired, in August she filed a complaint with the Department of Labor, which found evidence of discrimination in October. GE appealed the verdict. A year later an administrative law judge ordered GE to reinstate her to her original position and pay her $73,007 in damages plus back pay. GE appealed. In January 1987, the Secretary of Labor reversed the decision on the grounds that English had not filed the complaint within 30 days of being warned of the layoff. She appealed, arguing that she did complain within 30 days of being fired. After a number of other rehearings and appeals within the Labor Department, the secretary again dismissed her complaint.

But English had also sued GE in federal court. In February 1988, a federal district judge found that she had a valid claim, but dismissed it on a technicality. In June 1990, after two additional appeals, the U.S. Supreme Court ruled in her favor and returned the case to the lower court. In October her case was dismissed because she had not proven GE's actions to be "outrageous," a decision that was upheld on appeal. Amount of time spent fighting the case: 7 1/2 years with the Department of Labor; 5 1/2 years in court. Outcome: no damages recovered. A Tennessee Valley Authority whistle-blower concluded: "We all discovered that the process doesn't do anything but put a big bull's-eye on your back."

However, sometimes the outcome is different. David Lamb and James Dean, who raised safety concerns about a south Texas nuclear power plant run by Houston Lighting and Power (HLP), were fired in 1992. In late 1993 an administrative law judge in the Department of Labor ruled that they had been harassed and fired because of their whistle-blowing activities, but the company appealed the ruling to the Secretary of Labor. In November 1996, HLP paid a $160,000 fine to the NRC as a result of the allegations, and on November 19, 1996—the day before the Secretary of Labor was to announce his decision—the company reached an out-of-court settlement with the two for an undisclosed amount of money. Neither man has been able to find employment in the nuclear power industry, but Lamb concludes that "[the settlement takes] a big load off our backs.

(continued)

(continued from the previous page)

No amount of money will ever pay for what they did to us or what I believe they have done to other personnel. But it sure goes a long way."†

Applying What You've Learned

1. There is a good deal of evidence indicating that whistle-blowers' coworkers place intense pressure on them to withdraw their charges once they become public. What accepted assumptions in Western societies underlie this response?
2. What sources of power do whistle-blowers have available in their efforts to change organizational practices? How can those sources be used?

Questions to Think About and Discuss

1. Pretend that you are the manager of a nuclear plant and are not especially constrained by ethical considerations. Also pretend that an employee keeps making complaints about safety problems at the plant. The likelihood of these problems becoming public knowledge are quite slim, but they could be very expensive and embarrassing if they ever did. But solving the problems would be very expensive, and your supervisors already are pressuring you to reduce costs. So, the "rational" strategy seems to be to silence the dissenter. What strategies are available that would allow you to do so? What are the likely costs and effects of each of those strategies?
2. Now pretend that your efforts to suppress dissent failed, and the employee reported the problems to the Nuclear Regulatory Commission. What strategies are now available to you to deal with the problem? What are the likely costs and effects of each of those strategies?

---

*The primary source for this case study is a series of articles published by the *Houston Chronicle* during March and September 1993. For a broad analysis of issues regarding the release of low-level radioactivity, see Jay Gould, *Deadly Deceit: Low Level Radiation, High Level Coverup* (New York: Four Walls Eight Windows, 1990) and Jay Gould and Ernest Sternglass, *The Enemy Within: The High Cost of Living Near Nuclear Power* (New York: Four Walls Eight Windows, 1996).

†Jim Morris, "Whistle-blower Claims Settled," *Houston Chronicle,* Nov. 20, 1996, A24–25.

Muting Groups' Voices   One of the recurring themes of this chapter, indeed of this book, is that power and control in organizations depends on processes of perceiving and attributing meaning. Sense-making is guided by social and organizational power relationships; power relationships are managed strategically by creating shared sense-making. In turn, sense-making and strategic communication creates, reproduces, and sometimes transforms power relationships. At first glance, the interrelationships among meaning-creation, communication strategies, and power relationships appear to be the same for all groups of people. But a number of contemporary views of social and organizational power suggest that taking a closer look will reveal that there are important power inequalities embedded in meaning-creation and communication.

In short, in most U.S. organizations, what an act means is determined by the beliefs, values, and frames of reference of educated, white, male upper-level managers. Although employees who are nonwhite, lower-level, less educated, or female may make sense of an event or action in very different ways, the discourse of organizations tends to privilege to the sense-making processes of dominant groups. For example, the meaning that is typically attached to the job cuts that accompanied organizational downsizing during the 1990s is that they are unavoidable adaptations to the pressures of a global economy. They will increase efficiency and productivity, thus making U.S. firms more competitive in the long term and protecting Americans' jobs. Of course, many other interpretations are possible. For example, one could persuasively argue that downsizing primarily benefits upper management (recall Chapter 1), not workers, stockholders, or society as a whole; or that downsizing has had little positive effect on efficiency or productivity. Only 26 percent of downsized firms report efficiency increases; 19 percent report decreases, and 39 percent report no change. Eleven percent of downsized firms report increased absenteeism; 62 percent report lower morale, and 39 percent report increased voluntary turnover. So, for workers and middle managers—more of whom tend to be female, nonwhite, less well educated, and less wealthy than upper management—downsizing means lost income, reduced self-esteem, and increased stress and insecurity, not increased profits or a rosy future. But the discourse about downsizing, both within organizations and in the popular media focuses almost completely on the managerial interpretation and almost completely ignores or mutes other interpretations.[24]

Another alternative interpretation involves the criteria of "efficiency" and "effectiveness" themselves. Roger Jehensen has called these concepts ideological fictions that foster the interests of some groups over the interests of others. "Efficiency" is not itself a goal or outcome. It is a means of reaching some other goal or outcome. Driving fast, or driving in a fuel-efficient manner (two possible definitions of "efficient" travel), are meaningless unless doing so gets people somewhere, and gets them somewhere they want to go. Presumably, organizational efficiency is important, because it produces something else of value—profits or the continued existence of the organization, for example. If people define "efficiency" in this way, as a *means* to an end, it immediately raises questions about the value of the ends themselves. They will ask what communication theorist Jurgen Habermas has called **practical questions,** questions such as "What level of environmental damage are we willing to accept in order to increase profits?" or "What proportion of a firm's profits should be reinvested in the publicly funded infrastructure (roads, education systems, and so on) that the organization uses to produce its profits?" But when efficiency is defined as an *end* in itself, as it usually is, these value-laden questions are inappropriate. Instead, people only ask what Habermas calls **technical questions**, about how best to maximize efficiency. Defining efficiency as an end transforms value-laden questions about goals and

11111

1111111

111111111111111

social costs into seemingly value-neutral questions about technique. In the process, narrow, technical kinds of expertise—the expertise that managers are presumed to have—are elevated in importance. And the voices of people who ask *practical* questions that are based on nonmanagerial expertise, experiences, and values—workers and members of the communities in which our organizations exist—are silenced.[25]

Focusing on *technical* questions instead of *practical* ones, privileges the interests of some groups over others. So do the definitions of the key terms that make up the questions themselves. For example, the usual "technical" definition of "efficiency" is output per person hour. But what if "efficiency" is defined in terms of output per dollar of supervisory overhead? Both definitions are justifiable on economic grounds; but the former definition focuses attention on workers, places the burden for organizational success on controlling and motivating *them,* and legitimizes management's efforts to do so. It also suggests that the returns created through increased efficiency should be given largely to management because it was *their* skill at motivating and controlling workers that created the "efficiency." Similarly, the dominant definition justifies blaming workers for negative outcomes because it could only have been *their* lack of effort, ability, and productivity (inspite of management's best efforts) that caused the losses. This sense-making system further legitimizes management's efforts to motivate and control workers in the future. In contrast, the second definition of "efficiency" focuses attention on managerial overhead, places the burden for organizational success on management's shoulders, suggests that the number of managers and their compensation should be kept as small as possible, and assumes that nonmanagerial managerial personnel do the *real* work of the organization. The former definition elevates the interests and "voice" of managers over workers; the latter elevates the interests and voice of workers.

A number of feminist scholars have extended this concept of silencing voices to examine the ways in which organizational discourse privileges the meaning systems of males. The underlying assumptions of the perspective are that:

1.   The structure of Western economies divides labor into different categories by gender. (Men have tended to work for pay in public while women have tended to work without pay in private settings like the home.) This division means that men and women have different experiences and thus perceive the world differently.

2.   Men dominate the public realm (politics and organizations), so masculine constructions of reality dominate the public realm, preventing alternative meanings from being expressed or accepted.

3.   When women enter the public realm they are expected and pressured into adapting their meaning systems to "fit" the dominant (male) system.

As a result, women often have more difficulty expressing themselves in the public realm than men do, just as men often have greater difficulty expressing themselves in the "private" realm of emotions and interpersonal relationships. Men and women even learn to interpret symbolism differently. For example, men and women tend to laugh at different things and for different reasons. But, today women are required to learn the masculine language of the public realm to participate in masculine organizations. As a result, they often understand masculine communication better than men understand the language of the private realm. Women acting in public settings often do try to make the dominant meaning systems less masculine, but find it difficult to do so.

Masculine constructions of reality permeate the way people think as well as the way they communicate; language and thought are two sides of the same coin. For example, men (at least in Western societies) learn to think of interpersonal relationships in terms of hierarchy ("Who *is* the captain of this team, anyway?") while women tend to think in terms of "webs" of interconnected people.[26] Each of these metaphors suggests different definitions of achievement, ethics, power, effectiveness, and so on. For example, the hierarchy metaphor suggests that achievement means moving above others; power means being dominant *over* others; effectiveness means obtaining goals in the face of resistance; and "ethics" is defined in terms of the legal acceptability or success of an action. "Reality" is perceived in terms of discrete categories—policies are *either* good *or* bad; organizational issues are *either* "line" concerns *or* "staff" concerns; decisions are *either* rational *or* irrational. Once one metaphor is accepted as dominant within a society or social group, it is treated as *normal* and *natural*. It no longer needs to be justified, and any other metaphor is automatically defined as inferior and must constantly be justified.

Consequently, people who speak in the language of hierarchy are automatically heard; whereas people who speak in the language of connectedness constantly need to explain and legitimize themselves and their ideas. People who think and communicate in these terms (or who are *assumed* to do so) upset the dominant construction of "reality." Their presence alone is threatening, because it calls into question the entire set of accepted assumptions that define Western organizations. It is especially disruptive when they begin to enter the upper levels of organizations, because the essence of upper management is faith in power and hierarchy. Unless people believe that managers should be obeyed because they are managers, the power relationships that underlie bureaucratic organizations disappear. Stability can be maintained only if the threat to hierarchy is reduced. The most direct way to do that is to remove the threat, to suppress, ignore, or eliminate any different voices.

One means of muting these voices is to persuade potentially disruptive people to adopt the language and thought of the dominant members—to persuade women, members of minority groups, nonmanagerial employees—to become as normal (that is, as managerial) as possible. For example, women and minority managers are often advised to do everything possible to fit in to their organizations. Adopting the language of hierarchy, the values of upward mobility, the "power over" definition of power, and even the dress and mannerisms of middle- and upper-class white males, are depicted as the most direct avenue to organizational "success" (with success defined in terms of movement up the hierarchy). In short, employees are told that they will have influence only if they adapt their communication to the dominant power relationships of their organizations. But, ironically, adapting to those power relationships means communicating in the language of masculinity, which reproduces the dominance of masculine conceptions of reality and silences differing voices.

When people *do* speak in the language of connectedness and emotionality, their speech can be ignored or devalued ("Don't be so emotional," or "Of course it's important to consider the effects that our decision will have on the lives of our workers, but we really have to make a 'bottom-line' decision and we have to make it today," or "That's not a bad idea for a woman/African American/Latino/production worker/etc.") Different voices are also suppressed by treating people with professional credentials as if they were lower-level workers, as when women managers are assumed to be secretaries and treated as if they are, or African American and Latino managers are assumed to be and treated as if they were custodians. The voices of people who might deviate from the language of hierarchy can also be muted by placing those people where they are easy to ignore—outside of informal communication networks, in small offices that are hidden from public view, or in divisions of the organization that have little influence (for example, human resources or public relations). Issues that are particularly important to marginalized groups (for example, pay equity or sexual harassment) can be ignored, referred to a committee, or localized in powerless departments.

Claiming a Voice for Marginalized Groups   Three approaches have been suggested as means of claiming a voice for marginalized groups. One approach is the creation of alternative organizations that are grounded in collectivist metaphors, practices, and modes of thought. A number of these alternative organizations were described in Chapter 5. For example, feminist organizations usually attempt to substitute collectivist, truly participatory systems for hierarchy-based power. They strive to replace traditional, bureaucratic authority hierarchies with **hetrarchies,** in which authority is shared and formal leadership is rotated among the organization's members. They substitute a cooperative ethic for a competitive one in their talk and action. They try to replace domination with dialogue, in which all members have equal opportunities to present their ideas on important issues. Decisions are based on holistic considerations, including anticipated effects on the employees' lives and the surrounding community, rather than on narrow concerns like short-term profitability.[27] Of course, shifting to dialogue and hetrarchy in a society whose accepted assumptions value hierarchy and centralization, is difficult.

Even in organizations in which the members are committed to alternative forms of organizing there still is a tendency for the elites to emerge and use their positions in communication networks to reinforce their own positions of privilege.[28] In addition, alternative organizations almost always have to interact with traditional hierarchical organizations, and those external pressures make it difficult to operate in a truly nonheirarchical way. One way of managing these pressures is to identify a single person as the top manager; while organizing everyday activities around shared leadership. This strategy fulfills the expectations of outside organizations while allowing each member to achieve her (or his) own goals.[29]

Another approach to creating a voice for marginalized groups involves creating alternative systems within hierarchical organizations. For example, a number of studies have found that women faculty members are able to create and sustain collectivist informal groups within large, bureaucratic, masculine-dominated universities. Similarly, programs of legitimate participation in decision making serve to empower members of organizations whose voices have been muted. But internal strategies are difficult to implement. As Chapter 3 explained, formal programs of empowerment generate resistance from precisely those persons who have the greatest degree of organizational power, resistance that can take on a variety of subtle forms. Overcoming it may require employees to use the power sources and political strategies of hierarchical organizations in an effort to change those same sources and strategies.[30] Like much of organizational life, affecting change is a paradoxical activity.

A final approach to raising multiple voices involves the critical analysis of organizational discourse. One of the recurring themes of this book is that the taken-for-granted assumptions of a society or organization are powerful largely because they are taken for granted. Consequently, resistance can occur when those assumptions are raised to a conscious level and examined directly. One approach to doing this is called **deconstructing** organizational discourse. Deconstruction begins by recognizing that *all* organizational discourse, as all strategies of organizing, is strategic. Claims to truth, knowledge, expertise, and ethicality make sense only within particular views of reality, and those views of reality are strategic choices. So, deconstructing organizational discourse involves asking what it takes for granted, what it says, what it does not say, and how all of that influences organizational power relationships. We provided one example of deconstructing an organizational text earlier in this chapter when we discussed the different ways in which organizational "efficiency" could be defined.

Another example was provided by management professor JoAnne Martin. While conducting research at OZCO (her pseudonym for a Silicon Valley firm), Martin observed the CEO's response to a question about how the company helps women workers who have children. Initially he responded, "I'm not sure." When asked why the company had not made any provisions for day care, unlike many firms in the industry, he responded, "Well, I think we are, of course, concerned about family values. I think they are on the decline, and I think that is a problem." When pressed further he told a story:

> We have a young woman who is extraordinarily important to the launching of a major new [product]. We will be talking about it next Tuesday in its first worldwide introduction. She arranged to have her [baby born by a] Caesarean [operation] yesterday in order to be prepared for the event, so you—we have insisted that she stay home and this is going to be televised in a closed circuit television, so we're having this done by TV for her, and she is staying home three months.

The CEO interpreted the story as evidence of OZCO's commitment to helping mothers with managerial duties. He expressed pride in the company's willingness to incur the costs of granting her a three-month maternity leave and paying for a closed-circuit TV to her bedroom so she could perform her duties. Of course, a number of other interpretations of the story are possible.

For example, when Martin told the story to a group of employees, many hissed, and retorted that the story demonstrated how low the company would go to extract work from their employees. ("That baby deserved to be born when it was ready, not when OZCO scheduled it to be"). Others said that the organization's purported humanitarian policies were merely a cover for their low pay scale and lack of sensitivity to gender and family issues. There were no women in senior positions at OZCO, and those in managerial positions were not supportive of lower-level women. One of the dominant themes of the organization was that of the midwestern Mommy and Daddy: Daddy makes the decisions and takes care of the family and Mommy does the supplementary stuff. Others interpreted the discourse as showing just how out of touch upper management was with the needs of workers, or how confused they were about the policies that actually existed in the firm.

Martin's deconstruction of the story illustrates that there are a number of different ways in which one can interpret what the story says. But she goes even further to examine what was not said. For example, the first line of the story says "we *have* a young woman," not "we *employ* a young woman." The choice of the verb "have" suggests an exceptionally high degree of organizational control, and carries sexual implications. She suggests that the gender-related dimension of the story becomes clear if one substitutes a male manager having a coronary bypass operation for the pregnant manager. Interpretations of a firm arranging for *him* to have a closed-circuit TV system brought into his room the day after he returns home from surgery tend to be very different from the interpretations that are offered of the Caesarean story.[31] Organizational power relationships are grounded in deep structure, assumptions that are taken for granted. Deconstructing those assumptions in itself serves as resistance to hierarchical power and can serve as the basis of the many kinds of resisting discourse that have been discussed throughout this book.

CONCLUSION

Traditional models of organizational power define in terms of domination and through overt displays such as orders, threats, promises, and political strategizing. But power has additional, equally important dimensions. The "surface" structure of power also has a "hidden face," the conscious processes through which employees decide which battles to fight and how to fight them. And power has a deeper structure. Power is perception; it exists in the minds of social and organizational actors, not in a realm independent of our activities. It is inextricably linked to the taken-for-granted assumptions of our culture, both in general and in particular organizational cultures. It is exerted through disciplinary processes that permeate every corner of the organization.

Each of these dimensions of power must be considered if any one dimension is to be understood. Overt displays are influenced by the hidden face of power and its deep structure, *and* both of these dimensions are influenced by overt displays. Similarly, the hidden face is influenced by employees' perceptions of what actions are *normal* and *natural* in their cultures. Their decisions about which battles to fight and how to fight them determine how and when power is displayed in their organizations. Finally, the assumptions of a society are created, reproduced, and transformed by its members' overt actions and hidden decisions about power relationships. One dimension of power simply cannot be understood without simultaneously considering the others.

NOTES

[1] Abraham Zalzenik, "Power and Politics in Organizational Life," *Harvard Business Review* (May-June, 1970): 47–60; David Barber, *Power in Committees* (Chicago: Rand McNally, 1966). The literature on social and organizational power is almost overwhelmingly large, so much so that it would be impossible to list even a small proportion of the important works here. Particularly valuable items are Henry Mintzberg, *Power In and Around Organizations* (Englewood Cliffs, NJ: Prentice Hall, 1983); Jeffrey Pfeffer, *Managing with Power* (Boston: Harvard Business School, 1992); and Dennis Mumby, "Power in Organizations," in *The New Handbook of Organizational Communication,* Fredric Jablin & Linda Putnam, eds. (Thousand Oaks, CA: Sage, 2000).

[2] Fred Jablin, "An Exploratory Study of Subordinates' Perceptions of Supervisory Politics," *Communication Quarterly, 29* (1981): 269–275.

[3] See Angela Tretheway, "A Feminist Critique of Disciplined Bodies," in *Rethinking Organizational and Managerial Communication from Feminist Perspectives,* Patrice Buzzanell, ed. (Thousand Oaks, CA: Sage, 2000) and James Barker & George Cheney, "The Concept of Discipline in Contemporary Organizational Life," *Communication Monographs, 61* (1994): 19–43. These sources summarize Foucault's *Discipline and Punish,* A. Sheridan, trans. (New York: Vintage, 1977/1990) and *The History of Sexuality,* vol. I, A. Hurley, trans. (New York Vintage, 1978/1990).

[4] Multilevel models of power are developed in a large number of contemporary writings. They are summarized in Stewart Clegg, *Frameworks of Power* (Newbury Park, CA: Sage, 1989) and Charles Conrad, "Was Pogo Right?" in *Communication Research in the Twenty-first Century,* Julia Wood and Richard Gregg, eds. (Cresskill, NJ: Hampton Press, 1995). For applications of multilevel models to interpersonal relationships in organizations see Calvin Morrill, "The Private Ordering of Professional Relationships," in *Hidden Conflict in Organizations,* Deborah Kolb and Jean Bartunek, eds. (Newbury Park, CA: Sage, 1992); Robyn Clair, "The Use of Framing Devices to Sequester Organizational Narratives," *Communication Monographs, 60* (1993): 113–136.

[5] David Smith, "Stories, Values, and Patient Care Decisions," in *The Ethical Nexus,* Charles Conrad, ed. (Norwood, NJ: Ablex, 1992) and Marsha Vanderford, David Smith, and Willard Harris, "Value Identification in Narrative Discourse," *Journal of Applied Communication Research, 20* (1992): 123–161.

[6] Charles Berger, "Power, Dominance, and Social Interaction," in *Handbook of Interpersonal Communication,* Mark Knapp & Gerald Miller, eds. (Beverly Hills, CA: Sage, 1994).

[7] Michel de Certeau, *The Practices of Everyday Life* (Berkeley: University of California Press, 1984).

[8] Michel Foucault presents a somewhat different analysis of the relationship between power and knowledge in *Power/Knowledge,* C. Gordon, et al., trans. (New York: Pantheon, 1980).

[9] M. Crozier, *The Bureaucratic Phenomenon* (Chicago: University of Chicago Press, 1964).

[10] Linda Putnam, "Conflict in Group Decision Making," in *Communication and Group Decision Making,* Randy Hirokawa and M. Scott Poole, eds. (Newbury Park, CA: Sage, 1986).

[11] Classic studies of how interdependencies and power are inter-related include Andrew Pettigrew, "Information Control as a Power Resource," *Sociology, 6* (1972): 187–204. Richard M. Emerson, "Power-Dependence Relations," *American Sociological Review, 27* (1962): 31–41.

[12] Peter Monge and Noshir Contractor, "Emergent Communication Networks," in *New Handbook of Organizational Communication,* Fred Jablin and Linda Putnam, eds. (Thousand Oaks, CA: Sage, 2000) and Cynthia Stohl, *Organizational Communication: Connectedness in Action* (Thousand Oaks, CA: Sage, 1995).

[13] Jeffrey Pfeffer, *Power in Organizations* (Marshfield, MA: Pitman, 1981).

[14] Dennis Mumby, "Power, Politics, and Organizational Communication," in *New Handbook of Organizational Communication,* F. Jablin and L. Putnam, eds. (Thousand Oaks, CA: Sage, 2000).

[15] Peter Frost, "Power, Politics, and Influence," in *Handbook of Organizational Communication,* F. Jablin, L. Putnam, K. Roberts, & L. Porter, eds. (Newbury Park, CA: Sage, 1987); Karl Weick, *Sense-Making in Organizations* (Thousand Oaks, CA: Sage, 1995).

[16] Charles Redding, "Rocking Boats, Blowing Whistles, and Teaching Speech Communication," *Communication Education, 34* (1985): 245–258. Also see Marcia Miceli and Janet Near, *Blowing the Whistle: The Organizational and Legal Implications for Companies and Employees* (New York: Lexington Books, 1992).

[17] Amatai Etzioni, cited in C. Gorman, "Listen Here, Mr. Big!," *Time* (July 3, 1989): 40–45. The ADM case is summarized by Joseph Menn in "ADM Fine Criticized as Too Low," *Houston Chronicle,* December 1, 1996, C13.

[18] B.Z. Posner and W.H. Schmidt, "Values and the American Manager," *California Management Review, 26* (1984): 202–216. Also see Robert Sims, "The Challenge of Ethical Behavior in Organizations," *Journal of Business Ethics, 11* (1992) 501–513. The MBA study and the cost estimates are summarized in Jim Barlow, "Ethics Can Boost the Bottom Line," *Houston Chronicle,* October 31, 1996, C1.

[19] B.E. Toffler, *Tough Choices* (New York: John Wiley, 1986). Matthew Seeger has observed that when people *do* talk about ethics, it usually is to avoid taking responsibility for ethical choices "Responsibility in Organizational Communication," in *Proceedings of the 1992 National Communication Ethics Conference,* J. Jaska, ed. (Annandale, VA: Speech Communication Association, 1992).

[20] Herbert Kellman and L. Hamilton, *Crimes of Obedience* (New Haven, CT: Yale University Press, 1989).

[21] William G. Scott and D.K. Hart, *Organizational America* (Boston: Houghton Mifflin, 1979) and *Organizational Values in America* (New Brunswick, NJ: Transaction Publishers, 1989).

[22] Diane Vaughn, *Controlling Unlawful Organizational Behavior* (Chicago: University of Chicago Press, 1992). They also believed that they could get away with it.

[23] U.S. and Australian data are available in John McMillan, "Legal Protection of Whistleblowers," in *Corruption and Reform,* S. Prosser, R. Wear, & J. Nethercote, eds. (St. Lucia, Qld: University of Queensland Press, 1990) and Damien Grace & Stephen Cohen, *Business Ethics* (Melbourne, Australia: Oxford, 1995). The Lundwall interview is available in "Texaco Whistle-Blower: Much Trouble, Little Reward," *USA Today,* 20 December, 1999, 24A.

[24] The data presented is based on a September, 1996, survey of 5,000 companies by the Society for Human Resource Management. A summary was published in the October 1, 1996 *Houston Chronicle,* B1. Additional data is provided by Melissa Gibson & Nancy Schullery, "Shifting Meanings in a Blue-Collar Worker Philanthropy Program," *Management Communication Quarterly, 14* (2000): 189–236. An excellent summary of muted group theory is provided by Mark Orbe, "An Outsider Within Perspective to Organizational Communication," *Management Communication Quarterly, 2* (1998): 230–279.

[25] Roger Jehensen, "Effectiveness, Expertise, and Excellence as Ideological Fictions," *Human Studies, 7* (1984): 3–21 and Barker & Cheney, 1994. Habermas' work is treated at length in a number of sources. Two communication theorists have done an especially thorough job of developing these ideas: Dennis Mumby, *Communication and Power in Organizations* (Norwood, NJ: Ablex, 1988) and Stanley Deetz, *Democracy in an Age of Corporate Colonization* (Albany, NY: SUNY Press, 1992). For an analysis of the ways in which technical reason strengthens management's power see Dan Gowler & Karen Legge, "The Meaning of Management and the Management of Meaning," in *Understanding Management,* Stephen Linstead, R.G. Small, & P. Jeffcutt (London: Sage, 1996).

[26] See Judi Marshall, "Viewing Organizational Communication from a Feminist Perspective: A Critique and Some Offerings," in *Communication Yearbook 16*, S. Deetz, ed. (Newbury Park, CA: Sage, 1993) and *Rethinking Organizational and Managerial Communication from Feminist Perspectives*, Patrice Buzzanell, ed. (Thousand Oaks, CA: Sage, 2000).

[27] Patrice Buzzanell, "Gaining a Voice: Feminist Organizational Communication Theorizing," *Management Communication Quarterly, 7* (1994): 339–383.

[28] Tom Daniels, Barry Spiker, & Micahel Papa, *Perspectives on Organizational Communication,* 4th ed. Madison, WI: Brown & Benchmark, 1997; Albrecht and Bradford Hall, "Relational and Content Differences Between Elites and Outsiders in Innovation Networks," *Human Communication Research, 17* (1991): 535–561.

[29] K. Iannello, *Decisions without Hierarchy* (London: Routledge, 1993); Nancy Wyatt, "Shared Leadership in the Weavers' Guild," in *Women Communicating: Studies of Women's Talk*, Barbara Bate and Anita Taylor, eds. (Norwood, NJ: Ablex, 1988). For a similar example in a nonfeminist organization see George Cheney, *Values at Work* (Ithaca, NY: Cornell University Press, 1999).

[30] H. Gottfried and P. Weiss, "A Compound Feminist Organization," *Women and Politics, 14* (1994): 23–44; and Betsy Bach, "Making a Difference by Doing Differently: A Response to Putnam," paper presented at the Arizona State University Conference on Organizational Communication, Tempe, AZ, 1990. For an analysis of resistance to voicing strategies, see H. Eisenstein, *Gender Shock* (Boston: Beacon, 1991).

[31] Joanne Martin, *Cultures in Organizations* (New York: Oxford University Press, 1992). For additional examples, see Dennis Mumby and Cynthia Stohl, "Power and Discourse in Organization Studies," *Discourse and Society, 2* (1991): 313–332.

Chapter 9

COMMUNICATION AND DECISION MAKING: INDIVIDUAL, GROUP, AND ORGANIZATIONAL CONSIDERATIONS

Plans are important in organizations,
but not for the reasons people think.
—KARL WEICK

CENTRAL THEMES

- Both Western culture and traditional models of organizing view individual employees and organizations as rational actors. In contrast, many contemporary perspectives suggest that these assumptions are cultural myths and that actual decision-making processes are often not rational.

- Because our rationality is "bounded" and our choices are "intransitive," we cannot be rational actors. Consequently, we use communication to make choices that are acceptable and not necessarily rational.

- Traditional views of group decision making are straightforward applications of the rational actor model; contemporary models focus on the processes through which groups deviate from strict rationality.

- To make effective decisions, groups must exchange and analyze information in a critical fashion, maintain a balance between group cohesion and conflict, and counteract hidden agendas.

- Organizational groups make decisions through processes that are substantially different than those used in laboratory groups.

- A number of situational and interactional factors influence the extent to which a particular organizational decision can or should be made through strictly rational processes.

- Because rationality is a core value of Western cultures, people need to rationalize their nonrationality. However, doing so tends to privilege the interests of managers over those of workers.

KEY TERMS

Bounded rationality	Optimizing
Satisficing	Intransitivity
Retrospective sense-making	Consensus
Negotiation	Standard agenda
Group cohesion	Egocentric influence
Boundary-spanning activities	Intuition
Enactment-selection-retention	

Many people, especially in Western societies, view organizations as rational, cooperative enterprises. According to this perspective, organizations exist so that people can pursue their goals through the most efficient means, and organizations are efficient only if the people who comprise them are trained to make and rewarded for making rational decisions. Rational employees encounter problems or challenges; they systematically seek out the information and expertise needed to choose among courses of action and then make careful, objective decisions based on the available information. In this chapter we take a somewhat different position about individual, group, and organizational decision making. We first present the rational-actor model of decision making. Then we contrast that *theoretical* model with research on how individuals, groups, and organizations *actually do* make decisions. We conclude that, except in the simplest decision situations, people are not and cannot be strictly rational actors and may sacrifice a great deal by trying to be. Our goal is not to disparage the decision makers. Instead our objective is to suggest that strictly rational theories of decision making simply do not reflect the complex maze of personal, interpersonal, political, and ethical considerations that employees incorporate into their choices. In short, it is the "rational-actor" model that is in error, not the nonrational employees.

COMMUNICATION AND INDIVIDUAL DECISION MAKING

Instead of assuming that people are rational actors who should always strive to make strictly rational choices, we examine the ways in which real people manage complicated decision situations and propose that the "rationality" of a decision is only one of many viable evaluative criteria.

Communication and Rational Models of Individual Decision-Making

According to rational-actor models of decision making, people choose among all the available courses of action in a particular situation by comparing the probable outcomes of each alternative and selecting one that promises the greatest return. For example, if a person is trying to choose among three job

TABLE 9–1

A Rational Model of Career Decision-Making

	STOCK OPTIONS		FLEXIBILITY		SALARY		BONUS		TOTAL
Company X	.9(7)	+	.8(2)	+	.1(9)	+	.2(11)	=	11
Company Y	.1(7)	+	.5(2)	+	.1(9)	+	.1(11)	=	3.7
Company Z	.4(7)	+	.1(2)	+	.3(9)	+	.9(11)	=	15.6

offers, she or he will begin by selecting a set of evaluative criteria. (For the purposes of this example, we have chosen the flexibility in working conditions and three items included in offers given to recent college graduates in the early 2000's—stock options, signing bonuses, and initial salary). Next, our decision maker assigns a weight to each criterion and determines how important it is to him or her. Finally, she or he estimates the likelihood that accepting each offer will produce the outcomes that are implicit in each evaluative criterion. He or she then multiplies each weight by its associated probability, adds the products, and *voilà*, has her or his choice (see Table 9-1).

In our example, a hiring bonus is highly salient to our decision maker because she or he has large unpaid college loans and plans to change firms as soon as possible. So she or he gives it a weight of 11. Starting salary is almost as salient (a weight of 9) because he or she wants to invest the bulk of it to make enough money to start his or her own business quickly. Stock options are a bit less (a weight of 7) important because she or he anticipates that the firms' stocks will skyrocket in value in the short term, level off by the time she or he changes jobs, and plummet soon after (like dot.com companies did during the late 1990s and 2000). Flexibility of working conditions is relatively unimportant (a weight of 2) because he or she is single and plans to work incessantly before age 30 and then get a life.

He or she estimates that the probability of receiving handsome stock options from company X is quite high (and attaches a probability of 0.9); getting them from company Z is moderate (probability of 0.4), and the probability of getting them from company Y is quite low (probability 0.1). Negotiating for a large signing bonus is relatively easy with company Z, because a recent and successful I.P.O. (initial public offering of stock) has given it a lot of cash (probability of 0.9); but the likelihood is low for companies X and Y because they are cash-strapped at the moment. Company X has won a number of awards for its family-friendly policies and flexible scheduling (so it receives a likelihood score of 0.8). Company Y has just started its flextime and flexplace programs and still puts lots of limits on them (resulting in a score of .4), and company Z still is living in the 1950s on these issues (a score of .1). Starting salaries are comparable across the industry; but they are a little bit higher in company Z. So it receives a probability score of 0.3, while the other two companies receive scores of 0.1. When our decision maker performs all the necessary computations, company Z wins.

To use this system successfully, our decision maker must have a complete list of potential options (job offers) and criteria weightings, accurate and complete information about the companies in terms of the criteria (the probabilities), knowledge of all options and probabilities at the same time or the ability to use the same estimates during each of a series of choices, and sufficient time and computational skill. In the simplest life (and organizational) decision situations, these requirements may be met. But most of the choices people face are more complicated, and in those normal decision situations, one or more of these requirements will not be met.

Communication and Contemporary Models of Individual Decision Making

Studies of individuals' actions during decision-making situations indicate both that humans cannot act in accordance with this rational-actor model and that they do not do so. At most people act in ways that *appear* to be consistent with the model.[1]

Why Humans Cannot Be Rational Actors   People cannot be rational actors because they have limited analytical skills and because their decision making is handicapped by a variety of situational factors (the research says that our rationality is **bounded**). In real-world situations, the requirements of the rational-actor model are rarely met. Humans often choose the best possible course of action (a process that is called **optimizing**), but they make perfectly acceptable choices that allow them to "get by" quite well (a process that is called **satisficing**). They search through a haystack of complicated options looking for a needle that is sharp enough to sew with, not for the sharpest needle available.[2] Although the rationality of some people does seem to be more tightly bounded than others, and although some decision situations are more complex than others, people can rarely rely on strictly rational processes to make choices in real situations.

Human beings' rationality is bounded by other factors. Like Pollyanna, people overestimate the likelihood of "good" outcomes and underestimate the probability of "bad" ones. For example, no matter how much information students are given about past patterns of grading in a course and about their own academic records, they invariably seem to overestimate their chances of receiving A's and B's and underestimate their chances of getting C's, D's or F's. The criteria that people use to make decisions change in different situations (a process called **intransitivity**). This difference is partly because they shift their preferences, criteria, weightings, and probability estimates around between decisions. For example, if our mythical decision maker had received his or her job offers in a sequence, or even two at a time, he or she probably would have arrived at different scores for each offer than if they had been received all at once. Perceptions of the outcomes, weights, and probabilities would have changed. Potential long-term financial gains may outweigh lifestyle sacrifices for single "twentysomethings." But, the relative importance of the two considerations is likely to change when our decision maker has a family to support. Finally, when decisions are important to people and they have high levels of energy available, they tend to be very involved in the process. They are motivated to search actively for information, use their information-processing abilities to the greatest extent possible, and consider as wide a range of outcomes, criteria, and probabilities as they can. They will come as close as they can to being a rational actor. But when the decision is less emotionally involving or they have less energy available, their choice-making routine deviates from the rational-actor model even more than is usual.

For a variety of reasons, then, individuals cannot behave as rational actors. But we still have to make choices. To do so we must simplify the complicated situations that we face. We can do so largely because we are able to communicate. Once two of Charley Conrad's students (an engaged couple) sought advice about purchasing a new automobile. They said their goal was noble—to shift from their old gas guzzler to a fuel-efficient model to do their part to forestall a worldwide energy crisis. He suggested that this goal would be best achieved if they kept their old car. The amount of fuel they would save during the lifetime of their new car would be far less than the amount of energy and nonrenewable minerals that would be used in the manufacture of their new car. Besides, there was no guarantee that the person who purchased their old car would use it to replace an even less fuel-efficient vehicle. Thus the net effect of their buying a new car, regardless of how fuel-efficient it might be, would be to increase the depletion of nonrenewable resources, bringing the world even closer to eco-catastrophe.

Now, the rational actor model does not predict that the students would discover that Dr. Conrad was correct. But it does suggest that they should respond to his argument by seeking out information about the resources used in fabricating new automobiles, means of controlling the energy use of potential purchasers of their old car, and the relative scarcity of petroleum compared to the scarcity of the other resources used in the fabrication of cars. The model predicts that they would use their communicative and intellectual skills to obtain the information needed to find out whether he was right. However, the model fails to recognize that some of the needed information may either not exist or be so difficult to locate that it would not be worth the effort: that the decision makers could not care less about the effects that their actions might have on other people's actions, that their friends are committed to energy conservation, or that a host of other intangible factors may influence their decision making.

Eventually they chose a course of action that did incorporate some of these considerations. They returned after a lengthy discussion and produced the following changes in their position: They were going to be concerned only about gasoline (because it is too much work to determine the net effect of our purchase will have on other resources); they were going to ignore the effects that their decision has on anyone else's energy use; and they were going to buy a new fuel-efficient car, because doing so would symbolize their commitment to conservation whether it has that effect or not. So, in retrospect their interchange (and their private discussion) did not lead to a strictly rational decision, at least not as the rational-actor model defines that term. But their communication with one another did allow them to (1) simplify their decision situation and make it more manageable, (2) provide mutual validation of their new view of the situation and (3) provide social and emotional support for one another's decision-making processes. They were, in the end, able to make a decision and to make it with conviction. Communicating usually helps people make decisions, but not make strictly "rational" decisions.

Why Humans Are Not Rational Actors   The rational-actor model presumes that people determine decision criteria and seek out relevant information before they actually make a decision. Observations of human decision making, and especially of organizational decision making, suggest that they often reverse the sequence, first making choices and acting on them and then seeking out the information needed to *rationalize* their decisions. They make a decision that seems to be correct and then construct a picture of their decision-making process that makes them seem to be rational actors. This kind of backward thinking (the academic term is **retrospective sense-making**) seems to occur in almost all kinds of human decision making.[3]

COMMUNICATION AND MODELS OF GROUP DECISION MAKING

People form groups for a number of reasons, both inside and outside of organizations.[4] Many of these reasons have been discussed in earlier chapters—to get social and emotional support or stimulate creativity (Chapter 3), to exchange task-related information (Chapter 2), or for specific purposes, such as improving the quality of what they produce (Chapter 3). But a primary activity in groups, no matter what their purpose is decision making.

Traditional Views of Group Decision-Making Processes

Traditional models of group decision making are based on traditional (rational actor) models of individual decision making. Early twentieth century philosopher John Dewey argued that people confront personal problems through a five-step process: (1) a problem or general feeling of uneasiness is recognized, (2) the problem is located and defined, (3) the person sets standards by which to test a solution, (4) several response options are identified and tested, and (5) a solution is selected and implemented. From this individual model a standard-agenda model of group decision making developed. To make an effective decision, groups should follow these steps:

1. Define the task facing the group, making sure each member understands why the task is important, what its final product will look like, and what that product will be used for; then

2. Reach agreement on group and individual responsibilities (who is to do what about what); then

3. Seek out all the information needed by the group, arrange it for easy access, and evaluate its accuracy; then
4. Establish criteria for evaluating possible courses of action, including recognizing what options and outcomes are realistic; then
5. Discover and evaluate options; and finally
6. Prepare to present persuasively and defend its choice to people who will be involved in implementing it.

Each phase has characteristic goals, tasks that must be performed, and obligations for members and leaders. It is also important to define and understand the problem and establish criteria *prior* to considering options or solutions. Premature consideration of options or solutions may lead decision makers to attend to only those aspects of the situation or problem that pertain to the solution. This procedure is designed to promote open-minded and full exploration of the situation, and creative generation of apt solutions.

Determining How the Decision Will Be Made Most groups develop norms about how decisions should be made. Some groups attempt to make decisions by **consensus**—unanimous agreement of all members. Consensus is valuable because it can create unified support for the group's final decision. But it is time-consuming and may lead to weak decisions, because members may compromise on second-best decisions to find an outcome that is acceptable to everyone.

A second norm is **negotiation,** which involves bargaining to create a decision that honors each member's position on key issues. Unlike consensus, which leads to unanimous agreement on both a decision and its rationale, negotiation culminates in a decision that is acceptable without requiring agreement on goals and rationales. As the final sections of this chapter indicate, this procedure is common in organizational decision making. Negotiating takes less time than consensus and does not water down solutions, but can lead to piecemeal outcomes that are less coherent. When differing political interests make it difficult for members to agree on common goals, the group may decide to trade-off meeting one goal at present and the other in the future. "Smooth production" and "satisfying customers" may be impossible to achieve simultaneously, so the group focuses first on smoothing out production and agrees to turn to satisfying customers once production is worked out.[5]

A third method is voting. As well as being consistent with Western culture's acceptance of majority rule, voting is quick, efficient, and decisive. But it also reduces the information exchange necessary for good decisions; it may allow high-power members to force weaker members into accepting a decision they oppose and can polarize winner and losers, creating frustration and resentment. When it is imperative that every member actively support the group's decision after it is made, voting may be the least preferred decision form.

Leadership and Group Decision Making In Western societies people are taught to assume that groups must have a designated leader or leaders. In most organizations, the leader is identified before the group begins its work, either explicitly when person X is ordained as chairperson, or implicitly when members realize that person X is the group member who has the highest status in the organization. If no leader is appointed or selected for the group, the group has three options: Designate one person as leader from the outset; take a chance that a leader will emerge, or hope that the different members of the group can share leadership tasks efficiently and smoothly. The second and third options have their advantages, but they are also risky. When the group allows a leader to emerge naturally, the person best suited to the task and group often rises to the occasion. Emergent leaders are generally more effective than leaders appointed by management. However, the danger in the emergence option is that no leader will emerge or that competing candidates will split the group. Sharing among all members develops every member's skills and commitment to the group; but members must be very conscientious or important issues may slip through the cracks.[6]

Groups with clearly identified leaders are often more efficient, have fewer interpersonal problems, and produce better decisions, provided the leader is competent and effective at organizing the group. This does not mean that leaderless groups are doomed to failure. It just means that they will have problems unless members have the right mix of leadership skills and exercise them effectively. Another strategy for a leaderless group or self-managed teams is to rotate leadership; this builds all members' skills and also gives the team one clear point of responsibility without giving power to one person on a permanent basis.[7]

What role should a leader play in group decision making? Leaders have three options: They can make the decision themselves; they can consult with the group and make the decision themselves; or they can have the group make the decision. An important model developed by Victor Vroom and Peter Yetton advanced some rules to help leaders decide which method to use. According to their model, either consultation or group decision making should be used when quality of the decision is critical and when the leader does not have sufficient information to make the decision him or herself. The group model should also be used when members' acceptance of the decision is important. On the other hand, the leader should make the decision or consult if members do not share the organization's goals. If quality is not important, any of the methods can be used, depending on what seems best for the group at the time.[8] Two additional factors that must be considered are the amount of time the group has to make a decision and the cost of convening the group. If time is short and cost high, the recommendation is to have the leader make the decision or consult in an efficient manner.

When the group is making the decision, the leader's role should fulfill three functions. Leadership means influencing members' *perceptions of themselves*— motivating them to contribute to the group and to feel committed to it and its task. Leadership also involves influencing members' *perceptions of the group*. It means focusing the group's attention on the group's goals and the role that each step has in the group's meeting those goals. Making members feel that the group is an autonomous entity by minimizing references to outside pressures, involving members in decisions about tasks and procedures, taking each member's comments seriously, and building the group's confidence that it can make a good decision.

Finally, leadership means influencing the *pace* and *direction* of the discussion and the *decisions* made by the group. In general, leaders should avoid acting like advocates, especially early in the group's history; they should adopt a participative style that invites members' contributions and follows their ideas.[9] If the leader jumps in too early or too forcefully, members are discouraged from sharing their ideas and expertise, reducing the advantages of group decision making. However, leaders are generally selected because of their perspective or expertise, and there are times when the group needs to have that information made available.

Members who are not identified as leaders also play important roles. Group tasks are too large or complex to be performed by individuals. Consequently, the group needs the expertise and efforts of all members. But commitment is rarely high or equal among all members. One problem in groups, especially those larger than 6 or 7 members is the "free-rider" problem, where several members do not contribute their effort fairly and take advantage of other members' work[10] You may have experienced this yourself with classroom group projects. The opposite extreme, when members are excessively committed to the group, is equally damaging. Groups benefit from disagreement, from constructive conflict. When members agree for the sake of agreeing, the group does not benefit from their expertise or from the careful testing of ideas and evidence that comes from positive confrontation. The primary obligation of group members is to act as valuable members of a cooperative activity and to undertake communication functions, such as summarizing, contributing ideas, encouraging other members, and energizing the group.

Contemporary Models of Group Decision Making

Traditional models of group decision making are based on the assumption that groups should and do follow a **standard agenda** model of group process. This implies that the group's decision process should evolve in a simple, consistent, and straightforward manner and that model leaders and followers should adapt to the phase of decision making the group is in. Contemporary research indicates that these assumptions are only partly correct. Groups are systems in the sense that the concept was defined in Chapter 1. As such they are constantly dealing with pressures from their subsystems and suprasystems. Some of these pressures are constant throughout the decision-making process. For instance, the group's assigned task is a continual pressure. Other pressures are intermittent. They occur only at certain points during the process and pressure the group to change its direction, at least temporarily. Some are external, as when members discover and introduce new information from outside of the group. In organizational groups, external pressures are often political, and they often slow, sidetrack, or reverse decision-making processes.[11]

Other pressures are internal, developing out of the group discussion. Groups seem to participate in "reach testing," where they propose, develop, modify, drop, and then restart testing of ideas. As a result, the linear, step-by-step standard agenda rarely is—and rarely should be—implemented in the way that the traditional model envisioned. Instead, group processes are idiosyncratic and cyclical. Different phases overlap: Members move from one phase to another and back again; and roles change with the flow of the conversation. The key to effective participation is not adapting to the "phase" of group development, but adapting to the specific situations that emerge as the process continues. Participation is "strategic," in the sense that this book uses the term. Participation involves monitoring and interpreting the communication of the group, choosing productive ways of responding to that situation, and communicating effective strategic responses, while recognizing that each member's actions transform the situation and communication of the other members.

Each of the tasks envisioned in the traditional model—establishing criteria, evaluating alternatives, seeking and presenting information, and so on—must still be fulfilled, but are fulfilled only when doing so is appropriate to the communicative process. Fortunately, although almost everyone has been taught to follow the standard agenda, people are willing to deviate from its procedural norms when it is appropriate to do so.[12] In the case of group decision making, we tend to be strategic communicators in spite of our training.

Information Exchange   Regardless of the specific process that a decision-making group follows, it faces three problems: achieving effective information exchange, dealing with the consequences of group cohesion, and counteracting egocentric influences on decisions. Five information-related factors can lead a group to accept poor decisions:

1. The improper assessment of a situation
2. The establishment of inappropriate goals and objectives
3. The improper assessment of the strengths and weaknesses of various alternatives
4. The establishment of a flawed information base
5. Faulty reasoning based on the group's information base[13]

Improper information use sometimes results from errors in scanning. In complicated and ambiguous situations—the kind in which groups are better decision makers than individuals—members often do not know what kinds of information are useful or when they have sufficient amounts to make the choice. Thus, they often unknowingly collect too little information, the wrong information, or so much information that they cannot process it adequately. In other cases, they may not evaluate the information they obtain accurately. Organizational power relationships and political considerations may also lead members to withhold or distort the information they provide the group. In still other cases, groups may have to make a decision quickly, without sufficient time to properly understand the problem or the situation. This was the case for President Gerald Ford's response to the swine flu epidemic of the mid-1970s. Feeling intense pressure from what seemed to be an impending disaster, the Ford administration set up an inoculation program on an emergency basis. However, not only did it turn out that the inoculation program was unnecessary, because

the epidemic was overstated and did not materialize, but the vaccine led to ill-
nesses among some of those who were inoculated.

In addition, the communication processes that occur within the group may
create distortions. Groups collaborate in creating realities based on the information they have gathered (recall Chapter 1). Once these realities begin to be
shared, they influence subsequent interpretations of information. Citing Irving
Janis, Dennis Gouran noted that this kind of process seemed to influence U.S.
policy during the Korean War:

> The Chinese were seen by President Truman and his advisors as weak puppets
> of the Soviet Union. . . . The puppet like image created in presidential discus-
> sions, coupled with the belief that the Soviets were reluctant to become
> involved in a ground war, laid the foundation for predicting success in the con-
> templated action (crossing the border into North Korea). In reality, the decision
> proved to be one of the president's most costly. Something of the same mental-
> ity has been attributed to those in the Johnson administration who recom-
> mended increased military involvement (in Vietnam).[14]

Group Cohesion   **Group cohesion** refers to the degree to which members
are attracted and committed to the group. There are at least three sources of
group cohesion: *task cohesion,* which is due to members' beliefs that the group's
work is valuable and significant; *attraction-based cohesion,* which is due to lik-
ing for other members of the group, and *status cohesion,* which is due to the
rewards members receive based on the reputation and status of the group.
Research suggests that task cohesion is positively related to group effectiveness;
the other two forms of cohesion are unrelated to group performance but are
positively related to member satisfaction. Overall, the value of cohesion is curvi-
linear; that is, it is valuable up to a point, but beyond that point it begins to do
harm. In an important way "cohesion" is similar to "identification" as that term
was explained in Chapter 4. When people identify fully with their organizations,
they make decisions through the processes and based on the accepted premises
of their organizations. If those processes are inappropriate or if the premises are
incorrect or irrelevant in specific situations, people make choices that are inappropriate. When group members identify fully with one another, that is, when the
group is highly cohesive, they may make the same kinds of errors.

In all groups, but especially in highly cohesive groups, pressures develop
that may reduce the range and quality of information presented and thus eliminate the advantage of having decisions made by groups rather than by individuals. Often these pressures are not deliberate. Groups may develop *"norms of
concurrence,"* which pressure members into agreeing with other members
rather than seeking the best solutions. If an individual member dissents from
the group's position or questions the assumptions the other members seem to
share, others respond by arguing with, ignoring, or in extreme cases (or if the
deviant persists) expelling the dissenter from the group. As the discussion continues, the group shifts to the position initially taken by the majority or by its
most vocal members. These "choice shifts" depend not on the information available to the group, but on in-group communicative pressures. As a result groups

may make "extreme" decisions—ones that unquestioningly continue precedents and existing policies or that are inordinately risky. Since cohesion generates high levels of commitment to decisions and the high levels of motivation necessary to implement them, excessive cohesion may also lead groups to do everything they can to implement foolish decisions and to ignore or distort feedback indicating that their decision was unwise. The communicative processes that *should* lead to the generation of creative ideas, sharing of accurate and relevant information, and the critical analysis of options begin to support what often may be unwarranted and unwise decisions.[15]

Irving Janis and his associates have argued that these processes often dominate political decision making. Classic examples of groupthink include the 1941 decision to ignore warnings that Japan might attack Pearl Harbor, the 1961 decision to invade Cuba at the Bay of Pigs, and the Committee to Re-elect the President's 1974 decision to break into the Democratic Party's headquarters in the Watergate Hotel. In each case, extensive group deliberations preceded the decision, and ample information was available that suggested that the outcome was unwise. But as Wood, Phillips, and Peterson conclude: "The transcripts of these committees' discussion[s] clearly demonstrate that some members knuckled under to group opinion, others rationalized going along with the majority, and still others could not see beyond the 'party line.'"[16] The intelligence, extensive experience, and power of these groups did little to compensate for the communicative pressures that prevented constructive dissent.

Cohesive groups may also develop an illusion of invulnerability. Not only does this illusion hamper decision making, in organizational settings, it leads members to see themselves as separate from and better than other work groups. The competitive orientation that develops increases intergroup conflict. In time, the errors that highly cohesive groups make and the conflicts they have with other groups may create dissension. Members may respond by even more intensely suppressing disagreement, which increases cohesion and its disadvantages. In a continuing cycle, highly cohesive permanent groups may become less and less capable of making good choices. As these comments suggest, conflict can be a positive element of group communication. (Because the dynamics of conflict are examined at length in Chapter 10, it will be discussed only briefly here.)

Like cohesion, some conflict is valuable; but excessive conflict is damaging. In fact, a group's search for a mutually acceptable decision requires conflict if it is to succeed. Comparing and evaluating ideas—classifying, narrowing, refocusing, selecting, eliminating, and synthesizing—depend on the expression of divergent points of view. Properly managed, *substantive* conflict (over issues) aids group processes. When it is transformed into *affective* conflict (over emotions), productive conflict management becomes quite difficult.[17]

Counteracting Egocentric Influences on Decision Making   In some cases, one or more members of a group have a high need for control or are otherwise driven by a "hidden agenda" to push for a particular decision. Gouran and Hirokawa illustrate this **egocentric influence:**

As more than one observer has noted, former President Richard Nixon was ultimately responsible for his own political undoing in the Watergate case because of his inability to permit normal investigative processes to move forward in regard to the break-in at Democratic National Headquarters. Instead his need for control dominated discussions among members of his inner circle and culminated in the fateful decision to engage in a cover-up.[18]

Signs of egocentric influences on group decision making include (1) members adopting a win-lose orientation and appearing to be preoccupied with getting the group to adopt their particular solutions; (2) highly defensive members; and (3) statements such as "Please, don't question me, I know what I'm talking about," "I have been dealing with this kind of problem for over ten years," or "It's the principle of the thing."

To counteract egocentric influences, a group should adopt procedures that force it to approach the problem systematically and that do not give one member's viewpoint too much weight. It is also important that other members clearly indicate to the egocentric member that they are not going to knuckle under to him or her. Working out creative decisions that meet the member's needs but also guard against problems in the hidden agenda is another way of handling egocentric influences without creating serious fractures in the group.[19]

Group Decision Making in Organizational Settings

A key tenet of this book is that people adapt their communication to the situations they face. The situations faced by organizational decision-making groups are often very different from those of the isolated, laboratory groups involved in the research underlying the preceding sections. In organizational settings, groups are often larger than those in laboratory studies; members are often together for years rather than the short periods used in studies, and they must take other groups and managers into account. Three elements of organizations strongly shape group communication—*connectivity, hierarchical structure, and political considerations.*[20]

Group Connectivity   As Unit I pointed out, employees and units of organizations differ in terms of their "interdependence;" some employees/groups work independently of other employees/groups while others are highly dependent. This means that some units are tightly coupled. Each decision they make depends on information and expertise obtained from other groups and in turn influences the decisions of groups with which they are interdependent. Other groups are loosely coupled. Their decisions either do not influence other groups or do so only after considerable time and a number of intervening decisions. Loosely coupled groups make decisions independently, relying primarily on information and expertise from within the work group. When units are interdependent, their effectiveness depends on their "linking pins," members who actively communicate with outside people and units (see Chapter 3). In effective tightly coupled groups, linking pins talk more and have more impact on the group's decisions than other members. For these groups, centralized networks and leadership may be more productive than laboratory research would suggest. For loosely coupled groups, the general lessons of group communication may be more relevant.

Hierarchical Structure   Organizational group communication is also influenced by the hierarchical structure of the organization. As noted in Chapter 3, some work groups are ongoing while others are temporary—ad hoc committees formed to solve specific problems and project teams. In many cases, involvement in temporary groups is added to employees' normal responsibilities, making it difficult for them to be committed to those groups. Since they are outside of the normal organizational hierarchy, they have little formal power to implement the decisions they reach. Leaders of temporary groups face formidable problems creating and sustaining motivation, and the impact the group has may depend more on its members' being able to gain informal support outside of the group than on the quality of its own communication and decision making. If the issue is important to the organization, temporary groups may be able to make rapid and effective decisions.

But if the issue is not important, or if it threatens any established interests, the discussions may drag on forever, making morale and motivation even greater problems. A major university faced serious shortages of classroom space. The administration decided to help solve the problem by encouraging departments to schedule more evening classes. Eventually the administration took control of scheduling and started offering night classes without consulting the departments. Unfortunately, the daytime regulation of parking was not enforced after 5 P.M. and the city's bus service stopped running before evening classes were dismissed. Suddenly there was a serious shortage of night parking. A task force was appointed to find a solution to the problem. Even before their first meeting complaints started to be made; faculty members who were not teaching night classes were "concerned" that they would not have access to lots near the library and computer center if the committee voted to restrict evening parking. The theater and music departments complained that limiting parking would make their performances and concerts inconvenient to important patrons and their budgets would suffer.

As the committee's meetings continued, it seemed that every conceivable group had a vested interest in maintaining the chaos in night parking. They also learned that it was difficult to convince the upper administration that the problem was serious, in part because administrators had reserved spaces and "had never noticed any problems parking at night." Eventually, they found a way to reserve only a few lots for students and faculty who were involved in night classes, leaving the rest of the lots open to the interest groups. After two years of work, they implemented the new plan at the beginning of the spring semester. The system worked beautifully until January 13, the night of the first home basketball game. At this university, men's basketball is a serious—and very lucrative—business, and the administration suddenly received an avalanche of hostile calls from wealthy alumni who had driven all over campus searching for parking spaces. The new policy was canceled by the same administrator who formed the committee in the first place and the committee went back to the drawing board. For some reason attendance dropped off at recent committee meetings. For this and most ad hoc groups, the character and effectiveness of its internal communication is less important than its external communication. And, external pressures are so constraining that even superhuman leadership would do little to make the group ever again function as a cohesive, committed unit.

Organizational Groups and Political Considerations   A third reason why organizational groups differ from laboratory groups also involves considerations of organizational power and politics. Members may be appointed to the group as representatives of some other group or interests. Their communication reflects their out-group allegiances as much as it does their commitment to the group. Regardless of what happens within the group, members may have strong incentives to withhold or distort information or to protect their outside interests. The adverse effects of these pressures seem to be smaller when members represent groups that depend on one another, because everyone realizes that misleading or alienating other groups eventually will hurt them. In sum, whether external or internal, political considerations provide a powerful impetus for groups to move away from the traditional model of group decision making.

Boundary Spanning: A Key Component of Group Effectiveness in Organizations   Deborah Ancona and David Caldwell have conducted important research on factors that make groups effective in organizations[21]. They recognize that managing the group's internal decision-making processes well contributes to group effectiveness. However, in addition, their research establishes the importance of external, **boundary-spanning activities.** Groups must interact with individuals and groups in the organization who are important to the group's effectiveness, such as superiors who must evaluate the group, resource providers, customers and clients, and parties affected for good or ill by group activities. Four types of external activities that span the group's boundary with the organization are particularly important:

1. **Scouting or scanning activities** through which group members gather intelligence and information that can help them make better decisions.
2. **Liaison activities** with those who evaluate and consume the group's work or products to ensure that requirements are understood and needs met.
3. **Campaigns** to form good impressions of the group, its activities, and its products in the organization and external community.
4. **Buffering** activities that protect the group from external threats and events that might prevent it from attaining its goals. This includes a wide range of protective behavior, for example, keeping group activities secret until the group is ready to go or defending the group from negative comments made by a supervisor in another unit.

Depending on the group's context, some of these four types of activities may be more important than others.

COMMUNICATION AND ORGANIZATIONAL DECISION MAKING

When it is applied to organizations, the rational-actor model depicts decision making as a systematic process through which the following occurs:

1. An employee recognizes that a problem exists and that it is caused by some unexpected, or as yet, untreated change in the organization's environment or by the actions of some of its members.
2. Each member of the organization who, because of his or her formal position, expertise, or available information, has an interest in the problem is told about it and invited to help solve it.
3. Alternative courses of action are compared through open, problem-solving communication.
4. The optimal solution is chosen and implemented.
5. Its impact is monitored and information about its affects is gathered and stored for use in similar situations in the future.

Through this feedback process the rational decision process is able to correct itself.[22]

As in the case of individual decision making, in some cases employees can and do make decisions in this way—decisions that are simple and politically unimportant, for example. But in many other cases, organizational decision makers deviate from the rational-actor model, either by making decisions through "intuition" or through processes that are "nonrational" according to the rational-actor model.

Nonrational Organizational Decision Making

The rational-actor model assumes that making the best possible choice is always the best organizational strategy. In contrast, "nonrationality" models suggest that this kind of situation is quite rare in organizations. This perspective does not advocate *irrational* decision making—ignoring the realities of a situation—but neither does it exclude emotions. Instead, it proposes that organizational decision situations are complex and multidimensional and that decision-making processes should be adapted to the complexities of those situations. "Nonrationality" models are difficult to accept because they violate many of the taken-for-granted assumptions of modern Western societies. Consequently, fully understanding nonrational organizational decision making needs to involve an analysis of key societal myths.

Making Decisions through Intuition   According to the traditional mythology of Western organizations, managers make rational decisions, as do all adult men. In fact, it is rational decision making that differentiates the worlds of work and home. At home decisions are made by women, who base their decisions on emotion and "intuition."[23] However, there is a great deal of research indicating that managers, regardless of their gender, often make decisions by **intuition.**

Managers are often required to act quickly, especially in today's highly competitive global environments. Seeking out adequate and accurate information and devising and considering alternatives simply cannot be done. Markus Vodosek and Kathleen Sutcliffe succinctly summarize the dilemma that managers face: "Although in some cases extensive [rational] analyses may lead to better decision making. . . it consumes valuable time and resources, decreases the speed with which decisions can be made, and creates a false sense of security."[24]

Instead of trying to make rational choices when it is impossible to do so, managers play hunches. They are usually quite confident in the quality of those hunches and often make "intuitive" decisions that are quite successful because experience in any endeavor teaches people to recognize meaningful patterns. Without that experience, the events and conditions that make up a decision situation are just random bits of information. For example, present a chess champion and a chess novice a board with 25 pieces arranged at random. Let them study the board. Then, remove the pieces and ask the players to replace them in their correct positions. Both players will be able to replace about six pieces accurately. Later on, play a game of chess until there are about 25 pieces left on the board. Repeat the experiment. The novice will still be able to replace about 6 pieces, but the champion will correctly reposition 23 or 24 pieces. The difference lies in the champion's experience and the way that experience enables the recognition of meaningful patterns. When the pieces are randomly arranged, there are no patterns and the champion's experience does not help. Playing a game creates familiar patterns, which the champion can recognize instantly and intuitively. Managers' experience has the same effect. When confronted with a problem, they draw on experience, recognize the pattern, and recall solutions that worked before. Of course, intuition is not foolproof: Many situations only appear to be like past situations, and rapid recognition can be wrong recognition.[25]

But, in a great many situations, it is more important to *act* than to take the *best* action; accurate perceptions and decisions are nice, but often they are simply unnecessary. Acting also generates new information and encourages employees to communicate with one another in ways that correct misconceptions. As a result, organizations that prefer acting over rational decision making tend to understand the environmental pressures they face better; they are able to update their information more rapidly and do a better job of adapting quickly to future changes. In some cases acting may be the only way to solve a problem. Karl Weick tells a story about a small Hungarian military unit that became lost during maneuvers in the Swiss Alps. Snowbound for two days, one soldier finally found a map in his pocket, and using it, they found their way back to camp. Eventually, they discovered to their astonishment that the map was of the Pyrenees Mountains, not the Alps. Weick concludes:

> This incident raises the intriguing possibility that when you are lost, any old map will do. . . . [Maps and plans] animate and orient people. Once people begin to act (enactment), they generate tangible outcomes (cues) in some context (social), and this helps them discover (retrospect) what is occurring (ongoing), what needs to be explained (plausibility), and what should be done next (identity enhancement).

FIGURE 9–1
Acting, Coping, and Managing Ambiguity

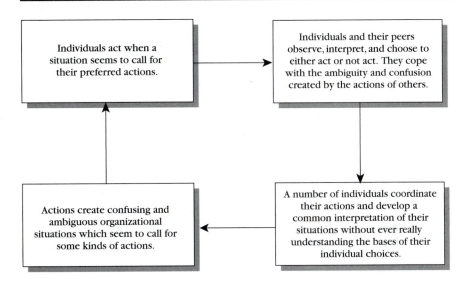

In short, intuition often generates effective solutions and may be the only form of decision making that is possible under intense time pressure or when other limiting factors are present.[26]

The Myth of Understanding   The rational actor model depicts communication as a process through which people obtain information to reduce uncertainty and ambiguity. According to nonrationality models of decision making, communication is a process through which people *manage* confusion and ambiguity. Employees encounter nonsensical situations and act in response to them. But in acting they change those situations.[27] These changes create confusion and ambiguity for other members of their organizations, and perhaps for themselves as well. Other employees act in response, which also changes the situation. In time, these cycles of acting and interacting transform the situation, creating new ambiguities and confusion and so on in a continuous cycle of acting, confusing, and coping (see Figure 9-1). The situation never really becomes clear; ambiguity is never eliminated and often is not even reduced. But ambiguity is managed; people are able to make choices and take actions that satisfy their needs and the needs of their organizations. Because the underlying causes of the problems are not eliminated, they crop up over and over again. But for people who are paid to make decisions, having a never-ending supply of problems to be solved may not be all that bad a thing.

As well as gathering information in nonrational ways, employees often manage information nonrationally. After all, organizational decision makers are people who are often acting in groups and thus are subject to all the pressures and nonrational processes described in the first parts of this chapter. They rationalize decisions already made, engage in groupthink, and persist in failing policies long after the available evidence makes it clear that they should be abandoned. Organizations are comprised of people who have a number of goals that are constantly changing, frequently inconsistent, and often not clear to anyone. The "intelligence" of an organization is more a loose and transient collection of impressions than a systematic and logical group of tightly interlocked preferences and procedures. Each employee has a set of preferred "solutions" when looking for problems; each person is a decision maker looking for work.[28] In normal organizational decision situations, employees make choices and then begin to construct, share, and publicize seemingly rational explanations and rationalizations of their choices. Like anyone else, managers often search more actively for relevant information after they make decisions than before they do so. Seventy-five years of research on the ways in which executives make decisions indicates that they are as likely as anyone else to use information to *rationalize* their decisions as they are likely to use it to make them. Even when their information searches precede decisions, they may use information as much because it is readily available as because it is accurate or relevant. Not only does it take time and effort to obtain information, seeking information usually involves admitting one's ignorance. In organizations in which appearing to be uninformed is punished, it may be wiser to rely on information that is easily accessible than to search for better information that cannot be obtained without publicly admitting one's ignorance.[29]

CASE STUDY:
MANAGING THE AMBIGUITY*

One of the key assumptions of nonrationality models of organizational decision making is that ambiguities can rarely be eliminated; but they can be managed. One of the most ambiguous roles played in a hospital is that of the social worker. Usually hospital social workers work with terminally ill patients and their families. But what they do with their clients is multidimensional and ambiguous. Some social workers say they "get families to communicate better when someone is dying;" others "help people live better when they are under stress;" still others "prepare people to leave the hospital as quickly as possible." Although almost all say that their primary concern is with providing the best possible care for their patients, the meaning of quality care depends on a number of factors. Sometimes quality care means playing the role of a bureaucrat—getting people out of the hospital as quickly as possible (or at least before their insurance or HMO coverage ends) or dealing with the mountains of paperwork that are part

(continued)

(continued from the previous page)

of helping a family move their loved one to a nursing home. Sometimes quality care involves providing psychotherapy, either for the family members or for the dying patient. Sometimes it involves helping people work through religious issues regarding death and afterlife. But always, there is a great deal of ambiguity about what a hospital social worker does.

A social worker's role in the medical organization also creates ambiguity. Most hospitals operate on the basis of a medical model, the view that medicine is about curing people—fixing what's broken, treating a disease through objective, emotionally detached, scientific methods, sending the patient home when she or he is cured. In this view of medical care everyone with the same condition should receive the same treatment, and only outcomes—getting the patient well—matter. But social workers have often been trained to operate on the basis of a very different view of reality, a psychosocial model that calls for treating each individual patient as a whole person who has psychological, medical, social, and economic needs. This model values empowering the patient, giving him or her as much control over what happens as possible. It treats emotions and emotional responses as central to the healing process. It tells social workers to be empathic and focus on the treatment process as well as its outcomes. But since hospital social workers practice in organizations that are dominated by the medical model, they often are caught in the middle between two different views of patient care and must find ways to manage the ambiguities and tensions that result.

Finally, authority relationships create ambiguities. Social workers are taught to value egalitarian relationships, but hospital social workers work in bureaucratic, authoritarian organizations. An egalitarian supervisor might be more comfortable to work with, but may not have sufficient credibility with the hospital administration to get the resources necessary for improving patient care. None of these ambiguities and tensions can be eliminated, because they are inherent in the nature of social work as a discipline and in hospitals as bureaucratic organizations. But managing them adds stress to an already stressful occupation. This does not mean that they cannot be managed. But the ways in which the tensions and ambiguities are managed have important implications, both for patients and for the social workers themselves.

One way of managing the ambiguity is through controlled chaos. In some social work units people all talk at the same time, come and go as they please, communicate as if no one else is in the room, and hold meetings that are unstructured free-for-alls. One social worker in these units described life at work as "like you're trying to find a place to stand in the middle of a kaleidoscope;" others said that "life is gray, not black and white. If you want black and white go to Macy's, not to a social work unit." Not only did their confusing, chaotic madness allow them to manage incongruities, it even contributed to their satisfaction with work and with their careers.

(continued)

(continued from the previous page)

Another way of coping was less chaotic, but still not traditional. In these units the social workers accepted the fact that they were part of a bureaucracy, but felt that their role was to keep an elbow in the system's side, to constantly advocate for individual patients and their unique needs in a context that was designed to treat everyone alike. They lacked the formal authority necessary to change the hospital's rules, so they had to affect change by working within the rules. For them, life involved constantly looking for opportunities to change the system from the inside, to rebel against the system while accepting their role in it. They coped with this contradiction by developing a healthy cynicism, using humor to diffuse the most frustrating situations, or expressing the group's shared emotions about unjustifiable policies that they knew could never be changed. Neither chaos nor cynicism eliminated the ambiguities or resolved the contradictions that hospital social workers faced, but they did allow them to manage their situations.

Social workers also seem to adopt one of two approaches to making sense out of their own experiences. Social work is a stressful occupation; stress that is sustained over long periods of time often leads to *burnout,* feelings of emotional exhaustion, and psychological withdrawal from one's job. Stress and burnout also are ambiguous experiences. They can be interpreted as either an individual employee's problem or as a symptom of the organizational situation. In most hospitals, social workers seem to use the medical model to make sense out of their own stress and burnout—they are abnormal responses, caused by individuals' inability to manage stress properly, that need to be treated and controlled. One social worker said, "I think that they [people that burn out] will have the same problem wherever they go. They probably had the problem before they came here. I see it as an internal problem. I don't see it as job-situated at all." Another concluded, "Yeah that's my professional job [to fight off burnout]. See, I would consider that if somebody said to me, 'I'm burned out' then I would call them a very nonprofessional person. I wouldn't deal with them anymore because they should quit." (1994: 643). Stress and burnout are understandable during times of crisis, organizational change, or when someone is new to a job. But it is something that can and should be cured. In the words of The Eagles, "get over it." Viewing stress as an individual weakness has a number of advantages for the organization: it means that the organization is not responsible for changing the conditions that create stress and gives supervisors permission to intervene in their subordinates' lives to fix their stress.†

But stress and burnout can be interpreted through a socio-psychological model that defines stress as a normal condition, a healthy response to stressful situations "there is no way not to have occasional bouts of burnout when you do this kind of work. . . . Burnout is the need to detach and I think that there's something healthy about needing to detach sometimes. . . . And just like stress, it's not a bad thing when you start to feel the signs and symptoms of stress, it's a warning signal to take care of yourself, and it can be a positive thing." It is an organizational and situational problem, not an individual pathology. It should be

(continued)

(continued from the previous page)

addressed by the organization, by providing time off for people who are burned out, offering retreats that provide training in stress management, and so on. One social worker noted that "I read something somewhere that hospice has the lowest turnover rate in social work because it's a place that honors that [stress and burnout]. If you get really depressed you can honor that, take a few days off for mental health days. That saves you in the long run" (1994: 648).

Although Meyerson does not indicate that any of the social workers in her study interpreted their experiences in this way, stress also can be viewed from a broad, social and political perspective.†† Social work is a predominantly female profession. Like other helping professions, it has relatively low social status and correspondingly low rates of pay. Because many of hospital social workers' activities are not directly related to the profit streams of their organizations, they are relegated to marginal positions in the organizational hierarchy and their problems are not treated as legitimate organizational concerns. Their clients—elderly, poor, chronically ill, or addicted people—are similarly relegated to the fringes of society. Treating social worker stress as an individual pathology tends to lump social workers and their clients together as sick people. Treating stress as evidence of how much they care about their careers and clients or as something that they should be allowed to get over quickly so that they can return to work defines them as means to organizational ends (profits). Both interpretations allow society and its organizations (hospitals) to keep social workers and their clients in marginalized positions. Their experiences can be treated as normal and natural elements of their career choices; their voices can easily be quieted or ignored (recall Chapter 8).

Applying What You've Learned

1. In Chapter 1 we argued that organizations and organizational communication is contextualized within the broader society. What assumptions must a society take for granted for the first interpretation of stress to make sense? The second interpretation? The final one?
2. Many scholars argue that organizational decision making can be better understood if it is treated as a ritual or ceremony rather than as an effort to solve problems. What kind of ceremony is stress management in these hospitals (recall Chapter 4)? What functions does that ritual play?

Questions to Think about and Discuss

1. Try to recall the most ambiguous or confusing experience you have ever had in an organization. Briefly describe the actions taken by members of the organization that caused your confusion. How did you manage the frustrations that you experienced? How did the other members of the organization manage the confusion that you caused them?

(continued)

(continued from the previous page)

2. Now try to recall the most confusing experience that you have had with an organization in which you were not a member. How did members of that organization deal with you (and thus with the confusion, ambiguity, and frustration that you caused them)? Why might they have chosen those ways of dealing with you instead of other ways?

*This case is based on Debra Meyerson, "'Normal' Ambiguity?" in Peter Frost, et al., *Reframing Organizational Culture* (Newbury Park, CA: Sage, 1991 and "Interpretations of Stress in Institutions," *Administrative Science Quarterly, 39* (1994): 628–653.
†Stephen Barley & D.B. Knight, "Towards a Cultural Theory of Stress Complaints," *Research in Organizational Behavior, 14* (1992): 1–48; Stephen Fineman, "Emotion and Organizing," in *Handbook of Organization Studies,* Stewart Clegg & Cynthia Hardy, eds. (Thousand Oaks, CA: Sage, 1999).
††Marifran Mattson, Robin Patric Clair, Pamela A. Chapman Sanger, & Adrianne Dennis Kunkel, "A Feminist Reframing of Stress," in *Rethinking Managerial and Organizational Communication from Feminist Perspectives*, Patrice Buzzanell, ed. (Thousand Oaks, CA: Sage, 2000).

The Myth of "Solving" Problems   The rational-actor model also presumes that the purpose of decision making is to solve problems. It may be more accurate to view them as political rituals in which members of organizations demonstrate their competence, power, and commitment to the organization by participating. To an observer who believes that decision making should be rational, it will seem that nothing ever gets done in these decision-making events. If the observer is an anthropologist or sociologist, he or she soon will realize that what gets done is the doing, the act of participating. If the observer is a recently hired college graduate who has been trained in strategic decision making, it may take years to realize that what goes on in meetings is meeting. When former students return to their alma maters and complain to their mentors that "I'm always going to meetings where nothing ever gets decided" (as they invariably seem to do), they provide testimony to the ritualized nature of organizational decision making.

Viewing decision-making events as rituals also helps explain the otherwise mystifying processes through which employees decide when and how to become involved in decision-making events. Employees have a variety of personal goals, favored actions, and pet plans. They move along during the day-to-day activities of their organizations until they discover a decision-making event relevant to one of their concerns. They then choose to participate in that event. Other members participate in the same event for different reasons. If they eventually do agree on a course of action, their consensus may be based on a long list of individual and often inconsistent goals. One supervisor may support a building plan, because it gives his subordinates more overtime. A department head may support it, because it gives her an opportunity to transfer two troublesome workers to another section. Other employees may agree because it diverts upper management's attention away from the large equipment purchases that they plan to make during the next week. They use the decision episode like a

FIGURE 9–2

Coping with Multiple Aims and Multiple Decision Events*

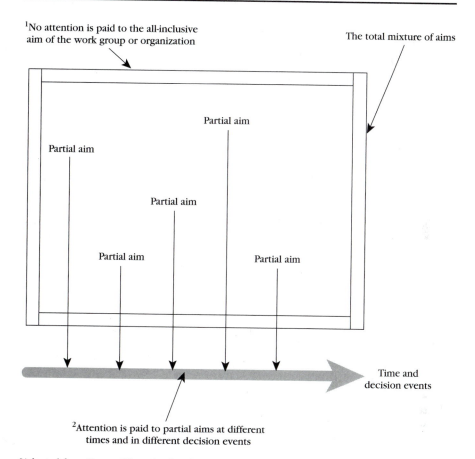

[1]No attention is paid to the all-inclusive aim of the work group or organization

The total mixture of aims

Partial aim

Partial aim

Partial aim

Partial aim

Partial aim

Time and decision events

[2]Attention is paid to partial aims at different times and in different decision events

*Adapted from Gunnar Westerlund and Sven-Erik Sjostrand, Organizational Myths (Harper & Row, 1979).

garbage can, dumping into the discussion a plethora of concerns, only some of which are logically related to the problem being discussed. Of course, it is not likely that the participants will admit their real motives in public. Instead, they search for a rationale for the building project that is acceptable to everyone and that can be stated in public. In this way, communication obscures the participants' real motivations rather than reveals them; but in the process, it also allows the participants to make what seems to be a rational decision. When an agreement is reached in organizations, it sometimes is an agreement over decisions and public justifications of them, not over the reasons or goals that lie behind the choice (see Figure 9-2).[30]

In fact, political considerations and power relationships may influence the decision-making process far more than does the goal of making the best deci-

sion (recall the hidden face of power discussed in Chapter 8). Powerful employees can push an issue through the process rapidly or can interrupt the process
by pressuring for a longer information search, demanding that other interested
parties be involved in the process, tabling the issue, or referring it to a subcom-
mittee. For example, the president of a subsidiary of a large multinational corporation chairs an eleven-person committee that includes the vice-presidents
and department heads (remember, organizational groups tend to be larger than
the optimal five to seven members because of political considerations). The
group must decide between the terms of an existing contract and a new pricing
system. After a half an hour it becomes clear that the president and executive
vice-president disagree on the proposal. One senior vice-president adds information about international market conditions, but no other members speak up,
because they realize that doing so may alienate one of the two top-ranking people in the organization. No action is taken, but another meeting is scheduled to
discuss the issue further (and then another, and another . . .).[31] In many organizations, employees attend meeting after meeting, year after year, where the same
issues are discussed and the same arguments and information are presented.
This repetitiveness is irritating primarily to employees who believe our cultural
myths that problem-solving rituals should solve problems once and for all.
For employees who realize that the purpose of meeting is meeting, repetitive
problem-solving is easy to understand.

The Myth of Plans as Solutions   Karl Weick has suggested that "plans are
important in organizations, but not for the reasons people think."[32] Plans serve
as s*ymbols,* signals to outsiders that the organization really does know what it is
doing. They also are a*dvertisements,* tools with which to attract investors or
mobilize workers. Plans also are g*ames,* means of determining how serious people are about their ideas. Planning takes time and energy. Unless a person or
group is really committed to the idea, they will not expend the effort needed to
plan. The 3M Company is famous for cutting off the funding for its new projects
at least six times, to cut their advocates back to the real fanatics.[33] Finally, plans
are often e*xcuses for further planning.* Because many decisions are too complex to be sorted out completely in a single decision-making episode, they must
be managed incrementally. Decision makers "muddle through" complex problems by making a series of small decisions. Eventually, the minor actions that
they take provide new information and help them make sense out of complicated problems. In the process they act, and by doing so, they convince others
that they really do understand those problems.[34]

   Over the long term, the decision makers do learn; but they do not do so
through strictly rational processes. Karl Weick has described organizational
learning as a process in which people first act (he calls this phase **enactment**);
then they observe their actions and the effects of their actions (he calls this
phase **selection**), and then they construct explanations of their actions (a
retention phase) (see Figure 9-3). Later, organizational decision makers remember the solutions (actions) that succeeded in the past, and a rough outline of the
situations in which they seemed to work. This list gives them guidelines about
when not to act and how and when to act. In fact, organizational learning and

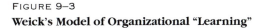

FIGURE 9–3

Weick's Model of Organizational "Learning"

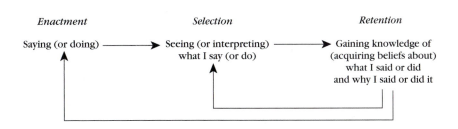

Enactment	Selection	Retention
Saying (or doing) →	Seeing (or interpreting) what I say (or do) →	Gaining knowledge of (acquiring beliefs about) what I said or did and why I said or did it

sense making is largely a process of constructing a link between the present and the past, of making decisions by intuition.[35]

A Contingency Model of Organizational Rationality

The goal of the preceding pages has been to suggest that people often do not act in ways that conform to the rational-actor model, either in everyday decision making or in their organizations. We do not intend to disparage employees. On the contrary, we want readers to understand that people violate societal myths of strict rationality for a number of good, understandable reasons. Some of these reasons involve the nature of the decision itself. It is possible to array organizational decision situations along a continuum. At one pole of the continuum are simple problems for which the effects of different courses of action can be quantified; where the information needed to make the decision is finite, well-defined, and readily available; where only a limited number of options are possible; and where the relevant communication networks are simple. At the other pole are decision situations that are so ambiguous, problems so complex, and information so inaccessible that rational decision making is impossible (see Table 9-2). Using strictly rational decision-making processes is both possible and preferable at the simple extreme; it is either inappropriate or impossible at the other.

A second continuum reflects the need to implement organizational decisions once they are made. It *is* important for organizational decision makers to make decisions of at least satisfactory quality. But it often is just as important to arrive at decisions that people will support actively. For example, in a six-year study of how hospitals make decisions about purchasing CAT scanners and other equipment costing millions of dollars, Alan Meyer uncovered a recurring decision-making process that combined rational and ritual processes in a complicated maze.[36] In general, the decision-making episodes started with careful consideration of program needs, equipment costs, projected payoff periods, and other objective factors. Necessary information was gathered before the decisions were made, important people were involved in the process, and so on. In short, the early phase of the decision-making process approximated the rational actor model.

But eventually, in most of the episodes, the process deviated from the rational model. Communication among participants became more vague and

TABLE 9-2
A Continuum of Forms of Decision Making

"RATIONAL DECISION MAKING"—BOTH POSSIBLE AND PREFERABLE	"RATIONAL DECISION MAKING"—EITHER IMPOSSIBLE OR INAPPROPRIATE
Quantifiable outcomes	Ambiguous outcomes
Clear decision-effect links	Ambiguous decision-effect links
"Finite" communication	Unknown or ill-defined parameters
Redundant available sources	"Infinite" communication
Defined information needs	Unknown or indefinite information
Limited communication networks	needs
Minimal organizational and	Diverse or undefined
environmental change	communication networks
Precedented and/or simple problems	Constant organizational and/or
	environmental change
	Unprecedented and/or complex
	problems

started to focus on abstract topics like the parties' shared beliefs, values, goals for the hospital, and vision of its future. Later the decision makers started to restructure and redefine what actually had taken place during the deliberations so that the events seemed to fit the myth of rational decision making. The later, nonrational (ritual) phase of the process served two important purposes for the hospitals' personnel. It allowed them to emerge from what often had been highly competitive, heated discussions with a revised image of themselves as tough but cooperative members of a functioning team. In addition, their symbolic strategies allowed them to gain a sense of psychological closure on the process—to feel that the decision had been made, the battle was over, and their attention could now turn toward using the new equipment effectively. In effect these groups had used the communication strategies that bind cultures together—myths, rituals, and ceremonies—to reunify themselves into a cohesive minisociety.

In hospitals where the decision makers used rational communication strategies throughout the process, the groups seldom reunified. Dissension continued, debates proliferated, and in some cases, key staff members resigned and expensive new equipment was left sitting in the basement. Meyer's research suggests that rational communication strategies are neither always superior to nor always inferior to less rational processes. Making rational decisions and making decisions that people will support are separate but interrelated elements of decision-making processes. Thus, as Figure 9-4 suggests, organizational decision situations can be described by two interrelated continua. One continuum reflects the extent to which rational decision making is possible and appropriate. The second involves the extent to which gaining commitment to and support for a decision is important. Different combinations of concern for rationality and concern for commitment call for different combinations of communication processes. What is important is that the mixture of these two factors be appropriate to a particular context, not that decision makers try to conform to social myths about how people ought to act or how organizational decisions ought to be made.

FIGURE 9–4
Continua of Organizational Decision Contexts

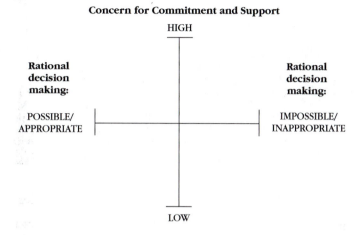

Concern for Commitment and Support

HIGH

Rational decision making:

POSSIBLE/ APPROPRIATE

Rational decision making:

IMPOSSIBLE/ INAPPROPRIATE

LOW

CASE STUDY:
KOALAS AND ROOS FLYING THROUGH CHAOS*

*"We're overrun with information,
but we're dying for lack of knowledge"*
—ALLAN MOORE,
QUANTAS' STRATEGIC PLANNING DIRECTOR (P. 133)

There probably is no industry that faces as chaotic an environment as airlines. The industry has faced a series of major, rapid, abrupt changes since the United States deregulated its airlines in 1979. By 1992 only three of the world's airlines (British Airways, Singapore Air, and Cathay Pacific) were profitable. Eastern Airlines, the largest carrier in the free world only ten years earlier, no longer existed. Worldwide deregulation of the industry was only one factor. Airport congestion, declining values of preowned airplanes, overcapacity created by the birth of a plethora of new airlines that were interested only in short-term profits, constant price wars (usually stimulated by the start ups who could undercut established airlines because they did not have to invest in the future), and a patchwork of government policies that gave preference to some airlines combined to create a situation that no airline decision maker had ever before encountered. To make matters worse, customers were also changing. Business travelers had started using new communication technologies to reduce overseas travel; they had started to combine multiple destinations into one long trip instead of a number of small ones,

(continued)

(continued from the previous page)

and they had started to demand low fares and enforce those demands by shopping around. To make matters worse, competitors had started to behave irrationally. For example, the management at Quantas once were able to predict what the management of Continental Airlines and Canadian Air would do. But, now they were going in and out of bankruptcy, announcing aircraft purchases and then changing their minds, and generally behaving irrationally, and thus unpredictably. Quantas' motto had become "make sense, and quickly (p. 122)."

Quantas faced its own sources of chaos. Because Australia is located at the end of international routes rather then in the middle, Quantas was effected more by the global chaos than other airlines. They also had recently merged with Australia Airlines and were coping with trying to integrate two very different organizational cultures. The Australia Airlines people were a mystery to the Quantas people. They feared that the newcomers would take over their territory, leaving them landing rights only at Hong Kong and Los Angeles. They thought the bushman's hats worn by AA's stewards were stupid, and felt that they were keeping them just to be different. In short, they felt, "We're different from them. We don't have the same history." Quantas management tried to deal with the culture clash by redistributing the workers so that all teams had members from both airlines. It seemed to be working, but the adjustment was slow, and the returns on the merger so small that the airline had to seek outside funding.

A bigger problem was a breakdown in the circulation of knowledge through the organization. Things had become so chaotic that employees had started to protect themselves by focusing inward, on their own, individual tasks and work groups. The communication networks that once extended throughout the organization had become fragmented; the organization's knowledge had become compartmentalized. Communication had become more formal, with all of the problems that accompany formalization (recall Chapter 2). Information, especially information that could be quantified, began to dominate decision making, because such information *seemed* to be stable. A new computer information system was installed to facilitate information flow; but it was so expensive that only a small percent of the workforce had access to it. As a result it became more of a status symbol than a decision-making tool. One employee confided, "When you don't know where you're going any more, you want to hear someone's voice, you don't want to read about it. And when nothing is going right, you want to be face to face, not looking at a screen (p. 132)."

But, knowledge was something that Quantas desperately needed. It faced one of the most important decisions it had ever made: deciding between merging with Singapore Airlines or British Airways. BA was easier to understand. It's strategy was to globalize, and to do so as quickly as possible. Its first step was to form an alliance with USAirways. Its second would be a merger with Quantas. SA's strategy was more ambiguous, even though it had made moves to globalize through alliances with Swissair and Delta Airlines. The key question for Quantas was, "How would the airline we don't merge with respond?" Time was short:

(continued)

(continued from the previous page)

Quantas' knowledge team had to make a recommendation to upper management soon. But, how could they sort through the piles of data they had and make sense out of it—how could they transform information into knowledge? After consulting with two outside advisors, the knowledge team decided to use a decision tree model: "We decided, I can't remember exactly when, to adopt the technique of decision trees. We were finally convinced that this was the direction to take" (Roger Robertson, Strategic Planning Manager). The decision was made in favor of British Airways; but Robertson admitted that "it is not easy to think strategically at difficult moments. Something occurs in the environment, and one has a tendency to use it as an excuse (p. 132)."

Applying What You've Learned

1. To what extent was Quantas' decision to merge with BA rational? Why?
2. What aspects of nonrational decision making were present in the situation they faced? How did they influence the decision process?

Questions to Think About and Discuss

1. How could Quantas' management have responded differently to the decision situations they faced?
2. What does your response imply about the possibility of rational organizational decision making?

---

*This case is based on Philippe Baumard, *Tacit Knowledge in Organizations* (London: Sage, 1999).

RATIONALIZING ORGANIZATIONAL NONRATIONALITY

Of course, we realize that the notion that good decisions need not be strictly rational decisions may seem counter to common sense. But, as we have suggested throughout this book, the common sense notions of a society are strategic, symbolic creations. And the notion that decision makers must be as rational as possible is a core assumption in Western societies. In a provocative article aptly entitled "The Technology of Foolishness," James March explained that Western societies embrace three primary articles of faith:

1. *The Preexistence of Purpose:* People begin with goals, make choices based on these goals, and can offer adequate explanations of their actions only in terms of their goals.
2. *The Necessity of Consistency:* People choose to act in ways that are consistent with their beliefs and with their roles in their social groups (families, organizations, communities, and so on).

3. *The Primacy of Rationality:* People make decisions by carefully project-
ing the probable effects of different courses of action, *not by intuition*
(in which they act without fully understanding why they do what they
do) or by tradition or faith (in which they do things because they always
have been done that way).[37]

A major part of acculturation involves learning these three commandments.
People learn that children act impulsively, irrationally, and playfully. Adults act
calmly and rationally, making decisions by carefully considering a number of
complicated factors and are spontaneous only when they have calmly and
rationally decided to be spontaneous. Because people are products of their
societies, their individual identities and self-esteem are linked to the belief that
they are rational people. As a result, when people do behave in ways that are not
strictly rational, they need to pretend that they have not. Everyone needs to save
face (recall Chapter 7), so people usually cooperate in maintaining the image
that they all are rational adults, even if they sometimes doubt that they, their
peers, and their organizations really are. People persist in pretending that they
are rational actors, because doing so allows them to gain comfort from the
knowledge that they live in a stable, predictable, rational world.

But, like all societal taken-for-granted assumptions, rationalizing human nonrationality has the effect of perpetuating social and organizational power relationships. Chapter 8 introduced social theorist Jurgen Habermas' distinction
between practical and technical reasoning. All societies can be defined by the
kind of balance they maintain between technical and practical reason. In traditional societies (some people use the more pejorative term primitive), practical
reason dominates technical reason. The experience of living is valued in itself;
the meaning of an act lies more in the act itself than in what it might allow people to obtain. In industrial societies, technical reason dominates practical reason.
For example, when Charley Conrad teaches time-management skills, he begins
by asking people to play a simple "priority clarification" game: "Pretend that you
just learned that you will live only one more year. Your situation will not change
markedly—you will not become richer or poorer, smarter or dumber, and so on.
What would you begin to do that you now do not do and what would you quit
doing that you now are doing?" When he asks students this question, at least 80
percent say, "I'd quit school and start to travel or spend time with my family."
Now, it is possible that they could be in college primarily for practical reasons, for
what school gives them in and of itself—because college piques and fulfills their
curiosity about life or because it meets their natural craving for knowledge
(remember, Habermas' definition of "practical" is *not* the usual definition). His students tell him, however, that they *really* are going to school for technical reasons—because getting a degree is a means for obtaining other goals like getting
a real job (recall Chapter 1), increasing their social status, or buying a BMW.
School is merely a means of obtaining something (knowledge or a diploma) that
is merely a means of obtaining something else. When these technical goals
become irrelevant because of their impending death, they have no reason to stay
in school. In Habermas' terms, technical reason dominates practical reason in
their lives, just as it does in the lives of everyone in "modern" societies.

But like other societal assumptions, the particular balance of technical and practical reason that exists in a society privileges some people and groups of people over others. In "traditional" societies those people who control symbolism—priests or shamans—are granted more power than other members of the culture. In technical societies people who control "rational" decision making are granted a privileged position. In the organizations of modern societies, the bias in favor of rational decision making favors managers. Upper-level male managers are in especially privileged positions. Men usually are assumed to be more rational than women. People in upper-level positions (usually men in U.S. organizations) have superior access to information. Their background and training give them greater facility with the language of rational decision making. So, they *seem* to have a superior ability to decide what should be done, when, where, and by whom. As long as modern societies privilege technical reason (rationality, efficiency, effectiveness, and so on) and as long as decision-making rituals allow managers to *appear* to be rational actors, their superior power positions will be protected. Low-power people will tend to perceive that they have less power because they are "naturally" and "normally" less rational (recall the discussion of "hegemony" in Chapter 1). Rationalizing nonrationality helps preserve the deep structure of power in modern organizations and modern societies.

SUMMARY AND CONCLUSIONS: COMMUNICATION AND DECISION MAKING

Contemporary models of decision making teach two important lessons about the functions of communication in organizations. They indicate that both the *processes* of communicating and the *products* of communication (decisions, plans, deals, and so on) allow members of organizations to *manage* ambiguous and confusing situations. If one embraces the assumptions of the rational actor model uncritically, the ambiguity-management function of communication will seem inefficient and perhaps a little bit perverse. But blending rational and nonrational elements of decision making together in the same decision-making episodes may be neither strange nor ineffective. Doing so allows employees to *act,* and acting is often more important than reaching *optimal* decisions.

The danger facing organizational decision makers is not that they will make decisions that are not strictly rational. Incorporating the ethical, political, personal, and interpersonal considerations that are excluded from the rational actor model often—perhaps usually—leads to more productive outcomes than blindly following the dictates of rationality. The danger is that decision makers may become trapped in their patterns of communicating and making decisions. Patterns of acting provide people with a great degree of stability. But, as Karl Weick has noted, the stability and predictability that come from tried and true ways of acting may themselves keep people from adapting to new needs and demands. Adaptation to past needs may prevent adaptability to future ones.

To avoid both of these problems—inappropriately imposing rational actor models of decision making and becoming trapped in patterns of acting—

employees must constantly monitor their communication and the communication patterns of their organizations, searching for strategies that can improve their ability to adapt. They must ask themselves, "Does strategy X work? Should I do it?" rather than asserting, "I know X works; it always has. We should use it." They must be able to obtain and accurately process information that casts doubts on their perceptions, beliefs, and interpretations. And they must be able to suspend their views of the "realities" of their organizations to understand how they can best respond to the situations they face.

NOTES

[1] Dennis Mumby & Linda Putnam, "The Politics of Emotion," *Academy of Management Review, 17* (1992): 465–487. For a summary of research on nonrational aspects of organizational decision making see Kathleen Sutcliffe, "Organizational Environments and Organizational Information Processing," in *The New Handbook of Organizational Communication,* Fredric Jablin & Linda Putnam, eds. (Thousand Oaks, CA: Sage, 2000) and Philippe Baumard, *Tacit Knowledge in Organizations* (London: Sage, 1999).

[2] James March and Herbert Simon, "The Concept of Rationality," in *Human Behavior and International Politics,* David Singer, ed. (Chicago: Rand-McNally, 1965), p. 343.

[3] Karl Weick, *The Social Psychology of Organizing* (Reading, MA: Addison-Wesley, 1979) and *Sense-Making in Organizations* (Thousand Oaks, CA: Sage, 1995); James March and Johann Olson, *Ambiguity and Choice in Organizations* (Bergen, Norway: Universitetsforlaget, 1970); and G. Westerlund and S. Sjostrand, *Organizational Myths* (New York: Harper & Row, 1979). These four works are important sources for the ideas presented in the remainder of this chapter.

[4] This survey is based largely on Randy Hirokawa and Marshall Scott Poole, eds., *Communication and Group Decision Making,* 2nd ed. (Thousand Oaks, CA: Sage, 1996). For more extensive summaries of research, see Randy Y. Hirokawa and Abran J. Salazar, "Task-Group Communication and Decision-Making Performance" in *Handbook of Group Communication Theory and Research,* Larry Frey, Dennis Gouran, & Marshall Scott Poole, eds. (Newbury Park, CA: Sage, 1999).

[5] David Hickson, W. Graham Astley, Richard Butler, and David Wilson, "Organizations as Power," in *Research in Organizational Behavior,* v. 3 (Greenwich, NJ: JAI Press, 1981) and Peter Abell, *Organizations as Bargaining and Influence Systems* (London: Heinemann, 1975).

[6] Martin Chemers, "Culture and Assumptions about Leadership," in *Small Group Communication,* Robert Cathcart and Larry Samovar, eds. (Dubuque, IA: William C. Brown, 1984). Ernest Bormann discusses the dynamics of leadership emergence very insightfully in *Small Group Communication: Theory and Practice,* 3rd ed (New York: HarperCollins, 1990). Also see Bernard M. Bass, *Bass & Stogdill's Handbook of Leadership: Theory, Research, and Managerial Applications,* 3rd edition (New York: Free Press, 1990), pp. 106–107.

[7] Bass, pp. 685–686.

[8] The classic source on this model, which is more complicated than the discussion here reflects, is Victor H. Vroom and Peter W. Yetton *Leadership and Decision Making* (Pittsburgh, PA: University of Pittsburgh Press, 1973). See Bernard M. Bass, *Bass & Stogdill's Handbook of Leadership, 3rd ed.* (New York: Free Press, 1990).

[9] Bass, pp. 452–455.

[10] John M. Levine and Richard L. Moreland, "Small Groups" in *Handbook of Social Psychology,* 4th edition, Daniel Gilbert, Susan Fiske, and Gardner Linzey, eds. (New York: Oxford University Press, 1998).

[11] Marshall Scott Poole and Carolyn Baldwin, "Developmental Processes in Group Decision-making," in Hirokawa and Poole, *Groups,* 2nd ed. Also see Marshall Scott Poole, "Decision Development in Small Groups," Parts I, II and III in *Communication Monographs 48* (1981): 1–24; *50* (1983): 206–232; and *50* (1983): 321–341; and Henry Mintzberg, Duru Raisinghani, and Andre Theoret, "The Structure of 'Unstructured' Decision Processes," *Administrative Science Quarterly, 21* (1976), 246–275.

[12] Linda Putnam, "Preference for Procedural Order in Task-oriented Small Groups," *Communication Monographs, 46* (1979), 193–218. Randy Hirokawa conducted a study that compared the relative effectiveness of groups that carried out the basic decision functions of problem definition, criteria development, thorough evaluation of options, and careful selection of an option, but did not do them in any particular order with groups that followed the standard agenda. The more of these functions groups carried out, the more effective their decision was, but the order in which they were carried out did not influence effectiveness. See R.Y. Hirokawa, "Discussion Procedures and Decision-Making Performance: A Test of a Functional Perspective," *Human Communication Research, 12* (1986): 203–224.

[13] Gouran and Randy Hirokawa, "Functional Theory and Communication in Decision-Making and Problem-Solving Groups: An Expanded Perspective," in Hirokawa and Poole, 2nd ed.

[14] Hirokawa and Poole, 2nd ed., p. 105. Also see Ernest Bormann, "Symbolic Convergence Theory and Communication in Group Decision-making," in Hirokawa and Poole, 2nd ed.

[15] David Seibold and Renee Meyers, "Communication and Influence in Group Decision-making," in Hirokawa and Poole. Also see Tim Cline and Rebecca Cline, "Risky and Cautious Decision Shifts in Small Groups," *Southern Speech Communication Journal, 44* (1979), 252–263; S.M. Alderton and Larry Frey, "Effects of Reactions to Arguments on Group Outcomes," *Central States Speech Journal, 34* (1983), 88–95; and Frank Boster and Michael Mayer, "Differential Argument Quality Mediates the Impact of Social Comparison Process of the Choice Shift," paper presented at the International Communication Association Convention, San Francisco, 1984; Irving Janis, *Victims of Groupthink* (Boston: Houghton Mifflin, 1972); "Sources of Error in Strategic Decision-making," in *Organizational Strategy and Change,* Johannes Pennings and Associates, eds. (San Francisco: Jossey-Bass, 1985); and Irving Janis and L. Mann, *Decision Making* (New York: Free Press, 1977).

[16] Wood, et al., p. 103.

[17] Nancy Harper and L. Askling, "Group Communication and Quality of Task Solution in a Media Production Organization," *Communication Monographs, 47* (1980), 77–100; Schiedel in Hirokawa and Poole, 1st ed.; Hirokawa and Scheerhorn; Harold Guetzkow and J. Gyr, "An Analysis of Conflict in Decision-making Groups," *Human Relations, 7* (1954), 367–381.

[18] "Functional Theory," p. 61.

[19] Many such procedures are available, including brainstorming, Nominal Group Technique, and Multi-Attribute Decision Making. See Susan Jarboe, "Procedures for Enhancing Group Decision Making," in Hirokawa and Poole, 2nd ed., for a good introduction and references to various group decision-making procedures.

[20] This section is based on Linda Putnam, "Understanding the Unique Characteristics of Groups within Organizations," in *Small Group Communication,* Robert Cathcart and Larry Samovar, eds. (Dubuque, IA: William C. Brown, 1984). Also see L.R. Hoffman, "Applying Experimental Research on Group Problem Solving to Organizations," *Journal of Applied Behavioral Science, 15* (1979), 375–391.

[21] Deborah G. Ancona and David F. Caldwell, "Beyond Task and Maintenance: Defining External Functions in Groups," *Group and Organization Studies, 13* (1988), 468–494; Ancona and Caldwell, "Demography and Design: Predictors of New Product Team Performance," *Organization Science, 3* (1992), 321–341.

[22] Karl Weick and Larry Browning, "Argument and Narration in Organizational Communication," *Yearly Review of Management of the Journal of Management, 12* (1986): 243–259. For a comparison of individual and organizational decision-making see C.R. Schwenk & M.A. Lyles, "Top Management, Strategy, and Organizational Knowledge Structures," *Journal of Management Studies, 29* (1992): 155–174.

[23] Linda L. Putnam & Deborah M. Kolb, "Rethinking Negotiation," in *Rethinking Organizational and Managerial Communication from Feminist Perspectives* (Thousand Oaks, CA: Sage, 2000).

[24] "Overemphasis on Analysis," in *Pressing Problems in Modern Organizations (That Keep Us Up at Night),* Robert Quinn, et al., eds. (New York: AMACOM, 2000).

[25] The chess example is from A. Newell & Herbert Simon, *Human Problem Solving* (Englewood Cliffs, NJ: Prentice Hall, 1972). Memory and managerial decision making is examined by Kathleen Sutcliffe in "Commentary on Strategic Sensemaking," in *Advances in Strategic Management,* J. Walsh & A. Huff, eds. (Greenwich, CT: JAI, 1997). Also see Henry Mintzberg, *The Rise and Fall of Strategic Planning* (New York: Free Press, 1994) and Vodosek & Sutcliffe.

[26] Weick, *Sensemaking,* p. 60.

[27] Charles O'Reilly, "Variations in Decision-makers' Use of Information Sources," *Academy of Management Journal, 25* (1982): 756–771. Analyses of how acting changes situations are available in Marshall Scott Poole and Andrew Van de Ven, "Using Paradox to Build Management and Organization Theories. *Academy of Management Review, 14:* 562–578 and Andrew Van de Ven and M.S. Poole, "Explaining Development and Change in Organizations," *Academy of Management Review, 20* (1995): 510–540.

[28] Alan Teger, *Too Much Invested to Quit* (New York: Pergamon, 1980); M. Cohen, J. March, and J. Olson, "A Garbage-can Model of Organizational Choice," *Administrative Science Quarterly, 17* (1972): p. 2.

[29] Karl Weick, *The Social Psychology of Organizing,* 2nd ed. (Reading, MA: Addison-Wesley, 1979).

[30] Cohen, March, and Olson; O'Reilly; and Richard Butler, David Hickson, David Wilson, and R. Axelsson, "Organizational Power, Politicking and Paralysis," *Organizational and Administrative Sciences, 8* (1977): 44–59. For a revision of the original garbage-can model, see Michael Masuch and Perry LaPotin, "Beyond Garbage Cans," *Administrative Science Quarterly, 34* (1989): 38–68.

[31] Richard Butler, Graham Astley, David Hickson, Geoffrey Mallory, and David Wilson, "Strategic Decision Making in Organizations," *International Studies of Management and Organization, 23* (1980): 234–249. The example is based on George Farris, "Groups and the Informal Organization," in *Groups at Work,* Roy Payne and Cary Cooper, eds. (New York: John Wiley, 1981).

[32] Weick, *Psychology:* p. 10. The first four of these functions are discussed by Weick; the fifth is drawn from C. Lindblom, "The Science of Muddling Through," *Public Administration Review, 19* (1959): 412–421.

[33] Peters and Nancy Austin, *A Passion for Excellence* (New York: Random House, 1985).

[34] Lindblom. Henry Mintzberg and Alexandra McHugh, "Strategy Formation in an Adhocracy," *Administrative Science Quarterly, 30* (1985): 160–197 provide an excellent example of a successful "muddling through" organization.

[35] Weick, *Psychology* and *Sensemaking.*

[36] Of course, our brief summary oversimplifies Meyer's research. See "Mingling Decision-Making Metaphors," *Academy of Management Review, 9* (1984): 231–246. Karl Weick takes an even more explicit position, concluding that a search for "accurate" conclusions sacrifices commitment and motivation (*Sensemaking,* p. 60).

[37] James March, "The Technology of Foolishness," in *Ambiguity and Choice in Organizations,* James March and Johann Olson, eds. (Bergen: Universitetsforlaget, 1970). Also see Michael Cohen and James March, *Leadership and Ambiguity,* 2nd ed. (Boston: Harvard Business School Press, 1974). Harrison Trice and Janice Beyer take an even more direct position, arguing that rationality is *the* core assumption of organizations in Western societies, including the United States. (See *The Cultures of Work Organizations,* Englewood Cliffs, NJ: Prentice-Hall, 1993, especially Chapter 2).

Chapter 10

COMMUNICATION AND THE MANAGEMENT OF ORGANIZATIONAL CONFLICT

*Not only do members of organizations use
communication to "work through" conflicts, they are
able to "work" through managing conflicts effectively.*
—ANNE MAYDAN NICOTERA

CENTRAL THEMES

- Conflicts are an inevitable part of relationships characterized by interdependence and interaction. People may perceive that a conflict exists when there is no realistic basis for one and vice versa.
- The ways in which people "frame" conflicts and the choices they make during the early phases of conflicts create parameters that guide and constrain the communication during overt conflicts.
- Overt conflicts are comprised of interactive cycles of communication, which tend to be self-perpetuating and self-reinforcing.
- Structuring strategies can be used to define an issue or guide a discussion in ways that favor a particular employee's position.
- The greatest barrier to productive conflict management is the tendency for conflict cycles to escalate.
- Destructive escalation occurs when major power imbalances exist. They can be prevented or controlled if all parties understand the communication strategies available to them.
- In productive conflicts many kinds of communication strategies are used; in destructive ones only a few strategies are employed.
- Conflicts escalate in three ways—expansion of issues, involvement of self, and dominance of emotion and symbol.
- An alternative view of conflict based on feminist principles views conflict and negotiation as an opportunity for communication and transformation rather than as issue-based problem solving.

KEY TERMS

Conflict resolution	Conflict
Latent conflict	Mixed-motive interactions
Conflict frames	Perceived conflict
Avoidance orientation	Accommodation orientation
Compromise orientation	Competitive orientation
Collaborative orientation	Felt conflict
Reflexive communication	Punctuation

This chapter examines another practical reality of organizational life: Disagreement and conflict are inevitable aspects of working relationships, and the need to manage conflicts is always with each of us. For many years researchers and managers viewed organizational conflict as an inherent evil. Conflicts revealed a weakness in the organization, a flaw in its design, operation, or communication. Conflicts needed to be resolved; that is, their sources had to be discovered and eliminated. Peace and stability had to be returned to the organization. The word conflict conjured up images of otherwise fair and equitable societies and rational organizations gone bad.[1]

However, contemporary views regard organizational conflicts as inevitable and potentially valuable, both for individuals and for organizations. Conflicts give employees opportunities to publicize, test, and refine their ideas and to demonstrate their competence and value to the organization. Conflicts also help organizations adapt to changes, foster innovation, and integrate their diverse constituent groups into a functioning whole.[2] Conflicts are neither inherently good nor intrinsically bad, although they do vary in the degree to which they are *productive*. Conflicts that are relatively productive for the organization as a whole may be destructive for some of the participants. Similarly, episodes that are disruptive and damaging to the organization may be productive for many of the participants.

THE BASES AND EARLY PHASES OF ORGANIZATIONAL CONFLICT

Typically when people hear the term *organizational conflict*, they imagine executives shouting at one another in a boardroom, giant oligopolies bidding for a majority share of a competitor's stock, or, for the more fanciful of us, secret meetings on foggy nights when technological secrets are exchanged for chalets on the Riviera. Although overt and sometimes hostile confrontations are part of organizational conflict, they are only one part. We will define **conflict** more broadly, as communication between people who depend on one another and who perceive that the others stand between them and the realization of their goals, aims, or values.[3] This definition encompasses each of the examples listed earlier, as well as everyday discussions of organizational policies and projects, negotiations between employees or groups of employees (for instance, labor-

management negotiations), and cooperative attempts to find mutually acceptable solutions to problems. In short, *conflicts* are communicative *interactions*
among people who are *interdependent* and who perceive that their interests
are *incompatible, inconsistent,* or *in tension.*

Theorist Louis Pondy has developed a model of the *bases* and *phases* of
organizational conflict. He observed that conflicts move through five phases:
latent, perceived, felt, overt, and *aftermath.* This chapter focuses mostly on the
overt phase, for it is in that phase that communication is most important and
complex. However, the earlier phases are also important, for they establish the
parameters within which the conflict will be played out, and parameters guide
and constrain communication in important ways.[4]

Latent Conflict

In the **latent conflict phase,** a situation arises in which there are grounds for
conflict, but the parties have not yet realized that the grounds exist. Grounds for
conflict stem from at least three different sources. The most important ground
for conflict is a real conflict of interests between parties. We noted in Chapters
2 and 3 that groups of people who must typically interact often have quite different interests. Management is pushed toward keeping the organization going
in the most efficient possible manner, often no matter what. Managers must
answer primarily to outside stakeholders, such as stockholders (in the case of
private organizations), legislators and citizens (in the case of government organizations), and boards of directors and donors (in the case of charitable organizations). The interests of employees, on the other hand, more often center on
personal concerns, such as compensation levels, amount of work required,
working conditions, and quality of work life. These two groups are thus put in a
position where conflicts of interest are likely to emerge.

Any time two different interest groups are created in an organization, latent
conflicts arise. The particular set of groups that arise differs across organizations
and over time in the same organizations. Possible oppositional groups include
employees from two previously separate organizations in a newly merged organization; employees of different genders, ethnicities, or backgrounds; recently
hired and experienced employees; and white-collar, blue-collar, and pink-collar
employees. Depending on the organizational culture, the particular history of the
organization, and trends in the surrounding society, any of these or dozens of
other oppositions could create latent conflict in an organization.

There is a widespread myth in our society that most conflicts are due to
"communication problems." While communication plays a vital role in conflicts,
and while a second source of latent conflict is misunderstandings or poor communication, it is a dangerous mistake to assume that most conflicts are due to a
lack of communication. In fact, organizations are shot through with conflicts of
interest that may develop into open conflict. Acknowledging this is often the
first step toward managing conflicts effectively.[5]

A third source of latent conflicts is the legacy of previous conflicts. Parties
usually have both a history of interacting with one another in the past and the

expectation that they will encounter one another in the future. Pondy noted that many latent conflicts are actually products of the aftermath of prior conflicts. A resolution in favor of one party may create resentment on the part of others that blooms into conflict at a later time. A mishandled conflict may sew seeds of discord at a later time. Unresolved grievances may suddenly reappear in the guise of issues completely unrelated to the original complaint.

Conflicts are most likely to develop among those employees who depend most on one another. Being interdependent means that there are many topics over which conflicts can arise—tangible objects, such as rewards and resources, or intangible factors, such as status and power. When people rarely interact with one another, they have few reasons or opportunities to fight. In organizational settings, the vast majority of conflicts are what theorists call **mixed-motive interactions.** This means that the parties have incentives to cooperate and to compete. Even if employees have little incentive to cooperate during the discussion of a single issue, the fact that they will have to depend on one another in the future means that they always have incentives to reach a cooperative outcome to conflicts.

Several factors influence or shape the emergence of latent conflicts. One factor is the culture and climate of the organization. Some strategies of organizing simply tend to generate more conflicts than others. Organizations dominated by traditional strategies are often rife with conflicts, because they exaggerate distinctions among employees and interest groups; they also rely on a slow and balky communication system that creates misunderstandings and rely on a structure that creates tensions among the different positions in the hierarchy. In contrast, using a relational strategy that is legitimately empowering is less likely to promote conflicts. Although no organizational strategy eliminates conflict situations altogether, because conflicts always emerge.

Relationships among parties also influence the development of latent conflict. Trust developed during past interactions decreases the number of latent conflicts, because parties assume that they will be able to work through issues effectively. The opposite is true of distrustful relationships, which tend to breed conflict. The climate of an organization may encourage the parties either to cooperate or compete with one another. Each of these factors is a latent aspect of the situation that surrounds a particular conflict.[6]

Ironically, attempts to improve communication can sometimes crystallize conflicts by surfacing or defining opposing interests. While still in graduate school, Charley Conrad was asked to mediate between a university administration (not his university) and the African American Students' Association. The more he talked with both sides, the clearer it became that they had almost no objective reason to cooperate and many reasons to compete with each other. They still were talking largely because they did not know how they really felt about each other. The situation was exceptionally volatile, because "getting them to talk to one another"—the task he had been called in to perform—almost certainly would have made it clear to everyone that a latent conflict actually did exist. If continued, "improving communication" easily could have transformed a latent conflict into a perceived one.

Another function of communication in organizations runs counter to open expression; communication often functions to hide and downplay latent conflicts, particularly conflicts of interest. Almost all organizations experience the conflicts of interest discussed earlier in this section. Dealing with them usually requires a large amount of time and resources, resulting in a decrease in resources devoted to organizational effectiveness and efficiency. As a result, management has incentives to paper over or obscure conflicts of interest. It may do this through messages that deny conflict and differences: Company newsletters, for example, may carry the theme "We're all in this together". Other messages may highlight different interests that draw attention away from oppositions between groups within the organization. One tactic is to define an outside threat that serves to unite people within the organization and focuses their attention on differences in interests between the organization and outside groups. For example, a school administration might inform teachers that the legislature is going to cut appropriations to public schools.

Perceived Conflict

Phase 2 in Pondy's model is *perceived conflict*. This stage exists when one or more parties believe that someone stands between them and achieving their goals. This perception can be created in a number of ways. Sometimes an outsider explicitly tells an employee that his or her interests are incompatible with someone else's. More often, the perception stems from a "precipitating event." One employee criticizes another or makes a demand that the second person perceives is not legitimate. Or an employee makes what she or he perceives is a legitimate request and is rebuffed. Or a long period of annoyance builds up until the employee realizes that a conflict exists. *Perceived* conflict can exist when *latent* conflict does not, as when siblings fight over a serving of rapidly melting ice cream so large that they cannot possibly eat all of it. There is no objective reason for conflict in this situation, although the children *believe* that their interests are incompatible. Also, *latent* conflict can exist without *perceived* conflict, as when siblings are given a seemingly (but not actually) inconsumable mound of ice cream.

In organizations, perceived conflict exists without latent conflict if employees believe that someone else is their enemy even when their interests really do coincide. Conflicts between "*line*" and "*staff*" personnel are quite common in all kinds of organizations. Often they exist because both groups ignore or deemphasize their need to cooperate and instead focus their attention on their incentives to compete. Latent conflict also exists without perceived conflict if people overlook minor day-to-day frictions or if they concentrate so completely on routine or easily resolved disagreements that they suppress major problems.

Perhaps more than any other factor, employees' perceptions influence what happens during conflicts and what effects conflicts have on organizations. Table 10-1 summarizes a number of ways in which employees may perceive a conflict. If they define the situation as all or nothing, or see only a small range of alternatives as acceptable solutions, or believe that they can win only if the

TABLE 10-1
Defining Conflict

DEFINITIONS THAT MAKE CONFLICTS EASIER TO MANAGE PRODUCTIVELY	DEFINITIONS THAT MAKE CONFLICTS DIFFICULT TO MANAGE PRODUCTIVELY
1. "Mixed motive" (or nonzero-sum) definitions: Each party perceives that it can obtain desired outcomes without the others losing the same amount of reward.	1. Zero-sum: Parties perceive that whatever one gains the other loses. The outcome will either grant them complete success or complete failure.
2. Empathic definition of the issue: Parties perceive the issue from both their own and the other parties' perspectives.	2. Egocentric definition of the issue: Parties perceive the issue only from their own frame of reference.
3. Broad contextualization of the issue: Parties search for underlying concerns that place the overt issue in a broad, organizational context.	3. Narrow focus on a single issue and its immediate effects.
4. "Commercial" issue: The issue defined as problem-centered.	4. "Ideological" issue: The conflict is defined as a moral struggle between forces of good and evil.
5. Large number of possible solutions are available.	5. Small number of alternative are available.

other parties lose, or believe that the difference of opinion has a strong moral or ethical dimension, they tend to try to impose their wills on others. They also perceive of others as hostile and untrustworthy and adopt a narrow and inflexible course of action during overt conflicts.[7]

An important influence on the perceived conflicts are the "*frames*" of reference that employees bring with them into conflict situations. Through past experiences, both in their organizations and in their outside lives, people develop certain ways of making sense out of situations and issues.[8] Conflict frames include preferences about how conflicts should be managed, which we label "*orientations*" to conflict. But conflict frames also include assumptions about what a conflict or issue is about, predictions about the costs and rewards associated with different outcomes, and definitions of one's position on a particular issue or group of issues. When people "frame" a conflict as an opportunity to achieve some kind of gain, they tend to use more open communicative strategies; when they "frame" it as an event that may lead to losses, their communicative strategies tend to be less flexible and the likelihood of the conflict reaching an impasse is increased.

Frames also involve a complex set of expectations—about how the parties in a conflict will and should act, what kinds of persuasive strategies can legitimately be used to influence the outcome of the conflict, and how the conflict episode will unfold. For example, employees' perceptions of how well they handled past conflicts seem to influence the way they handle future conflicts. People who expect to handle a conflict well tend to employ more open and cooperative orientations and communication strategies; people who expect that they will not handle conflicts well tend to avoid conflicts or adopt competitive orientations and strategies.

However, this does not mean that conflict frames automatically determine the communication strategies that people use in conflicts. Instead, they provide parameters within which people initially make sense out of a conflict situation. As conflicts proceed, the ambiguities change. As new issues are raised and old ones are abandoned, different aspects of one's past experiences become salient and others disappear from one's view. As other parties act in unexpected ways, people adjust their assumptions and expectations. Frames guide and constrain communicative acts, and communicative action leads to new frames. Framing is a *process* through which situations are reframed over and over and new guidelines and constraints are constantly being created.[9] Nonetheless, some frames constrain parties' actions more tightly than others, making it more difficult to productively manage conflict.

In addition to perceiving conflicts in different ways, employees also differ in their perceptions of how conflicts ought to be managed. Kenneth Thomas developed a model of five "typical" *orientations* to conflict, although he recognized that an infinite number of possible orientations exists (see Table 10-2). These "orientations" describe the approaches that people *intend* to pursue if an overt conflict begins.[10]

1. **Avoidance:** Believing that unassertive and uncooperative behavior is the best approach, either because the issues are not worth fighting about, the potential costs of open confrontation are greater than the potential gains, or the issue will go away if it is left alone. Requires little communication.

2. **Accommodation:** Acquiescing to the perceived goals of the other(s). Requires little communication.

3. **Compromise:** Searching for a resolution that partly satisfies both parties. In our society compromise generally means splitting the difference fifty-fifty. Requires some degree of willingness to sacrifice individual goals, some communication, and some degree of assertiveness.

4. **Competition:** Seeking to dominate others and impose one's preferences on them. Involves some communication, though not as much as compromise.

5. **Collaboration:** All parties believe they should assertively seek a mutually acceptable solution and are willing to spend large amounts of time and effort to reach such an outcome.

The orientation an employee takes depends on a number of factors (see Table 10-3). Employees high in the organizational hierarchy avoid conflicts less than people lower in the hierarchy.[11] Supervisors tend to use competition more often than the other orientations during conflicts with their subordinate. This is

TABLE 10–2
Orientations to Conflict: Continuum

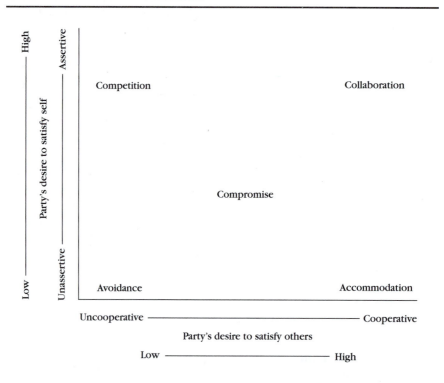

especially true when *their* supervisors have made it clear that they prefer a certain outcome to the conflict. In contrast, supervisors tend to adopt nonassertive orientations (accommodation or avoidance) with their supervisors. In general, people try to avoid overt conflicts, even in Western organizations. Both the anticipation of conflict and the act of communicating are stressful. For employees that find conflicts to be especially stressful, the less assertive orientations—avoidance, accommodation, and compromise—are attractive, because they promise to minimize tense or prolonged communication. The quality of interpersonal relationships between parties—the legacy of past interactions, current feelings toward one another, and anticipation of future interactions—also seems to influence orientations. These interpersonal factors may operate subconsciously, as when one party accommodates a favored coworker without realizing it. Or they may be quite explicit, as when one party decides to support another on a current issue to influence that person better in the future. Of course, the orientation that a person takes to a particular conflict should (and usually does) change as a conflict progresses, because the parties obtain more information about the other person, their own goals, and their own priorities.[12]

TABLE 10-3
Orientations to Conflict: Characteristics

ORIENTATION	DEFINITION	STRENGTHS	WEAKNESSES
Collaboration (also known as problem solving)	Seeking resolution through face-to-face confrontation to find a mutually acceptable definition of and solution to the problem; most appropriate when there are common goals that cannot be achieved without the cooperation of all parties	Effective when the conflict stems from communication breakdowns or misunderstanding; when use repeatedly, establishes norms that support collaborative problem solving	Time-consuming and inappropriate when there are legitimate differences among the parties or when they have different goals or values
Avoidance	Includes withdrawal and suppression; sometimes can be coupled with expansion of the rewards available	Natural, simple response to conflict; avoids labeling parties as winner and loser, thus reducing the negative legacy that sometimes accompanies conflicts	Usually provides no productive resolution of differences, a temporary expedient, even when combined with expansion of available rewards
Accommodation (also known as smoothing)	plays down differences while emphasizing common features; responds to emotions that accompany conflicts while ignoring the base; includes compromise	Exploits cooperative elements that exist in all conflicts	Temporary expedient; leaves legacy of unresolved issues, unmanaged emotions, outcome depends more on relative power of the parties than on the legitimacy of their complaints or wisdom of the solution
Competition (also called forcing or autocratic)	Solution imposed by most powerful party	Effective when members recognize and accept power relationships; time efficient	Fails to treat base of conflict; temporary, with residue of unmanaged emotions; fails to address real problems

CASE STUDY:
DARNED BIRD HUGGERS*

This chapter focuses on conflicts that take place within organizations. However, conflicts also occur between organizations and outsiders and among organizations. "Framing" processes often have an even more pronounced effect on these conflicts than they do on intraorganizational conflicts.† And, they often illustrate the ways in which conflict frames influence perceptions of risks, potential solutions, and the relevance of different kinds of information.††

One such conflict has pitted the U.S. Fish and Wildlife Service (USFWS) and the Environmental Protection Agency against the farmers and ranchers of central Texas for the past decade. The Golden Cheeked Warbler is an endangered species that inhabits the cedar (really juniper) and oak woodlands of central Texas. For ranchers and farmers, juniper is a nuisance—it grows so thickly that it chokes out grass and spreads rapidly, so rapidly that it cannot really be eliminated. But efforts to control its spread by burning or bulldozing reduce the amount of habitat available to the warbler, and thus threaten its continued existence. To complicate the situation further, most of its habitat is on privately owned land, in a state in which private property rights are taken very seriously. The Republic of Texas agreed to enter the Union only if no lands were owned by the federal government, and, with the exception of some land that has been purchased in west Texas, the stipulation has been honored for a century and a half. The law allows the federal government to force landowners to sell land in the warbler's range; but the government does not have the money to buy it. At the time of the study, the Nature Conservancy was negotiating to purchase a small proportion of the habitat, probably not enough to maintain a viable warbler population. Those negotiations were successful. In short, it is a classic environmental conflict.

Government organizations (primarily the USFWS) have framed the conflict in familiar terms: The endangered species is the property of all Americans and the government's obligation is to protect it by representing the interests of all Americans, not just the local landowners who are directly affected by its presence. Doing so requires them to base their decisions on a broad, cosmopolitan knowledge base grounded in the best scientific information available. One USFWS manager noted: "We got real good reasons and we got real good laws that tell us how we will operate the refuge system . . . (unlike the ranchers who make) decisions based on what you've seen within 15 miles of your home for all your life" (p. 162).

In contrast, the farmers and ranchers frame the conflict as a battle between outsiders and "good stewards" of the land. Ranchers (the stewards) make decisions by common sense, grounded in their individual experiences and the experiences of previous generations of their families who lived on the land. Common sense is contrasted with "scientific" knowledge based on supposedly objective research conducted by or imposed on them by city-dwelling outsiders. Their

(continued)

(continued from the previous page)

identity is linked to *living* on the land, and their ability to independently act to protect and preserve it. They take a holistic view of ecosystems, but also see meeting the needs of human beings as a central part of ecosystem management. They talk about nature in what they believe is a *realistic* way—including its constant and sometimes violent change, its disease, birth, death, and predation: "When you're from the country, you understand the normal things that happen through life, but people in the cities don't see those things, and when they see . . . animals that are sick or dying or dead, they become overly emotional" (p. 153). The farmers and ranchers view themselves as good stewards of the land—managers who voluntarily restrain their actions to preserve the land for the future, who are actively present, daily walking the land, and who accept accountability for their actions. But they believe that to be fully accountable, they also have to be independent of government regulation. And they admit that some ranchers and farmers are bad stewards of the land; they often are absentee owners; they do not accept accountability for their actions because they have not been on and of the land for generations and are not concerned about the effects of their action on future generations; and they see the land as something that should be conquered or subdued, not cared for.

But the farmers and ranchers believe that theirs is a voice that seldom is heard. They believe "that the broader culture no longer accommodates their interests" (p. 141) and rarely participate in the political arena directly, although many do support politically active organizations such as the Texas Farm Bureau. As a result, public hearings about the issue tend to involve only representatives of formal organizations—government agencies, environmental organizations, and associations that claim to speak for them.

Applying What You've Learned

1. How do the parties to this conflict perceive it differently? How do these perceptions contribute to the conflict and how it unfolds.
2. What interests underlie this conflict? Are they potentially compatible? If so, how?

Questions to Think About and Discuss

1. Peterson and Horton seem to believe that conflicts like the Golden Cheeked Warbler controversy can be managed through open, collaborative discourse: "Exchanges between (opposing groups) are necessary for moving beyond factionalism to the potential for convergence across perspectives. . . . Dialogue holds great potential for U.S. environmentalism" (pp. 142, 163). Given what you know about the controversy and about the role that framing plays in conflict management, do you agree or disagree? Why or why not?

(continued)

(continued from the previous page)

2. At the time of the study many of the ranchers in the warbler's habitat obtained substantial income from a federal mohair subsidy program that was started during World War II to ensure an adequate supply of fiber for military clothing (the subsidy program ended in April 1996, and reinstated in 1998). Would introducing evidence of their "dependence" on the government make the conflict more or less manageable? Why or why not?

---

*This case is based on Tarla Rai Peterson and Christi Choat Horton, "Rooted in the Soil," *The Quarterly Journal of Speech, 81* (1995): 139–166.

†See J. Chase and I. Panagopoulous, "Environmental Values and Social Psychology," in Y. Gurrier, M. Alexander, J. Chase, and M. O'Brien, eds., *Values and the Environment* (Chichester, UK: John Wiley, 1995) and E. Vaughn and M. Siefert, "Variability in the Framing of Risk Issues," *Journal of Social Issues, 48* (1992): 119–135.

††See Michael Papa and Wendy Papa, "Competence in Organizational Conflicts," in W. R. Cupach and D. J. Canary, eds. *Competence in Interpersonal Conflict* (New York: McGraw-Hill, 1996).

An important influence on perceptions of conflict is a party's gender.[13] Literally dozens of studies have been conducted on the affects of gender on conflict. However, the results of this research have been mixed. Some studies have found that women prefer cooperative and passive orientations. However, other studies have found that women view conflicts as wars and thus adopt a stereotypically male perspective, especially when the situation leaves no other option. A clue to the differences between male and female response to conflicts is found in several studies in which a party's partner starts cooperatively, shifts to competition, and then shifts back into cooperation. These studies show that women generally start out more cooperative than men and, other things being equal, they prefer to stay that way. However, both male and female behavior changes in a more competitive direction when the other party shifts to competition. When the other party reverts to cooperation, females are slower than males to change to a cooperative approach in response.

These apparently puzzling findings have been explained as a function of the different degrees of interpersonal orientation men and women typically exhibit. Males are typically oriented more to the task at hand and interpret others' behavior in terms of how it relates to the task. Females, on the other hand, are typically oriented more to relationships with others in the situation and interpret others' behavior in terms of relationships between parties. The finding that males tend to favor competition at the outset can be explained by the fact that most tasks posed in conflict studies seem to require competition. Females start out more cooperatively in the same studies because they are trying to forge a relationship with the other party. When the other party suddenly shifts from cooperative to competitive behavior, men and women have different reactions. Men, oriented to the task at hand, shift to competition because it seems the best way to win, or at least to hold their own; women, oriented to others, shift to competition because they feel the relationship has deteriorated and they want to punish the other for betrayal. When the other switches back to cooperation—ostensibly because of the negative impacts of the party's competitive behavior on other—males tend to respond cooperatively sooner than do females. Again this can be explained on the basis of task versus interpersonal orientation: Males revert to cooperation because they see that now they can profit most in the study through mutual cooperation, whereas females revert to cooperation more slowly because they have been distrustful of the other and feel a need to test and build the cooperative relationship.

These differences in orientation are important because they imply that men and women may perceive conflict in different terms. Later in this chapter we consider an alternative model of conflict and negotiation based on women's viewpoints. This feminist view of conflict differs considerably from the issue-oriented, problem-solving approach that is assumed in most of this chapter.

Orientations are important because they influence the ease with which conflicts can be managed. When the parties are oriented in complementary ways, conflicts tend to be more productive. For instance, if two parties have misunderstood each other's communication or goals, but they really do have good reasons to cooperate and intend to do so, collaboration is an appropriate orientation for both of them. By collaborating they will discover mutual, important goals, and will learn to understand each other better and resolve their differences. In other situations, collaboration may lead them to suppress legitimate differences of opinion or to spend much time and energy searching for a mutually acceptable solution when one simply does not exist. Each orientation also has characteristic strengths and weaknesses (see TABLE 10-3). Perhaps most important, orientations toward conflict seem to be only loosely related to the actual communicative acts of people in conflict. Orientations are just that—intentions about how one will communicate—and they may be changed or abandoned immediately after the conflict begins. Human beings are social animals; they are influenced as much by the characteristics of immediate interactions with others as by their generalized beliefs about how conflicts should be handled. Although some orientations seem to be more stable than others, there is little reason to believe that knowing someone's general orientation to conflict will predict their communication strategies.[14]

Parties are especially prone to deviate from their intended orientations when the conflict involves an emotionally hot topic. For example, after much delay and the gathering of a great deal of evidence, Elias decided to confront one of his subordinates about his use of illegal drugs. Elias' orientation was collaborative; he wanted to help the man get professional help for what seemed to be a serious addiction and was willing to go to great lengths to see that he could keep his job during and after the treatment. Elias called the worker in and explained his concerns. The worker denied using drugs, which made Elias a little angry; but Elias' emotions were tempered by his knowledge that drug and alcohol addicts almost always deny their dependence. He presented all the evidence that he had collected, assuming that doing so would help facilitate an open and honest discussion of the problem. Suddenly the worker blew up, shouting about Elias' dual standard. Everyone knew, he said, that Elias had taken a three-month leave of absence in 1982 to enter a treatment program for alcoholism after the company had tolerated his tardiness, absenteeism, and excuses for three years.

Elias, he said, had a "lot of gall" confronting him. As suddenly, Elias lost his temper. He had been promised that the referral would be kept secret and thought that it had been. He felt betrayed and projected his quite justifiable anger on the employee. He started screaming too and ended the episode by firing the worker and throwing him out of the office. His intention to be cooperative and collaborative had disappeared in the face of a communicative interaction that he could never have predicted. Few organizational conflicts are over as serious an issue as drug dependency, and relatively few involve as radical a shift between intention and communication as this example involved. But often, communication in conflicts only vaguely reflects the generalized intentions of the parties.

Felt Conflict

Phase 3 of Pondy's model is *felt conflict,* the point at which the parties begin to personalize perceived conflict. Differences of opinion and interests that once were only vaguely perceived begin to be focused and defined, and internal tensions and frustrations begin to crystallize around specific issues. During this phase employees start to make choices about the *communication strategies* they will use to manage the conflict, and what *range of possible solutions* they are willing to accept. In short, they establish *plot lines,* expectations about how the conflict will be played out. They may even construct complicated step-by-step imaginary scenarios of what they will say, how the other parties will respond, and so on. This process of rehearsing arguments and responses can lead to a productive outcome, but only under certain circumstances. First, parties' strategic plans must not be so *constraining* that they keep the parties from listening to one another and adapting to the information they gain.[15] Second, they must not lead a party to confuse what she or he imagines will happen during the episode with what actually does. Third, parties must realize that their rehearsed plot lines are always capable of being *altered without loss of face.* No one has yet said anything to which they feel they must remain committed. The felt conflict stage is the final point before communication itself becomes the dominant influence on the conflict. Consequently, it is often the final opportunity for the parties to use cooperative strategies.

The felt conflict phase is also the point at which employees decide to *openly confront* someone about the situation, *accept it,* or resort to *covert resistance.* These decisions are influenced by their general orientations to conflict and the quality of the interpersonal relationships they have with the other people who might become involved. But their choices also depend on the power relationship that employees perceive exists. *Open confrontation* is a risky choice. It can alienate powerful people and, if the confronters lose the battle, it may reduce their status in the eyes of others. Both of these outcomes reduce their organizational power. However, confrontation can also have productive results. Winning battles or arguing positions effectively can enhance employees' power and self-esteem, lead the organization to make good decisions, and dissipate destructive emotions and pent-up hostilities. But provoking open confrontations or actively participating in them is wise only when the potential gains outweigh the probable risks (unless ethical or other personal considerations make it imperative that an employee oppose offensive policies or actions). It is for these reasons that confronting a difference in an open and productive way seems to occur only when power relationships are in balance. When there are major power differences, high power employees tend to impose autocratically an outcome on the other parties.[16]

Accepting a situation is a viable approach when the risks of confrontation are far greater than the potential benefits and when employees have not so completely personalized the issue that acquiescing will damage their self-esteem. When acquiescence is unacceptable, low power employees may resort to *covert resistance*—malicious gossip, theft, sabotage, filing grievances, or any of the other resistance strategies that have been described in this book. Consequently, many experts believe that equalizing power relationships is necessary for productive conflict management to occur.[17]

Employees make two more specific decisions during the felt conflict phase. They adopt *goals* for the conflict as they decide on the range of outcomes they are willing to accept. They also *make preliminary decisions about the communicative strategies they will use.* Of course, the goals, their relative importance, and strategic choices change as conflicts progress.[18] But participants' initial choices are important because they guide and constrain subsequent choices. If the employee accepts only total victory or decides to be aggressive from the outset, the probability that the conflict will escalate is increased. For example, historians' analyses of U.S. strategy in World War II indicate that after President Franklin D. Roosevelt announced that we would accept only the complete surrender of Japan, we were committed to use every weapon at our disposal to obtain that outcome. Consequently, once the atomic bomb was developed, it was almost inevitable that it would be used against Japan.

To summarize, the three preliminary stages of organizational conflict are important because they establish the plot lines within which the conflict will be played out. *Definitions, orientations,* and *choices* influence the course the conflict will take, the communicative strategies that will be used to manage it, and, eventually, the degree to which the conflict is productive or destructive.

COMMUNICATION AND OVERT CONFLICT

Sometimes all the potential parties to a conflict accept the situation as it is and never raise the issue in public. In other cases, the conflict becomes overt. When that happens communication is the primary determinant of the outcome and effect of the conflict. Conflicts are made up of communication, of *interactive* cycles of messages, responses, and counterresponses. Once these cycles begin, their development and outcomes are not within the control of any one participant. A conflict tends to have a *momentum* all its own; it is a co-creation of the parties, their interpretations, arguments, definitions, and strategies. Parties make choices about how they respond (communicate) based in part on their interpretations of the communicative strategies used by the other parties. They look to the other parties' communication for clues about how they are likely to respond to available communicative strategies.

Communication Strategies in Conflict

In conflicts that have productive outcomes, communication is both flexible and strategic. Parties begin with a wide range of acceptable outcomes and believe that everyone will be able to get something out of the episode (a "win-win" orientation). Initially, all parties generally do (and should) make lengthy statements that clearly state their positions on the key issues and the reasons for those positions (in the jargon of conflict research they "*differentiate*" their positions from those of the other parties). The parties engage in short cycles of different kinds of communication. Periods of coercion, cooperation, joking, relaxation, threats, and promises are mixed together as the parties move toward a solution that will be mutually acceptable. Of course, the movement is rarely smooth or easy. Tension between the parties' incentives to cooperate and to compete lasts throughout the interaction. As a result, the balance shifts back and forth, and the parties' communication also shifts from cooperative strategies to competitive strategies and back again. As long as it seems that progress is being made, a positive interchange will continue. When the interaction turns in a positive direction, parties respond with supportive statements or tension-reducing strategies, such as jokes, which in turn move the interaction in productive directions.

If, however, one party seems to be excessively stubborn or noncompliant, the other party is likely to shift to more competitive communication strategies, especially if he or she has more power in the organization. If the other parties reciprocate, they all may suddenly become trapped in escalating cycles of competitive communication, transforming a productive interaction into a destructive one.[19] It is this fear of uncontrolled escalation that encourages people to try to avoid conflicts. Ironically, avoiding conflicts tends to make uncontrolled escalation more likely, because it allows people to develop a deeply held anger that may explode once a conflict does occur. The same thing may happen if two parties have accommodative orientations and real differences. They tend to repeatedly ignore their problems and over time build up a large reservoir of unexpressed hostility.

In contrast, in *destructive* conflicts, the parties usually begin with a win-lose orientation and view only a small number of outcomes as acceptable. Their

TABLE 10-4
Communication Strategies in Conflicts

CONFRONTIVE STRATEGIES	AVOIDANT STRATEGIES

1. Coercion: Overt
   Displays of Power
     Formal rank
     Coalitions
     Expertise
2. Coercion: Threats or Promises
3. Personalization
     Moral accusations
     Ad hominem
     Revelation of secrets
4. Toughness
   Pure form
   Reformed sinner
5. Problem solving
6. Superordinate goal
	1. Delay/Procrastination
	     Manipulating
	     procedures
	     "Putting off"
	     communication
	     Focusing on rules of interaction
	2. Regression
	3. Commitments to Revenge
	4. Refusing to Admit
	     Existence of Conflict

communication is rigid and *reflexive* (mirroring the other parties' communication) rather than flexible and strategic.[20] Long periods of competitive strategies dominate the interaction, with little or no periods of joking, relaxation, or cooperation. For example, a labor union that used *Robert's Rules of Order* called a meeting to decide whether to stop work in support of a grievance against the plant's management. Although most of the members favored the proposal, a minority used parliamentary tactics long past the point where the outcome was in any doubt. The longer they argued against the proposal, the more polarized the group became and the more committed the majority became to winning the battle. The dispute left such a bitter legacy that the minority group eventually left the organization. Although the parties' orientations to the conflict set the stage for a destructive escalation, it was their way of communicating that led to a negative outcome.

Avoidant Strategies   Table 10-4 summarizes the communicative strategies that have most often been observed in organizational conflicts.[21] One group of strategies allows parties to *avoid* a divisive issue. Delaying or procrastinating can be overt ("I don't have time to talk about it now") or subtle. Employees can manipulate procedural rules to delay or avoid sustained confrontations. For instance, they can refer an issue to a committee or manipulate agendas so that it is either excluded from the discussion or discussed too late in a session to be taken seriously. Or they can focus the discussion so completely on establishing proper rules of interaction that the issue itself is never addressed. For example, when peace talks started during the Vietnam War, the two sides argued for months about the shape of the bargaining table, proper display of flags, and rules for speaking times and turns. Although these topics were important for symbolic reasons (round tables symbolize that the participants are of equal status; rectangular tables do not), discussion of them delayed the consideration of key differences.

Sometimes parties regress to childlike tactics or quietly make commitments to "let this one go by but get revenge later on." Commitments to get revenge, silently obsessing about felt conflicts, running away, unproductively worrying, begging, and pouting all are far too common among adults and children alike. Often one or more parties avoid conflicts by refusing to admit that there is an issue between them, either through statements like "I really think we basically are in agreement on this" or transcend to a level at which agreement does exist: "I know we both have the welfare of the students at heart."[22]

Southern High School is a rural school led by a principal who makes virtually every decision and watches teachers and students like a hawk. Like many small, service-oriented organizations, it had a family atmosphere. However, an issue arose over a failing grade given an all-state fullback in a required history course. The principal, who was also the football coach, asked the teacher to let the student do some remedial work. When she refused, he quietly changed the student's grade in the main office. Eventually the faculty member discovered the change (on Friday night, when she saw the fullback start an important game) and confronted the principal in private. The principal minimized the event, arguing that the fullback would drop out of school if he could not play, and that his dropping out would weaken the teachers' negotiating position in upcoming contract talks. He apologized but argued that for the good of the student, and for the good of the family, he had little choice.

Unconvinced, the teacher brought the issue up at the next meeting of the history department. Many of them agreed with the teacher, feeling that all of them had been insulted when the principal went over the teacher's head. They also were concerned about the contract talks, however, and encouraged her to forget the matter. But the anger didn't go away. Eventually the history teachers started to take sides over the issue and fight among themselves over what really were trivial issues. Others became quietly dissatisfied and started to disengage from their work. Morale dropped, as did the quality of teaching. But they did win the state football championship.

The moral of this story is really quite simple. There are cases in which avoidant strategies are productive. Avoidance may be the best response if issues really are trivial, if organizational power relationships make successful resistance impossible, if the parties lack the communication skills necessary to prevent destructive escalation, if the circumstances surrounding the issue are likely to change in ways that will eliminate the bases of the conflict, or if there is insufficient time to work through the issue adequately. But, avoidant strategies usually only delay confrontations; they do not manage or resolve differences. When people use avoidant strategies, the people who raised the issue are frustrated. They have taken risks without having an opportunity to realize any gains. Consequently, avoidant strategies may only generate hostilities that will come out in conflicts over other issues, making it more difficult to manage them productively.

Confrontative Strategies Another strategy is *confronting* the conflict directly. Though confrontation sounds competitive, it refers to directly addressing the issues at hand. It can be done in a competitive manner or in an integrative, problem-solving manner. Both competitive and integrative confrontation can work hand in hand: In some cases, for example, to motivate another party to cooperate in an integrative solution, one must show them that one is willing to compete and will extract considerable costs unless they cooperate.

First, consider the more competitive approaches to confrontation. *Personalization* and *coercion* probably are best known, more because they are so often used than because they are the strategically wisest or most productive. Attacking the *person* of one's opponent(s), especially when the attack impugns morals, reveals secrets, or makes accusations of assorted "-isms" (racism, sexism, fascism, communism, and so on), denies that person any defense except counterattacking or acquiescing. *Coercion* comes in two forms, *overt displays of power* and *threats or promises*.[23] These function in essentially the same way; they depend on the same conditions for their success and are, in effect, two sides of the same coin. Three conditions must be present for coercion, threats, or promises to succeed. First, the *sources* must be perceived to have sufficient organizational power to be able to carry out the threat/promise. The threat or promise must also be communicated in a way that makes the *desired responses clear and specific* and the *consequences of compliance or noncompliance "vivid."* Both "I'm gonna cover you with honey and tie you to a hill of biting red ants in a glaring Arizona sun" and "I'm gonna cover you with whipped cream and . . ." are vivid threats or promises. Finally, the consequence must be *perceived as being fair, equitable, and appropriate to the magnitude of the action that is requested.* Consequences that are either trivial or horrendous compared to the request will not be taken seriously.

Threats are risky because they always insult the other party (although if they are worded as promises, the insult is reduced). They do help the other party understand the threatener's priorities and thus may increase the potential to avoid misunderstandings. The problem with threats and promises is that people's perceptions about what is credible, equitable, fair, and appropriate differ widely. In addition, the *act* of threatening or promising may influence those perceptions in unpredictable ways. Threats and promises tend to provoke counterthreats and promises, creating a sometimes comical response ("My mommy will beat up your daddy.") They often lead to destructive cycles of escalation.

A final competitive strategy is *"taking a tough stance."* In its pure form, where all parties initially refuse to concede their positions, it can lead to productive results. Because no party appears to be willing to acquiesce or be intimidated, all parties are forced to take one another seriously and search for a mutually acceptable resolution of their differences. The key is knowing when to make an initial concession. If it is made too early the other parties will see it as a sign of weakness and become more intransigent. If made too late, the conflict already may have escalated to a destructive level. If the parties are careful not to fall into a cycle of escalation, for example, by pausing and thinking strategically for a while before matching the other party's offer, matching can allow both parties to appear simultaneously to be both tough and reasonable.[24]

A more integrative, but related, strategy has been called *playing the reformed sinner.* In the reformed sinner strategy, one party takes a tough stance until the negotiation reaches an impasse and then makes a significant concession. This signals that the party could compete, but is willing to cooperate. Generally the issue on which the concession is made is important, but not vital to the party. In societies with strong norms of reciprocity, the act of conceding creates strong psychological pressures for the other parties to concede something in response. In 1982, during the worst housing market in recent memory (mortgage interest rates were around 21 percent), Charley Conrad's wife's career led the Conrads to decide to move. Fortunately, BJ (Charley's wife) had purchased a nice, middle-priced, brick ranch house that had appreciated a bit, thanks primarily to her renovation work. She also had negotiated a 6.5 percent loan that was assumable by any buyer. In short, as long as they asked a somewhat reasonable price, they had a strong negotiating position. Their first potential buyer was a newly hired assistant professor in the psychology department of a major private southeastern university whose primary research area was conflict management. This situation created a wonderful opportunity to watch conflict strategies in action.

He and his wife said they were delighted with the house, but somewhat concerned with the deterioration of an exterior brick staircase into the basement. But they would go home and talk about it and call the next day. Because this concern was over what could be perceived as a major problem, but actually was not, it provided an excellent opportunity for the new professor to use the reformed sinner strategy—taking a tough stance and then conceding on the staircase to force a reciprocal concession on a more important issue, like price. The next day Charley Conrad had two contractors come by and give him written estimates for repairing the stairs ($200 and $800, which should tell you something about why you should always get multiple bids on construction and home repair projects). That night the assistant professor called, explained that they were excited about the house but very concerned about the stairs and what they might suggest about the structural integrity of the foundation. They had talked about the problem with his father-in-law, who "knew a lot about construction," and learned that it could cost $4,000 or $5,000 to repair it. So, they would be happy to buy the house for $3,000 below the asking price. After the Conrads told the buyer about their written estimates, the buyers quickly agreed that they would love to move in next week (after paying the asking price, of course).

We provide this example for two reasons. One is to explain the "reformed sinner" strategy. In studies of conflict and negotiation, it has proven to be a useful strategy for motivating others to shift from competitive to cooperative (integrative) approaches. We also discuss the reformed sinner strategy because being able to identify the communication strategies that are being used by other parties is often as important as being able to use those strategies oneself. There is substantial evidence that conflicts become destructive when there is a major power imbalance between the parties. Understanding communication strategies in conflicts provides a potent source of power, which can lead to unfair domination of powerless people. Empowerment—the creation of the power balances that generate productive outcomes in conflicts—begins with training all parties in the use of strategic communication.

There are also more cooperative confrontative strategies. One of these is *problem solving,* in which the parties utilize one of the decision-making models defined in Chapter 8 to work jointly through the conflict issues and identify options that meet both parties' needs.

Another integrative approach is to identify a *superordinate goal* in which parties find a common goal significant to both that gives them some common ground. A classic experiment by Sherif was one of the first studies of this technique.[25] Sherif and his colleagues first created two opposing groups in a summer camp, the Bulldogs and the Red Devils. These groups engaged in a number of competitions, and members developed a strong sense of the value of their own group, while devaluing the competing group. Sherif and colleagues then created several emergencies that required both groups to work together to overcome problems at the camp. For example, they had to work together to get a truck unstuck from the mud. This common activity in service of a valued shared goal significantly reduced competition between the groups, as well as undermined the strong boundaries between them. The superordinate goal approach works only if the goal is truly desired by both parties and if accomplishing it is beyond the capacities of any single party or group. Moreover, it is not a foolproof integrator: If the parties fail to achieve the superordinate goal, they may go back to blaming one another for the failure, polarizing even more.

In summary, conflicts are not made up of one party using one strategy. They are made of interactions, of patterns of communication, response, and counterresponse. In *productive conflicts* these patterns consist of a number of brief episodes during which the parties adopt a wide range of strategies. Coercion, threats, promises, redefinition, relational comments, digressions, joking, and relaxing are intermixed in a variety of proportions. No single strategy takes over; no sustained cycle of threat and counterthreat, coercion and regression distorts parties' perceptions or clouds their analysis of the situation. In *destructive conflicts* a narrow range of communicative strategies is used. Escalating cycles of threat, coercion, expansion of issues, and personalization lock parties into competitive, zero-sum patterns of interaction. Sometimes—perhaps often—destructive cycles are accidentally initiated by more powerful employees. They misperceive less powerful people as jealous, resentful, or hostile and overreact, adopting confrontative, competitive strategies when other approaches would have been more appropriate. Or they inadvertently place weaker people in positions where they feel they must either fight or be humiliated. But conflict cycles are never under any one member's control. It is the participants' ability to manage and control tendencies for escalation that determines whether a conflict will be productive or destructive.[26]

Case Study:
The Bargaining Case

Bargaining is a special kind of conflict management. It looks like compromise, but involves negotiating shared rules and cooperation within these rules to gain a competitive advantage. It focuses on the exchange of formal offers; but making offers is only one kind of communicative interaction in bargaining sessions. As Chapter 1 explains, a major function of communication is the creation of "realities" that guide and constrain further communication. But "realities" are constantly changing throughout processes of communicative interaction. These processes—and the way in which "history" is defined and redefined through communication—is illustrated nicely in the following case study of bargaining between teachers and the school board in a small rural, midwestern district. It is based on the research of Linda Putnam and her associates.*

The state teachers association provided the 133 teachers with a professional bargainer, Doug. The school board hired its own pro. Usually teacher bargaining (and most formal labor–management negotiation) is limited to an exchange of money (salaries and fringe benefits) versus teacher control over their working conditions. The teachers' "reality-creation" process involved three stories (see Chapter 4). One story was about "the bad old days" of bargaining. For years the two sides had experienced hostile bargaining: long and heated arguments over rules of negotiation, making threats, fist-pounding, name-calling, and refusals to settle had dominated yearly discussions. One year the two sides' initial offers were thinly veiled insults: The board offered a $1 raise; the teachers demanded a 25 percent increase. Four years ago the hostility erupted into a strike.

The townspeople supported the teachers—telephoning the board members at home and insulting and haranguing them as they walked down the streets. But the story the teachers told one another was about the immaturity that they had shown during the strike. They prided themselves in their newfound maturity, which essentially meant that they would cooperate with the board and do everything possible to avoid another strike. Their reasoning was simple and self-fulfilling: We must avoid antagonistic bargaining because it could result in a strike, which is unacceptable because it would show that we are immature bargainers. Because we have matured we will not strike. Of course, accepting this story eliminated the only threat the teachers had; but it created a comfortable reality that would guide and constrain their communication. The second story was about Doug. He had started working with the teachers during the strike, and although no one remembered exactly what he did to achieve it, he negotiated an acceptable settlement. Telling this story reinforced the teachers' trust for Doug and led them to accept his goals, strategies, and decisions throughout the negotiation. Doug told the third story. He had faced Jim, the board's pro, many times in the past and found him to be "a bear" on power issues—he just would not give in on these issues. The teachers adapted the story and applied it to their board. One said, "It'll be a cold day in hell

(continued)

(continued from the previous page)

before that board will give us any policy issues (control)." The fact that Doug failed to tell them that their district was far behind the other districts in the state in terms of teacher control of working conditions added to the power of the story. So the teachers decided to introduce power issues but drop them early during the bargaining. Unfortunately, the "reality" they had created was inaccurate. Jim had advised the board to be ready to give up some policy issues to minimize financial costs in the new contract. In fact, the board was surprised when Doug dropped these items; but of course it had no reason to say so.

The teachers told and retold these three stories throughout the bargaining session. They asked for, and thus received, less than they could have gotten. But they communicated in a way that maintained the reality that they had created— they behaved maturely, reached an acceptable settlement (70–75 percent of the teachers supported the final contract), and avoided a strike. Of course, if you consider only the offers they made and accepted, they took a very soft bargaining position. But they compensated for that kind of softness through a ritual that proved they were tough negotiators. Negotiations regularly continued night after night, extending into the early morning hours. The bargaining team even enjoyed going to breakfast together after a long night of negotiations, arriving at school just in time to go to class. This ritual, repeated every year, proved to the negotiators and the other teachers that their representatives were tough bargainers. (Sometimes late-night negotiations are more than ritual. Charley Conrad once was on a teacher bargaining committee that stayed late to exhaust the opposition. We enlarged the teachers' committee so that no one member had to attend more than one late-night meeting, knowing that the school board did not have this flexibility. After five weeks of negotiating, when rumor had it that four board members were on the verge of divorce, we obtained what we wanted: the transfer of a much-hated principal, and the largest salary increase in the district's history. But that was a different situation, a very different "reality.")

Applying What You've Learned

1. How did the parties' definitions of "reality" influence communication? The relative power of the bargainers?
2. In this situation, could an individual teacher or member have argued successfully for taking a tougher negotiating position?

Questions to Think About and Discuss

1. What functions did the "staying-all-night" ritual play in addition to demonstrating toughness?

(continued)

(continued from the previous page)

2. What long-term effects is this negotiation likely to have on the teachers' perceptions of reality? Doug's image and role? the board's negotiating strategies? the outcomes of subsequent negotiations?

---

*See similar analyses in the following papers and publications: Linda Putnam and Shirley Van Hoeven, "Teacher Bargaining as a Cultural Rite of Conflict Reduction," paper presented at the Central States Speech Association Convention, Cincinnati, 1986; Linda Putnam and Shirley Van Hoeven, "The Role of Narrative in Teachers' Bargaining," paper presented at the Temple University Discourse Conference on Conflict Intervention, Philadelphia, 1987; Linda Putnam, Shirley Van Hoeven, and Connie Bullis, "The Role of Rituals and Fantasy Themes in Teachers' Bargaining," *Western Journal of Speech Communication, 55* (1991): 85–103; and Linda Putnam, "Negotiation of Intergroup Conflict in Organizations," Hallie Mande Neff Wilcox Published Lecture. Waco, TX: Baylor University, 1987.

Communication and Conflict Escalation

Conflicts escalate in three ways—*expansion of issues, involvement of self and "face,"* and *dominance of emotion and symbol.*[27] The first is self-explanatory. When episodes of conflict begin, they revolve around a small number of issues that immediately concern the participants. Sometimes the nature of these issues leads the parties to consider other, more basic issues. In fact, a number of models of conflict management recommend careful, systematic broadening of the issue being discussed. As long as the parties continue to focus on the central problem while taking new and different perspectives on it, this approach may lead to the consideration of a wider range of potential solutions.

However, issues in conflicts often expand in a very different way. The archetypal example of destructive escalation is a standard fare of television sitcoms. The cycle begins when the husband complains about a burned pot roast. The wife responds that if he doesn't like it he can cook it himself. Before the interchange ends with one of the two storming out of the room (usually after walking into a closet by mistake), they will have discussed each spouse's parents (who are lazy, bad cooks, or whatever), stereotypical sex roles, housecleaning and repair needs, their relative incomes, and their sex lives. In these conflicts the expansion of issues obscures the initial problem, reveals no possible solutions, and redefines the problem in ways that make it impossible to arrive at any productive resolution of the initial (pot roast) disagreement.[28]

Conflicts also escalate when they begin to involve the *self-esteem or self-images* ("faces") of the participants. When one party personalizes a conflict, it creates a need for others to defend themselves, to save face. To complicate face saving even more, in Western cultures negotiators must appear to be tough, fair, and competent if they are to save face. Because it is difficult to simultaneously do all of these things, face management is especially complicated. Typically they do so by adopting their own personalizing strategies, which creates pressure for others to save face, and an escalating cycle of personalization begins.[29]

In non-Western cultures saving face is even more important. Stella Ting-Toomey has described the complicated saving face system that characterizes Japanese approaches to conflict management. One principle of this system is the concept of *Nemawashi,* the subtle process of achieving consensus and support for a proposal. Extensive informal communication eventually involves every relevant member of the organization, but never includes a "group confrontation" in which everyone meets in a formal negotiating session. The second principle is the Ringi System, a way of preventing open conflicts by circulating a document widely and getting everyone's seals of approval. This system diffuses responsibility and saves face for those people who initially may oppose the proposal, and it saves face for everyone should the proposal fail. The third principle is the go-between system, in which people with different opinions seek out a third party to mediate. This complex, time-consuming, indirect system of conflict management is appropriate for Japanese organizations, because the demands and constraints of Japanese culture make it more important to prevent conflicts than to manage them in the open. Confrontation is characteristic of more open, individualistic societies.[30]

The final form of escalation involves breakdowns in *strategic thinking,* the balanced consideration of situations, self-interests, and others' interests (discussed in Chapter 7). Once conflict episodes begin, they create their own realities. Participants often begin to base their choices only on the communication taking place during the episode. As the conflict continues, participants begin to mirror the other person's communication rather than focus on the situation and choose strategies appropriately. They lose sight of the larger organizational situation—the parties' organizational roles, the importance of the issue and reaching a productive resolution of it, and the need to maintain effective working relationships. Winning the *conflict* takes on a *symbolic* importance that transcends the other dimensions of the situation. In trying to win, actors lose sight of their desires to arrive at a satisfactory solution. They begin to focus wholly on their incentives to compete and forget their incentives to cooperate.

Although these three forms of escalation differ in some respects, they are similar in two important ways. First, they tend to go unnoticed by the participants. Communication strategies generate counterstrategies in a seemingly natural and appropriate sequence. Conflicts begin to become more destructive than productive; parties begin to make choices about how to communicate without realizing how their choices contribute to the escalation; and they become progressively more immersed in escalating cycles. They perceive that their increasingly hostile actions are merely responses; that if anyone is responsible for the escalation, it is someone else. Paul Watzlawick and his colleagues call this process ***punctuation.***

Think of childhood conflicts that end in both children defending their actions by claiming that the other child started it. Regardless of which one struck the first blow in the current battle, the other can recall an earlier insult, an earlier fight, or some proof that they were only defending themselves. In conflicts between adults, the parties also each choose a different starting point for the sequence of communication and response. By perceiving that someone else started it, they can blame the conflict on others and justify their own contributions to the escalation as just and proper. They begin to employ nonproductive avoidant or aggressive strategies and ignore potentially productive collaborative approaches. Communication becomes a weapon with which they can win the battle, not a process through which differences can be managed productively.[31]

The second similarity among different forms of escalation is that they can be recognized by the same cues:

1. Parties argue emotionally for their preferred outcome rather than calmly explain it and its implications.
2. Parties use individual or coalition-related pronouns rather than group or organization-oriented ones.
3. The time and emotional energy devoted to a topic is much greater than its importance. (Parties may begin to ask themselves "Why is this so important?" and not be able to produce sensible answers.)
4. Parties cannot (or can only vaguely) remember the issue that started the discussion or the links between it and the topic currently being debated.
5. Parties find themselves thinking more about persons, positions, and strategies than about problems and solutions.

When any of these cues is present, participants should step back from the interaction and consciously search for and use appropriate de-escalating strategies. Sometimes this withdrawal may be physical, as when formal cooling-off periods are imposed on labor–management negotiations. At other times the withdrawal may be purely cognitive. But unless the parties are able to separate themselves from the cycle of communication, the escalation will continue.

Unfortunately, the previous comments about escalation processes make them sound aberrant, almost perverse. The potential for escalation, however, exists in all conflicts and for understandable reasons. Some bases of escalation are related to the nature of organizations. Typically, employees are rewarded for competing and achieving. Every organizational conflict also carries a legacy of past conflicts and the anticipation of future conflicts. The perfectly managed organizational conflict—in which every participant and the organization find an acceptable solution and relationships are strengthened by the interaction— is quite rare, perhaps nonexistent. Each conflict leaves its own legacy. When organizations adopt norms that suppress or repress overt conflicts, or when parties inappropriately use avoidant orientations or strategies, this legacy of hidden dissatisfaction is intense. When overt conflicts do occur, the legacy provides impetus to "win this one because I may never get another chance" or "win this one because I lost the last one."

Escalation also is supported by the two faces of organizational power (recall Chapter 8). Whenever employees decide to enter into an overt conflict, they incur risks. These risks can be offset only if the employees gain power or rewards from the outcome of the conflict. For this reason, they have an absolute incentive to push the conflict to a point where they win. Similarly for power-holders, the existence of an open conflict threatens them and their position in the power structure. Once an overt conflict begins, the hidden face of power is being attacked. Because this face allows powerholders to maintain their dominance, they must defend it. "Winning" the conflict allows them to reestablish their superior position. Losing the battle, or compromising on the issues, diminishes their power. The interrelationships between conflict and power relationships establish a motive for employees to adopt a win-lose orientation, increasing the potential for escalation.

Still another base of escalation is the nature of human communication. Chapter 7 explained that all messages have both content and relational dimensions. If the parties in a conflict focus on the relational dimension of one another's communication, the conflict becomes personalized and escalation is quite probable. Perceptual processes also contribute. If an interaction is tense, as conflicts are, parties focus their attention on the evidence of hostility and competition present in other parties' communication. People perceive their opponents as more competitive than they really are and perceive themselves as being more cooperative than they really are. As conflicts escalate, parties begin to see themselves, their allies, and their ideas as wholly good and their opponents and their ideas as wholly evil. Trust begins to dissolve and participants begin to listen less and argue more. Eventually communication breaks down; little information is exchanged; more information is distorted, and hostility and distrust grow. Parties begin to narrow the range of communication strategies they use and the number of outcomes they will accept. Escalation continues.[32]

For example, workers at one plant became so angry about what they perceived as arbitrary and inflexible management and intolerable working conditions that they launched a wildcat strike (a local strike not sanctioned by the national union). Management perceived that the strike was an attempt to take over the organization, not a response to grievances. They responded defensively, becoming more intransigent, less flexible, and more hostile. Management's communication convinced the workers that their initial perceptions had been correct, which led them to become even more hostile and to make stronger demands for control of working conditions, which supported management's perceptions that the real issue was power, and so on.[33] When combined, *organizational,* and *communicational* factors make escalation an inevitable problem in overt conflicts.

When escalation gets out of hand, or when parties come to an impasse that seems insurmountable, organizations often call in third parties to intervene in conflicts. The labor mediators who are brought in to try to avert strikes and resolve labor disputes are the most familiar interveners to most people. However, interveners need not have such a high profile. Often they are informal third parties—managers or others who are trusted by both parties and have experience with disputes. In other cases, organizations have created their own professional dispute resolution or mediation services. The University of Michigan, for example, established a dispute resolution office to address grievances between its employees and administration. This service provides trained media-tors to assist in the resolution of conflicts that have escalated to the point that they can no longer be handled with traditional means.[34]

THE AFTERMATH OF CONFLICTS

This chapter began with a summary of Pondy's three preliminary phases of con-flict—*latent, perceived,* and *felt.* The fourth phase in his model, *overt conflict,* has been examined at length. The final phase is the *aftermath* of the conflict. Two criteria are appropriate for evaluating the short-term effects of conflicts: the quality of the final decision and the effect of the conflict on working rela-tionships. If a sensible solution emerges that meets the needs of every party or is supported by a legitimate consensus, the short-term effects will be positive. However, such integrative solutions are difficult to attain, and consensus is often elusive. In fact, in many cases a conflict will move from issue to issue with no real resolution. When new issues arise, the same patterns of communicative interaction recur.[35]

The more common modes of managing conflicts—compromise, majority vote, or acquiescence by one or more parties—leave residual frustrations that prompt future conflicts and complicate their management. Similarly, the dynamics of conflict episodes may leave behind changed perceptions of each party, unman-aged emotions, and commitments to get revenge, all of which influence working relationships. If they are repeated often, escalating conflicts may lead employees to view their relationships with one another as competitive rather than coopera-tive. Because their tasks are interdependent, competitive relationships may under-mine the participants' performance and the organization's success.[36]

This potential for long-term negative effects on working relationships has led many organizations to use formal procedures and make structural changes to minimize the impact of unproductive conflicts. Some have tried to reduce unit or employee interdependence, both to minimize the number of issues over which differences might occur and to decrease the adverse effects of long-term relational problems. But interdependence cannot be reduced beyond a certain point, and when it is reduced, the parties' incentives to cooperate with one another are also reduced. Other organizations create formal conflict managers or formal procedures for handling even minor disagreements. Third-party inter-ventions *can* prevent escalation, as long as the third party is skilled in conflict management and has sufficient formal power.[37] Formal rules and procedures can structure conflicts in ways that reduce ambiguity and prevent the use of the communication strategies that prompt escalation. Although there are limits to the effectiveness of structural changes, their use accents the need to evaluate the productiveness of each episode within the long-term perspective of the organization's operation.

Conflicts can be valuable and productive for organizations and employees alike. For organizations, conflict can stimulate creative problem solving; it can generate or publicize superior ideas and adjust perceived power relationships to better fit the skills and abilities of employees. For individual employees, conflict can provide opportunities to test, expand, and demonstrate their skills; better understand their organizations; and develop their self-esteem and confidence. If conflicts are kept within civil bounds and if satisfactory solutions to problems can be found, the total impact of each conflict can be positive.

Two implications emerge from the preceding discussion. First, organizational conflicts must be evaluated in terms of many considerations. Open conflicts are invariably disruptive and leave behind negative legacies. But their impact on the long-term effectiveness of the organization may on balance be favorable. Attempting to suppress or repress conflicts often damages organizations more than allowing them to surface and be managed. Second, controlling processes of escalation is the key to productive conflict management. The aftermath of organizational conflicts depends on maintaining patterns of communication that simultaneously allow people to demonstrate their competencies and solve problems. Escalation robs the participants of these opportunities and establishes the bases of nonproductive legacies. The strategic use of communication is the key to productive conflict management.

A FEMINIST VIEW OF COMMUNICATION AND CONFLICT

Linda Putnam and Deborah M. Kolb recently articulated a view of conflict and negotiation that represents a significant departure from the approach to conflict taken so far in this chapter.[38] Traditional perspectives on negotiation and conflict management rest on a limited set of taken-for-granted assumptions about the nature of conflict, negotiation, and conflict management. This set of assumptions and related understandings reflects the predominant perspective in the United States and Western Europe. It underlies almost all the hundreds of studies and books that have been published on conflict in the past 40 years. Those assumptions are as follows:

1. The goals of parties in conflict is mutual gain that helps them achieve their interests.
2. Conflicts are best managed through setting up conditions whereby parties can make tradeoffs that enable them to realize their goals. The ultimate outcomes of conflicts should be assessed in terms of winning and losing, with the preferred outcome being win-win results (i.e. all parties gain).
3. Relationships between parties in conflicts are seen in terms of one party related to another with different interests. Parties view each other instrumentally, in terms of how they are either a barrier against or means for achieving their goals. Trust, which refers to the degree to which parties uphold their agreed upon bargains, is a critical dimension of relationships.
4. Conflict management and negotiation occurs in the form of proposals and counterproposals, with each side suggesting courses of action that

benefit their own interests. The conflict is regarded as a problem that must be solved by parties or third parties brought in to help them reach an acceptable resolution.

5. Communication in conflicts functions largely to exchange information about parties' positions and interests that can be used to develop a final solution. Communication should play a largely informational role in effective conflict management and should not inflame the situation by injecting counterproductive emotions.

However, like all accepted assumptions, this frame automatically excludes other legitimate perspectives. Based on feminist perspectives, Putnam and Kolb argue that the goal of conflict management and negotiation can be more than achieving a mutually beneficial outcome in the short term. It also can transform a situation so that parties understand themselves and their world better and develop stronger relationships for the long term. This alternative view criticizes the traditional perspective on conflict for its short-sighted and overly narrow focus on satisfying immediate interests. Instead, the alternative view would advocate that the entire point of engaging in conflict and negotiation is not simply to fulfill immediate needs, but to work toward a better life. Focus on immediate needs may in fact detract from bettering oneself.

For example, in the Bargaining Case introduced previously, the negotiators took a traditional approach to their conflict, assuming that it had to be settled in terms of a contract that addressed the issues that the parties thought important. Doug and Jim worked out a contract that resulted in a mutually acceptable solution. However, as the case shows, the stories the teachers told themselves led them finally to obtain less than they might have. Consider what might have happened if the parties had taken the alternative view offered here: They would not have focused on immediate, concrete issues, but rather on the nature of the relationship between teachers and the board. Both parties would have entered the negotiation interested in improving their relationship and in understanding the best ways to educate children. This would have eventually led the discussion to the degree of control teachers should have over working conditions. Teachers would likely have argued that they needed more control over their work to have the flexibility needed to meet student needs. The board would have had to face the hard fact that though keeping control was comfortable for them, the degree of control they had was probably too great. The end result might have been that the board granted the teachers more control, and that the teachers in turn would have increased respect for the board for giving up something that gave it a clear advantage. This admittedly hypothetical discussion could not have occurred if the parties had restricted themselves to talking about issues only, because control over work would be reduced to an issue—recall that this is exactly how Doug had treated it—and therefore as something to trade away or win rather than discuss.

The longer-term, more general goals of the alternative perspective imply that the ultimate end of negotiation is not a settlement of immediate issues, but instead transformation of the situation and the people in it. Conflict and negotiation aim to transform the situation by creating new understandings and new ways for members to work together. It aims to transform the parties by giving them insights into themselves, into how they are contributing to the conflict and how they might change to improve the situation and also deeper insights that help them live their lives better. The emphasis shifts from winning and losing to how to develop actions that parties can undertake together to a new level of collaboration. It also assumes that there may be no fundamentally opposed interests, in the sense that novel, transforming actions may allow seemingly different interests to be reconciled. In our hypothetical extension of the bargaining case, this is exactly what would happen. Through open discussion, parties come to understand each other better and see the situation differently. The result was that the board of its own accord would give up some of its power, thus fundamentally transforming how education occurred in the district. It would also fundamentally transform and build the relationship between teachers and board.

In the Bargaining Case the board and teachers—through their intermediary bargainers Doug and Jim—viewed each other in instrumental terms. Each viewed the other as someone who could be convinced or enticed to give in on one or more issues of interest, or, if the worst happened, as a barrier to achieving their ends. Trust had been achieved between Doug and Jim; but it was not a trust based on appreciation of each other and on the importance of the relationship between board and teachers; instead trust was based on living up to prior commitments on issues and on a contract hammered out in the negotiations. On the alternative view of conflict, the board and teachers would try to understand each others' motivations and needs, not with an aim of finding out what sort of offer to make, but with true concern for the other as someone each had a long term relationship with. Their communication would not aim at finding points of agreement, but of understanding the other and with figuring out how to improve the current situation and relationship. This could then be the basis for future cooperation that went well beyond the immediate contract negotiations.

Conflict management and negotiation are viewed as problem-solving processes in the traditional perspective: Each side has to define the requirements for a good solution, and these then constitute a problem that the sides have to solve by finding a course of action that meets the requirements. The alternative perspective would not give problem solving primacy, but rather dialogue between the parties whereby they communicate with the goal of achieving understanding and transformation. This communication might take the form of a deep I and thou discussion in which parties bare their souls; but it could also be more restrained as parties regard their counterpart as other and try to appreciate this other from their own point of view. Once effective communication has been established, the best course of joint action might simply suggest itself in the flow of discussion. Problem solving would be reserved for jointly defined issues that did not have readily apparent solutions.[39]

In the Bargaining Case the teachers and the board might have promoted communication by demoting (in a sense) their professional bargainers to one of a team of people who met in an open communication forum to simply discuss their points of view. The goal of this forum would be to understand, not to solve things or define problems, or any other instrumental goal. Simple understanding is the goal, and it is expected that this understanding will lead to sympathetic interactions that generate joint actions endorsed by all parties.

The alternative, feminist view of conflict is fundamentally different from the confrontative, problem-oriented "let's-make-a-deal" traditional approach. In fact, it is so different that it may seem Utopian in a world full of hard bargainers. However, traditional strategies often fail. Instead of leading to mutually acceptable outcomes, they often produce conflict situations that are increasingly difficult to resolve. The intransigence and polarization that results often has disastrous consequences for organizations and for their employees. Perhaps a different perspective is needed, one that would not make it more difficult to manage conflicts by restricting the flexibility of negotiators. Unfortunately, the traditional perspective is so deeply imbedded in the political, societal, and legal context surrounding organizations that it is difficult to implement or even imagine any alternative. But in an era of globalization, where alternative forms of organizing are rapidly emerging, alternative forms of conflict management may be viable. For example, the alternative perspective seems particularly well suited for the network strategies of organizing described in Chapter 5. In these organizations, open communication and the establishment of long-term relationships is of fundamental importance. In view of the complexity of their structures and how often they must change them, network organizations are best coordinated in exactly the sort of communicative exchanges that the alternative model envisions. This enables them to continuously improve and address the actual, often ill-defined problems the network encounters, rather than simply react to well-defined issues handed down from previous groups and leaders.

CONCLUSION

Conflicts are inevitable parts of organizational life. Whenever people depend on one another and interact with one another, grounds for cooperation and competition exist. Although there is substantial evidence that it is counterproductive to try to avoid or suppress conflicts, especially in the long term, our fear of conflict escalation and the accepted assumptions of some organizational cultures make it difficult to deal with conflicts openly and productively. Fortunately, a wide variety of communicative strategies are available to employees before and during overt conflicts. Understanding those strategies and using them *strategically* determines whether a particular conflict will be productive or destructive.

NOTES

[1] This section is based primarily on four sources: Louis Pondy, "Organizational Conflict: Concepts and Models," *Administrative Science Quarterly, 12* (1967):296–320; Morton Deutsch, *The Resolution of Conflict* (New Haven: Yale University Press, 1973); Linda Putnam, "Conflict and Dispute Management," in *New Handbook of Organizational Communication,* Fredric Jablin and

Linda Putnam, eds. (Thousand Oaks, CA: Sage, 1997); and Joseph Folger, Marshall Scott Poole, and Randall Stutman, *Working Through Conflict,* 4th ed. (New York: Longman, 2001).

[2] Stella Ting-Toomey, "Toward a Theory of Conflict and Culture," in *Communication and Culture*, William Gudykunst, ed. (Beverly Hills, CA: Sage, 1985).

[3] Putnam, *Handbook;* Charles Franz and K. Gregory Jin, "The Structure of Group Conflict in a Collaborative Work Group During Information Systems Development," *Journal of Applied Communication Research, 23* (1995): 108–127.

[4] Pondy. For an excellent summary of phase models and their strengths and weaknesses, see Linda Putnam, "Reframing Integrative and Distributive Bargaining," in Blair Shepard, M. Bazerman, and R. Lewicki, eds., *Research on Negotiation in Organizations,* vol. 2 (Greenwich, CT: JAI Press, 1990); Michael Holmes, "Phase Structure in Negotiation," in L. Putnam and M. Roloff, eds., *Communication and Negotiation* (Newbury Park, CA: Sage, 1993). A number of phase models are summarized in Folger, Poole, and Stuttman.

[5] See Folger, Poole, and Stuttman, Ch.1.

[6] Psychological models of conflict call this process "displacement" (see Folger, Poole, and Stuttman). It is examined at length later in this chapter, in "The Bargaining Case" and in the section entitled "Aftermath." Also see Steven R. Wilson, "Face and Facework in Negotiation," in L. Putnam and M. Roloff, eds., *Communication and Negotiation* (Newbury Park, CA: Sage, 1993). An excellent book on mediation that points to its transformative potential is R. Baruch Bush and Joseph P. Folger, *The Promise of Mediation: Responding to Conflict Through Empowerment and Recognition* (San Francisco: Jossey-Bass, 1994).

[7] M. Neale and M. Bazerman, *Cognition and Rationality in Negotiations* (New York: The Free Press, 1991).

[8] T. Simons, "Speech Patterns and the Concept of Utility in Cognitive Maps," *Academy of Management Journal, 36* (1993): 139–156. An excellent summary of frame-oriented conflict research is available in Linda Putnam and Majia Holmer, "Framing and Reframing," in L. Putnam and M. Roloff, *Communication and Negotiation* (Newberry Park, CA: Sage, 1992). For summaries of the impact that frames have on conflict behavior, see R. Fisher and W. Ury, *Getting to Yes* (Boston: Houghton Mifflin, 1981); Linda Putnam, S. Wilson and D. Turner, "The Evolution of Policy Arguments in Teachers' Bargaining, *Argumentation, 4* (1990): 129–152; Daniel Canary and Brian Spitzberg, "A Model of the Perceived Competence of Conflict Strategies," *Human Communication Research, 15* (1990): 630–649; and Linda Putnam, "Reframing Integrative and Distributive Bargaining," in *Research on Negotiation in Organizations,* vol. 2 R.J. Lewicki, B.H. Sheppard, and M.H. Bazerman, eds. (Greenwich, CT: JAI Press, 1990).

[9] W.L. Felsteiner, R.L. Abel, and A Sarat, "The Emergence and Transformation of Disputes," *Law and Society Review, 33* (1980/1981): 631–654; Linda Putnam, "Reframing."

[10] Thomas, "Conflict." Kenneth Thomas, "Where Do We Go from Here?" *Management Communication Quarterly, 1* (1988): 301–305. A number of scales have been developed to measure orientations toward conflict. See the special issue of *Management Communication Quarterly, 2* (1988) edited by Linda Putnam.

[11] Phillip Tompkins, J. Fisher, D. Infante, and E. Tompkins, "Conflict and Communication within the University," in *Perspectives on Communication and Social Conflict,* G. Miller and H. Simons, eds. (Englewood Cliffs, NJ: Prentice-Hall, 1974).

[12] Dean Morley and Pamela Shockley-Zalabak, "Conflict Avoiders and Compromisers," *Group and Organizational Behavior, 11* (1986): 387–402; and M. Rahim, "Referent Role and Styles of Handling Interpersonal Conflict," *Journal of Social Psychology, 126* (1986): 79–86; Charles Conrad, "Power, Performance and Supervisors' Choices of Strategies of Conflict Management," *Western Journal of Speech Communication, 47* (1983): 218–228; Putnam, "Reframing."

[13] See Nancy Burrell, Patrice Buzzanell, and J.J. McMillan, "Feminine Tensions in Conflict Situations as Revealed by Metaphoric Analysis," *Management Communication Quarterly, 6* (1992): 115–149; Charles Conrad, "Communication in Conflict: Style-Strategy Relationships, *Communication Monographs, 58* (1991): 135–155; Folger, Poole, and Stuttman; Barbara Mae Gayle, "Sex Equity in Workplace Conflict Management," *Journal of Applied Communication Research, 19* (1991): 152–169; Folger, Poole, Stutman, p. 236.

[14] Thomas, "Where Do We Go?"; Putnam, *Handbook*. This is especially true if we conceive of orientations as stable "personality traits" or "usual" responses to conflicts. Because people also adapt to one another's communication, our actual behaviors tend to deviate further and further away from our orientations as conflicts progress (Folger, Poole, and Stutman). Also see Conrad, "Conflict" and "Style-Strategy."

[15] Michael Roloff and Jerry M. Jordan, "Achieving Negotiation Goals," in L. Putnam and M. Roloff, eds., *Communication and Negotiation* (Newbury Park, CA: Sage, 1993).

[16] Folger, Poole, and Stutman provide an extended analysis of the relationship between power and conflict. See especially Chapter 4.

[17] See Berger; D.G. Pruitt, J. Rubin, and S. Kim, *Social Conflict* (New York: McGraw Hill, 1994); and J. Tucker, "Some Everyday Forms of Employee Resistance," *Sociological Forum, 8* (1993): 25–45.

[18] L. Kriegsberg, *The Sociology of Social Conflicts* (Englewood Cliffs, NJ: Prentice-Hall, 1973); Folger, Poole, and Stuttman.

[19] Donnellon and Gray; Putnam and Holmer; V. Sambamurthy and M.S. Poole, "The Effects of Level of Sophistication of Computer Support on Conflict Management in Groups," *Information Systems Research*, (1991) 224-251, Folger, Poole, and Stutman label this process "trained incapacity," and define the concept much as it was defined in Chapter 2 of this book. Also see Putnam, "Reframing"; Marshall Scott Poole, "Decision Development in Small Groups I," *Communication Monographs, 48* (1981):1–24; and Marshall Scott Poole and Jonelle Roth, "Decision Development in Small Groups IV," *Human Communication Research, 15* (1989): 323–356.

[20] Timothy Leary, *Interpersonal Diagnosis of Personality* (New York: Ronald, 1957); Kenneth Thomas and Richard Walton, *Conflict-handling Behavior in Interdepartmental Relations* (Los Angeles: UCLA Graduate School of Business Administration, 1971).

[21] This summary is based on a number of sources. The most important are Alan Sillars, "Stranger and Spouse as Target Persons for Compliance-gaining Strategies," *Human Communication Research, 6* (1980): 265–279; Bertram Raven and Arie Kruglanski, "Power and Conflict," in *The Structure of Conflict,* Paul Swingle, ed. (New York: Academic Press, 1970); and Folger, Poole, and Stutman.

[22] David F. Bush, "Passive-aggressive Behavior in the Business Setting," in *Passive-Aggressiveness,* Richard Parsons and Robert Wicks, eds. (New York: Brunner-Mazel, 1983). Also see Deborah Kolb, ed., *Hidden Conflict in Organizations* (Newbury Park, CA: Sage, 1991). The list of regressive strategies is taken from Michael Roloff, "Roloff's Modes of Conflict Resolution and Their Items," in *Explorations in Interpersonal Communication,* Gerald Miller, ed. (Beverly Hills, CA: Sage, 1976).

[23] Julia Wood and Barnett Pearce, "Sexists, Racists and Other Classes of Classifiers," *Quarterly Journal of Speech, 66* (1980): 239–250. Also see Wilson; Tedeschi; "Threats and Promises," in *The Structure of Conflict,* Paul Swingle, ed. (New York: Academic Press, 1970); and W. Schenck-Hamlin and G. Georgacarakos, "Response to Murdock, Bradac, and Bowers," *Western Journal of Speech Communication, 50* (1986): 200–207.

[24] Wilson; R. Axelrod, *The Evolution of Cooperation* (New York: Basic Books, 1984). Also see Folger, Poole, and Stutman.

[25] Muzafer Sherif, O. J. Harvey, B. J. White, W. R. Hood, and Carolyn W. Sherif, *Intergroup Conflict and Cooperation: The Robber's Cave Experiment* (Norman, OK: University Book Exchange, 1961). Also see Folger, Poole, and Stutman, p. 262.

[26] Raven and Kruglanski; S.S. Komorita, "Negotiating from Strength and the Concept of Bargaining," *Journal of the Theory of Social Behavior, 7* (1977): 56–79. Of course, a number of such books have been written. See especially Folger, Poole, and Stutman; and Putnam and Roloff.

[27] Morton Deutsch and Robert Krauss, "Studies in Interpersonal Bargaining," *Journal of Conflict Resolution, 61* (1962): 52–76; Folger, Poole, and Stutman; Linda Putnam and T. Jones, "Reciprocity in Negotiations," *Communication Monographs, 49* (1982): 171–191; and William Donohue, M. Diez, and M. Hamilton, "Coding Naturalistic Negotiation Interaction," *Human Communication Research, 10* (1984): 403–425.

[28] Margaret Neale and Max Bazerman have observed that organizational negotiators often engage in the same kinds of not strictly rational processes that are described in the discussion of decision-making in Chapter 8. In particular they are (1) overly influenced by the form/presentation of information rather than its content, (2) remain stubbornly committed to their initial positions when it is inappropriate, (3) assume a zero-sum posture when the situation is mixed motive, (4) make decisions on irrelevant information, (5) rely on readily available information rather than high-quality information to make strategic decisions, (6) don't take the perspective of the other party, and (7) are overconfident about ease of obtaining favorable outcomes (see "Negotiating Rationally," *Academy of Management Executive, 6* [1992]: 42–65). As conflicts escalate, the degree of irrationality also increases.

[29] Wilson; also see T. Lim and J.W. Bowers, "Face-work: Solidarity, Approbation, and Face," *Human Communication Research, 17* (1990): 415–450 and Roloff and Jordan.

[30] Ting-Toomey.

[31] Paul Watzlawick, Janet Beavin, and Don Jackson, *Pragmatics of Human Communication* (New York: W.W. Norton, 1967); Linda Putnam and Charmaine Wilson, "Communicative Strategies in Organizational Conflicts," in *Communication Yearbook 6,* M. Burgoon, ed. (Newbury Park, CA: Sage, 1982); Sillars, "Stranger"; Roy Lewicki, "Lying and Deception," in *Negotiating in Organizations,* Max Bazerman and R. Lewicki, eds. (Newbury Park, CA: Sage, 1983).

[32] Folger, Poole, & Stutman.

[33] A. Gouldner, *Wildcat Strike* (Yellow Springs, OH: Antioch Press, 1954).

[34] See Folger, Poole, and Stutman, Ch. 9 for a discussion of the third party intervention process.

[35] For an excellent explanation of this process and case study, see Kenwyn Smith, "The Movement of Conflict in Organizations," *Administrative Science Quarterly, 34* (1989): 1–20.

[36] William Donohue and R. Kolt, *Managing Interpersonal Conflict* (Newbury Park, CA: Sage, 1992).

[37] Putnam, *Handbook.*

[38] Linda L. Putnam and Deborah M. Kolb, "Rethinking Negotiation: Feminist View of Communication and Exchange," in Rethinking Organizational and Managerial *Communication from Feminist Perspectives,* Patrice Buzzanell, ed. (Thousand Oaks, CA: Sage, 2000).

[39] See Bush and Folger.

Chapter 11

COMMUNICATION AND DIVERSE WORKPLACES

*As a result of changes in economic policy and technologies,
economies that were once separated . . . now are linked in
an increasingly dense network of economic interactions.
This veritable economic revolution over the last 15 years
has come upon us so suddenly that its fundamental
ramifications for economic growth, the distribution of
income and wealth, and patterns of trade and finance
in the world economy are only dimly understood.*
—JEFFREY SACHS

*By the end of the 1980s, over two thirds of the American [U.S.]
workforce was employed in organizations with international
connections. . . . Indeed, it is now virtually impossible to conceive
of a completely domestic, unicultural organization or organizational communication practices that do not have intercultural dimensions. The Hudson report,* Workforce 2000,
*highlights the increasing racial, gender, ethnic, cultural,
lifestyle, and age mix of American organizations; the open
borders of the European Union have diversified their
workforces; the political upheavals across Europe, Asia, and
Africa have increased immigration, and communication
technologies have minimized the saliency of
geographical boundaries and national borders.*
—CYNTHIA STOHL[1]

CENTRAL THEMES

• The dominant perspective on organizations focuses on homogeneity and
separation. Managers are separated from workers; organizations are sepa-

rated from their environments, and employees are separated from their families and members of other organizations.

- Two processes—diversification and globalization—have challenged the dominant perspective by collapsing time and space. Organizations are increasingly heterogeneous, and "*different*" peoples are working in closer and closer proximity with one another.
- Organizational responses to increased diversification can be arrayed along a continuum from *denying* that it has occurred, to reducing its impact by attempting to *homogenize* the "*others*," to accepting their presence but *marginalizing* them, to confronting it as a positive development.
- In the long term, strategies of balanced innovation may affect significant change. They are sufficiently subtle to generate little resistance; although they make small changes, they can have major unintended consequences. Eventually, these small wins may actually change the dominant perspective and the power structure of organizations.
- Societal expectations and organizational processes combine to limit the organizational power and upward mobility of *other* employees.
- Confronting the dominant perspective begins in legitimate efforts to value "*others*" ways of acting and leading and by treating flexibility as more important than consistency.
- A number of factors have combined to make it increasingly difficult to balance home and work. Both organizations and individuals can take steps to enhance that balance.

KEY TERMS

Essentializing	Hostile environment/sexual
Quid pro quo sexual harassment	harassment
Glass ceilings	Glass walls
Familialism	*Machismo*
Simpatia	Flextime
Flexplace	Face time
Maquiladora	

Chapter 1 of this book introduced the concept of *hegemony,* the idea that the hierarchical relationships that exist in a society come to be treated as if they are *natural* (that is, inevitable) and *normal* (that is, expected and morally correct). As people *internalize* the values and assumptions of their societies they also internalize its class, race, gender, and ethnicity-based hierarchies. In Western societies, educated Anglo, middle- and upper-class men have traditionally been (and often still are) assumed to be superior to everyone else, at least in the public venues of organizations. But broad societal assumptions are only part of the story. Another part involves dominant assumptions about organizations and organizational life. At least since the industrial revolution, and especially since traditional strategies of organizing were first articulated (recall Chapter 2), organizations

have been defined as sites where managers control workers in an effort to maximize performance through rational decision making and the efficient use of
resources. In them, thinking is separated from doing, and the people responsible
for one activity are assumed to be very different from the people charged with
the other. Each group is relatively homogeneous in gender, education, class, and
race. This homogeneity enhances communication within each group and makes
it unlikely that a member of one group will ever occupy a position within the
other. Of course, neither societies nor their organizations have to be structured
and operated in accord with these assumptions. They reflect a group of *choices*
that societies and their members have made and reinforce through their everyday activities. People come to and view the choices they have made as normal
and natural and tend to forget that other forms of organizing are possible.

However, this dominant perspective has not gone unchallenged. One does
not have to observe organizations closely to realize that the doers possess a
great deal of task-related expertise and that the thinkers often act in nonrational
ways. Personal interests and political considerations often lead them to sacrifice
efficiency and organizational performance. Organizational power and managerial control are constantly resisted in many different ways. Instead of being the
smoothly oiled machines depicted in the dominant perspective, organizations
are sites where contradictions, fissures, and tensions are constantly being played
out. Relational, cultural, and networking strategies of organizing make it clear
that other options are available, and successful alternative forms of organizing
indicate that the assumptions themselves may be inaccurate.

During the past two decades, this dominant perspective has been challenged further by two processes—*diversification* and *globalization.* In many
ways the dominant view is based on notions of *distance* and *separation.* Managers are physically, sociologically, and psychologically separated from workers.
Each group tends to view the "*other*" as fundamentally different people with different tasks, interests, personalities, and motivations. Organizations are viewed
as "containers," separated from their environments and from "*other*" organizations.[2] Of course, every member of an organization recognizes that other people are out there, supplying their organization with raw materials, purchasing
the organization's products or services, regulating its activities, competing with
it in the market, and welcoming its members home at the end of the day. But,
each organization is separated from the "*others*" in its environment, and each
group of employees is separated from the "*other*" groups by space and time.

This way of viewing organizational reality simplifies and stabilizes everyone's organizational world and provides them with a degree of comfort and predictability. But, today's organizations are becoming increasingly heterogeneous,
especially in parts of the industrialized world. Moreover, the internal separation
between workers and managers—primarily white, educated, middle-to-upper
class, heterosexual males—has started to dissolve as women and nonwhite
employees have moved into professional and managerial positions. Simultaneously, many employees have rejected the arbitrary elevation of work over home
that characterizes the dominant view. For many people, relationships and family
take precedence over work and career and balancing the two has become a sig-

nificant challenge. Organizations are becoming increasingly *diversified*. And, increasingly since the breakup of the Soviet Union, organizations have been *globalized*. New technologies and the elimination of cold war barriers to economic activity have created global competition. Increasing levels of education in the non-Western world, especially among women, have combined with the creation of a truly global flow of capital and trade to create a new environment for organizations the world over.[3]

Each of these changes has increased the *proximity* between groups of "*others*," creating new challenges, new opportunities, and new demands on communicative processes. White, male, middle-to-upper class managers are no longer separated from nonwhite people or from women. These "*others*" comprise an increasing percentage of their employees and sit with them in executive dining rooms. Workers compete directly with people half a world away as well as with people down the street. The insulation, comfort, and predictability provided by traditional barriers is rapidly disappearing and the "*others*" who once were so far away are now right next door. Unfortunately, increased proximity does not automatically produce increased understanding or increased cooperation. It does mean that the dominant perspective is under increasing pressure. Modes of operating, social and organizational power relationships, systems of control and resistance, all are being changed. As the quotation by Jeffrey Sachs at the beginning of this chapter indicates, it is far too early to be able to predict the outcomes of these changes with any certainty. So, our goal in these final chapters is to help readers understand the processes that are at work. In this chapter we focus on proximity within organizations—the challenges of diversification. In Chapter 12 we focus on a broader definition of proximity and examine the challenges of globalization.

RESISTING "OTHERS"

During the 1960s, women started to move into professional and managerial roles throughout northern Europe. During the 1970s and 1980s these trends reached the United States, United Kingdom, and former Commonwealth countries (Canada, Australia, and New Zealand). Almost simultaneously, white women were joined by members of racial and ethnic minority groups. Today virtually every economy in the world is experiencing workforce diversification to some degree. Organizational responses can be arrayed along a continuum from *denying* that it has occurred, to trying to reduce its impact by attempting to homogenize the "*others*," to accepting their presence but attempting to marginalize them, to confronting it as a positive development. Different organizations and different societies respond in their own unique ways to the presence of different "*others*," just as different employees have unique experiences with diversification and develop distinctive strategies for dealing with resistance to the process. When discussing diversification, it is important to not **essentialize** the widely varying experiences and responses of individual members of different organizations, genders, classes, races, or individuals. Broad generalizations invariably obscure important differences in the experiences of the members of different societal groups. Employees' perceptions and actions are influenced by their culture, gender, race, and economic class; but they also are influenced by family values, personality characteristics, life history and a host of other individual attributes. Conversely, it is also important to recognize that there are similarities in the strategic options that are available to employees in different organizations and different societies. Consequently, their strategic choices also may be quite similar.[4]

Denying "Others" a Legitimate Place in the Organization

The simplest response to diversification, and the one that seems to be most common when an organization or economy is just beginning the process, is to deny the legitimacy of "*others*" presence in organizations. Denial is accomplished through exclusion, overt discrimination and/or through harassment. Its goal is to keep "*others*" out of the organization, persuade them to leave it prematurely, or force them to submit completely to the demands of dominant employees. In the West, discrimination usually is thought of in terms of overt bias in hiring and promotion decisions. First in northern Europe, then in Canada, the United States, and later in Australia, New Zealand, and southern Europe, a number of laws have been passed that make this kind of discrimination illegal. However, as the 1996 Texaco Oil case (recall Chapters 7 and 8) indicated, organizations often devise complicated strategies to circumvent or ignore these laws. Major corporations worldwide are regularly convicted of discriminating on the basis of race, sex, age, religion, or disability, or choose to settle cases out of court. Perhaps the most visible case in the United States in the year 2000 involved Coca Cola, which in November accepted a record $192.5 million out-of-court settlement of a case in which 2,000 current and former employees alleged that they were "systematically bypassed for raises and promotions" because of their race (the previous U.S. record was $176 million in the Texaco case). The plaintiffs complained of a closed promotion system in which job openings were filled by less qualified and experienced white employees without ever being announced in public. Plaintiffs also complained of Coca Cola's strategy of refusing promotions for minority employees on the grounds of budget constraints while finding ways to circumvent those constraints to promote whites. Plaintiff Elvenyia Barton-Gibson noted that "it's so unfortunate that in the year 2000, we are still fighting this kind of case. These should be dead issues."[5]

However, discrimination often goes far beyond formal hiring and promotion decisions, and in many countries, employees have little legal recourse when they are discriminated against. For example, during the 1980s and 1990s many governments in Asia (for example, Hong Kong, Taiwan, South Korea, and Singapore) and Latin America acted to weaken labor movements and legal protections afforded workers, sometimes in the guise of anticommunism. Their goal was to create the "industrial peace" necessary to attract investment by Western organizations. In turn, Western corporations who were moving their production operations to Latin America and Asia sought out a labor force of young, single women, who they believed would be easy to control. For example, a manager of a *maquiladora* (a plant owned by a U.S. firm but located in Mexico out of the reach of U.S. labor and environmental laws) on the U.S. Mexican border said that he preferred young and inexperienced female workers because they are "easier to shape to our requirements" and have a higher capacity for "eating bitterness."[6] Supervisors and labor contractors, almost all of whom are men, refer to women workers as "daughters," and treat them as "children" who should always "obey their parents (supervisors)." In societies where daughters are viewed as poor long-term investments, families and organizations often collude to have workers work long hours at low pay because a substantial proportion of their income is returned to the family. These payments help compensate for the expenses of raising a "low-worth" (female) child. A Taiwanese worker reported that the system left her feeling trapped, like a "frog beneath a coconut shell."

However, all control systems also spawn resistance. Workers often view their jobs and income as a means of gaining independence, a measure of self-esteem, and as a way to improve their technical skills and obtain better jobs. Outside of work, they reject traditional mores regarding dress; they form friendships with coworkers from communities with very different societal standards and demand the right to select their own husbands and begin to act like Western consumers. For example, in Malaysia sales of cosmetics quadrupled in only two years, in spite of a traditional link between cosmetics and prostitution. (Asia is now by far the fastest growing market for Avon products). Of course, with this increased independence has come an increase in economic and personal insecurity, and increased efforts by their local societies to more tightly control their behavior. In Asia and Latin America, the creation of a large, single, female labor force has led to increased public pressure for women to behave "properly." Malay women, as well as women workers in West Java and Thailand, are perceived as invading male (public) places, and their social activities are closely monitored and controlled. Transnational companies in Islamic countries hold religious classes in the workplace in an effort to enhance "moral discipline," including working hard and obeying orders without question. In both Latin American and Asian countries, multinational corporations control workers by appealing to feminine sex roles through beauty pageants and cooking classes.[7]

In industrialized economies, denial is more frequently expressed in various forms of harassment than in overt discrimination. Racial harassment and **quid pro quo sexual harassment** (where a person is promised rewards in exchange for sexual activity or threatened with punishment or job loss if they reject sexual proposals) have been illegal for some time. In 1994, Australia, following Europe, Canada, and the United States also made "**hostile environment**" harassment illegal. Two landmark cases from Australia help explain this concept. In 1989, a woman who was employed by Effective Cleaning Services to clean the Brisbane K-Mart store was told by K-Mart manager Brian Drysdale that she was a "naughty little girl who needed her bare bum smacked." He forced her to kneel beside him, ostensibly to clean under some cooking equipment, placed a hand on her head, lifted her t-shirt, and pulled down her pants and panties. On other occasions he lifted her off the ground, chased her around the room, made comments about her legs and bottom and repeatedly referred to her as a "naughty girl." When she complained to upper management, they believed Drysdale's denials of the events. The worker, who had been sexually abused as a child and adult, took her case to the Human Rights and Equal Opportunity Commission and won her case. Since Drysdale never demanded sexual activity, her case was not covered under laws regarding *quid pro quo* harassment. But, his behavior clearly created a hostile work environment based on her sex.

In virtually all Western countries, hostile environment laws were eventually expanded to encompass actions by coworkers that are known to management.[8] Again, Australia provides a typical case. Heather Horne and Gail McIntosh received compensation after being subjected to two years of verbal abuse, graffiti, and the display of soft- and hard-core pornography in their workplace, some of which the Western Australian Equal Opportunity Tribunal found to be grossly offensive and degrading. The worker's union sided with the organization, but the Tribunal did not. Damien Grace and Stephen Cohen explain the basis of the decision and why harassment often should be interpreted as a denial strategy:

> The display of pornography was anything but innocent. The two workers were bullied because they were different. This difference happened to be one of sex. It might as easily have been one of religion. . . . [T]he harassment is a particularly nasty display of sexism; the women were attacked as *women*. There was a clear assumption that women did not qualify for equal esteem with men . . . that they were powerless, and that they could be degraded through ridicule of their sex [emphasis in the original].[9]

As in similar cases in other industrialized countries, episodes such as these helped establish the illegality of hostile environment sexual harassment. Unfortunately, as the following case study indicates, harassment is still prevalent in organizations in the industrialized world, and the legal system is still emerging. In the United States, same-sex harassment was not ruled illegal until 1999, and educational institutions were not held liable for harassment of students until 2000. Laws regarding religious and age-based harassment are only now emerging in the United States and Canada as workforces become more diverse. Many societies—in Scandanavia, Southern Europe, Africa, and Asia—attempt to create conditions in which the distinctive contributions made by both male and female contributions can be combined and rewarded. But, in the United States, United Kingdom, and Commonwealth countries, treating members of different groups in similar ways is valued, and those values are enforced through antidiscrimination law. Consequently, legal gaps and inequities create greater disadvantages than they might in more communitarian societies.

In addition, there is some evidence that harassment—in both nonviolent and violent forms—is increasing in Europe and in the United States. Overt hostility in the workplace—racist, sexist, and homophobic slurs in conversations, hate mail/graffiti/faxes, sabotage of work projects and computer files, and physical assaults—may be increasing, suggesting that attitudinal barriers to diversity may be on the upswing.[10]

CASE STUDY:
THE HARASSMENT CASE

The 1990s provided substantial, repeated evidence of how pervasive sexual and racial harassment are in U.S. organizations. Professor Anita Hill's testimony during the U.S. Senate confirmation hearings for Supreme Court Justice Clarence Thomas brought the problem into the living rooms of everyone who owns a television set; the U.S. Navy's Tailhook scandal, in which a number of female officers were shoved down a crowded Las Vegas hotel hallway and molested by a large group of Navy aviators; and the forced resignation of Senator Robert Packwood for repeatedly harassing female staff members over more than a decade provided compelling evidence of the extent of the problem for those people who had doubted the veracity of Professor Hill's testimony. By the middle of the decade media reports of allegations of sexual harassment, out-of-court settlements, or convictions became commonplace. In August 1995, Del Labs of Farmingdale, New York, agreed to pay $1.2 million to settle a lawsuit in which CEO Dan Wasong was charged by fifteen employees with touching their breasts and buttocks, asking for oral sex, and using abusive sexual language. In April 1996, the U.S. Equal Employment Opportunity Commission filed a lawsuit against Mitsubishi Motors Corporation for allowing sexual harassment to continue at its Normal, Illinois, assembly plants. In November 1996, charges of rape, coerced sex, and sexual harassment of women trainees at the U.S. Army's Aberdeen (Maryland) Proving Ground led to the publication of past or ongoing sexual harassment cases at Fort Leonard Wood (Missouri) and Fort Hood (Texas). A toll-free hotline set up by the Army after the Aberdeen case became public received more than 4,000 calls reporting cases of harassment during its first ten days of existence. In January 1997, the Publix Grocery store chain announced an out-of-court settlement of a sexual discrimination and harassment case that dwarfs the Del Labs settlement, and, in turn, will be dwarfed by the Mitsubishi case should the plaintiffs eventually be awarded only a fraction of their $150 million claim.

However, our purpose in this case study is not to examine the frequency of racial or sexual harassment. The available evidence suggests that virtually all women and persons of color work in a hostile environment much of their lives. Surveys indicated that at least one-third of female students and employees experience overt sexual harassment; the figure increases to 70–90 percent if researchers explain the legal definition of sexual harassment to their respondents (Wagner, 1992). While *quid pro quo* harassment is widely understood and unambiguously illegal, *hostile environment* harassment is more difficult to define and prevent. During the late 1990s, U.S. courts consistently ruled that repeated physical affronts—touching, groping, or pinching—are illegal. Symbolic actions—written or oral comments including sexual jokes or lewd comments, or displays like nude pinups or obscene/pornographic displays in electronic media—are especially difficult to interpret. These activities are illegal only if they are sufficiently

(continued)

(continued from the previous page)

extreme and pervasive that a reasonable person would conclude that they create a *hostile and intimidating work environment,* they were unwanted, and they were known by the plaintiff's supervisors, or reasonably could be expected to have been known by them. Consequently, what constitutes a hostile environment varies across different courts and different cases. Some courts still use a reasonable person standard—would a reasonable person interpret the behaviors in question as constituting a hostile work or educational environment. Other courts have substituted a "reasonable woman" standard, because there is clear research evidence indicating that women generally perceive a wider range of symbols and behaviors to be unwanted, hostile, or intimidating than do men. The Mitsubishi Motors case provided an excellent example of the range of activities that may be illegal. The suit alleged that male workers called their female peers "sluts, whores and bitches;" they placed drawing of genitals and breasts and various sexual acts labeled with female employees' names on car fenders and cardboard signs along the assembly lines; explicit sexual graffiti such as "kill the slut Mary" were scrawled on rest-area and bathroom walls and one supervisor declared "I don't want any bitches on my line. Women don't belong in the plant;" anonymous callers made threats like "You better watch your back, bitch" or "Die bitch, you'll be sorry." Women were subjected to groping, forced sex play, and male flashing; one complainant found her car defaced; another was forced off the road as she drove home from work; and in another case a worker put an air gun between a woman worker's legs and pulled the trigger. However, only one of these actions—the supervisor's comment—is *in itself* illegal. Peer harassment is illegal only if supervisors are directly involved or know about, or could be expected to know about, the harassment. The allegations at Mitsubishi also claimed that plant management was repeatedly told of the actions and failed to take corrective measures.

Because of the threat of retaliation and intimidation if they complain, and because of the low likelihood of winning harassment cases (it is *very* difficult to produce sufficient evidence to meet the legal requirements) only about 10 percent of targets of harassment actually report the incidents. Fewer still file formal complaints. But our goal is not to examine the legal barriers that exist when women or persons of color attempt to find redress for their grievances; although those barriers are significant and important. The sources listed at the end of this case study provide excellent analyses of both of these issues. Instead, our goal is to briefly summarize the ways in which organizations hide harassment and suppress complaints of harassment. Not all cases of organizational efforts to suppress complaints are as blatant as Rear Admiral John Snyder's response to helicopter pilot Paula Coughlin's complaints about behavior at the Tailhook convention: "That's what you get when you go to a hotel party with a bunch of drunk aviators." Once Coughlin told her story to the press, the Navy conducted an investigation that was so sloppy that a year later the Navy was not even certain which of its pilots were among the seventy or so involved in the incident. In

(continued)

(continued from the previous page)

the end, the Navy investigation recommended punishment for only two aviators, one Australian and one U.S. Marine. Eventually, and again in response to public reports about the sloppiness of the investigation and resulting pressure from the House Armed Services Committee, a number of officers (including Admiral Snyder) were dismissed, and the Pentagon took over the investigation (Violanti, 1996). Because few readers of this case are autoworkers or ever will be naval officers, these examples of harassment may not seem terribly relevant. But there is substantial evidence that college and university students are frequent targets of racial and sexual abuse, and that their experiences and their university's responses are very much like those faced by career women. In all kinds of organizations, harassment is most likely when the organization accepts and reinforces what we have called the "dominant perspective"—that the "normal" employee is white and male, the number of "other" employees is small and people who are not Anglo men have few sources of support, the organization is loosely coupled (recall Chapter 8), making it difficult to obtain timely corrective action, and the power relationships between supervisors and their subordinates are highly unequal. Of course, each of these factors is present in most colleges and universities. In 1992 the *Journal of Applied Communication* (Eadie & Wood, eds.) published a special issue on sexual harassment that included 20 extended verbatim narratives written by people in the discipline of communication who have been sexually harassed. These stories are quite typical of instances of harassment in the academic (and organizational) world. Some of the cases provided summaries of the responses of the survivors' peers and of university administrations that are not unlike the response of the Navy or Mitsubishi's management; three are illustrative.

One new graduate student experienced three instances of unwanted sexual advances by professors. Soon after the third event, she confided in a senior Ph.D. student. Unknown to her, he called a meeting of the other doctoral students to discuss sexual harassment in the department. Although he protected the names of the professors, he revealed her identity. The doctoral students took no action, because many of them were working closely with a professor who had a reputation for harassment, and they did not want to make him uncomfortable. (He was not one of the three.) Because she could not even count on support from her peers, she decided not to pursue the matter any further (p. 367).

In a second case, the chair of a department told about a case that is still in progress. A woman student complained about actions by a professor that were both improper and illegal, although she did not file criminal charges. When the department chair first heard about the charge, she did not believe it. After all, the professor projected the image of an innocent choirboy and had recently published an essay in the school newspaper that provided a "feminist" analysis of sexual harassment. His outspoken support of women's issues had earned him strong support among women faculty. After a lengthy hearing, during which the professor received a leave of absence with pay (in most universities, these are

(continued)

(continued from the previous page)

highly sought-after awards, not punishments), he signed a statement admitting guilt and was allowed to return to normal duties provided he had no further contact with the student, would do nothing else to create an intimidating environment for women students, and would not socialize with students for a year. Although he has already violated the latter two terms, the administration has taken no action. His department chair has been "gagged" by the university's administration. If she were to warn any potential employers about his history she could lose her job; although she now knows he has been guilty of similar behavior at other universities. He was even dismissed from graduate school for sexual harassment; but that case too was kept confidential. Soon he will be looking for a new professorship. She concludes: "He will do a wonderful interview. You (other professors) will like him. Chances are you will hire him."

In a third case, a new assistant professor accepted a job in a department with a department chair who was reputed to be politically liberal. After two years on the job she felt secure enough to complain about her chair's repeated sexist comments and jokes: "Once, when I was advising a senior major, he stopped by my opened door, looked at me, and then turned and asked the student, 'Are there any cute girls in your (sorority) house?' She blushed and turned to me. 'You shouldn't say that!' I retorted. 'Oh, I'm sorry. Are there any cute tarts? Are there any cute wenches?' He quipped. I yelled his name emphatically, 'You know that's inappropriate.' 'I guess you think it's harassment (it is) and you're writing it down.' He responded as he smiled and walked away." The professor complained about the event in a private meeting with the affirmative action officer and asked specifically that her identity not be revealed. Less than an hour later, the officer revealed her identity to the department chair. Eventually she was not reappointed to her position, although her performance had been excellent, and she was refused access to written evaluations of her work. The university administration alerted the professor to irregularities in her case, but it did not want to overrule the department and granted her a probationary contract. Shortly before her final tenure review, one of her female colleagues filed a sexual harassment complaint against the chair. The female provost (a position equivalent to vice president in private-sector organizations) advised the professor not to support her colleague. With no support, her colleague resigned. The following year the professor was denied tenure. But in this case, the university administration overruled the department's decision and appointed the professor chair of her department.

As these cases suggest, successful complaints against professors for sexual harassment are quite rare. By the time action is taken, students have often completed their coursework with the harasser or have graduated. Universities often conduct harassment investigations in private; they do not notify victims of the date and times of hearings or allow them to testify and fail to inform the students of any actions taken against the harasser. The rationale for maintaining secrecy typically is that the matter is a personnel action and that the accused harasser

(continued)

(continued from the previous page)

deserves the protection of academic due process. If the university is a public institution, the professor also may be afforded some protection by the free speech considerations. But given the unequal power relationship that exists between harassers and targets, this conspiracy of silence primarily protects the university and the harasser from public embarrassment. More important, it lulls people into a complacent view that harassment is not a problem, creates skepticism and mistrust of the system among students (which mitigates against victims filing complaints), and leads victims to believe that they are alone in having been harassed, thus encouraging them (and others) to blame themselves. A Latina university employee explained that nonfaculty/nonstudent women have similar experiences:

> Everyone likes to pretend it doesn't happen. When you go from one position to the next in this university it's so small that bosses know each other and say, "Hey, this woman—watch out for her." So, you get blackmailed that way.

The cult of secrecy ensures that the university will never face any organized pressure to eliminate harassment of students.

For these reasons, in the landmark *Meritor v. Vincent* case, the U.S. Supreme Court ruled that targets of harassment can take legal action against their employers (or universities, in later rulings) without following internal procedures, although not doing so makes it more difficult to demonstrate that supervisors knew or should have known about the harassment. The reason for the court's decision is simple: It realized that those procedures rarely work.

Applying What You've Learned

1. What is *quid pro quo* harassment? *Hostile environment* harassment?
2. Why is harassment considered to be an issue of power/coercion?

Questions to Think About and Discuss

1. At a number of points in this book we have suggested that bureaucratic organizations typically suppress dissent, avoid conflicts, and restrict the flow of negative information. To what extent is the silence surrounding sexual or racial harassment simply another example of communication breakdowns in organizations? To what extent is it a function of racist or sexist attitudes? How might the two be interrelated?
2. Recently the U.S. Supreme Court ruled that sexual harassment of students violates Title IX of the Civil Rights Act and that women can now collect monetary damages from universities if they are harassed. What impact is this ruling likely to have on universities and their handling of sexual harassment cases?

(continued)

(continued from the previous page)

General Sources:

S. Bingham, ed., *Conceptualizing Sexual Harassment as Discursive Practice* (Westport, CT: Praeger, 1994).

Robin Clair, "The Use of Framing Devices to Sequester Organizational Narratives," Communication Monographs, 60 (1993): 113–136.

William Eadie and Julia Wood, eds., *Journal of Applied Communication Research*, 20 (1992): v–418.

G. Kreps (Ed.), *Sexual Harassment: Communication Implications* (Cresskill, NJ: Hampton Press, 1993).

David Terpstra and Douglas Baker, "Outcomes of Sexual Harassment Charges," *Academy of Management Journal, 31* (1988): 185–194.

Specific Cases:

Michelle Violanti, "Hooked on Expectations: An Analysis of Influence and Relationships in the Tailhook Reports," *Journal of Applied Communication Research, 24* (1996): 67–82.

Colleges and Universities:

Robin Clair, "The Bureaucratization, Commodification, and Privatization of Sexual Harassment Through Institutional Discourse," *Management Communication Quarterly, 7* (1993): 12–157.

Charles Conrad and Bryan Taylor, "The Contexts of Sexual Harassment: Power, Silences and Academe," in *Conceptualizing Sexual Harassment as Discursive Practice,* Shereen Bingham, ed. (Westport, CT: Praeger, 1994).

B.W. Dziech, *Sexual Harassment in Higher Education* (New York: Garland, 1998).

B.W. Dziech, and L. Weiner, *The Lecherous Professor,* 2nd ed. (Urbana, IL: University of Illinois Press, 1990).

Steve Lash, "Court Holds Educators Liable for Harassment," Houston *Chronicle,* 25 May, 1999: A1.

Paul Mongeau and Jennifer Blalock, "Student Evaluations of Instructor Immediacy and Sexually Harassing Behaviors: An Experimental Investigation," *Journal of Applied Communication Research, 22* (1994): 256–272.

M.A. Paludi and R.B. Barickman, *Academic and Workplace Sexual Harassment* Albany, NY: SUNY, (1991).

Denise Segura, "Chicanas in White-Collar Jobs," in *Situated Lives,* Louise Lamphere, Helena Razone, and Patricia Zavella, eds. (New York: Routledge, 1997).

Differences in Perceptions of What Constitutes Harassment

Denise Haunani Solomon & Mary Lynn Miller Williams, "Perceptions of Social-Sexual Communication at Work," *Journal of Applied Communication Research, 25*(1997): 196–216 and "Perceptions of Social-Sexual Communication at Work as Harassing," *Management Communication Quarterly, 11* (1997): 147–184.

Joann Keyton & Steven Rhodes, "Organizational Sexual Harassment," *Journal of Applied Communication Research, 27* (1999): 158–173.

Homogenizing "Others"

A second possible form of resistance to diversification is to accept it while trying minimize its impact. If "*other*" employees can be persuaded (or forced) to mimic the beliefs, values, and actions of organizational powerholders, their entry into organization will lead to little or no change. As Chapter 7 explained, "oldtimers" have a number of reasons for wanting newcomers to change to "fit in" to existing organizational roles and practices. These incentives are especially strong when the newcomer is "different."

The Discourse of Accommodation Regardless of the country that is involved, one of the most common responses to "different" employees is to encourage them to minimize their "differentness," to accommodate themselves to the norms of their organizations, to learn and use the communicative strategies of Anglo men. But people who are different (and in U.S. organizations this term encompasses people from lower socioeconomic classes, as well as African Americans, Latinos, Asian Americans, people with disabilities, and women) all find it immensely difficult to fit in. They clearly **are** different than the educated, middle-to-upper class, white males who dominate their organizations. In many cases, their lack of familiarity with the communication style of bureaucratic discourse makes fitting in all the more difficult.[11]

One means of doing so is always to *appear to be rational.* Because societal myths depict women, African American men, and Latinos as emotional (nonrational), using highly rational (that is, unemotional) forms of communication is especially important. A key part of the language of rationality is justifying decisions or proposals in data-based terms (recall Chapter 9) or in terms of the dominant values of the organizational culture. A second way of fitting in is to create an image of loyalty to the organization. In an era of rapid job turnover (recall the Generation X case study in Chapter 1), perceived loyalty is an even more powerful image. The most common way of creating perceptions of loyalty is to repeatedly signal that the organization is one's highest priority. Although the symbols of loyalty differ in various organizations, there seems to be one common component: sublimating all other activities and relationships to one's career and one's working relationships. Consistently taking work home, seeking and accepting promotions or transfers even when they would be disadvantageous to one's family and limiting social ties to business contacts all seem to be widely accepted indices of loyalty. Of course, there is little evidence that these activities are either a reliable sign of loyalty or necessary to the successful operation of organizations. But they are part of the symbolic reality that guides perceptions. In traditionally structured middle-and-upper class families (Ward and June Cleaver of *Leave It to Beaver* or Reverend and Mrs. Camden of *7th Heaven*), creating these impressions is possible. The professional's wife is available to serve as hostess, secretary, child-care specialist, and therapist. But for unmarried professionals or married women professionals, there often is no one available to play this "wifely" role.

Presumably the husbands of women professionals could assist in home activities. However, studies of time allocation have found that they often spend no more time doing home-related work than husbands whose wives do not work outside of the home. In many families, women are able to negotiate more equitable distributions of household work. For example, in separate studies Denise Segura and Beatri'z Pesquera examined how Latinas negotiated workload arrangements at home. Since Latin cultures strongly support traditional sex-role arrangements, they expected that Latinas would find these negotiations to be especially difficult. They did find that it was a struggle for Latinas to negotiate more equitable arrangements, just as it is a struggle for non-Latin women to do so. The title to Pesquera's study is taken from a comment made by one of the women she interviewed: "In The Beginning He Wouldn't Even Lift a Spoon or, as they say in Spanish, *no levanta ni una cuchara.* But, both researchers found that over time, couples often do negotiate more equitable task sharing, and that the dominant factors in their being able to do so are income and task requirements as much as culture.

White-collar Latinas bring a great deal of work home and have frequent evening meetings. Blue-collar Latinas often work evening or night shifts, or work more than one job. In both cases, the visible evidence of work spillover into family life makes it easier for them to negotiate more equitable arrangements with their husbands. Similarly, the closer a wife's income is to her husband's, the more bargaining power she has. But, they still have to negotiate. Pesquera observed that "women also utilize a variety of strategies in their daily struggle: they retrain, coach, and praise husbands for a job well done. At times they resort to slowdowns or work stoppages, so that eventually men are forced to contribute more to household labor." Husbands respond by stalling, doing slipshod work, or discrediting their wives by comparing about them to women who do even more household work.[12] Many women find it easier to give up the struggle and do the work themselves. In fact, the total number of nonleisure hours worked by women employed full time is almost double the total for traditional housewives.[13] As a result, the Center for Creative Leadership found that 25 percent of the women they interviewed said that balancing work and family concerns was one of the greatest challenges they faced, while only 10 percent of the men shared this concern

Of course, discourse that advises women and minority employees to strive to fit in rarely recognizes the complications that are involved in doing so. Employees are told to actively seek promotions that involve relocation and assignments that involve travel, to stay with the same firm for long periods of time, and to make decisions about their non-organizational life that put their careers and organizations first—choosing not to marry, to delay marriage, or to wait to begin a family until after they are well established in their careers.[14] If they do marry or form long-term partnerships, they are advised to negotiate a lifestyle with their partners that allows them to pursue their careers and simultaneously participate in a fulfilling family life.

Given the very real difficulties involved in following this advice, it is somewhat surprising that so many women in U.S. firms have been able to do so. Executive women change jobs for career, not family, reasons and are as likely or more likely to relocate to further their careers than are male executives; and they take the same number of vacation days. But ironically, in spite of this evidence, upper managers still *perceive* that women put family before career and *believe* they will turn down assignments involving travel or relocation, and so on. So, when women *do* experience career interruptions, they have a disproportionately negative effect on their careers. Women lose seniority, opportunities for training, and salary: "The first year back your wages are 33 percent lower than women who didn't leave. Over time, that difference diminishes (to 20 percent over 3–5 years and 10 percent after 11–20 years) but it never disappears."[15]

A final strategy that women and minority employees are told will help them fit in is to develop an exceptional performance record. Virtually all studies of the upward mobility of successful women and African Americans and Latinos in

U.S. firms have found that their performance had to be better and more consistent than the performance of Anglo men. A Latina white-collar worker told Denise Segura that:

> "I've seen it! In interviews with a white candidate, they see it written on the paper and they say, "Isn't this great!" But, when you bring a Latina in, it's almost like they're drilled: "Tell us;" "Give us examples;" "How long did you do it?" . . . You always have to prove yourself. . . . You almost have to fight harder to demonstrate that you can do a job just as well."[16]

This pattern is explained in part by overt discrimination. But it also is related to the weak link between performance and rewards that exists in most organizations. Excellent performance is rewarded only if it also is *visible* to the organization's powerholders and only if they *perceive* that it provides evidence of exceptional competence. But, how does one make his or her performance visible? The simplest way is to tell others about it. Even simple strategies are complicated by societal assumptions. In many societies, openly talking about one's successes is unacceptable. An employee must rely on communication through informal networks. But, "*different*" employees often are excluded from those networks. In Western societies, men typically learn to be more comfortable talking about their exploits than most women do. In fact, they tend to exaggerate their successes ("I caught a fish/made a sale/won a case that was *this* big") and to express them in comparative and competitive terms. Women brag less frequently; they tend to understate their accomplishments and attribute their successes to other members of their team. As a result, males' bragging creates impressions of competence, confidence, pride, and success (all positively valued in managerial settings) while females' bragging makes people like them more and praise them for being sensitive, not for being successful.[17]

For women and members of minority groups, visibility is paradoxical in other ways. In organizations or units that have small numbers of women, African Americans, or Latinos (Rosabeth Moss Kanter has suggested that 15 percent is a crucial level), the ones who are there often live in "glass houses". As one woman executive explained, "There is an element of derailment built into the system for women—the pressure created by having to be a role model and a 'first' along with personal competency. Men don't have to deal with this added pressure." Another admitted that "I feel that if I fail, it will be a long time before they hire another woman for the job. . . . Carrying that burden can lead women to play it safe, to be ultraconservative, to opt out if a situation looks chancy." Everyone makes mistakes. If powerholders focus on an employee's mistakes instead of successes, or if they attribute an occasional error to a person's race or sex, visibility becomes a barrier, not an advantage.[18]

Differential Perceptions and Attributions   The visibility paradox is further complicated by perceptual and attributional processes. Societal myths about race, gender, and ethnicity create perceptual sets through which people *interpret* events and actions. Researchers have long recognized that, in general, subordinates receive significantly higher ratings from persons of their own race and sex, even when objective performance standards are used. This results in part from the continuation of overtly racist attitudes and behaviors, as the Texaco, Coca Cola, and other cases so clearly indicate. But differential evaluation also seems to occur even when overt racial biases are not evident.[19]

Societal assumptions also influence attributions. Even when excellent performance by women, African American men, or Latinos is made visible, it may be attributed to factors outside of the employee's control—luck, special advantages, the help of other employees, the effectiveness of the organization as a whole, or high motivation and effort (which cannot be sustained over the long term)—rather than to skill and expertise. Even when performance is attributed to the same factors, it may have different effects. If a white male's success is attributed to hard work, it usually helps his career because evaluators assume that he is also competent. But when a woman's or minority employee's success is attributed to hard work, evaluators tend to assume that it disguises limits to her or his competence, so it may do little to help him or her advance in the organization.[20] In addition, supervisors also seem to feel and express less confidence in their evaluations of women and minority subordinates than of their white male subordinates. When evaluators express a lack of confidence in their judgments about an employee's performance, it creates less positive perceptions than the performance merits. In organizations, as in the rest of life, perceptual "realities" are more important than actual performance.

Finally, Anglo male supervisors tend to base their evaluations of African American and Latino/Latina subordinates more on the extent to which they *conform* to the organization's norms of behavior than on their performance (the reverse is true for Anglo subordinates). As a result, "fitting in" is transformed from a means to an end. In general, Anglo male supervisors and employers feel more comfortable with people who they perceive as similar to them and tend to promote similar people. Because Latinas and African American women are most dissimilar, they are least likely to be promoted. To complicate matters further, Anglo male supervisors are often unaware of their perceptions or the role that those perceptions play in their actions toward and evaluations of women and African Americans and Latinos.[21] "*Different*" employees experience a complex web of double binds as they try to fit in to organizations in which being a white male is perceived to be "normal" and "natural."

Dealing with Homogenization   There is substantial evidence that white women in Northern European, U.S., and Commonwealth organizations are beginning to break through the **glass ceiling** successfully. Although the concept is most often associated with women, it also applies to members of ethnic and religious minority groups and to people with disabilities. And, it is a worldwide phenomenon.[22] Progress for Latino, African American and Asian American men has been slower, but still is substantial. Members of all four groups seem to have found ways to balance the conformity demands of organizations while maintaining their own distinctive styles of leading and managing. They may accept the overall constraints imposed by their organizations but find ways to create cohesive, high-performing work groups within those constraints. For example, they may maintain a highly structured, unemotional mode of communicating with people outside of their units, but encourage openness and honest communication with their subordinates while providing them with support for creative risk taking.[23] Educated Muslim immigrants in U.S. firms seem to adopt the attitudes and behaviors of their organizations while at work, but retain their original culture outside of work (especially if they are highly committed to their faith).

African American and Asian American women, as well as Latinas, have experienced less progress, in part because they are doubly (or triply, if socio-economic class is included) "*different*" from the white male norm. Consequently, even politically conservative commentators admit that the progress has been slow and mixed. The glass ceiling once was assumed to be located at the level of middle management. Above that point in an organization's hierarchy, the number of openings falls rapidly, and performance evaluation becomes much more subjective. However, recent research has found that the ceiling is even lower than middle management for Anglo women, and lower still for African Americans and Latinos/Latinas. This does not mean that the ceiling cannot be penetrated—there are a number of noted successes—but it does suggest that the combination of differences in opportunity and societal attitudes make it difficult to do so. And "the barriers to the upper rungs of the corporate ladder for minority women appear to be nearly impenetrable;" the percent of Latinas, African American and Asian women in the corporate offices of Fortune 500 firms (1.3 percent) has not changed in recent years.[24]

In the long term, these strategies of balanced innovation have the potential for effecting significant change. They are sufficiently subtle to generate little resistance, while making small changes that over the long term will have major unintended consequences. Eventually, these small wins may actually change the power structure of bureaucratic organizations. For example, if the supervisor of one division of an organization successfully implements structural changes, such as **flextime** (allowing employees to work schedules that fit their needs) or **flexplace** (allowing people to work at home whenever possible), it may serve as a model for other divisions and eventually for the organization as a whole. When significant numbers of "*different*" employees enter organizations they *will* truly be different, and they eventually and *inevitably will* have to make fundamental changes. When the upper levels of organizational hierarchies begin to include some people who are not Anglo men, new perspectives, values, and ideas will become part of the discourse of upper management. When substantial numbers of Anglo men have worked successfully with women and persons of color as peers below the glass ceiling, they will bring more positive attitudes with them when *they* move into upper management.[25]

Marginalizing "Others"

A third possible organizational response to increased diversification is to accept "different" others presence in the organization, but to isolate them in "spaces" that have relatively low levels of power. In some societies these spaces often are literal—in Mongolia, South America, India, the Philippines, and North Africa, women workers tend to be segregated in homes or "out-of-the-way" places in their organizations—and serve to isolate them from potential sources of power and influences. In U.S. organizations, they are more likely to be placed in relatively powerless departments.[26] Obtaining power is crucial to upward mobility. It also is necessary to achieve a number of other personal and career goals, such as effectively serving one's customers and clients, successfully obtaining and completing challenging and meaningful projects, and so on. As Chapter 8 explained, power is closely related to one's place in the formal structure of one's organization.

Manipulating Opportunity Structures   Latinos, African Americans, and Anglo women often are in industries that provide little opportunity for advancement and divisions of organizations that have low levels of power. This location results in part from broad socialization processes. From preschool through graduate school, women are encouraged to enter "nurturing" or "people-oriented" fields, and African Americans and Latinos are encouraged to pursue "applied" or "practical" (as opposed to theoretical or managerial) careers. As a result, women, Latinos, and African American men often choose careers in service organizations—finance, real estate, or retail trade—or staff-oriented specializations, such as personnel administration or corporate communication. Service organizations tend to have flat structures that provide few opportunities for advancement. Staff positions have relatively low levels of organizational power and staff managers tend not to be given significant assignments or receive advanced training. Even when African American men, Latinos, and women do not "choose" staff-related careers, organizations tend to shunt them in those directions anyway. For example, only 7.3 percent of *line* divisions (those that contribute directly to the profitability of the firm) in the Fortune 500 (the largest 500 firms in the United States) have women managers, although this represents a significant increase over the 5.3 percent in 1997. Because virtually all organizations require upper managers to have line experience, being limited to staff positions reduces one's organizational power and may preclude one being promoted. Virtually all the 1,622 women among the 12,945 corporate officers (12.5 percent, up from 8.7 percent in 1995) Fortune 500 firms have had substantial line experience. Staff positions seem to be surrounded by "**glass walls**" and these walls may be the greatest barrier to upward mobility for women and minority managers.[27]

Of course, creating racially and gender-segregated sectors of an organization also reduces organizational effectiveness. People who have the same backgrounds and experiences are more prone to problems of "trained incapacity," "groupthink," and communication breakdowns. Organizations with one unit or subculture composed of all upper-class Anglo males and other units or subcultures made up of people with widely differing attributes and experiences tend to have low levels of cross-sector cooperation and high levels of cross-unit communication breakdowns.[28] But upper managers' preferences for coworkers with whom they are comfortable seem to be more important in promotion decisions than concerns about efficient communication or "objective" decision making.

Dealing with Marginalization   To compensate for "glass walls," women and members of racial/ethnic minority groups actively prepare for, seek out and accept assignments in traditionally Anglo male occupations, industries, and specializations. Although doing so often means that they will suffer temporary financial losses or personal dislocation and will have to deal with more extensive sexism/racism and sexual/racial harassment than they would experience in service/staff positions, their long-term career prospects will increase.[29] Interestingly, many women seem to have recognized that these barriers continue to exist and have responded by starting organizations of their own. During the 1980s a much larger number of women—one of three MBAs in one study— have left large organizations to start their own businesses. These decisions were motivated in part by anticipation of the freedom, excitement, and feelings of achievement that accompany succeeding in running one's own business in a highly competitive environment. But they also stemmed from frustration with gender-related barriers in their old firms that kept them from being rewarded adequately and equitably for their contributions, and from moving into positions of greater challenge and creativity.

The growth has been remarkable. In 1980, there were two million women-owned businesses with $25 billion in sales or receipts; in 1999 there were 9.1 million with 27.5 million employees and $3.6 trillion in sales or receipts. Thirty-eight percent of U.S. businesses are now owned by women. In California the number of women-owned companies has increased 164 percent since 1992. In 1996, 405,200 African American women owned businesses with 261,400 employees and sales of $24.7 billion, a 137 percent increase over 1986. In Australia about one-half of small businesses are owned by women, and their growth rate is double that of small businesses owned by men. Women entrepreneurs are just as successful as male entrepreneurs; they provide better benefits packages for their employees (especially in the United States and Mexico) and play an increasing role in traditionally male sectors of the economy such as construction, transportation, agriculture, and manufacturing.[30] Consequently, as a result of their inability or unwillingness to meet the personal and career needs of professional women, large, complex organizations have lost a great deal of talent and expertise and in the process have created a large number of effective competitors. Unfortunately, limited access to investment capital makes it difficult for women or persons of color to become entrepreneurs; but they are slowly overcoming those barriers. Banks are reticent to make loans to women entrepreneurs, and only two percent of loans made by venture capitalists (the individuals or organizations who fund start ups) go to women (far less than one percent go to minority entrepreneurs). As a result, most women draw on personal assets or loans from friends and family to start their businesses in the United States, Europe, and the Commonwealth countries.[31]

CONFRONTING THE DOMINANT PERSPECTIVE

Organizations have a variety of strategies available to resist workforce diversification. Each of these strategies sacrifices the potential benefits of diversity, but allows the organization to avoid making changes. "*Other*" employees use an equally varied group of strategies to overcome organizational resistance. An alternative approach is for organizations to recognize the potential benefits of diversity, and devise strategies for confronting the dominant perspective.

Valuing "Others'" Ways

A number of researchers have noted that the people who make up the workforce of today's organizations in the industrialized world have a different set of core values than those that are included in the dominant perspective. Virtually absent are an unquestioning loyalty to the organization and an obsession with the pursuit of money. Instead, today's workers value recognition, feelings of accomplishment, being treated with respect and dignity, psychological involvement and pride in meaningful work (recall Chapter 3), and quality of life, including opportunities for self-development, health, and wellness. These values are inconsistent with traditional, bureaucratic strategies of organizing and are consistent with the more flexible, relationship-, culture-, and network-oriented strategies that were described in Unit I. They underlie a pattern of acting and a set of leadership strategies that are especially appropriate to the turbulent and globally competitive environments faced by modern organizations.

Others' Ways of Communicating and Acting   All employees, but especially supervisors, need to develop a high level of awareness of cultural differences and a positive view of diversity. Achieving this change in attitudes will be difficult in societies that still resist racial integration of schools and public accommodations, maintain largely segregated housing patterns, demand that others adopt the language and mores of the dominant perspective, and incorporate little international/intercultural education into their school curricula. For example, in 1979 the first major U.S. government report that advised academic organizations to increase training in foreign (non-English) language and international cultures was published. A decade later only 23,000 U.S. college students were studying Japanese, while 20 million Japanese were studying English. Today the figures are not significantly different, although the number of Anglos learning Spanish has increased in the five states with large Latino populations (NY, CA, TX, FL, and AZ). Change has been almost as slow in noneducational organizations. U.S. firms spend a small percent of their training budgets on international/intercultural education (10–15 percent). Even though American employees are critical of their international colleagues' errors when speaking English and believe that these breakdowns hurt productivity, they make no attempt to learn even the most simple foreign phrases.[32] In contrast, international firms take language learning much more seriously. In fact, the two major Japanese banks spend 50 percent of their training funds on international training.

Although, the cultural myopia of U.S. citizens is widely known and criticized, lack of cross-cultural understanding is a worldwide problem. A survey of 1,300 Japanese managers and their Southeast Asian subordinates found that the managers thought their local colleagues were illogical, indecisive, and inflexible, and the local managers perceived that their Japanese supervisors were secretive, intolerant, and inflexible. And, major cultural differences exist within countries.[33] For example, important linguistic and cultural differences have existed between northern and southern China for centuries, and between rural and urban China for decades. Rice University in Houston, Texas conducts popular training programs that are designed to explain Texas and Texan culture to "expatriates" who have been transferred to the Republic from the rest of the United States.

Fortunately, resistance to diversity can be reduced to some extent through education. Sensitivity training helps employees become aware of their own cultural biases and helps them more accurately interpret "*other*" employees' actions. For example, an Anglo male supervisor may misinterpret an Asian Americans' (or Latino/Latinas') respect for modesty and deference to authority as evidence of lack of leadership skills or managerial competence.[34] To succeed, diversity training must help participants understand at least six key concepts that differentiate cultures:

• Individualistic and communitarian orientations
• High- and low-context meaning systems
• Different versions of time and time consciousness
• Relational definitions, including the role of hierarchy in relationships
• Distinctive values and behavioral norms
• Different work habits and practices, including communication

We have examined the contrast between individualism and communitarianism throughout this book. Chapter 7 examined high and low context meaning systems and the role that listening plays in each. Cultures also differ in the time orientation that is taught to their members. Some value precision and exactness (e.g., Germany) and view violations of "normal" schedules as a serious affront (recall the expatriate case in Chapter 7); others value flexibility (e.g., Latin societies, although the influx of multinational employees is rapidly changing this norm in urban areas). In some cultures, obeying "promptness" rules depends on one's rank, age, or status; in others everyone is expected to use the same clock. When New York's Corning corporation began collaborating with Mexican firm Vitro, Mexican employees sometimes felt that Corning moved too fast to integrate the two operations. (They also found the Americans to be too blunt and direct.) The Americans felt that Vitro was moving too slowly (and that their dogged pursuit of politeness kept them from acknowledging problems that needed to be dealt with).[35]

In some cultures, relationships are defined solely by organizational rank and expertise; in others they are influenced by non-organizational considerations, such as age, kinship, sex, and wealth. In some societies, intimate relationships are expected to be monogamous; in others polygamy (multiple wives) and polygandry (multiple husbands) is normal. In some, providing access to alcohol and prostitutes is a normal part of business entertaining; in others it is a capital offense. In short, people in different cultures are pleased, worried, annoyed, and embarrassed by different things; conventions and rituals mean different things, and showing respect and deference vary in importance. A final dimension of intercultural organizational communication involves work: Different societies socialize their members to accept different attitudes about work, tasks, the division of labor, and various practices, punishments, and rewards.

Well-designed diversity programs also focus on communication itself. For example, the Canadian International Development Agency's predeparture program for its expatriates provides training in seven core communication skills:

- Communicating respect (in the language/behavior of the host society)
- Being nonjudgmental (of others' attitudes, beliefs, and behaviors)
- Recognizing the influence of one's own perceptions and knowledge
- Being empathic (trying to understand the others' point of view and life situation)
- Being flexible (being able to accomplish a task in a manner and time that is appropriate to the host culture and the other's needs)
- Demonstrating reciprocal concern (actually listening and promoting shared communication)
- Tolerating ambiguity, especially about cultural differences

The goal of these programs is to convince managers not to define "*differences*" as "*deficiencies.*" All organizational change efforts are difficult to implement; diversification training is even more difficult. After years of designing and conducting such programs Carnevale and Stone warn that

> In most organizations, valuing and managing diversity requires nothing less than cultural transformation. This is a prodigious task, for it requires people— especially those in the dominant culture—to let go of the assumptions about the universal rightness of their own values and customary ways of doing things in order to become receptive to other cultures.[36]

And even well-designed and conducted diversity training can have negative, unintended consequences. If they focus solely on *differences* among employees, the values, beliefs, and experiences that they have *in common* may be obscured. The result is to perpetuate stereotypes and polarize the workforce. For example, Ellen Castro became a successful consultant after she left her job as a manager of 500 employees in a $90 million retail profit center in response to her boss's use of ethnic slurs. She explains how her experience led to her current approach to consulting:

> [At first] I did it the man's way, the Anglo man's way. I've [since] learned that if you don't let people be who they are, they won't be authentic or creative. I know what it's like to be in an environment where you can't be yourself. It took a toll on my spirit. I don't think employers can afford to do that today. . . . [So, you have to value differences. But] what you [often] do with these programs is emphasize how we're different, that people can get their feelings hurt. But what about how we're alike? All employees want respect. We all want to be involved in decision making. By emphasizing "diversity" we've created a chasm. Instead, let's look at people for who they are, what's their best skill? What can she bring to the table as a female? Diversity is not going to work until you have a culture where everyone is given respect and dignity.[37]

Others' Ways of Leading   In a now-classic study, Sally Helgessen compared the day-by-day work activities of (primarily Anglo) male managers to those of (primarily Anglo) female managers. She found that males tend to work at an unrelenting pace, with no scheduled breaks during the day. Their days are characterized by interruptions, discontinuity, and fragmentation. They spend little time in long-term planning or reflecting on their goals or the effectiveness of the strategies they use. They prefer face-to-face communication to written messages, but have difficulty sharing information with coworkers and subordinates. Anglo women, Helgessen observed, also tend to prefer face-to-face interactions. They work at a steady pace and schedule small breaks during the day; they take a broader and long-term perspective instead of focusing solely on day-to-day activities; they actively share information with others and gain satisfaction from *both* the process of working *and* its results. They define power as the ability to *act with* others to accomplish goals that could not be achieved by individuals acting alone, rather than as *power over* others (recall Chapter 8). Leadership involves empowering others, being at the *center* of a group rather than in front of it. Leaders' claims to expertise and authority must be justified continually and be explained to other employees in terms they can readily understand.[38]

Research with Latinos and Latinas also suggests a preference for a particular form of leadership. Latin cultures are grounded in the concepts of familialism, *machismo*, and *simpatía*. **Familialism** involves strong values attached to family and community, and a commitment to hard work and achievement as a way of honoring one's family. It also involves aiding others who are in need. It is for this reason that having a job that pays low wages is even more stressful for Latinos than for other males. **Machismo,** a concept that is widely misunderstood by non-Latinos/Latinas, embraces a strong sense of loyalty and duty to other members of the community and a sense of honor and duty, not to an impersonal organization, but to other people. **Simpatía** is a complex concept that involves engaging in positive, agreeing behaviors whenever possible, showing respect for one's superiors by conforming to their wishes, and avoiding conflict and confrontation *in public settings*. But it does not mean conformity and blind obedience, because it also requires superiors to show respect to their subordinates, especially in public. These values lead to a high level of concern for interpersonal relationships and the feelings of other people, a participatory, open-door leadership style, and a preference for face-to-face communication. They also generate a desire for fair treatment and high levels of freedom and autonomy. Latino/Latina supervisors tend to feel a responsibility for developing their subordinates' skills and abilities. Latin culture also encourages a high level of flexibility in leadership strategies, including a willingness to ignore the formal chain of command when it is inefficient. African Americans and Asian Americans also seem to lead by developing cooperative work teams, openly sharing information, encouraging participation in decision making, and helping to develop all employees' expertise.[39]

In sum, Anglo men tend to use what Chapter 2 called "transactional leadership." Women, Latinos, African American, and Asian American men prefer what Chapter 4 called "transformational leadership," an approach that is particularly well suited to the turbulent environment of a competitive, global economy. Of course, individual employees have had their own distinctive developmental experiences and may have developed leadership styles that deviate from both their general cultural backgrounds and the norms of their organizations. However, if organizations pressure "*others*" to adopt transactional leadership styles, as they seem to do much more frequently in U.S. firms than in European organizations, they sacrifice the strengths that can come with diversity.[40]

Challenging the Underlying Attitudes of the Dominant Perspective

Instead of resisting diversification, organizations can confront the dominant perspective directly by valuing attitudes that are appropriate to a diverse workforce in a global environment. The key assumptions of the dominant perspective were that thinking and doing should be separated; the thinking function should be treated as superior and should be conducted by a group of people who were similar to one another in every possible respect, and actions should be guided by stable policies and procedures that are arrived at through rational decision making. Employees should be chosen based largely on how well they fit into the existing organization, and once they arrive, they should be encouraged to adapt to an existing organizational role. Of course, attempting to assimilate employees into existing organizational practices and valuing diversity are contradictory ideas.[41]

The most important attitudinal change in confronting the dominant perspective is to celebrate *flexibility*. It has two components: *Recognizing* that achieving goals of equity and effectiveness does not mean treating everyone in the same way, but means treating them all fairly; and *believing* that organizations should be adapted to fit the needs and develop the talents of every *individual* employee, instead of *demanding* that every employee adapt to the organization. An organization needs to make very different adjustments to utilize fully the talents of a single mother of two preschoolers, a computer programmer who is confined to a wheelchair, a deaf investment counselor, a group of Latina production workers, or a middle-aged Anglo male who has "*plateaued*" (reached the highest level in the organization that he will ever reach). For example, the Aluminum Company of America (ALCOA) hired Kevin Kennedy, an operations engineer who had a degenerative eye condition that restricted his peripheral vision and would eventually lead to blindness. Instead of declaring that Kevin inevitably would be incapable of doing his job, ALCOA's management asked how the organization could enable Kevin to continue to contribute. They assigned an assistant to help him when his job involved operating large industrial machinery or visiting plants with which he was unfamiliar. When his vision deteriorated further, the organization responded by redefining his duties so that they focused on computer modeling; they provided special lighting for his workspace and a large magnifying glass to help him read and purchased a large-screen computer and software for converting written texts to Braille. In this way the company was able to retain a highly competent employee at a cost far below what it would take to hire and train a replacement.[42] In the process, they discovered what researchers have known for some time—meeting the needs of disabled workers is far less expensive than managers tend to believe that it will be.

The Hallmark Corporation no longer encourages members of its artistic staff to specialize. Instead it rotates new employees through a number of different assignments to give them a wide range of actual job experiences. If potential candidates for a promotion lack a specific set of skills, the organization may assign them to a different department for six months or so to give them a chance to develop the skills necessary to move up. In some cases, the employees may discover that they are better suited for the division to which they are temporarily assigned, and the organization does everything possible to facilitate a move to that division. Traditionally, promotion has meant abandoning one's technical specialty and becoming a manager. But many people who have exceptional technical skills do not have the interests or abilities necessary for them to be successful managers. So, they are forced to either remain in the same unchallenging positions or move into a role with which they are uncomfortable. Diversity management proposes that organizations create alternative career paths, in which people stay within their specialties but receive promotions and increasingly complex technical assignments, or which allow people to cycle in and out of management positions.

Another attitudinal change involves focusing on *outcomes* instead of constraints. Different employees produce the best outcomes if they are enabled to do their jobs in their own ways. Jim James, a research engineer, had promised his wife that he would retire in two months. He knew he would not be able to finish the project that he was working on in that amount of time. His supervisor decided that his expertise on the project was too valuable to lose, so he arranged to have James spend 20 hours a week as a consultant to the firm and to be assigned a co-op student from the local university as a research assistant. He was able to arrange his own working schedule, keep his commitment to his wife, and offer his firm expertise on specified projects that only he could provide.

CASE STUDY:
THE CASE OF ROSA N.*

In many parts of the world the kind of blatant racism, sexism, and discrimination described in the denial section of this chapter is becoming less common. Two such places are The Netherlands and California, both of which have the reputation of being racially progressive and tolerant when compared to other European countries or U.S. states. People articulate the virtues of pluralism, deny the presence of racism in their communities, and condemn its presence in other societies. One would expect them, and the organizations that operate within them, to be sites in which race is not an important part of people's everyday experiences. Philomena Essed

(continued)

(continued from the previous page)

decided to test this assumption through a very simple process—conducting extensive interviews with 55 black women about their everyday experiences, both at work and outside of their organizations. Rosa N. was typical of these women.

She was born in Suriname in 1951, but lost both parents before age 10. Her mother's sister adopted her and raised her along with four other daughters. After finishing high school in Suriname she receives a scholarship to study medicine in The Netherlands where she specialized in geriatrics. She married a Dutch man. When Essed interviewed her, she was an intern in a medical research complex. She had never been physically molested; her life had never been threatened. She rarely has had to deal with blatant "bigots;" has been called a "black whore" only once; is gifted and successful. So, as Essed says, "What is the problem?" Her answer, based on all of her interviews, is that race is subtly woven into the fabric of everyday life. And dealing with is complicated by the notion that "racism just doesn't happen here" and with her coworkers' fervent belief that they are not racist. As Rosa says, "If you want to say something about racism, you've got to state your case very well. . . otherwise they tackle you. . . and they make you look ridiculous." You appear to be overly sensitive, and overly emotional.

For the only Black woman in her med school (and the only black woman physician in her medical center), "fitting in" was almost impossible for Rosa. Even when she didn't feel different than the Dutch, her fellow students reminded her that she wasn't like them. She remembered making a phone call in a dorm when a Dutch man said "There's Rosa with that laugh of hers." She was laughing loudly, as Surinamese people do. But, she doesn't do it anymore, except when she is alone with her husband Rob; nor does she use any of the other aspects of the communicative style of her homeland: "It was always getting thrown in my face."

Rosa was more often offended by the way in which other members of minority groups—especially Turks and Moroccans—were treated than by the way she was treated. In a surgery class a professor talked about an industrial accident in which a Turk had sliced open his hand (which eventually became so infected that it had to be amputated). He repeatedly insulted his patient: "That stupid Turk. His hand is not a can!" He made fun of another "stupid foreigner" who had lost his heel in an industrial accident. He never explained that "foreigners" are more prone to industrial accidents because the Dutch do not do dangerous factory work, foreigners do. Rosa recalled:

> The students thought it was real funny. They don't give it much thought, because it arouses a kind of hilarity when it's told that way. Then everybody laughs about it. . . . I waited until the man was finished. The lights went on, I told him he should make remarks like that again because they are offensive, and I chose that attitude because I thought: I must not become uncontrolled, agitated, or aggressive (1991, pp. 149-150).

> And then one time in a general health class, this extremely stupid civil servant blamed the foreigners for overpopulation. I said something about that then, but

(continued)

(continued from the previous page)

> what struck me was that someone said: oh, there's Rosa with that racism again. . . . And I thought, I'll turn in a complaint. But—and that really disappointed me—when I asked a few people I got on well with if they would testify, the one said, like no, because I have a child and a job I don't want to lose. . . . Then I spoke with my advisor, and he gave me some literature which showed that it has never been demonstrated that foreigners cause overpopulation. [However, because the Dutch reproduction rate is negative and their immigration policy allows immigrants into the country to do menial jobs, the proportion of foreigners in the population is growing]. I very politely sent the man a letter. He sent such a nasty letter back. It was a totally degrading letter that . . . attacked me on personal points: that I had used my boss's FAX number—while my boss had even approved my letter (1991, p. 50).

In fact, race infused comments were made directly to her in strange ways. A student introduced a patient who had genital herpes by noting that she was Surinamese. Then "he looked at me and said: sorry. I thought, what's all this? Why in God's name does he say 'sorry?!' Then another student patted me on the back [in sympathy]." The student went on to say, "Oh, yeah women in Suriname have more than one man. I jumped in immediate with, then everyone in Suriname must have herpes!" When Rosa came back after lunch, her boss "came up and said: you reacted in a way in which you did not want to react. That was true enough. . . . But afterward, what surprised me was [that] he said it's because I'm Surinamese. Anything at all can happen, and [people interpret it as me] reacting as a Surinamese [rather than me reacting as *me*].

Sometimes race was reflected in pronoun choice. The Dutch language has a formal form of address, used with people who are older or of higher social status or organizational rank ("*U*") and an informal form ("*jij*"), used with younger or lower-status persons (much like the words "*vous*" and "*tu*" in French). But, Rosa found that the Dutch used *jij* to refer to her, even when they knew she was a physician. And, even when she was addressed formally, the same people treated other Surinamese employees as children. Rosa concluded her interview with Essed with the following statement:

> I used to think, when I am a doctor, this will be in the past, then I'll have proved myself, but no such thing. Then the long, hard road begins. Then you start to notice that you aren't there yet, that the fight has just begun. I would really like for it to be over, because I'd like to just be able to live. I'd find it wonderful if I could just feel good with my job and not have a third-rate position in the job. If you spend all your time competing, then it never stops. I participate in this consciously and take care that I don't backslide. I think: just keep it up. I read a lot more about discrimination now—but then, not so much about Holland, because you don't' get any further if you keep on thinking only about how they do that and they do that and they do that (1991, p. 156).

Rosa's story is echoed by other minority women in other cultures. The black women that Essed interviewed in California all told of experiences like Rosa's. Many of the Latinas that Denise Segura interviewed talked about subtle discrim-

(continued)

(continued from the previous page)

ination, comments that devalue their culture or their gender/ethnicity—"that subtle baloney that people pass over you because they think that women of color aren't as brilliant as they [Anglos] are," as one phrased it. A Latina with a light complexion recalled that people tell her "you have a funny accent. And I say, 'I'm Mexican.' And people are really surprised. They say, 'You don't look Mexican.' And so I ask, 'How many Mexican people do you know? And they say, "Oh, just you. (p. 303).'"†

Applying What You've Learned
1. Which of the taken-for-granted assumptions of Rosa's society influence her experiences? How do those influences operate?
2. Can Rosa fit in to her society/organization? What effects would trying to do so have on her and her work relationships?

Questions to Think About and Discuss
1. What kind of "diversity" training programs should Rosa's organization develop to deal with "everyday racism?" Why would you make those choices?
2. What intended and unintended consequences is a program like the one you've described likely to have? Why?

---

*This case is based on Philomena Essed, *Everyday Racism* (San Francisco: Hunter House, 1990) and *Understanding Everyday Racism* (Newbury Park, CA: Sage, 1991).
†Denise Segura, "Chicanas in White-Collar Jobs," in *Situated Lives,* Louise Lamphere, Helena Razone, and Patricia Zavella, eds. (New York: Routledge, 1997).

Developing Supportive Policies

The single most important step that an organization can take to challenge the dominant perspective is to change its reward system. Rewarding employees for conforming to organizational norms merely serves to perpetuate dominant attitudes and behaviors. Rewarding them for performance not only generates change, it adds credibility to change efforts. Performance-based systems involve collecting data on the number and proportion of people who are promoted, breaking that data down by gender, race, and ethnicity, and *publicizing* that data throughout the firm. This is because upper managers tend to *overestimate* the success of diversity programs, leading to complacency, and Anglo males who are competing with newcomers tend to *underestimate* their own opportunities, leading to unnecessary resistance and backlash. Like all organizational change efforts, diversity will succeed only if it is strongly, honestly, and openly supported by upper management. *They* must establish policies and procedures that target women, African American men, and Latinos for recruitment, professional development, and advancement. *They* must support the development of internal advocacy groups and task forces to provide emotional support for diverse groups of employees and *they* must keep the organization's diversification goals at the forefront of everyday activities. Policies and programs alone are meaningless. After all, Texaco and Coca Cola had a number of diversity management and fair employment practices, policies, and procedures on the books, and had even won a number of awards for them. So did San Diego Gas and Electric Company when, in 1994, the courts ordered it to pay $3 million to a former worker who had been repeatedly called "nigger," "coon," or "boy," and subjected to threats and racial and sexual graffiti about him. So did Walmart when it recently lost a $50 million sexual harassment suit (later reduced to $5 million on appeal) in spite of the company's "strong" commitments, policies, and procedures. In all of these cases, there was no evidence that the commitments and policies had ever been translated into action—no one had been disciplined for any of the activities included in the cases.[43]

TAKING A HOLISTIC PERSPECTIVE

The final element of the dominant perspective is the notion that organizations are "containers," places that are separated by time and space from the places where employees live their nonwork lives. Of course, this notion has never been accurate for professional and managerial employees. Taking work home, being on call, and spending sleepless nights thinking about work-related problems have all been normal parts of white-collar employees' lives in the industrialized world. However, the advent of many new technologies—laptop computers, the Internet, cell phones, paging systems, and so on—mean that many people never actually leave work. It is ironic that historically technologies that promised people more control over their time—from the telephone to the personal computer—usually have not provided the promised control. Instead they often have increased organizations' ability to limit or invade employees' private time. Organizational downsizing throughout the world has created a situation in which a smaller number of workers are available to complete the same amount of work. Increased organizational demands to work overtime during the past decade have created a situation in which balancing work and family is one of the greatest problems faced by modern employees. Overall, the average U.S. workweek increased only two hours between 1982 and 1996, but that figure is misleading. The vast majority of new workers added during that time were women, who average less than forty hours per week. Underemployment among blue-collar workers also artificially reduces the average. As a result, as the new century started the U.S. workforce was divided into two disparate groups: those who are unable to work full time because the jobs are not there, and those whose workload has skyrocketed. For the latter group the experience of Elizabeth Oaks, a lawyer who works in the oil and gas industry is typical: "We come home, we barely get something to eat, and we're exhausted. . . I can't imagine what people do who have children."[44]

For example, in the United States, one third of adults average less than seven hours of sleep a night while most people need eight or nine hours. Bureau of Labor Statistics show that the average number of paid vacation days in U.S. firms is 6.8, rising to 10 for professional employees. These figures are comparable to those of the Philippines, Hong Kong, and Mexico, but substantially below Saudi (15 days), German (18), Italian (28–42), or British (35) workers. The rapid movement of women into the professional labor force during the past 20 years has significantly increased the number of people who experience work-home spillover. The percentage of women who chose to not have children almost doubled between 1976 and 1995, a figure that is even higher among women with college degrees. More than half of new mothers return to the workforce within a year of giving birth. Two-thirds of women with some college do so; as do three-quarters of women with graduate or professional degrees. In general, mothers with higher incomes are more likely to return (two-thirds of those making $75,000 or more do so compared to half of those earning less than $20,000). These differences result in part from personal goals; educated, upper-income mothers have usually postponed having children until they have completed their education, become established in their careers, and moved up through their organizational hierarchies. The high level of career commitment that results gives them extra incentives to return to work. But it also results from their greater ability to afford high-quality child care and their enhanced bargaining power with their employers.

"Family-friendly" policies are rarely made available to all members of an organization. Instead they are offered to employees who are difficult to replace and/or who have other sources of organizational power.[45] Lower-level, lower-income workers, those who need benefits the most, often are not eligible for them. It is for this reason that *Working Mother* magazine, whose annual list of the "100 Best Companies for Mothers to Work For" is the most comprehensive survey of "family-friendly" policies, entitled its 2000 study "Nice Perks, If You Can Get 'Em." In short, employees have multidimensional lives, each part of which demands their time, energy, and commitment. Unfortunately, some organizations refuse to take a holistic perspective, one that recognizes these multiple responsibilities. Fortunately, some do.

Organizational Choices and Family-Work Balance   One of the easiest ways to get a sense of the kinds of programs and policies that can be valuable to a diverse workforce is to peruse *Working Mother's 100 -best* list. Firms are evaluated in part on the fairness of their salary schedules and their record of promoting women. But they also gain points for having programs, such as child care assistance (including back up day care for children who are ill, out of school for a holiday, vacation, or snow day), flextime, flexplace, and flexible benefits plans. But *Working Mother* also warns readers about surveys that look *only* at a company's policies, because they are often either not implemented or implemented in a way that penalizes employees who use them. As Jennifer Chatman, a professor in the school of business at the University of California-Berkeley notes, "The policies provide a good image and attract employees, but they're not practiced because people get informally penalized for doing anything that takes away from a one-hundred-percent effort." Even if upper management supports the policies—and a growing percentage do because it is very clear that these policies really do increase productivity and reduce costs related to absenteeism and turnover—middle- or lower-level managers may not. For example, Dupont has struggled for years to persuade their managers to support family friendly policies. In 2000, they spent $200,000 to train managers in locations away from the home office to assess their employees' needs and develop appropriate policies.

Policies are often limited to white-collar employees, even though lower-level workers need them most. And, even well-intentioned programs can create problems if they are not administered in a fair and flexible way. For example, many firms are experiencing increasing tensions between parents and childless workers. Flextime, flexplace, and parental leave arrangements can easily increase the workload of single employees.[46]

But, in spite of these challenges, there are many examples of programs and policies that seem to have been implemented successfully. Ben and Jerry's Homemade (Ice Cream), Inc., pays health club fees and reimburses parents for adoption fees (up to the cost of a hospital delivery of a baby); Beth Israel Hospital in Boston provides breast pumping stations for returning mothers who are nursing their babies; Arthur Andersen and Company provides on-site day care for employees during the peak tax preparation season; Barnett Bank in Florida provides round-trip transportation for employees' children to summer day camp at the local YMCA; Lincoln National Insurance has trained 300 family day care providers to be employed by their workers; and Colgate-Palmolive pays the full cost of in-home emergency care for ill children for its employees. At the Bureau of National Affairs, Inc., employees with ten years of service are eligible for six-month sabbaticals at half-pay, and Consolidated Edison of New York has a new training program to attract women to higher-paying jobs traditionally held by men (such as utility repair work).[47] The list could be extended almost endlessly.

Even small and medium-sized businesses can help. They often lack the funds to establish expensive benefits, such as on-site day care or scholarships for employees' children. But, they can provide flexibility. Cross Country Staffing, a Boca Raton, Florida firm with only 284 employees (84 percent of whom are women) made the *Working Mother* list for the first time in 2000. They instituted job-sharing in 1991 and a variety of flextime systems during the 1990s. Since more than half of U.S. employees work in small companies (those with less than 500 employees), and two thirds of the new jobs created in the next five years will be in small firms, these steps are especially important. And they demonstrate that any organization can consult with employees about what *their* needs are and design flexible programs that *individualize* policies, procedures, and benefits, while staying within the constraints imposed by budgets and concerns for fairness.

Individual Choices and Family-Work Balance   Employees can influence the level of work overload they experience by making strategic choices. On the one hand, many people consciously choose careers or organizational roles that they know will be exhausting. Some white-collar workers thrive in a high-pressure environment; many blue-collar workers actively seek out overtime to build up cash reserves in anticipation of layoffs. In many careers, excessive time demands are simply taken for granted. In the United States, these careers include the law, medicine, and high tech firms. Sociologist Neal Bull, an expert on leisure time, concluded that "they would love employees to work 24 hours a day in technology firms." People who want to be able to devote a substantial amount of time to their families, communities, or self, should avoid these careers.

When people look for jobs, they should search through job descriptions carefully for required travel or overtime; actively seek out information about a company's "family friendly" policies and programs and the extent to which those policies are used; and inquire about the organization's willingness to support flexible work arrangements. In many organizations, evaluations of employee performance are based on **"face time"** (the number of hours they are at the workplace) rather than by output. Ironically, a series of studies have found that "face time" is not related to productivity—people who are rested and energized get more work done in a shorter time and the quality of their work is greater.[48] In addition, errors are reduced and safety is enhanced. In September 2000, safety concerns led the state of Maine to enact the first maximum overtime regulations in the United States (80 hours in a two-week period). But, as we have suggested throughout this book, organizational policies and practices are often based more on mythology than on evidence, so demands regarding face time persist.

Once people accept a job, they should closely monitor the organization's practices to see whether "family-friendly" rhetoric is actually followed and to determine the extent to which the organization rewards managers for being flexible. They should also make their own values clear to their coworkers. Although these strategies are often thought of as relevant only for women, they may be even more important for men. Chicago *Tribune* columnist Carol Kleiman summarizes the available evidence rather bluntly: "The workplace gives a lot of lip service to family-friendly policies, but when it comes to crunch time and a male employee isn't there, he's considered disloyal. In fact, if he puts his family first, he's considered a wimp."[49] When Maryland State Trooper Kevin Knussman won a four-year legal battle for paternity leave in 1999, only a few coworkers congratulated him and many made snide comments. As a result of these pressures, only one-half million of the two million people who have taken parental leave under the 1993 Family and Medical Leave Act (U.S.) have been men.

The average amount of time that U.S. fathers spend with their children has increased from 1.8 hours a day in 1977 to 2.3 hours in 1996 (compared to 9-17 minutes a day in Japan and less than one hour in Britain and Germany). But, the change is mixed—there is an increasing number of U.S. men who have nothing to do with their children and an increasing number who are becoming more involved. The ones who are spending more time do it because they want to be more involved in their children's lives than their fathers were involved in theirs, because their wives are working full time, and because they can do so. Sometimes being involved in one's family requires creative resistance. One new father parks his car at the far corner of the parking lot so that he can disappear (to home) at 5:00; another leaves his desk lamp and computer on when he takes his child to the physician; many cobble together vacation and sick leave time so that they can spend time with their children without admitting it. One noted, "I know other men who are doing the same thing" and compared their group to Alcoholics Anonymous: "We know who we are and why we're doing this, but we don't give our names."[50]

Choosing to have family as a top priority is a difficult decision because it often requires people to violate powerful social norms. For example, while Japanese workers are officially allotted eighteen paid vacation days each year, on average they only take nine. They have learned to see vacation time as a burden on their coworkers, not as an entitlement they have earned. When holidays are institutionalized—meaning that everyone takes them off—Japanese workers actually take them. Even in northern Europe, where lengthy paid vacations have been mandated by law for decades, people hesitate to take them for fear that they will be viewed as disloyal. But, in the United States, a trend toward maintaining a greater balance between work and family seems to be taking hold. Generation X and Generation Y employees consistently list work-family balance as a high priority, suggesting that there will be increasing pressure for organizations to change. But, it also is clear that many organizations will strongly resist those changes, so choosing an organization with similar values will continue to be important.

CONCLUSION

On the one hand, in the United Stated and many other countries, substantial progress has been made in changing organizations to meet the challenges of a diverse workforce. Today there are far more women, African Americans, and Latinos in entry-level professional and managerial positions than there were twenty years ago. Between 1970 and 1985 the proportion of female managers in the U.S. economy as a whole increased from 15 percent to 36 percent, and the number of female managers grew 400 percent. Two-thirds of all managers hired between 1965 and 1985 were women. In 1992, 55 percent of the people earning bachelor's degrees were women, as were 35 percent of new M.D.s and 42 percent of new attorneys, suggesting that there are sufficient numbers of women receiving advanced training to continue these trends. The percentage of women in upper management grew from 3.5 in 1970 to 6.8 in 1980 to 14 percent in 1996 (the latest date for which reliable data is available).

However, people who are not Anglo males are still concentrated at the lower levels of organizations and in sectors with lower salaries and mobility opportunities. In 1991, 25 percent of officers and managers in small firms were

Anglo women; 5 percent were African Americans; 3 percent were Latinos or Latinas; and 2 percent were Asian Americans. In very large (*Fortune* 100) firms, fewer officers and managers are women (about 18 percent), and only 7 percent are African Americans, Latinos, or Asian Americans. Upper management still is almost exclusively the province of Anglo males—90 percent of *Fortune* 500 firms do not have a woman among the five most compensated officers.[51]

Salaries for all women in the labor force have hovered around 69 percent of men's salaries for decades. In 1992 the figure reached a high of 72 percent. Subsequently it fell back to 69 percent, and in 1999 reached it's highest level ever, 74 percent. The gap is even smaller for women aged 25–34 (82 percent) and smaller still for women aged 27–33 who have never had children (98 percent). Among professional occupations, the gap is smallest in finance, law, and computers. When age and experiences are factored in, the gap for executives is less than 5 percent. In contrast, African American men still earn approximately 50 percent of Anglo men's salaries; African American women earn approximately 30 percent of Anglo men's incomes and approximately 60 percent of the income of Anglo women. Overall, Latinos earned two-thirds of the salaries of Anglo men. Of course, many of these gaps are still significant, even if the data are corrected for education, experience, or seniority within the firm.

Attitudes about a diverse workforce also have improved but still serve as barriers to change. And, as the U.S. workforce becomes more diverse, other groups of employees have started to confront the dominant perspective. For example, age discrimination has become an increasing problem during the 1990s and is likely to grow in importance as the baby boomers age. Like other forms of differential treatment, ageism is both pervasive and subtle. It is grounded in the cultural assumption that older people are inherently less capable than younger workers. For example, when managers described 30–year-old and 60–year-old workers, they used the terms "more productive, capable of working under pressure, flexible, able to learn, and decisive" for the younger workers and "reliable, honest, committed to quality, have good attendance records, and use good judgment" for the older ones in spite of consistent research evidence indicating that intellectual skills do not decline substantially with age. They also tend to assume that younger workers will stay with the company for 25 to 30 years, in spite of substantial evidence that long-term connections to a single organization no longer can be assumed of *any* group of employees (recall the Generation X case study in Chapter 1).[52] Negative attitudes about gay and lesbian employees persist even though a number of organizations have taken steps to reduce differential treatment. In 1996, IBM announced that it would extend health benefits to partners of its homosexual employees, joining 470 other companies (up from 250 in 1995 and including Apple Computer, Ben and Jerry's, Dayton Hudson, Eastman Kodak, Fox Broadcasting, Glaxo-Wellcome, Hewlett-Packard, Seagram and Sons, Levi Strauss, Microsoft, NYNEX, Time Warner, Walt Disney, Wells Fargo, and Xerox).

So, at least in the United States, Europe, and the Commonwealth countries, there is evidence that some organizations have started to confront the dominant perspective while others engage in resistance. The barriers that traditionally have separated different groups of employees have started to dissolve. But, it is not yet clear whether the vestiges of those barriers will continue to exist, new barriers will be created, or the dominant perspective will disappear.

NOTES

[1] Jeffrey Sachs, "International Economics: Unlocking the Mysteries of Globalization," *Foreign Policy, 110* (Spring, 1998): 168–206; Cynthia Stohl, "Globalizing Organizational Communication," in *The New Handbook of Organizational Communication,* Fredric Jablin & Linda Putnam, eds. (Thousand Oaks, CA: Sage, 2000), p. 324.

[2] Steve Axley, "Managerial and Organizational Communication in Terms of the Conduit Metaphor," *Academy of Management Review, 9* (1984): 428–437.

[3] See Anthony Giddens, *The Consequences of Modernity* (Cambridge, UK: Polity Press, 1990), *Modernity and Self-Identity* (Cambridge, U.K.: Polity Press, 1991), and *Beyond Left and Right* (Cambridge, U.K.: Polity Press, 1994); John Tomlinson, *Globalization and Culture* (Chicago: University of Chicago Press, 1999). An excellent introduction to the related issues is provided by a special issue of *The Annals of the American Academy of Political and Social Science,* edited by Louis Ferleger & Jay Mandle (July, 2000).

[4] Radha S. Hegde, "A View from Elsewhere," *Communication Theory, 8* (1998): 271 - 297; John Oetzel & Keri Bolton-Oetzel, "Exploring the Relationship Between Self-Construal and Dimensions of Group Effectiveness," *Management Communication Quarterly, 10* (1997): 289–315; A.R. Jan Mohamed & J. Lloyd, eds. *The Nature and Context of Minority Discourse* (Oxford, U.K.: Oxford University Press, 1990). J. Sullivan & S. Taylor's study of Korean and Japanese employees illustrates the combined influence of cultural and individual characteristics "A Cross-Cultural Test of Compliance-Gaining Theory," *Management Communication Quarterly, 5* (1991): 220–239.

[5] David Ivanovich, "$192.5 Million Settles Coca-Cola Race Suit," *Houston Chronicle,* 17 Nov., 2000,. 1A, 20A. As is typical in out-of-court settlements, Coca Cola's management denied that discrimination was systematic or consistent with the values of the organization. Also see Sheri Prasso, "Study: Stereotypes Hinder Female Executives," *Houston Chronicle,* 29 Feb., 1996, B1.

[6] This hiring preference came as a surprise to local governments who had hoped that the new factories would provide jobs for a potentially much more troublesome group—young males who recently had migrated from rural areas to the cities in search of employment.

[7] The most sophisticated studies of these changes are by Aihwa Ong. See *Spirits of Resistance and Capitalist Discipline* (Albany, NY: SUNY Press, 1987); "The Gender and Labor Politics of Postmodernity," *Annual Review of Anthropology,* 20 (1991); and "Spirits of Resistance," in *Situated Lives,* Louise Lamphere, Helena Razone, and Patricia Zavella, eds. (New York: Routledge, 1997). Also see Stohl, "Globalizing."

[8] And in some countries, coworker actions that could reasonably have been expected to be known by management.

[9] Damian Grace & Stephen Cohen, *Business Ethics* (Melbourne, Australia: Oxford, 1995), pp. 42,148.

[10] Susan Faludi, *Backlash: The Undeclared War Against American Women* (New York: Crown, 1991); Charlene Solomon, "Keeping Hate Out of the Workplace," *Personnel Journal* (July, 1992): 30–36; M.W. Zak, "It's Like a Prison in There," *Journal of Business and Technical Communication, 8* (1994): 282–298; Kathleen Kelley Reardon, *They Don't Get It, Do They?* (Boston: Little, Brown and Co., 1995); Michele Galen and Ann Therese Palmer, "White, Male and Worried," *Business Week* (January 31, 1994): 50–55; Edwards and Polite; and Anne Fisher, "When Will Women Get to the Top," *Fortune* (Sept. 21, 1992): 44–56.

[11] A. Rizzo and C. Mendez, *The Integration of Women in Management* (New York: Quorum Books, 1990); Barbara Reskin & Irene Padavic, *Women and Men at Work* (Thousand Oaks, CA: Pine Forge Press, 1994).

[12] Beatri'z Pesquera, "In the Beginning He Wouldn't Even Lift a Spoon" and Denise Segura, "Chicanas in White-Collar Jobs," both in *Situated Lives,* Louise Lamphere, Helena Razone, and Patricia Zavella, eds. (New York: Routlege, 1997).

[13] See Arlie Hochschild & Anne Machung, *The Second Shift* (New York: Avon Books, 1997); A. Hochschild, *The Time Bind* (New York: Metropolitan Books, 1997); Janie Carter, *He Works, She Works* (New York: AMACOM, 1995); and Jean Potuchek, *Who Supports the Family?* (Palo Alto, CA: Stanford University Press, 1997).

[14] See Ann Morrison, Randall White, and Ellen Van Velsor, *Breaking the Glass Ceiling* (Greensboro, NC: Center for Creative Leadership, 1992).

[15] Korn/Ferry International, "The Decade of the Executive Woman," (New York: 1993); *Houston Chronicle,* 2/19/96, B1.

[16] "Chicanas in White-Collar Jobs," in *Situated Lives,* Louise Lamphere, Helena Razone', and Patricia Zavella, eds. (New York: Routledge, 1997), p. 301.

[17] Lynn Miller, Linda Cooke, Jennifer Tsang, & Faith Morgan, "Should I Brag," *Human Communication Research, 18* (1992): 364–399.

[18] Morrison, White, and Van Velsor. For extended analyses of the visibility paradox, see Daniels, et al; Katherine Miller, *Organizational Communication,* (Belmont, CA: Wadsworth, 1994); Philomena Essed, *Everyday Racism,* trans. Cynthia Jaffe, (Claremont, CA: Hunter House, 1990) and *Understanding Everyday Racism* (Newbury Park, CA: Sage, 1991).

[19] This is likely to also be true for Latinos/Latinas, but there is little directly relevant research. See John Dovidio, Samuel Gaertner, Phyllis Anastasio, and Rasyid Sanitioso, "Cognitive and Motivational Bases of Bias," in Knouse, et al., eds., *Hispanics;* and Essed, *Everyday.*

[20] Karsten; Marjorie Nadler and Larry Nadler, "Feminization of Public Relations," in Cynthia Berryman-Fink, D. Ballard-Reich, and L.H. Newman, eds., *Communication and Sex-Role Socialization* (New York: Garland Publishing Company, 1993). Supervisors' confidence in their evaluations is examined in Stella Nkomo, "The Emperor Has No Clothes: Rewriting Race in Organizations," *Academy of Management Review, 17* (1992): 487–512. Problems related to perceptions and explanations of success are the bases of advice often given women who enter careers in sales or merchandising. The assumption is that these occupations provide employees with quantifiable and easily communicated evidence of their success. To the extent that objective data are available, differential attribution of success is a less serious problem.

[21] Martin, *Hearings,* p. 29. For summaries of perceptions of women and persons of color, see Denise Segura, "Walking on Eggshells: Chicanas in the Labor Force," and Dovidio, et al., both in Knouse, et al., eds., *Hispanics.*

[22] Grace & Cohen, p. 143. For data on U.S. workers breaking through the glass ceiling see Marianne Bertraud, "Female Executives Make What Men Do," *Houston Chronicle,* 21 Oct., 2000, C2.

[23] Dickens and Dickens argue that eventually all African American employees will need to confront their supervisors over issues of racism and provide extended advice about when, how, and over what specific issues to do so. Many of the other sources cited in this chapter provide similar advice. Interestingly, self-help books oriented toward white women rarely provide advice about how subordinates should confront their supervisors over issues of sexism, except perhaps in cases of overt sexual harassment, perhaps because they are written from a more completely accommodationist perspective. For an analysis of how African American women implement the balancing act, see Ella Louise Bell, "The Bicultural Life Experience of Career-Oriented Black Women," *Journal of Organizational Behavior, 11* (1990): 459–477.

[24] See Khalid Mohammed Alkhazraji, et al., "The Acculturation of Immigrants to U.S. Organizations," *Management Communication Quarterly, 11* (1997): 217–265; "Number of Female Executives Continues to Rise, Survey Says," *Houston Chronicle,* 14 Nov., 2000, C3; Cindy Reuther & Gail Fairhurst, "Chaos Theory and the Glass Ceiling," in *Rethinking Organizational and Managerial Communication from Feminist Perspectives,* Patrice Buzzanell, ed. (Thousand Oaks, CA: Sage, 2000); Patrice Buzzanell, "Reframing the Glass Ceiling as a Socially Constructed Process," *Communication Monographs, 62* (1995): 327–354; Peter T. Kilborn, "For Many in Work Force, Glass Ceiling Still Exists," *New York Times,* 16 March, 1995; Pan Suk Kim and Gregory Lewis, "Asian Americans in the Public Service," *Public Administration Review, 54* (1994): 285–290; Paul Page, "African Americans in Executive Branch Agencies," *Review of Public Personnel Administration, 14* (1994): 24–51; U.S. Department of Labor, *The American Workforce: 1992–2005* (Washington, D.C.: Government Printing Office, USDL Bulletin N. 2452, 1994; Gary Powell and D.A. Butterfield, "Investigating the 'Glass Ceiling' Phenomenon," *Academy of Management Journal, 37* (1994): 68–86; see Patrice Buzzanell, "Reframing the Glass Ceiling as a Socially Constructed Process," *Communication Monographs, 62* (1995): 327–354; Peter T. Kilborn, "For Many in Work Force, Glass Ceiling Still Exists," *New York Times,* 16 Mar., 1995; Pan Suk Kim and Gregory Lewis, "Asian

Americans in the Public Service," *Public Administration Review, 54* (1994): 285–290; Paul Page, "African Americans in Executive Branch Agencies," *Review of Public Personnel Administration, 14* (1994): 24–51.

[25] See Linda Putnam, "Feminist Theories, Dispute Processes, and Organizational Communication" and Betsy Bach, "Making a Difference by Doing Differently," papers presented at the Arizona State University Conference on Organizational Communication: Perspectives for the 1990s, Tempe, AZ, April 1990; and Connie Bullis, "At Least It's a Start," in *Communication Yearbook 16,* Stanley Deetz, ed. (Newbury Park, CA: Sage, 1993).

[26] D. Spain, *Gendered Spaces* (Chapel Hill, NC: University of North Carolina Press, 1992).

[27] "Just 10% of Senior Managers for Fortune 500 Are Women," *Houston Chronicle,* 7 Jan., 2000, 3C; Eileen Alt Powell, "Women are Hitting the 'Glass Wall,'" *Houston Chronicle,* 12 Nov., 1999, C1; "Number of Female Executives Continues to Rise, Survey Says," *Houston Chronicle,* 14 Nov., 2000, 3C. Also see G. Moore, "Structural Determinants of Men's and Women's Personal Networks," *American Sociological Review, 55* (1990): 726–735; Sonia Ospina, *Illusions of Opportunity* (Ithaca, NY: Cornell University Press, 1996); Reskin & Padavic; and L. Smith-Lovin and M.J. McPherson, "You Are Who You Know," in *Theory on Gender/Feminism on Theory,* Paula England, ed. (New York: Aldine, 1993).

[28] Jorge Chapa, "Creating and Improving Linkages Between the Tops and Bottoms," paper presented at the Organizational Innovation Conference, Humphrey Institute of Public Affairs, University of Minnesota, Minneapolis, Sept., 1992; Ospina; B. Schneider, S. Gunnarson, and J. Wheeler, "The Role of Opportunity in the Conceptualization and Measurement of Job Satisfaction," in C.J. Crannay, et al., eds. Job Satisfaction (New York: Lexington Books, 1992); *Houston Chronicle,* 10/18/96, 3C; Korn/Ferry; Julie Lopez Amparano, "Study Says Women Face Glass Walls as Well as Glass Ceilings," *Wall Street Journal,* 3 March, 1992.

[29] Morrison, White, & van Velsor; Laura Mansnerus, "Why Women are Leaving the Law," *Working Woman,* Apr. 1993.

[30] The best single source of information on women-owned businesses in the United States is the Website of the National Foundation of Women Business Owners, www.nfwbo.org. Australian data is presented in Grace & Cohen. Also see Anita Blair, *Houston Chronicle,* 7/8/96, 15A; Charles Boisseau, "Ranks of Female Businesses Soar," *Houston Chronicle,* 1/30/96, 1c); Arne Kalleberg and Kevin Leicht, "Gender and Organizational Performance," *Academy of Management Journal,* 34 (1991): 157; "Women Owned Firms See Huge Growth," *Houston Chronicle,* 11 May, 1999, C5.

[31] "Financing," *Houston Chronicle,* 23 May, 1999, D5; Grace & Cohen.

[32] C. Hilton, " International Business Communication," *Journal of Business Communication,* 29 (1992): 253–265; Charles Bantz, "Cultural Diversity and Group Cross-Cultural Team Research," *Journal of Applied Communication Research,* 20 (1993): 1–19. Both Richard Shuter ("Communication in Multinational Organizations," in *Communication and Multinational Organizations,* R. Wiseman & R. Shuter, eds. [Thousand Oaks, CA: Sage, 1994]) and Fred Casmir ("Third Culture Building," in *Communication Yearbook* 16, Stanley Deetz, ed. [Newbury Park, CA: Sage, 1993]) have argued that intercultural effectiveness depends on building blended or multicultural workplaces in which ethnic, racial, and cultural differences are celebrated.

[33] Philip Harris & Robert Moran, *Managing Cultural Differences,* 5th ed. (Houston: Gulf Publishing, 2000). For an excellent case study of cross-cultural conflict between Japanese managers and Anglo-U.S. engineers and human resource officers see Stephen Banks & Patricia Riley, "Structuration Theory as an Ontology for Communication Research," in Stanley Deetz, ed., *Communication Yearbook* 16 (Newbury Park, CA: Sage, 1992).

[34] Dovidio, et al. Jamieson and O'Mara list Hewlett-Packard and Hallmark as organizations with especially effective training programs. Unfortunately, there is little evidence that education itself will overcome racism or sexism (K. Kraiger & J. Ford, "A Meta-Analysis of Ratee Race Effects in Performance Ratings," *Journal of Applied Psychology,* 70 (1985): 56–65.

[35] A. DePalma, "It Takes More than a Visa to do Business in Mexico," *New York Times,* 26 June, 1994), 16–17A.

[36] A.P. Carnavale & S.C. Stone, "Diversity: Beyond the Golden Rule," *Training and Development* (Oct., 1994): p. 24.

[37] Hector Cantu, "Racial Slur Helped Form New Career," *Houston Chronicle,* 21 March, 1999, 3D. Also see Stephen Paskoff, "Ending the Workplace Diversity Wars," *Training: The Human Side of Business* (August, 1996), p. 3. Also see Al Gonzalez, et al., "Cultural Diversity and Organizations," in Peggy Yuhas Byer, ed. *Organizational Communication* (Boston: Allyn and Bacon, 1997).

[38] Sally Helgessen, *The Female Advantage: Women's Ways of Leadership* (New York: Double-day, 1990). Also see Judith Rosener, "Ways Women Lead," *Harvard Business Review* (Nov.-Dec., 1990): 119–125 and Marlene Fine & Patrice Buzzanell, "Walking the High Wire," in *Rethinking Organizational and Managerial Communication from Feminist Perspectives* (Thousand Oaks, CA: Sage, 2000).

[39] For a summary of Latino/Latina leadership styles, see Bernardo Ferdman and Angelica Cortes, "Culture and Identity Among Hispanic Managers in an Anglo Business," in *Hispanics in the Workplace*, S. Knouse, P. Rosenfeld, and A. Culbertson, eds. (Newbury Park, CA: Sage, 1992), especially p. 265. Also see G. Marin and B.V. Marin, *Research with Hispanic Populations* (New-bury Park, CA: Sage, 1991); Richard Cervantes, "Occupational and Economic Stressors Among Immigrant and United States-Born Hispanics," in Knouse, et al.; and Floyd Dickens and Jacqueline B. Dickens, *The Black Manager* (New York: AMACOM, 1991).

[40] B.W. Wilkins & P.A. Anderson, "Gender Differences and Similarities in Management Com-munication," *Management Communication Quarterly*, 5 (1991). Also see Ann Harriman, *Women—Men—Management* (Westport, CT: Greenwood Press, 1996); Gary Powell, *Women and Men in Management* (Newbury Park, CA: Sage, 1993); Frederica Olivares, "Ways Men and Women Lead," *Harvard Business Review* (January-February, 1991).

[41] D.P. Blanchette, "Technology Transfer in a Culturally Diverse Workforce (Part I)," *Indus-trial Management* (July/Aug, 1994): 31–32.; and H. Sussman, "Is Diversity Training Worth Main-taining?" *Business and Society Review*, 89 (1994): 48–49.

[42] David Jamieson and Julie O'Mara, *Managing Workforce 2000* (San Francisco: Jossey-Bass, 1991), p. 89.

[43] Ann Morrison, *The New Leaders* (San Francisco: Jossey-Bass, 1992).

[44] Daniel Creson, cited in Jeannie Kever, "Life in the Tired Lane," *Texas Magazine*, 13 Aug. 2000, p. 8; also see "Overworked America?" 6 Sept., 1999. The Online (P.B.S.) Newshour, ww.pbs.org/newshour/bb/business/july-dec99/overwork_9–6a.html.

[45] See Faye Fiore, "New Mothers Now Return to Work Sooner, Study Says," *Houston Chron-icle*, 27 Nov., 1997, 2A and "More New Mothers Returning to Work," *Houston Chronicle*, 24 Oct., 2000, 6A.

[46] The survey's results are presented in the October, 2000 issue. In that year the top ten orga-nizations were (listed alphabetically with the number of years they have been on the Top 100 list in parentheses) Allstate Insurance, Northbrook , IL (10); Bank of America, Charlotte, NC (2); Eli Lilly & Co., Indianapolis, IN (6); Fannie Mae, Washington, D.C. (7); IBM Corporation, Armonk, NY (15); Life Technologies, Rockville, MD (5); Lincoln Financial Group, Philadelphia (14); Merrill Lynch & Co., New York (5); Novant Health, Inc., Winston-Salem, NC (1); Prudential, Newark, NJ (11).

[47] Many of these policies have been mandated by law for decades outside of the United States. In Ecuador, for example, firms must provide women with three months of paid maternity leave and schedule them for only six hours of work at time during the next three months so that they can nurse their babies. Most European and Canadian firms have on-site day care and provide special breaks for nursing mothers.

[48] Rex Huppke, "Study: Success Possible Despite Working Less," Bryan/College Station Eagle, 31 Jan., 1999, 3E; "Workers in a Land of Plenty See a Scarcity of Vacation Time," *Houston Chron-icle*, 24 Nov., 2000, 2C; "Japanese Have Lots of Time Off, But Taking it is Another Matter," *Hous-ton Chronicle*, 24 Nov., 2000, 2C; Tom Mooney, "U.S. Fathers Give More Time to Kids Than Many Dads—Even Their Own," *Houston Chronicle*, 20 June, 1999, 6A.

[49] "Men Still Suspect if Priority is Family," *Houston Chronicle*, 9 April, 2000, p. 2D; also see Suzanne Braun Levine, *Father Courage* (New York: Harcourt, 2000).

[50] "Dad Wins Legal Fight for Time Off," *Houston Chronicle*, 5 Feb., 1999, 19A.

[51] Jennifer Holt, "Women's Status Improving, But Slowly," *Houston Chronicle*, 16 Nov., 2000, 2C; L.M. Sixel, "Pay Gap Narrower, But Far From Closed," *Houston Chronicle*, 26 February, 1999, 12C. "Female Executives Make When Men Do," *Houston Chronicle*, 21 Oct., 2000, 2C.

[52] L.M. Sixel, *Houston Chronicle*, 19 July, 1996; L.J. Bradford & C. Raines, *Twentysomething* (New York: Master Media, Ltd., 1992).

Chapter 12

COMMUNICATION, ORGANIZATIONS, AND GLOBALIZATION

The times, they are a changin'
—BOB DYLAN

All of this [globalization] creates a problem for democracies. Democracy and capitalists have very different core values. Democracy is founded on equality—one vote per citizen regardless of his [sic] intelligence or work ethic. Capitalism, however, is motivated by inequality: differences in economic returns create the incentive structure which encourages hard work and wise investment. . . . The economically fit are expected to drive the economically unfit out of existence; there are no equalizing feedback mechanisms in capitalism.
—LESTER THUROW

[Today] is the first time in history that virtually every individual at every level of society can sense the impact of international changes. . . . [D]uring the next decade [the global labor pool] will absorb nearly 2 billion workers from emerging markets, a pool that currently includes close to 1 billion unemployed and underemployed workers. . . These people will be earning a fraction of what their counterparts in developed countries earn and will be only marginally less productive. You are either someone who is threatened by this change or someone who will profit from it, but it is almost impossible to conceive of a significant group that will be untouched by it.
—DAVID ROTHKOPF

How we learn to strike the right balance between globalization's inherently empowering and humanizing aspects and its inherently disempowering and dehumanizing aspects will determine whether is it reversible or irreversible, a passing phase or a fundamental revolution in the evolution of human society.
—THOMAS FRIEDMAN[1]

CENTRAL THEMES

- The theoretical basis for globalization is *laissez-faire* capitalism and the doctrine of free trade. The former stipulates that government should stay out of the economic realm; the latter rests on the theory of comparative advantage.
- Globalization has shifted power away from individuals and governments toward multinational corporations and financiers. In the developing world, it has encouraged the development of democratic structures.
- As the theory of comparative advantage predicts, globalization has led to massive increases in economic inequality, both within and between nations.
- Globalization forces organizations to become *responsive,* not just reactive.
- Over time, capitalists and scholars alike have struggled to deal with the moral and ethical dilemmas created by *laissez faire* capitalism. Their approach to these dilemmas have ranged from notions of corporate social responsibility to corporate social responsiveness to multiple stakeholder models.
- It is too early to predict the effects that globalization will have on local cultures. Some observers predict increasing cultural homogenization; others fear heightened polarization; still others believe that cultures will be slowly hybridized.

KEY TERMS

Laissez-faire capitalism	Futility thesis
Perversity thesis	Jeopardy thesis
Theory of comparative advantage	Responsive organizations
Heterarchy	Charity principle
Stewardship principle	

One of the dominant themes of this book is that there is an important and complex relationship between organizations and the societies from which they draw their members. To this point we have focused on one side of that relationship—the ways in which societal assumptions, structures, and processes influence organizations and organizational communication. For millennia, those processes encouraged homogeneity, separation, and often antagonism—workers versus managers; men versus women; racial/ethnic majorities versus minorities; Europeans versus Americans versus Africans, versus Asians; upper- versus middle- versus lower classes. Homogeneity and separation were sustained through a number of human-made social barriers and through the seemingly natural realities of time and space.

However, at least since the time of the industrial revolution and the democratization of Europe and North American, there also have been pressures toward heterogeneity. During the past 20 years, those pressures have become progressively more potent. Workforces have become more diverse and the barriers that exist within organizations to separate "different" groups of "*others*" have started to break down. As a result, new assumptions, structures, and processes are beginning to emerge. As Chapter 11 explained, this increased proximity *within* organizations demands the development of new systems and communicative strategies.

At least since the beginning of the 1980s, organizations and their members have been forced to deal with a second kind of proximity, an unprecedented collapsing of the barriers of time and space. Of course, the late twentieth and early twenty-first century is not the first time that economic activity has taken on a global dimension. Extensive trade networks among Asia, Africa, and Europe existed at the time of Alexander the Great (around 300 B.C.) and were expanded during the Roman Empire. The mercantile system of the fifteenth through the nineteenth centuries established a worldwide economic system dominated by Europe.[2] But, the current situation seems to be historically unique. Technological developments have fundamentally changed the way that information and expertise is disseminated around the globe (recall Chapter 6). As important, the level of education provided people throughout the world has substantially increased. For example, in the 13 largest poor countries, male illiteracy rates fell from 19 percent to 12 percent between 1980 and 1997; for women they fell by more than one-third, from 36 percent to 22 percent. In China and Indonesia, illiteracy declined by more than 75 percent. Similar increases in school enrollment suggest that the trends will continue. Thus, even in the so-called "Third World," populations are increasingly capable of using new technologies and the information and expertise that they provide.[3]

As a result, today it is almost impossible to predict where a given organization (or its many divisions) will be located. People who log on to AOL's help desk to straighten out a bill or correct a technical glitch will be talking to a Filipino techie working at what used to be Clark Air Force Base in the shadow of Mount Pinatubo. People who dial the Mexico tourism hotline will talk with someone who is located in Bend, Oregon and employed by Destination Ventures. The odds are less than 50–50 that she or he is from Mexico. McDonald's Restaurants of Canada and the Moscow (Russia) City Council have established joint ventures. Managerial decisions made in small savings and loans in Ohio are tightly linked to British oil stocks. Swissair moved its entire accounting division to India to take advantage of lower labor costs for secretaries, accountants, and programmers; British Air's office that corrects reservation errors and keeps track of frequent flyer miles is located in Mumbai, India. IBM may have the most complex global network: Programmers at Tsinghua University in Bejing write Java-based software; they send it to an IBM facility in Seattle via the Internet, where the programming is revised and sent to the Institute of Computer Science in Balarus and the Software House Group in Latvia, where it is sent back to Bejing and the process starts over in a never-ending cycle. IBM calls the system "Java Around the Clock" and prides itself at having created a "forty-eight hour day" via the Internet.[4]

While globalization has been driven by technology and increased education, it has been guided and directed by institutions of international trade and finance. Within a decade, the barriers to global production and economic activity that existed during the Cold War have largely disappeared, to be replaced by international economic bodies (largely controlled by the United States and Europe) like the World Trade Organization (WTO) and the International Monetary Fund (IMF). Both critics and defenders of globalization have noted that these changes have significantly shifted power away from individual citizens and governments and toward large multinational organizations.[5] The effects of these changes have been decidedly mixed—some people, countries, and societies have benefited in many ways; others have suffered. Whatever the specific results of globalization may become, it is clear that organizations now have a significantly increased ability to influence the societies from which they draw their members.

It is too early to make any firm predictions about the outcomes of globalization. Instead, our goal in this chapter is to outline the changes that have taken place and to explore the ongoing debate about their consequences. We begin by briefly describing the set of beliefs, values, and economic theories that underlie globalization. Then we examine its economic, organizational, and cultural effects.

ECONOMIC THEORY AND GLOBALIZATION

The intellectual justification of globalization is free market capitalism, the theory that the more a society lets market forces rule and the more it opens its economy to free trade and competition, the more its economy will flourish. The essence of free market capitalism is a process of "*creative destruction*," a perpetual cycle in which less efficient institutions, organizations, and practices are destroyed and replaced by more efficient ones. It is a distinctively Anglo model, in that the underlying economic theory was largely developed in the United Kingdom; while the underlying ethical theory is a product of U.S. thinkers.

Laissez-Faire Capitalism and Free Trade

Laissez-faire **capitalism** is based on the assumption that a free-market economic system has sufficient checks and balances in place to ensure that the legitimate interests of all members of a society will be met. Individuals compete with other individuals, and organizations compete with other organizations in pursuit of their own self-interests, and an invisible hand ensures that over the long term good individuals and organizations will triumph and bad ones will disappear. If left alone, markets will move toward an equilibrium, and an equilibrium is the most efficient way for a society to allocate its resources. The competitive dynamics of a free marketplace ensure that no individuals or organizations can unfairly impose their own wills on others. In this theory, government should have only a limited role in the economy. It may sometimes need to ensure that economic markets remain competitive (through antimonoply laws, for example) or that property rights are protected. But, with these few exceptions, government is best when it does the least.

This view of government's role in the economy is grounded in three assumptions. A **futility thesis** states that governments simply cannot effectively direct a society or economy. The presumed "miracle" of the free market is that its processes work "invisibly," and thus do not have to be understood or managed. The presumed lesson of the demise of the Soviet Union is that centralized economic planning by a government is doomed to fail. When governments act, they do so on the basis of an incomplete understanding of social and economic processes and often base their decisions on considerations other than market values (that is, what one person is willing to pay another in a free economic exchange). In very rare instances, governments may actually do what the market needs to have done at a particular moment, but these instances are purely accidental. It is much more likely that government "intervention" will worsen the condition that the action is designed to solve (a **perversity thesis).** Even more important, government activities inevitably produce serious, perverse, unintended, and unanticipated consequences. As a result, whenever government acts, it is likely to jeopardize the virtues of a society or the economic gains that have been achieved through the free market (a **jeopardy thesis).**[6]

Although these concepts were developed for a nation's internal economic system, they are easily applied to international economics. The key link is a concept called the "**theory of comparative advantage.**" This theory starts with the observation that different areas of the globe have different *natural* economic advantages. Some areas have abundant natural resources; some have an especially productive labor force; some are strategically located on trade routes, and so on. If the economy of an area relies on its natural advantages, it will be more efficient than if it tries to develop industries in which it does not have an advantage. With increased efficiency comes increased profits, incomes, and wealth. If every area focuses on its advantages and refuses to develop industries in which it does not have a comparative advantage, the entire global economy benefits. Conversely, if governments interfere with these natural processes by adopting tariffs, quotas, or currency values that artificially support industries in which their country does not have an advantage, or if they create artificial barriers to the free flow of trade, finance, and labor, they reduce the wages and wealth of their own people and make the whole world's economy less efficient than it otherwise would be.[7]

Of course, free trade may be socially disruptive and create serious economic inequities for short periods of time. Industries in which an area does not have a competitive advantage will be unable to compete. Companies in nonadvantaged industries will go bankrupt, and workers will either have to shift to advantaged industries or move to areas where their old companies have a comparative advantage. These areas are likely to have lower standards of living and incomes than workers enjoyed when their companies were being artificially supported. Capital will flow to advantaged industries or to countries that are effectively exploiting their advantages. Eventually each area will be dominated by organizations that produce the products or provide the services in which it has a comparative advantage.

If the wealth that is created by these new-found advantages is invested wisely, each economy will begin to capitalize on their advantages. The system will self-correct, and wage rates will rise, eventually creating an equilibrium. For example, there is evidence that many counties are investing more in their educational systems to more effectively compete in a global market. In the industrialized countries, this means increasing the percentage and number of residents who go to college and to encourage college students to focus on technologically-oriented careers. Doing so gives them and their countries a comparative advantage in the high-tech sectors of the world economy. In developing countries, it means increasing literacy rates and the number and percent of their residents who are in school. In both cases, the primary beneficiaries of these trends are women, for they have historically received weaker educations, especially in technical fields. In both the developed and developing world, these strategies already seem to be increasing incomes and wealth. However, the correction occurs only if the newly acquired capital stays in the home country. Since investors can now easily shift their funds to any country in the world at the touch of a button, much of the wealth created by exploiting a country's comparative advantage leaves the country. From south Asia to Europe, the fruits of economic advantage in the global economy largely have wound up in the U.S. stock and bond markets.[8] Without increased capital, development is stunted and the corrective functions of the free market are short-circuited.

Of course, in some cases there may be good noneconomic reasons for violating the tenets of free trade. For example, a government may wish to support its own computer or steel industry as a matter of national defense, or it may want to protect a fledgling industry from foreign competition until it is sufficiently well-established to compete successfully, or it may wish to restrict migration across its borders for political reasons. But, any artificial barrier reduces the efficiency of the national (and world) economy, and reduces wealth, wages, profits, and employment in the long run. They should be continued only as long as the noneconomic advantages clearly outweigh the economic disadvantages. Too many barriers to the free movement of trade, capital, and labor—whether imposed by government, labor organizations, or cultural norms—upset the global free market and reduce the total amount of wealth that is created. It is for this reason that some proponents of free trade, such as American philosopher-educator John Stuart Mill, advocated having governments pay compensation to workers and industries that lose out to global competition. Doing so reduces social costs and potential social unrest, but does not interfere with market processes. The modern version of this argument comes when governments invest funds for retraining of employees who have lost their jobs due to globalization.[9]

Economic Theory and the Effects of Globalization

The economic theory of *laissez faire* capitalism and free trade is not new. But, historically its influence on the world economy has waxed and waned as powerful governments based their policies on other considerations. During the Cold War, governments protected themselves by building economic (and sometimes physical) walls around themselves and creating generous social support systems for their citizens and their friends in other nations. When the Cold War ended, these protections were both unnecessary and counterproductive because they made it difficult for their residents to compete in the rapidly-emerging global economy. In this new economic reality, governments protect their residents by *removing* political and economic barriers, forming economic agreements with other countries, and using the resources of the state to help their core organizations compete.

Governments and Government-Organization Relationships   In the process of adapting to globalization, governments themselves are changed. For the "core" countries in the global economy (the United States, Europe, and the British Commonwealth countries) the greatest change has involved a shift in the power of government. For the peripheral countries (the rapidly-developing economies of Asia and Latin America) the shift has been toward a form of democracy.

Globalization began in the core countries, and their economies have benefited most from it. But, this does not mean that they are in control of the process. Once international agreements are made, they must be implemented. By signing on, governments give up some of their sovereignty to multinational corporations and international organizations, such as the International Monetary Fund (IMF) and World Bank. This shift is clearest in the experience of developing countries (or, in the case of Russia, redeveloping countries). When a country goes to the IMF or to the global capital market for financing, they receive the needed funds only if they adopt a strict series of economic reforms: raise interest rates and reduce government spending, reduce economic regulation, reduce or eliminate barriers to foreign trade and investment by foreign countries and corporations, privatize state-owned industries, and do everything possible to eliminate corruption.

Countries that are more dependent on the international markets for funds have no choice but to accept the dictates of the financial community and its institutions. If these changes address the causes of a particular country's economic problems, making the changes will be beneficial, especially in the long run. But, if they are not appropriate to the country's situation (for example, in Russia during the 1990s), the economic crisis will deepen, because the country has to grow its economy and simultaneously pay its international debts. But, if the government does not make the required changes, the country does not receive the needed funds, and private investors refuse to invest in it (as happened to much of south Asia during the late 1990s). The worsening economic crisis that results may actually topple governments, as it did in Indonesia in 1997. In some cases, the effects are devastating for local peoples. African nations that accepted IMF aid during the 1980s and 1990s saw their living standards fall, unemployment rates increase, and ecosystems deteriorate. In sub-Saharan Africa, more than one half of World Bank projects failed, leaving the countries with massive debt and no improvements in their economies. Austerity measures imposed on Mexico and east Asian countries by the IMF during the 1980s led to massive increases in income inequality that have not yet been offset.

Of course, the governments of wealthy countries give up less control to international organizations than the governments of developing countries. But, even they are not immune. In 1996, the developed nations attempted to include a clause in the WTO's charter that mandated a minimal list of social rights (freedom of association, a ban on forced labor and employment discrimination, and restrictions on child labor). The effort was abandoned after intense opposition from developing countries that argued that the clause would rob them of their primary comparative advantage, and multinational corporations that feared that it would restrict free trade.[10] In 1999, the IMF's staff recommended that the United States enact a policy of additional financial austerity—no tax cuts, new investments in education or health care, reductions in Social Security and Medicare benefits—a recommendation that was rejected as an unwanted intrusion into U.S. affairs. However, all but the richest countries in the world have little choice but to accept the requirements of international financial institutions and the global financial market. Together they create what Thomas Friedman has labeled the "Golden Straightjacket."[11]

Globalization will never eliminate government power. For example, in 2000 the U.S. and British governments successfully persuaded the five largest oil companies and two multinational mining companies to sign a code of conduct pledging to discourage local police and private security companies from abusing people who live near their oil fields. The code is voluntary, to be enforced only by public opinion. It also is ironic because it is largely a response to situations in which MNCs are accused of collaborating with local governments to violate human rights (Unocal in Myanmar's use of forced labor, Chevron and Shell in Nigeria, Freeport McMoran in Irian Jaya, for example). But it does suggest that the governments of the largest economies are able to influence organizational practices. Still, even in the richest economies, globalization seems to be limiting and changing government's role. Of the world's 100 largest economies, more than half are corporations, not countries. The 200 largest corporations account for 28 percent of the world's economic activity, although they employ only three-fourths of one percent of its people. The 500 largest corporations account for 70 percent of world trade. No country can ignore that kind of economic power. M.I.T. economist Lester Thurow concludes:

> The knowledge-based economy is fundamentally transforming the role of the nation-state. Instead of being a controller of economic events within its borders, the nation-state is increasingly having to become a platform builder to attract global economic activity to locate within its borders. . . . Because countries need corporations more than corporations need countries, the relative bargaining power of governments and multinational corporations is shifting. High profile multinational companies . . . no longer pay taxes to governments. Governments pay taxes to them.[12]

Just as cities and states within the U.S. compete with one another to attract new industries, nations also offer multinational corporations major financial incentives. Israel paid $600 million (in grants, facility construction, and tax rebates) to land an Intel plant; Brazil promised to pay Ford $700 million, and so on. Similarly, the tax burden felt by corporations has declined significantly throughout the developed world. In the late 1950s, approximately one half of U.S. federal income tax receipts came from corporations; by 1996 that figure had fallen to around 10 percent. Financier George Soros concludes that, while the proportion of a country's income that goes to taxes has not changed substantially, "the taxes on capital and employment have come down while other forms of taxation, particularly on consumption, have been increasing. In other words, the burden of taxation has shifted from capital to citizens."[13]

In the periphery of the global economy, the form of governments has changed, usually toward more democratic forms. In some ways, this is a curious development because democracy and *laissez-faire* capitalism are not especially compatible with one another. Democracy is based on equality—one vote per person regardless of his or her intelligence, wealth, or work ethic. *Laissez-faire* capitalism, on the other hand, is motivated by inequality—differences in economic returns create incentives to work hard and invest resources wisely. Capitalism is designed to serve individual, private interests; democracy is designed to serve shared, public ones. Consequently, the success of the Western capitalist democracies is something of a marvel to behold. It has occurred because of a unique combination of factors—a large middle class whose economic future and upward mobility depends on social stability, a relatively homogeneous population with limited (and largely nonviolent) ethnic divisions, a set of cultural values that support capitalism (as Max Weber brilliantly demonstrated), and natural resources that provided the basis for a strong economy and an opportunity for citizens to accumulate wealth.[14]

Many countries on the periphery of globalization have adopted the *structure* of democracy—popular election of most government officials. If democracy is defined in these terms, 118 of the world's 193 countries, encompassing more than half of its people, now are democratic. But, *legitimate* democracy involves more than just a structure that includes elections. It includes having free and fair elections in which the vast majority of competent adults are allowed to vote, where everyone's vote counts equally, and citizens are afforded adequate education and sufficient amounts of unbiased information to be able to make informed choices. Democracy also involves a commitment by elected officials to implement the will of the people and rule of law, to a separation of powers, and to protection of basic liberties of free speech, assembly, religion, and property.[15] Many of the peripheral democracies lack one or more of these characteristics. Some Latin American counties, most of the Asian countries that once were part of the Soviet Union, and many of the democracies of the Middle East, Pacific Rim, and north Africa have chief executives who rule with little regard for the preferences of representative bodies.

It should not be surprising that emerging democracies differ from those of the core countries. It is much more difficult to establish and maintain democratic institutions in countries that are *developing* a middle class, dealing with limited natural resources, *growing* their economies but still burdened with a lower standard of living than the core countries, and *trying* to manage racial and ethnic divisions. In addition, the demands of multinational corporations complicate democratization. MNC's prefer a capitalist economy and a democratic government, but also demand social and economic stability. In the core countries, with their centuries-old democratic traditions, democracy can provide stability. But, in emerging democracies (for example, Burma, Singapore, South Africa, China, and so on) a democratic-totalitarian hybrid may be the only way to meet the demands of multinational corporations and the global capital market. In both the core and the periphery of the global economy, globalization has changed the nature of government and its relationship to formal organizations.

National Economies and Individual Citizens   Although it is difficult to predict the long-term effects that globalization will have on individual countries and their citizens, it is clear that the process is already having a major impact. Developing countries that have put on the "golden straightjacket" have often experienced remarkable economic growth. Living standards in the developing world have grown two-to-five fold since 1950. Most of that improvement has come in the last 29 years, and most of it has taken place in countries that are tightly linked to the global economy. The improvement has been uneven—living standards in sub-Saharan Africa have improved very little, while they have skyrocketed in some countries in Asia and Latin America. And, living standards in the developing world are less than one-fifth of those in the developed world; in India and sub-Saharan Africa, they are less than one-tenth as high. But, there is no question that some countries and their peoples have benefited significantly from globalization.

There also is no question that economic inequality has also skyrocketed, both within countries and between them (recall the Generation X case study in Chapter 1). Among the developed countries, these trends have been most pronounced in the United States: "Among men, wage inequalities are larger than they ever have been. Real inflation-adjusted median family incomes are slightly below where they were in 1973. Economic uncertainty is very high, and a majority of Americans expect their children to have real incomes below what they have."[16] Globalization has significantly increased the incomes and wealth of educated Americans, particularly those with advanced training and jobs in high-tech industries, while reducing the employment and incomes of workers in traditional production-oriented firms. Moving production jobs offshore, declining union membership and influence, and the shift to a service economy have combined to create a distribution of income and wealth that is more unequal in the United States than in any other developed country. The trends have been particularly pronounced in the inner-cities and some rural areas. The real incomes of the poorest one fifth of U.S. families fell 21 percent between 1979 and 1995; the decline for the lowest-paid ten percent was 15 to 20 percent between 1980 and 1995. Thirty-one million U.S. residents live in households that suffer from hunger; requests for emergency food aid rose 18 percent from 1998 to 1999, with most of the increase going to families in which parents are employed, often in multiple jobs. These declines occurred while the income of the richest fifth jumped 30 percent. At the very top of the scale the differences are staggering. The richest 1 percent of U.S. citizens received 20–25 percent of the nation's income in 1998, about the same percentage that the French nobility received in Marie Antoinette's day.

The real incomes of the lowest-paid 10 percent of U.S. workers fell 15 to 20 percent between 1980 and 1995 (depending on the study) while they rose in the United Kingdom, which ranks second among industrialized countries in wage inequality. The poorest 10 percent of American workers earn about 45 percent of the income of the poorest 10 percent of German workers, 54 percent of the poorest Norwegians, half as much as the poorest Italians, and so on. Since European workers receive a much higher proportion of their compensation in benefits than U.S. workers, and the overall tax system in the United States is more regressive than in Europe, comparing wage rates almost certainly *underestimates* the discrepancy. Although the gap narrowed a bit during1998 and 1999, almost a quarter of U.S. children live in poverty (around 15 percent of Anglo children, 40 percent of Latino children, and 50 percent of African American children). Wealth is even more concentrated than income. The richest 1 percent of U.S. citizens currently hold 39 percent of the nation's wealth, more than twice as much as the bottom 80 percent. In 1996, Bill Gates' fortune was equal to the wealth of the poorest 106 million Americans *combined* (roughly 45 percent of the population).

However, unemployment rates in the United States are currently lower than they ever have been in peacetime. While Europe seems to have paid for globalization with increased unemployment, the United States has paid for it with lower wages for production employees and increased inequalities in income and wealth. Of course, these "choices" are not surprising, given the individualistic orientation of U.S. society and the more communitarian values of northern Europe. Richard Freeman concludes:

> Compared with most advanced countries, the United States does well in job creation, but not in pay; it does well in flexibility and [internal] mobility but not in job security or workers representation. This country rates high in productivity and earnings but has alarmingly low rates of growth in productivity and real wages. And the United States pays less skilled workers lower wages than in many other advanced countries.[17]

Similar trends toward inequality are taking place on a global scale. In Africa, unemployment has increased *and* incomes have fallen. In Asian countries, whose primary comparative advantage is low labor costs, "aggressive strategies of low-labor-cost production are in full bloom. Child labor, sweatshops, and oppressive domestic outwork proliferate."[18] In Brazil the poorest half of the population receive less than 12 percent of the income while the richest 10 percent take home almost two-thirds. In 1960, the 20 percent of the world's people who live in the 10 richest countries had 30 times the income of the people who lived in the poorest 20 percent; in 1995 the figure was 82 times as much. The wealthiest one-fifth of the world's population consumes 45 percent of all meat and fish, and use 58 percent of all energy; the poorest one fifth consume 5 percent of the meat and fish and use 4 percent of the world's energy supply. Globalization is exaggerating each of these trends.

All of these trends are predicted by economic theory—they are the (hopefully) short-term dislocations mentioned in the theory of comparative advantage. However, the free flow of capital among countries has exaggerated the dislocations created by free trade. Developing countries simply cannot provide the education and infrastructure required by multinational companies quickly enough to keep investors from moving their capital elsewhere.

In addition, some government policies, such as restrictions on immigration, have short-circuited the corrective effects of the economic system. For example, soon after negotiating a series of "free trade" policies (for example, NAFTA), the United States significantly increased its efforts to *reduce* immigration, particularly from Latin America. In doing so, Congress responded to polls indicating that 70 percent of U.S. citizens supported immigration restrictions by tripling the budget of the Immigration and Naturalization Service (INS), making it the largest federal law enforcement agency. It allowed the INS to detain suspected illegal immigrants indefinitely with none of the rights afforded suspected criminals—a right to see an attorney or judge or receive released time for good behavior. However, even with more than 20,000 people in INS prisons and 180,000 deportations annually, the INS has barely dented the estimated 5 million illegal immigrants currently working in the United States. Even though the theory of comparative advantage specifies that labor mobility is necessary for the global economy to successfully reach and maintain an equilibrium position, restricting immigration continues to be popular, even among staunch supporters of free trade. For example, immediately after being elected, Mexico's new President Vincente Fox, himself educated in the United States as a *laissez faire*/free trade economist, proposed eliminating immigration restrictions between his country and the United States. No politician north of the *Rio Del Norte* (Rio Grande) took his suggestion seriously. Instead, the newly elected President, George W. Bush, responded that his goal is to find "a humane way" to crack down on migration from "our friendly neighbor to the south." Many European governments have taken similar positions about immigration. Economists argue that governments will eventually have to confront this inconsistency in their policies if free trade is to succeed, but there is little evidence that they will do so very soon.[19]

Multinational corporations (MNCs) also are able to short-circuit the corrective mechanisms of free trade. When a developing economy does begin to grow and wages begin to rise, MNCs can simply shift their operations to more economically undeveloped areas. For example, like most shoe companies, Nike moved its production operations out of the United States during the early 1990s, primarily to South Korea (the United States lost 65,000 jobs in the shoe manufacturing business). When the Korean economy improved and wage rates started to rise (as predicted by the theory of comparative advantage), Nike shifted its operations to Indonesia, China, and Malaysia, where wages are about one seventh of the South Korean rate. Until the wage rates increase in the *entire* developing world, multinational firms will be able to shift production to even lower-wage countries, erasing the gains of developing countries, and short-circuiting the corrective effects of free trade. In the process, they are able to increase the incomes of their nonproduction workers and their investors. (Nike's profits in 1994 were about $323 million; it's CEO's compensation was well over $1 million.)[20]

Some countries are attempting to cushion or offset the adverse effects of globalization. The European Economic Union and European Trade Union Confederation are implementing a number of strategies designed to increase productivity (and thus support wages) and attract investment capital while reducing the size of their social support programs. Developing countries, primarily in Latin America, are discussing ways to pool their resources to insulate themselves against currency fluctuations and the capital markets, much as Europe has done with the Euro. Developed nations in Asia are taking similar steps. But, at this point no region has devised strategies that promise to protect their economies from the pressures of globalization successfully over the long term.

CASE STUDY:
STUDENTS, SWEATSHOPS, AND GLOBALIZATION

The U.S. anti-sweatshop movement was born in 1995 and 1996 when a series of news reports found that sweatshops were producing clothing for The Gap in Central America, Kathy Lee Gifford's line of clothing sold at Walmart in Honduras, and Nike shoes in Indonesia. Raids of domestic sweatshops continued the adverse publicity. In response, the Clinton administration created the Apparel Industry Partnership (AIP), which issued a final report in 1998. Part of that report was a Collegiate Code of Conduct (CCC), which proposed that colleges and universities license their products only to companies that met specific standards for working hours, child labor, forced overtime, discrimination, harassment, abuse, and rights of freedom of association and collective bargaining. As negotiations over the terms of the CCC continued, the initial draft was changed in many ways. Instead of requiring that companies pay a "living wage," the final draft required them to pay the locally prevailing "minimum wage," which is so low in many developing countries that it leaves recipients in dire poverty (Brakken, 1999). Monitoring and enforcement by an independent external group was replaced with corporate self-monitoring and self-enforcement. In protest of these changes, three of the organizations originally involved in the AIP quit—both union members, and the Interfaith Center on Corporate Responsibility. Michael Shellenberger, a spokesman for Global Exchange (an anti-sweatshop organization), said "this is a step backwards. These companies will be able to market their products as sweatshop-free—without actually making changes to sweatshop practices abroad" (cited in Dobnik, 1988: p. 5). If the company produces apparel in U.S. territories such as Saipan, which is outside of U.S. minimum wage and worker protection laws, they also can sew "Made in the USA" labels in their products. But, more than 100 universities, including Duke and Notre Dame signed on. Others refused to do so because of

(continued)

(continued from the previous page)

the weaknesses—the University of Michigan, University of Wisconsin, and University of California. In April 1999, the University of California added clauses to its agreement that required firms to pay a living wage, allow collective bargaining, and obey applicable environmental and health and safety laws.

The economics of college apparel are simple. There is a high-fashion market that caters to high-income customers and shifts in their tastes. It needs to remain close to its retail markets, and thus cannot move its operations offshore (although it can contract with sweatshops in New York City and Paris for some of its production). The rest of the market need not concern itself with fashion pressures, and production for colleges and universities is most insulated from market trends. Fans and alumni buy the same designs decade after decade; in fact universities lose market when they change designs, not when they repeat them. Between 1980 and 1992, 850,000 jobs were lost in the apparel industry in the developed world while 850,000 new jobs were created in the developing world, mostly in Asia. (500,000 new jobs were created in Bangladesh, Thailand, Indonesia, and the Philippines.) Specific relocation decisions were based primarily on wage rates—$0.10–0.18 in Bangladesh and Myanmar (Burma), $0.20–0.68 in China, Pakistan, Vietnam, India, Sri Lanka, and Indonesia), and $1.00–2.00 per hour in Latin America. Of the $20.00 that a customer pays for a university baseball cap, approximately $1.50 will go to the university and $0.08 will go to the worker who produced it. Corporations will attempt to pay workers the lowest wage they can and place them in the least expensive working conditions, and that wage/working condition is set by the maximum wage available to the worker in other industries or occupations. Since the countries mentioned here are primarily agricultural, and agriculture pays very low wages, corporations need not pay higher wages to attract a workforce. When a developing economy improves and higher-paid jobs become available, apparel manufacturers either pay those higher wages, or move their operations to even less developed countries. "Artificial" processes, such as government pressure or labor unions, could increase local wage rates, but apparel manufacturers tend to locate in countries with little or no unionization and governments that are either weak or strongly pro-employer.

Student anti-sweatshop groups seek to create an alternative source of power for apparel workers. College and university licenses provide manufacturers with a virtually guaranteed market and are incredibly lucrative, bringing profits of as much as 1000 percent. Student groups have found strong allies in U.S. labor unions, primarily the Union of Needletrades and the Industrial and Textile Employees (UNITE), and grass-roots organizations such as Global Exchange. Like Miriam Joffe-Block, a 21-year-old activist at Penn, students recognize that "it's a very complex issue—global economic justice—but this is a very tangible way for students to see themselves connected to the issue." And, they have had some success. Joffe-Block says that the Penn campaign "really has taken off."

(continued)

(continued from the previous page)

The first target of their activities, Nike, has altered its contracting and oversight processes. The newest target is Gap, which is particularly vulnerable since the primary market of Gap, Banana Republic, and Old Navy stores, is college students and young adults. Emily Pope, a 20-year old student at the University of Delaware who helped start the local Student Labor Action Committee, said "It's just another way that companies try to rip us off. We shouldn't let that happen."*

Applying What You've Learned

1. What economic pressures encourage multinational firms to contract with sweatshops? To what extent can the students' tactics counteract those pressures?

2. To what extent do these student activists fit the stereotype of "Generation X" students (recall Chapter 1)? Why or why not?

Questions to Think About and Discuss

1. Is it appropriate for U.S. citizens to apply their own values to the actions of global corporations?

2. Since most (but not all) of the people who work in sweatshops do so "voluntarily," don't the students actions impinge on their right to choose their own lives?

---

*Jennifer Lin, "Students Create Groups to Fight Sweatshops," Houston *Chronicle*, 5 Dec., 1999, 12C. Also see John Cavanagh, "The Global Resistance to Sweatshops," in *No Sweat*, Andrew Ross, ed. New York: Verso, 1997 and Randy Shaw, *Reclaiming America* (Berkeley: University of California Press, 1999).

Background information:
The Collegiate Code is available at www.sweatshopwatch.org.
Verena Dobnik, "Employees Sign Sweatshop Pact." Available at www.cleanclothes.org.
Eric Brakken, "Critical Analysis of the Fair Labor Association." Available at www.asm.wisc.edu/asas/.
UNITE Report on Campus Caps. Available at www.uniteunion.org/sweatshops/.

Organizational Practices and Strategies of Organizing   Globalization has also had a major impact on organizations themselves. Throughout this book, we have noted that some strategies of organizing are better suited for turbulent, highly competitive environments than others. Relational, cultural, and networking strategies all increase the speed of information flow and the quality of organizational decisions. Each strategy creates a communication system that allows an organization to rapidly respond to environmental pressures. But, in a global economy, being able to *react* quickly and decisively may not be enough. Globalization "requires that an organization *anticipate* change and move *proactively*. In a **responsive organization** (in contrast to a reactive one) structures and procedures must enhance the organization's ability to take advantage of changes in the environment to increase its competitive advantage."[21] One of the realities of globalization is that minor differences in an organization's ability to exploit its environment have major effects on its performance. The most effective firm in a given sector of the economy can completely dominate the market; being second best may not mean having a smaller share of the market, it can mean having no share at all.[22] Global organizations have two options—to become *the* dominant force in their field, or to become a highly selective niche player. Organizational size has a number of advantages—it allows an organization to dominate governments, suppliers, and workers. This is why corporate mergers, both within the core countries and between them, today occur on almost a daily basis. But, historically, size also has meant bureaucratization, and bureaucratization has meant inflexibility. So, the optimal strategy for global organizations is to be both large and nimble, a combination that requires new and different strategies of organizing. It means that some activities need to be centralized while others need to be decentralized; an organizational form called an **heterarchy.** For example, Dell Computer Corporation has centralized the billing, inventory management, and distribution networks for its European operations in a single site in Ireland. But, it has decentralized decision making to its individual sales and service centers in each European country. A large European food corporation requires all its European branches to interact with the Italian branch for their own ice cream marketing because the Italian market is so complex. But, the Italian director of manufacturing must interact with his or her French colleague who is responsible for European manufacturing. Every national manager has several bosses worldwide, and also is a worldwide supervisor for some specific practices.

Monsanto still is searching for the optimal mix of centralization and decentralization, specialization and "global vision." It's CEO Robert Shapiro, realizes that any strategy that denies information to its employees, or encourages the firm to hire people because they take orders well, will not survive. He also realizes that the final strategy will reduce his control over the organization and even reduce his awareness of "what's going on." Monsanto has not yet settled on a final strategy, but it is clear that it cannot be a traditional bureaucracy. It will involve a form of "radical decentralization," one that focuses on enhancing internal and external communication. Globalization does not mean that every organization will develop radically new strategies of organizing. For example, the family business model that long has dominated Taiwan and Hong Kong seems to be especially well-suited to globalization—their members are highly motivated, more committed, more flexible, and less bureaucratic than the state-owned businesses with which they compete. In China, where government agents still operate as supervisors, the challenge is to find ways to combine the socialist model and the family firm in a way that balances "the modern and the traditional while remaining competitive in the global economy."[23] Whatever strategy a given organization develops, it must deal effectively with the pressures of globalization.

In sum, the economic theories underlying *laissez-faire* capitalism and free trade predict many of the observed effects of globalization. While these theories predict that the resulting economic dislocations will eventually be corrected,

there is reason to doubt those predictions. Neither theory adequately anticipates the effects of a free market in capital, and both assume that multinational
organizations will be less monopolistic than they are becoming. Both factors
may undermine the corrective mechanisms noted in economic theory. If these
mechanisms do fail, economic inequality is likely to increase further; social tensions are likely to continue to grow, and the democratizing pressures of globalization will be undermined. Organizations and their members could find themselves in a world that is both chaotic and increasingly hostile and divided.

GLOBALIZATION, ETHICS, AND ORGANIZATIONAL DEMOCRACY

Historically, U.S. organizations have been decidedly undemocratic institutions.
And throughout U.S. history formal organizations have exerted strong influences on political decision making, increasingly out of sight of the public eye.
When combined with widespread acceptance of the assumptions underlying
laissez-faire capitalism, these realities have created a social situation in which
powerful organizations can operate freely, without being held responsible to
the larger society. For example, Stanley Deetz concludes that in the contemporary United States "commercial corporations function as public institutions but
without public accountability." Given U.S. residents' commitments to openness
and democracy, this is somewhat surprising. The tension between democracy
and autonomous, nondemocratic organizations is the basis of a distinctive view
of corporations' responsibilities to the larger society.[24]

Laissez-Faire Capitalism and Stakeholder Interests

Over time, capitalists and scholars alike have struggled to deal with the moral
and ethical dilemmas created by *laissez faire* capitalism. Their approach to
these dilemmas have ranged from notions of corporate social responsibility to
corporate social responsiveness to multiple stakeholder models.

The "Robber Barons" and Corporate Social Responsibility   During an
earlier era of economic globalization, Andrew Carnegie, founder of U.S. Steel,
argued that two principles needed to be accepted if *laissez-faire* capitalism was
to succeed over the long term. One was the **charity principle,** which required
more fortunate members of the society to assist its less fortunate members,
either directly through philanthropy or indirectly through corporate support of
social service organizations. Carnegie roundly criticized other "captains of
industry" (the term "robber barons" was an equally popular adjective at the
time) for ignoring broader social concerns in their narrow pursuit of wealth
and power. Somewhat ironically, Carnegie seemed to be less concerned about
the wealthy industrialists' treatment of their employees, but his commitment to
the society as a whole was clear. Carnegie was also committed to the **stewardship principle,** which suggested that businesses and wealthy people had an

obligation to try to increase the wealth of the society as a whole by wisely investing the resources they controlled. For the following fifty years, Carnegie's assumptions were accepted and codified into a concept of "corporate social responsibility," a belief that organizations had a responsibility to assist in the solution of social problems in addition to making money, especially if they had helped to create those problems. But, by the 1960s the social responsibility perspective was being challenged.

Conservative U.S. economist Milton Friedman (among others) argued that the only responsibility corporations have is to pursue their own economic self-interest. Managers have no particular expertise in defining social problems, no incentives for trying to solve them, and capitalism provides no means of holding them accountable for the effects of their purportedly "socially responsible" activities. To the extent that they *do* invest the organization's capital in such activities, they make it vulnerable to competitors who invest all their resources in enhancing the firm's economic position. Thus, in the long run, they threaten the jobs of their employees and violate the trust of their investors. In short, Friedman argued, Carnegie's two principles are contradictory—in an economy defined by competitive, *laissez-faire* capitalism, corporate *charity* reduces the economic viability of a firm, thus violating the *stewardship* principle. In a democratic society, only government is responsible for dealing with social problems, because only government can be held accountable for doing or not doing so. Organizations should be concerned with *generating* wealth and government should not interfere in that process. Governments should concern themselves with *distributing* wealth and not leave that task to corporations.[25] When government tries to solve social problems, it must do so without interfering with the operation of economic markets.

Corporate Social Responsiveness   Debates over the social responsibility doctrine continued until the late 1970s, eventually leading to a new doctrine of "social responsiveness." In the social responsiveness perspective, managers are responsible for monitoring an organization's environment and strategically responding to environmental pressures. Most of these pressures are economic, as Unit I explained. But others are more social than economic. For example, the growing environmental movement of the 1970s and 1980s placed new pressures on managers, pressures that, ironically, were enforced by governmental action. The advantage of the social responsiveness perspective is that it does give managers some guidelines for making socially relevant choices: Obey the law, fulfill regulations, and placate powerful external interest groups.

But the social responsiveness doctrine is problematic in a number of ways. First, it establishes an adversarial relationship between managers and both government agencies and external interest groups. Instead of fostering a cooperative effort to deal with social and economic problems, it encourages competitive and hostile orientations. Second, it encourages managers to find ways to proactively manage external pressures. In many cases, it is easier to circumvent or overpower external pressures than to be responsive to them. Contributing to the political campaigns of candidates who promise to weaken environmental standards is often much less expensive than meeting those standards. Exploiting weaknesses in governmental monitoring or the legal system may be more cost effective than acting in legal and ethical ways. For example, in late 1996, Archer Daniels Midland was fined $100 million by the U.S. Justice Department for illegally fixing the prices of citric acid and lysine (an additive in animal feeds). It was the largest fine ever levied against a U.S. organization. Since price fixing short-circuits the competitive mechanisms of the free market, this is precisely the kind of governmental action that is sanctioned by *laissez faire* economic theory. The government's ability to punish ADM paled in comparison to the estimated $200–$600 million in extra profits that the company made by engaging in the illegal activities.

From Social Responsiveness to Multiple Stakeholders   Problems with the corporate social responsibility doctrine eventually led to the development of "multiple-stakeholder" models of organizational ethics. Advocates of multiple-stakeholder perspectives argue that many groups have a legitimate stake in the decisions made by managers and the actions taken by the organizations they control. Management is responsible for finding ways to meet the needs and interests of all legitimate stakeholders in the company. Workers, suppliers, consumers, host communities, stockholders, and the general community often have taken more risks and made greater long-term investments in their organizations than upper management has. Through their taxes, *they* have paid to educate the workers hired by the organization, built the infrastructure needed for the organization to function (roads, airports, electric systems, etc.), and invested *their* labor and capital in the organization. And *they* are harmed most when the organization downsizes, despoils the environment, engages in discriminatory actions, and so on.

At a number of points in this book, we have observed that owners, managers, and workers have distinct and competing interests (see especially Chapter 3). Different strategies of organizing manage these differences in distinctive ways. They also create particular kinds of power relationships among the three groups. Globalization has exaggerated differences in the interests of the three groups because it has led to important shifts in their relative power. Since the time of Frederick Taylor, managers or organizations in developed countries have had more power than either workers or owners, particularly in the United States. Entrepreneur-owners largely handed control of their organizations over to professionally-trained managers because of their presumably superior expertise. In publicly owned organizations, stockholders are the legal owners; but they were so dispersed that they had little, if any, direct influence on organizational policies or practices. Managers tended to retain much of the money their organizations made and reinvested it in plants, equipment, and personnel. Although there were tensions between management and labor, particularly in the United States, systems were created to assure at least acceptable levels of labor peace and assure stable employment and wages.

Since 1980, stockholders have radically increased their influence on managerial decisions, usually through the mechanism of institutional investments. Legal barriers continue to make it difficult for shareholders to exercise direct control over organizational operations, but they have increasingly linked management compensation to stock values. In response, managers have focused on finding ways to maximize short-term profits and shareholder returns, particularly in the United States. Downsizing, shifting production off-shore, outsourcing, heavy reliance on part-time workers, and taking steps to weaken labor organizations all serve to maximize shareholder returns (recall the Generation X case study in Chapter 1). Each of these strategies also increase managerial power over workers and enhances managerial incomes. On average, the compensation given to U.S. CEOs increased from 44 times the average factory worker's wage in 1995 to 419 times the workers' income in 1998. In countries with stronger systems of employee representation (for example, Germany) the trends have not been as extreme, but they have been in the same direction. The "Anglo-American model of corporate governance that generates pressures . . . to maximize shareholder value as their primary objective" is now firmly entrenched throughout the developed world.[26]

At the same time, worker power has declined substantially. This results in part from structural factors—labor organizations are highly bureaucratic and thus are unable to respond rapidly to changes in overall power relationships. In addition, they have traditionally relied on political action. As governments have become progressively less powerful relative to multinational organizations, workers' ability to influence corporate practices through political action has declined. The policy decisions that are most important to workers now are made by international organizations, not national governments. Corporations have shifted their operations to areas in which labor's influence is weak, for example, the developing world and the southern U.S. International trade; economist Dani Rodrik concludes:

> Employers are less willing to provide the benefits of job security and stability, partly because of increased competition but also because their enhanced global mobility makes them less dependent on the good-will of their local work force. Governments are less able to sustain social safety nets, because an important part of their tax base has become footloose because of increased mobility of capital. . . . Globalization creates an inequality in bargaining power that 60 years of labor legislation in the U.S. has tried to prevent.[27]

As a result, a two-tiered labor force has emerged throughout the developed and developing world. One tier is composed of highly educated workers in stable, high-paying jobs that provide substantial benefits and job security. Their skills and their ability to move from company to company provide them with relatively strong bargaining positions, as long as the economy is strong. The other tier is composed of workers who typically (but not always) have less education or education that is not relevant to high-tier jobs, and who are in various kinds of contingent positions that may (but often do not) provide high salaries, but no benefits or job security. Of course, even in the United States, there have been notable instances of labor resistance to the creation of a two-tiered system—successful strikes against United Parcel Service and General Motors over the use of part-time workers and outsourcing and Microsoft's multimillion settlement in December, 2000 with "permatemp" workers who had long-term jobs with the company but were denied fringe benefits, such as health insurance and stock options. But, the global trend toward a two-tiered workforce seems to be quite clear. Although different stakeholders are increasingly affected by the actions of MNCs, they are increasingly powerless to affect those actions.

Stakeholder Interests and Organizational Democracy

Consequently, the needs of multiple stakeholders will be met only if organizations themselves strive to meet them. Ironically, globalization may provide the impetus for democratizing organizations, at least among "first-tier" employees. To be responsive to global pressures, organizations must legitimately empower their core employees. But, democratizing MNCs will not be easy. Democratization requires taking two simple but radical steps: First, it requires encouraging open and honest debate about the accepted assumptions about organizations and economic justice that dominate contemporary U.S. society, and second it requires the creation of systems, structures, and practices through which the voices of multiple stakeholders are raised and heard. Democratization can succeed only if people challenge the societal myth that democratic governance is too inefficient to be used by organizations in highly competitive environments.

Challenging this assumption begins by recognizing the inefficiencies that are built into traditional, nondemocratic, strategies of organizing—the inevitable communication breakdowns described in Chapter 2; the alienation and resistance described in Unit I, the nonrational nature of organizational decision making, and suppression of conflicts described in Chapters 8 and 9; and the orientation toward short-term profit maximization and managerial control that are part of the traditional strategies of organizing (Chapter 2).

However, challenging the assumptions also involves taking a new look at instances in which democratic processes have succeeded even within nondemocratic organizations (Chapters 5 and 11). For example, the Saturn automobile corporation was designed to foster a cooperative relationship between labor and management that focused on finding ways to increase product quality. This system was a radical departure from the adversarial, bureaucratic strategy that had long characterized U.S. auto manufacturers in general and General Motors in particular. The Saturn experiment was so successful that by 1992 the company needed to increase production substantially. Operating on the assumptions of traditional strategies of organizing, management proposed a strategy of short-term cost containment that would reduce economic rewards to workers and reduce product quality. Workers protested the strategy and responded with a work slowdown, forcing management to eventually negotiate systems that improved the production process, protected worker income, maintained high product quality, and ensured long-term customer satisfaction and loyalty. But the solution emerged only because workers had sufficient power to make their voices heard (recall Chapter 7), and because both sides used integrative, problem-solving conflict management strategies to move beyond the preferences for short-term profit maximization that long have typified U.S. management.

Once the assumption that democracy is inefficient is challenged, a number of steps can be taken to represent the interests of multiple stakeholders better. For example, limiting the size of organizations or units of organizations seems to encourage open debate and foster opportunities for multiple voices to be heard. Systems of employee empowerment, including different versions of participatory decision making (Chapter 3), are a first step toward democratizing organizations; but if they are employed within nondemocratic organizations, they tend to punish or unethically manipulate workers. But the key shift is to take the long-standing U.S. preference for democratic governance seriously, so seriously that systems of empowerment and democracy are applied *even* to formal organizations.[28]

GLOBALIZATION AND CULTURE

Just as globalization is transforming economics and politics, it is also influencing cultures around the world. When multinational organizations enter an area, they bring with them a distinctively Western set of values—individualism, commercialism, separation of church and state, liberty, and *laissez-faire* economics—that are alien to Islamic, Confucian, Japanese, Hindu, Buddhist, or Orthodox cultures. Many of their products, from rock music to fast food to cosmetics, are also distinctively Western. Some observers argue that these trends will lead to *cultural homogenization*, a bland world in which the rich cultural diversity of the world will be squeezed into a single, standardized, Western or American pattern. Different writers have created their own clichés for these trends—McWorld, Coca-Colonization, McDonaldization, or McDisneyization—but they all refer to the same processes. Other observers warn that people in non-Western societies will be progressively more alienated and angered by this cultural invasion, resulting in an increasingly hostile world (a *polarization thesis*). A third group argues that culture is far more resilient and flexible than either of the extreme positions suggest. Historically peoples throughout the world have accepted some aspects of "invading" cultures, modified others to fit their core values, and maintained their distinctive character. This *hybridization thesis* suggests that the challenge imposed by globalization is for countries and individuals to find a healthy balance between preserving a sense of identity, home, and community while living and acting within a global economic system.[29]

The Homogenization Thesis

There is a great deal of anecdotal evidence to support the globalization thesis—McDonalds, Walmarts, Coca-Cola, and so on now exist in every conceivable corner of the world. Western consumerism is distinctively oriented toward consistency and name-brand identification. Everyone who discusses globalization has his or her own story. Sociologist Peter Berger, who you met in Chapter 4, talks about a recent visit to Hong Kong. He went into a Buddhist temple and found a middle-aged man in a business suit and stocking feet, standing in front of an altar, facing a large statue of Buddha, burning incense and talking on a cell phone. Cultural homogenization is fueled by mass advertising and the status that accompanies Western (or American) products in much of the world. In fact, the phenomenon seems to be closely linked to the emergence of a global economic elite, people who have become wealthy as a result of the global economy and who are increasingly tied to one another and increasingly isolated from non-elite people in their own societies.

Even people who fear McWorld admit that some degree of homogenization is good. For example, societies that allow slavery are now quite rare (with some notable exceptions such as Sudan) and the anti-tobacco movement that started in the West (primarily in the United States) is now becoming a world-wide success.[30] And, the extent of cultural globalization and of American dominance of global culture has probably been overstated. Many cross-cultural similarities existed prior to globalization and the Internet. Baseball and American football have not become world sports; the Coca-Cola consumed in Africa is imported from Europe, not the United States; Paris still is the world's cultural magnet, not New York or Los Angeles; and there has been extensive and quite successful resistance to dominance by the U.S. media. Cultural power is not like economic power. It is not arranged in a core-periphery structure, but has multiple centers and very complex patterns of diffusion. But, participating in a global culture is important because it influences core values and views of reality. As local taken-for-granted assumptions become less powerful, the bases of social cohesion decline in power and are not replaced by alternatives. Shared economic preferences and common media experiences simply do not provide a stable basis for social cohesion: "global society could never satisfy... individuals' need to belong. It could never become a community."[31] In that sense, cultural homogenization may have a major impact.

The Polarization Thesis

Other observers see much more negative forces at work in the class divisions and resistance that seem to accompany cultural globalization. As Western culture permeates non-Western societies, it is seen as more and more immoral and pathologically individualist, as a threat to moral order and community. Differences between cultures are much more fundamental and emotional than differences in politics or economics. When the world becomes a smaller place, these differences become *more visible* and people's consciousness of cultural differences becomes more pronounced. Cultural conflicts are much more difficult to resolve than economic or political ones—compromise on the terms of a trade contract is a fundamentally different thing than compromise on moral or religious truths. As countries form regional associations to protect themselves from the negative effects of economic globalization, the cultural ties that unify them may separate them from other regions.

In the process of regionalizing, people of non-Western cultures may find that they have much more in common with one another than with the West (for example, Islam and Confucianism).[32] When combined with the wide disparities of wealth and income that have accompanied economic globalization, these cultural differences may lead to an increasing polarization both within societies and between them. There are many sources of the current backlash against globalization, some economic, some cultural. This backlash is most intense in societies suffering both economic and cultural dislocation, and it tends to be focused on the United States. Whether it is accurate or fair to single out the United States, it is quite clear that polarization is significant, and in some areas, growing. And, ironically, the same forces that created globalization can be used to resist it. The 1999 protests of the WTO meeting in Seattle were organized via the Internet, and the size and scope of those demonstrations was transmitted instantaneously throughout the world by CNN.

DISNEY GOES GLOBAL*

Disneyland now is a global operation. By all counts, Disney Tokyo has been a resounding success. Opening in 1983, in 1991 it drew 5 million more customers than the original Disneyland. In contrast, Euro-Disney initially was a financial and public relations bust, losing more than $900 million in its first year. The Magic Kingdom's international operations reveal a great deal about the complexities of global operations and the nuances of cultural resistance.

Disney Tokyo was a success largely because it allowed the Japanese to reinterpret core American symbols and make them their own. In some ways, Japanese culture made Tokyo Disney a natural. Many observers of modern Japan note the country's penchant for importing the very best of anything foreign in an effort to make Japan a composite of "the best in the world." Disneyland/World clearly is the "best" of the United States. In addition, many of its core values are "Japanese," a belief in technological wizardry, a philosophy that emphasizes high-quality service, happiness, harmony, and hospitality, and an obsession with clean and orderly operations. The park itself is an almost perfect replica of Disneyland. It is run by a Japanese firm, the Oriental Land Company, which gives the Disney empire a 10 percent cut of its profits. A small American management team (known locally as "Disnoids") and a few "cast members" (entertainers, crafts people, and characters) supplement the Japanese workforce. Unlike Japanese workers, all of whom wear a tag displaying their last names, these *gajin* (foreign) employees have none. They are merely "others," nameless and faceless people who are clearly not part of the Japanese community. And, just as blacks are notably absent from visible positions at Disneyland, non-Japanese Asians (Koreans, and Chinese) are absent from Tokyo Disneyland.

There are differences, of course. The park is larger than Disneyland, which gives it a spaciousness that simply does not exist in the rest of Tokyo. There are few pushcart food vendors, but many more restaurants, reflecting Japanese beliefs that it is rude to walk while eating. There are no Nautilus-style submarines,

(continued)

(continued from the previous page)

reflecting Japanese sensitivity to all things nuclear. Drivers wear white gloves, like those of Tokyo taxi and bus drivers; security is "loose" by U.S. standards, allowing people to move in much closer proximity. Main Street, USA has been transformed into the World Bazaar, a shopping mall where the products of five continents are brought together in a collage that is distinctively Japanese. Disneyland's "Meet Mr. Lincoln," which provides an unabashedly sentimental journey through U.S. history culminating in a sing-along of "America the Beautiful" becomes "Meet the World." In it a crane guides a boy and his sister through Japan's past, focusing on what makes Japan unique. A "Magic Journey" movie takes guests across five continents, returning them dramatically to "our beloved Japan, where our hearts always remain." John van Maanen concludes that, just as "the nostalgia, patriotism, and historical narratives provide the context of meaning for visitors to Disneyland. . . . Tokyo Disneyland serves as something of a shrine in Japan to Japan itself, an emblem of the self-validating beliefs as to the cultural values and superiority of the Japanese" (pp. M-10, M-11). Both parks are shrines to their own culture's superiority. In short, what makes Disneyland the "happiest place on earth" for U.S. citizens makes Tokyo Disneyland the happiest place on earth for Japanese.

Euro-Disney is a different story entirely. Many of the initial decisions were based solely on financial considerations. Disney was determined to not let a local company keep most of the profits, as they had done in Tokyo. So, they set up a very complex ownership system that kept most of the money in a separate company set up to run the park. In spite of these moves, the French government, eager to attract jobs and development spillover (Disney also was considering a site in Spain), sold Disney 4,800 acres of land at below market prices (and allowed them to resell the land at whatever price they could get), gave them low-interest loans from state banks, and extended a high-speed rail line to the park at government expense. To gain support from the French, Disney offered more than 30 percent of the stock in Euro Disney to the public. However, when it was learned that their offering price ($11.50 a share) was almost ten times the price that Disney charged itself for its shares, any good-will that might have been prompted by the offer disappeared.

Things went downhill from there. When Michael Eisner went to Paris to launch the project he was met with egg-throwing protesters. To make Euro Disney as much like the other Disney parks as possible, it required the same dress code. Employees protested, and the park was charged with violating French labor law. Journalist Jacques Neher asked in the New York *Times,* "how could these brash Americans be so insensitive to French culture, individualism, and privacy." For the French, regulating employees' hair color and length, make-up and jewelry, and undergarments was "an attack on individual liberty" (as leaflets handed out at the park by the General Confederation of Labor claimed) and a violation of "human dignity," as the Democratic Confederation of Labor claimed in its appeal to have the Labor Ministry halt Disney's dress code. Standard Disney

(continued)

(continued from the previous page)

control practices (recall Chapter 4) also violated French sensibilities and French labor law. Using part-time and contingent workers who are not paid benefits, rewarding the most reliable and malleable workers with perks like overtime pay, and speedily dismissing workers who failed to meet Disney standards, all created ill-will and immersed Disney in costly litigation.

Although Disney tried to placate European sensibilities by tracing Disney fairytales back to their roots (Snow White speaks German, Peter Pan takes place in London, the Caribbean Pirates speak French, and so on), the French cultural elite was appalled. One called Euro Disney a "cultural Chernobyl," another proclaimed that it was a "horror made of cardboard, plastic, and appalling colors, a construction of hardened chewing gum, and idiotic folklore taken straight out of comic books written for obsese Americans."† More important, at least to Disney, it lost money. Attendance was high, as high as management had predicted. But, Europeans vacation differently than Americans or the Japanese. Many were "day-trippers" who spent most of their time in Paris instead of staying in Disney hotels (which cost more than three-star hotels in the city). Admissions prices were higher than in the other parks, and souvenirs were prohibitively expensive by French standards. Initially, Disney banned alcohol at the park, but relented after being met with intense pressure. Unlike the other parks, they allowed guests to bring box lunches with them, but this cut into restaurant revenues. A recovery process was started in 1994, when the park was renamed Disneyland Paris, but a great deal of damage had already been done. Today the park is making money, but its returns pale in comparison to Disneyland and Disney Tokyo.

Applying What You've Learned

1. France and the United States are supposedly "individualistic" cultures; Japan is a "communitarian" one. This generalization would lead one to expect that a U.S. firm operating in France would have fewer cultural conflicts than one operating in Japan. But, Disney had the opposite experience? Why?
2. Some observers complain that people who resist globalization tend to confuse cultural and economic factors. Which of the two was most responsible for Disney's success in Tokyo? Its failure in France?

Questions to Think About and Discuss

1. In the "Trouble in the Happiest Place on Earth" case study (Chapter 4) management and workers at Disneyland developed very different ways of interpreting key symbols. What factors led management to misinterpret workers perceptions? Were the same factors present at Euro Disney?
2. What, if anything, could Disney have done differently to make the early years of Euro-Disney more successful? Why would those steps have succeeded?

(continued)

(continued from the previous page)

*This case is based on Pyrra Alnot & Mary Yoko Brannen, "Cultural Misunderstanding," in *Pressing Problems in Organizations (That Keep Us Awake at Night),* Quinn, et al., eds. (New York: AMACOM, 2000) and John van Maanen, "Displacing Disney," in Ancona, et al., *Organizational Behavior and Processes* (Cincinnati: Southwestern College Publishing, 1999).
†Richard Pells, *Not Like Us* (New York: Basic Books, 1997).

The Hybridization/Glocalism Thesis

A third group of observers argue that the most likely outcome of cultural globalization will be the development of a number of hybrid societies that combine local and Western cultural characteristics. This, they argue, has been the primary lesson of history. From Hellenization to Christianization, local societies have found ways to accept some aspects of "invading" cultures while retaining the core of their culture. Thomas Friedman calls this process "glocalizing," a term that originally was developed in Japan as a label for marketing products to fit local tastes. John Tomlinson explains:

> Culture simply does not transfer in this [simple linear] way. Movement between cultural/geographical areas always involves interpretation, translation, mutation, adaptation . . . as the receiving culture brings its own cultural resources to bear . . . upon cultural imports.[33]

The use of English as the global language of commerce provides an excellent example. On the one hand, it is obvious that English dominates the global economy. There is no inherent reason for English to dominate—it is not easier to learn, more precise, more flexible, or more capable of expressing emotions. One third of the world's population (1.6 billion people) use English in some form today. 80 percent of the content posted on the Internet is in English (although the percent is declining), even though one half of Internet users speak a different language at home. Corporations in English-speaking countries account for 40 percent of the world's economic activity. English dominance reflects the political, economic, and military power of English-speaking countries. In many ways, it has created a new system of global haves and have-nots. Being able to speak and read English opens up opportunities for knowledge and career advancement that are not available to people who do not speak the language. Career ads in French newspapers published in Belgium are in English, because MNCs increasingly require English-language skills of their professional employees.

But, regional languages have not disappeared. In fact, differences among dialects of non-English languages are becoming more pronounced, and regional languages are increasingly popular ways of bridging linguistic differences. Mulitlingualism is becoming the world-wide norm, everywhere except in the

United States. The language that a person uses with family and friends may be different than the one used with coworkers, which may be different than the one used with bosses or government. Many countries have reacted to the growing use of English by forbidding its use in settings where it is not required. As a result, local language use is becoming hybridized, just as local cultures are becoming "glocalized." Instead of becoming impoverished, as the homogenization thesis suggests, world cultures are being enriched by processes of hybridization. Instead of creating an increased potential for hostility, globalization has provided more opportunity for connection. Cultural hybridization is a slow, highly selective, and context-dependent process.[34]

Epilogue

The 1990s were dominated by a realization that the organizations of today's global economy are both very different than they were a generation ago and even less like they will be a generation from now. As in all times of social and cultural change, the 1990s and early 2000s have witnessed a great deal of anxiety and controversy about the directions that societies, economies, and organizations will take. It is clear that people now work in closer proximity to one another than ever before. Increased proximity comes in the form of a diverse workforce and in the form of a global economy. Some of the strategies of organizing that were discussed in Unit I may soon become obsolete; others may experience a resurgence. Alternative forms will emerge, dominate some sectors for a time and then be eclipsed by others. Each of the challenges described in Unit II will become more relevant and more pronounced. Technological change will continue; managing organizational membership will become more difficult; organizational power and politics will become more complex; decision making will be more difficult; and conflict-management will be more important.

Organizations and their members throughout the world will continue to face a number of crucial challenges. This conclusion should not be especially surprising because it results from the fundamental tensions described in Chapter 1. The problem—and the challenge—is that a society and its organizations can deal with these fundamental tensions in one of two ways. They can focus on *individuality,* domination, and control, become more competitive and divided, with one group of members turning against another and magnifying long-held antagonisms based on organizational rank, nationality, class, race, ethnicity, and gender. Or they can focus on creating a meaningful *global community* that represents the interests of multiple stakeholders and meets the needs of all of its members. But "societies" and "organizations" do not make choices—people do. Human beings are, after all, choice-making beings. It is our choices that will determine the road our society and our organizations take. The strategies that *all of us* choose will determine the kind of organizations that *we* live in for the rest of our lives, and the kind of society that *we* will create for ourselves and for our children. Make good choices.

NOTES

[1] Lester Thurow, "New Rules: The American Economy in the Next Century. In book on globalization, p. 250. Orig. in *Harvard International Review* (Winter 1997/1998); David Rothkopf, "In Praise of Cultural Imperialism?" in book on globalization, p. 443. Orig. in *Foreign Policy, 107* (Summer, 1997); Thomas Friedman, *The Lexus and the Olive Tree* (New York: Farrar, Straus, & Giroux, 1999).

[2] John Parry, ed. *The Establishment of the European Hegemony, 1415–1715* (New York: HarperCollins, 1967); Kevin O'Rourke & Jeffrey Williamson, *Globalization and History* (Cambridge, MA: M.I.T. Press, 1999); Louis Uchitelle, "Some Economic Interplay Comes Nearly Full Circle," *New York Times on the Web,* 30 Apr., 1998.

[3] Alan Heston & Neil Weiner, "Dimensions of Globalization," *The Annals of the American Academy of Political and Social Science, 570* (2000): 8–18. However, substantially less progress has been made in sub-Saharan Africa.

[4] These examples are taken from Cynthia Stohl, "Globalizing Organizational Communication," in *The New Handbook of Organizational Communication,* Fredric Jablin & Linda Putnam, eds. (Thousand Oaks, CA: Sage, 2000); Harry Shattuck, "Mexico Offers Better Assistance," *Houston Chronicle,* 12 Nov., 2000, 1G; and Thomas Friedman, "You've Got Mail—from the Philippines," *Houston Chronicle,* 30 Sept., 2000, 36A and *Lexus.*

[5] Dani Rodrik, "Has Globalization Gone Too Far?" *Challenge, 41*(1998): 81–94. Also see Gary Burless, et al., *Globaphobia* (Washington, D.C.: Brookings Institution Press, 1998); Thomas Friedman, *Lexus;* and George Soros, *The Crisis of Global Capitalism* (New York: Public Affairs, 1998) and *The Open Society* (New York: Public Affairs, 2000).

[6] Albert Hirschman, *The Rhetoric of Reaction* (Cambridge, MA: Belknap Press, 1991). For an extended summary of this argument and an excellent application of it to the recurring debate in the United States about increasing the minimum wage, see James Aune, *Selling the Free Market* (New York: Guilford Press, 2001), esp. Chapter 1.

[7] The theory of comparative advantage was first proposed in 1817 by David Ricardo in *Principles of Political Economy and Taxation* (Buffalo, NY: Prometheus Books, 1996). It is summarized at length in any good economics textbook and is examined at length by Douglas Irwin in *Against the Tide* (Princeton, NJ: Princeton University Press, 1996).

[8] Richard Freeman & Lawrence Katz, "Rising Wage Inequality," in *Working Under Different Rules* (New York: Russell Sage Foundation, 1994); Jim Hoagland, "Can't Leave Backyard Politics Out of Globalization," *Houston Chronicle,* 22 Oct., 2000, 3C; and Soros.

[9] Irwin.

[10] Ross, "Labor;" Yves DeZalay & Bryant Garth, *Dealing in Virtue* (Chicago: University of Chicago Press, 1996).

[11] Robert Borosage, "Small Wonder the IMF is Universally Reviled," *Houston Chronicle,* 28 Sept., 2000, 27A. For an extended analysis of the inappropriateness of U.S. attempts to impose *laissez faire* capitalism on Russia see Stephen Cohen, *Failed Crusade* (New York: W.W. Norton, 2000) and Robert Daniels, *Russia's Transformation* (New York: Rowman & Litchfield, 1998). George Ross discusses these issues in "Labor Versus Globalization," *Annals of the American Academy of Political and Social Science, 570* (2000): 78–91. Also see Lester Thurow, "Globalization," Annals of the American *Academy of Political and Social Science, 570* (2000): 19–31; Soros, *Global Capitalism;* Friedman, *Lexus.*

[12] Thurow, "Globalization," pp. 21, 22. Also see Robert D. Kaplan, "Was Democracy Just a Moment?" *The Atlantic Monthly* (December, 1997).

[13] Soros, *Global,* p. 112. For a summary of the human rights accord see Norman Kempster, "Five Oil Leaders Agree to New Conduct Code," *Houston Chronicle,* 21 Dec., 2000, C1–2.

[14] *Ibid,* p. 111. Lester Thurow, "New Rules," *Harvard International Review* (Winter, 1997/98): 7–42; and David Held, *Models of Democracy* (Palo Alto, CA: Stanford University Press, 1987).

[15] Robert Dahl, *A Preface to Economic Democracy* (Cambridge, U.K.: Polity Press, 1985); Fareed Zakaria, "The Rise of Illiberal Democracy," *Foreign Affairs, 76*(1997); Kaplan, "Moment."

[16] Ibid, p. 27. The primary sources for the following section are Kevin Phillips, "The Wealth Effect," *Houston Chronicle, 8 Aug., 1999, 1C;* York Bradshaw & Michael Wallace, *Global Inequalities* (Thousand Oaks, CA: Pine Forge Press, 1996); Richard B. Freeman, ed., *Working Under Different Rules* (New York: Russell Sage Foundation, 1994); Lawrence Mishel, Jared Bernstein, & John

Schmidt, *The State of Working America* (Ithaca, NY: Cornell University Press, 1998), and Mary O'Sullivan, *Contests for Corporate Control* (Oxford, U.K.: Oxford University Press, 2000). Data on emergency food aid was collected by the U.S. Conference of Mayors and is summarized in a New York *Times* report entitled "Food Banks Across the U.S. Report Record Requests," *Houston Chronicle,* 19 Dec., 2000, 11A.

[17] Freeman, p. 25.

[18] Ross, p. 88.

[19] Anti-immigration policies are very popular, in part because they are linked to racial and ethnic divisions. See "Fox's Open-Border Dream Impossible, Mexicans Say," Bryan/College-Station *Eagle,* 3 Dec., 2000, 9A and a series on the INS in the December 15, 2000 *Houston Chronicle,* pp. 48–53A. For superb analyses of global immigration policies see Saskia Sassen, *Losing Control?* (New York: Columbia University Press, 1996); *Globalization and its Discontents* (New York: New Press, 1998) and *Guests and Aliens* (New York: The New Press, 1999).

[20] See Soros, *Crisis;* Frank Rampersad, "Coping With Globalization," *Annals of the American Association of Political and Social Science, 570* (2000): 115–125; and Jeffrey Sachs, "Making it Work," *Economist,* 12 Sept., 1998, available at http://www.economist.com.

[21] Lynda St. Clair, Robert Quinn, & Regina O'Neill, "The Perils of Responsiveness in Modern Organizations," in *Pressing Problems in Organizations (That Keep Us Awake at Night),* Robert Quinn, et al., eds. (New York: AMACOM, 2000), p. 245.

[22] Robert Frank & Philip Cook, *The Winner Take All Society* (Reading, MA: Addison-Wesley, 1998).

[23] Ling Chen, "Connecting to the World Economy," *Management Communication Quarterly,* 14 (2000): 152–160. The other examples in this paragraph are from Ruggero Cesaria, "Organizational Communication Issues in Italian Multinational Corporations," *Management Communication Quarterly,* 14 (2000): 161–172; and Friedman, *Lexus.*

[24] Stanley Deetz, "Transforming Communication, Transforming Business," *The International Journal of Value-Based Management* (1995, in press), p. 2. Also see Stanley Deetz. *Transforming Communication; Transforming Business* (Creskill, NJ: 1995).

[25] Milton Friedman, *Capitalism and Freedom* (Chicago: University of Chicago Press, 1962) and "The Social Responsibility of Business Is to Increase Profits," *New York Times Magazine,* September 13, 1970, pp. 122–126. Also see Thomas Friedman, *Olive* and *Lexus,* p. 86.

[26] Stakeholder models are discussed by Stanley Deetz in *Transforming Organizations* (with Tanni Haas) and in "Between the Generalized and the Concrete Other," in *Rethinking Organizational and Managerial Communication from Feminist Perspectives* (Thousand Oaks, CA: Sage, 2000). Also see Mary O'Sullivan, "Corporate Governance and Globalization," *Annals of the American Academy of Political and Social Science,* 570 (2000): 153–171. Also see O'Sullivan, *Contests* and David Gordon, *Fat and Mean* (Ithaca, NY: Cornell University Press, 1996); and William Greider, *One World, Ready or Not* (New York: Simon & Schuster, 1997).

[27] Dani Rodrik, "Sense and Nonsense in the Globalization Debate," *Foreign Policy,* 107 (Summer, 1997), pp. 17, 19.

[28] Deetz & Haas; Peter Bacharach & Aryeh Botwinik, *Power and Empowerment* (Philadelphia, PA: Temple University Press, 1992); Carol Pateman, *The Problem of Political Obligation* (Cambridge, U.K.: Polity Press, 1995); Cheney, "Democracy."

[29] Key advocates of the homogenization thesis are D. Howes, ed., *Cross-Cultural Consumption* (London: Routledge, 1996), George Ritzer, *The McDonalization of Society* (Newbury Park, CA: Pine Forge Press, 1993); George Ritzer & A. Liska, "McDisneyization and Post-Tourism," in *Touring Cultures,* C. Rojek & J. Urry, eds. (London: Routledge, 1997). Advocates of the polarization thesis include B.R. Barber, Jihad vs. McWorld (New York: Random House, 1995); Edward Said, *Orientalism* (New York: Penguin, 1978); and Samuel Huntington, *The Clash of Civilizations and the Remaking of World Order* (New York: Simon & Schuster, 1996). Advocates of the hybridization thesis include Friedman, *Lexus;* and Ulf Hannerz, *Cultural Complexity* (New York: Columbia University Press, 1992).

[30] Peter Berger, "Four Faces of Global Culture," *Annals of the American Academy of Political and Social Science,* 570 (2000): 419–427; Jon Mandle, "Globalization and Justice," *Annals of the American Academy of Political and Social Science, 570* (2000): 126–139.

[31] Soros, p. 93.

[32] Samuel Huntington, "The Clash of Civilizations?" *The Annals of the American Academy of Political and Social Sciences, 570* (2000): 3–22; Benjamin Barber, "Jihad vs. McWorld," *The Annals of the American Academy of Political and Social Sciences, 570* (2000): 23–33; Robert D. Kaplan, "The Coming Anarchy," *The Annals of the American Academy of Political and Social Sciences,* 570 (2000):34–60.

[33] John Tomlinson, *Globalization and Culture* (Chicago: University of Chicago Press, 1999), p. 84.

[34] Madeline Drohan and Alan Freeman, "English Rules," *Annals of the American Academy of Political and Social Science, 570* (2000): 428–434; Joshua Fishman, "The New Linguistic Order," *Foreign Policy, 113* (Winter 1998/1999).

BIBLIOGRAPHY

+*Indicates particularly appropriate for graduate students.*

Abell, Peter. *Organizations as Bargaining and Influence Systems.* London: Heinemann, 1975.

Abrahamson, E. "Management Fashion." *Academy of Management Review* 21 (1996): 254–85.

Abrahamsson, B. *Bureaucracy or Participation.* Beverly Hills, Calif.: Sage, 1977.

Acker, J. "Feminist Goals and Organizing Processes." In *Feminist Organizations,* edited by M. Marx Ferree and Y. Martin. Philadelphia: Temple University Press, 1995.

———. "The Gender Regime In Swedish Banks." *Scandinavian Journal of Management* 10 (1994): 116–42.

Adams, R., and R. Parrot. "Pediatric Nurses' Communication of Role Expectations of Parents to Hospitalized Children." *Journal of Applied Communication Research,* 22 (1994): 36–47.

Adler, G.S. and P. Tompkins. "Electronic Performance Monitoring." *Management Communication Quarterly* 10 (1997): 259–88.

Adler, N. *International Dimensions of Organizational Behavior.* 2d ed. Boston: Kent, 1991.

Aiello, J.R. "Computer-Based Work Monitoring." *Journal of Applied Social Psychology* 23 (1993): 499–507.

Aiello, J.R., and C.M. Svec. "Computer Monitoring of Work Performance." *Journal of Applied Psychology* 23 (1993): 537–48.

+Aktouf, O. "Defamiliarizing Management Practice." In *Understanding Management,* edited by S. Linstead, R.G. Small, and P. Jeffcutt. London: Sage, 1996.

Albert, R. "Cultural Diversity and Intercultural Training in Multinational Organizations." In *Communicating In Multinational Organizations,* edited by R.L. Wiseman and R. Shuter. Thousand Oaks, Calif.: Sage, 1994.

Albrecht, T. "Communication and Personal Control." In "Empowering Organizations." In *Communication Yearbook 11,* edited by J. Anderson. Beverly Hills, Calif.: Sage, 1987.

+———. "An Overtime Analysis of Communication Patterns and Work Perceptions." In *Communication Yearbook 8,* edited by R. Bostrom. Beverly Hills, Calif.: Sage, 1984.

Albrecht, T., and M. Adelman. *Communicating Social Support.* Newbury Park, Calif.: Sage, 1988.

Albrecht, T., and B. Bach. *Organizational Communication.* Ft. Worth, Tex: Harcourt, 1996.

+Albrecht, T., and B. Hall. "Facilitating Talk about New Ideas." *Communication Monographs* 58 (1991a): 273–88.

———. "Relational and Content Differences between Elites and Outsiders in Innovation Networks." *Human Communication Research* 17 (1991b): 535–61.

Albrecht, T., and J. Halsey. "Mutual Support in Mixed Status Relationships." *Journal of Social and Personal Relationships* 9 (1992): 237–52.

Alderton, S.M., and L. Frey. "Effects of Reactions to Arguments on Group Outcomes." *Central States Speech Journal* 34 (1983): 88–95.

Aldrich, H.E. *Organizations and Environments.* Englewood Cliffs, N.J.: Prentice Hall, 1979.

Alexander, E., L. Penley, and I.E. Hernigan. "The Effect of Individual Difference on Managerial Media Choice." *Management Communication Quarterly* 5 (1991): 155–73.

+Alkhazraji, K., W. Gardner, J. Martin, and J. Paolillo. "The Acculturation of Immigrants to U.S. Organizations." *Management Communication Quarterly* 11 (1997): 217–65.

Allen, B. "A Black Feminist Standpoint Analysis." In *Rethinking Management and Organization Communication from Feminist Perspectives,* edited by P. Buzzanell. Thousand Oaks, Calif.: Sage, 2000.

+———. "Feminist Standpoint Theory." *Communication Studies* 47 (1996): 257–71.

Allen, M.W. "The Relationship between Communication, Affect, Job Alternatives, and Voluntary Turnover Intentions." *Southern Communication Journal* 61 (1996): 198–209.

Alnot, P., and M.Y. Brannen. "Cultural Misunderstanding." In *Pressing Problems in Organizations (That Keep Us Awake at Night)*, edited by R. Quinn, R. O'Neill, and L. St. Clair. New York: AMACOM, 2000.

+Alvesson, M. "Cultural-Ideological Modes of Management Control: A Theory and a Case Study of a Professional Service Company." In *Communication Yearbook 16*, edited by S. Deetz. Newbury Park, Calif.: Sage, 1994.

+———. "Organizations, Culture and Ideology." *International Studies of Management and Organization* 17 (1987): 4–18.

+———. *Organization Theory and Technocratic Consciousness.* New York: Walter de Gruyter, 1987.

+Alvesson, M., and H. Wilmott, eds. *Critical Management Studies.* Newbury Park, Calif.: Sage, 1992.

Amparano, J.L. "Study Says Women Face Glass Walls as Well as Glass Ceilings." *Wall Street Journal*, 3 March 1992.

+Ancona, D.G., and D.F. Caldwell. "Beyond Task and Maintenance: Defining External Functions in Groups." *Group and Organization Studies* 13 (1988): 468–94.

———. "Demography and Design: Predictors of New Product Team Performance." *Organization Science* 3 (1992): 321–41.

Ancona, D.G., T. Kuchan, J. Van Maanen, M. Scully, and D. Westney. "The New Organization: Taking Action in an Era of Organizational Transformation." In *Managing for the Future: Organizational Behavior and Processes.* Cincinnati: South-Western College Publishing, 1999.

Andrews, P. H., and R. Herschel. *Organizational Communication.* Geneva, Ill.: Houghton Mifflin, 1996.

Ansari, S., and K. Euske. "Rational, Rationalizing, and Reifying Uses of Accounting Data in Organizations." *Accounting, Organizations, and Society* 12 (1987): 549–70.

Arendt, H. *The Human Condition.* Chicago: University of Chicago Press, 1958.

Aronowitz, S. *False Promises.* New York: McGraw-Hill, 1973.

Ashford, B.E., and R.H. Humphrey. "Emotional Labor in Service Roles." *Academy of Management Review* 18 (1993): 88–115.

Aune, J. *Selling the Free Market.* New York: Guilford Press, 2001.

Axelrod, R. *The Evolution of Cooperation.* New York: Basic Books, 1984.

+Axley, S. "Managerial and Organizational Communication in Terms of the Conduit Metaphor." *Academy of Management Review* 9 (1984): 428–37.

Bach, B. "The Effect of Multiplex Relationships upon Innovation Adoption." *Communication Monographs* 56 (1991): 133–48.

———. "Making a Difference by Doing Differently: A Response to Putnam." Paper presented at the Arizona State University Conference on Organizational Communication, Tempe, Ariz., February 1990.

Bacharach, P., and A. Botwinik. *Power and Empowerment.* Philadelphia: Temple University Press, 1992.

Bailey, F.G. *The Tactical Uses of Passion.* Ithaca, N.Y.: Cornell University Press, 1983.

Balitis, J.J., Jr. "Care Needed with Electronic Monitoring." *Business Journal (Phoenix)* 18 (1988): 71–78.

+Banks, S., and P. Riley. "Structuration Theory as an Ontology for Communication Research." In *Communication Yearbook 16*, edited by S. Deetz. Newbury Park, Calif.: Sage, 1992.

Bantz, C. "Cultural Diversity and Group Cross-Cultural Team Research." *Journal of Applied Communication Research* 20 (1993): 1–19.

Barber, B. "Jihad vs. McWorld." *The Annals of the American Academy of Political and Social Sciences* 570 (2000): 23–33.

Barber, B.R. *Jihad vs. McWorld.* New York: Random House, 1995.

Barber, D. *Power in Committees.* Chicago: Rand McNally, 1966.

+Barge, J.K. *Leadership.* New York: St. Martin's, 1994.

Barge, J.K., and G.W. Musambria. "Turning Points in Chair-Faculty Relationships." *Journal of Applied Communication Research* 20 (1992): 54–77.

+Barker, J.R. "Tightening the Iron Cage: Concertive Control in Self-Managing Teams." *Administrative Science Quarterly* 38 (1993): 408–37.

Barker, J., and G. Cheney. "The Concept and Practices of Discipline in Contemporary Organizational Life." *Communication Monographs* 61 (1994): 20–43.

Barker, J. and Tompkins, P. "Identification in the Self-Managing Organization: Characteristics of Target and Tenure." *Human Communication Research* 21 (1994): 223–40.

+Barker, J.R., C.W. Melville, and M.E. Pacanowsky. "Self-Directed Teams at Xel: Changes IN Communication Practices during a Program of Cultural Transformation." *Journal of Applied Communication Research* 21 (1993): 297–313.

Barley, S., and D.B. Knight. "Towards a Cultural Theory of Stress Complaints." *Research in Organizational Behavior* 14 (1992): 1–48.

+Barley S., and G. Kunda. "Design and Devotion: Surges of Rational and Normative Ideologies of Control in Managerial Discourse." *Administrative Science Quarterly* 37 (1992): 363–99.

+Barley, S., G.W. Meyer, and D. Gash. "Cultures of Culture." *Administrative Science Quarterly* 33 (1988): 24-60.

Barlow, J. "Ethics Can Boost the Bottom Line." *Houston Chronicle,* 31 October 1996.

Bartunek, J.M., and M. Moch. "Multiple Constituencies and the Duality of Working Life." In *Reframing Organizational Culture,* edited by P. Frost, L. Moore, M.R. Louis, C. Lundberg, and J. Martin. Newbury Park, Calif.: Sage, 1991.

Bass, B. *Bass and Stogdill's Handbook of Leadership.* 3d ed. New York: Free Press, 1993.

———. *Leadership and Performance beyond Expectations.* New York: Free Press, 1985.

Bastien, D. "Change in Organizational Culture." *Management Communication Quarterly* 5 (1992): 403-42.

Baumard, P. *Tacit Knowledge in Organizations.* London: Sage, 1999.

Baxter, L. "Talking Things Through" and "Putting It in Writing." *Journal of Applied Communication Research 21* (1994): 313-28.

Bell, E.L. "The Bicultural Life Experience of Career-Oriented Black Women." *Journal of Organizational Behavior* 11 (1990): 459-77.

Bellah, R., R. Madsen, W. Sullivan, and S. Tipton. *Habits of the Heart.* 2d ed. Berkeley: University of California Press, 1995.

Bennis, W., Parikh, J., and Lessem, R. *Beyond Leadership: Balancing Economics, Ethics, and Ecology.* Cambridge, Mass.: Basil Blackwell, 1994.

Benson, S. "The Clerking Sisterhood." In *Gendering Organizational Analysis,* edited by A.J. Mills and P. Tancred. Newbury Park, Calif.: Sage, 1992.

+Berger, C. "Power, Dominance, and Social Interaction." In *Handbook of Interpersonal Communication,* edited by M. Knapp and G. Miller. Beverly Hills, Calif.: Sage, 1994.

Berger, P. "Four Faces of Global Culture." *Annals of the American Academy of Political and Social Science 570* (2000): 419-27.

Bertraud, M. "Female Executives Make What Men Do." Houston *Chronicle,* 21 October 2000.

Bettman, J., and B. Weitz. "Attributions in the Board Room." *Administrative Science Quarterly* 28 (1983): 165-83.

+Bingham, S., ed. *Conceptualizing Sexual Harassment as Discursive Practice.* Westport, Conn.: Praeger, 1994.

Bitzer, L. "Functional Communication." In *Rhetoric in Transition,* edited by Eugene White. University Park: Pennsylvania State University Press, 1980.

———. "The Rhetorical Situation." *Philosophy and Rhetoric* 1 (1968): 1-14.

Blair, A. *Houston Chronicle,* 8 July, 1996, p. 15A.

Blanchette, D.P. "Technology Transfer in a Culturally Diverse Workforce (Part I)." *Industrial Management* (July/August 1994): 31-32.

Blau, J. *Illusions of Prosperity.* New York: Oxford University Press, 1999.

Boisseau, C. "Ranks of Female Businesses Soar." *Houston Chronicle,* 30 January 1996.

Boje, D. "The Storytelling Organization." *Administrative Science Quarterly* 36 (1991): 106-26.

Bokeno, R.M., and V. Gantt. "Dialogic Mentoring." *Management Communication Quarterly 14* (2000): 237-70.

Bormann, E. *Small Group Communication: Theory and Practice.* 3d ed. New York: HarperCollins, 1990.

+———. "Symbolic Convergence Theory and Communication in Group Decision-making." In *Communication and Group Decision Making,* edited by R. Hirokawa and M.S. Poole. 2d ed. Thousand Oaks, Calif.: Sage, 1996.

Borosage, R. "Small Wonder the IMF Is Universally Reviled." *Houston Chronicle,* 28 September 2000.

Boster, F., and M. Mayer. "Differential Argument Quality Mediates the Impact of Social Comparison Process of the Choice Shift." Paper presented at the International Communication Association Convention, San Francisco, May 1984.

Botan, C. "Communication, Work and Electronic Surveillance." *Communication Monographs 63* (1996): 294-313.

———. "Examining Electronic Surveillance in the Workplace." Paper presented at the International Communication Convention, Acapulco, Mexico, May 2000.

Bradford, L.J., and C. Raines. *Twentysomething.* New York: Master Media, Ltd., 1992.

Bradshaw, Y., and M. Wallace. *Global Inequalities.* Thousand Oaks, Calif.: Pine Forge Press, 1996.

Brakken, E. "Critical Analysis of the Fair Labor Association." http://www.asm.wisc.edu/ass/, 6 January 2001.

Braverman, H. *Labor and Monopoly Capital.* New York: Monthly Review Press, 1974.

Brewin, B. "Garment Maker Donning Wireless." *Computerworld,* 11 September 2000.

Bridge, K., and L. Baxter. Blended Relationships: Friends as Work Associates. *Western Journal of Communication* 56 (1992): 200-25.

Brockner, J., T.R. Tyler, and R. Cooper-Schneider. "The Influence of Prior Commitment to an Institution of Reactions to Perceived Unfairness." *Administrative Science Quarterly* 37 (1992): 254-71.

+Browning, L. "Lists and Stories in Organizational Communication." *Communication Theory 2* (1992): 281–302.

Bryant, S. "Texaco Initiates Scholarship Program to Help Minorities." Houston *Chronicle,* 12 November 1996.

Bullis, C. "At Least It's a Start." In *Communication Yearbook 16,* edited by Stanley Deetz. Newbury Park, Calif.: Sage, 1993.

+Bullis, C. and B.W. Bach. "Socialization Turning Points." *Western Journal of Speech Communication* 53 (1989): 273–93.

Bullis, C., and P. Tompkins. "The Forest Ranger Revisited." *Communication Monographs* 56 (1989): 287–306.

+Burawoy, M. *Manufacturing Consent.* Chicago: University of Chicago Press, 1979.

Burgoon, J., D. Buller, and W.G. Woodall. *Nonverbal Communication: The Unspoken Dialogue.* New York: Harper & Row, 1995.

Burless, G., R. Lawrence, and R. Shapiro. *Globaphobia.* Washington, D.C.: Brookings Institution Press, 1998.

+Burns, T., and G.M. Stalker. *The Management of Innovation.* London: Tavistock, 1961.

+Burrell, N., P. Buzzanell, and J.J. McMillan. "Feminine Tensions in Conflict Situations as Revealed by Metaphoric Analysis." *Management Communication Quarterly 6* (1992): 115–49.

Bush, D.F. "Passive-Aggressive Behavior in the Business Setting." In *Passive-Aggressiveness,* edited by R. Parsons and R. Wicks. New York: Brunner-Mazel, 1983.

+Bush, S.B., and J.P. Folger. *The Promise of Mediation: Responding to Conflict Through Empowerment and Recognition.* San Francisco: Jossey-Bass, 1994.

+Butler, R., G. Astley, D. Hickson, G. Mallory, and D. Wilson. "Strategic Decision Making in Organizations." *International Studies of Management and Organization* 23 (1980): 234–49.

+Butler, R., D. Hickson, D. Wilson, and R. Axelsson. "Organizational Power, Politicking and Paralysis." *Organizational and Administrative Sciences* 8 (1977): 44–59.

Buzzanell, P. "Gaining a Voice: Feminist Organizational Communication Theorizing." *Management Communication Quarterly* 7 (1994): 339–83.

———. "The Promise and Practice of the New Career and Social Contract." In *Rethinking Organizational and Managerial Communication from Feminist Perspectives,* edited by P. Buzzanell. Newbury Park, Calif.: Sage, 2000.

———. "Reframing the Glass Ceiling as a Socially Constructed Process." *Communication Monographs* 62 (1995): 327–54.

———, ed. *Rethinking Organizational and Managerial Communication from Feminist Perspectives.* Thousand Oaks, Calif.: Sage, 2000.

Cameron, K., and M. Thompson. "The Problems and Promises of Total Quality Management." In *Pressing Problems in Modern Organizations (That Keep Us Awake at Night).* edited by R. Quinn, R. O'Neill and L. St. Clair. New York: AMACOM, 2000.

Campbell, J., and R. Pritchard. "Motivation Theory." In *Handbook of Industrial and Organizational Psychology,* edited by M. Dunnette. Chicago: Rand-McNally, 1976.

Canary, D., and B. Spitzberg. "A Model of the Perceived Competence of Conflict Strategies." *Human Communication Research* 15 (1990): 630–49.

Cantu, H. "Racial Slur Helped Form New Career." *Houston Chronicle,* 21 March 1999.

Carnavale, A.P., and S.C. Stone. "Diversity: Beyond the Golden Rule." *Training and Development* 48 (October 1994): 21–26.

Carnegie, S. "The Hidden Emotions of Tourism: Communication and Power in the Caribbean." Master's thesis, Texas A&M University, 1996.

Carter, J. *He Works, She Works.* New York: AMACOM, 1995.

Casmir, F. "Third Culture Building." In *Communication Yearbook 16,* edited by S. Deetz. Newbury Park, Calif.: Sage, 1993.

Cavanagh, J. "The Global Resistance to Sweatshops." In *No Sweat,* edited by A. Ross. New York: Verso, 1997.

Cawelti, J. *Apostles of the Self-Made Man.* Cambridge, Mass.: Harvard University Press, 1974.

Celente, G. "The Millennial Generation." *Parade Magazine,* 10 September 2000, p. 19.

Cervantes, R. "Occupational and Economic Stressors among Immigrant and United States-Born Hispanics." In *Hispanics in the Workplace,* edited by S. Knouse, P. Rosenfeld, and A. Culbertson. Newbury Park, Calif.: Sage, 1992.

Cesaria, R. "Organizational Communication Issues in Italian Multinational Corporations." *Management Communication Quarterly* 14 (2000): 161–72.

Chang, H.C., and G.R. Holt. "More than Relationship." *Communication Quarterly* 39 (1991): 251–71.

Chapa, J. "Creating and Improving Linkages between the Tops and Bottoms." Paper presented at the Organizational Innovation Conference, Humphrey Institute of Public Affairs, University of Minnesota, Minneapolis, September 1992.

Chase, J. and I. Panagopoulous. "Environmental Values and Social Psychology." In *Values and the Environment,* edited by Y. Gurrier, M. Alexander, J. Chase, and M. O'Brien. Chichester, U.K.: John Wiley & Sons, 1995.

Chemers, M. "Culture and Assumptions about Leadership." In *Small Group Communication,* edited by R. Cathcart and L. Samovar. Dubuque, Iowa: William C. Brown, 1984.

Chen, L. "Connecting to the World Economy." *Management Communication Quarterly* 14 (2000): 152–60.

Cheney, G. "Democracy in the Workplace." *Journal of Applied Communication Research* 23 (1995): 167–200.

+———. *Rhetoric in an Organizational Society: Managing Multiple Identities.* Columbia: University of South Carolina Press, 1991.

———. *Values at Work.* Ithaca, N.Y.: Cornell University Press, 1999.

Cheney, G., and G. Frenette. "Persuasion and Organization." In *The Ethical Nexus,* edited by C. Conrad. Norwood, N.J.: Ablex, 1992.

Chiles, A.M. and T. Zorn. "Empowerment in Organizations: Employees' Perceptions of the Influences on Empowerment." *Journal of Applied Communication Research* 23 (1995): 1–25.

Clair, R.P. "The Bureaucratization, Commodification, and Privatization of Sexual Harassment through Institutional Discourse." *Management Communication Quarterly* 7 (1993): 128–57.

———. "The Political Nature of the Colloquialism, 'A Real Job.'" *Communication Monographs* 63 (1996): 249–67.

+———. "The Use of Framing Devices to Sequester Organizational Narratives." *Communication Monographs* 60 (1993): 113–36.

———. "Ways of Seeing." *Communication Monographs* 66 (1999): 374–81.

Clair, R.P., and K. Thompson. "Pay Discrimination as a Discursive and Material Practice." *Journal of Applied Communication Research* 24 (1996): 1–20.

Clampitt, P., and C. Downs. "Employee Perceptions of the Relationship between Communication and Productivity." *Journal of Business Communication* 30 (1993): 5–28.

+Clegg, S. *Frameworks of Power.* Newbury Park, Calif.: Sage, 1989.

+———. *Modern Organizations.* Newbury Park, Calif.: Sage, 1990.

+———. *Power, Rule and Domination.* London: Routledge and Kegan Paul, 1975.

+———. "Power, Theorizing and Nihilism." *Theory and Society* 3 (1976): 65–87.

+Cline, T., and R. Cline. "Risky and Cautious Decision Shifts in Small Groups." *Southern Speech Communication Journal* 44 (1979): 252–63.

+Cohen, M., and J. March. *Leadership and Ambiguity.* 2d ed. Boston: Harvard Business School Press, 1974.

+Cohen, M., J. March, and J. Olson. "A Garbage-Can Model of Organizational Choice." *Administrative Science Quarterly* 17 (1972): 1–25.

Cohen, S. *Failed Crusade.* New York: W.W. Norton, 2000.

Collins, P.H. "Comment on Hekman's 'Truth and Method.'" *Signs* 22 (1997): 375–81.

Collinson, D. *Managing the Shop Floor.* New York: DeGruyter, 1992.

Comer, D. "Organizational Newcomers' Acquisition of Information from Peers." *Management Communication Quarterly* 5 (1991): 64–89.

Conrad, B.W. "The Moving Experience." *The Waiting Room* 2 (1985): 12–18.

+Conrad, C. "Communication in Conflict: Style-Strategy Relationships." *Communication Monographs* 58 (1991): 135–55.

———. "Power, Performance and Supervisors' Choices of Strategies of Conflict Management." *Western Journal of Speech Communication* 47 (1983): 218–28.

———. "Review of *A Passion for Excellence.*" *Administrative Science Quarterly* 30 (1985): 426–29.

———. "Was Pogo Right? Communication, Power and Resistance." In *Communication Research in the 21st Century,* edited by J. Wood and R. Gregg. Creskill, N.J.: Hampton Press, 1995.

Conrad, C. and B. Taylor. "The Contexts of Sexual Harassment: Power, Silences and Academe." In *Conceptualizing Sexual Harassment as Discursive Practice,* edited by Shereen Bingham. Westport, Conn.: Praeger, 1994.

Contractor, N. "Inquiring Knowledge Networks on the Web. Conceptual Overview." http://www.tec.spcomm.uiuc.edu/nosh/IKNOW/sld001.ht, 6 January 2001.

Contractor, N., B. O'Keefe, and P.M. Jones. "IKNOW: Inquiring Knowledge Networks on the Web." http://iknow.spcomm.uiuc.edu, 6 January 2001.

Coolidge, S.D. "Boomers, Gen-Xers Clash." http://www.abcnews.go.com/sections/business, 1 September 1999.

Coopersmith, J. "Facsimile's False Starts." *IEEE Spectrum* (February 1993): 46–49.

"Corporate Women." *Business Week,* 8 June 1992.

Courtright, C., G. Fairhurst, and L.E. Rogers. "Interaction Patterns in Organic and Mechanistic Systems." *Academy of Management Journal* 32 (1989): 773–802.

Cox, T., C. Lobel, and P. McLeod. "Effects of Ethnic Cultural Differences on Cooperative and Competitive Behavior on a Group Task." *Academy of Management Journal* 34 (1991): 827–47.

Crozier, M. *The Bureaucratic Phenomenon.* Chicago: University of Chicago Press, 1964.

Cupach, W. and S. Metts. *Facework.* Newbury Park, Calif.: Sage, 1994.

+Czarniawska-Joerges, B. *Exploring Complex Organizations.* Newbury Park, Calif.: Sage, 1992.

"Dad Wins Legal Fight for Time Off." *Houston Chronicle,* 5 February 1999.

Daft, R. *Organization Theory and Design.* 3d ed. St. Paul, Minn.: West, 1989.

Daft, R., and R.H. Lengel. "Information Richness." In *Research in Organizational Behavior,* edited by L. Cummings and B. Staw. Vol. 6. Greenwich, Conn.: JAI Press, 1984.

Dahl, R. *A Preface to Economic Democracy.* Cambridge, U.K.: Polity Press, 1985.

Dana, L.P. "Small Business as a Supplement in the People's Republic of China (PRC)." *Journal of Small Business Management* 37 (1999): 76–81.

+Dandeker, C. *Surveillance, Power and Modernity.* New York: St. Martin's Press, 1984.

Daniels, R. *Russia's Transformation.* New York: Rowman & Litchfield, 1998.

Daniels, T., B. Spiker, and M. Papa. *Perspectives on Organizational Communication.* 4th ed. Madison, Wis.: Brown & Benchmark, 1997.

Davis, K. "Management Communication and the Grapevine." *Harvard Business Review,* 31 (September-October 1953): 43–49.

+de Certeau, M. *The Practice of Everyday Life.* Berkeley: University of California Press, 1984.

Deal, T., and A. Kennedy. *Corporate Cultures.* Reading, Mass.: Addison-Wesley, 1982.

DeBrosse, J. "The Y's Have It." *Houston Chronicle,* 17 February 1998.

+Deetz, S. "Critical Theories of Organizational Communication." In *The New Handbook of Organizational Communication,* edited by Fredric Jablin and Linda Putnam. Thousand Oaks, Calif.: Sage, 2000.

+———. *Democracy in the Age of Corporate Colonization.* Albany: State University of New York Press, 1992.

———. *Transforming Communication, Transforming Business.* Creskill, N.J.: Hampton Press, 1995.

———. "Transforming Communication, Transforming Business." *The International Journal of Value-Based Management* (1995): 1–18.

+Deetz, S., and T. Haas. "Between the Generalized and the Concrete Other." In *Rethinking Organizational and Managerial Communication from Feminist Perspectives,* edited by P. Buzzanell. Thousand Oaks, Calif.: Sage, 2000.

DePalma, A. "It Takes More Than a Visa to Do Business in Mexico." *New York Times,* 26 June 1994.

+DeSanctis, G., and B. Gallupe. "A Foundation for the Study of Group Decision Support Systems." *Management Science* 33 (1987): 589–609.

Deutsch, M. *The Resolution of Conflict.* New Haven: Yale University Press, 1973.

Deutsch, M., and R. Krauss. "Studies in Interpersonal Bargaining." *Journal of Conflict Resolution* 61 (1962): 52–76.

DeWine, S., J. Pearson, and C. Yost. "Intimate Office Relationships and Their Impact on Work Group Communication." In *Communication and Sex Role Socialization,* edited by D. Berryman-Fink, A. Ballard-Reisch, and D.H. Newman. New York: Garland Publishing Company, 1993.

DeZalay, Y., and B. Garth. *Dealing In Virtue.* Chicago: University of Chicago Press, 1996.

Dickens, F. and J. Dickens. *The Black Manager.* New York: AMACOM, 1991.

Dillard, J., J.L. Hale, and C. Segrin. "Close Relationships in Task Environments." *Management Communication Quarterly* 7 (1994): 227–55.

Dillard, J., and K. Miller. "Intimate Relationships in Task Environments." In *Handbook of Personal Relationships,* edited by S. Duck. Chichester, N.Y.: John Wiley & Sons, 1997.

DiSanza, J., and C. Bullis. "Everybody Identifies with Smokey the Bear." *Management Communication Quarterly* 12 (1999): 347–99.

Dobnik, V. "Employees Sign Sweatshop Pact." http://www.cleanclothes.org, 6 January 2001.

Donohue, W., and R. Kolt. *Managing Interpersonal Conflict.* Newbury Park, Calif.: Sage, 1992.

+Donohue, W., M. Diez, and M. Hamilton. "Coding Naturalistic Negotiation Interaction." *Human Communication Research* 10 (1984): 403–25.

Dovidio, J., S. Gaertrer, P. Anastasio, and R. Sanitioso. "Cognitive and Motivational Bases of Bias." In *Hispanics in the Workplace,* edited by P. Knouse, P. Rosenfeld, and A. Culberson. Newbury Park, Calif.: Sage, 1992.

Downs, A. *Corporate Executions.* New York: AMACOM, 1995.

Downs, C., and C. Conrad. "A Critical Incident Study of Effective Subordinancy." *Journal of Business Communication* 19 (1982): 27–38.

Drohan, M., and A. Freeman. "English Rules." *Annals of the American Academy of Political and Social Science* 570 (2000): 428–34.

Drucker, P. "The Age of Transformation." *Atlantic Monthly* (September 1994): 53.

Duncan, R.B. "Characteristics of Perceived Environments and Perceived Environmental Uncertainty." *Administrative Science Quarterly* 17 (1972): 313–27.

Dziech, B.W. *Sexual Harassment in Higher Education.* New York: Garland, 1998.

Dziech, B.W., and L. Weiner. *The Lecherous Professor.* 2d ed. Urbana: University of Illinois Press, 1990.

Eadie, W., and J. Wood, eds. *Journal of Applied Communication Research* 20 (1993): 349–436.

Edwards, A., and C. Polite. *Children of the Dream: The Psychology of Black Success.* New York: Doubleday, 1992.

+Edwards, R. *Contested Terrain.* New York: Basic Books, 1978.

Edwards, R. "Sensitivity to Feedback and the Development of Self." *Communication Quarterly* (1990): 101–11.

Eichenwald, K. *New York Times,* 4 November 1966.

Eisenberg, E. "Ambiguity as Strategy in Organizational Communication." *Communication Monographs* 51 (1984): 227–42.

Eisenberg, E., P. Monge, and K. Miller. "Involvement in Communication Networks as a Predictor of Organizational Commitment." *Human Communication Research* 10 (1983): 179–201.

Eisenberg, E., and S. Phillips. "Miscommunication in Organizations." In *"Miscommunication" and Problematic Talk,* edited by N. Coupland, H. Giles, and J. Wieman. Newbury Park, Calif.: Sage, 1991.

Eisenberg, E., and P. Riley. "Organizational Culture." In *The New Handbook of Organizational Communication,* edited by F. Jablin and L. Putnam. Thousand Oaks, Calif.: Sage, 2000.

Eisenstein, H. *Gender Shock.* Boston: Beacon, 1991.

Ellis, B. "The Effects of Uncertainty and Source Credibility on Attitude about Organizational Change." *Management Communication Quarterly* 6 (1992): 34–57.

Emerson, R.M. "Power-Dependence Relations." *American Sociological Review* 27 (1962): 31–41.

Emmett, R. "Vnet or Gripenet." *Datamation* 27 (1981): 48–58.

Eng, S. "Love in the Office Can Be Risky Affair." *Houston Chronicle,* 14 March 1999.

Essed, P. *Everyday Racism.* Translated by Cynthia Jaffe. Claremont, Calif.: Hunter House, 1990.

———. *Understanding Everyday Racism.* Newbury Park, Calif.: Sage, 1991.

"Executive Pay Remains Tops." http://abcnews.go.com/sections/business, 30 August 1999.

Eyer, D.E. *Mother-Infant Bonding: A Scientific Fiction.* New Haven, Conn.: Yale University Press, 1992.

+Fairhurst, G. "Dialectical Tensions in Leadership Research." In *The New Handbook of Organizational Communication,* edited by F. Jablin and L. Putnam Thousand Oaks, Calif.: Sage, 2000.

Fairhurst, G., and Sarr, R. *The Art of Framing: Managing the Language of Leadership.* San Francisco: Jossey-Bass, 1996.

Falbe, C., and G. Yukl. "Consequences of Managers Using Single Influence Tactics and Combinations of Tactics." *Academy of Management Journal* 32 (1992): 638–52.

Faludi, S. *Backlash: The Undeclared War against American Women.* New York: Crown, 1991.

Farrell, A.Y. "Like a Tarantula on a Banana Boat." In *Feminist Organizations,* edited by M.M. Ferree and P.Y. Martin. Philadelphia: Temple University Press, 1995.

Farris, G. "Groups and the Informal Organization." In *Groups at Work,* edited by R. Payne and C. Cooper. New York: John Wiley & Sons, 1981.

Fayol, H. *General and Industrial Management.* London: Pitman, 1949.

+Felsteiner, W.L., R.L. Abel, and A. Sarat. "The Emergence and Transformation of Disputes." *Law and Society Review* 33 (1980/1981): 631–54.

"Female Executives Make What Men Do." *Houston Chronicle,* 21 October 2000.

Ferdman, B., and A. Cortes. "Culture and Identity among Hispanic Managers in an Anglo Business." In *Hispanics in the Workplace,* edited by S. Knouse, P. Rosenfeld, and A. Culbertson. Newbury Park, Calif.: Sage, 1992.

Ferleger, F., and J. Mandle. Special Issue on Globalization. *Annals of the American Academy of Political and Social Science* 557, July 2000.

Ferree, M.M., and P.Y. Martin. *Feminist Organizations.* Philadelphia: Temple University Press, 1995.

Fiebig, G., and M. Kramer. "A Framework for the Study of Emotions in Organizational Contexts." *Management Communication Quarterly* 11 (1998): 536–72.

"Financing." *Houston Chronicle,* 23 May 1999.

Fine, M., and P. Buzzanell. "Walking the High Wire." In *Rethinking Organizational and Managerial Communication from Feminist Perspectives,* edited by P. Buzzanell. Thousand Oaks, Calif.: Sage, 2000.

Fineman, S. "Emotion and Organizing." In *Handbook of Organization Studies,* edited by Stewart Clegg, Cynthia Hardy, and Walter Nord. Thousand Oaks, Calif.: Sage, 1999.

———. "Organizations as Emotional Arenas." In *Emotions In Organizations,* edited by Stephen Fineman. London: Sage, 1993.

Finholt, T., and L. Sproull. "Electronic Groups at Work." *Organization Science* 1 (1990): 41-64.

Fiore, F. "New Mothers Now Return to Work Sooner, Study Says." *Houston Chronicle,* 27 November 1997.

Fisher, A. "When Will Women Get to the Top?" *Fortune,* 21 September 1992, 44-56.

Fisher, C. "On the Dubious Wisdom of Expecting Job Satisfaction to Correlate with Performance." *Academy of Management Review* 5 (1980): 607-12.

Fisher, M. "What's the Proper Etiquette for a Scarlet E-Mail?" *Houston Chronicle,* 1 June 1999.

Fisher, R. and W. Ury. *Getting to Yes.* Boston: Houghton Mifflin, 1981.

Fisher, W. "Narration as a Human Communication Paradigm." *Communication Monographs* 51 (1984): 1-22.

Fishman, J. "The New Linguistic Order." *Foreign Policy* 113 (Winter 1998/1999): 116-42.

Flam, H. "Fear, Loyalty, and Greedy Organizations." In *Emotion in Organizations,* edited by Stephen Fineman. Newbury Park, Calif.: Sage, 1993.

+Fleishman, E., and Assoc., eds. *Studies in Personnel and Industrial Psychology.* Homewood, Ill.: Dorsey, 1961 and 1967.

Folger, J., M.S. Poole, and R. Stutman. *Working through Conflict.* 4th ed. New York: Longman, 2001.

"Food Banks across the U.S. Report Record Requests." *Houston Chronicle,* 19 December 2000.

"Ford, Union to Open 30 Child-Care and Family-Service Centers for Workers." *Houston Chronicle,* 22 November 2000.

Foreman, C. "The Reality of Workplace Democracy: A Case Study of One Company's Employee Involvement Process." Paper presented at the International Communication Association Convention, Chicago, Illinois, May 1996.

+Forester, J. *Planning in the Face of Power.* Berkeley: University of California Press, 1989.

Foss, S., and C. Griffin. "Beyond Persuasion." *Quarterly Journal of Speech* 62 (1995): 2-18.

+Foucault, M. *Discipline and Punish.* Translated by A. Sheridan. New York: Vintage, 1977, 1990.

+———. *The History of Sexuality,* translated by A. Hurley. Vol. 1. New York: Vintage, 1978, 1990.

+———. *Power/Knowledge.* Translated by C. Gordon. New York: Pantheon, 1980.

+———. *The Practice of Everyday Life.* Berkeley: University of California Press, 1984.

"Fox's Open-Border Dream Impossible, Mexicans Say." *Bryan/College Station Eagle,* 3 December 2000.

Francis, B. "Tune In to Cheaper Videoconferencing." *Datamation* 39 (1993): 48-51.

Frank, R., and P. Cook. *The Winner Take All Society.* Reading, Mass.: Addison-Wesley, 1998.

Franken, S. "Corporations' Quest to Create a Happy Workplace." *Houston Chronicle,* 15 October 2000.

+Franz, C., and K.G. Jin. "The Structure of Group Conflict in a Collaborative Work Group during Information Systems Development." *Journal of Applied Communication Research* 23 (1995): 108-27.

Freeman, R., ed. *Working under Different Rules.* Washington, D.C.: Russell Sage Foundation, 1994.

Freeman, R., and L. Katz. "Rising Wage Inequality." In *Working under Different Rules.* New York: Russell Sage Foundation, 1994.

Friedman, M. *Capitalism and Freedom.* Chicago: University of Chicago Press, 1962.

———. "The Social Responsibility of Business Is to Increase Profits." *New York Times Magazine,* 13 September 1970, 122-26.

Friedman, T. *The Lexus and the Olive Tree.* New York: Farrar, Straus, & Giroux, 1999.

———. "You've Got Mail—From the Philippines." *Houston Chronicle,* 30 September 2000.

+Frost, P. "Power, Politics, and Influence." In *Handbook of Organizational Communication,* edited by F. Jablin, L. Putnam, K. Roberts, and L. Porter. Newbury Park, Calif.: Sage, 1987.

Frost, P., L. Moore, M.R. Louis, C. Lundberg, and J. Martin, eds. *Reframing Organizational Culture.* Newbury Park, Calif.: Sage, 1991.

Fukuyama, F. "The End of History?" *National Interest* 481 (1989): 117-42.

+Fulk, J., and L. Collins-Jarvis. "Wired Meetings: Technological Mediation of Organizational Gatherings." In *The New Handbook of Organizational Communication,* edited by F. Jablin and L. Putnam. Thousand Oaks, Calif.: Sage, 2000.

+Fulk, J., and G. DeSanctis. "Articulation of Communication Technology and Organizational Form." In *Shaping Organization Form: Communication, Connection, and Community,* edited by G. DeSanctis and J. Fulk. Newbury Park, Calif.: Sage.

Fulk, J., and S. Mani. "Distortion of Communication in Hierarchical Relationships." *Communication Yearbook 9,* edited by M. McLaughlin. Newbury Park, Calif.: Sage, 1986.

Fulk, J., C. Steinfield, and J. Schmitz. "A Social Information Processing Model of Media Use in Organizations." *Communication Research* 14 (1987): 529-52.

Galbraith, J. "Organizational Design." In *Handbook of Organizational Behavior,* edited by J. Lorsch. Englewood Cliffs, N.J.: Prentice Hall, 1987.

Galen, M., and A.T. Palmer. "White, Male and Worried." *Business Week,* 31 January 1994, 50-55.

Gallupe, B., L. Bastianutti, and W.H. Cooper. "Unblocking Brainstorms." *Journal of Applied Psychology* 76 (1991): 137-42.

Gardner, W., and D. Cleavenger. "The Impression Management Strategies Associated with Transformational Leadership at the World-Class Level." *Management Communication Quarterly* 12 (1998): 3-41.

Garko, M. "Persuading Subordinates Who Communicate in Attractive and Unattractive Styles." *Management Communication Quarterly* 5 (1992): 289-315.

Garson, B. *The Electronic Sweatshop: How Computers Are Transforming the Office of the Future into the Factory of the Past.* New York: Penguin, 1988.

Gayle, B.M. "Sex Equity in Workplace Conflict Management." *Journal of Applied Communication Research* 19 (1991): 152-69.

Geertz, C. "Common Sense as a Cultural System." In C. Geertz, *Local Knowledge.* New York: Basic Books, 1983.

George, C. *The History of Management Thought.* Englewood Cliffs, N.J.: Prentice Hall, 1972.

Gibson, M., and M. Papa. "The Mud, The Blood, and the Beer Guys." *Journal of Applied Communication Research* 28 (2000): 72-91.

Gibson, M., and N. Schullery. "Shifting Meanings in a Blue-Collar Worker Philanthropy Program." *Management Communication Quarterly* 14 (2000): 189-236.

+Giddens, A. *Beyond Left and Right.* Cambridge, U.K.: Polity Press, 1994.

+———. *The Consequences of Modernity.* Cambridge, U.K.: Polity Press, 1990.

+———. *Modernity and Self Identity.* Palo Alto, Calif.: Stanford University Press, 1991.

+Gioia, D., and H. Sims. "Cognition-Behavior Connections: Attribution and Verbal Behavior in Leader-Subordinate Interactions." *Organizational Behavior and Human Performance* 37 (1986): 197-229.

Goffman, E. "On Face Work." *Psychiatry* 18 (1955): 213-31.

———. *The Presentation of Self in Everyday Life.* New York: Doubleday, 1959.

Goldberg, L. "Slowdowns Hit Airlines." *Houston Chronicle,* 6 December, 2000.

+Golding, D. "Management Rituals." In *Understanding Management,* edited by S. Linstead, R.G. Small, and P. Jeffcutt. London: Sage, 1996.

Goleman, D. *Emotional Intelligence.* New York: Bantam Books, 1995.

Gonzalez, A., et al. "Cultural Diversity and Organizations." In *Organizational Communication,* edited by P.Y. Byer. Boston: Allyn and Bacon, 1997.

Gordon, D. *Fat and Mean.* Ithaca, N.Y.: Cornell University Press, 1996.

Gorman, C. "Listen Here, Mr. Big!" *Time,* 3 July 1989, 40-45.

Gorry, G.A., and M.S. Scott-Morton. "A Framework for Management Information Systems." *Sloan Management Review* 13 (Fall 1971): 55-70.

+Gottfried, H., and P. Weiss. "A Compound Feminist Organization." *Women and Politics* 14 (1994): 23-44.

Gould, J. *Deadly Deceit: Low Level Radiation, High Level Coverup.* New York: Four Walls Eight Windows, 1990.

Gould, J., and E. Sternglass. *The Enemy Within: The High Cost of Living near Nuclear Power.* New York: Four Walls Eight Windows, 1996.

Gouldner, A. *Wildcat Strike.* Yellow Springs, Ohio: Antioch Press, 1954.

+Gowler, D., and K. Legge. "The Meaning of Management and the Management of Meaning." In *Understanding Management,* edited by S. Linstead, R.G. Small, and P. Jeffcutt. London: Sage, 1996.

Grace, D., and S. Cohen. *Business Ethics.* Melbourne, Australia: Oxford, 1995.

Granovetter, M. *Getting a Job.* Cambridge, Mass.: Harvard University Press, 1974.

Grant, A., and J.H. Meadows, eds. *Communication Technology Update VI.* Boston: Focal Press, 2000.

Greene, C., and P. Podsakoff. "Effects of Withdrawal of a Performance-Contingent Reward on Supervisory Influence and Power." *Academy of Management Journal* 24 (1981): 527-42.

Greenhaus, J.H., S. Parasuraman, and W.M. Wormley. "Effects of Race on Organizational Experiences, Job Performance Evaluations, and Career Outcomes." *Academy of Management Journal* 33 (1990): 64-86.

+Gregory, K. "Native-View Paradigms." *Administrative Science Quarterly* 28 (1983): 360-72.

Greider, W. *One World, Ready or Not.* New York: Simon & Schuster, 1997.

+Guetzkow, H., and J. Gyr. "An Analysis of Conflict in Decision-Making Groups." *Human Relations* 7 (1954): 367–81.

Guzley, R. "Organizational Climate and Communication Climate." *Management Communication Quarterly* 5 (1992): 379–402.

+Habermas, J. *Communication and the Evolution of Society.* London: Heinemann Educational Books, 1979.

+———. *Knowledge and Human Interests.* London: Heinemann Educational Books, 1972.

Hackman, J.R. *Groups That Work (And Those That Don't).* San Fransisco: Jossey-Bass, 1990.

Hackman, M.Z., and C.E. Johnson. *Leadership: A Communication Perspective.* Prospect Heights, Ill.: Waveland Press, 1991.

Hancock, M., and M. Papa. "Employee Struggles with Autonomy and Dependence: Examining the Dialectic of Control through a Structurational Account of Power." Paper presented at the International Communication Association Convention, Chicago, Illinois, May 1996.

Handy, C. "Trust In Virtual Organizations." *Harvard Business Review* 73 (1995): 40–51.

Hannerz, U. *Cultural Complexity.* New York: Columbia University Press, 1992.

Harper, N., and L. Askling. "Group Communication and Quality of Task Solution in a Media Production Organization." *Communication Monographs* 47 (1980): 77–100.

Harriman, A. *Women—Men—Management.* Westport, Conn.: Greenwood Press, 1996.

Harris, P., and R. Moran. *Managing Cultural Differences.* 3d. ed. Houston, Tex.: Gulf, 1991.

+Harris, S., and R. Sutton. "Functions of Parting Ceremonies in Dying Organizations." *Academy of Management Journal* 29 (1986): 5–30.

Harrison, T. "Communication and Interdependence in Democratic Organizations." *Communication Yearbook 17,* edited by Stanley Deetz. Newbury Park, Calif.: Sage, 1995.

———. "Communication and Participative Decision-Making." *Personnel Psychology* 38 (1985): 93–116.

+Hegde, R.S. "A View from Elsewhere." *Communication Theory* 8 (1998): 271–97.

+Held, D. *Introduction to Critical Theory.* London: Hutchinson, 1980.

———. *Models of Democracy.* Palo Alto, Calif.: Stanford University Press, 1987.

Helgessen, S. *The Female Advantage: Women's Ways of Leadership.* New York: Doubleday, 1990.

Hellman, P. "Her Push for Prevention Keeps Kids out of ER." *Sunday Examiner and Chronicle Parade Magazine,* 19 April 1995, 8–10.

Hess, J. "Maintaining Nonvoluntary Relationships with Disliked Partners." *Human Communication Research* 26 (2000): 458–88.

Heston, A., and N. Weiner. "Dimensions of Globalization." *The Annals of the American Academy of Political and Social Science* 570 (2000): 8–18.

+Hickson, D., W. Astley, R. Butler, and D. Wilson. "Organizations as Power." In *Research in Organizational Behavior.* Vol. 3. Greenwich, N.J.: JAI Press, 1981.

Hilton, C. "International Business Communication." *Journal of Business Communication* 29 (1992): 253–65.

Hiltz, S.R., and M. Turoff. *The Network Nation: Human Communication via Computer.* Reading, Mass.: Addison-Wesley, 1978.

Hine, D.C. "The Future of Black Women in the Academy." In *Black Women in the Academy,* edited by L. Benjamin. Gainesville: University of Florida Press, 1997.

Hirokawa, R. "Discussion Procedures and Decision-Making Performance: A Test of a Functional Perspective." *Human Communication Research* 12 (1986)*:* 203–24.

Hirokawa, R., and A. Miyahara. "A Comparison of Influence Strategies Used by Managers in American and Japanese Organizations." *Communication Quarterly* 34 (1986): 250–65.

Hirokawa, R., and M.S. Poole, eds. *Communication and Group Decision-Making.* 2d ed. Thousand Oaks, Calif.: Sage, 1996.

+Hirokawa, R., and A. Salazar. "Task-Group Communication and Decision-Making Performance." In *Handbook of Group Communication Theory and Research,* edited by L. Frey, D. Gouran, and M.S. Poole. Newbury Park, Calif.: Sage, 1999.

Hirschman, A. *The Rhetoric of Reaction.* Cambridge, Mass.: Belknap Press, 1991.

Hitt, M., et al. "Rightsizing: Building and Maintaining Strategic Leadership and Long-Term Competitiveness." *Organizational Dynamics* 23 (1994): 18–32.

Hoagland, J. "Can't Leave Backyard Politics Out of Globalization." *Houston Chronicle,* 22 October 2000.

Hochschild, A. "Ideology and Emotion Management." In *Research Agendas in the Sociology of Emotions,* edited by T.D. Kemper. Albany: State University of New York Press, 1990.

———. *The Managed Heart.* Berkeley: University of California Press, 1983.

———. *The Time Bind.* New York: Metropolitan Books, 1997.

Hochschild, A., and Machung, A. *The Second Shift.* New York: Avon Books, 1997.

Hoffman, L.R. "Applying Experimental Research on Group Problem Solving to Organizations." *Journal of Applied Behavioral Science* 15 (1979): 375–91.

Hollihan, T., and P. Riley. "The Rhetorical Power of a Compelling Story." *Communication Quarterly* 35 (1987): 15.

Holmes, M. "Phase Structure in Negotiation." In *Communication and Negotiation,* edited by L. Putnam and M. Roloff. Newbury Park, Calif.: Sage, 1993.

Holsapple, C., and D. Joshi. "In Search of a Descriptive Framework for Knowledge Management: Preliminary Delphi Results." *Kentucky Initiative for Knowledge Management,* Research Paper No. 118. Lexington: University of Kentucky.

Holt, J. "Women's Status Improving, But Slowly." *Houston Chronicle,* 16 November 2000.

Homans, G. *The Human Group.* New York: Harcourt Brace, 1950.

Houston Chronicle, 18 October 1996.

+Howes, D., ed. *Cross-Cultural Consumption.* London: Routledge, 1996.

Huntington, S. "The Clash of Civilizations?" *The Annals of the American Academy of Political and Social Sciences* 570 (2000): 3-22.

———. *The Clash of Civilizations and the Remaking of World Order.* New York: Simon & Schuster, 1996.

Huppke, R. "Study: Success Possible Despite Working Less." *Bryan/College Station Eagle,* 31 January 1999.

+Huspek, M. "The Language of Powerlessness." Ph.D. diss., University of Washington, 1987.

Iannello, K. *Decisions without Hierarchy.* London: Routledge, 1993.

Ibarra, H. "Personal Networks of Women and Minorities in Management." *Academy of Management Review* 18 (1993): 56-87.

———. "Race, Opportunity, and Diversity of Social Circles in Managerial Settings." *Academy of Management Journal* 38 (1995): 673-703.

Infante, D., and W. Gordon. "How Employees See the Boss." *Western Journal of Speech Communication* 55 (1991): 294-304.

Irwin, D. *Against the Tide.* Princeton, N.J.: Princeton University Press, 1996.

Irwin, H. *Communicating With Asia.* Sydney, Australia: University of New South Wales, 1997.

Ivanovich, D. "$192.5 Million Settles Coca-Cola Race Suit." *Houston Chronicle,* 17 November 2000.

+Jablin, F. "Communication Competence and Effectiveness." In *The New Handbook of Organizational Communication,* edited by F. Jablin and L. Putnam. Thousand Oaks, Calif.: Sage, 2000.

+———. "An Exploratory Study of Subordinates' Perceptions of Supervisory Politics." *Communication Quarterly* 29 (1981): 269-75.

+———. "Formal Organizational Structure." In *Handbook of Organizational Communication,* edited by F. Jablin, L. Putnam, K. Roberts, and L. Porter. Newbury Park, Calif.: Sage, 1987.

+———. "Organizational Entry, Assimilation and Exit." In *The New Handbook of Organizational Communication,* edited by F. Jablin and L. Putnam. Newbury Park, Calif.: Sage, 2000.

———. "Superior-Subordinate Communication." In *Communication Yearbook 2,* edited by B. Ruben. New Brunswick, N.J.: Transaction Books, 1979.

+———. "Task/Work Relationships." In *Handbook of Interpersonal Communication,* edited by G. Miller and M. Knapp. Beverly Hills, Calif.: Sage, 1985.

+Jablin, F., and M. Kramer. "Communication-Related Sense-Making and Adjustment during Job Transfers." *Management Communication Quarterly* 12 (1998): 155-82.

Jackall, R. "Life above the Middle." *Harvard Business Review* 60 (September-October, 1982): 47-54.

Jackson, M. "Business Bends to Include Generation X Workforce." *Bryan/College Station Eagle,* 31 January 1999.

Jamieson, D., and J. O'Mara. *Managing Workforce 2000.* San Francisco: Jossey-Bass, 1991.

Janis, I. "Sources of Error in Strategic Decision-making." In *Organizational Strategy and Change,* edited by J. Pennings and associates. San Francisco: Jossey-Bass, 1985.

———. *Victims of Groupthink.* Boston: Houghton Mifflin, 1972.

Janis, I., and L. Mann. *Decision Making.* New York: Free Press, 1977.

Jan Mohamed, A.R., and J. Lloyd, eds. *The Nature and Context of Minority Discourse.* Oxford, U.K.: Oxford University Press, 1990.

"Japanese Have Lots of Time Off, but Taking It Is Another Matter." *Houston Chronicle,* 24 November 2000.

Jarboe, S. "Procedures for Enhancing Group Decision Making." In *Communication and Group Decision Making,* edited by R. Hirokawa and M.S. Poole. 2d ed. Thousand Oaks, Calif.: Sage, 1996.

+Jehensen, R. "Effectiveness, Expertise, and Excellence as Ideological Fictions." *Human Studies* 7 (1984): 3-21.

Johansen, R. *Teleconferencing and Beyond.* New York: McGraw-Hill, 1984.

Johansen, R., J. Vallee, and K. Spangler. *Electronic Meetings: Technological Alternatives and Social Choices.* Reading, Mass.: Addison-Wesley, 1979.

Johnson, B., and R. Rice. *Managing Organizational Innovation: The Evolution from*

Word Processing to Office Information Systems. New York: Columbia University Press, 1987.

Johnson, K. "Many Companies Turn Workers into High-Tech Nomads." *Minneapolis Star-Tribune* 3 April 1994.

"Just 10% of Senior Managers for Fortune 500 Are Women." *Houston Chronicle,* 7 January 2000.

Kalleberg, A., and K. Leicht. "Gender and Organizational Performance." *Academy of Management Journal* 34 (1991): 155–63.

Kaplan, A. "Was Democracy Just a Moment?" *The Atlantic Monthly* 274 (December, 1997): 3–18.

Kaplan, R.D. "The Coming Anarchy." *The Annals of the American Academy of Political and Social Sciences* 570 (2000): 34–60.

Kanter, R.M. *Men and Women of the Corporation.* New York: Harper & Row, 1977.

———. *A Tale of "O": On Being Different in an Organization.* New York: Harper & Row, 1980.

Karsten, M.F. *Management and Gender.* Westport, Conn.: Quorum Books, 1994.

Katzenbach, J.R., and D.K. Smith. *The Wisdom of Teams.* New York: HarperCollins, 1993.

Keen, P.W.G. "Ready for 'new' B2B?" *Computerworld,* 11 September 2000, 17.

Kellman, H., and L. Hamilton. *Crimes of Obedience.* New Haven, Conn.: Yale University Press, 1989.

Kennedy, G. *Classical Rhetoric in Its Christian and Secular Traditions from Ancient to Modern Times.* Chapel Hill: University of North Carolina Press, 1980.

Keough, C. "The Case of the Aggrieved Expatriate." *Management Communication Quarterly* 11 (1998): 453–59.

Kerr, J., and J. Slocum. "Managing Corporate Culture through Reward Systems." *Academy Management Executive* 1 (1987): 99–108.

Kerr, K., and R.H. Starr. *Computer-Mediated Communication Systems.* New York: Academic Press, 1982.

Kerr, S. "On the Folly of Rewarding A While Hoping for B." *Academy of Management Journal* 19 (1975): 769–83.

Kersten, A. "Culture, Control, and the Labor Process." In *Communication Yearbook 16,* edited by S. Deetz. Newbury Park, Calif.: Sage, 1993.

Kever, J. "Life In the Tired Lane." *Texas Magazine,* 13 August 2000, 8.

Keyton, J., and S. Rhodes. "Organizational Sexual Harassment." *Journal of Applied Communication Research* 27 (1999): 158–73.

Kidwell, R.E., Jr., and N. Bennett. "Employee Reactions to Electronic Control Systems." *Group and Organization Management* 19 (1994): 203–19.

+Kiesler, S., J. Siegel, and T.W. McGuire. "Social Psychological Aspects of Computer-Mediated Communication." *American Psychologist* 39 (1984): 1123–34.

Kilborn, P.T. "For Many in Work Force, Glass Ceiling Still Exists." *New York Times,* 16 March 1995.

+Kim, K., H.-J. Park, and N. Suzuki. "Reward Allocations in the United States, Japan, and Korea." *Academy of Management Journal* 33 (1990): 188–98.

Kim, M., J. Hunter, A. Miyahara, A. Horvath, M. Bresnahan, and H. Yoon. "Individual- vs. Culture-Level Dimensions of Individualism and Collectivism." *Communication Monographs* 63 (1996): 29–49.

Kim, P.S., and G. Lewis. "Asian Americans in the Public Service." *Public Administration Review* 54 (1994): 285–90.

+Kim, Y.Y., and K. Miller. "The Effects of Attributions and Feedback Goals on the Generation of Supervisor Feedback Message Strategies." *Management Communication Quarterly* 4 (1990): 6–29.

Knouse, S. "The Mentoring Process for Hispanics." In *Hispanics in the Workplace,* edited by S. Knouse, P. Rosenfeld, and A. Culberson. Newbury Park, Calif.: Sage, 1992.

+Knuf, J. "'Ritual' in Organizational Culture Theory." In *Communication Yearbook 16,* edited by S. Deetz. Newbury Park, Calif.: Sage, 1994.

Koenig, D. *More Mouse Tales.* Irvine, Calif.: Bonaventure Press, 1999.

———. *Mouse under Glass.* Irvine, Calif.: Bonaventure Press, 1997.

Kogut, B., W. Shan, and G. Walker. "Knowledge in the Network and the Network as Knowledge: Structuring of New Industries." In *The Embedded Firm: On the Socioeconomics of Industrial Networks,* edited by G. Grabher. New York: Rutledge, 1993.

Kolb, D. and J. Bartunek, ed. *Hidden Conflict in Organizations.* Newbury Park, Calif.: Sage, 1991.

+Komorita, S.S. "Negotiating from Strength and the Concept of Bargaining." *Journal of the Theory of Social Behavior* 7 (1977): 56–79.

Korn/Ferry International. "The Decade of the Executive Woman." New York: 1993: *Houston Chronicle,* 2/19/96, B1.

+Kraiger, K., and J. Ford. "A Meta-Analysis of Ratee Race Effects in Performance Ratings." *Journal of Applied Psychology* 70 (1985): 56–65.

Kram, K. *Mentoring.* Chicago: Scott, Foresman, 1986.

+Kramer, M. "Communication after Job Transfers: Social Exchange Processes in Learning New Roles." *Human Communication Research* 20 (1993): 147–74.

+————. "Communication and Uncertainty Reduction during Job Transfers: Leaving and Joining Processes." *Communication Monographs* 60 (1993): 178-98.

+Kramer, M. "A Longitudinal Study of Superior-Subordinate Communication during Job Transfers." *Human Communication Research* 22 (1995): 39-64.

+Kramer, M., R.R. Callister, and D.B. Turban. "Information-Receiving and Information-Giving during Job Transitions." *Western Journal of Communication* 39 (1995): 151-70.

Kramer, M., and V. Miller. "A Response to Criticisms of Organizational Socialization Research." *Communication Monographs* 66 (1999): 360-69.

Kreps, G., ed. *Sexual Harassment: Communication Implications.* Cresskill, N.J.: Hampton Press, 1993.

Krone, K., L. Chen, D. Sloan, and L. Gallant. "Managerial Emotionality in Chinese Factories." *Management Communication Quarterly* 11 (1997): 6-50.

+Kunda, G. *Engineering Culture.* Philadelphia: Temple University Press, 1992.

Lamude, K., T. Daniels, and K. White. "Managing the Boss." *Management Communication Quarterly* 1 (1987): 232-59.

Larkey, L., and C. Morrill. "Organizational Commitment as Symbolic Process." *Western Journal of Communication* 59 (1995): 193-213.

Larson, C.E., and F.M.J. LaFasto. *TeamWork: What Must Go Right/What Can Go Wrong.* Newbury Park, Calif.: Sage, 1989.

Lash, S. "Court Holds Educators Liable for Harassment." *Houston Chronicle,* 7 September 1999, C25.

Leary, T. *Interpersonal Diagnosis of Personality.* New York: Ronald, 1957.

Legg, N.A. "Other People's Kids: Decision-Making about Sexual Education." Master's thesis, Texas A&M University, 1992.

Levine, J.M. and R.L. Moreland. "Small Groups." In *Handbook of Social Psychology,* edited by D. Gilbert, S. Fiske, and G. Linzey. 4th ed. New York: Oxford University Press, 1998.

Levine, S.B. *Father Courage.* New York: Harcourt, 2000.

Lewicki, R. "Lying and Deception." In *Negotiating in Organizations,* edited by M. Bazerman and R. Lewicki. Newbury Park, Calif.: Sage, 1983.

Leyden, P. "Teleworking Could Turn Our Cities Inside Out." *Minneapolis Star-Tribune,* 5 September 1993.

Likert, R. *New Patterns of Management.* New York: McGraw-Hill, 1961.

+Lim, T., and J.W. Bowers. "Face-Work: Solidarity, Approbation, and Face." *Human Communication Research* 17 (1990): 415-50.

Lin, J. "Students Create Groups to Fight Sweatshops." *Houston Chronicle,* 5 December 1999.

Lindblom, C. "The Science of Muddling Through." *Public Administration Review* 19 (1959): 412-21.

"Little Upward Help for Minority Females: Executive Women Say Mentors Needed." *Houston Chronicle,* 14 July 1999.

Locke, E. "The Ideas of Frederick Taylor." *The Academy of Management Review* 7 (1982): 14-24.

————. "The Nature and Causes of Job Satisfaction." In *Handbook of Industrial and Organizational Psychology,* edited by M. Dunnette. Chicago: Rand-McNally, 1976.

"The Lordstown Auto Workers." In *Life In Organizations,* edited by R.M. Kanter and B. Stein. New York: Basic Books, 1979.

Louis, M.R. "Acculturation in the Workplace." In *Organizational Climate and Culture,* edited by B. Schneider. San Francisco: Jossey-Bass, 1990.

————. "Surprise and Sense-Making in Organizations." *Administrative Science Quarterly* 25 (1980): 226-51.

+Lucas, H.C. *The T-Form Organization: Using Technology to Design Organizations for the 21st Century.* San Francisco: Jossey-Bass, 1996.

Mandle, J. "Globalization and Justice." *Annals of the American Academy of Political and Social Science* 570 (2000): 126-39.

Mansnerus, L. "Why Women Are Leaving the Law." *Working Woman,* April 1993: 21-24.

+Mantovani, G. "Is Computer-Mediated Communication Intrinsically Apt to Enhance Democracy in Organizations?" *Human Relations* 47 (1994): 45-62.

Manusov, V., and J.M. Billingsley. "Nonverbal Communication in Organizations." In P. Y. Byers, ed. *Organizational Communication: Theory and Behavior.* Boston: Allyn and Bacon, 1997.

March, J. "The Technology of Foolishness." In *Ambiguity and Choice in Organizations,* edited by J. March and J. Olson. Bergen, Norway: Universitetsforlaget, 1970.

+March, J., and J. Olson, J. *Ambiguity and Choice in Organizations.* Bergen, Norway: Universitetsforlaget, 1970.

+March, J., and G. Sevon. "Gossip, Information, and Decision Making." In *Advances in Information Processing In Organizations,* edited by L. Sproull and P. Larkey. Vol. 1. Greenwich, Conn.: JAI Press, 1982.

+March, J., and H. Simon. "The Concept of Rationality." In *Human Behavior and International Politics,* edited by D. Singer. Chicago: Rand-McNally, 1965.

Marin, G., and B.V. Marin. *Research with Hispanic Populations*. Newbury Park, Calif.: Sage, 1996.

Marrow, A., D. Bowers, and S. Seashore. *Management by Participation*. New York: Harper & Row, 1967.

Marshall, J. "Viewing Organizational Communication from a Feminist Perspective: A Critique and Some Offerings." In *Communication Yearbook 16*, edited by S. Deetz. Newbury Park, Calif.: Sage, 1993.

Marshall, J. *Women Managers Moving On*. London: Routledge, 1995.

Martin, J. *Cultures in Organizations*. New York: Oxford University Press, 1992.

Martin, J., and M. Powers. "Truth or Corporate Propaganda: The Value of a Good War Story." In *Organizational Symbolism*, edited by L. Pondy. Greenwich, Conn.: JAI Press, 1983.

Martin, L. *Pipelines of Progress*. Washington, D.C.: U.S. Department of Labor, August 1992.

Masuch, M., and P. LaPotin. "Beyond Garbage Cans." *Administrative Science Quarterly* 34 (1989): 38–68.

Mattson, M., et al. "A Feminist Reframing of Stress." In *Rethinking Managerial and Organizational Communication from Feminist Perspectives*, edited by P. Buzzanell. Thousand Oaks, Calif.: Sage, 2000.

Maynard, M. "Diversity Programs Work, Where They Exist." *USA Today*, 15 September 1994.

Mayo, E. *Social Problems of an Industrial Civilization*. Boston: Graduate School of Business Administration, Harvard University, 1945.

McAllister, D.J. "Affect- and Cognition-Based Trust as Foundations for Interpersonal Cooperation in Organizations." *Academy of Management Journal* 38 (1995): 24–59.

McFarlin, C., and P. Sweeney. "Distributive and Procedural Justice as Predictors of Satisfaction with Personal and Organizational Outcomes." *Academy of Management Journal* 35 (1992): 626–37.

McLaughlin, M. *Conversation*. Beverly Hills, Calif.: Sage, 1984.

+McLeod, R., Jr. *Management Information Systems*. 6th ed. New York: Macmillan, 1990.

McMillan, J. "Legal Protection of Whistleblowers." In *Corruption and Reform*, edited by S. Prosser, R. Wear, and J. Nethercote. St. Lucia, Queensland: University of Queensland Press, 1990.

+McPhee, R. "Vertical Communication Chains: Toward an Integrated View." *Management Communication Quarterly* 1 (1988): 455–93.

McPhee, R., and S. Corman. "An Activity-Based Theory of Communication Networks in Organizations, Applied to a Local Church." *Communication Monographs* 62 (1995): 132–51.

+McPhee, R., and M.S. Poole. "Organizational Structure, Configurations, and Communication." In *The New Handbook of Organizational Communication*, edited by F. Jablin and L. Putnam. Thousand Oaks, Calif.: Sage, 2000.

Meindl, J. "Managing to Be Fair." *Administrative Science Quarterly* 34 (1989): 252–76.

"Men Still Suspect If Priority Is Family." *Houston Chronicle*, 9 April 2000.

Menn, J. "ADM Fine Criticized as Too Low." *Houston Chronicle*, 1 December 1996.

+Meyer, A. "Mingling Decision-Making Metaphors." *Academy of Management Review* 9 (1984): 231–46.

Meyer, M. "Here's a 'Virtual' Model for America's Industrial Giants." *Newsweek*, 13 August 13, 1993.

Meyerson, D. "Interpretations of Stress in Institutions." *Administrative Science Quarterly* 39 (1994): 628–53.

———. "Normal" Ambiguity?" In *Reframing Organizational Culture*, edited by P. Frost, L. Moore, M.R. Louis, and J. Martin. Newbury Park, Calif.: Sage, 1991.

Meyerson, D., and J. Martin. "Cultural Change: An Integration of Three Different Views." *Journal of Management Studies* 24 (1987): 623–47.

Miceli, M., and J. Near. *Blowing the Whistle: The Organizational and Legal Implications for Companies and Employees*. New York: Lexington Books, 1992.

Miller, K. *Organizational Communication*. Belmont, Calif.: Wadsworth, 1994.

Miller, L., L. Cooke, J. Tsang, and F. Morgan. "Should I Brag?" *Human Communication Research* 18 (1992): 364–99.

+Miller, V., and F. Jablin. "Information Seeking during Organizational Entry." *Academy of Management Review* 16 (1991): 92–120.

Mills, K. "Northwest on a Flier-Satisfaction Mission." *Houston Chronicle*, 14 May 2000.

Milwid, B. *Working with Men*. East Rutherford, N.J.: Berkley, 1992.

+Mintzberg, H. *Mintzberg on Management*. New York: Basic Books, 1989.

+———. *Power in and around Organizations*. Englewood Cliffs, N.J.: Prentice Hall, 1983.

+———. *The Rise and Fall of Strategic Planning*. New York: Free Press, 1994.

+Mintzberg, H., and A. McHugh. "Strategy Formation in an Adhocracy." *Administrative Science Quarterly* 30 (1985): 160–97.

+Mintzberg, H., D. Raisinghani, and A. Theoret. "The Structure of 'Unstructured' Decision Processes." *Administrative Science Quarterly* 21 (1976): 246-75.

Mishel, L., J. Bernstein, and J. Schmidt. *The State of Working America.* Ithaca, N.Y.: Cornell University Press, 1998.

Moch, M.K., and J. Bartunek. *Creating Alternative Realities at Work.* New York: Harper Business, 1990.

+Mohrman, S.A., S.G. Cohen, and A.M. Mohrman. *Designing Team-Based Organizations: New Forms for Knowledge Work.* San Francisco: Jossey-Bass, 1995.

+Monge, P., and N. Contractor. "Emergent Communication Networks." In *The New Handbook of Organizational Communication,* edited by F. Jablin and L. Putnam. Thousand Oaks, Calif.: Sage, 2000.

Mongeau, P., and J. Blalock. "Student Evaluations of Instructor Immediacy and Sexually Harassing Behaviors: An Experimental Investigation." *Journal of Applied Communication Research* 22 (1994): 256-72.

Mooney, T. "U.S. Fathers Give More Time to Kids Than Many Dads—Even Their Own." *Houston Chronicle,* 20 June 1999.

Moore, G. "Structural Determinants of Men's and Women's Personal Networks." *American Sociological Review* 55 (1990): 726-35.

Morand, D.A. "The Role of Behavioral Formality and Informality in the Enactment of Bureaucratic versus Organic Organizations." *Academy of Management Review* 20 (1995): 831-72.

"More New Mothers Returning to Work." *Houston Chronicle,* 24 October 2000.

Morely, D., and P. Shockley-Zalabak. "Conflict Avoiders and Compromisers." *Group and Organizational Behavior* 11 (1986): 387-402.

Morrill, C. "The Private Ordering of Professional Relationships." In *Hidden Conflict in Organizations,* edited by D. Kolb and J. Bartunek. Newbury Park, Calif.: Sage, 1992.

+Morris, G.H., S.C. Gaveras, W.L. Baker, and M.L. Coursey. "Aligning Actions at Work." *Management Communication Quarterly* 3 (1990): 303-33.

Morris, J. "Whistle-Blower Claims Settled." *Houston Chronicle,* 20 November 1996.

Morrison, A. *The New Leaders.* San Francisco: Jossey-Bass, 1992.

Morrison, A., R. White, and E. Van Velsor. *Breaking the Glass Ceiling.* Greensboro, N.C.: Center for Creative Leadership, 1992.

Mulder, M. "Power Equalization through Participation?" *Academy of Management Journal* 16 (1971): 31-38.

Mulder, M., and H. Wilke. "Participation and Power Equalization." *Organizational Behavior and Human Performance* 5 (1970): 430-48.

+Mumby, D. *Communication and Power in Organizations.* Norwood, N.J.: Ablex, 1988.

+———. "Communication, Organization, and the Public Sphere." In *Rethinking Organizational and Managerial Communication from Feminist Perspectives,* edited by P.M. Buzzanell. Thousand Oaks, Calif.: Sage, 2000.

+———. "Organizing Men." *Communication Theory* 8 (1998): 164-83.

+———. "Power, Politics, and Organizational Communication." In *New Handbook of Organizational Communication,* edited by F. Jablin and L. Putnam. Thousand Oaks, Calif.: Sage, 2000.

———. ed. *Narrative and Social Control: Critical Perspectives.* Newbury Park, Calif.: Sage, 1993.

+Mumby, D., and L. Putnam. "The Politics of Emotion." *Academy of Management Review* 17 (1992): 465-86.

+Mumby, D., and C. Stohl. "Power and Discourse in Organization Studies." *Discourse and Society* 2 (1991): 313-32.

Murphy, A. "Hidden Transcripts of Flight Attendant Resistance." *Management Communication Quarterly* 11 (1998): 499-535.

Nadler, M., and L. Nadler. "Feminization of Public Relations." In *Communication and Sex-Role Socialization,* edited by C. Berryman-Fink, D. Ballard-Reich, and L.H. Newman. New York: Garland Publishing Company, 1993.

Nathan, B., A. Mohrman, and J. Milliman. "Interpersonal Relations as a Context of the Effects of Appraisal Interviews." *Academy of Management Journal* 34 (1991): 352-69.

National Foundation of Women Business Owners, http://www.nfwbo.org, 6 January 2001.

Neale, B., and M. Bazerman. *Cognition and Rationality in Negotiations.* New York: Free Press, 1991.

———. "Negotiating Rationally." *Academy of Management Executive* 6 (1992): 42-65.

Nelson, R. *1001 Ways to Take Initiative.* New York: Workman, 1999.

Neumark, D., ed. *On the Job: Is Long-term Employment a Thing of the Past?* New York: Russell Sage Foundation, 2000.

Newell, A., and H. Simon. *Human Problem Solving.* Englewood Cliffs, N.J.: Prentice Hall, 1972.

+Nkomo, S. "The Emperor Has No Clothes: Rewriting Race in Organizations." *Academy of Management Review* 17 (1992): 487-512.

Nohria, N., and J.D. Berkley. "Allen-Bradley's ICCG Case Study." In *The Post-Bureaucratic Organization: New Perspectives on Organizational Change,* edited by C. Heckscher and A. Donnellon. Newbury Park, Calif.: Sage, 1994.

"Number of Female Executives Continues to Rise, Survey Says." *Houston Chronicle,* 14 November 2000.

+Nunamaker, J.F., A. Dennis, J. George, J. Valacich, and D. Vogel. "Electronic Meeting Systems to Support Group Work." *Communications of the ACM* 34 (1991): 40–61.

O'Conner, E. "Discourse at Our Disposal." *Management Communication Quarterly* 10 (1997): 395–432.

O'Reilly, C. "Variations in Decision-Makers' Use of Information Sources." *Academy of Management Journal* 25 (1982): 756–71.

Oetzel, J., and K. Bolton-Oetzel. "Exploring the Relationship between Self-Construal and Dimensions of Group Effectiveness." *Management Communication Quarterly* 10 (1997): 289–315.

Olivares, F. "Ways Men and Women Lead." *Harvard Business Review* 69 (January-February 1991): 2–11.

Olson, D.L., and J.F. Courtney Jr. *Decision Support Models and Expert Systems.* Houston: Dame, 1998.

Ong, A. "The Gender and Labor Politics of Postmodernity." *Annual Review of Anthropology* 20 (1991): 196–214.

———. "Spirits of Resistance." In *Situated Lives,* edited by L. Lamphere, H. Razoné, and P. Zavella. New York: Routledge, 1997.

———. *Spirits of Resistance and Capitalist Discipline.* Albany: State University of New York Press, 1987.

Orbe, M. "An Outsider Within Perspective to Organizational Communication." *Management Communication Quarterly* 2 (1998): 230–79.

Organ, D. "Linking Pins between Organizations and Environments." *Business Horizons* 14 (1971): 73–80.

+Orlikowski, W.J., J. Yates, K. Okamura, and M. Fujimoto. "Shaping Electronic Communication: The Metastructuring of Technology in the Context of Use." *Organization Science* 6 (1995): 423–44.

O'Rourke, K., and J. Williamson. *Globalization and History.* Cambridge, Mass.: MIT Press, 1999.

Ospina, S. *Illusions of Opportunity.* Ithaca, N.Y.: ILR/Cornell University Press, 1996.

O'Sullivan, M. *Contests for Corporate Control.* Oxford, U.K.: Oxford University Press, 2000.

———. "Corporate Governance and Globalization." *Annals of the American Academy of Political and Social Science* 570 (2000): 153–71.

Ouchi, W. "The Relationship between Organizational Structure and Control." *Administrative Science Quarterly* 22 (1977): 95–113.

———. *Theory Z.* Reading, Mass.: Addison-Wesley, 1981.

Ouchi, W., and A. Jaeger. "Type Z Organization." *Academy of Management Review* 3 (1978): 305–14.

Ouchi, W., and A. Wilkins. "Efficient Cultures." *Administrative Science Quarterly* 28 (1983): 468–81.

"Overworked America?" *The Online (PBS) Newshour,* http://www.pbs.org/neshour/bb/business/july-dec99/overwork_9-6a.html, 6 September 1999.

Pacanowsky, M. "Communication in the Empowering Organization." In *Communication Yearbook 11,* edited by James Anderson. Beverly Hills, Calif.: Sage, 1987.

———. "Creating and Narrating Organizational Realities." In *Rethinking Communication,* edited by Brenda Dervin et al. Vol. 2. Beverly Hills, Calif.: Sage, 1989.

Page, P. "African Americans in Executive Branch Agencies." *Review of Public Personnel Administration* 14 (1994): 24–51.

Paludi, M.A., and R.B. Barickman. *Academic and Workplace Sexual Harassment.* Albany: State University of New York Press, 1991.

+Papa, M., and W. Papa. "Competence in Organizational Conflicts." In *Competence in Interpersonal Conflict,* edited by W.R. Cupach and D.J. Canary. New York: McGraw-Hill, 1996.

Parker, P.S., and D. Ogilvie. "Gender, Culture, and Leadership." *Leadership Quarterly* 7 (1996): 189–214.

Parry, J., ed. *The Establishment of the European Hegemony, 1415–1715.* New York: HarperCollins, 1967.

Paskoff, S. "Ending the Workplace Diversity Wars." *Training: The Human Side of Business* (August 1996): 2–8.

+Pateman, C. *The Problem of Political Obligation.* Cambridge, U.K.: Polity Press, 1995.

Paulson, N. "The Intergroup Context of Communication in Organizations." Paper presented at the International Communication Association Convention, Acapulco, Mexico, 6 June 2000.

+Pavitt, C., G.G. Whitchurch, H. McClurg, and N. Petersen. "Melding the Objective and Subjective Sides of Leadership: Communication and Social Judgments in Decision-Making Groups." *Communication Monographs* 62 (1995): 243–64.

Pells, R. *Not Like Us.* New York: Basic Books, 1997.

Pena, D. "Tortuodidad." In *Women on the U.S.-Mexican Border,* edited by V.L. Ruiz and S. Tiano. Boston: Allen & Unwin, 1987.

Perrow, C. "A Framework for the Comparative Analysis of Organizations." *American Sociological Review* 32 (1967): 194-208.

+Perrow, C. *Complex Organizations.* 3d ed. New York: Random House, 1986.

Pesquera, B. "In the Beginning He Wouldn't Even Lift a Spoon." In *Situated Lives,* edited by L. Lamphere, H. Razoné, and P. Zavella. New York: Routledge, 1997.

Peters, T., and N. Austin. *A Passion for Excellence.* New York: Random House, 1985.

Peters, T., and R. Waterman. *In Search of Excellence.* New York: Harper & Row, 1982.

Peterson, T.R., and C.C. Horton. "Rooted In the Soil." *The Quarterly Journal of Speech* 81 (1995): 139-66.

Pettigrew, A. "Information Control as a Power Resource." *Sociology* 6 (1972): 187-204.

+Pfeffer, J. *Managing with Power.* Boston: Harvard Business School, 1992.

+———. *Power in Organizations.* Marshfield, Mass.: Pitman, 1981.

+Pfeffer, J. and A. Davis-Blake. "The Effect of the Proportion of Women on Salaries." *Administrative Science Quarterly* 32 (1987): 1-24.

+Pfeffer, J., and N. Langton. "Wage Inequality and the Organization of Work." *Administrative Science Quarterly* 33 (1988): 588-606.

Phillips, D. *Houston Chronicle,* 12 July 1996.

Phillips, K. "The Wealth Effect." *Houston Chronicle,* 8 August 1999.

Phillips, K.R. "The Spaces of Public Dissension." *Communication Monographs* 63 (1996): 231-48.

Planalp, S. *Communicating Emotion.* Cambridge, U.K.: Cambridge University Press, 1999.

———. "Communicating Emotion." *Communication Theory* 9 (1999): 216-28.

Planalp, S., S. Hafen, and A.D. Adkins. "Messages of Shame and Guilt." In *Communication Yearbook 23,* edited by M. Roloff. Thousand Oaks, Calif.: 1999.

Pollock, T., R. Whitbred, and N. Contractor. "Social Information Processing and Job Characteristics." *Human Communication Research* 26 (2000): 292-330.

Pondy, L. "Organizational Conflict: Concepts and Models." *Administrative Science Quarterly* 12 (1967): 296-320.

———. "The Role of Metaphors and Myths in the Organization and the Facilitation of Change." In *Organizational Symbolism,* edited by L. Pondy, P. Frost, G. Morgan, and T.D. Dandridge. Greenwich, Conn.: JAI Press, 1993.

+Poole, M.S. "Decision Development in Small Groups I." *Communication Monographs* 48 (1981): 1-24.

+———. "Decision Development in Small Groups II." *Communication Monographs* 50 (1983): 206-32.

+———. "Decision Development in Small Groups III." *Communication Monographs* 50 (1983): 321-41.

———. "Organizational Challenges for the New Forms." In *Shaping Organization Form: Communication, Connection, and Community,* edited by G. DeSanctis and J. Fulk. Newbury Park, Calif.: Sage, 1999.

+Poole, M.S., and C. Baldwin. "Developmental Processes in Group Decision-Making." *Communication and Group Decision Making,* edited by R. Hirokawa and M.S. Poole. Thousand Oaks, Calif.: Sage, 1996.

+Poole, M.S., and J. Roth. "Decision Development in Small Groups IV." *Human Communication Research* 15 (1989): 323-56.

+Poole, M.S., and A. Van de Ven. "Using Paradox to Build Management and Organization Theories." *Academy of Management Review* 14 (1995): 562-78.

Posner, B.Z., and W.H. Schmidt. "Values and the American Manager." *California Management Review* 26 (1984): 202-16.

Potuchek, J. *Who Supports the Family?* Palo Alto, Calif.: Stanford University Press, 1997.

Powell, E.A. "Women Are Hitting the 'Glass Wall.'" *Houston Chronicle,* 12 November 1999.

Powell, G. *Women and Men in Management.* Newbury Park, Calif.: Sage, 1993.

Powell, G., and D.A. Butterfield. "Investigating the 'Glass Ceiling' Phenomenon." *Academy of Management Journal* 37 (1994): 68-86.

Powers, D. *The Office Romance.* New York: AMACOM, 1999.

Prasso, S. "Study: Stereotypes Hinder Female Executives." *Houston Chronicle,* 29 February 1996.

Pratt, M. "The Good, The Bad, and the Ambivalent." *Administrative Science Quarterly* 45 (2000): 456-93.

Pruitt, D.G., J. Rubin, and S. Kim. *Social Conflict.* New York: McGraw-Hill, 1994.

+Putnam, L. "Conflict and Dispute Management." In *The New Handbook of Organizational Communication,* edited by F. Jablin and L. Putnam. Thousand Oaks, Calif.: Sage, 1997.

———. "Conflict in Group Decision Making." In *Communication and Group Decision Making,* edited by R. Hirokawa and M.S. Poole. Newbury Park, Calif.: Sage, 1986.

+———. "Feminist Theories, Dispute Processes, and Organizational Communication." Paper presented at the Arizona State University Conference on Organizational Communication: Perspectives for the 1990s, Tempe, Arizona, April 1990.

———. "Negotiation of Intergroup Conflict in Organizations." Hallie Mande Neff Wilcox Published Lecture. Waco, Tex.: Baylor University, 1987.

+———. "Preference for Procedural Order in Task-Oriented Small Groups." *Communication Monographs* 46 (1979): 193-218.

+———. "Reframing Integrative and Distributive Bargaining." In *Research on Negotiation in Organizations,* edited by B. Shepard, M. Bazerman, and R. Lewicki. Vol. 2. Greenwich, Conn.: JAI Press, 1990.

———. "Understanding the Unique Characteristics of Groups within Organizations." In *Small Group Communication,* edited by R. Cathcart and L. Samovar. Dubuque, Iowa: William C. Brown, 1984.

+———, ed. Special Issue on Communication and Conflict. *Management Communication Quarterly* 2 (1988).

Putnam, L., and M. Holmer. "Framing and Reframing." In *Communication and Negotiation,* edited by L. Putnam and M. Roloff. Newbury Park, Calif.: Sage, 1992.

+Putnam, L., and T. Jones. "Reciprocity in Negotiations." *Communication Monographs* 49 (1982): 171-91.

+Putnam, L. and D.M. Kolb. "Rethinking Negotiation: Feminist Views of Communication and Exchange." In *Rethinking Organizational and Managerial Communication from Feminist Perspectives,* edited by P. Buzzanell. Thousand Oaks, Calif.: Sage, 2000.

Putnam, L., and S. Van Hoeven. "The Role of Narrative in Teachers' Bargaining." Paper presented at the Temple University Discourse Conference on Conflict Intervention, Philadelphia, Pennsylvania, 1987.

———. "Teacher Bargaining as a Cultural Rite of Conflict Reduction." Paper presented at the Central States Speech Association Convention, Cincinnati, Ohio, October 1986.

+Putnam, L., and C. Wilson. "Communicative Strategies in Organizational Conflicts." In *Communication Yearbook 6,* edited by M. Burgoon. Newbury Park, Calif.: Sage, 1982.

Putnam, L., S. Van Hoeven, and C. Bullis. "The Role of Rituals and Fantasy Themes in Teachers' Bargaining." *Western Journal of Speech Communication* 55 (1991): 85-103.

Putnam, L., S. Wilson, and D. Turner. "The Evolution of Policy Arguments in Teachers' Bargaining." *Argumentation* 4 (1990): 129-52.

Rafaeli, A., and R. Sutton. "The Expression of Emotion in Organizational Life, II." *Research in Organizational Behavior* 11(1989): 1-42.

Rafaeli, S. *Electronic Message to Computer-Mediated Hotline.* Comserve Electronic Information Service, 26 April 1990.

+Rahim, M. "Referent Role and Styles of Handling Interpersonal Conflict." *Journal of Social Psychology* 126 (1986): 79-86.

Ralston, S., and W. Kirkwood. "Overcoming Managerial Bias in Employment Interviewing." *Journal of Applied Communication Research* 23 (1995): 75-92.

Rampersad, F. "Coping with Globalization." *Annals of the American Association of Political and Social Science* 570 (2000): 115-25.

+Raven, B., and A. Kruglanski. "Power and Conflict." In *The Structure of Conflict,* edited by P. Swingle. New York: Academic Press, 1970.

Reardon, K.K. *They Don't Get It, Do They?* Boston: Little, Brown, 1995.

Redding, W.C. "Rocking Boats, Blowing Whistles, and Teaching Speech Communication." *Communication Education* 34 (1985): 245-58.

Remland, M. "Leadership Impressions and Nonverbal Communication." *Communication Quarterly* 19 (1987): 108-28.

Reskin, R., and I. Padavic. *Women and Men at Work.* Thousand Oaks, Calif.: Pine Forge Press, 1994.

+Reuther, C., and G. Fairhurst. "Chaos Theory and the Glass Ceiling." In *Rethinking Organizational and Managerial Communication from Feminist Perspectives,* edited by P. Buzzanell. Thousand Oaks, Calif.: Sage, 2000.

Reynolds, C.W., and R.V. Norman, eds. *Community in America: The Challenge of Habits of the Heart.* Berkeley: University of California Press, 1988.

+Ricardo, D. *Principles of Political Economy and Taxation.* Buffalo, N.Y.: Prometheus Books, 1996.

Rice, R. "Evaluating New Media Systems." In *Evaluating the New Information Technologies,* edited by J. Johnstone. San Francisco: Jossey-Bass, 1984.

———. *New Communication Technologies.* Beverly Hills, Calif.: Sage, 1984.

+Rice, R., and C. Aydin. "Attitudes toward New Organizational Technology." *Administrative Science Quarterly* 36 (1991): 219-44.

+Rice, R., and U. Gattiker. "Communication Technologies and Structures." In *The New Handbook of Organizational Communication,* edited by F. Jablin and L. Putnam. Thousand Oaks, Calif.: Sage, 2000.

+Rice, R., and G. Love. "Electronic Emotion." *Communication Research* 14 (1987): 85-108.

Richmond, V.P., and J.C. McCroskey. "The Impact of Supervisor and Subordinate Immediacy on Relational and Organizational Outcomes." *Communication Monographs* 67 (2000): 85-95.

Richmond, V.P., and K.D. Roach. "Willingness to Communicate and Employee Success in U.S. Organizations." *Journal of Applied Communication Research* 20 (1992): 95-115.

Ritzer, G. *The McDonaldization of Society.* Newbury Park, Calif.: Pine Forge Press, 1993.

Ritzer, G., and A. Liska. "McDisneyization and Post-Tourism." In *Touring Cultures,* edited by C. Rojek and J. Urry. London: Routledge, 1997.

Rizzo, A., and C. Mendez. *"The Integration of Women in Management."* New York: Quorum Books, 1990.

+Roberts, N. "Organizational Power Styles." *The Journal of Applied Behavioral Science* 22 (1986): 443-55.

Rodrik, D. "Has Globalization Gone Too Far?" *Challenge* 41 (1998): 81-94.

Rodrik, D. "Sense and Nonsense in the Globalization Debate." *Foreign Policy* 107 (Summer 1997): 15-24.

Rogers, E.M. *Communication of Innovations.* 4th ed. New York: Free Press, 1994.

+Roloff, M. "Roloff's Modes of Conflict Resolution and Their Items." In *Explorations in Interpersonal Communication,* edited by Gerald Miller. Beverly Hills, Calif.: Sage, 1976.

+Roloff, M., and J.M. Jordan. "Achieving Negotiation Goals." In *Communication and Negotiation,* edited by L. Putnam and M. Roloff. Newbury Park, Calif.: Sage, 1993.

Rosen, M. "Breakfast at Sprio's." In *Reframing Organizational Culture,* edited by Peter Frost, L. Moore, M.R. Louis, C. Lundberg, and J. Martin. Newbury Park, Calif.: Sage, 1991.

———. "You Asked for It: Christmas at the Bosses' Expense." *Journal of Management Studies* 25 (1988): 463-80.

Rosener, J. "Ways Women Lead." *Harvard Business Review* 68 (November-December 1990): 119-25.

Rosner, R. *Working Wounded.* New York: Warner Books, 1999.

Ross, G. "Labor Versus Globalization." *Annals of the American Academy of Political and Social Science* 570 (2000): 78-91.

Rothschild-Whitt, J., and J.A. Whitt. *The Cooperative Workplace.* Cambridge: Cambridge University Press, 1986.

Russo, T.C. "Organizational and Professional Identification." *Management Communication Quarterly* 12 (1998): 72-111.

Sachs, J. "International Economics: Unlocking the Mysteries of Globalization." *Foreign Policy* 110 (Spring 1998): 168-206.

———. "Making It Work." *Economist,* 12 September 1998, available at http://www.economist.com.

+Said, E. *Orientalism.* New York: Penguin, 1978.

+Sambamurthy, V., and M.S. Poole. "The Effects of Variations in Capabilities of GDSS Designs on Management of Cognitive Conflict in Groups." *Information Systems Research* 3 (1993): 224-51.

Sampson, E.E. "Justice, Ideology, and Social Legitimation." In *Justice In Social Relations,* edited by H.W. Bierhoff, R.L. Cohen, and J. Greenberg. New York: Plenum, 1986.

Sassen, S. *Globalization and its Discontents.* New York: New Press, 1998.

———. *Guests and Aliens.* New York: New Press, 1999.

———. *Losing Control?* New York: Columbia University Press, 1996.

Sayles, L. "Work Group Behavior and the Larger Organization." In *Research in Industrial Human Relations,* edited by W.F. Whyte. New York: Harper, 1957.

+Schenck-Hamlin, W., and G. Georgacarakos. "Response to Murdock, Bradac, and Bowers." *Western Journal of Speech Communication* 50 (1986): 200-207.

Scherer, R. "First National Survey of Minority Views Shows Deep Racial Polarization." *Christian Science Monitor,* 16 March 1994.

Schneider, B., S. Gunnarson, and J. Wheeler. "The Role of Opportunity in the Conceptualization and Measurement of Job Satisfaction." In *Job Satisfaction,* edited by C.J. Crannay, P. Smith, and E. Stone. New York: Lexington Books, 1992.

Schneider, M. "Life Isn't So Magical for Some Workers." *Houston Chronicle,* 2 January 1999.

+Schweiger, D., and A. Denisi. "Communication with Employees Following a Merger." *Academy of Management Journal* 34 (1991): 110-35.

+Schwenk, C.R., and M.A. Lyles. "Top Management, Strategy, and Organizational Knowledge Structures." *Journal of Management Studies* 29 (1992): 155-74.

Scott, C. "Identification with Multiple Targets in a Geographically Dispersed Organization." *Management Communication Quarterly* 10 (1997): 491-522.

———. "Communication Technology and Group Communication." In *Handbook of Group Communication Theory and Research,* edited by L. Frey, D. Gouran, and M.S. Poole. Newbury Park, Calif.: Sage, 1999.

+Scott, C., S. Connaughton, H. Diaz-Saenz, K. McGuire, R. Ramirez, B. Richardson, S. Shaw, and D. Morgan. "The Impacts of Communication and Multiple Identifications on Intent to Leave." *Management Communication Quarterly* 12 (1999): 400-435.

+Scott, C., S. Corman, and G. Cheney. "Development of a Structurational Model of Identification in the Organization." *Communication Theory* 8 (1998): 298-336.

Scott, J. *Domination and the Arts of Resistance.* New Haven, Conn.: Yale University Press, 1990.

Scott, W.G., and Hart, D.K. *Organizational America.* Boston: Houghton Mifflin, 1979.

———. *Organizational Values in America.* New Brunswick, N.J.: Transaction Publishers, 1989.

Seeger, M. "Responsibility in Organizational Communication." In *Proceedings of the 1992 National Communication Ethics Conference,* edited by J. Jaska. Annandale, Va.: Speech Communication Association, November 1992.

Segura, D. "Chicanas in White-Collar Jobs." In *Situated Lives,* edited by L. Lamphere, H. Razoné, and P. Zavella. New York: Routledge, 1997.

+Seibold, D., and R. Meyers. "Communication and Influence in Group Decision-Making." In *Communication and Group Decision Making,* edited by R. Hirokawa and M.S. Poole. 2d ed. Thousand Oaks, Calif.: Sage, 1996.

+Seibold, D., and C. Shea. "Participation and Decision-Making." In *The New Handbook of Organizational Communication,* edited by F. Jablin and L. Putnam. Thousand Oaks, Calif.: Sage, 2000.

Senge, P. *The Fifth Discipline.* New York: Doubleday, 1990.

Series on the INS. *Houston Chronicle,* 15 December 2000.

Shattuck, H. "Mexico Offers Better Assistance." *Houston Chronicle,* 12 November 2000.

Shaw, R. *Reclaiming America.* Berkeley: University of California Press, 1999.

Sherif, M., O.J. Harvey, B. White, W. Hood, and C.W. Sherif. *Intergroup Conflict and Cooperation: The Robber's Cave Experiment.* Norman, Okla.: University Book Exchange, 1961.

Shuler, S., and B.D. Sypher. "Seeking Emotional Labor." *Management Communication Quarterly* 14 (2000): 50–89.

Shuter, R. "Communication in Multinational Organizations." In *Communication and Multinational Organizations,* edited by R. Wiseman and R. Shuter. Thousand Oaks, Calif.: Sage, 1994.

+Sias, P. "Constructing Perceptions of Differential Treatment." *Communication Monographs* 63 (1996): 171–87.

+Sias, P., and F. Jablin. "Differential Superior-Subordinate Relations, Perceptions of Fairness, and Coworker Communication." *Human Communication Research* 22 (1995): 5–38.

+Sillars, A. "Stranger and Spouse as Target Persons for Compliance-Gaining Strategies." *Human Communication Research* 6 (1980): 265–79.

Simons, T. "Speech Patterns and the Concept of Utility in Cognitive Maps." *Academy of Management Journal* 36 (1993): 139–56.

Sims, R. "The Challenge of Ethical Behavior in Organizations." *Journal of Business Ethics* 11 (1992): 501–13.

+Sitkin, S.B., K.M. Sutcliffe, and J.R. Barrios-Choplin. "A Dual-Capacity Model of Communication Medium Choice in Organizations." *Human Communication Research* 18 (1992): 563–98.

Sixel, L.M. *Houston Chronicle,* 19 July 1996.

———. "Pay Gap Narrower, But Far from Closed." *Houston Chronicle,* 26 February 1999.

———. "Workplace Racism Cases Hard to Win." *Houston Chronicle,* 13 November 1996.

Sless, D. "Forms of Control." *Australian Journal of Communication* 14 (1988): 57–69.

Smith, D. "Stories, Values, and Patient Care Decisions." In *The Ethical Nexus,* edited by C. Conrad. Norwood, N.J.: Ablex, 1992.

+Smith, K. "The Movement of Conflict in Organizations." *Administrative Science Quarterly* 34 (1989): 1–20.

Smith, K., and V. Simmons. "The Rumpelstiltskin Organization." *Administrative Science Quarterly* 28 (1983): 377–92.

Smith, R. "How to Be a Good Subordinate." *New York Times,* 25 November 1970.

Smith, R.C., and E. Eisenberg. "Conflict at Disneyland: A Root-Metaphor Analysis." *Communication Monographs* 54 (1987): 367–80.

+Smith-Lovin, L. and M.J. McPherson. "You Are Who You Know." In *Theory on Gender/Feminism on Theory,* edited by Paula England. New York: Aldine, 1993.

+Snyder, R., and J. Morris. "Organizational Communication and Performance." *Journal of Applied Psychology* 69 (1984): 461–65.

Solomon, C. "Keeping Hate out of the Workplace." *Personnel Journal* 71 (July 1992): 30–36.

Solomon, D.H., and M.L.M. Williams. "Perceptions of Social-Sexual Communication at Work." *Journal of Applied Communication Research* 25 (1997): 196–216.

———. "Perceptions of Social-Sexual Communication at Work as Harassing." *Management Communication Quarterly* 11 (1997): 147–84.

Soros, G. *The Crisis of Global Capitalism.* New York: Public Affairs, 1998.

———. G. *The Open Society.* New York: Public Affairs, 2000.

Spain, D. *Gendered Spaces.* Chapel Hill, N.C.: University of North Carolina Press, 1992.

Spence, L. *The Politics of Social Knowledge.* University Park: Pennsylvania State University Press, 1978.

+Sproull, L., and S. Kiesler. *Connections: New Ways of Working in the Networked World.* Cambridge, Mass.: MIT Press, 1992.

+————."Reducing Social Context Cues." *Management Science* 32 (1986): 1492–1512.

St. Clair, L., R. Quinn, and R. O'Neill. "The Perils of Responsiveness in Modern Organizations." In *Pressing Problems in Organizations (That Keep Us Awake at Night),* edited by Robert Quinn, R. O'Neill, and L. St. Clair. New York: AMACOM, 2000.

+Staw, B., P. McKechnie, and S. Puffer. "The Justification of Organizational Performance." *Administrative Science Quarterly* 28 (1983): 582–600.

Steinfeld, C. "Computer-Mediated Communication in the Organizations." In *Cases In Organizational Communication,* edited by Beverly Sypher. New York: Guilford, 1991.

Stohl, C. "Bridging the Parallel Organization: A Study of Quality Circle Effectiveness." In *Communication Yearbook 10,* edited by Judee Burgoon. Beverly Hills, Calif.: Sage, 1985.

————. "Globalizing Organizational Communication." In *The New Handbook of Organizational Communication,* edited by F. Jablin and L. Putnam. Thousand Oaks, Calif.: Sage, 2000.

————. *Organizational Communication.* Thousand Oaks, Calif.: Sage, 1995.

+————. "The Role of Memorable Messages in the Process of Organization Socialization." *Communication Quarterly* 34 (1983): 231–49.

Stolberg, S.G., and J. Gerth. "Drug Makers Fight Generic Rivals and Raise Questions of Monopoly." *Houston Chronicle,* 23 July 2000.

+Sullivan, J., and S. Taylor. "A Cross-Cultural Test of Compliance-Gaining Theory." *Management Communication Quarterly* 5 (1991): 220–39.

Sussman, H. "Is Diversity Training Worth Maintaining?" *Business and Society Review* 89 (1994): 48–49.

Sutcliffe, K. "Commentary on Strategic Sensemaking." In *Advances in Strategic Management,* edited by J. Walsh and A. Huff. Greenwich, Conn.: JAI Press, 1997.

+————. "Information Processing and Organizational Environments." In *The New Handbook of Organizational Communication,* edited by F. Jablin and L. Putnam. Thousand Oaks, Calif.: Sage, 2000.

Tannenbaum, A. "Control in Organizations." *Administrative Science Quarterly* 7 (1962): 17–42.

Taylor, F. "The Principles of Scientific Management." In *Classics of Organizational Theory,* edited by J. Shafritz and P. Whitbeck. Oak Park, Ill.: Moore, 1978.

+Tedeschi, J. "Threats and Promises." In *The Structure of Conflict,* edited by P. Swingle. New York: Academic Press, 1970.

Tegar, A. *Too Much Invested to Quit.* New York: Pergamon, 1980.

+Terpstra, D., and D. Baker. "Outcomes of Sexual Harassment Charges." *Academy of Management Journal* 31 (1988): 185–94.

"Texaco Reeling from Racial Scandal." *Houston Chronicle,* 5 November 1996.

"Texaco Whistle-Blower: Much Trouble, Little Reward." *USA Today,* 20 December 1999.

+Therborn, G. *The Ideology of Power and the Power of Ideology.* London: Verso, 1980.

Thomas, D., and C. Alderfer. "The Influence of Race on Career Dynamics." In *Handbook of Career Theory,* edited by M. Arthur, D. Hall, and B. Lawrence. New York: McGraw-Hill, 1989.

Thomas, K. "Where Do We Go from Here?" *Management Communication Quarterly* 1 (1988): 301–5.

Thomas, K., and R. Walton. *Conflict-handling Behavior in Interdepartmental Relations.* Los Angeles: UCLA Graduate School of Business Administration, 1971.

+Thompson, J. *Organizations in Action.* New York: McGraw-Hill, 1967.

Thurow, L. "Globalization." *Annals of the American Academy of Political and Social Science* 570 (2000): 19–31.

————. "In Praise of Cultural Imperialism?" *Foreign Policy* 107 (Summer 1997): 107–19.

————. "New Rules: The American Economy in the Next Century." *Harvard International Review* 19 (Winter 1997/1998): 7–42.

Ting-Toomey, S. "Toward a Theory of Conflict and Culture." In *Communication and Culture,* edited by W. Gudykunst. Beverly Hills, Calif.: Sage, 1985.

Toffler, B.E. *Tough Choices.* New York: John Wiley & Sons, 1986.

Tomlinson, J. *Globalization and Culture.* Chicago: University of Chicago Press, 1999.

Tompkins, P. *Organizational Communication Imperatives: Lessons from the Space Program.* Los Angeles: Roxbury House, 1993.

Tompkins, P., J. Fisher, D. Infante, and E. Tompkins. "Conflict and Communication within the University." In *Perspectives on Communication and Social Conflict,* edited by G. Miller and H. Simons. Englewood Cliffs, N.J.: Prentice Hall, 1974.

Tompkins. P.K., and G. Cheney. "Communication and Unobtrusive Control in Organizations." In *Organizational Communication: Traditional Themes and New Directions,* edited by R.D. McPhee and P. Tompkins. Beverly Hills, Calif.: Sage, 1985.

"Top, Junior Officers Vie, Study Says." *Houston Chronicle,* 19 November 2000.

Toth, E.L., and R. Heath, eds. *Rhetorical and Critical Approaches to Public* Relations. New York: Praeger, 1992.

+Tracy, K., and E. Eisenberg. "Giving Criticism." *Research on Language and Social Interaction* 24 (1990/1991): 37-70.

Tracy, S.J. "Becoming a Character for Commerce." *Management Communication Quarterly* 14 (2000): 90-128.

Tracy, S., and K. Tracy. "Emotion Labor at 911." *Journal of Applied Communication Research* 26 (1998): 390-411.

+Tretheway, A. "A Feminist Critique of Disciplined Bodies." In *Rethinking Organizational and Managerial Communication from Feminist Perspectives,* edited by P. Buzzanell. Thousand Oaks, Calif.: Sage, 2000.

+Trevinio, L., R. Lengel, and R. Daft. "Media Symbolism, Media Richness, and Media Choices in Organizations." *Communication Research* 14 (1987): 553-74.

Trice, H., and J. Beyer. *The Cultures of Work Organizations.* Englewood Cliffs, N.J.: Prentice Hall, 1993.

———. "Studying Organizational Cultures through Rites and Ceremonials." *Academy of Management Review* 9 (1984): 653-69.

Tucker, J. "Some Everyday Forms of Employee Resistance." *Sociological Forum* 8 (1993): 25-45.

U.S. Department of Labor. *The American Workforce: 1992-2005.* Washington, D.C.: Government Printing Office, USDL Bulletin N. 2452, 1994.

Uchitelle, W. "Some Economic Interplay Comes Nearly Full Circle." *New York Times on the Web,* www.nytimes.com, 30 April 1998.

UNITE Report on Campus Caps. http://www.uniteunion.org/sweatshops/, 6 January 2001.

Vanderford, M., D. Smith, and W. Harris. "Value Identification in Narrative Discourse." *Journal of Applied Communication Research* 20 (1992): 123-61.

+Van de Ven, A., and M.S. Poole. "Explaining Development and Change in Organizations." *Academy of Management Review* 20 (1995): 510-40.

van Maanen, J. "Displacing Disney." In *Managing for the Future: Organizational Behavior and Processes,* edited by D. Ancona, T. Kochan, J. Van Maanen, M. Scully, and D. Westney. Cincinnati: Southwestern College Publishing, 1999.

———. "The Smile Factory." In *Reframing Organizational Culture,* edited by P. Frost, L. Moore, M.R. Louis, C. Lundberg, and J. Martin. Newbury Park, Calif.: Sage, 1991.

+van Maanen, J., and G. Kunda. "Real Feelings: Emotional Expression and Organizational Culture." In *Research In Organizational Behavior,* edited by L.L. Cummings and B.M. Staw. Vol. 11. Greenwich, Conn.: JAI Press, 1989.

van Maanen, J., and E. Schein. "Toward a Theory of Socialization." In *Research in Organizational Behavior,* edited by B. Staw. Vol. 1. Greenwich, Conn.: JAI Press, 1979.

Vaughn, D. *The "Challenger" Launch Decision.* Chicago: University of Chicago Press, 1996.

———. *Controlling Unlawful Organizational Behavior.* Chicago: University of Chicago Press, 1992.

———. "NASA and the 'Challenger.'" *Administrative Science Quarterly* 35 (1990): 225-57.

Vaughn, E., and M. Siefert. "Variability in the Framing of Risk Issues." *Journal of Social Issues* 48 (1992): 119-35.

Verton, D. "Employers OK with E-Surfing." *Computerworld,* 18 December 2000.

———. "Senator Attacks Data Sharing." *Computerworld,* 11 December 2000.

Violanti, M. "Hooked on Expectations: An Analysis of Influence and Relationships in the Tailhook Reports." *Journal of Applied Communication Research* 24 (1996): 67-82.

Vodosek, M., and K.M. Sutcliffe. "Overemphasis on Analysis." In *Pressing Problems In Modern Organizations (That Keep Us Up at Night),* edited by R. Quinn, R.M. O'Neill, and L. St. Clair. New York: AMACOM, 2000.

Vroom, V.H., and P.W. Yetton. *Leadership and Decision Making.* Pittsburgh: University of Pittsburgh Press, 1973.

+Waldron, V. "Achieving Communication Goals in Supervisor-Subordinate Relationships." *Communication Monographs* 58 (1991): 289-306.

+Waldron, V., and K. Krone. "The Experience and Expression of Emotion in the Workplace." *Management Communication Quarterly* 4 (1991): 287-309.

Walker, Chip, and E. Moses. "The Age of Self-Navigation." *American Demographics* 18 (September 1996): 36-42.

Walsh, S. "Plaintiffs Say Texaco Tough in Bias Cases." *Houston Chronicle,* 14 November 1996.

Ware, B.L., and W.A. Linkugel. "They Spoke in Defense of Themselves." *The Quarterly Journal of Speech* 59 (1973): 273-83.

Walther, J.B. "Interpersonal Effects in Computer-Mediated Interaction." *Communication Research* 19 (1992): 52–90.

+Watzlawick, P., J. Beavin, and D. Jackson. *Pragmatics of Human Communication.* New York: W.W. Norton, 1967.

+Weber, Max. *The Protestant Ethic and the Spirit of Capitalism.* New York: Charles Scribner's and Sons, 1958.

Weick. K. "Organizational Culture and High Reliability." *California Management Review* 29 (1987): 112–27.

+———. *Sense-Making in Organizations.* Thousand Oaks, Calif.: Sage, 1995.

+———. *The Social Psychology of Organizing.* 2d ed. Reading, Mass.: Addison-Wesley, 1979.

+Weick, K., and L. Browning. "Argument and Narration in Organizational Communication." *Yearly Review of Management of the Journal of Management* 12 (1986): 243–59.

+Westerlund, G., and S. Sjostrand. *Organizational Myths.* New York: Harper & Row, 1979.

+Westley, F. "Middle Managers and Strategy." *Strategic Management Journal* 11 (1990): 339.

Wilkins, A. *Managing Corporate Character.* San Francisco: Jossey-Bass, 1989.

Wilkins, B.W., and P.A. Anderson. "Gender Differences and Similarities in Management Communication." *Management Communication Quarterly* 5 (1991): 186–211.

Wilson, S. "Face and Facework in Negotiation." In *Communication and Negotiation,* edited by L. Putnam and M. Roloff. Newbury Park, Calif.: Sage, 1993.

+Wilson, S.R., J.O. Greene, and J.P. Dillard. "Introduction to the Special Issue on Message Production." *Communication Theory* 10 (2000): 135–38.

+Wilson, S., and L. Putnam. "Interaction Goals in Negotiation." In *Communication Yearbook 13,* edited by James Anderson. Newbury Park, Calif.: Sage, 1990.

+Winstead, B.A., V.J. Derlega, M.J. Montgomery, and C. Pilkington. "The Quality of Friendships at Work and Job Satisfaction." *Journal of Social and Personal Relationships* 12 (1995): 199–215.

+Winter, S.J., and S.L. Taylor. "The Role of Information Technology in the Transformation of Work: A Comparison of Post-Industrial, Industrial, and Proto-Industrial Organizations." In *Shaping Organization Form: Communication, Connection, and Connectivity,* edited by G. DeSanctis and J. Fulk. Newbury Park, Calif.: Sage, 1999.

Wolfson, B. "For Disneyland, Boss is Wish upon a Star Come True." *Houston Chronicle,* 5 December 1999.

"Women Owned Firms See Huge Growth." *Houston Chronicle,* 11 May 1999.

Wood, J. "Engendered Relationships." In *Processes in Close* Relationships, edited by S. Duck. Vol. 3. Beverly Hills, Calif.: Sage, 1993.

+———. *Gendered Lives.* Belmont, Calif.: Wadsworth, 1994.

Wood, J., and B. Pearce. "Sexists, Racists and Other Classes of Classifiers." *Quarterly Journal of Speech* 66 (1980): 239–50.

"Workers in a Land of Plenty See a Scarcity of Vacation Time." *Houston Chronicle,* 24 November 2000.

Wyatt, N. "Shared Leadership in a Weavers' Guild." In *Women Communicating,* edited by B. Bate and A. Taylor. Norwood, N.J.: Ablex, 1988.

+Yammarino, F.J., and A.J. Dubinsky. "Superior-Subordinate Relationships." *Human Relations* 45 (1992): 575–600.

+Yates, J., and W.J. Orlikowski. "Genres of Organizational Communication." *The Academy of Management Review* 17 (1992): 299–326.

Youker, R. "Organization Alternatives for Project Managers." *Project Management Journal* 8 (March 1977): 18–24.

+Young, E. "On the Naming of the Rose." *Organization Studies* 10 (1989): 187–206.

Young, G. "Gender Identification and Working-Class Solidarity Among *Maquila* Workers in Cuidad Juarez." In *Women on the U.S.-Mexican Border,* edited by V.L. Ruiz and S. Tiano. Boston: Allen & Unwin, 1987.

Zak, M.W. "It's Like a Prison in There." *Journal of Business and Technical Communication* 8 (1994): 282–98.

Zakaria, F. "The Rise of Illiberal Democracy." *Foreign Affairs* 76 (1997): 187–219.

Zalzenik, A. "Power and Politics in Organizational Life." *Harvard Business Review* 48 (May-June 1970): 47–60.

+Zand, D.E. "Trust and Managerial Problem-Solving." *Administrative Science Quarterly* 17 (1972): 229–39.

Zipkin, A. "Bosses Become Nice to Try to Keep Employees from Leaving." *Houston Chronicle,* 4 June 2000.

Zorn, T., D. Page, and G. Cheney. "Nuts about Change." *Management Communication Quarterly* 13 (2000): 515–66.

+Zuboff, S. *In the Age of the Smart Machine.* New York: Free Press, 1988.

INDEX